Ulrich Sieber / Konstanze Jarvers / Emily Silverman (eds.)

National Criminal Law in a Comparative Legal Context

Schriftenreihe des Max-Planck-Instituts für
ausländisches und internationales Strafrecht

Strafrechtliche Forschungsberichte

Herausgegeben von Ulrich Sieber

Band S 128.1.5

Max-Planck-Institut für ausländisches
und internationales Strafrecht

National Criminal Law in a Comparative Legal Context

Volume 1.5

Introduction to National Systems

National characteristics, fundamental principles, and history of criminal law

India, Italy, Romania, Spain

edited by

Ulrich Sieber • Konstanze Jarvers • Emily Silverman

Duncker & Humblot • Berlin

Bibliografische Information der Deutschen Nationalbibliothek

Die Deutsche Nationalbibliothek verzeichnet diese Publikation in der Deutschen Nationalbibliografie; detaillierte bibliografische Daten sind im Internet über <http://dnb.ddb.de> abrufbar.

Redaktion: Petra Lehser

c/o Max-Planck-Institut für ausländisches und internationales Strafrecht
Günterstalstraße 73, 79100 Freiburg i.Br.
http://www.mpicc.de
Vertrieb in Gemeinschaft mit Duncker & Humblot GmbH, Berlin
http://www.duncker-humblot.de

Umschlagbild: © Martin Langhorst, Köln
Druck: Stückle Druck und Verlag, Stückle-Straße 1, 77955 Ettenheim
Printed in Germany

ISSN 1860-0093
ISBN 978-3-86113-785-6 (Max-Planck-Institut)
ISBN 978-3-428-15569-9 (Duncker & Humblot)
Gedruckt auf alterungsbeständigem (säurefreiem) Papier
entsprechend ISO 9706 ♾

Foreword

The research program launched in 2004 by the Department of Criminal Law at the Max Planck Institute for Foreign and International Criminal Law is devoted to analyzing the changing face of criminal law in today's global risk society. The projects it has inspired are based in large part on the comparative criminal law method, the quintessence of Prof. Dr. Dr. h.c. mult. *Hans-Heinrich Jescheck's* vision for the Institute. Since the founding of the Max Planck Institute in Freiburg, comparative criminal law has been both one of its principal research methods as well as a key subject of its research. At the heart of the Institute's comparative legal research, the *International Max Planck Information System for Comparative Criminal Law* is one of the first projects begun under the aegis of the 2004 research program. This volume is one of the fruits of this project.

I.

In the fields of national and international law, changes attributable to globalization have led to an increase in the importance of *comparative criminal law* and its methodological underpinnings. In order to take account of the changes to criminal law around the world, develop general legal principles, and shape criminal policy, there is a growing need for a comprehensive, systematic comparison of criminal law that encompasses numerous legal systems. The question of whether this kind of "universal comparison of criminal law" involving a multitude of highly diverse legal systems is possible, in practice, is as yet unanswered. In many countries, data have not been collected in such a way as to enable a systematic comparative legal analysis.

A *primary objective* of the project *International Max Planck Information System for Comparative Criminal Law* thus encompasses the development of a *universal meta-structure of criminal law* that can serve as the basis for the organization of the material based on a common outline, enable systematic comparisons, and further the development of an international criminal law doctrine. This meta-structure is also a prerequisite for analyzing the various approaches taken around the world to shared criminal law-related problems, identifying general legal principles, and drafting international model codes. Therefore, the study must first determine whether, given the diversity of criminal law systems, it is possible to pinpoint an overarching structure that can serve as the basis of a systematic and functional legal comparison.

A *second goal of this project* is to provide access to data from the participating legal systems in the form of country reports organized on the basis of a universal meta-structure. At the 1999 conference "Die deutsche Strafrechtswissenschaft vor der Jahrtausendwende" (German Criminal Law Science at the Turn of the Millennium), Prof. Dr. Dr. h.c. mult. *Claus Roxin* rightly defined such a *compendium of criminal law* as "the future task of global criminal law science." The highly-structured presentation of data in the form of detailed country reports contributes not only to the development and verification of the project outline but is also a prerequisite for the project's more far-reaching research goals and potentialities: comparative legal analysis of the country reports, elucidation of different approaches taken in the countries under study, and identification of general legal principles and their contribution to an international criminal law doctrine.

In addition to these basic research aims, the project has a *third practical, application-oriented objective*; namely, the development of a *computer-based information system for the comparison of criminal law*. The project's meta-structure has led to a complex systematization that has undergone feasibility-testing on the basis of extensive data. Thus, the data mined from the individual legal systems not only provide the foundation for a comprehensive encyclopedia of criminal law on a global scale, they have also been used to engineer a database with which new types of computer-assisted legal comparisons – also via the Internet – can be executed. The development of this tool is sure to enable innovative comparative legal analyses.

II.

Towards these ends, the project *International Max Planck Information System for Comparative Criminal Law* started with a pilot project carried out to analyze, structure, and present the general part of the criminal law in twelve legal systems. The results were published in five volumes from 2008 to 2010 under the title *Nationales Strafrecht in rechtsvergleichender Darstellung* (vols. S 114.1–S 114.5 of this series). In the meantime, the number of legal systems included in the study has grown considerably – with contributions from researchers at the Max Planck Institute as well as from external research partners. At a later date, a decision will be taken as to how far the scope of the project can be extended (content-wise) to the special part of the criminal law and to criminal procedure and (with regard to the project's objectives) to the development of general legal principles and model codes.

Due to this methodological approach the country reports are organized according to the *universal meta-structure* developed within the framework of the pilot project by a working group led by *Ulrich Sieber* and *Karin Cornils* and modified slightly under the leadership of *Susanne Forster*, *Konstanze Jarvers*, and *Emily Silverman*.

The meta-structure takes account of distinctive national features while at the same time overcoming the limits and peculiarities of country-specific systems. In order to achieve this aim, the group established a new level separate and detached from national criminal law doctrine, a level that accommodates the varying rules, theories, and approaches found in the legal systems under study. The independence of the meta-structure from the constraints of any particular national system is apparent, for example, in the discussion of the definitions and internal structure of the criminal offense (Chapter II.C.). The discussion is not organized in terms of a tripartite offense system as employed, for example, in the German system. Instead, the discussion is based on a "common denominator," namely, the differentiation between objective and subjective aspects of the offense. Also, since a distinction between justification and excuse is unknown in many legal systems, these phenomena are largely dealt with from the broad perspective of grounds excluding criminal liability (Chapter II.J.). They are further distinguished by means of functional comparisons based on frequently encountered scenarios. The terminology chosen often does not contain terms typically used in individual countries.

The quest for a universal meta-structure of criminal law, that is, a single structure that accommodates all legal systems, was made all the more difficult by the fact that this pursuit was not merely an exercise in structuring the material in response to specific questions of interest; rather, a *comprehensive system* capable of handling all potential issues arising in the context *of the entire general part* was the goal. In light of the practical aim of ultimately entering the findings into a database, a detailed outline was essential so that future queries to the database would consistently elicit discrete, directly comparable elements from the various legal systems. This effort has paid off. The country reports prepared to date share four structural levels, thus ensuring their comparability.

The difficulties encountered during the design of a universally applicable framework for the general part of the criminal law as well as the need to make allowance for trial and error contributed to the decision to carry out the pilot project in *German*, a language with a specialized terminology familiar to all participants in the pilot phase. Once this outline was developed and translated, it was possible to change the *project language* to *English.*

It was clear from the very beginning that intense personal cooperation during the pilot phase of the project would be necessary. Thus, all participants in the project had to be physically present at the Institute. Consequently, the *countries considered for the pilot study* were determined to a large extent by the expertise of researchers employed by the Institute. Within these constraints, countries were chosen so as to maximize the diversity of participating legal systems: *China* and *South Korea* were chosen to represent Asian legal systems, whereby Chinese criminal law exhibits socialist tendencies and South Korean criminal law reflects the early reception of German criminal law. The criminal law of *Côte d'Ivoire* is based in part on the law of France, its former colonial power, and in part on traditional tribal law. While both *England and Wales* and *Scotland* belong to the common law family, they display some significant differences. *France*, *Italy*, and *Spain* are part of the Romanic family of legal systems. *Poland* is an example of a former socialist country, and *Sweden* represents the Nordic countries. *Austrian* criminal law exhibits characteristics typical of the German-speaking world, and *Turkey*, with the introduction of a new criminal code in 2005, has emancipated itself to a large extent from previous influences.

The selection of *additional countries* for the *second phase* of the project was based primarily on the contribution specific legal systems could make to the already-existing roster: *Switzerland* was added as an example of a legal system that integrates various continental European approaches to criminal law. *Greece* and *Portugal* supplement the southern European countries. *Bulgaria*, the *Czech Republic*, *Hungary*, *Romania*, and *Russia* represent four additional formerly socialist systems – countries that differ markedly, to be sure, in their approaches. *Bosnia and Herzegovina* is the first country from the territory of the former Yugoslavia to be included in the project. Outside of Europe, *Japan* and *Thailand* were chosen to augment representation of Asian legal systems, and *Uruguay* is the first Latin American country to participate. From the Middle East, the criminal law of *Iran* exhibits a most interesting blend of Islamic law and continental European influences. Finally, with *Australia*, *India*, *Uganda*, and the *United States of America*, four more common law legal systems on four different continents join the project. New countries are joining the project on a regular basis.

Parallel to the preparation and print-publication of the country reports, the abovementioned *IT-based expert system* was developed. Work on the conceptualization and basic algorithm of the system began in 2005. The first fully operational prototype, dating to 2012, was subsequently transformed into a more user-friendly and sophisticated system that has been freely accessible via the Internet since the fall of 2015 (infocrim.org). In its current form, it allows the user to choose one or more national legal orders and to combine the selected legal orders with a specific topic. The system responds by displaying the appropriate chapter. The user then has the option of selecting additional legal orders. Two chapters can be shown simultaneously on the screen, side-by-side, and compared directly. Additional functions include, for example, the possibility of scrolling all the way through each country report, from start to finish, and the possibility of carrying out a full-text search of the entire data set. This information system proves not only the successful achievement of the concept of a universal meta-structure for the complete general part of criminal law. It also shows the ingenuity of such a meta-structure: direct comparison of complex issues is easily achieved since each participating legal order has addressed the same issues in the same place in the structure.

III.

This volume, S 128.**1**.5, contains reports on four countries: two of them (*India* and *Romania*) were originally written in English; the other two (*Italy* and *Spain*) are translations of the country reports written in German during the pilot phase of the project. The latter have been revised and updated since they were first published in 2009. Volume S 128.**1**.5 is devoted to *introductory chapters* on national characteristics, constitutional parameters, criminal law theory, the development of criminal law throughout history, and other areas that promote the understanding and comparison of the participating legal systems. Introductory chapters from additional countries will be published in future volumes (S 128.**1**.6 ff.).

Additional volumes originating from this project contain *chapters on the general limitations on the application of criminal law* (the principle of legality and the scope of extraterritorial jurisdiction, vols. S 128.**2**.1 ff.), *chapters on the definition of criminal conduct*, namely, the concept and systematization of the criminal offense, the objective aspects of the offense, and the subjective aspects of the offense (vols. S 128.**3**.1 ff.), *chapters on special forms of criminal liability* (punishable conduct prior to the completion of an offense, parties to crime, and criminal liability for crimes in companies, associations, and other collective legal entities, vols. S. 128.**4**.1 ff.), and *chapters on the grounds for rejecting criminal liability* (vols. S 128.**5**.1 ff.).

IV.

We would like to thank all participants in the preparation of this volume for their commitment to its success. We are especially grateful to the authors (a list of whose names can be found on page XI) who form the backbone of the project and help advance ongoing research with their detailed depictions and discussions; they are responsible for the content of their reports. Our special thanks go to Dr. phil. *Yvonne Shah-Schlageter*, *Jan Schwab*, M.A., and *Karen Huber-Guida*, J.D., for their work on the translation of the reports on Italy and Spain. Mr. *Sebastian Heni*, our student assistant, earned our gratitude by providing welcome assistance throughout the editing process. Ms. *Petra Lehser* is to be commended for her editorial and technical finesse, and we thank her for her patience in preparing this volume for publication. Finally, we are deeply indebted to Dr. Dr. h.c. mult. *Karin Cornils* for her invaluable contribution to the pilot project and the meta-structure.

The driving force of globalization, the need to prevent transnational crime, and the aspiration to universal protection of human rights have led to a significant increase in the importance of comparative criminal law. It is our hope that the volumes of the *International Max Planck Information System for Comparative Criminal Law* will take the development of an international criminal law doctrine one step further – a crucial step towards the integration of national and international legal systems into a globally functioning system of criminal justice and human rights protection.

Freiburg, June 2018 *Ulrich Sieber*, *Konstanze Jarvers, Emily Silverman*

List of countries included and contributing authors

India	*Neha Jain*
Italy	*Konstanze Jarvers*
Romania	*Johanna Rinceanu*
Spain	*Teresa Manso Porto*

Comprehensive overview of project
(structure of the country reports)

I. Introduction

Vol. 1: A. National characteristics

B. Comparative legal classification and international ties

C. Constitutional parameters of criminal law

D. Fundamentals of criminal law

E. Nature, form, and boundaries of criminal law

F. Sources of criminal law and interpretation aids

G. Developments in criminal law, criminal procedure, and the execution of punishment

II. Foundations of criminal law
(general part of criminal law)

Vol. 2: A. Principle of legality

B. Extraterritorial jurisdiction – the applicability of domestic criminal law to activities undertaken abroad

Vol. 3: C. The criminal offense – definitions and internal structure

D. Objective side of the offense

E. Subjective side of the offense

Vol. 4: F. Punishable conduct prior to the completion of an offense

G. Parties to crime

H. Criminal liability for crimes in companies, associations, and other collective legal entities

Vol. 5: J. Grounds for excluding criminal liability

K. Grounds for terminating or expunging criminal liability

Detailed outline of country reports in volume 1.5

Introduction to national systems

A. National characteristics

1. Geography
2. Population
    a) Population and demographics
    b) Language
    c) Religion
3. Economy
4. System of government
5. Crime and criminal prosecution
    a) Investigating authorities
    b) Prosecuting authorities
    c) Criminal courts
    d) Criminal penalties
    e) Execution of custodial penalties

B. Comparative legal classification and international ties

1. Comparative legal classification
2. Effects of international ties
    a) Membership in international and regional organizations
    b) Signature and ratification of international treaties and conventions

C. Constitutional parameters of criminal law

1. Supra-statutory rules as repositories of criminal law principles
2. Fundamental rights and freedoms and the criminal law
3. Other supra-statutory norms relevant to criminal law and criminal procedure

Table of contents

National characteristics, fundamental principles, and history of criminal law in

India

Neha Jain

Contents

A. National characteristics

1. Geography

The Republic of India is located in the northern hemisphere on the Asian continent. It forms a distinct peninsula that is separated from the rest of the Asian continent by the Himalayas in the north and is surrounded by the Bay of Bengal in the east, the Arabian Sea in the west, and the Indian Ocean to the south. India is the seventh largest country in the world, covering an area of 3,287,263 sq km. The total length of the land frontier is 15,200 km, while the coastline, which encompasses the mainland, the Lakshadweep Islands, and the Andaman and Nicobar Islands, is 7,517 km. The capital of India is New Delhi.[1]

India dominates the South Asian sub-continent and is bordered by Afghanistan and Pakistan to the northwest; China, Bhutan, and Nepal to the north; and Myanmar and Bangladesh to the east. A narrow channel of sea comprising the Palk Strait and the Gulf of Mannar separates India from Sri Lanka. The Indian mainland consists of four main geographical regions: the great mountain zone, the plains of the Ganga and the Indus rivers, the desert region, and the southern peninsula.[2]

2. Population

a) Population and demographics

India is a multi-ethnic, multilingual, and multicultural society. According to the provisional population data compiled by the most recent decennial census (2011), the total population of India was approximately 1.2 billion at the time of the census, with 623.7 million males and 586.4 million females.[3] A more recent population estimate (July 2016) is closer to 1.3 billion.[4] India is the second most populous country in the world, outranked only by China.[5] At 382 persons per sq km, it has one of the highest population densities amongst the world's populous nations: while it accounts for only 2.4 % of the world's total surface area, it supports 17.5 % of the world's population.[6]

---

1 Know India, National Portal of India: Profile.

2 Know India, National Portal of India: Profile.

3 Know India, National Portal of India: Profile.

4 CIA World Factbook, India: People and Society.

5 CIA World Factbook, India: People and Society.

6 Census 2011, Provisional Population Totals, Paper 1, India, pp. 38–39, 78.

India's rapid growth in population is a matter of considerable concern. In absolute terms, India registered an increase of 181 million people during the decade 2001–2011, which is only slightly lower than the total population of the fifth most populous country in the world, Brazil.[7] There are indications, though, that with the slow tapering off of the growth rate in population (an estimated 1.19 % in 2016)[8] and the decline in fertility, India could achieve a stable population in the future.[9]

India has a sizeable young population. According to the 2011 census, the total number of children in the age group of 0 to 6 years was 158.8 million (about 5 million less than in 2001), which constituted 13.1 % of the total population. The sex ratio in India has been historically negative and was 940 females per 1000 males in the 2011 census provisional population tables.[10]

In 2015, India's urban population was 32.7 %, while the majority of the population (67.3 %) continues to live in rural areas. India has several large cities with sizeable populations: New Delhi (25.7 million); Mumbai (21.0 million); Kolkata (11.8 million); Chennai (9.62 million); and Hyderabad (8.94 million) (2015 estimates).[11]

b) Language

According to the 2001 census (data from the 2011 census are not available), a total of 122 languages are spoken. Of these, 22 are scheduled languages officially recognized by the Eighth Schedule to the Constitution (Const.) of India. In 2001, 96.6 % of the population had one of the scheduled languages as its mother tongue. Hindi, the predominant language, was spoken by 41 % of the population. Other languages spoken by significant numbers of people were Bengali (8.1 %), Telugu (7.2 %), Marathi (7.0 %), Tamil (5.9 %), Urdu (5.0 %), Gujarati (4.5 %), Kannada (3.7 %), Malayalam (3.2 %), Oriya (3.2 %), Punjabi (2.8 %), Assamese (1.3 %), and Maithili (1.2 %).[12]

Hindi in Devanagari script is designated by the Constitution as the official language of the Union (Art. 343(1)). States may legislate any one or more of the languages in use in the state or Hindi as the language(s) to be used for official purposes (Art. 345 Const.). Originally, the Constitution also provided for English as a secondary official language of the Union, which was to be gradually phased out

---

[7] Census 2011, Provisional Population Totals, Paper 1, India, p. 38.

[8] CIA World Factbook, India: People and Society.

[9] Census 2011, Provisional Population Totals, Paper 1, India, pp. 38, 45, 58–59.

[10] Census 2011, Provisional Population Totals, Paper 1, India, pp. 62–67, 80–81.

[11] CIA World Factbook. India: People and Society.

[12] Census Data 2001, General Note and Statement 5 on Comparative Speakers' Strength of Scheduled Languages – 1971, 1981, 1991 and 2001.

over a fifteen-year period, starting from the entry into force of the Constitution (Art. 343(2)) in 1950. The Official Languages Act, 1963, however, provides that English shall continue to function as the secondary official language until resolutions for its discontinuance have been passed by all states that do not have Hindi as the official language, following which each House of Parliament must pass a resolution to this effect (Sec. 3). Notwithstanding its subsidiary official status, English is the most important language for purposes of commerce, politics, and national communication.[13]

As per the provisional population totals of the 2011 census, the literacy rate for persons ages seven and above was 74.0 %. There was a marked gender disparity in literacy levels (males: 82.1 %; females 65.5 %), though the census data 2011 indicates that this gender gap is shrinking.[14] According to a 2015 estimate, 81.3 % of males and 60.6 % of females ages 15 and over could read and write.[15]

c) Religion

The Preamble to the Constitution declares India a secular republic. Arts. 25–28 Const. further provide for the fundamental right to freedom of religion.

India is home to a bewildering array of religions and faiths. Hinduism is professed by the majority of the population, commanding 828 million followers (80.5 % of the population) as per the 2001 census. Other prominent religions are Islam (13.4 %), Christianity (2.3 %), Sikhism (1.9 %), Buddhism (0.80 %), and Jainism (0.4 %). In the 2001 census, over 6 million people also reported professing other religions and faiths, including tribal religions.[16]

3. Economy

As of 1 June 2017, the Indian economy was the seventh largest in the world measured in nominal US dollars, but the third largest according to purchasing power parity exchange rates.[17] India has a highly diversified economy, with a sizeable private sector that co-exists with a large public sector.[18] The 1990s saw a wave of economic reforms towards liberalization being introduced by the government, including the deregulation of industries, privatization of state-owned enterprises,

---

13 CIA World Factbook, India: People and Society.

14 Census 2011, Provisional Population Totals, Paper 1, p. 101.

15 CIA World Factbook, India: People and Society.

16 Census Data 2001, India at a glance, Religious Composition.

17 The Economist Intelligence Unit. India: Country fact sheet.

18 The Economist Intelligence Unit. India: Country fact sheet.

and reduced controls on foreign investment and trade.[19] These reforms have borne fruit, as evidenced by robust economic growth, which enabled India to withstand the global financial crisis of 2007–2008: the estimated level of growth in real GDP in 2012–2016 was 5.7 %.[20] In 2015–2016, general inflation declined for the second straight year.[21]

While almost half of the population was employed in the agricultural sector in 2012 (2012 estimate),[22] the main driver of economic growth is the services sector: the services sector registered a growth of 9.2 % in 2015–2016 (advanced estimate), following growth of 10.3 % in 2014–2015 and 7.8 % in 2013–2014.[23]

According to the Employment Survey 2015-16, the unemployment rate (i.e., the percentage of persons ages 15 and above who were available for work but could not get work during the reference period) was estimated to be 5.0 %, with unemployment in the rural sector at 5.1 % and in the urban sector at 4.9 %. The unemployment rate was significantly higher among women (8.7 %) than among men (4.0 %).[24] Long-term economic concerns for India include widespread poverty and the lack of adequate infrastructure and social, educational, and health services.[25]

4. System of government

The Constitution of India, which came into force on 26 January 1950, declares India a sovereign, socialist, secular, democratic republic (Preamble). It provides for a parliamentary form of government. India is a union of states (Art. 1 Const.); it is a federal republic, which has distinct unitary features.[26]

India is administratively divided into 29 states and seven centrally administered union territories. These are Andhra Pradesh, Arunachal Pradesh, Assam, Bihar, Chhattisgarh, Goa, Gujarat, Haryana, Himachal Pradesh, Jammu and Kashmir, Jharkhand, Karnataka, Kerala, Madhya Pradesh, Maharashtra, Manipur, Meghalaya, Mizoram, Nagaland, Odisha, Punjab, Rajasthan, Sikkim, Tamil Nadu, Telangana, Tripura, Uttar Pradesh, Uttarakhand, West Bengal (states) and Andaman and

---

19 CIA World Factbook. India: Economy.

20 The Economist Intelligence Unit. India: Country fact sheet.

21 Government of India, State of the Economy, in: Economic Survey 2015-16, p. 16.

22 CIA World Factbook: India. Economy.

23 Government of India, Services Sector, in: Economic Survey 2015-16, pp. 155–156.

24 Government of India. Report on Fifth Annual Employment-Unemployment Survey (2015-16), pp. v, 32.

25 CIA World Factbook: India. Economy.

26 Government of India: Constitution. National Portal of India.

Nicobar Islands, Chandigarh, Dadra and Nagar Haveli, Daman and Diu, Delhi, Lakshadweep, Puducherry (union territories).[27]

The central government is divided into three main organs: the legislature, the executive, and the judiciary, each performing distinct but interrelated functions.

– *Legislature*

The Parliament[28] is the supreme legislative body of India and consists of a bicameral legislature – comprising the *Lok Sabha* (House of the People) and the *Rajya Sabha* (Council of States) – and the president of India (Art. 79 Const.). The *Lok Sabha*, the lower house, consists of representatives of the people who are directly elected on the basis of universal adult suffrage. The maximum strength of the *Lok Sabha* is 552 members (at most 530 representing the states, at most 20 representing the union territories, and at most two members nominated by the president from the Anglo-Indian community) (Arts. 81, 331 Const.). The general term of the House is five years, but if the government loses its majority, the president may dissolve it earlier and call for elections. Its term may also be extended in yearly increments by Parliament during a proclamation of emergency (Arts. 83, 85 Const.).

The *Rajya Sabha*, the upper house, is a permanent body consisting of a maximum of 250 members: at most 238 representing the states and union territories and 12 members nominated by the president for their expertise in fields such as literature, science, art, and social service (Art. 80 Const.). The term of each member is six years, and one-third of the members retire every second year to be replaced by newly elected members (Art. 83 Const.).

The *Rajya Sabha* plays a generally subordinate role to the *Lok Sabha* in the legislative process, as money bills involving taxation and expenditure can only be introduced in the *Lok Sabha* (Arts. 107, 109 Const.). Furthermore, the Council of Ministers, the highest policy-making body in the government, is responsible to the *Lok Sabha* (Art. 75 Const.).

The Constitution distributes legislative powers between the central Parliament and the state legislatures as per the lists of entries in the Seventh Schedule to the Constitution (Art. 246): List I (Union List), List II (State List), and List III (Concurrent List). The residuary powers vest in the Parliament. The Parliament has the exclusive authority to make laws on any matter pertaining to the subjects in the Union List, which includes defence, foreign affairs, interstate commerce, banking, communications, and transportation. Moreover, on any matter falling within the Concurrent List, laws made by Parliament enjoy precedence over those passed by state legislatures (Art. 254 Const.). The Parliament is also vested with the authority

---

[27] Know India, States and Union Territories.

[28] See generally Library of Congress, Country Profile: India, pp. 15–16.

to impeach the president (Art. 61 Const.) and to remove judges of Supreme and High Courts (Arts. 124, 217 Const.), the chief election commissioner (Art. 324 Const.), and the comptroller and auditor general (Art. 148 Const.) in accordance with the procedure laid down in the Constitution. It can also initiate amendments to the Constitution (Art. 368 Const.).

– *Executive*

The president exercises the executive power of the Union[29] and is the supreme commander of the armed forces (Art. 53 Const.). He or she is elected for a term of five years by an electoral college consisting of elected members of both Houses of Parliament and elected members of the legislative assemblies of the states and union territories (Arts. 54–56 Const.). The president appoints the prime ministers and the cabinet of ministers (Art. 7 Const.), governors of states and union territories (Arts. 155, 239 Const.), judges of the Supreme Court and High Courts (Arts. 124, 217 Const.), and diplomatic representatives. Presidential ordinances issued when Parliament is not in session have the force of acts of Parliament (Art. 123 Const.). The president also summons and prorogues Parliament and has the authority to dissolve the *Lok Sabha* as well as dismiss state governments (Arts. 85, 352 and 356 Const.).

In practice, however, the president's powers are fairly limited, as he or she is required to act in accordance with the advice of the Council of Ministers headed by the prime minister, in whom the real executive authority rests (Art. 74 Const.). The prime minister is generally appointed by the president from the party that commands a majority in the Parliament. The president also appoints members of the Council of Ministers selected by the prime minister who are either members of the Parliament, or must become members within six months of their selection (Art. 75 Const.).

– *Judiciary*

The Supreme Court is the highest judicial authority in the country[30] and is the ultimate interpreter of the Constitution and the laws of the land. It has original and exclusive jurisdiction to resolve disputes between the central government and one or more states and union territories as well as between different states and union territories (Art. 131 Const.). It can also hear appeals from all civil and criminal proceedings in the High Courts that involve a substantial question of law concerning the interpretation of the Constitution (Arts. 132–134 Const.). The president can refer matters to the Supreme Court for an advisory ruling on issues of fact and law

---

29 See generally Library of Congress, Country Profile: India, pp. 15–16.

30 See generally Library of Congress, Country Profile: India, p. 16.

that are of public importance (Art. 143 Const.). In addition, the Court can grant special leave to appeal on any matter from any court except those relating to the armed forces (Art. 136 Const.).

The Supreme Court consists of the chief justice, who is appointed by the president of India, and 30 other judges appointed by the president in consultation with the chief justice and with other judges of the Supreme Court and High Courts as the president deems necessary (Art. 124 Const. and The Supreme Court [Number of Judges] Amendment Act, 2008). Judges hold office until they reach the mandatory retirement age of 65; they can only be removed from office by a presidential order after a formal statement charging "proved misbehaviour or incapacity" that is supported by a majority of the total membership of each House of Parliament and by a majority of at least two-thirds of the members in attendance has been passed (Art. 124 Const.).

The organization of government at the state level mirrors the structure at the central level. Each state has a Legislative Assembly (the counterpart to the *Lok Sabha*) and some states also have an upper house called the State Legislative Council (Art. 168 Const.). Executive power vests in the governor, who is the head of the state appointed by the president (Arts. 154, 155 Const.). The governor is advised by the Council of Ministers headed by the chief minister in the exercise of his or her executive functions (Art. 163 Const.). The Council of Ministers is collectively responsible to the Legislative Assembly (Art. 164 Const.).

5. Crime and criminal prosecution

a) Investigating authorities

The Code of Criminal Procedure, 1973 (CrPC) defines investigation in the following terms:

Sec. 2 CrPC Definitions

(a)–(g) […]

(h) "Investigation" includes all the proceedings under this Code for the collection of evidence conducted by a police officer or by any person (other than a Magistrate) who is authorized by a Magistrate in this behalf.

(i)–(y) […]

The chief investigative agency is the police, which is tasked with maintaining public order and preventing and detecting crime. Under Art. 246 Const. read with the Seventh Schedule, the police is designated a state subject; thus, each state has its own police force governed by the rules framed by the respective state governments and contained in each state's police manual. Despite this decentralization, there are strong common elements in the diverse police forces for a number of reasons: first, the organization and operation of the state police forces are governed by the Police Act, 1861, a central piece of legislation that is still applicable in most parts of the country, or by State Police Acts that are modelled largely on the 1861 Act; second, the main laws dealing with crime, including the Indian Penal Code, 1860 (IPC), the Code of Criminal Procedure, and the Indian Evidence Act, 1872, are also almost uniformly applied throughout the country; third, the majority of senior offices in the state police forces is supplied by the Indian Police Service, which is one of the three all-India civil services managed by the central government; fourth, due to India's federal polity, the central government plays a coordinating role in police matters.[31]

At the state level, the director general is the head of the police. States are divided into administrative units called districts with the district police force headed by the superintendent. A group of districts forms a range, which is under the command of the deputy inspector general, and in some states two or more ranges comprise a zone, which is looked after by an inspector general. Districts are divided into subdivisions in the charge of an assistant or deputy superintendent of police. Each subdivision is further divided into a number of police stations that constitute the basic unit of police administration in a district. The inspector is the officer in charge of a police station, especially in cities and metropolitan areas, whereas rural areas and smaller police stations are usually headed by a sub-inspector.[32] The total strength of the state police forces has increased steadily over the years and was 2.28 million in 2016.[33]

Recruitment to the state police generally takes place at three levels – constable, sub-inspector/assistant sub-inspector, and deputy superintendent. Furthermore, the assistant superintendent is recruited through the Indian Police Service. The constable is the lowest rank in the police force and is recruited directly; other positions are filled through direct recruitment or promotion. The qualifications for recruitment to the rank of constable can differ: while some states require high school level education, for others, primary or middle school level education is sufficient. This is despite the recommendations of the Committee on Police Training (1973) and the National Police Commission (1980) prescribing the high school examination as the minimum qualification. Sub-inspectors and deputy superintendents are generally required to be college graduates, though states such as Andhra Pradesh, Sikkim, and Tripura relax this requirement. The National Police Commission recommends a minimum age of 17 for a constable's recruitment, with 21 years as the maximum, but again, the implementation of these recommendations varies from state to state.

---

[31] Commonwealth Human Rights Initiative, Police Organisation in India 2015, p. 6.

[32] Commonwealth Human Rights Initiative, Police Organisation in India 2015, pp. 7, 18.

[33] Bureau of Police Research and Development, Data on Police Organisations: Basic Police Data (2016), Table 3.1, p. 31.

For sub-inspectors, the minimum age limit is 19 to 21 years whereas the maximum varies from 24 to 31 years.[34]

Pursuant to the Code of Criminal Procedure, all offences must be registered at the police station, which then forms the centre for all subsequent preventive and investigative work (Secs. 154–155).[35] The procedure for investigation differs depending on the classification of the offence. In the case of cognizable offences, the police officer can arrest an alleged offender without a warrant and can investigate the matter without orders or directions from a magistrate (Secs. 156(1) and 157 CrPC). For non-cognizable offences, the police officer generally needs a warrant to carry out an arrest and can only commence investigation after authorization from a judicial magistrate (Sec. 155(2) read with Sec. 3(1)(a) CrPC). A judicial magistrate may order the police to investigate a non-cognizable offence if warranted (Sec. 155(2) and (3) CrPC).[36]

The state police forces usually have specialized departments, such as the Intelligence Department, the State Armed Police, and the State Crime Records Bureau, in order to efficiently discharge their functions.[37] The most important of these is the Criminal Investigation Department, which is the premier investigative agency of the state police and generally investigates specialized crimes, such as organized and inter-state crime, and other major crimes that may be transferred to it by the government or the head of the police force.[38]

While the police and public order are state subjects under the Constitution, as per Art. 246 read with the Seventh Schedule, the central government through the Ministry of Home Affairs nonetheless possesses the competence to legislate with respect to central paramilitary forces (List I, Entry 2A), the Central Bureau of Intelligence and Investigation (List I, Entry 8), the union agencies responsible for training of police officers and providing research or assistance related to crime investigation (List I, Entry 65), the all-India services (List I, Entry 70), and extension of jurisdiction of members of state police forces (List I, Entry 80).[39]

The central government has thus established a number of central police organisations under the Ministry of Home Affairs. One set of these consists of the Central Armed Police Forces, such as the Assam Rifles, Border Security Force, Central Industrial Security Force, Central Reserve Police Force, Indo-Tibetan Border Police, and the National Security Guards. These are specialized forces set up under

---

34 Commonwealth Human Rights Initiative, Police Organisation in India 2015, pp. 41–45.

35 Commonwealth Human Rights Initiative, Police Organisation in India 2015, p. 23.

36 On the categories of crimes, see generally II.C.1.b.

37 Commonwealth Human Rights Initiative, Police Organisation in India 2015, pp. 31–35.

38 Commonwealth Human Rights Initiative, Police Organisation in India, pp. 31–32.

39 Commonwealth Human Rights Initiative, Police Organisation in India 2015, pp. 59–60.

different central legislations and have specific mandates.[40] The other set comprises organisations such as the Bureau of Police Research and Development, the Central Bureau of Investigation (CBI), Directorate of Coordination of Police Wireless, Intelligence Bureau, National Crime Records Bureau, National Institute of Criminology and Forensic Science, and the National Police Academy.[41]

Of these, the CBI is the elite investigating agency set up under the Delhi Special Police Establishment Act, 1946. It investigates crimes that are specified by the central government under Sec. 3 of the Act. Specialized divisions within the CBI are in charge of some of the most high-profile cases that significantly impact the nation: the Anti-Corruption Division, the Economic Offences Division, and the Special Crimes Division.[42]

The total number of reported cognizable crimes in India in 2015 was 7,326,099, comprising 2,949,400 offences under the IPC (40.3 %) and 4,376,699 offences under special and local laws (59.7 %). The number of persons arrested was 8,493,826 (3,636,596 for IPC crimes and 4,857,230 for crimes under special and local laws). Violent crimes accounted for 11.4 % of IPC crimes, while property crimes constituted 21.2 % of IPC crimes. The conviction rate for crimes under the IPC was 46.9 %.[43]

b) Prosecuting authorities

List III of the Seventh Schedule of the Constitution (Concurrent List) contains items subject to legislation by both the central and the state legislatures. All matters relating to criminal procedure, including the prosecution system, are concurrent subjects (List III, Entry 2). The Code of Criminal Procedure designates the public prosecutor as the prosecuting agency in respect of cognizable offences; in the case of non-cognizable offences, a private party may launch a prosecution by filing a private complaint in the court of the judicial magistrate.[44]

A public prosecutor is any person who is so appointed under Sec. 24 CrPC and includes any person acting under the directions of a public prosecutor (Sec. 2(u) CrPC). In the case of High Courts, the central or the state government appoints a public prosecutor and one or more additional public prosecutors in consultation with the High Court for conducting prosecutions, appeals, and other proceedings on

---

40 Commonwealth Human Rights Initiative, Police Organisation in India 2015, pp. 61–70.

41 Commonwealth Human Rights Initiative, Police Organisation in India 2015, pp. 61, 72–81.

42 Commonwealth Human Rights Initiative, Police Organisation in India 2015, pp. 73–75.

43 National Crime Records Bureau, Crime in India 2015. Snapshots, pp. 1–7.

44 *Palkar*, in: Dupont/Fijnaut (eds.), International Encyclopaedia of Laws: Criminal Law, p. 33. See below 5.c. on the structure of criminal courts. See also II.C.1.b. on the categorisation of offences.

behalf of the central or state governments. Public prosecutors may also be appointed by the central government for conducting cases in any district or local area, and state governments must appoint a public prosecutor and if needed, an additional public prosecutor for the district. State governments may make this appointment either from a panel of persons prepared by the district magistrate in consultation with the sessions judge, or, in cases where a regular cadre of prosecuting officers exists, from that cadre. In order to be appointed a public prosecutor or an additional public prosecutor, a person must have been in practice as an advocate for at least seven years; a special public prosecutor appointed by the central or state government for the purposes of a specific case or class of cases must have been in practice as an advocate for at least ten years (Sec. 24 CrPC).

In the courts of magistrates, one or more assistant public prosecutors shall be appointed by the state government in every district for conducting prosecutions. The central government may also appoint one or more assistant public prosecutors for conducting any case or class of cases. In the event that no assistant public prosecutor is available for a case, the district magistrate may appoint any other person to the position for the case, including a police officer, as long as he or she has not been involved in the investigation with respect to the case and is at least of the rank of inspector (Sec. 25 CrPC).

The prosecutor's role in the criminal trial is not merely to secure a conviction at all costs; rather, the prosecutor is expected to act impartially and to place all the evidence, irrespective of whether it favours the accused, before the court to assist the court in arriving at a decision.[45]

While the settled jurisprudence of the courts emphasizes the independence of the prosecutor from the executive as well as from the investigative agencies, the precise nature of the relationship between the prosecutor and these other authorities has been an issue of repeated controversy.[46] This is despite the fact that one of the intentions behind the enactment of the current provisions of the Code of Criminal Procedure was to do away with the previous system, under which prosecutors functioned under the control of the police department, and to render the prosecution and the police completely independent of each other.[47]

c) Criminal courts

The structure of criminal courts consists of the Supreme Court at the apex, the High Courts of states, and a series of subordinate courts provided for in the Code of

---

[45] *Pillai*, R.V. Kelkar's Criminal Procedure, pp. 27–28.

[46] See Law Commission of India, 197th Report on Public Prosecutor's Appointments (2006); Government of India, Ministry of Home Affairs, Report of the Committee on Reforms of Criminal Justice System (2003), pp. 125–129.

[47] *Menon*, in: Asian Development Bank, Strengthening the Criminal Justice System, p. 28.

Criminal Procedure. The following categories of criminal courts are recognized: courts of session; judicial magistrates of the first class and, in any metropolitan area, metropolitan magistrates; judicial magistrates of the second class; and executive magistrates (Sec. 6 CrPC). The hierarchy of the criminal courts is as follows:[48]

Supreme Court ↓				
High Courts ↓				
Sessions Courts (Sessions Judge, Additional Sessions Judge)				
Assistant Sessions Judge	Chief Metropolitan Magistrate ↓		Chief Judicial Magistrate ↓	
	(Additional Chief Metropolitan Magistrate)		Sub-Divisional Judicial Magistrates	
	Metropolitan Magistrates	Special Metropolitan Magistrates (Honorary) (Additional Chief Judicial Magistrate)	Judicial Magistrates of first class	Special Judicial Magistrates of first class
			Judicial Magistrates of second class	Special Judicial Magistrate of second class

In addition, special criminal courts may be authorized under special criminal laws to deal with the cases that arise under them. An example are the special courts constituted under Sec. 11 of the National Investigation Agency Act, 2008, which have jurisdiction over the offences in the Act.

For each offence contained in the Indian Penal Code, the First Schedule to the CrPC enumerates the courts by which it may be tried. The court of sessions is the highest court at the district level and has the power to impose any sentence, including capital punishment. In each district, the High Court appoints a judicial magistrate of the first class as the chief judicial magistrate (Sec. 12 CrPC), who may pass a sentence of imprisonment of up to seven years and a fine. A judicial magistrate of the first class has the power to pass a sentence of imprisonment of up to three years and a fine of up to Rupees 5,000 (USD 77.3)[49] whereas the corresponding authority of a judicial magistrate of the second class is a sentence of imprisonment up to one

---

48 *Pillai*, R.V. Kelkar's Criminal Procedure, p. 18.

49 64.7 Rupees = 1 USD (as of 31 March 2017, source: U.S. Department of the Treasury, https://www.fiscal.treasury.gov/fsreports/rpt/treasRptRateExch/currentRates.htm [last visited June 2017]).

year and a fine of up to Rupees 1,000 (USD 15.5). Executive magistrates perform mainly police or administrative functions.[50]

In 2015, there were 10,502,256 cases for trials (including pending cases from the previous years). The percentage of cases in which trial was completed was 12.6. The total number of crimes under the IPC that were compounded/withdrawn from trial or for which trial was completed in 2015 was 1,325,989, of which 11.4 % were violent crime cases.[51]

d) Criminal penalties

Chapter III IPC provides for the following categories of punishment: death, life imprisonment, rigorous (with hard labour) and simple imprisonment, forfeiture of property, and fine (Sec. 53).

The death penalty is a matter of some controversy in India; it is imposed only exceptionally, in the rarest of rare cases.[52] Under the IPC, capital punishment may be awarded for specific offences against the government (Secs. 121, 132), offences against lawful justice (Secs. 194, 195A), and offences against persons (Secs. 302, 303, 305, 307, 364A and 396). In addition, a number of special legislations primarily dealing with offences related to the armed forces, narcotic substances, and terrorism also provide for the death penalty.[53] According to prison statistics compiled by the National Crime Records Bureau, 101 persons were sentenced to death in 2015.[54]

Imprisonment for life generally connotes imprisonment for the natural life term of a convict (Sec. 45 IPC),[55] though as per the provisions of the Penal Code and the Code of Criminal Procedure, the appropriate government has the power to commute the punishment to a term not exceeding 14 years (Sec. 55 IPC and Sec. 433A CrPC).

The IPC provides for a range of the sentence that may be imposed for each offence, and within these limits, the courts have wide discretion to impose sentences depending on the circumstances of the case. A minimum sentence is prescribed only for a few offences, such as murder (Sec. 302 IPC) and waging war against the

---

50 *Palkar*, in: Dupont/Fijnaut (eds.), International Encyclopaedia of Laws: Criminal Law, pp. 34–35.

51 National Crime Records Bureau, Crime in India 2015, Table 4(B), p. 76, Table 3(A), p. 55.

52 *Bachan Singh v State of Punjab*, (1983) 1 SCR 145.

53 Amnesty International India and People's Union for Civil Liberties, Lethal Lottery: the Death Penalty in India (2008), pp. 28, 30–31.

54 National Crime Records Bureau, Prison Statistics India 2015, pp. ii, 117.

55 *Ramraj v State of Chhattisgarh*, 2009(14) SCALE 533.

government (Sec. 121 IPC).[56] In the case of offences punishable with rigorous imprisonment involving hard labour, the court has the discretion to order that the offender serve some part of it, not exceeding a period of three months, in solitary confinement. If the term of imprisonment is six months, the period of solitary confinement cannot exceed one month; for imprisonment ranging from six months to one year, solitary confinement cannot exceed two months; the maximum period of solitary confinement is three months for imprisonment that exceeds one year (Sec. 73 IPC).

The distribution of the length of sentences of the total prison population in 2015 was as follows: death penalty (0.3 %); life imprisonment (55.8 %), 10–13 years (13.8 %), 7–9 years (8.5 %), 5–6 years (5.9 %), 2–4 years (5.4 %), 1–2 years (3.7 %), 6 months to 1 year (2.5 %).[57]

While forfeiture of property is provided as a punishment for relatively few offences – for example, committing depredation on territories of power at peace with the government of India (Sec. 126 IPC) and receiving property taken by war or depredation (Sec. 127 IPC) – fines are generally permissible as penalties for every offence under the IPC, usually alongside other forms of punishment but in exceptional cases as the only punishment, for example, illegal payments in connection with an election (Sec. 171H IPC).[58]

In addition to these generally applicable punishments, certain special penalties, such as confiscation of property, publication of the sentence, and deprivation of certain civil and political rights (such as the right to hold political office), may be imposed for conviction of specific offences or under special legislations.[59]

Furthermore, certain provisions of the Indian Penal Code, the Code of Criminal Procedure, and some special acts provide for preventive and corrective measures that may be applied as an alternative to, or as a substitute for, traditional penal sanctions. For instance, the Juvenile Justice (Care and Protection of Children) Act, 2000 (JJA) has been enacted with a view to the provision of proper care, treatment, and protection of juveniles and the establishment of institutions to facilitate their rehabilitation.[60] If a juvenile is found to have committed an offence by the Juvenile Justice Board, the Board may pass a series of orders ranging from counselling to confinement in a special home (Sec. 15 JJA): the Board may allow the juvenile to go home after advice or admonition; may direct group counselling and participation in other similar activities; may order community service; may order the juvenile or

---

[56] *Gaur*, Textbook on Indian Penal Code, pp. 105–106.

[57] National Crime Records Bureau, Prison Statistics India 2015, p. 117.

[58] See *Palkar*, in: Dupont/Fijnaut (eds.), International Encyclopaedia of Laws: Criminal Law, pp. 126–127.

[59] See *Palkar*, in: Dupont/Fijnaut (eds.), International Encyclopaedia of Laws: Criminal Law, pp. 127–131.

[60] Preamble, Juvenile Justice (Care and Protection of Children) Act, 2000.

his or her parent to pay a fine; may direct release on probation of good conduct and place juvenile under the care of a parent, guardian, or any fit institution; or may order the juvenile to be sent to a special home.

In 2015, 39,074 juveniles were arrested for crimes under the Indian Penal Code (94.4 %) and 2,311 were arrested for crimes under special and local laws (5.6 %) and sent to various courts.[61] Of these, 38.2 % were awaiting trial at the end of 2015; 13.0 % were disposed of after advice or admonition; 15.6 % were placed under care of parents or guardians; 3.4 % were sent to institutions; 17.1 % were sent to special homes; 4.6 % were fined; and 8.1 % were either acquitted or their cases were otherwise dealt with.[62]

Special measures may also be applied to individuals such as mentally ill offenders, habitual offenders, and vagrants and beggars. For example, a police officer may take a person believed to be mentally ill into custody and produce the person before a magistrate for medical examination and subsequent detention in a psychiatric hospital or nursing home (Secs. 23 and 24 Mental Health Act, 1987). Habitual offenders, who accounted for 3.0 % of the total number of admitted convicts in 2015,[63] may be required by a judicial magistrate to execute a bond with or without surety as a security for good behaviour for a period not exceeding three years as a preventive measure (Sec. 110 CrPC). State legislation, such as the Bombay Prevention of Begging Act, 1959, provides for certified institutions for the detention, training, and employment of beggars and their dependants.[64]

e) Execution of custodial penalties

The primary institutions for the execution of custodial penalties in India are prisons. While the main legislations governing prisons, the Prisons Act, 1894 and the Prisoners Act, 1900, are central legislations, prisons, reformatories, and borstal institutions are classified as a state subject under the Constitution (Seventh Schedule [Art. 246], List II, Entry 4).

Prisons thus fall within the exclusive management and administration of state governments, and the states have the authority to frame laws, rules, and regulations with respect to prison administration. Prison establishments in India fall into several categories: the most common institutions are central jails, district jails, and sub jails, and the various states and union territories have different criteria for the clas-

---

61 National Crime Records Bureau, Crime in India 2015, p. 132.

62 National Crime Records Bureau, Crime in India 2015, p. 135.

63 National Crime Records Bureau, Prison Statistics 2015, p. 32.

64 See *Palkar*, in: Dupont/Fijnaut (eds.), International Encyclopaedia of Laws: Criminal Law, pp. 133–136.

sification of institutions into these categories. Other institutions include women jails, borstal schools, open jails, and special jails.[65]

According to the 2015 Crime Statistics provided by the National Crime Records Bureau, the total number of jails in India was 1,401. Central jails, which have larger capacities than other jails and generally house prisoners with longer sentences, numbered 134. They also have rehabilitation facilities. There were 379 district jails serving as the main prisons in some of the states and union territories, and 741 sub jails. Only 13 states/union territories had women jails exclusively for women prisoners, numbering 18. There were 63 open jails, which are minimum security prisons where prisoners with good behaviour who satisfy certain norms are confined and engage in agricultural activities. Special jails house particular classes of prisoners, including habitual and violent offenders. In 2015, India had 43 special jails. There were also 20 borstal schools, which are not jails proper and whose primary purpose is the care and rehabilitation of young offenders. These provide education and various kinds of vocational training to delinquents. Finally, there were three "other" jails in various states/union territories in 2015.[66]

Overcrowding is a matter of significant concern for Indian prisons. While the total prison capacity at the end of 2015 was 366,781,[67] the total number of inmates at the end of 2015 was recorded as 419,623 (with males accounting for 95.7 % and females for 4.3 % of the population).[68] The occupancy level, based on official capacity) was 114.4 %.[69] The prison population rate (the number of persons per 100,000 of the national population) at the end of 2015 was 33.[70] The prisons house different categories of inmates: convicts, that is, prisoners serving sentences (32.0 %); undertrial prisoners, that is, persons kept in judicial custody while the charges against them are being tried (67.2 %); and detenues, that is, persons who are detained in prisons under relevant preventive detention laws (0.6 %).[71] The large number of undertrial prisoners also constitutes a worrying feature of prisons.

At the end of 2015, out of a total of 118,746 prisoners convicted of various crimes under the IPC, 59.6 % were convicted of murder. There were 15,217 prisoners who had been convicted of offences under special and local laws, with 47.5 % having been convicted under the Narcotic Drugs and Psychotropic Substances Act, 1985.[72]

---

65 Commonwealth Human Rights Initiative, the Prison System in India.

66 National Crime Records Bureau, Prison Statistics 2015, Table 1.2, p. 10.

67 National Crime Records Bureau, Prison Statistics 2015, Table 2(A), p. 15.

68 National Crime Records Bureau, Prison Statistics 2015, Table 2.1, p. 20.

69 National Crime Records Bureau, Prison Statistics 2015, Table 2.1, p. 20.

70 World Prison Brief, India.

71 National Crime Records Bureau, Prison Statistics 2015, p. 29.

72 National Crime Records Bureau, Prison Statistics 2015, p. 73.

Bibliography and further reading

General references:

CIA World Factbook: India, https://www.cia.gov/library/publications/the-world-factbook/geos/in.html [last visited June 2017].

National Portal of India, https://india.gov.in [last visited June 2017].

Geography:

CIA World Factbook: India, Geography, https://www.cia.gov/library/publications/the-world-factbook/geos/in.html [last visited June 2017].

Know India, National Portal of India: Profile, https://india.gov.in/india-glance/profile [last visited June 2017].

Population:

Census 2011, Provisional Population Totals Paper 1, http://www.censusindia.gov.in/2011-prov-results/prov_results_paper1_india.html [last visited June 2017].

Census Data 2001, General Note, http://www.censusindia.gov.in/Census_Data_2001/Census_Data_Online/Language/gen_note.html [last visited June 2017].

Census Date 2001, Statement on Comparative Speakers' Strength of Scheduled Languages – 1971, 1981, 1991 and 2001, http://www.censusindia.gov.in/Census_Data_2001/Census_Data_Online/Language/Statement5.aspx [last visited June 2017].

Census Data 2001, India at a glance, Religious Composition, http://censusindia.gov.in/Census_Data_2001/India_at_glance/religion.aspx [last visited June 2017].

CIA World Factbook. India: People and Society, https://www.cia.gov/library/publications/the-world-factbook/geos/in.html [last visited June 2017].

Know India, National Portal of India: Profile, https://india.gov.in/india-glance/profile [last visited June 2017].

Economy:

CIA World Factbook. India: Economy, https://www.cia.gov/library/publications/the-world-factbook/geos/in.html [last visited June 2017].

The Economist Intelligence Unit, India, Country fact sheet. 1 June 2017, http://country.eiu.com/article.aspx?articleid=614574245&Country=India&topic=Summary&subtopic=Fact+sheet [last visited June 2017].

Government of India (Labour Bureau), Report on Fifth Annual Employment-Unemployment Survey, 2015-16, vol. I, http://labourbureaunew.gov.in/UserContent/EUS_5th_1.pdf [last visited June 2017].

Government of India, Services Sector. In: Economic Survey 2015-16, vol. II, http://www.indiabudget.nic.in/budget2016-2017/es2015-16/echapvol2-07.pdf [last visited June 2017].

Government of India, State of the Economy: An Overview. In: Economic Survey 2015-16, vol. II, http://indiabudget.nic.in/es2015-16/echapvol2-01.pdf [last visited June 2017].

System of government:

Government of India (Ministry of Law and Justice): Constitution. National Portal of India, http://lawmin.nic.in/olwing/coi/coi-english/coi-4March2016.pdf [last visited June 2017].

Know India, States and Union Territories, http://knowindia.gov.in/knowindia/state_uts.php [last visited June 2017].

Library of Congress, Federal Research Division, Country Profile: India, Dec. 2004. https://www.loc.gov/rr/frd/cs/profiles/India.pdf [last visited June 2017].

Investigating authorities:

Bureau of Police Research and Development, Data on Police Organizations: Basic Police Data (2016), http://bprd.nic.in/content/62_1_DataonPoliceOrganizations.aspx [last visited June 2017].

Commonwealth Human Rights Initiative, Police Organisation in India, Dec. 2015. http://www.humanrightsinitiative.org/publication/police-organisation-in-india [last visited June 2017].

National Crime Records Bureau, Crime in India 2015. Snapshots, http://ncrb.nic.in/StatPublications/CII/CII2015/FILES/Snapshots-11.11.16.pdf [last visited June 2017].

Prosecuting authorities:

Law Commission of India, 197th Report on Public Prosecutor's Appointments (2006).

Menon, N.R. Madhava, Public Prosecution Service in India: An Institution in Need of Reform. In: Asian Development Bank, Strengthening the Criminal Justice System. 2006, pp. 24–33. http://www.adb.org/sites/default/files/publication/29047/strengthening-criminal-justice-system.pdf [last visited June 2017].

National Crime Records Bureau, Crime in India 2015 (Disposal of Cases by Police and Courts), http://ncrb.nic.in/ [last visited June 2017].

Palkar, Vineeta Vinayak, India. In Liewen Dupont/Cyrille Fijnaut (eds.), International Encyclopaedia of Laws: Criminal Law. Vol 3, Suppl. 22. The Hague 2001.

Pillai, K.N. Chandrasekharan, R.V. Kelkar's Criminal Procedure. 5th ed. Lucknow 2008 (repr. 2011).

Criminal courts:

Palkar, Vineeta Vinayak, India. In Liewen Dupont/Cyrille Fijnaut (eds.), International Encyclopaedia of Laws: Criminal Law, vol 3, Suppl. 22. The Hague 2001.

Pillai, K.N. Chandrasekharan, R.V. Kelkar's Criminal Procedure. 5th ed. Lucknow 2008 (repr. 2011).

National Crime Records Bureau, Crime in India 2015, http://ncrb.nic.in/ [last visited June 2015].

Criminal penalties:

Amnesty International India and People's Union for Civil Liberties, Lethal Lottery: the Death Penalty in India. 2008, https://www.amnesty.org/en/documents/ASA20/007/2008/en/ [last visited June 2017].

Bachan Singh v State of Punjab, (1983) 1 SCR 145.

Gaur, K.D., Textbook on Indian Penal Code. 4th ed. New Delhi 2009 (repr. 2011).

National Crime Records Bureau, Crime in India 2015, http://ncrb.nic.in/ [last visited June 2015].

National Crime Records Bureau, Prison Statistics India 2015, http://ncrb.nic.in/Stat Publications/PSI/Prison2015/PrisonStat2015.htm [last visited June 2017].

Palkar, Vineeta Vinayak, India. In Liewen Dupont/Cyrille Fijnaut (eds.), International Encyclopaedia of Laws: Criminal Law, vol 3, Suppl. 22. The Hague 2001, pp. 124–136.

Ramraj v. State of Chhattisgarh, 2009(14) SCALE 533.

Execution of custodial penalties:

Commonwealth Human Rights Initiative, the Prison System in India. http://humanrights initiative.org/old/index.php?option=com_content&view=article&id=109&Itemid=122 [last visited June 2017].

National Crime Records Bureau, Prison Statistics 2015. http://ncrb.nic.in/StatPublications/ PSI/Prison2015/PrisonStat2015.htm [last visited June 2017].

World Prison Brief, India, http://www.prisonstudies.org/country/india [last visited June 2017].

B. Comparative legal classification and international ties

1. Comparative legal classification

India is a common law country.[1] The common law has been defined as a body of law that "consists in the applying to new combinations of circumstances those rules of law which we derive from legal principles and judicial precedents."[2] Some of the most prominent features of the common law system are trial by jury, the adversarial system of trial, and the system of precedents. These features can be found to greater or lesser degrees in most of the legal systems generally considered to belong to the common law family.[3]

The penetration of the common law into India began with the advent of the British East India Company and its trading activities in India. The Company was established in 1600 and granted the authority to administer justice in the areas of operation of its factories in India by the British Crown.[4] The period leading up to 1726 saw the rise of its factories in Bombay, Madras, and Calcutta, which grew into the three Presidency towns that played a primary role in the common law's reception into India.[5] Over the next 50 years, the Company's courts presided over the Presidency towns and the factories subordinate to them, applying a combination of English law and Company regulations.[6] Initially, disputes between the natives were outside the jurisdiction of these courts, but during the latter part of the 18th century, Hindu and Mahomedan law were applied as the personal law of native litigants on matters such as inheritance, succession, and contracts.[7]

In 1765, the Company was granted Diwani rights (the right to collect revenue) over Bengal, Bihar, and Orissa, and within a decade, an English-style court system was established.[8] The Regulating Act of 1773, passed by the British Parliament, established a Supreme Court in each Presidency town with complete jurisdiction over residents. The Act of Settlement, passed in 1781, established a system of Adalat courts for the regions outside the Presidency towns known as the mofussils. These were independent of the Supreme Courts, and staffed by Indian administrators under Company control.[9] Thus a dual system of courts came into existence,

---

1 On the common law in general, see *Goodhart*, 76 L.Q. Rev. 39–40, 45–48 (1960); *Maxwell Fyfe*, (Viscount *Kilmuir*), 76 L.Q. Rev. 41–44 (1960); *Bose*, 76 L.Q. Rev. 59–63 (1960).

2 *Mirehouse v. Rennell* (1833) 6 Engl. Rep. (HL) 1015, 1023 (appeal taken from Eng.).

3 See *Setalvad*, The Common Law in India, pp. 35–53.

4 *Setalvad*, The Common Law in India, p. 4.

5 *Setalvad*, The Common Law in India, p. 11.

6 *Skuy*, 32 Modern Asian Stud. 513, 520 (1998).

7 *Lipstein*, 8 Int'l Soc. Sci. Bull. 85, 86 (1956).

8 *Skuy*, 32 Modern Asian Stud. 513, 521 (1998).

9 *Skuy*, 32 Modern Asian Stud. 513, 522 (1998).

with different courts applying distinct criminal laws, that is, English law and Company regulations, Mahomedan law, and Hindu law.[10]

This chaotic state of the law prompted the British Parliament to enact the Charter Act of 1833 and establish the Indian Law Commission to rectify the deficiencies in the legal system operating in territories under the Company's control.[11] The first task of the Commission was to codify the criminal law of India, and the main architect of the Indian Penal Code (IPC), 1860 was *Thomas Babbington Macaulay*, one of its Commissioners. The IPC, in its substance, is heavily based on English law.[12] The form and structure of the Code bears the stamp of utilitarian thinking, which was prominent in the English codification movement during the same period.[13]

The Code of Criminal Procedure (CrPC), the procedural counterpart to the IPC, was enacted immediately after it in 1861 and subsequently amended in 1872, 1882, and 1898. Trial by jury was initially introduced by the East India Company and continued to be provided for in the 1898 Code, but the practice never quite took root in India. There were calls for its abolition by successive Law Commission Reports[14] for several reasons including the following: influence of extraneous factors on verdicts, delays in trial, the accused's limited right of appeal, and the susceptibility of jurors to financial incentives.[15] The jury system is no longer in operation. The current Code of Criminal Procedure, which was introduced in 1973, has several common law features, including the adversarial system of trial. The accused is presumed to be innocent, and the burden is on the prosecution to prove the accused's guilt beyond reasonable doubt. The judge is a neutral and passive arbiter who must decide the dispute based on the competing claims put forward by the prosecution and the defence in the course of a confrontational trial.[16]

India also follows the doctrine of precedent. According to Art. 141 Const., the law declared by the Supreme Court is binding on all courts. The Supreme Court has consistently held the view that the doctrine of stare decisis, denoting "to stand by decisions and not to disturb what is settled," is a valuable principle of precedent

---

10 *Skuy*, 32 Modern Asian Stud. 513, 522–523 (1998); *Setalvad*, The Common Law in India, pp. 118–122.

11 *Skuy*, 32 Modern Asian Stud. 513, 516 (1998); *Setalvad*, The Common Law in India, p. 122.

12 *Setalvad*, The Common Law in India, pp. 122–129; *Skuy*, 32 Modern Asian Stud. 513, 541–545 (1998).

13 *Skuy*, 32 Modern Asian Stud. 513, 524, 539–540 (1998).

14 Law Commission of India, 14th Report vol. 2, p. 873; Law Commission of India, 41st Report, p. 184.

15 See Law Commission of India, 37th Report, p. 23, citing the findings of the Law Commission of India, 14th Report vol. 2, p. 873.

16 Government of India, Ministry of Home Affairs, Report of the Committee on Reforms of Criminal Justice System (2003) pp. 23–24, http://www.mha.nic.in/hindi/sites/upload_files/mhahindi/files/pdf/criminal_justice_system.pdf [last visited Feb. 2017].

that should be departed from only in exceptional cases.[17] Thus, when a court of law makes a decision on a question of law that is necessary for the determination of the case before it, this decision constitutes a binding precedent not only for the same court, but also for other courts of equal or lower rank when they are faced with the same question, and it may be deviated from only when necessary for considerations of public policy.[18]

2. Effects of international ties

a) Membership in international and regional organizations

India has played an active role in international and regional organizations ever since its independence from British rule in 1947. Indeed, even before achieving independence, during the period 1919 to 1947, India occupied an anomalous position as a subject of international law, and was quasi-independent in her international relations with the capacity to exercise treaty-making power in her own right. Thus, India was an original member of the League of Nations, which was founded in 1919, and became a founding member of the United Nations in 1945.[19]

In the post-independence era, India's relationship to international organizations has taken one of three forms: full membership, observer status, and dialogue partner. The following organizations of which India is a member are most relevant to its human rights and humanitarian law standards or its efforts to tackle issues of crime and security: the International Atomic Energy Agency,[20] the Organization for the Prohibition of Chemical Weapons,[21] the Conference on Disarmament,[22] the International Criminal Police Organization (Interpol),[23] and the International Organization for Migration.[24]

---

[17] See, e.g., *Manganese Ore (India) Ltd. v. Regional Assistant Commissioner of Sales Tax*, (1976) 4 SCC 124, 127; *Ganga Sugar Corporation v. State of U.P.*, (1980) 1 SCC 223, 233; *Central Board of Dawoodi Bohra Community and Anr. v. State of Maharashtra and Anr.*, (2005) 2 SCC 673.

[18] *Krishena Kumar v. Union of India*, (1990) 4 SCC 207, 233.

[19] See *Anand*, 23 Leiden J. Int'l L. 5–21 (2010).

[20] Member States of the IAEA, https://www.iaea.org/about/governance/list-of-member-states [last visited Feb. 2017].

[21] OPCW Member States, http://www.opcw.org/about-opcw/member-states/ [last visited Feb. 2017].

[22] Conference on Disarmament, Member States http://www.unog.ch/cd [last visited Feb. 2017].

[23] Interpol: Member countries, https://www.interpol.int/Member-countries/World [last visited Feb. 2017].

[24] IOM, Member States, http://www.iom.int/member-states [last visited Feb. 2017].

India is one of the 54 members of the Commonwealth of Nations, which is a "voluntary association of independent sovereign states [...] consulting and cooperating in the common interests of their peoples and in the promotion of international understanding and world peace."[25] In addition, it is one of the founding members of the South Asian Association for Regional Cooperation (SAARC), which was established in 1985 to facilitate regional co-operation between the member states on a range of economic, social, and cultural matters.[26] Regional counter-terrorism cooperation measures have featured prominently on the SAARC agenda ever since its inception.[27]

b) Signature and ratification of international treaties and conventions

Art. 253 Const. provides Parliament with the exclusive authority to legislate to give effect to any international obligation entered into:

Constitution of India 1950

Article 253

Notwithstanding anything in the foregoing provisions of this Chapter, Parliament has power to make any law for the whole or any part of the territory of India for implementing any treaty, agreement or convention with any other country or countries or any decision made at any international conference, association or other body.

This is in accordance with Parliament's power under Art. 246 Const. read with the List I (Union List) of the Seventh Schedule to make laws with respect to any of the subjects contained in the List: participation in international conferences, associations, and other bodies, and implementing of decisions made thereat (List I, Entry 13); entering into treaties and agreements with foreign countries and implementation of treaties, agreements, and conventions with foreign countries (List I,

---

25 Declaration of Commonwealth Principles, 22 Jan. 1971, http://thecommonwealth.org/sites/default/files/history-items/documents/Singapore%20Declaration.pdf [last visited Feb. 2017].

26 Charter of the South Asian Association for Regional Co-operation, 1985, http://saarc-sec.org/SAARC-Charter/5/ [last visited Feb. 2017].

27 See, e.g., SAARC Regional Convention on Suppression of Terrorism, 1987, http://saarc-sec.org/areaofcooperation/detail.php?activity_id=21 [last visited Feb. 2017]; Terrorism featured prominently in the first few SAARC summits: Joint Press Release, First SAARC Summit (Dhaka, 7–8 Dec. 1985); Second Summit Declaration (Bangalore, 17 Nov. 1986); Third Summit Declaration (Kathmandu, 4 Nov. 1987); Fourth Summit Declaration (Islamabad, 31 Dec. 1988). It continues to be emphasized in more recent summits: Thirteenth Summit Declaration (Dhaka, 13 Nov. 2005); Fifteenth Summit Declaration (Colombo, 2–3 Aug. 2008); Sixteenth Summit Declaration (Thimpu, 28–29 Apr. 2010); Seventeenth Summit Declaration (Addu City, 10–11 Nov. 2011); Eighteenth Summit Declaration (Kathmandu, 26–27 Nov. 2014). Summit declarations are available at http://www.saarc-sec.org/SAARC-Summit/7/ [last visited Feb. 2017].

Entry 14). While Art. 51 Const. provides that the state must endeavour to "foster respect for international law and treaty obligations," India is a dualist state. Thus, international treaties do not become enforceable automatically upon ratification; rather, they must be incorporated into domestic law by enabling municipal law. In the case of a conflict between municipal law and international law, the former prevails, though courts attempt to interpret domestic statutes harmoniously with international obligations.[28]

– Human rights

India is party to almost all the main human rights instruments at the international level, including the following (for each treaty, the year of ratification is noted in parentheses): the Universal Declaration of Human Rights 1948 (in the drafting of which India played a prominent role),[29] the International Covenant on Civil and Political Rights (ICCPR) 1966 (1979), and the International Covenant on Economic, Social and Cultural Rights (ICESCR) 1966 (1979). In addition, it has ratified the International Convention on the Elimination of All Forms of Racial Discrimination 1966 (1968), the Slavery Convention 1926 (1954), the Convention on the Rights of the Child 1990 (1992), and the Convention on the Elimination of All Forms of Discrimination Against Women 1979 (1993). While India has not ratified the Convention against Torture and Other Cruel, Inhuman or Degrading Treatment or Punishment 1984, it has signed the Convention (14 Oct. 1997). Similarly, it has only signed the International Convention for the Protection of All Persons from Enforced Disappearance 2006 (6 Feb. 2007) but has not yet ratified it.[30]

– International humanitarian law and international criminal law

India is party to the 1949 Geneva Conventions I, II, III, and IV (1950) and has given effect to the obligations under them through the enactment of the Geneva Conventions Act, 1960;[31] it has failed to sign or ratify Additional Protocols I, II, and III to the Geneva Conventions. It has ratified the Convention for the Protection of Cultural Property in the Event of Armed Conflict 1954 (1958) and the First Protocol to the Convention 1954 (1958), the Optional Protocol to the Convention on the Rights of the Child on the Involvement of Children in Armed Conflict 2000 (2005), the Convention on the Non-Applicability of Statutory Limitations to War

---

[28] *Kashyap*, in: Patel (ed.), India and International Law, pp. 20–21.

[29] National Portal of India, http://archive.india.gov.in/spotlight/spotlight_archive.php?id=73 [last visited Feb. 2017].

[30] For the status of the Slavery Convention, see UNTC, Status of Treaties: Chapter XVIII (Penal Matters); for all other treaties cited in this paragraph, see UNTC, Status of Treaties: Chapter IV (Human Rights), https://treaties.un.org/Pages/ParticipationStatus.aspx?clang=_en [last visited Feb. 2017].

Crimes and Crimes Against Humanity 1968 (1971), and the Genocide Convention 1948 (1959).[32] Despite significant lobbying by civil society organizations, however, India has not signed the Rome Statute to the International Criminal Court, partly because of concerns related to the operationalisation of the complementarity principle and the inclusion of war crimes occurring in non-international armed conflicts within the jurisdiction of the court.[33]

India is also party to a range of international instruments dealing with weapons, including the Protocol for the Prohibition of the Use of Asphyxiating, Poisonous or Other Gases, and of Bacteriological Methods of Warfare 1925 (1930), the Convention on the Prohibition of the Development, Production and Stockpiling of Bacteriological (Biological) and Toxin Weapons and on their Destruction 1972 (1974), Convention on the Prohibition of the Development, Production, Stockpiling and Use of Chemical Weapons and on their Destruction 1992 (1996), Convention on Prohibitions or Restrictions on the Use of Certain Conventional Weapons Which May be Deemed to be Excessively Injurious or to Have Indiscriminate Effects 1980 (1984), and Protocols I–V to the Convention.[34]

– *Terrorism*

Terrorism is a matter of significant concern for India, and it has ratified a number of international and regional instruments related to anti-terrorism measures. These include the International Convention Against the Taking of Hostages 1979 (1994), the International Convention for the Suppression of the Financing of Terrorism 1999 (2003), the International Convention for the Suppression of Terrorist Bombings 1997 (1999), the International Convention for the Suppression of Acts of Nuclear Terrorism 2005 (2006),[35] the Tokyo Convention on Offenses and Certain Other Acts Committed on Board Aircraft 1963 (1975), the Hague Convention for

---

31 Gazette of India, http://egazette.nic.in/WriteReadData/1960/E-1970-1960-0007-88740.pdf [last visited Feb. 2017].

32 For information on the status of all treaties mentioned in this paragraph, see Geneva Academy of International Humanitarian Law and Human Rights, Rule of Law in Armed Conflicts Project, International Treaties Adherence: India, http://www.adh-geneve.ch/RULAC/international_treaties.php?id_state=107 [last visited Feb. 2017].

33 See *Ramanathan*, 3 J. Int'l Crim. Just. 627–634 (2005).

34 For information on the status of treaties dealing with weapons, see Geneva Academy of International Humanitarian Law and Human Rights, Rule of Law in Armed Conflicts Project, International Treaties Adherence: India, http://www.adh-geneve.ch/RULAC/international_treaties.php?id_state=107 [last visited Feb. 2017]; for information on the status of most of the these treaties, see UNTC, Status of Treaties: Chapter XXVI (Disarmament), https://treaties.un.org/Pages/ParticipationStatus.aspx?clang=_en [last visited Feb. 2017].

35 For information on the status of these treaties, see UNTC, Status of Treaties: Chapter XVIII (Penal Matters), https://treaties.un.org/Pages/ParticipationStatus.aspx?clang=_en [last visited Feb. 2017].

the Suppression of Unlawful Seizure of Aircraft 1970 (1982), and the Montreal Convention for the Suppression of Unlawful Acts against the Safety of Civil Aviation of 1971 (1982).[36] The main regional counter-terrorism instruments to which India is party are the SAARC Regional Convention on Suppression of Terrorism 1987 and the Additional Protocol to the SAARC Regional Convention on Suppression of Terrorism 2004.[37]

India has enacted several laws pursuant to these treaties, including the Anti-Hijacking Act, 2016, the Suppression of Unlawful Acts against Safety of Civil Aviation Act, 1982, the Tokyo Convention Act, 1975, the SAARC Convention (Suppression of Terrorism) Act, 1993, and the National Investigation Agency Act, 2008.

– Organized crime and white collar crime

India has ratified some of the most important instruments dealing with organized crime and trafficking in persons, weapons, and drugs. These include the UN Convention against Transnational Organized Crime 2000 (2011) and the Protocols to the Convention: the Protocol to Prevent, Suppress and Punish Trafficking in Persons, Especially Women and Children 2000 (2011), the Protocol against the Smuggling of Migrants by Land, Sea and Air 2000 (2011) and the Protocol against the Illicit Manufacturing of and Trafficking in Firearms, their Parts and Components and Ammunition 2001 (2011).[38] It is party to the UN Convention against Illicit Traffic in Narcotic Drugs and Psychotropic Substances 1988 (1990).[39] India has also ratified regional instruments on organized crime, including the SAARC Convention on Combating and Prevention of Trafficking in Women and Children for Prostitution 2002[40] and the SAARC Convention on Narcotic Drugs and Psychotropic Substances 1990.[41]

---

36 International Civil Aviation Organization, Working Paper, Assembly – 37th session Legal Commission, Notification of Acts of Signature, Ratification, or Accession to International Air Law Instruments by India (2010), http://www.icao.int/Meetings/AMC/Assembly37/Working Papers by Number/wp095_en.pdf [last visited Feb. 2017].

37 IPCS: Countering Terrorism, http://www.ipcs.org/project/countering-terrorism-building-a-common-approach-in-saarc-25.html [last visited Feb. 2017]. See also SAARC Conventions, http://saarc-sec.org/SAARC-Conventions/63/ [last visited Feb. 2017].

38 UNTC, Status of Treaties: Chapter XVIII (Penal Matters), https://treaties.un.org/Pages/ParticipationStatus.aspx?clang=_en [last visited Feb. 2017].

39 UNTC, Status of Treaties: Chapter VI (Narcotic Drugs and Psychotropic Substances), https://treaties.un.org/Pages/ParticipationStatus.aspx?clang=_en [last visited Feb. 2017].

40 UN Women, http://evaw-global-database.unwomen.org/en/countries/asia/india/2002/south-asian-association-for-regional-cooperation [last visited Feb. 2017].

41 U.S. Department of State, Bureau of International Narcotics and Law Enforcement Affairs, 2011 International Narcotics Control Strategy Report, Country Reports: India, http://www.state.gov/j/inl/rls/nrcrpt/2011/vol1/156361.htm#india [last visited Feb. 2017].

Corruption is a pervasive feature of political and social life, and India has been ranked 76th of 168 countries in Transparency International's Corruption Perceptions Index in 2015.[42] India has, however, signed and recently ratified the United Nations Convention against Corruption 2003 (2011).[43]

Extradition and mutual legal assistance in criminal matters are governed by treaty law, the Extradition Act, 1962, and Sections 166A and 166B of the Code of Criminal Procedure, 1973. The Prevention of Money Laundering Act, 2002 also provides for mutual legal assistance if there is an applicable treaty.[44] As of 2017, India had signed bilateral extradition treaties with 37 countries (e.g., Canada, the United States of America, United Kingdom, South Africa, Germany, France, Kuwait, and Oman) and also had extradition arrangements with 8 others (including Italy, Singapore, and Sri Lanka).[45] In addition, it was party to 39 Mutual Legal Assistance Treaties (with countries such as the United States of America, United Kingdom, Singapore, South Korea, France, and Turkey).[46] India has also ratified the SAARC Convention on Mutual Assistance in Criminal Matters, 2008.[47]

Bibliography and further reading

Anand, R.P., The Formation of International Organizations and India: A Historical Study. 23 Leiden J. Int'l L. 5–21 (2010).

Bose, Vivian, The Migration of the Common Law: 5. India. 76 L.Q. Rev. 59–63 (1960).

Goodhart, A.L., The Migration of the Common Law: Preface. 76 L.Q. Rev. 39–40 (1960).

– The Migration of the Common Law: 2. What is the Common Law. 76 L.Q. Rev. 45–48 (1960).

Government of India, Ministry of Home Affairs, Report of the Committee on Reforms of Criminal Justice System (2003).

---

42 Transparency International, Corruption Perceptions Index 2015, http://www.transparency.org/cpi2015 [last visited Feb. 2017].

43 UNTC, Status of Treaties: Chapter XVIII (Penal Matters), https://treaties.un.org/Pages/ParticipationStatus.aspx?clang=_en [last visited Feb. 2017].

44 *ADB/OECD Anti-Corruption Initiative for Asia and the Pacific*, Mutual Legal Assistance, Extradition and Recovery of Proceeds of Corruption in Asia and the Pacific, p. 153, http://www.oecd.org/dataoecd/28/47/37900503.pdf [last visited Feb. 2017].

45 Interpol Delhi: Extradition, http://cbi.nic.in/interpol/extradition.php [last visited Feb. 2017].

46 Interpol Delhi: MLATS, http://cbi.nic.in/interpol/mlats.php [last visited Feb. 2017].

47 International Cooperation, http://mha.nic.in/International_Cooperation [last visited Feb. 2017].

Kashyap, Subhash C., The Constitution of India and International Law. In: Bimal N. Patel (ed.), India and International Law. Leiden 2005, pp. 9–32.

Law Commission of India, 41st Report on the Code of Criminal Procedure, 1898 (1969).

– 37th Report on the Code of Criminal Procedure, 1898 (1967).

– 14th Report on the Reform of Judicial Administration, vol. II (1958).

Lipstein, Kurt, The Reception of Western Law in India. 8 Int'l Soc. Sci. Bull. 85–95 (1956).

Maxwell Fyfe, David (Viscount *Kilmuir*), The Migration of the Common Law: 1. Introduction. 76 L.Q. Rev. 41–44 (1960).

Ramanathan, Usha, India and the ICC. 3 J. Int'l Crim. Just. 627–634 (2005).

Setalvad, Molital Chimanlal, The Common Law in India. London 1960.

Skuy, David, Macaulay and the Indian Penal Code of 1862: The Myth of the Inherent Superiority and Modernity of the English Legal System Compared to India's Legal System in the Nineteenth Century. 32 Modern Asian Stud. 513–557 (1998).

Table of cases

Central Board of Dawoodi Bohra Community and Anr. v. State of Maharashtra and Anr. (2005) 2 SCC 673

Ganga Sugar Corporation v. State of U.P. (1980) 1 SCC 223

Krishena Kumar v. Union of India. (1990) 4 SCC 207

Manganese Ore (India) Ltd. v. Regional Assistant Commissioner of Sales Tax. (1976) 4 SCC 124

Mirehouse v. Rennell (1833) 6 Eng. Rep. 1015

C. Constitutional parameters of criminal law

1. Supra-statutory rules as repositories of criminal law principles

The Constitution of India constitutes the supreme law of the land[1] and the primary source of supra-statutory criminal law principles. It came into effect on 26 January 1950 in the aftermath of India's independence from British rule in August 1947. Its immediate predecessor was the Government of India Act, 1935, enacted by the British Parliament, which conferred a limited right to self-government and sought to establish a federation consisting of autonomous British Indian provinces and Indian states governed by native princes. The structure for governance introduced by this enactment did not sit well with increasing political aspirations for full independence. A Constituent Assembly was set up in 1946 to draft a Constitution for the future governance of India and, after three years, officially adopted the Constitution on 26 November 1949.[2]

The Indian Constitution is a comprehensive document consisting of 395 articles and 12 schedules. Some of its provisions have been heavily influenced by other constitutional traditions and legal texts: for example, the Government of India Act, 1935 (the distribution of legislative power), British constitutional law (British parliamentary procedure and model of the executive), the American Bill of Rights (Fundamental Rights, Part III of the Constitution), and the Constitution of the Irish Free State (Directive Principles of State Policy, Part IV of the Constitution).[3]

The Preamble to the Constitution expresses the aspirations and objectives of the Constitution: India is declared to be a sovereign, socialist, secular, and democratic republic[4] that aims to secure justice, liberty, and equality for all its citizens and to promote fraternity and the unity and integrity of the nation. Above all, it affirms the principles of equality and human dignity.[5] Further, the invocation to "We, the people of India [...] give to ourselves this Constitution" emphasises that the people of India constitute the political sovereign and source of constitutional power and authority, which they exercise through their elected representatives.[6]

---

1 *G.M., ONGC Shilchar v. ONGC Contractual Workers Union*, (2008) 8 SCALE 665; *U.P. State Electricity Board v. Pooran Chandra Pandey*, (2007) 11 SCC 92; *Teesta Setalvad v. State of Gujarat*, (2004) 10 SCC 88.

2 See *Ramaswamy*, Constitutional Developments in India, pp. 331–338; *Jain*, Outlines of Indian Legal and Constitutional History, pp. 591–596. For details on the drafting process and the work of the Constituent Assembly, see *Rao*, The Framing of India's Constitution.

3 *Seervai*, Constitutional Law of India, pp. 157–171, 174; *Jain*, Outlines of Indian Legal and Constitutional History, p. 596.

4 The words "socialist" and "secular" were added to the Preamble by the Forty-Second Amendment to the Constitution in 1976.

5 *Nandini Sundar v. State of Chhattisgarh*, (2011) 7 SCC 547; *Secretary, State of Karnataka v. Umadevi*, AIR 2006 SC 1806.

6 *Singh*, V.N. Shukla's Constitution of India, pp. A21–A23; *Jain*, Outlines of Indian Legal and Constitutional History, p. 598.

The Preamble, together with the fundamental rights in Part III, the directive principles of state policy in Part IV, and the fundamental duties in Part IV-A, embody a vision of the citizen as a bearer of individual and collective rights and obligations. While the fundamental rights conferred in Part III are enforceable by the courts (Art. 32), the directive principles are non-enforceable prescriptions that place obligations on the government to strive towards economic and social welfare and provide education, health, and employment for its citizens (Arts. 36–51). The Supreme Court has played a pivotal role in the development and expansion of the scope of these rights and directives, for example, by means of creative interpretation of the right to life (Art. 21),[7] by liberally construing the requirement of enforceability only against the state,[8] and by giving effect to directive principles by reading them into fundamental rights.[9] The fundamental duties (Art. 51-A) were added to the Constitution by the Forty-Second Amendment. The duties are not self-executing; they can be implemented through the introduction of specific laws.[10]

In addition to the Constitution, international treaties to which India is party form an important source of criminal law. Art. 51 Const. provides that the state must endeavour to "foster respect for international law and treaty obligations." India is, however, a dualist state: international treaties do not become enforceable automatically upon ratification; rather, they must be incorporated into domestic law by enabling municipal law. In case of a conflict between municipal law and international law, the municipal law prevails, though courts attempt to interpret domestic statutes harmoniously with international obligations.[11] The Supreme Court has read international treaty obligations that are not inconsistent with domestic law into the rights guaranteed by Part III, even in the absence of an enabling domestic law, to enhance their meaning and promote their purposes.[12]

2. Fundamental rights and freedoms and the criminal law

The events leading to the enactment of the Constitution – the movement for independence and the struggle for political and civil rights, in particular – deeply influenced the demand for fundamental rights to be constitutionally guaranteed. Following the precedent of the Bill of Rights in the United States, legally enforcea-

---

[7] See below 2.

[8] *Mohini Jain v. State of Karnataka*, AIR 1992 SC 1858. See below 2.

[9] *Singh*, V.N. Shukla's Constitution of India, pp. 366–371 (citing *Akhil Bharatiya Soshit Karamchari Sangh (Rly.) v. Union of India*, (1981) 1 SCC 246; *Unni Krishnan v. State of Andhra Pradesh*, (1993) 1 SCC 645).

[10] *Singh*, V.N. Shukla's Constitution of India, p. 388.

[11] *Kashyap*, in: Patel (ed.), India and International Law, pp. 20–21. See I.B.

[12] *Vishaka v. State of Rajasthan*, (1997) 6 SCC 241; *Apparel Export Promotion Council v. A.K. Chopra*, (1999) 1 SCC 759.

ble fundamental rights were provided in Part III of the Constitution.[13] Art. 13 prohibits the state from making any law that contravenes or abridges fundamental rights, and any law is void to the extent of such inconsistency. Fundamental rights may be violated directly by the state as well by its officials and agencies. In addition to this "vertical application" of the fundamental rights (between state and citizen), certain pronouncements by the Supreme Court countenance the possibility of their "horizontal application," that is between citizens.[14]

The fundamental rights in Part III of the Constitution can be grouped under the following headings:[15]

- right to equality – equality before law (Art. 14); prohibition of discrimination on grounds of religion, race, caste, sex, or place of birth (Art. 15); equality of opportunity in matters of public employment (Art. 16); abolition of untouchability (Art. 17); abolition of titles (Art. 18);
- right to freedom – protection of certain rights regarding freedom of speech, association, assembly, movement, residence, and profession (Art. 19); protection in respect of conviction for offences (Art. 20); protection of life and personal liberty (Art. 21); protection against arrest and detention in certain cases (Art. 22);
- right against exploitation – prohibition of traffic in human beings and forced labour (Art. 23); prohibition of employment of children in factories and any other hazardous employment (Art. 24);
- right to freedom of religion – freedom of conscience and free profession, practice, and propagation of religion (Art. 25); freedom to manage religious affairs (Art. 26); freedom as to payment of taxes for promotion of any particular religion (Art. 27); freedom as to attendance at religious instruction or religious worship in certain educational institutions (Art. 28);
- cultural and educational rights – protection of interests of minorities (Art. 29); right of minorities to establish and administer educational institutions (Art. 30);
- right to property (Art. 31), which was repealed by the Forty-Fourth Amendment to the Constitution, 1978;
- right to constitutional remedies – remedies for enforcement of rights conferred by Part III (Art. 32); power of Parliament to modify the rights under Part III in their application to armed forces and other such forces (Art. 33); and restrictions on the rights while martial law is in force (Art. 34).

---

13 *Seervai*, Constitutional Law of India, pp. 158–159, 349.

14 *Singh*, V.N. Shukla's Constitution of India, pp. 25–26 (citing *M.C. Mehta v. Union of India*, (1987) 1 SCC 395; *Ashok v. Union of India*, (1997) 5 SCC 10; *Bandhua Mukti Morcha v. Union of India*, (1984) 3 SCC 161; *Bodhisattwa Gautam v. Subhra Chakraborty*, (1996) 1 SCC 490; *Mr. "X" v. Hospital "Z,"* (1998) 8 SCC 296).

15 *Seervai*, Constitutional Law of India, p. 370.

While certain rights, such as the right to freedom (Art. 19 Const.), are conferred only on citizens, others, such as the right to equality (Art. 14 Const.), are conferred on all persons, irrespective of citizenship.[16]

The Supreme Court has followed a policy that favours a broad and expansive interpretation of the fundamental rights.[17] In particular, the term "life" in Art. 21 Const. has been given a liberal construction to include the right to life with dignity and all that this entails, such as the bare necessities of life.[18] Thus, the court has interpreted Art. 21 Const. to encompass the right to livelihood, the right to a clean environment, the right to shelter, the right to a reasonable accommodation for living, the right to reputation, the right to self-preservation, the right to water, and the right to education till fourteen years of age.[19] Similarly, the court has also accorded an expansive interpretation to the term "liberty" in Art. 21 Const., bringing within its scope the right to privacy, the right to travel abroad, and the right of a person under preventive detention to meet with friends and family.[20] Some of the most important rights that pertain to the criminal law and process have also been read into Art. 21 Const., including the right to legal aid, the right to speedy trial, the right against cruel and unusual punishment, the right to fair trial, prisoners' rights, and the right to compensation for violation of the rights.[21]

3. Other supra-statutory norms relevant to criminal law and criminal procedure

An important procedural development of interest to criminal law that has been initiated and championed by the Supreme Court is public interest litigation (PIL).[22] Under this rubric, the Court has relaxed the requirements for *locus standi* as well as the forms of proceedings for enforcement of fundamental rights.[23] According to the traditional rules on standing, a petition alleging violations of fundamental rights can only be filed by the individual who has suffered this violation. This narrow rule has been relaxed by the Court, and any member of the public who has sufficient interest can file a petition seeking redress for public injury that arises from a breach

---

[16] *Seervai*, Constitutional Law of India, p. 370.

[17] *Jain*, Outlines of Indian Legal and Constitutional History, p. 602 (citing *Maneka Gandhi v. Union of India*, AIR 1978 SC 597).

[18] *Francis Coralie v. Union Territory of Delhi*, (1981) 1 SCC 608.

[19] *Singh*, V.N. Shukla's Constitution of India, pp. 209–211 and cases cited therein; *Sripati*, Am. U. Int'l L. Rev. 413, 445–448 (1998) and cases cited therein.

[20] *Singh*, V.N. Shukla's Constitution of India, pp. 211–215 and cases cited therein.

[21] *Singh*, V.N. Shukla's Constitution of India, pp. 222–228 and cases cited therein; *Sripati*, Am. U. Int'l L. Rev. 413, 442–444 (1998) and cases cited therein.

[22] *Bhagwati*, 23 Colum. J. Transnat'l L. 561 (1985).

[23] *Cassels*, 37 Am. J. Comp. L. 495, 497–501 (1989).

of a legal duty or from the violation of a constitutional provision.[24] The rationale is that fundamental rights protections should be available equally to the poor or oppressed, who may be prevented from petitioning the court because of poverty, lack of awareness, or social and economic disadvantage. Thus, any member of the public acting in good faith should be able to bring a petition for the enforcement of the rights.[25] Much of PIL has focused on exposing repressions by state agencies, such as the police and custodial authorities, on ensuring fulfilment of legal obligations by state authorities, and on asserting new constitutional rights (e.g., under Art. 21).[26]

Another innovation introduced by the Supreme Court that is relevant to criminal law has centred on giving more teeth to the directive principles of State Policy. Under Art. 37, the directive principles are not enforceable by any court but nonetheless embody principles that are fundamental in the governance of the country. The Supreme Court has diluted this unenforceability, however, by emphasising the balance between the directive principles and fundamental rights, whereby they supplement each other and must be construed harmoniously.[27] It has also held that the fundamental rights should be interpreted in light of the directive principles and that these principles should, where possible, be read into the former.[28]

Apart from these creative developments by the judiciary, the Constitution contains several provisions pertaining to the criminal law. Most of these relate to the conduct of public officials. For instance, no criminal proceeding or process for arrest or imprisonment may be instituted against the president of India or the governors of states during their terms of office (Art. 361). The president and the governors have the power to grant pardons and to suspend, remit, or commute sentences in certain cases (Arts. 72 and 161).[29] Members of Parliament cannot be subjected to any proceedings in courts in respect of statements or votes in Parliament or any committee thereof and are not liable for any publication under the authority of the Parliament (Art. 105).

In addition to the Constitution, international law obligations entered into by India, to the extent that they are not inconsistent with municipal law, can be read into

---

[24] *Singh*, V.N. Shukla's Constitution of India, pp. 354–355; *S.P. Gupta v. Union of India*, AIR 1982 SC 149.

[25] *Cassels*, 37 Am. J. Comp. L. 495, 499 (1989); *Bandhua Mukti Morcha v. Union of India*, AIR 1984 SC 802.

[26] *Baxi*, Third World Legal Stud. 107 (1985), p. 119.

[27] *Minerva Mills Ltd. v. Union of India*, (1980) 2 SCC 591; *Singh*, V.N. Shukla's Constitution of India, pp. 366–368; *Narain*, 27 J. Indian L. Inst. 198 (1985).

[28] *Singh*, V.N. Shukla's Constitution of India, p. 371 (citing *Akhil Bharatiya Soshit Karamchari Sangh (Rly.) v. Union of India*, (1981) 1 SCC 246).

[29] See further II.K.

fundamental rights guarantees by the courts.[30] India has ratified a number of important human rights instruments, including the International Covenant on Civil and Political Rights (ICCPR) 1966.[31] While some of the rights protected by the ICCPR are similar to those in Part III of the Constitution, the ICCPR additionally provides some rights that are not expressly granted by the fundamental rights: right to be tried without delay (Art. 14), right to free legal services (Art. 14), prohibition on imprisonment for mere non-fulfilment of contractual obligations (Art. 11), right to travel abroad (Art. 12), right against unlawful interference with privacy (Art. 17), right against torture and other forms of cruel and degrading treatment or punishment (Art. 7), the right to compensation for victims of unlawful arrest and detention (Art. 9),[32] and the right of aliens against unlawful expulsion (Art. 13).

Bibliography and further reading

Baxi, Upendra, Taking Suffering Seriously: Social Action Litigation in the Supreme Court of India. 4 Third World Legal Stud. 107–132 (1985).

Bhagwati, P.N., Judicial Activism and Public Interest Litigation. 23 Colum. J. Transnat'l L. 561–577 (1985).

Cassels, Jamie, Judicial Activism and Public Interest Litigation in India: Attempting the Impossible? 37 Am. J. Comp. L. 495–519 (1989).

Jain, M.P., Outlines of Indian Legal and Constitutional History. 6th ed. 2006 (repr. Gurgaon 2009).

Kayshap, Subhash C., The Constitution of India and International Law. In: Bimal N. Patel (ed.), India and International Law, vol. I. Leiden 2005, pp. 9–32.

Narain, Jagat, Judicial Law Making and the Place of Directive Principles in the Indian Constitution. 27 J. Indian L. Inst. 198–222 (1985).

Ramaswamy, M., Constitutional Developments in India 1600–1955. 8 Stan. L. Rev. 326–387 (1956).

Rao, B. Shiva, The Framing of India's Constitution: A Study. New Delhi 1968.

Seervai, Hormasji Manekji, Constitutional Law of India, vol. I. 4th ed. Bombay 1991.

Singh, Mahendra P., V.N. Shukla's Constitution of India. 12th ed. Lucknow 2016.

Sripati, Vijayashri, Toward Fifty Years of Constitutionalism and Fundamental Rights in India: Looking Back to See Ahead (1950–2000). 14 Am. U. Int'l L. Rev. 413–495 (1998).

---

[30] See above 1.

[31] See I.B.2.b.

[32] *Sripati*, Am. U. Int'l L. Rev. 413, 461–462 (1998).

Table of cases

Akhil Bharatiya Soshit Karamchari Sangh (Rly.) v. Union of India, (1981) 1 SCC 246

Apparel Export Promotion Council v. A.K. Chopra, (1999) 1 SCC 759

Ashok v. Union of India, (1997) 5 SCC 10

Bandhua Mukti Morcha v. Union of India, (1984) 3 SCC 161

Bodhisattwa Gautam v. Subhra Chakraborty, (1996) 1 SCC 490

Francis Coralie v. Union Territory of Delhi, (1981) 1 SCC 608

G.M., ONGC Shilchar v. ONGC Contractual Workers Union, (2008) 8 SCALE 665

M.C. Mehta v. Union of India, (1987) 1 SCC 395

Maneka Gandhi v. Union of India, AIR 1978 SC 597

Minerva Mills Ltd. v. Union of India, (1980) 2 SCC 591

Mohini Jain v. State of Karnataka, AIR 1992 SC 1858

Mr. "X" v. Hospital "Z," (1998) 8 SCC 296

Nandini Sundar v. State of Chhattisgarh, (2011) 7 SCC 547

S.P. Gupta v. Union of India, AIR 1982 SC 149

Secretary, State of Karnataka v. Umadevi, AIR 2006 SC 1806

Teesta Setalvad v. State of Gujarat, (2004) 10 SCC 88

U.P. State Electricity Board v. Pooran Chandra Pandey, (2007) 11 SCC 92

Unni Krishnan v. State of Andhra Pradesh, (1993) 1 SCC 645

Vishaka v. State of Rajasthan, (1997) 6 SCC 241

D. Fundamentals of criminal law

1. Functions of criminal law

It is difficult to find any comprehensive discussion of the function of criminal law in India; courts, commentators, and law reform commissions instead make scattered references to the functions, aims, or objectives of the criminal law, sometimes mingled with references to the purposes of punishment. Nonetheless, some discrete strands of thought can be identified. For instance, criminal law is perceived as serving the purpose of discharging the obligation of the state to protect the life, liberty, and property of its citizens.[1] Its ultimate aim is to ensure the protection of primary personal rights against intentional harm by third parties. These rights include the right to life, the right to inviolability of the person, the right to freedom of movement, and the rights to security of person, habitation, and enjoyment of property.[2] The criminal law performs this function through the enactment of punitive and preventive measures, which in turn ensure the maintenance of law and order and a peaceful society by preventing private retribution.[3]

While there is no explicit mention of the criminal law as a tool for the protection of recognized legal interests, the categorization of offences under the Indian Penal Code (IPC) can be analogized to the recognition of specific interests the violation of which is subject to punitive sanctions. Some of the legal interests thus recognized include the preservation of public tranquillity and the common welfare, the protection of the human body and property against harm, and the preservation of the safety and security of the state.[4]

A related function of the criminal law is to protect citizens against arbitrary deprivations of their civil and political rights by governmental authorities. Thus, the criminal law contains guarantees against self-incrimination, unreasonable search and seizure, and cruel and unusual punishment and provides for rights of fair trial and due process.[5]

The functions of the criminal law have also been expressed as a modern approach to the conception of crime, as contrasted with the traditional approach, which focused on defining a crime. Thus, the positive functions of the criminal law have been identified as the preservation of public order and decency and the protection of citizens from offensive and injurious conduct and from exploitation and corrup-

---

[1] Report of the Committee on Reforms of Criminal Justice System, p. 23; *Gaur*, Textbook on Indian Penal Code, p. 70; see also *Selvi v. State of Karnataka*, (2010) 7 SCC 263.

[2] *Gaur*, Crime: Aims and Objects, in: K.D. Gaur (ed.), Criminal Law and Criminology, p. 12.

[3] Report of the Committee on Reforms of Criminal Justice System, p. 23.

[4] See II.C.2.a.

[5] *Gaur*, Crime: Aims and Objects, in: K.D. Gaur (ed.), Criminal Law and Criminology, p. 13.

tion by others. These functions apply particularly strongly in the case of the young, weak, inexperienced, or dependent. The negative function of the criminal law, on the other hand, has been expressed thus: the law's function is not to interfere in citizens' private lives or enforce particular conduct except to the extent that doing so fulfils its positive purposes.[6]

Criminal law has also been alluded to as a general means of regulating conduct, such as discouraging behaviour motivated by avarice, primarily in the context of social and economic offences.[7] These are offences such as adulteration of food and drugs or hoarding and black marketing. Here, the function of the law is to protect the social interest in the preservation of national resources and the health and wealth of members of the society as well as the preservation of the general economic system from waste and exploitation. In these cases, even though there may be an individual direct victim, the actual harm is suffered by the state or society.[8]

2. Limits on criminal law imposed by the rule of law

The rule of law is considered one of the core features of the Constitution in a democratic system of government.[9] It ensures equality before the law as well as equal protection of laws to citizens[10] and acts as a check against the arbitrary exercise of state power.[11] This implies that laws must be applied and enforced equally, in an unbiased fashion, and without discrimination.[12] The rule of law is pervasive in every field of administration and governs all state organs that are required to act in a fair and just manner in the performance of their functions.[13] The principles enshrined by the rule of law thus apply to all areas of the law, including the criminal law. The courts have also at times alluded to specific aspects of the rule of law that are relevant to criminal law, for example, the accused's right to legal assistance

---

6 *Nigam*, Law of Crimes in India, p. 36; *Naz Foundation v. Government of NCT*, 2010 Cri LJ 94.

7 Law Commission of India, 47th Report on the Trial and Punishment of Social and Economic Offences, p. 10.

8 Law Commission of India, 47th Report on the Trial and Punishment of Social and Economic Offences, pp. 1–3.

9 *Singh*, V.N. Shukla's Constitution of India, p. A54.

10 *Singh*, V.N. Shukla's Constitution of India, p. A54; *State of Haryana v. Mahabir Vegetable Oils Pvt. Ltd.*, (2011) 3 SCC 778; *M/s. Motilal Padampat Sugar Mills Co. (P) Ltd. v. State of U.P.*, (1979) 2 SCC 409.

11 *State of Orissa v. Mamata Mohanty*, (2011) 3 SCC 436; S.*G. Jaisinghani v. Union of India*, AIR 1967 SC 1427.

12 *M. Nagaraj v. Union of India*, (2006) 8 SCC 212; *Noida Entrepreneurs Association v. Noida*, (2011) 5 SCALE 505.

13 *Justice P.D. Dinakaran v. Hon'ble Judges Inquiry Committee*, 2011 (6) SCALE 797; *A.K. Kraipak v. Union of India*, (1969) 2 SCC 262.

during interrogation;[14] the requirement of a fair, transparent, and judicious investigation;[15] the punishment of the guilty irrespective of status and authority;[16] prohibition of custodial violence;[17] and the authority to impose preventive detention only in exceptional circumstances.[18]

Adherence to the rule of law invites commitment to several principles of criminal law that may be part of it or entailed by it. The first amongst these is the principle of legality. The animating spirit behind the principle of legality in Indian criminal law is twofold: the requirement of fair warning – the state should not punish its citizens in the absence of specific laws giving them prior notice that certain conduct will be punishable in a particular matter; and prevention of arbitrary state action.[19] Laws that violate the principle of legality are considered inequitable and unjust and are repugnant to universal notions of fairness and justice.[20] The principle of legality finds expression in the constitutional prohibition against retroactive application of the law (Art. 20(1)) and in the constitutional right to be deprived of life and liberty only in accordance with the procedure established by law (Art. 21).[21] In addition, courts have held that the terms of a penal statute should be relatively clear and unambiguous; in the event of any ambiguity, a strict construction of the penal statute is favoured.[22]

The principle of personal responsibility or culpability is not mentioned as such by courts and does not feature in academic opinions. However, it is reflected in the importance accorded to the element of *mens rea* in order for conduct to constitute an offence. The IPC includes the mental element required for an offence within the definition of the particular offence in most cases.[23] While academic opinion supports the view that where no state of mind is specified, the presumption is that such an omission is deliberate and that *mens rea* would be inapplicable,[24] the Supreme Court has held that unless a statute explicitly or by necessary implication excludes *mens rea* as a constituent part of a crime, *mens rea* should be imported into the

---

14 *Senior Intelligence Officer v. Jugal Kishore Samra*, MANU/SC/0731/2011.

15 *Babubhai v. State of Gujarat*, (2010) 12 SCC 254; *Manu Sharma v. State (NCT of Delhi)*, (2010) 6 SCC 1.

16 *Narmada Bai v. State of Gujarat*, (2011) 4 SCALE 469.

17 *Mehboob Batcha v. State rep. by Supdt. of Police*, (2011) 4 SCALE 20; *Haricharan v. State of M.P.*, (2011) 4 SCC 159; *D.K. Basu v. State of West Bengal*, (1997) 1 SCC 416.

18 *Rekha v. State of Tamil Nadu Through Sec. to Government*, (2011) 4 SCALE 387.

19 *Pillai*, General Principles of Criminal Law, p. 85; see II.A.1.

20 *Rao Shiv Bahadur Singh v. State of Vindhya Pradesh*, 1953 SCR 1188; see II.A.1.

21 See II.A.2., II.A.3.a., and II.A.3.d.

22 See II.A.3.b. and II.A.3.c.

23 See II.C.2.a. and II.E.1.

24 *Gaur*, Principles of Criminal Liability, in: Gaur (ed.), Criminal Law and Criminology, p. 27; *Mayne*, Criminal Law in India, p. 9; *Setalvad*, The Common Law in India, p. 139. See II.E.4.

definition of the crime as a general principle.[25] There are nonetheless cases of strict liability offences where an exception to the general requirement of *mens rea* is made.[26]

The principle of proportionality as an essential element of the rule of law has been recognized by Indian courts, whereby the punishment imposed must fit the crime and the level of culpability.[27] The imposition of a sentence that is disproportionate is considered arbitrary and irrational and hence violative of the constitutional requirement of reasonableness under Arts. 14, 19, and 21.[28] In addition to being unjustified, such a punishment is recognized as having undesirable practical consequences.[29] While judges have broad discretion in the determination of sentences, the proportionality principle plays an influential role in this determination. Nonetheless, in practice, departures from the principle are not uncommon for other relevant considerations, such as the correctional needs of the perpetrator, the desirability of keeping the perpetrator out of circulation, or the tragic results of his or her crime.[30]

While there is no explicit reference to the principle of humanity, according to which punishment should not be a tool of revenge but should be designed to rehabilitate, the principle is manifested in the Supreme Court's pronouncements that the aim of punishment should not be to wreak vengeance but to reform and rehabilitate the offender.[31]

3. Purposes of punishment

Punishment is a form of sanction meted out to the offender for violating the established norms and rules of society.[32] The object of punishment is societal protection through deterring potential offenders, preventing the offender from repeated commission of crimes, extracting retribution for the crime committed, and rehabilitating the offender.[33]

---

[25] See, e.g., *State of Gujarat v. D.P. Pandey*, AIR 1971 SC 866, 868. For more detailed examination, see II.E.4.

[26] See II.E.4.

[27] *Bachan Singh v. State of Punjab*, (1982) 3 SCC 24.

[28] *Bachan Singh v. State of Punjab*, (1982) 3 SCC 24.

[29] *Mohan Anna Chavan v. State of Maharashtra*, (2008) 7 SCC 561; *Bantu v. State of U.P.*, (2008) 11 SCC 113.

[30] *State of M.P. v. Basodi*, AIR 2009 SC 3081; *State of M.P. v. Ghanshyam Singh*, AIR 2003 SC 3191; *Ruli Ram v. State of Haryana*, AIR 2002 SC 3360.

[31] *State of Haryana v. Jagdish and Harpal*, AIR 2010 SC 1690; *Mohammad Giasuddin v. State of A.P.*, AIR 1977 SC 1926; *Nadella Venkatakrishna Rao v. State of A.P.*, AIR 1978 SC 480.

[32] *Gaur*, Textbook on Indian Penal Code, p. 70.

[33] *Gaur*, Textbook on Indian Penal Code, p. 70.

The retributive theory of punishment embodies two related concepts: the satisfaction by the state of the victim's desire for vengeance, and the state's expression of disapproval of the violation of its laws through sanctions that are proportionate to the gravity of the offence.[34] Closely connected to the theory of retribution is the concept of expiation: the offender must atone for the crime through suffering, and balance must be restored by punishment that is equal to the offender's culpability.[35] Expiation is a largely discredited basis for punishment in modern penology, both due to the recognition that the concepts of crime and sin are not necessarily related and due to problems with accurately measuring culpability and suffering.[36] Concern is also expressed about retribution's associations with revenge and revulsion. Nonetheless, retribution remains present in discussions on the aims of punishment, even though the present trend is to give more weight to deterrence and reformation.[37]

Deterrence is considered one of the main functions of punishments and has two aspects. The first is general deterrence, whereby punishing the offender serves as a warning to deter other persons from committing crimes. The second is individual deterrence or prevention, which physically prevents the offender him- or herself from the commission of further crimes.[38] Some doubts have been expressed about the value of deterrence[39] – in particular, the assumption that human beings are rational creatures who base their decisions on a cost-benefit analysis has been questioned.[40] Deterrence continues to play an important role in considerations of punishment, however, and its utility has been especially emphasized in the context of socio-economic offences.[41]

The approach that has become increasingly important is the reformative or corrective theory. Pursuant to this theory, punishment is inflicted on the offender with a view to restoring him or her to society as a better person and a good citizen. Thus, while punished by being detained, the offender is given education and training in order to mould his or her character and facilitate his or her social and psychological

---

34 *Nigam*, Law of Crimes in India, p. 226.

35 *Nigam*, Law of Crimes in India, p. 228; *Chabra*, in: Gaur (ed.), Criminal Law and Criminology, pp. 686–687.

36 *Nigam*, Law of Crimes in India, p. 229; *Chabra*, in: Gaur (ed.), Criminal Law and Criminology, p. 687.

37 *Nigam*, Law of Crimes in India, pp. 227–229; *Chabra*, in: Gaur (ed.), Criminal Law and Criminology, pp. 688–689; Law Commission of India, 156th Report on the Indian Penal Code, pp. 15–16.

38 *Nigam*, Law of Crimes in India, pp. 229–230; *Gaur*, Textbook on Indian Penal Code, p. 71; Law Commission of India, 156th Report on the Indian Penal Code, p. 18.

39 *Gaur*, Textbook on Indian Penal Code, p. 71; Law Commission of India, 156th Report on the Indian Penal Code, pp. 16, 18.

40 *Chabra*, in: Gaur (ed.), Criminal Law and Criminology, p. 689.

41 Law Commission of India, 156th Report on the Indian Penal Code, p. 17.

re-orientation.[42] The reformative theory is particularly prominent within the framework of juvenile delinquency, where two points are emphasized: first, that harsh punishment would only turn the juvenile into a hardened criminal, and second, that the juvenile can be rehabilitated through the employment of educational and other corrective measures.[43]

Indian courts have not been uniform in their approach to the aims of punishment, though the general trend is to give more emphasis to the reformative theory.[44] In certain cases, the Supreme Court has denounced retribution and stated that deterrence and reformation are the primary purposes for which deprivation of life and personal liberty may be justified.[45] The value of reformation has been especially highlighted in cases concerning juvenile offenders.[46] There have been exceptions to this approach,[47] however, and the Court has at times displayed a retributive stance by stating that the punishment should fit the crime so that it reflects public abhorrence of the crime.[48]

4. Fundamental principles of criminal procedure

The Constitution of India is the ultimate source of fundamental principles governing criminal procedure, and several additional procedural protections have been developed by the courts based on a liberal construction of constitutional provisions. The Code of Criminal Procedure, 1973 (CrPC) is intended to be a comprehensive code concerning all matters related to criminal procedure, including the fundamental principles of procedure.

The Constitution guarantees several procedural rights to the accused, including rights relating to due process. Art. 21 provides that no one shall be deprived of life and personal liberty except according to procedure established by law. The initial interpretation of the phrase "procedure established by law" was simply that there

---

42 *Chabra*, in Gaur (ed.), Criminal Law and Criminology, pp. 691–693; *Nigam*, Law of Crimes in India, pp. 230–231.

43 Law Commission of India, 156th Report on the Indian Penal Code, p. 17.

44 See *Balasubrahmanyam*, in: Pillai/Aquil (eds.), Essays on the Indian Penal Code, pp. 239–243.

45 *Bachan Singh v. State of Punjab*, (1982) 3 SCC 24; *Rajendra Prasad v. State of U.P.*, (1979) 3 SCC 646; *Mohammad Giasuddin v. State of A.P.*, (1977) 3 SCC 287; *State of Haryana v. Jagdish and Harpal*, AIR 2010 SC 1690.

46 *Satto v. State of U.P.*, (1979) 2 SCC 628; *Munna v. State of U.P.*, AIR 1982 SC 806.

47 See *Maru Ram v. Union of India*, (1981) 1 SCC 107 (questioning the validity of the reformative theory). See also *Om Prakash v. State of Uttaranchal*, (2003) 1 SCC 648; *Sushil Murmu v. State of Jharkhand*, (2004) 2 SCC 338 (deeming the accused beyond reformation due to the cruel and brutal nature of the offence).

48 *Dhananjoy Chatterjee v. State of West Bengal*, (1994) 2 SCC 220.

must be a valid law enacted by the state and that the deprivation must be strictly in keeping with the procedure prescribed by the law.[49] The Supreme Court later expanded this guarantee to include due process protections, however, by reading Art. 21 along with Arts. 14 and 19 Const. to state that the process must, in addition, be just, fair, and reasonable.[50] Art. 21 Const. has increasingly been given an expansive construction to encompass several fundamental rights of the accused at the pre-trial, trial, and post-conviction stages.[51] These include the right to legal aid,[52] the right to an expeditious trial (encompassing all stages – investigation, inquiry, trial, appeal, revision, and retrial),[53] and the right against cruel and unusual punishment.[54] The right to a fair trial has also been considered inherent in Art. 21 Const. It consists not only in the observance of the forms of the law but also in the just application of its substantive principles so as to facilitate the discovery of truth and to prevent miscarriages of justice.[55] The rights of prisoners have also been read into Art. 21 Const.:[56] prisoners are entitled to all fundamental rights unless their liberties have been constitutionally curtailed.[57] Furthermore, prisoners have the right to be protected against co-prisoners,[58] detainees facing a trial may not be handcuffed without adequate reasons,[59] and the rights of women and children must be especially safeguarded.

Art. 20(2) Const. recognizes the prohibition against double jeopardy: a person cannot be prosecuted and punished for the same offence more than once. In order for Art. 20(2) Const. to apply, the previous proceedings must have been of "a criminal nature instituted or continued before a court of law or tribunal in accordance with the procedure prescribed in the statute which creates the offence and regulates the procedure."[60] Art. 20(3) Const. embodies the constitutional protection against

---

[49] *Singh*, V.N. Shukla's Constitution of India, p. 215; *A.K. Gopalan v. State of Madras*, AIR 1950 SC 27; *Bishan Das v. State of Punjab*, AIR 1961 SC 1570; *Kharak Singh v. State of U.P.*, AIR 1963 SC 1295.

[50] *Singh*, V.N. Shukla's Constitution of India, pp. 216–221; *Maneka Gandhi v. Union of India*, (1978) 1 SCC 248.

[51] *Singh*, V.N. Shukla's Constitution of India, pp. 222–228.

[52] *M.H. Hoskot v. State of Maharashtra*, (1978) 3 SCC 544; *Hussainara Khatoon v. State of Bihar*, (1980) 1 SCC 98.

[53] *Singh*, V.N. Shukla's Constitution of India, p. 226; *Abdul Rehman Antulay v. R.S. Nayak*, (1992) 1 SCC 225; *Supreme Court Legal Aid Committee v. Union of India*, (1994) 6 SCC 731.

[54] *Singh*, V.N. Shukla's Constitution of India, p. 226.

[55] *Singh*, V.N. Shukla's Constitution of India, p. 228; *Zahira Habibullah Shaikh (5) v. State of Gujarat*, (2006) 3 SCC 374.

[56] *Singh*, V.N. Shukla's Constitution of India, pp. 222–223.

[57] *State of A.P. v. Challa Ram Krishna Reddy*, (2000) 5 SCC 712.

[58] *Kewal Pati v. State of U.P.*, (1995) 3 SCC 600; *Murti Devi v. State of Delhi*, (1998) 9 SCC 604.

[59] *Prem Shankar v. Delhi Admn.*, (1980) 3 SCC 526; *Sunil Gupta v. State of M.P.*, (1990) 3 SCC 119.

[60] *Raja Narayanlal Bansilal v. M.P. Mistry*, AIR 1961 SC 29.

self-incrimination: no person who is accused of an offence can be compelled to be a witness or give evidence against him- or herself.

In addition to the Constitution, the provisions of the CrPC are also aimed at ensuring that the accused gets a fair trial in accordance with well-established principles of law that fulfil the requirements of natural justice.[61] The rights of fair trial relate to "the character of the court, the venue, the mode of conducting the trial [...] rights of the accused in relation to defence, and other rights."[62] The CrPC envisages an adversarial system of trial. The accused is presumed innocent (presumption of innocence) and the burden is on the prosecution to prove his or her guilt beyond reasonable doubt.[63] The judge is a neutral and passive arbiter who must decide the dispute based on the competing claims put forward by the prosecution and the defence in the course of a confrontational trial.[64] There has been some modification of this system by the CrPC, which allows a more active role by the judge in protecting public interests as well as the interests of the accused. For instance, charges against the accused are not framed by the prosecution but by the judge (Secs. 228 and 240 CrPC); the judge may call any person as a witness (Sec. 311 CrPC); and the court has the discretion to accept or refuse the guilty plea of the accused (Secs. 229, 241, and 252 CrPC).[65]

The CrPC also ensures that the trial is conducted by an independent, impartial, and competent judge by providing for a separation of the judiciary from the executive (judicial independence),[66] recognizing that the judge must not be connected with the prosecution in any matter (Sec. 479), and requiring a public hearing (Sec. 327). Other fair trial rights incorporated in the CrPC[67] include the right of the accused to be informed of the charges against him or her (Secs. 228, 240, 246, 251); the requirement of the accused's presence throughout the trial (exception: Sec. 317); the requirement that – barring certain exceptions – evidence be taken in the presence of the accused (Sec. 273); the accused's right to cross-examine prosecution witnesses (Sec. 243);[68] and the requirement of a reasoned decision.[69]

---

61 *Thakker/Thakker*, Takwani Criminal Procedure, p. 2; Willie *Stanley v. State of M.P.*, AIR 1956 SC 116; V.C. *Shukla v. State*, AIR 1980 SC 962.

62 Law Commission of India, 37th Report on the Code of Criminal Procedure, 1889, pp. 2–3.

63 *Babu Singh v. State of Punjab*, (1964) 1 Cri LJ 566; *K.M. Nanavati v. State of Maharashtra*, AIR 1962 SC 605.

64 Government of India, Ministry of Home Affairs, Report of the Committee on Reforms of Criminal Justice System (2003) pp. 23–24. See I.B.1.

65 *Pillai*, R.V. Kelkar's Criminal Procedure, pp. 336–337.

66 *Pillai*, R.V. Kelkar's Criminal Procedure, pp. 10–11, 339.

67 *Pillai*, R.V. Kelkar's Criminal Procedure, pp. 340–346.

68 *Habeeb Mohd. v. State of Hyderabad*, AIR 1954 SC 51; *Ronald Wood Mathams v. State of West Bengal*, AIR 1954 SC 455.

69 *Mukhtiar Singh v. State of Punjab*, (1995) 1 SCC 760.

Bibliography and further reading

Balasubrahmanyam, V., Punishment. In: K.N. Chandrasekharan Pillai/S. Aquil (eds.), Essays on the Indian Penal Code. New Delhi 2005, pp. 236–277.

Chabra, K.S., Theories of Punishment. In: K.D. Gaur (ed.), Criminal Law and Criminology. New Delhi 2003, pp. 686–695.

Gaur, K.D., Textbook on Indian Penal Code. 5th ed. New Delhi (2014 repr. 2015).

– Crime: Aims and Objects. In: K.D. Gaur (ed.), Criminal Law and Criminology. New Delhi 2003, p. 3–20.

– Principles of Criminal Liability. In: K.D. Gaur (ed.), Criminal Law and Criminology. New Delhi 2003, pp. 21–29.

Government of India, Ministry of Home Affairs, Report of the Committee on Reforms of Criminal Justice System (2003).

Law Commission of India, 156th Report on the Indian Penal Code vol. I, (1997).

– 47th Report on the Trial and Punishment of Social and Economic Offences (1972).

– 37th Report on the Code of Criminal Procedure, 1889 (1967).

Nigam, R.C., Law of Crimes in India, vol I: Principles of Criminal Law. London 1965.

Pillai, K.N. Chandrasekharan, R.V. Kelkar's Criminal Procedure. 5th ed. Lucknow 2008 (repr. 2011).

– General Principles of Criminal Law. 2d ed. Lucknow 2011.

Singh, Mahendra P., V.N. Shukla's Constitution of India. 12th ed. Lucknow 2016.

Thakker, C.K./Thakker, M.C., Takwani Criminal Procedure. 4th ed. Gurgaon 2015.

Table of cases

A.K. Gopalan v. State of Madras, AIR 1950 SC 27

A.K. Kraipak v. Union of India, (1969) 2 SCC 262

Abdul Rehman Antulay v. R.S. Nayak, (1992) 1 SCC 225

Babu Singh v. State of Punjab, (1964) 1 Cri LJ 566

Babubhai v. State of Gujarat, (2010) 12 SCC 254

Bachan Singh v. State of Punjab, (1982) 3 SCC 24

Bantu v. State of U.P., (2008) 11 SCC 113

Bishan Das v. State of Punjab, AIR 1961 SC 1570

D.K. Basu v. State of West Bengal, (1997) 1 SCC 416

Dhananjoy Chatterjee v. State of West Bengal, (1994) 2 SCC 220

Habeeb Mohd. v. State of Hyderabad, AIR 1954 SC 51

Haricharan v. State of M.P., (2011) 4 SCC 159

Hussainara Khatoon v. State of Bihar, (1980) 1 SCC 98

Justice P.D. Dinakaran v. Hon'ble Judges Inquiry Committee, 2011 (6) SCALE 797

K.M. Nanavati v. State of Maharashtra, AIR 1962 SC 605

Kewal Pati v. State of U.P., (1995) 3 SCC 600

Kharak Singh v. State of U.P., AIR 1963 SC 1295

M. Nagaraj v. Union of India, (2006) 8 SCC 212

M.H. Hoskot v. State of Maharashtra, (1978) 3 SCC 544

M/s. Motilal Padampat Sugar Mills Co. (P) Ltd. v. State of U.P., (1979) 2 SCC 409

Maneka Gandhi v. Union of India, (1978) 1 SCC 248

Manu Sharma v. State (NCT of Delhi), (2010) 6 SCC 1

Maru Ram v. Union of India, (1981) 1 SCC 107

Mehboob Batcha v. State rep. by Supdt. of Police, (2011) 4 SCALE 20

Mohammad Giasuddin v. State of A.P., (1977) 3 SCC 287

Mohan Anna Chavan v. State of Maharashtra, (2008) 7 SCC 561

Mukhtiar Singh v. State of Punjab, (1995) 1 SCC 760

Munna v. State of U.P., AIR 1982 SC 806

Murti Devi v. State of Delhi, (1998) 9 SCC 604

Nadella Venkatakrishna Rao v. State of A.P., AIR 1978 SC 480

Narmada Bai v. State of Gujarat, (2011) 4 SCALE 469

Naz Foundation v. Government of NCT of Delhi, 2010 Cri LJ 94

Noida Entrepreneurs Association v. Noida, (2011) 5 SCALE 505

Om Prakash v. State of Uttaranchal, (2003) 1 SCC 648

Prem Shankar v. Delhi Admn., (1980) 3 SCC 526

Raja Narayanlal Bansilal v. M.P. Mistry, AIR 1961 SC 29

Rajendra Prasad v. State of U.P., (1979) 3 SCC 646

Rao Shiv Bahadur Singh v. State of Vindhya Pradesh, 1953 SCR 1188

Rekha v. State of Tamil Nadu Through. Sec. to Government, (2011) 4 SCALE 387

Ronald Wood Mathams v. State of West Bengal, AIR 1954 SC 455

Ruli Ram v. State of Haryana, AIR 2002 SC 3360

S.G. Jaisinghani v. Union of India, AIR 1967 SC 1427

Satto v. State of U.P., (1979) 2 SCC 628

Senior Intelligence Officer v. Jugal Kishore Samra, MANU/SC/0731/2011

Selvi v. State of Karnataka, (2010) 7 SCC 263

State of A.P. v. Challa Ram Krishna Reddy, (2000) 5 SCC 712

State of Gujarat v. D.P. Pandey, AIR 1971 SC 866, 868

State of Haryana v. Jagdish and Harpal, AIR 2010 SC 1690

State of Haryana v. Mahabir Vegetable Oils Pvt. Ltd., (2011) 3 SCC 778

State of Madhya Pradesh v. Basodi, AIR 2009 SC 3081

State of Madhya Pradesh v. Ghanshyam Singh, AIR 2003 SC 3191

State of Orissa v. Mamata Mohanty, (2011) 3 SCC 436

Sunil Gupta v. State of M.P., (1990) 3 SCC 119

Supreme Court Legal Aid Committee v. Union of India, (1994) 6 SCC 731

Sushil Murmu v. State of Jharkhand, (2004) 2 SCC 338

V.C. Shukla v. State, AIR 1980 SC 962

Willie Stanley v. State of M.P., AIR 1956 SC 116

Zahira Habibullah Shaikh (5) v. State of Gujarat, (2006) 3 SCC 374

E. Nature, form, and boundaries of criminal law

1. Nature and form of criminal law

A formal or legal definition of criminal law does not exist in Indian law. Statutes, courts, and commentators instead focus on the definition of an "offence." Thus, the concern is with defining a "crime" rather than the concept of "criminal law."[1] Nonetheless, a functional definition of the criminal law has been proposed: the function of the criminal law is to preserve public order and decency, to protect individuals from offensive and injurious conduct, and to safeguard against exploitation and corruption of others, especially the young, weak, inexperienced, or dependent. The law's function is not to interfere in the private lives of individuals or enforce particular conduct except to the extent it fulfills the aforementioned purposes.[2]

Since the law concerns itself more with defining "crime" and not "criminal law," the distinction between criminal law and other areas of law is also couched in terms of differentiating crimes from other kinds of wrongs. While the purpose behind the law's recognition of civil wrongs is indemnification or making good the loss to the party injured by the wrong, crimes are wrongs that are visited with punishment, that is, infliction of pain upon the actor committing the wrong.[3] In this vein, there are discrete references by courts distinguishing between criminal law and the law of torts: whereas both areas of law have a deterrent function in relation to wrongdoing, criminal law seeks to protect the public interest and punish wrongdoers, while tort law aims at vindicating individual rights and compensating victims for the loss or injury they have suffered. The distinction between the two is not always clear cut – for instance, the practice of awarding exemplary damages in the law of torts signals the law's punitive function.[4]

Criminal law in India is subdivided into substantive criminal law, the law of criminal procedure, and the law of evidence. Substantive criminal law is found primarily in the Indian Penal Code, 1860 (IPC), which is a comprehensive legislation that contains the general principles of jurisdiction, criminal responsibility, exemptions from liability, and the definitions of offences. The Code of Criminal Procedure, 1973 (CrPC) consolidates the law on the establishment of criminal courts and regulates the procedure for investigation, inquiry, and trial of offences and determination of guilt.[5] The law relating to punishment and sentencing is part

---

1 See II.C.1.a.

2 *Nigam*, Law of Crimes in India, p. 36; *Naz Foundation v. Government of NCT*, 2010 Cri LJ 94. See I.D.1.

3 *Huda*, Principles of the Law of Crimes, p. 2; *Nigam*, Law of Crimes in India, p. 34. See II.C.1.

4 *Destruction of Public and Private Properties v. State of A.P.*, AIR 2009 SC 2266.

5 *Gaur*, Textbook on Indian Penal Code, pp. 8–10.

of the law of criminal procedure and is contained in the Code of Criminal Procedure. The Indian Evidence Act, 1872, provides the rules of evidence that are applicable in all judicial proceedings in or before any court, with the exception of courts-martial convened under specific legislation (Sec. 1).

In additional to these primary sources, the Indian Penal Code is supplemented with local and special statutes that punish specific categories of conduct.[6] Examples include the Explosive Substances Act (VI of 1908), the Customs Act (LII of 1962), and the Indian Arms Act (LIV of 1959). Finally, the Constitution is the supreme law of the land and also contains specific provisions that relate to criminal law, including the principle of legality (Arts. 20 and 21)[7] and fundamental rights of the accused, including the right to fair trial (Arts. 20, 21 and 22). Some of these have been developed by courts through an expansive interpretation of the fundamental rights protections under Part III of the Constitution.[8]

2. Boundaries between criminal law and other areas of law with a criminal or quasi-criminal function

The boundaries between criminal law and other areas of law with a criminal or quasi-criminal function are not always rigid or immutable.[9] Nonetheless, three distinct areas of law that also serve a quasi-criminal function are the law of torts, administrative law, and the law relating to the military. While tort law and criminal law have distinct ends, the Supreme Court has sanctioned the award of exemplary damages, which are punitive in nature, to deter people against rioting and engaging in vandalism that results in damage or destruction of public and private property.[10]

Administrative law comprises the rules and regulations that concern the function of administration and the relations between administrative authorities and the individual as well as with other state authorities. The powers and duties of government departments, public officials, statutory bodies, public corporations, administrative tribunals, and local authorities all fall within the scope of administrative law.[11] The legislature may confer administrative powers on the government, any government department or official, individuals, bodies of individuals, such as universities, municipalities, and other local authorities, or public corporations, for various public purposes. Where such authorities are tasked by statute with discharging various duties, the failure to do so is considered a specific wrong. Thus, the statute may

---

6 *Gaur*, Textbook on Indian Penal Code, p. 9.

7 See II.A.

8 See I.C.2.

9 See *Destruction of Public and Private Properties v. State of A.P.*, AIR 2009 SC 2266.

10 *Destruction of Public and Private Properties v. State of A.P.*, AIR 2009 SC 2266.

11 *Basu/Nandi*, Administrative Law, pp. 4–5.

prescribe a specific remedy for non-performance, such as a fine, forfeiture, or other monetary penalty. Alternatively, in the absence of a specific remedy, the breach may give rise to a claim for damages under the common law. In the case of the former, a proceeding for the enforcement of the penalty shares certain characteristics with a criminal proceeding, including the requirements of strict construction and clarity of the statutory provision.[12]

Certain statutes may create administrative tribunals to settle any disputes that arise under them. Administrative tribunals are adjudicating authorities vested with judicial powers under a statute or statutory rule[13] that possess some of the characteristics of ordinary courts. Their subject matter jurisdiction is statutorily conferred and limited to specific cases, and they are not generally bound by strict rules of procedure and evidence.[14] Some of the administrative tribunals in India are the Industrial Tribunals (Industrial Disputes Act, 1947), the Income Tax Tribunal (Income Tax Act, 1961), the Central Administrative Tribunal (Administrative Tribunals Act, 1985), and National and State Consumer Commissions (Consumer Protection Act, 1986), all of which have the power to enforce various penalties prescribed by the corresponding statutes.[15]

The military in India is governed by the Armed Forces Act, 1950.[16] The Act provides for the convening of a court martial, which has the authority to hold a trial and convict any person who is subject to the Act (Sec. 2) and who commits an offence under the Act (Secs. 34–64) or any "civil offence" (Secs. 69, 70), that is, an offence triable by a criminal court (Sec. 3(ii)). While the court-martial has exclusive jurisdiction in relation to offences that are created by the Act, in the case of civil offences, this jurisdiction is concurrent with that of ordinary criminal courts (Secs. 125, 126). Sanctions that may be imposed by a court-martial include death, imprisonment, transportation, cashiering in the case of officers, dismissal from service, reduction in rank or grade, forfeiture of seniority of rank, reprimand, and forfeiture or stoppage of pay and allowances (Sec. 71). The Act also gives a commanding officer and certain other officers the authority to impose specific sanctions (Secs. 80 to 85). The procedural rules for investigation and trial by court-martial are specified in the Army Rules, 1954. Appeals against any order, finding, decision, or sentence passed by a court-martial lie before the Armed Forces Tribunal, which was established by the Central Government under the Armed Forces Tribunal Act, 2007 (Sec. 17). Appeals against orders passed by the Tribunal can be filed before the Supreme Court with the leave of the Tribunal.

---

12 *Basu/Nandi*, Administrative Law, pp. 189–212.

13 *Bharat Bank Ltd. v. Employees*, AIR 1950 SC 188; *Jaswant Sugar Mills Ltd. v. Lakshmi Chand*, AIR 1963 SC 677.

14 *Thakker*, Lectures on Administrative Law, pp. 230–236.

15 *Thakker*, Lectures on Administrative Law, pp. 236–244.

16 For details, see *Sharma*, Military Law in India, pp. 49–112.

In addition to these areas of the law, specific statutes impose liability that is quasi-criminal in nature. In considering whether the prohibition against *ex post facto* laws applies to the liability provided in these statutes, courts have held that the liability is civil rather than criminal in nature.[17] For instance, in *Hatisingh Manufacturing Co. v. Union of India*, the Supreme Court considered a provision of the Industrial Disputes Act which required employers closing their undertakings to pay compensation to their employees. Failure to discharge this liability could result in imprisonment. The Court held that the liability to pay compensation was civil and the failure to perform it could not be considered an offence.[18] Similarly, a penalty under a tax law that is retrospective also does not violate Art. 20(1) Const. since the penalty is a civil liability that is enforced by the tax authorities, even though it may be penal in character.[19]

3. Special regimes connected to the status of the offender

In general, the Indian Penal Code's provisions on punishment do not distinguish between offenders based on their status (Sec. 53). There are certain exceptions to this: for instance, certain offences under Chapter XII (Offences Relating to Coins and Government Stamps) and Chapter XVII (Offences Against Property) warrant enhanced punishment in cases of recidivism. Thus, if an accused who has been convicted of an offence under these Chapters punishable by imprisonment for a term of three or more years is found guilty of an additional offence under the Chapters punishable by imprisonment for the same term, for every such subsequent offence, the accused shall be subject to either imprisonment for life or for a term exceeding ten years (Sec. 75 IPC). Habitual offenders may also be required by a judicial magistrate to execute a bond with or without surety as a security for good behaviour for a period not exceeding three years as a preventive measure under Sec. 110 CrPC.

The Indian Penal Code also has special provisions relating to children and persons of unsound mind. Conduct by a child under the age of seven or a child seven to eleven years of age who does not understand the nature and consequences of his or her actions is not considered an offence (Secs. 82 and 83 IPC).[20] Similarly, conduct by a person who, due to unsoundness of mind, was unaware of the nature of his or her act or that it was wrong or contrary to the law will not be an offence (Sec. 84 IPC).[21]

---

17 On the prohibition of retroactivity, see II.A.3.d.

18 AIR 1960 SC 923.

19 *Shiv Dutt Rai Fateh Chand v. Union of India*, AIR 1984 SC 1194.

20 See II.J.6.

21 See II.J.7.

There are also special legislative acts that create specific regimes for specific categories of offenders.[22] For instance, by virtue of Sec. 8 of the Representation of the People Act, 1951, a person may be disqualified from becoming a member of Parliament or state legislature if he or she has been convicted of certain offences under the IPC or special laws, such as the Protection of Civil Rights Act, 1955, the Unlawful Activities (Prevention) Act, 1967, the Narcotic Drugs or Psychotropic Substances Act, 1985, and the Prevention of Corruption Act, 1988.

Furthermore, certain provisions of the Code of Criminal Procedure as well as special acts provide for preventive and corrective measures that may be applied as an alternative or as a substitute for traditional penal sanctions in the case of certain classes of offenders. Sec. 360 CrPC provides that, if they have no previous convictions, the following three categories of accused persons may be released on probation instead of being sentenced to punishment: persons under the age of 21 who are convicted of an offence punishable with fine only or with imprisonment for a period of up to seven years; persons under the age of 21; and women who are convicted of an offence not punishable with death or imprisonment for life.

The Juvenile Justice (Care and Protection of Children) Act, 2015, was enacted with a view to the provision of proper care, treatment, social re-integration and protection of juveniles and the establishment of institutions to facilitate their rehabilitation.[23] If a juvenile is found to have committed an offence by the Juvenile Justice Board, the Board may pass a series of orders ranging from counselling to confinement in a special home (Sec. 18). Juveniles ages 16 and 17 can be tried as adults for heinous offences before the Children's Court (Secs. 15, 18(3), and 19).

Similarly, under the Immoral Traffic (Prevention) Act, 1956, if a female offender is found guilty of soliciting or prostitution, the court may, in lieu of a sentence of imprisonment, pass an order of detention in a corrective institution for a term of two to five years, as long as the court is satisfied that given the character, health, and mental condition of the offender and the circumstances of the case, she is likely to benefit from the discipline and instruction at the institution (Sec. 10A). A person engaged in prostitution may also make an application to a magistrate for an order to be kept in a protective home, a corrective institution, or under supervision of a person appointed by the magistrate (Sec. 19).

Individuals such as mentally ill offenders, vagrants, and beggars may also be subject to special measures. For example, the Mental Health Act, 1987, governs the treatment and care of mentally ill persons (Preamble). Under Secs. 23 and 24 of the Act, a police officer may take a person believed to be mentally ill into custody and produce the person before a magistrate for medical examination and subsequent

---

22 See *Palkar*, in: Dupont/Fijnaut (eds.), International Encyclopaedia of Laws, pp. 127–131. See I.A.5.d.

23 Preamble, Juvenile Justice (Care and Protection of Children) Act, 2015.

detention in a psychiatric hospital or nursing home. State statutes such as the Bombay Prevention of Begging Act, 1959, provide for certified institutions for the detention, training, and employment of beggars and their dependants.[24]

Bibliography and further reading

Basu, Durga Das/Nandi, A.K., Administrative Law. 6th ed. Kolkata 2004 (repr. 2006).

Gaur, K.D., Textbook on Indian Penal Code. 4th ed. Delhi 2009 (repr. 2011).

– Crime: Aims and Objects. In: K.D. Gaur (ed). Criminal Law and Criminology. New Delhi 2003, pp. 3–20.

Huda, Syed Shamsul, The Principles of the Law of Crimes in British India: Tagore law lectures 1902. Calcutta 1919.

Nigam, Ram Chandra, Law of Crimes in India, vol. I: Principles of Criminal Law. London 1965.

Palkar, Vineeta Vinayak, India. In: Lieven Dupont/Cyrille Fijnaut (eds.), International Encyclopaedia of Laws: Criminal Law, vol. 3, Suppl. 22. The Hague 2001.

Sharma, Om Parkash, Military Law in India. 2d ed. Bombay 1990.

Thakker, C.K./Thakker, M.C., Lectures on Administrative Law. 4th ed. Lucknow 2008 (repr. 2010).

Table of cases

Bharat Bank Ltd. v. Employees, AIR 1950 SC 188

Destruction of Public and Private Properties v. State of A.P., AIR 2009 SC 2266

Hatisingh Manufacturing Co. v. Union of India, AIR 1960 SC 923

Jaswant Sugar Mills Ltd. v. Lakshmi Chand, AIR 1963 SC 677

Naz Foundation v. Government of NCT of Delhi, 2010 Cri LJ 94

Shiv Dutt Rai Fateh Chand v. Union of India, AIR 1984 SC 1194

---

[24] See *Palkar*, in: Dupont/Fijnaut (eds.), International Encyclopaedia of Laws, pp. 133–136. See I.A.5.d.

F. Sources of criminal law and interpretation aids

1. Overview

The primary sources of criminal law are the Constitution and statutory law as applied and interpreted by the courts. The Constitution represents the supreme law of the land[1] and is the primary source of supra-statutory criminal law principles. The substantive criminal law is found primarily in the Indian Penal Code, 1860 (IPC), whereas the Code of Criminal Procedure, 1973 (CrPC) is a comprehensive legislation governing the procedural aspects of criminal law.[2] International treaties to which India is party form an important source of criminal law, but they must be incorporated into domestic law by enabling domestic law.[3]

The judiciary is tasked with the interpretation and application of the Constitution and statutory law. Case law thus comprises an important source of Indian criminal law.[4] While neither executive orders nor academic opinion constitutes a source of law, both have an influence on the application of the criminal law. The executive may be granted discretion to regulate activities that are subject to criminal sanctions.[5] Academic opinion may be referred to by the courts[6] or by committees tasked with law reform.

2. Legislation and other written laws

The Constitution also contains specific provisions that relate to the criminal law, including the principle of legality (Arts. 20 and 21)[7] and fundamental rights of the accused, such as the right to fair trial (Arts. 20, 21 and 22). Some of these provisions have been developed by the courts through an expansive interpretation of the fundamental rights protections under Part III of the Constitution.[8] The main source of substantive criminal law is the Penal Code, which is a comprehensive legislation containing the general principles of jurisdiction, criminal responsibility, exemptions from liability, and definitions of offences. The Code of Criminal Procedure consolidates the law on the establishment of criminal courts and regulates the pro-

---

1 *G.M., ONGC Shilchar v. ONGC Contractual Workers Union*, (2008) 8 SCALE 665; *U.P. State Electricity Board v. Pooran Chandra Pandey*, (2007) 11 SCC 92; *Teesta Setalvad v. State of Gujarat*, (2004) 10 SCC 88. On the Constitution, see I.C.

2 See I.E.1.

3 See I.B.2.b.

4 *Yeo*, in: Heller/Dubber (eds.), The Handbook of Comparative Criminal Law, p. 290.

5 *Yeo*, in: Heller/Dubber (eds.), The Handbook of Comparative Criminal Law, p. 291.

6 *Yeo*, in: Heller/Dubber (eds.), The Handbook of Comparative Criminal Law, p. 291.

7 See II.A.

8 See below 4.

cedure for investigation, inquiry, and trial of offences and determination of guilt.[9] The Indian Evidence Act, 1872 provides the rules of evidence that are applicable in all judicial proceedings before any court, with the exception of court-martial (Sec. 1).[10]

In addition to these primary sources, the Penal Code is supplemented by local statutes that are applicable within specific areas and special statutes that punish particular categories of conduct.[11] These statutes include the Explosive Substances Act (VI of 1908), the Customs Act (LII of 1962), and the Indian Arms Act (LIV of 1959).[12] India also has special legislation governing the administration of criminal justice, including the Prisons Act, 1894 and the Prisoners Act, 1900.

Under the Constitution, both Parliament as well as state legislatures can enact laws dealing with substantive criminal law and criminal procedure (Art. 246, Seventh Schedule, List III (1) and (2)). State legislatures may enact amendments to the Penal Code and Code of Criminal Procedure and promulgate special laws that apply within their jurisdiction.[13]

In addition to the Constitution, international treaties to which India is party form an important source of criminal law. The Constitution provides that the state must endeavour to "foster respect for international law and treaty obligations" (Art. 51). India is, however, a dualist state: international treaties do not become enforceable automatically upon ratification; rather, they must be incorporated into domestic law by enabling domestic law. In case of a conflict between domestic law and international law, the domestic law prevails, though courts attempt to interpret domestic statutes harmoniously with international obligations.[14] Even in the absence of an enabling domestic law, the Supreme Court has read international treaty obligations that are not inconsistent with domestic law into the rights guaranteed by Part III in order to enhance their meaning and promote their purposes.[15]

The power to enact criminal law falls within the exclusive domain of the legislature; however, the legislature may delegate powers to the executive to regulate activities that are subject to criminal sanction. For instance, the central government has broad powers under special laws such as the Unlawful Activities (Prevention) Act, 1967 to declare an organization "unlawful" (Sec. 3).[16]

---

[9] *Gaur*, Textbook on Indian Penal Code, pp. 8–10.

[10] See I.E.1.

[11] *Gaur*, Textbook on Indian Penal Code, p. 9.

[12] See I.E.1.

[13] *Palkar*, in: Dupont/Fijnaut (eds.), International Encyclopaedia of Laws, p. 55.

[14] *Kashyap*, in: Patel (ed.), India and International Law, pp. 20–21. See I.B.

[15] *Vishaka v. State of Rajasthan*, (1997) 6 SCC 241; *Apparel Export Promotion Council v. A.K. Chopra*, (1999) 1 SCC 759.

[16] *Yeo*, in: Heller/Dubber (eds.), The Handbook of Comparative Criminal Law, p. 291.

Under the General Clauses Act, 1897, if legislation does not expressly state when it is to come into operation, it is deemed to do so on the day on which it receives the assent of the president of India (Sec. 5). The courts have held that principles of natural justice require that statutory law be promulgated or published in order to become operative. This stems from the recognition that persons should not be punished for infractions of which they had no knowledge and indeed could not have acquired knowledge, even with exercise of reasonable diligence.[17] The requirement of publication also applies to delegated or subordinate legislation. In this case, the parent statute or the subordinate legislation itself may prescribe a specific method of publication. In the absence of such a prescription, the legislation must generally be published through the customarily recognised official channel, that is, the Official Gazette.[18]

The general principle for construction of statutes, especially those that impose criminal sanctions, is that if the language of the statute is clear and unambiguous, the words must be taken to indicate the legislative intent and given effect to as such. However, if the words are ambiguous and capable of multiple meanings, the court may look at various aids to interpretation, including the legislative history, the basic framework of the statute, its object and purpose, and the consequences that would be entailed by the adoption of one interpretation over another.[19]

3. Customary law

Custom occupied a very important position in ancient Hindu law as a material source of law. There are conflicting schools of thought on its place vis-à-vis written law in the sources-of-law hierarchy. Nonetheless, it is acknowledged as having played a vital role in the development of Hindu law through absorption into the law. In addition, the written law was interpreted skilfully to bring it into harmony with existing customs and usages.[20] The importance of custom was briefly eclipsed by the preference accorded to textual personal law based on the religion of the community in the initial period of British rule over India.[21] However, custom's preeminence was soon reinstated as evidenced by the Privy Council's ruling in 1868 that "[u]nder the Hindoo system of law, clear proof of usage will outweigh the

---

[17] *Harla v. State of Rajasthan*, AIR 1951 SC 467; *Balbir Singh v. State of Punjab*, AIR 1975 P&H 83.

[18] *B.K. Srinivasan v. State of Karnataka*, AIR 1987 SC 1059.

[19] *Chief Justice of A.P. v. L.V.A. Dixitulu*, [1979] 1 SCR 26; *Kehar Singh v. State (Delhi Admn.)*, 1989 Cri LJ 1; *Reema Aggarwal v. Anupam*, AIR 2004 SC 1418.

[20] *Jain*, 3 Jaipur L.J. 96, 99–100 (1963); *Jain*, Outlines of Indian Legal and Constitutional History, pp. 556–557.

[21] *Galanter*, 24 J. Soc. Issues (1968), 73; *Jain*, Outlines of Indian Legal and Constitutional History, pp. 557–558.

written text of the law."[22] Various kinds of custom were applied by the courts during this period, including general, tribal, sectarian, local, and family custom.[23]

In the course of time, the application of custom became increasingly restrictive. Custom was required to be reasonable, ancient, certain, and in keeping with public policy and justice, equity, and good conscience. It also had to be established by formal methods of proof, including clear and cogent evidence.[24] Having lost its status as a living source of law, its role has been reduced considerably in modern India through the enactment of legislation such as the Hindu Marriage Act, 1955 and the Hindu Adoptions and Maintenance Act, 1956.[25] These Acts give overriding effect to the provisions contained in the legislation with respect to matters governed by the Act, thus abolishing custom unless the Act provides otherwise (Sec. 4 Hindu Marriage Act; Sec. 4 Hindu Adoptions and Maintenance Act). Hence, customary law has been abrogated to a large extent.[26]

Custom does not have an analogous position in traditional Muslim law, where it is not regarded as an independent source of law and is considered invalid if it contravenes textual law or the consensus of opinion among the jurists.[27] While it was recognised as a source of law during the British administration and at times even given precedence over other sources of Muslim law,[28] customary Muslim law was virtually abrogated by the Muslim Personal Law (Shariat) Application Act, 1937 (Sec. 2).[29]

Thus, custom continues to play a very limited role in Indian law and pertains primarily to civil rather than criminal matters.[30] It is accepted as a source of law in Art. 13(3)(a) Const., but it cannot violate any of the fundamental rights contained in Part III of the Constitution.[31]

---

[22] *Collector of Madura v. Mootoo Ramalinga*, 12 MIA 397, 436 (1868). See also *Jain*, 3 Jaipur L.J. (1963), 103–104.

[23] *Jain*, 3 Jaipur L.J. (1963), 107–111; *Jain*, Outlines of Indian Legal and Constitutional History, p. 559.

[24] *Galanter*, 24 J. Soc. Issues 65, 73–74 (1968); *Jain*, 3 Jaipur L.J. 96, 112–123 (1963).

[25] *Jain*, 3 Jaipur L.J. 96, 124 (1963); *Jain*, Outlines of Indian Legal and Constitutional History, pp. 560–561.

[26] *Jain*, Outlines of Indian Legal and Constitutional History, p. 560.

[27] *Jain*, 3 Jaipur L.J. 96, 101 (1963); *Jain*, Outlines of Indian Legal and Constitutional History, p. 561.

[28] *Jain*, 3 Jaipur L.J. 96, 104–105 (1963); *Jain*, Outlines of Indian Legal and Constitutional History, pp. 561–562.

[29] *Jain*, 3 Jaipur L.J. 96, 123–124 (1963); *Jain*, Outlines of Indian Legal and Constitutional History, p. 563.

[30] See *Jain*, 3 Jaipur L.J. 96, 125 (1963).

[31] *Dashratha Rama Rao v. State of A.P.*, AIR 1961 SC 564; *Sant Ram v. Labh Singh*, AIR 1965 SC 314; *Singh*, V.N. Shukla's Constitution of India, p. 43.

In addition to domestic customary law, customary international law also constitutes a source of law in the legal system. Under the Constitution, the state must foster respect for treaty obligations as well as for "international law" (Art. 51). The latter phrase is generally recognised as referring to customary international law.[32] The Supreme Court has held that customary international law principles that are not contrary to domestic law shall be deemed to have been incorporated in the domestic law.[33] Thus, customary international law principles in environmental law, such as the "precautionary principle," have been held to be part of domestic environmental law.[34]

4. Case law and judicial opinion

The Indian legal system adheres to the common law tradition.[35] Thus, case law and judicial opinion play a central role in the interpretation and development of the law. This role manifests itself primarily in two ways: through the doctrine of precedent and by virtue of the Supreme Court's constitutional authority to declare law that is binding on all courts within the territory of India (Art. 141 Const.).

The Supreme Court has consistently held the view that the doctrine of *stare decisis* – denoting "to stand by decisions and not to disturb what is settled" – is a valuable principle of precedent that should be departed from only in exceptional cases.[36] Thus, when a court of law makes a decision on a question of law that is necessary for the determination of the case before it, this decision constitutes a binding precedent not only for the court itself but also for other courts of equal or lower rank when they are faced with the same question, and it may be deviated from only when necessary for considerations of public policy.[37] This authoritative status of the court's decision only applies, however, to that part of the judgment that is considered the *ratio decidendi*,[38] that is, the reason or ground of a judicial decision.[39] *Obiter dictum* – casual statements or observations made in the course of

---

32 See *Alexander*, 1 Int'l & Comp. L.Q. 289, 291 (1952).

33 *Vellore Citizens Welfare Forum v. Union of India*, AIR 1996 SC 2715; *Gramophone Company of India Ltd. v. Birendra Bahadur Pandey*, AIR 1984 SC 667.

34 *Vellore Citizens Welfare Forum v. Union of India*, AIR 1996 SC 2715.

35 See I.B.1.

36 See, e.g., *Manganese Ore (India) Ltd. v. Regional Asstt. CST*, (1976) 4 SCC 124, 127; *Ganga Sugar Corpn. v. State of U.P.* (1980) 1 SCC 223, 233; *Central Board of Dawoodi Bohra Community and Anr. v. State of Maharashtra and Anr.*, (2005) 2 SCC 673. See I.B.1.

37 *Krishena Kumar v. Union of India*, (1990) 4 SCC 207, 233. See I.B.1.

38 *Girnar Traders v. State of Maharashtra*, (2007) 7 SCC 555; *Arun Kumar Aggarwal v. State of M.P.*, AIR 2011 SC 3056.

39 *Saxena*, 3 Jaipur L.J.96, 188, 205 (1963).

the decision that are not essential to the settlement of the issue before the court – does not have this binding effect.[40]

A corollary to the importance of precedent is that decisions must be published and that there must be reliable records of the propositions of law laid down in them. This has been accomplished through a system of law reports that constitute the primary source of case law.[41] India has a number of official as well as private law reports. For instance each High Court has a series of official Indian Law Reports (ILRs) where decisions of the court are reported. Similarly, the Supreme Courts Reports (SCR) is the official report for Supreme Court cases. The All India Reporter (AIR) – the most prominent private publication – publishes High Court as well as Supreme Court cases. There are also specialised law reports for specific areas of the law, such as the Criminal Law Journal, the Taxation Law Reports, and the Income Tax Reports.[42]

Case law and judicial decisions have played a vital role in the development of criminal law by virtue of an expansive construction of constitutional fundamental rights protections and a creative approach to statutory interpretation. For instance, the dominant opinion is that if the Penal Code does not provide for a particular mental state within the definition of the offence, the presumption is that such an omission is deliberate and that *mens rea* would be inapplicable in such a case.[43] However, the Supreme Court has consistently held that unless a statute explicitly or by necessary implication excludes *mens rea* as a constituent part of an offence, *mens rea* should be imported into the definition of the offence as a general principle.[44] Similarly, some of the most important rights that pertain to the criminal law and process have also been read into Art. 21 Const., which guarantees the right to life and liberty. These include the right to legal aid, the right to a speedy trial, the right against cruel and unusual punishment, the right to fair trial, prisoners' rights, and the right to compensation for violation of the rights under Art. 21 Const.[45]

---

[40] *State of Haryana v. Ranbir*, (2006) 5 SCC 167; *Divisional Controller, KSRTC v. Mahadeva Shetty*, (2003) 7 SCC 197; *Arun Kumar Aggarwal v. State of M.P.*, AIR 2011 SC 3056.

[41] *Jain*, Outlines of Indian Legal and Constitutional History, p. 655.

[42] *Jain*, Outlines of Indian Legal and Constitutional History, pp. 661–664.

[43] *Setalvad*, The Common Law in India, p. 139; *Mayne*, Criminal Law in India, p. 9; *Gaur*, in: Gaur (ed.), Criminal Law and Criminology, p. 27. See II.E.4.

[44] See, e.g., *State of Gujarat v D.P. Pandey*, AIR 1971 SC 866, 868. See II.E.4.

[45] *Singh*, V.N. Shukla's Constitution of India, pp. 222–228 and cases cited therein; *Sripati*, 14 Am. U. Int'l L. Rev. 413, 442–444 (1998) and cases cited therein. See I.C.2.

5. Legal literature and academic opinion

Legal literature and academic opinion are not a formal source of law in India. There are, however, comprehensive and fairly established commentaries on the Penal Code, the Code of Criminal Procedure, and some of the special laws dealing with crime, which may be cited in judicial decisions.[46]

There are also law reform bodies such as the Law Commission of India and other specialized bodies that are occasionally set up to recommend revisions to specific areas of the law. These bodies, which sometimes have a significant impact on legislative reform and may even be referred to in judicial decisions,[47] may be composed of retired judges, practicing lawyers, and academics.[48]

6. Other

Different religious communities in India continue to be governed by their personal laws in specific cases, usually pertaining to civil rather than criminal matters such as marriage, inheritance, adoption, etc.[49] However, some aspects of these laws may have criminal law implications. For instance, under Muslim personal law, a divorced wife has the right to claim maintenance from her husband only until the expiry of the *iddat* period (generally three months after the divorce). However, in the case of *Mohd. Ahmed Khan v. Shah Bano*,[50] the Supreme Court held that a Muslim woman was nonetheless entitled to maintenance beyond this period pursuant to the Code of Criminal Procedure, which obligates a man of sufficient means to maintain his divorced wife if she is unable to provide for herself (Sec. 125 CrPC).[51] This decision was followed by the enactment of the Muslim Women (Protection of Rights on Divorce) Act, 1986, making Muslim law applicable to divorced Muslim women. However, some High Courts have taken the position that the right to maintenance under Sec. 125 CrPC persists, and the Supreme Court has held[52] that a reasonable and fair provision for the future of the divorced wife beyond the *iddat* period must be made by the husband within the *iddat* period under the Act.[53]

---

46 See *Yeo*, in: Heller/Dubber (eds.), The Handbook of Comparative Criminal Law, p. 291.

47 See *Jain*, Outlines of Indian Legal and Constitutional History, p. 515. For examples of cases that have cited Law Commission Reports, see *Hussainara Khatoon v. Bihar*, AIR 1979 SC 1360; *Jagmohan Singh v. Uttar Pradesh*, AIR 1973 SC 947.

48 On the composition of the Law Commission of India, see, e.g., *Jain*, Outlines of Indian Legal and Constitutional History, p. 506.

49 *Jain*, Outlines of Indian Legal and Constitutional History, p. 530.

50 *Mohd. Ahmed Khan v. Shah Bano*, (1985) 2 SCC 556.

51 *Pillai*, R.V. Kelkar's Criminal Procedure, pp. 804, 810.

52 *Daniel Latifi v. Union of India*, (2001) 7 SCC 740.

53 *Pillai*, R.V. Kelkar's Criminal Procedure, pp. 804–805, 810–811.

Bibliography and further reading

Alexander, C.H., International Law in India. 1 Int'l & Comp. L.Q. 289–300 (1952).

Galanter, Marc, The Displacement of Traditional Law in Modern India. 24 J. Soc. Issues 65–91 (1968).

Gaur, K.D., Textbook on the Indian Penal Code. 4th ed. Delhi 2009 (repr. 2011).

– Principles of Criminal Liability. In: K.D. Gaur (ed.), Criminal Law and Criminology. New Delhi 2003, pp. 21–29.

Jain, M.P., Outlines of Indian Legal and Constitutional History. 6th ed. (repr. Gurgaon 2009).

– Custom as a Source of Law in India. 3 Jaipur L.J. 96–130 (1963).

Kashyap, Subhash C., The Constitution of India and International Law. In: Bimal N. Patel (ed.), India and International Law. Leiden 2005, pp. 9–32.

Palkar, Vineeta Vinayak, India. In: Lieven Dupont/Cyrille Fijnaut (eds.), International Encyclopaedia of Laws: Criminal Law, vol. 3, 22d Suppl. The Hague 2001.

Pillai, K.N. Chandrasekharan, R. V. Kelkar's Criminal Procedure. 5th ed. Lucknow 2008 (repr. 2011).

Saxena, Ishwar Chandra, The Doctrine of Precedent in India: A Study of Some of its Aspects. 3 Jaipur L.J. 188–214 (1963).

Setalvad, Motilal Chimanlal, The Common Law in India. London 1960.

Singh, Mahendra P., V.N. Shukla's Constitution of India. 12th ed. Lucknow 2016.

Sripati, Vijayashri, Toward Fifty Years of Constitutionalism and Fundamental Rights in India: Looking Back to See Ahead (1950–2000). 14 Am. U. Int'l L. Rev. 413–495 (1998).

Yeo, Stanley, India. In: Kevin Jon Heller/Markus D. Dubber (eds.), The Handbook of Comparative Criminal Law. Stanford 2011, pp. 288–319.

Table of cases

Apparel Export Promotion Council v. A.K. Chopra, (1999) 1 SCC 759

Arun Kumar Aggarwal v. State of M.P., AIR 2011 SC 3056

B.K. Srinivasan v. State of Karnataka, AIR 1987 SC 1059

Balbir Singh v. State of Punjab, AIR 1975 P&H 83

Central Board of Dawoodi Bohra Community and Anr. v. State of Maharashtra and Anr., (2005) 2 SCC 673

Chief Justice of A.P. v. L.V.A. Dixitulu, [1979] 1 SCR 26

Collector of Madura v. Mootoo Ramalinga, 12 MIA 397, 436 (1868)

Daniel Latifi v. Union of India, (2001) 7 SCC 740

Dashratha Rama Rao v. State of A.P., AIR 1961 SC 564

Divisional Controller, KSRTC v. Mahadeva Shetty, (2003) 7 SCC 197

G.M., ONGC Shilchar v. ONGC Contractual Workers Union, (2008) 8 SCALE 665

Ganga Sugar Corpn. v. State of U.P., (1980) 1 SCC 223

Girnar Traders v. State of Maharashtra, (2007) 7 SCC 555

Gramophone Company of India Ltd. v. Birendra Bahadur Pandey, AIR 1984 SC 667

Harla v. State of Rajasthan, AIR 1951 SC 467

Hussainara Khatoon v. Bihar, AIR 1979 SC 1360

Jagmohan Singh v. Uttar Pradesh, AIR 1973 SC 94

Kehar Singh v. State (Delhi Admn.), 1989 Cri LJ 1

Krishena Kumar v. Union of India, (1990) 4 SCC 207

Manganese Ore (India) Ltd. v. Regional Asstt. CST, (1976) 4 SCC 124

Mohd. Ahmed Khan v. Shah Bano, (1985) 2 SCC 556

Reema Aggarwal v. Anupam, AIR 2004 SC 1418

Sant Ram v. Labh Singh, AIR 1965 SC 314

State of Gujarat v. D.P. Pandey, AIR 1971 SC 866

State of Haryana v. Ranbir, (2006) 5 SCC 167

Teesta Setalvad v. State of Gujarat, (2004) 10 SCC 88

U.P. State Electricity Board v. Pooran Chandra Pandey, (2007) 11 SCC 92

Vellore Citizens Welfare Forum v. Union of India, AIR 1996 SC 2715

Vishaka v. State of Rajasthan, (1997) 6 SCC 241

G. Developments in criminal law, criminal procedure, and the execution of punishment

1. Overview

The history of the development of criminal law in India is closely connected to British colonial policy and administration. The primary legislation that regulates modern criminal law is the Indian Penal Code, 1860 (IPC), which is still in force today. Prior to the enactment of the Penal Code, criminal law was not administered uniformly across the country and was a mixture of Hindu law and Muslim law.[1] A comprehensive account of the various models of criminal law in pre-colonial India is beyond the scope of this Chapter. However, it is important to note the most significant steps that led to the adoption of the IPC and the goals it set out to accomplish.

Prior to the advent of the East India Company, Muslim law was the dominant criminal law of the land under the Mughal dynasty (1526–1707). After the Company acquired *diwani* rights (right to harvest the revenue) over the provinces of Bengal, Bihar, and Orissa in 1765, it opted to continue to administer Muslim criminal law but gradually modified it through regulations leading to a distinctive form of Anglo-Islamic law.[2] The reforms in Indian criminal law carried out by the British colonial administration during the 19th century were inspired both by a liberal and utilitarian impulse, on the one hand, and as a way to secure British colonial interests and sovereignty, on the other.[3]

The first systematic attempts to reform Muslim criminal law were undertaken during the period 1790 to 1793 by Lord *Cornwallis* acting as the governor-general. Changes were introduced in particular to the law of homicide, punishments, and evidence with a view to curbing cruel and arbitrary sanctions and converting murder from a private injury to a public wrong.[4]

The East India Company adopted a different policy in the province of Bombay, large parts of which had not been governed by Muslim law. Criminal law administration in Bombay thus saw the parallel application of different criminal law systems: English law applied to Christians and Parsees, while for Hindus and Muslims, "native expositors" of law were asked about the punishment that would have been prescribed for the offence under Hindu or Muslim law.[5] Conscious of the need for some uniformity, *Elphinstone*, the Governor of Bombay, enacted a series of

---

1 *Yeo*, in: Heller/Dubber (eds.), The Handbook of Comparative Criminal Law, p. 289.

2 *Jain*, Outlines of Indian Legal History, pp. 405, 430.

3 *Wright*, in: Chan/Wright/Yeo (eds.), Codification, Macaulay and the Indian Penal Code, pp. 23–24.

4 *Jain*, Outlines of Indian Legal History, pp. 417–420.

5 *Jain*, Outlines of Indian Legal History, p. 430.

regulations in 1827 that came to be known as the *Elphinstone* Code.[6] Regulation XIV of this Code included a penal code, which remained operative until its replacement in 1860 by the Indian Penal Code.[7] Yet another system of criminal law prevailed in the three presidency towns of Calcutta, Madras, and Bombay, where the English law of crimes formed the basis of the criminal jurisdiction exercised by the Supreme Courts.[8]

This heterogeneous system of laws and the resulting confusion prompted the enactment of the Charter Act of 1833, which established a single legislature for the governance of British India with the authority to legislate for the presidency towns as well as the provinces.[9] The Charter Act contemplated the setting up of Law Commissions to enquire into the state of law and administration in British India and make reports and suggest reforms.[10] Criminal law was indeed specifically chosen as one of the first areas of law to be codified due to the colonial lawmakers' understanding of crime as "universal" as compared to civil law, which was more likely to impinge upon local peculiarities, fears, and prejudices.[11]

The first Law Commission was appointed in 1834 and, spearheaded by *T.B. Macaulay*, took up the task of drafting a penal code for India.[12] The first draft of the penal code was submitted in 1837, and, after a series of delays caused partly by political upheaval, the Penal Code was enacted in 1860; it entered into force on 1 January 1862.[13] Various steps were also taken to systematize the law of criminal procedure. Separate legislation was initially passed to consolidate the various rules and regulations related to procedure in the provinces and the presidency towns, culminating in a uniform law of procedure for the whole of India in the form of the Code of Criminal Procedure, 1882.[14] Similar attempts were made to systematize the law of evidence: while English rules of evidence modified by various Acts of the Indian legislature prevailed in the presidency towns, the provinces were governed by a patchwork of rules based on the practice of courts. These laws were consolidated and overhauled with the passage of the Indian Evidence Act, 1872 prepared under the leadership of Sir *James Fitzjames Stephen*.[15]

---

[6] *Setalvad*, The Common Law in India, pp. 119–120.

[7] *Setalvad*, The Common Law in India, p. 120.

[8] *Setalvad*, The Common Law in India, p. 121.

[9] *Setalvad*, The Common Law in India, p. 120.

[10] *Patra*, in: Pillai/Aquil (eds.), Essays on the Indian Penal Code, p. 34.

[11] *Kolsky*, 23 Law & Hist. Rev. 631, 659 (2005).

[12] *Patra*, in: Pillai/Aquil (eds.), Essays on the Indian Penal Code, pp. 34–35.

[13] *Patra*, in: Pillai/Aquil (eds.), Essays on the Indian Penal Code, pp. 38–41.

[14] Law Commission of India, Report No. 37 on the Code of Criminal Procedure, 1898 (1967), pp. 7–10.

[15] Law Commission of India, Report No. 69 on the Indian Evidence Act, 1872 (1977), pp. 4–12.

The Penal Code, Code of Criminal Procedure, and the Indian Evidence Act have undergone major revisions since their enactments through a variety of avenues. In some cases, special legislation on specific subjects such as terrorism, corruption, or information technology have led to modifications or refinements. Additionally, important amendments targeting various subjects under the codes have been passed, amongst them the recently enacted Criminal Law (Amendment) Act, 2013 dealing with the law related to sexual offenses.[16]

The Law Commission of India has played an important role in a large number of these efforts. A significant proportion of the reports on law reform by the Law Commission deal with recommendations for reforms in criminal law. Several of these have been highly influential in generating a list of issues in the criminal law where reform is needed or in instigating amendments to the law, including: Report No. 29 on the Proposal to Include Certain Social and Economic Offences in the Indian Penal Code, 1860 (1967); Report No. 35 on Capital Punishment (1967); Report No. 37 on the Code of Criminal Procedure, 1898 (1967); Report No. 39 on Punishment for Imprisonment for Life Under the Indian Penal Code (1968); Report No. 40 on Law Relating to Attendance of Prisoners in Courts (1969); Report No. 41 on the Code of Criminal Procedure, 1898 (1969); Report No. 42 on the Indian Penal Code, 1860 (1971); Report No. 43 on Offences Against the National Security (1971); Report No. 47 on the Trial and Punishment of Social and Economic Offences (1972); Report No. 48 on Some Questions under the Code of Criminal Procedure Bill, 1970 (1972); Report No. 64 on the Suppression of Immoral Traffic in Women and Girls Act, 1956 (1975); Report No. 78 on Congestion of Under-Trial Prisoners in Jails (1979); Report No. 84 on Rape and Allied Offences – Some Questions of Substantive Law, Procedure and Evidence (1980); Report No. 87 on Identification of Prisoners Act, 1920 (1980); Report No. 91 on Dowry Deaths and Law Reform (1983); Report No. 94 on Evidence Obtained Illegally or Improperly (1983); Report No. 113 on Injuries in Police Custody (1985); Report No. 142 on Confessional Treatment for Offenders Who on Their Own Initiative Choose to Plead Guilty Without Any Bargaining (1991); Report No. 152 on Custodial Crimes (1994); Report No. 154 on the Code of Criminal Procedure, 1973 (Act No. 2 of 1974) (1996); Report No. 155 on the Narcotics Drugs and Psychotropic Substances Act, 1985 (Act No. 61 of 1985) (1997); Report No. 156 on the Indian Penal Code (1997); Report No. 172 on Review of Rape Laws (2000); Report No. 173 on Prevention of Terrorism Bill, 2000 (2000); Report No. 177 on Law Relating to Arrest (2001); Report No. 185 on Review of the Indian Evidence Act, 1872 (2003); Report No. 187 on Mode of Execution of Death Sentence and Incidental Matters (2003); Report No. 197 on Public Prosecutor's Appointments (2006); Report No. 198 on Witness Identity Protection and Witness Protection Programmes (2006); Report No. 210 on Humanization and Decriminalization of Attempt to Sui-

[16] See below 2.

cide (2008); Report No. 226 on the Inclusion of Acid Attacks as Specific Offences in the Indian Penal Code and a Law for Compensation for Victims of Crime (2009); Report No. 237 on Compounding of (IPC) Offences (2011); Report No. 243 on Sec. 498A, IPC (2012); and Report No. 262 on the Death Penalty (2015).

2. Developments in substantive criminal law

Developments in substantive criminal law have occurred primarily through one of three routes: amendments to the Penal Code, case law, and the introduction of special legislation concerning particular offences. The Penal Code has undergone various piecemeal revisions over the course of its history and there is no consistent philosophy or trend that can be seen as underlying these changes. Nonetheless, specific areas of law stand out as having been the focus of substantial reform efforts.

Amongst these areas, the law relating to sexual offences and other crimes against women deserves special attention. One of the practices that has been criminalized is the dowry system. Initially, the Dowry Prohibition Act, 1961 provided for penalties in the form of imprisonment and fines for any person convicted of demanding, receiving, giving, or abetting the practice of dowry (Secs. 3 and 4). Subsequently, the Penal Code was amended in 1983 to insert Sec. 498A that specifically penalized cruelty to a woman by her husband or his relatives. In 1986, a new offence of "dowry death" was introduced into the Penal Code (Sec. 304B) through the enactment of the Dowry Prohibition (Amendment) Act, 1986. The offence of dowry death criminalizes the causing of the death of a woman within seven years of her marriage where the death does not occur under normal circumstances and there is evidence to demonstrate that she was harassed in connection for a demand for dowry. Recently, due to concerns about the misuse of Sec. 498A IPC voiced by the judiciary[17] and the Law Commission of India,[18] a proposal to make the offence compoundable is being considered by the government. In other words, if the law is amended, a case can be withdrawn if a settlement is reached by the couple and the court gives its permission.[19]

The criminalization of rape and related sexual offences has also been deemed inadequate, leading to a spate of amendments. The Criminal Law Amendment Act, 1983 modified the definition of rape in the Penal Code to include situations of "ag-

[17] *Sushil Kumar Sharma v. Union of India*, (2005) 6 SCC 281; *Preeti Gupta v. State of Jharkhand*, AIR 2010 SC 3363.

[18] Law Commission of India, Report No. 243 on Section 498A IPC (2012).

[19] *Marapakwar*, Anti-Dowry Law Likely to be Amended Soon, The Times of India, 19 Apr. 2015.

gravated rape" under Secs. 376A–E IPC, including custodial rape. The criminalization of sexual offences against children has been strengthened through the enactment of special legislation, The Protection of Children from Sexual Offences Act, 2012, which seeks to protect children from sexual assault, sexual harassment, and pornography. The brutal rape and subsequent death of a young medical student in the capital city of Delhi in 2012 has led to further changes. The Justice *Verma* Committee established in the wake of the incident recommended an overhaul of the definition of rape and the explicit recognition of various other offences of a sexual nature that target women and other vulnerable sections of society as victims: acid attacks against women, a separate offence of sexual assault in addition to the offence of rape, voyeurism, stalking, and a comprehensive prohibition on trafficking.[20] Most of these recommendations were implemented through the Criminal Law (Amendment) Act, 2013.

The law related to suicide and euthanasia has also seen major revisions. While suicide is not criminalized, the attempt to commit suicide is an offence (Sec. 309 IPC), as is the abetment of suicide (Sec. 306 IPC) and the abetment of attempted suicide (Sec. 309 in conjunction with Sec. 107 IPC).[21] The constitutional validity of the crimes of attempt to commit suicide and abetment of suicide was challenged on the ground that their criminalization violates the right to life guaranteed under Art. 21 Const. However, the Supreme Court rejected this argument by holding that the right to life does not include the right to die.[22]

The Law Commission of India has unsuccessfully recommended the decriminalization of the attempt to commit suicide on a number of occasions.[23] A limited exception to the offence of assisting suicide has now been judicially recognized by the Supreme Court in the form of passive euthanasia. In *Aruna Ramchandran Shanbaug v. Union of India*,[24] the Supreme Court distinguished between passive euthanasia, defined as a "withholding of medical treatment for the continuance of life," and active euthanasia, which involved the "use of lethal substances or forces to kill a person." Only the former conduct, pending legislation by Parliament, is permitted in specific circumstances and under judicial supervision.[25] The Law Commission has subsequently endorsed the decriminalization of passive euthanasia and recommended the enactment of suitable legislation to this effect.[26]

---

[20] Report of the Committee on Amendments to Criminal Law (2013), Appendix 4.

[21] *Yeo*, in: Heller/Dubber (eds.), The Handbook of Comparative Criminal Law, p. 313.

[22] *Gian Kaur v. State of Punjab*, AIR 1996 SC 1257.

[23] Law Commission of India, Report No. 42 on the Indian Penal Code, 1860 (1971), paras 16.31–16.33; Law Commission of India, Report No. 210 on Humanization and Decriminalization of Attempt to Suicide (2008).

[24] (2011) 4 SCC 454.

[25] *Aruna Ramchandran Shanbaug v. Union of India*, (2011) 4 SCC 454.

[26] Law Commission of India, Report No. 241 on Passive Euthanasia – A Relook (2012). See also Law Commission of India, Report No. 196 on Medical Treatment to Terminally Ill Patients (Protection of Patients and Medical Practitioners) (2006).

Significant advances have also taken place in the area of corporate criminal liability.[27] Notwithstanding its antiquity, the Penal Code envisages the possibility of holding a corporation criminally responsible for an offence.[28] Sec. 2 IPC provides that every person shall be liable to punishment under the Code and Sec. 11 IPC defines "person" to include "any Company or Association or body of persons, whether incorporated or not." Nevertheless, the earlier jurisprudence of the Supreme Court did not permit the punishment of a company if the punishment for an offence consisted of mandatory imprisonment.[29] This position was reversed in the landmark case of *Standard Chartered v. Directorate of Enforcement*, where the court held that a company is liable to be prosecuted for offences that are punishable by mandatory imprisonment and a fine. However, since the sentence of imprisonment cannot be enforced against the company, it would be within the court's discretion to only impose the sentence of a fine.[30] The court also left open the issue of whether, in addition to statutory strict liability offences,[31] a corporation may also be punished for crimes that require *mens rea*.[32] This question was finally settled in the case of *Iridium India Telecom Ltd. v. Motorola Incorporated & Ors.*, where the Supreme Court held that a corporation, much the same as any individual, can be held liable for the commission of offences that require a *mens rea* element. The criminal intent of the "alter ego" of the corporation, that is, the persons or persons through whom the company can be said to think and act and who control its affairs, would be attributable to the corporation.[33]

Important developments should also be noted in the law related to terrorism and organized crime. Special legislation dealing with terrorism and organized crime legislation has been enacted at both the central and the state level, in most cases to initially deal with a specific event in political history. The Terrorist and Disruptive Activities (Prevention) Act, 1985 and 1987 (TADA) was initially introduced by Parliament primarily to counter the separatist movement in the state of Punjab and neighbouring regions.[34] TADA was widely criticized for violating fair trial rights and was permitted to lapse in 1995 amidst serious and continuing allegations of abuse.[35] Subsequently, the 2001 attack on the Indian Parliament led to the passage of the Prevention of Terrorism Act, 2002 (POTA). POTA fared no better in its adherence to fundamental criminal law principles relating to the requirement of legal-

---

27 On corporate criminal liability, see II.H.2.

28 *Yeo*, in: Heller/Dubber (eds.), The Handbook of Comparative Criminal Law, p. 297.

29 *Assistant Commissioner v. Velliappa Textiles Ltd.*, (2003) 11 SCC 405.

30 AIR 2005 SC 2622.

31 On strict liability, see II.E.4.

32 See *Naniwadekar/Umakanth*, 23(1) National Law School of India Review 109, 111 (2011).

33 AIR 2011 SC 20.

34 *Singh*, in: Ramraj et al. (eds.), Global Anti-Terrorism Law and Policy, p. 421.

35 *Singh*, in: Ramraj et al. (eds.), Global Anti-Terrorism Law and Policy, pp. 423–428.

ity and procedural guarantees. It was repealed in 2004, though several trials pending under the legislation are yet to be concluded.[36]

POTA's repeal coincided with the enactment of the Unlawful Activities Prevention (Amendment) Act, 2004, which incorporated specific terrorism-related provisions into the erstwhile Unlawful Activities Prevention Act, 1967 (UAPA), an act that was directed towards the prevention of unlawful conduct of a general character.[37] Alongside the UAPA, which currently constitutes the primary anti-terrorism law, a host of anti-terrorism and organized crime laws have proliferated at the state level. Prominent amongst them are the Maharashtra Control of Organised Crime Act, 1999, the Karnataka Control of Organised Crime Act, 2000, and the Chhattisgarh Special Public Safety Act, 2006.[38]

3. Developments in criminal procedure

The first consolidated Code of Criminal Procedure, 1882 was replaced by the Code of Criminal Procedure, 1898 to take into account changes concerning procedure introduced by other Acts, deal with other matters brought to the notice of the government of India, and remove difficulties in its administration and implementation.[39] Amending Acts were enacted in 1923 and 1955 to incorporate changes in certain matters of policy, include developments in case law, simplify procedure, and increase the speed and efficiency of trials.[40] A comprehensive review of the Code of Criminal Procedure, 1898 was undertaken in the 41st Report of the Law Commission in 1969, leading to the enactment of the Code of Criminal Procedure, 1973 (CrPC).

The Code of Criminal Procedure has subsequently been amended several times, often in response to Law Commission Reports recommending changes on specific issues, including delays in the trial process, the condition of prisoners and detainees, and procedural issues related to rape and related offences.[41] The government

---

36 Vidhi Centre for Legal Policy, Anti-Terror Law in India: A Study of Statutes and Judgments, 2001–2014 (2015), pp. 6–7.

37 Vidhi Centre for Legal Policy, Anti-Terror Law in India: A Study of Statutes and Judgments, 2001–2014 (2015), pp. 7–8.

38 *Singh*, in: Ramraj et al. (eds.), Global Anti-Terrorism Law and Policy, pp. 441–442; Vidhi Centre for Legal Policy, Anti-Terror Law in India: A Study of Statutes and Judgments, 2001–2014 (2015), p. 8.

39 Law Commission of India, Report No. 37 on the Code of Criminal Procedure, 1898 (1967), p. 5.

40 Law Commission of India, Report No. 37 on the Code of Criminal Procedure, 1898 (1967), p. 5. On the comparative legal classification of Indian criminal procedure, see I.B.1.

41 Law Commission of India, Report No. 154 on the Code of Criminal Procedure, 1973 (1996), p. 1.

has also set up high-level committees from time to time to recommend comprehensive changes to the law of criminal procedure, which have influenced developments in the law. One of the most comprehensive proposals on reforms to the law of criminal procedure was advocated by the 2003 Report of the Justice *Malimath* Committee on Reforms of the Criminal Justice System.[42] The Committee advocated the adoption of some of the features of the inquisitorial model of criminal proceedings into the trial process.[43] These included a specific provision in the Code of Criminal Procedure imposing a duty on the court to "seek the truth," enhancing the court's role in securing evidence and regulating investigations for this purpose, and increasing victim participation in trial proceedings.[44] It also proposed significant changes to the rights of the accused, including the permission to draw an adverse inference from the accused's silence during trial.[45]

Pursuant to the *Malimath* Committee's recommendations, the government established a committee in 2006 headed by *N.R. Madhava Menon* to draft a National Policy Paper on Criminal Justice. The Draft National Policy, submitted in 2007, suggested further reforms, including a comprehensive scheme for victim compensation,[46] the establishment of a central agency with independent powers of investigation, prosecution, and control over serious offences affecting national security,[47] an overhaul of the law and institutional machinery on sentencing,[48] and systematization of standards on arrest, interrogation, detention and bail developed through case law.[49] The Policy Paper also emphasized the need for professionalizing the work of the police, prosecution, and defence services,[50] ensuring effectiveness and efficiency in trial proceedings,[51] and facilitating better use of scientific techniques in criminal investigations and forensic evidence.[52]

Some recent amendments to the Code of Criminal Procedure that deserve special mention relate to the position of victims and to the law of sexual offences. Prior to 2008, the Code recognized a limited provision for compensation in the form of

---

42 Government of India, Ministry of Home Affairs, Report of the Committee on Reforms of Criminal Justice System (2003).

43 Report of the Committee on Reforms of Criminal Justice System, para. 2.15.

44 Report of the Committee on Reforms of Criminal Justice System, paras. 2.16.10, 2.18.8, 2.19.3, 2.20.2.

45 Report of the Committee on Reforms of Criminal Justice System, paras. 3.40–3.42.

46 Government of India, Ministry of Home Affairs, Report of the Committee on Draft National Policy on Criminal Justice (2007), s. 5.2.

47 Report of the Committee on Draft National Policy on Criminal Justice, s. 5.4.

48 Report of the Committee on Draft National Policy on Criminal Justice, s. 5.5.

49 Report of the Committee on Draft National Policy on Criminal Justice, s. 6.4.

50 Report of the Committee on Draft National Policy on Criminal Justice, ss. 6.3, 6.7, 6.8.

51 Report of the Committee on Draft National Policy on Criminal Justice, s. 6.9.

52 Report of the Committee on Draft National Policy on Criminal Justice, ch. 7.

Sec. 357(1) CrPC, whereby if a fine was imposed as part of a sentence, the court could order the amount of the fine to be paid as compensation to the victim. Additionally, under Sec. 357(3) CrPC even in the absence of a fine, the court could order the defendant to pay compensation the amount of which was determined taking into account all circumstances, including the capacity of the accused to pay the amount.[53] Since these provisions were inadequate to deal with a situation where the compensation amount was insufficient to rehabilitate the victim and/or cases where the wrongdoer's liability could not be established, the Code of Criminal Procedure was amended in 2008 to include an expanded right to compensation under Sec. 357A.[54] Sec. 357A CrPC signifies the shift towards a state-funded system for victim compensation under which state governments must allocate money towards and establish a fund for the compensation and rehabilitation of victims. State-level victim compensation schemes that have been established under Sec. 357A CrPC include the Delhi Victims Compensation Scheme, 2011, the Odisha Victim Compensation Scheme, 2012, and the Tamil Nadu Victim Compensation Scheme, 2013.[55] Nevertheless, as noted in the Supreme Court's ruling in *Suresh v. State of Haryana*,[56] the compensation amounts under some of these schemes are fairly low. The court emphasized the need for upward revision of the scale for compensation as well as for the courts to grant interim compensation pending the determination of the final award. Further refinements to the provision for victim compensation were introduced by the Criminal Law Amendment Act, 2013, which requires all hospitals, whether public or private, to provide free medical treatment to victims of certain offences under the Penal Code (Sec. 357C CrPC).

The Criminal Law Amendment Act, 2013 also introduced various changes to the law of procedure in the case of sexual offences. These include provisions for speedy trial, including insofar as possible, the completion of a trial within two months of the filing of the charge sheet (Sec. 309 CrPC) and special procedures for recording information and gathering evidence in the case of sexual offences committed against persons who are either temporarily or permanently physically or mentally disabled (Secs. 54A, 154, 160, 164 CrPC). Provisions of the Indian Evidence Act, 1872 related to the establishment of consent in sexual offences have also been amended to exclude the relevance of evidence as to character and previous sexual experience of the victim (Sec. 53A) and to shift the burden of proof in certain cases (Sec. 114A).

In addition to amendments to the Code of Criminal Procedure, significant procedural developments have taken place by means of judicial interpretation of the Constitution, which enumerates several procedural rights, including due process

[53] *Ankush Shivaji Gaikwad v. State of Maharashtra*, AIR 2013 SC 2454.

[54] Law Commission of India, Report No. 262 on the Death Penalty (2015), pp. 102–103.

[55] Law Commission of India, Report No. 262 on the Death Penalty (2015), p. 103.

[56] (2015) 2 SCC 227.

guarantees.[57] Art. 21 Const. prohibits the deprivation of life and personal liberty except according to procedure established by law. The Supreme Court initially held that the phrase "procedure established by law" only required that the deprivation be strictly in accordance with a valid law enacted by the state.[58] However, this interpretation has subsequently been expanded to provide that the process shall in addition be just, fair, and reasonable.[59] Art. 21 Const. now encompasses numerous procedural rights at the pre-trial, trial, and post-conviction stages.[60] These include the right to legal aid,[61] the right to an expeditious trial (encompassing all stages – investigation, inquiry, trial, appeal, revision, and retrial),[62] and the right against cruel and unusual punishment.[63] The Supreme Court has championed the right to fair trial under Art. 21 Const., holding that it includes the just application of the law so as to discover the truth and prevent miscarriage of justice.[64] The rights of prisoners have also been read into Art. 21 Const.:[65] prisoners are entitled to all fundamental rights unless their liberties have been constitutionally curtailed.[66] Furthermore, detainees facing a trial may not be handcuffed without adequate reasons,[67] and the rights of women and children must be especially safeguarded.[68]

4. Developments in the execution of punishment

The Penal Code forms the basis for the law of punishment in modern India. However, it has been supplemented in important respects by the jurisprudence of the Supreme Court, in particular on capital punishment.

---

57 See I.D.4.

58 *Singh*, V.N. Shukla's Constitution of India, p. 215; *A.K. Gopalan v. State of Madras*, AIR 1950 SC 27; *Bishan Das v. State of Punjab*, AIR 1961 SC 1570; *Kharak Singh v. State of U.P.*, AIR 1963 SC 1295.

59 *Singh*, V.N. Shukla's Constitution of India, pp. 216–221; *Maneka Gandhi v. Union of India*, (1978) 1 SCC 248.

60 *Singh*, V.N. Shukla's Constitution of India, pp. 222–228.

61 *M.H. Hoskot v. State of Maharashtra*, (1978) 3 SCC 544; *Hussainara Khatoon v. State of Bihar*, (1980) 1 SCC 98.

62 *Singh*, V.N. Shukla's Constitution of India, p. 226; *Abdul Rehman Antulay v. R.S. Nayak*, (1992) 1 SCC 225; *Supreme Court Legal Aid Committee v. Union of India*, (1994) 6 SCC 731.

63 *Singh*, V.N. Shukla's Constitution of India, pp. 226–227.

64 *Singh*, V.N. Shukla's Constitution of India, p. 228; *Zahira Habibullah Shaikh (5) v. State of Gujarat*, (2006) 3 SCC 374.

65 *Singh*, V.N. Shukla's Constitution of India, pp. 222–223.

66 *State of Andhra Pradesh v. Challa Ram Krishna Reddy*, (2000) 5 SCC 712.

67 *Prem Shankar v. Delhi Admn.*, (1980) 3 SCC 526; *Sunil Gupta v. State of M.P.*, (1990) 3 SCC 119.

68 See I.D.4.

The Penal Code provisions on punishment reflect the political and philosophical outlook of its principal architect, *Macaulay*, who was highly influenced by the utilitarian philosophy of *Bentham.*[69] The driving spirit behind the infliction of punishment was economy and efficaciousness, with an emphasis on less harsh penalties (for the time) and exceptional resort to capital punishment.[70] The Penal Code envisages the following categories of punishment (Sec. 53): death, transportation (replaced by life imprisonment), penal servitude (abolished in 1949), imprisonment (rigorous and simple), forfeiture of property, and fines.[71] Punishment in the form of dismissal from office, pillory and exhibition of the convicted person on a donkey, and flogging were considered by the drafters but rejected as unreasonable and unnecessarily cruel.[72]

Pursuant to the recommendations of the Law Commission of India, the Indian Penal Code (Amendment) Bill, 1978 proposed additional kinds of punishments in order to achieve deterrence: community service, victim compensation, public censure, and disqualification from public office. However, the Bill was never implemented.[73] An expansion of the categories of punishment has nonetheless occurred through amendments to the Code of Criminal Procedure and case law. For instance, Sec. 357 CrPC authorizes the court to order the defendant to pay compensation to the victim for certain offences and in limited circumstances. Lower level courts have been parsimonious in their application of this discretion, notwithstanding exhortations by the Supreme Court for liberal application of the power to grant compensation.[74] Similarly, under Sec. 8(3) of the Representation of People Act, 1951, a defendant who has been convicted of certain offences may be disqualified from contesting an election to hold office in the central and state legislatures for a limited period.

The Penal Code generally prescribes the maximum punishment for an offence and, in very few instances, also the minimum sentence, but otherwise grants discretion to the courts on the measure of punishment to be awarded. The jurisprudence of the courts on the criteria for sentencing has been far from uniform, leading to disparities in sentencing.[75] The courts have also proposed various theories for the

---

[69] *Smith*, in: Gordon/Fergus (eds.), Legal History in the Making: Proceedings of the Ninth British Legal History Conference Glasgow 1989, p. 159.

[70] *Smith*, in: Gordon/Fergus (eds.), Legal History in the Making: Proceedings of the Ninth British Legal History Conference Glasgow 1989, p. 159.

[71] On the categories of punishments, see in detail I.A.5.d.

[72] *Nigam*, Law of Crimes in India, pp. 233–234.

[73] *Gaur*, Textbook on Indian Penal Code, p. 74.

[74] *Gaur*, Textbook on Indian Penal Code, p. 76 citing *Sarwan Singh v. State of Punjab*, AIR 1978 SC 1525; *Harikishan and State of Haryana v. Sukhbir Singh*, AIR 1988 SC 2131.

[75] *Nigam*, Law of Crimes in India, p. 252.

purposes of punishment, including retribution,[76] deterrence, prevention, and the reformation and rehabilitation of the offender.[77]

There has been some evolution on the practice of capital punishment. In *Bachan Singh v. State of Punjab*, a constitutional bench of the Supreme Court upheld the constitutionality of the death penalty with the caveat that it should be awarded only in the "rarest of rare" cases and that in the event of a conviction for murder, life imprisonment should be the norm and the death penalty the exception. It also introduced guidelines that required the court to consider a number of factors before imposing capital punishment, including the circumstances of the offender and the crime, and the balance to be struck between well recognized standards for aggravating and mitigating circumstances.[78] Further refinements on the circumstances warranting capital punishment were introduced in *Machhi Singh v. State of Punjab*, which identified five categories of cases based on "the motive for, or the manner of commission of the crime, or the anti-social or abhorrent nature of the crime."[79]

Notwithstanding these guidelines, as the Supreme Court has noted in a series of cases, the imposition of the death penalty has been arbitrary and prone to error.[80] In its 2015 report on the death penalty, the Law Commission conducted a comprehensive survey of the jurisprudence on death penalty, the reality of its implementation, and the world-wide trend towards its abolition and recommended the abolition of capital punishment for all crimes with the exception of offences related to terrorism and waging war.[81] Notwithstanding this general trend towards the recognition of the exceptional nature of capital punishment, the death penalty has been authorized for various offences in recent legislation such as the Criminal Law (Amendment) Act, 2013, which permits capital punishment in situations where the crime of rape leads to the death of the victim or causes her to be in a permanent vegetative state (Sec. 376A IPC), and for certain repeat offenders in the case of rape (Sec. 376E IPC).

The Supreme Court has also sought to mitigate the harshness of the punishment of solitary confinement under Sec. 73 IPC, emphasizing its exceptional nature that is justified only in crimes of excessive brutality.[82] Any imposition of solitary con-

---

[76] *Dhananjoy Chatterjee v. State of West Bengal*, (1994) 2 SCC 220.

[77] *State of Gujarat v. Hon'ble High Court of Gujarat*, AIR 1998 SC 3164. *See* PSA Pillai's Criminal Law, pp. 287–289.

[78] (1980) 2 SCC 684.

[79] (1983) 3 SCC 470.

[80] See, e.g., *Santosh Kumar Satishbhushan Bariyar v. State of Maharashtra*, (2009) 6 SCC 498; *Sangeet v. State of Haryana*, (2013) 2 SCC 452; *Swamy Shraddhananda v. State of Karnataka*, (2008) 13 SCC 767; *Shankar Kisanrao Khade v. State of Maharashtra*, (2013) 5 SCC 546.

[81] Law Commission of India, Report No. 262 on the Death Penalty (2015).

[82] *Kishore Singh Ravinder Dev v. State of Rajasthan*, AIR 1981 SC 625.

finement must adhere to strict procedural safeguards.[83] Despite these judicial safeguards, the practice of solitary confinement of prisoners, especially those on death row, is rampant.[84]

Under Entry 4, List II (State List) of the Seventh Schedule to the Constitution, "Prisons, reformatories, Borstal institutions and other institutions of a like nature" are a state subject. Thus, the administration and management of prisons and allied institutions is the responsibility of the state governments and is carried out through rules and regulations enacted under the Prisons Act, 1894, and the Prison Manuals of the respective state governments. Nonetheless, due to the political significance of the matter and in order to promote uniformity across states, the central government has taken various prison reform initiatives to assist the state governments in this function.[85] These include the enactment of a Model Prison Manual in 2016.[86]

Prison reforms in India have focused on a number of key issues, such as overcrowding, poor prison conditions, including prisoner security, safety, and hygiene, and the needs of special classes of prisoners, such as women.[87] For instance, according to the 2015 Prison Statistics released by the National Crime Records Bureau, the occupancy rate in prisons stands at 114.4 %, with 67.2 % of the prison population consisting of undertrials.[88] Several measures have been proposed, both by the central government and the Supreme Court, to tackle overcrowding and the consequent problems with prison conditions, in part by reducing the numbers of undertrial prisoners. The 2007 National Policy on Prison Reforms and Correctional Administration prepared by the Bureau of Police Research and Development recommended reducing the prison population by expediting the construction of new prisons while simultaneously disposing of undertrial cases more efficiently through fast track courts, operationalizing plea bargaining, and implementing liberalized bail procedures.[89] The Policy also made specific recommendations to improve sanitation, accommodation, nutrition, and medical and recreational facilities in prisons.[90]

---

83 *Sunil Batra v. Delhi Administration*, (1978) 4 SCC 494.

84 *Shatrughan Chauhan v. Union of India*, (2014) 3 SCC 1.

85 *Pande*, in: van Zyl Smit/Dünkel (eds.), Imprisonment Today and Tomorrow, pp. 375, 379.

86 Government of India, Ministry of Home Affairs, Prison Reforms – Center State Division.

87 *Pande*, in: van Zyl Smit/Dünkel (eds.), Imprisonment Today and Tomorrow, pp. 380–398.

88 National Crime Records Bureau, Prison Statistics India 2015, p. i.

89 Bureau of Police Research and Development, 2007 National Policy on Prison Reforms and Correctional Administration, Part III.

90 Bureau of Police Research and Development, 2007 National Policy on Prison Reforms and Correctional Administration, Part III.

Special guidelines and institutional arrangements have also been proposed for different classes of offenders such as women and children. The Report of the All India Committee on Jail Reforms (1980–83) suggested a variety of special prisons or annexes for categories of offenders, including women, juveniles, and undertrials.[91] The National Expert Committee on Women Prisoners (1986–87) conducted a detailed evaluation of the procedures for the handling of women offenders in detention and in custody and recommended a series of administrative and legislative reforms relating to their custody and rehabilitation as well as rules for their superintendence and management.

The Supreme Court has also played an active role in introducing prison reforms and highlighting the fundamental rights of prisoners.[92] Early on in its jurisprudence, the court emphasized the therapeutic role of punishment and the Gandhian approach to treating offenders as patients and prisons as mental and moral hospitals.[93] The Court has lauded the institution of open prisons as a way to further the aims of correctional treatment and restore a sense of dignity and citizenship in the prisoner.[94] It has pioneered a fundamental right to compensation for prisoners for violations of the right to life and personal liberty under Art. 21 Const. and ordered compensation in cases of illegal detention and severe ill-treatment of prisoners.[95] The Court has also advocated the urgent resolution of the problem of prison overcrowding and its effect on the basic needs of prisoners, including health and hygiene.[96] In this process, it has issued a number of guidelines and rulings to various branches of the legislature and executive to institute and implement prison reforms.[97]

Early release and review of cases of undertrials have been a major focus of reform efforts by the central government and the Supreme Court. The Ministry of Home Affairs took the initial lead in this respect by issuing advisories in 2011 and 2013, providing for the setting up of Under Trial Review Committees in every district. These committees, which are headed by the district judge as chairman and the district magistrate and district superintendent of police as members, are expected to

---

91 Report of the All India Committee on Jail Reforms (1980–83) vol. I, pp. 110–111, 174, 187.

92 *Gaur*, Textbook on Indian Penal Code, pp. 900–910; *Bhuvan Mohan Patnaik v. State of A.P.*, AIR 1974 SC 2092.

93 *Mohammad Giasuddin v. State of A.P.*, AIR 1977 SC 1926.

94 *Dharambir v. State of U.P.*, AIR 1979 SC 1595.

95 *Rudul Sah v. State of Bihar*, AIR 1983 SC 1086; *Khatri v. State of Bihar*, AIR 1981 SC 928.

96 *Ramamurthy v. State of Karnataka*, AIR 1997 SC 1739.

97 See, e.g., *Ramamurthy v. State of Karnataka*, AIR 1997 SC 1739; *Inhuman Conditions in 1382 Prisons, In Re*, (2016) 3 SCC 700; *Inhuman Conditions in 1382 Prisons, In Re*, (2016) 14 SCC 815; *Inhuman Conditions in 1382 Prisons (II), In Re*, (2016) 10 SCC 17.

meet every three months and review the cases of undertrials.[98] The Supreme Court has been at the forefront of issuing directions to the executive to ensure the speedy establishment and efficient functioning of the Under Trial Review Committees.[99]

Special legislation has also been enacted for the punishment of certain classes of offenders such as juveniles. The Juvenile Justice (Care and Protection of Children) Act, 2015 provides for the following categories of sanctions for a juvenile found by the Juvenile Justice Board to have committed an offence: advice and admonition; participation in counselling; community service; payment of a fine; release on probation of good conduct for a maximum three-year period; stay in a special home established or certified by the state government for three years.[100] A juvenile may not be sentenced to death or imprisonment for life without the possibility of release (Sec. 21). However, juveniles ages 16 and 17 can be tried as adults for heinous offences before the Children's Court (Secs. 15, 18(3), and 19).

Bibliography and further reading

Bureau of Police Research and Development, 2007 National Policy on Prison Reforms and Correctional Administration. http://bprd.nic.in/content/196_1_NPPRCA.aspx [last visited June 2017].

Gaur, K.D., Textbook on Indian Penal Code. 5th ed. New Delhi 2014 (repr. 2015).

Government of India, Ministry of Home Affairs, Prison Reforms – Center State Division. http://mha1.nic.in/PrisonReforms/home.html [last visited June 2017].

– Report of the All India Committee on Jail Reforms (1980–83).

– Report of the Committee on Reforms of Criminal Justice System, vol. I (2003).

– Report of the Committee on Draft National Policy on Criminal Justice (2007).

Jain, M.P., Outlines of Indian Legal History. 3d ed. Bombay 1972, pp. 403–431.

Kolsky, Elizabeth, Codification and the Rule of Colonial Difference: Criminal Procedure in British India. 23 Law & Hist. Rev. 631–683 (2005).

Law Commission of India, Report No. 262 on the Death Penalty (2015).

– Report No. 243 on Section 498A IPC (2012).

– Report No. 241 on Passive Euthanasia – A Relook (2012).

– Report No. 210 on Humanization and Decriminalization of Attempt to Suicide (2008).

---

98 Ministry of Home Affairs Advisory, vide No. 17011/2/2010-PR (May 2011); Ministry of Home Affairs Advisory, vide No. V-13013/70/2012-IS(VI) (Jan. 2013).

99 *Inhuman Conditions in 1382 Prisons, In Re*, (2016) 3 SCC 700; *Inhuman Conditions in 1382 Prisons, In Re*, (2016) 14 SCC 815.

100 Juvenile Justice (Care and Protection of Children) Act, 2000, Sec. 18.

– Report No. 196 on Medical Treatment to Terminally Ill Patients (Protection of Patients and Medical Practitioners) (2006).

– Report No. 154 on the Code of Criminal Procedure, 1973 (1996).

– Report No. 69 on the Indian Evidence Act, 1872 (1977).

– Report No. 42 on the Indian Penal Code, 1860 (1971).

– Report No. 37 on the Code of Criminal Procedure, 1898 (1967).

Marapakwar, Prafulla, Anti-Dowry Law Likely to be Amended Soon. The Times of India, 19 Apr. 2015.

Naniwadekar, Mihir/Umakanth, V., Corporate Criminal Liability and Securities Offerings: Rationalizing the Iridium-Motorola Case. 23 Nat'l L. Sch. India Rev. 109–132 (2011).

National Crime Records Bureau, Prison Statistics 2015. http://ncrb.nic.in/StatPublications/PSI/Prison2015/PrisonStat2015.htm [last visited June 2017].

Nigam, R.C., Law of Crimes in India, vol I: Principles of Criminal Law. London 1965.

Pande, Bhuvan, India. In: Dirk van Zyl Smit/Frieder Dünkel (eds.), Imprisonment Today and Tomorrow. 2d ed. The Hague 2001, pp. 373–399.

Patra, A.C., Historical Introduction to the Indian Penal Code. In: K.N. Chandrasekharan Pillai/Shabistan Aquil (eds.), Essays on the Indian Penal Code. Delhi 2005, pp. 33–43.

Setalvad, M.C./Vibhufhan, Padma, The Common Law in India: The Hamlyn Lectures. London 1960.

Singh, Mahendra P., V.N. Shukla's Constitution of India. 12th ed. Lucknow 2016.

Singh, Ujjwal Kumar, Mapping Anti-Terror Legal Regimes in India. In: Victor V. Ramraj/Michael Hor/Kent Roach/George Williams (eds.), Global Anti-Terrorism Law and Policy. Cambridge 2012, pp. 420–446.

Smith, K.J.M., Macaulay's "Utilitarian" Indian Penal Code: An Illustration of the Accidental Function of Time, Place and Personalities in Law-Making. In: W.M. Gordon/T.D. Fergus (eds.), Legal History in the Making: Proceedings of the Ninth British Legal History Conference Glasgow 1989. London 1991, pp. 147–164.

Suresh, V./Nagasaila, D., PSA Pillai's Criminal Law. 9th ed. Delhi 2005, pp. 286–324.

Verma, J.S./Seth, Leila/Subramanium, Gopal, Report of the Committee on Amendments to Criminal Law (2013).

Vidhi Centre for Legal Policy, Anti-Terror Law in India: A Study of Statutes and Judgments, 2001–2014 (2015).

Wright, Barry, Macaulay's Indian Penal Code: Historical Context and Originating Principles. In: Wing-Cheong Chan/Barry Wright/Stanley Yeo (eds.), Codification, Macaulay and the Indian Penal Code: The Legacies and Modern Challenges of Criminal Law Reform. Surrey 2011, pp. 19–55.

Yeo, Stanley, India. In: Kevin Jon Heller/Markus D. Dubber (eds.), The Handbook of Comparative Criminal Law. Stanford 2011, pp. 288–319.

Table of cases

A.K. Gopalan v. State of Madras, AIR 1950 SC 27

Abdul Rehman Antulay v. R.S. Nayak, (1992) 1 SCC 225

Ankush Shivaji Gaikwad v. State of Maharashtra, AIR 2013 SC 2454

Aruna Ramchandran Shanbaug v. Union of India, (2011) 4 SCC 454

Assistant Commissioner v. Velliappa Textiles Ltd., (2003) 11 SCC 405

Bachan Singh v. State of Punjab, (1980) 2 SCC 684

Bhuvan Mohan Patnaik v. State of A.P., AIR 1974 SC 2092

Bishan Das v. State of Punjab, AIR 1961 SC 1570

Dhananjoy Chatterjee v. State of West Bengal, (1994) 2 SCC 220

Dharambir v. State of U.P., AIR 1979 SC 1595

Gian Kaur v. State of Punjab, AIR 1996 SC 1257

Harikishan and State of Haryana v. Sukhbir Singh, AIR 1988 SC 2131

Hussainara Khatoon v. State of Bihar, (1980) 1 SCC 98

Inhuman Conditions in 1382 Prisons, In Re, (2016) 3 SCC 700

Inhuman Conditions in 1382 Prisons, In Re, (2016) 14 SCC 815

Inhuman Conditions in 1382 Prisons (II), In Re, (2016) 10 SCC 17

Iridium India Telecom Ltd. v. Motorola Incorporated & Ors., AIR 2011 SC 20

Kewal Pati v. State of U.P., (1995) 3 SCC 600

Kharak Singh v. State of U.P., AIR 1963 SC 1295

Khatri v. State of Bihar, AIR 1981 SC 928

Kishore Singh Ravinder Dev v. State of Rajasthan, AIR 1981 SC 625

M.H. Hoskot v. State of Maharashtra, (1978) 3 SCC 544

Machhi Singh v. State of Punjab, (1983) 3 SCC 470

Maneka Gandhi v. Union of India, (1978) 1 SCC 248

Mohammad Giasuddin v. State of A.P., AIR 1977 SC 1926

Murti Devi v. State of Delhi, (1998) 9 SCC 604

Preeti Gupta v. State of Jharkhand, AIR 2010 SC 3363

Prem Shankar v. Delhi Admn., (1980) 3 SCC 526

Ramamurthy v. State of Karnataka, AIR 1997 SC 1739

Rudul Sah v. State of Bihar, AIR 1983 SC 1086

Sangeet v. State of Haryana, (2013) 2 SCC 452

Santosh Kumar Satishbhushan Bariyar v. State of Maharashtra, (2009) 6 SCC 498

Sarwan Singh v. State of Punjab, AIR 1978 SC 1525

Shankar Kisanrao Khade v. State of Maharashtra, (2013) 5 SCC 546

Shatrughan Chauhan v. Union of India, (2014) 3 SCC 1

Standard Chartered v. Directorate of Enforcement, AIR 2005 SC 2622

State of Andhra Pradesh v. Challa Ram Krishna Reddy, (2000) 5 SCC 712

State of Gujarat v. Hon'ble High Court of Gujarat, AIR 1998 SC 3164

Sunil Batra v. Delhi Administration, (1978) 4 SCC 494

Sunil Gupta v. State of M.P., (1990) 3 SCC 119

Supreme Court Legal Aid Committee v. Union of India, (1994) 6 SCC 731

Suresh v. State of Haryana, (2015) 2 SCC 227

Sushil Kumar Sharma v. Union of India, (2005) 6 SCC 281

Swamy Shraddhananda v. State of Karnataka, (2008) 13 SCC 767

Zahira Habibullah Shaikh (5) v. State of Gujarat, (2006) 3 SCC 374

List of abbreviations in country report India

AIR	All India Reporter
Am. J. Comp. L.	American Journal of Comparative Law
Am. U. Int'l L. Rev.	American University International Law Review
Anr.	Another
A.P.	Andhra Pradesh
CBI	Central Bureau of Investigation
Colum. J. Transnat'l L.	Columbia Journal of Transnational Law
Cri LJ	Criminal Law Journal
CrPC	Code of Criminal Procedure
Eng. Rep.	English Reports
GDP	Gross Domestic Product
G.M.	General Manager
IAEA	International Atomic Energy Agency
ICCPR	International Covenant on Civil and Political Rights
ICESCR	International Covenant on Economic, Social and Cultural Rights
Int'l & Comp. L.Q.	International and Comparative Law Quarterly
Int'l Soc. Sci. Bull.	International Social Science Bulletin
Interpol	International Criminal Police Organization
IOM	International Organization for Migration

IPC	Indian Penal Code
IPCS	Institute of Peace and Conflict Studies
Jaipur L.J.	Jaipur Law Journal
J. Indian L. Inst.	Journal of the Indian Law Institute
J. Int'l Crim. Just.	Journal of International Criminal Justice
J. Int'l L.	Journal of International Law
JJA	Juvenile Justice (Care and Protection of Children) Act, 2000
J. Soc. Issues	Journal of Social Issues
KSRTC	Karnataka State Road Transport Corporation
Law & Hist. Rev.	Law and History Review
L.Q. Rev.	Law Quarterly Review
MIA	Moore's Indian Appeals
M.P.	Madhya Pradesh
Nat'l L. Sch. India Rev.	National Law School of India Review
NCT	National Capital Territory
ONGC	Oil and Natural Gas Commission
OPCW	Organization for the Prohibition of Chemical Weapons
P&H	Punjab & Haryana
PIL	Public Interest Litigation
POTA	Prevention of Terrorism Act, 2002
Rly.	Railway
SAARC	South Asian Association for Regional Cooperation
SC	Supreme Court
SCALE	Supreme Court Almanac
SCC	Supreme Court Cases
SCR	Supreme Court Reports
Stan. L. Rev.	Stanford Law Review
Stud.	Studies
TADA	Terrorist and Disruptive Activities (Prevention) Act, 1985 and 1987
Third World Legal Studies	Third World Legal Stud.
UAPA	Unlawful Activities Prevention Act, 1967
UNTC	United Nations Treaty Collection
U.P.	Uttar Pradesh

National characteristics, fundamental principles, and history of criminal law in

Italy*

Konstanze Jarvers

---

* This country report first appeared in the German version of the project as "Rahmenbedingungen, Vorgaben, Grundlagen und Entwicklung des Strafrechts in Italien." In: Ulrich Sieber/Karin Cornils (eds.), Nationales Strafrecht in rechtsvergleichender Darstellung, vol. 1. Berlin 2009, pp. 277–339. It was translated, revised, and updated for this publication.

For constructive comments and valuable suggestions, the author would like to thank Dr. *Till Bettels* (Office of the Prosecutor, Offenburg), Ms. stud. jur. *Marie Endres* (University of Freiburg), Prof. *Luigi Foffani* (University of Modena and Reggio Emilia), and Dr. *Donato Vozza* (University of Naples II).

Contents

A. National characteristics

1. Geography

Italy is located in southern Europe, primarily on the Apennine peninsula, which extends into the Mediterranean Sea. With a coastline of 8,970 km,[1] the country extends from the Alps to the central Mediterranean and borders France in the northwest, Switzerland and Austria in the north, and Slovenia in the northeast.[2] Except for the Po Valley, its terrain is generally mountainous, with the Alps in the North and the Apennine Mountains as the country's backbone. At 652 km, the Po is the longest of Italy's rivers. There are several volcanoes, some of which are still active, including the highest, Mount Etna, at 3,340 m, and the second highest, Mount Vesuvius, at 1,277 m. The associated seismic danger is considerable: since 1997, there have been a number of serious earthquakes with a local earthquake magnitude (Richter) above 5.0 (1997, 1998, 2002, 2009, and 2012); in 2016, there was an earthquake with a magnitude above 6.0.[3] The capital of Italy is Rome (Art. 114 para. 3 Constitution of the Italian Republic, *Costituzione della Repubblica italiana*, Cost.).

Along with its two largest islands, Sicily and Sardinia, Italian territory encompasses many more islands and island groups. In addition, Italy possesses an exclave in Switzerland: the community of Campione. The Republic of San Marino *(Repubblica di San Marino)* and Vatican City *(Città del Vaticano)* are two sovereign microstates within Italy. The country's total area is 302,073 sq km,[4] ranking it seventh in the European Union behind France, Spain, Sweden, Germany, Finland, and Poland.

---

1 Istituto nazionale di statistica – annuario statistico italiano 2016, p. 8.

2 CIA World Factbook: Italy, Geography.

3 Istituto nazionale di statistica – annuario statistico italiano 2016, p. 9.

4 Istituto nazionale di statistica – annuario statistico italiano 2016, p. 3.

2. Population

a) Population and demographics

With a population of almost 61 million (31 December 2015),[5] Italy ranks fourth in the European Union behind Germany, France, and the United Kingdom. Its population density is 201 per sq km.[6]

69 % of Italians live in cities.[7] In the 1950s and 1960s, in particular, Italy experienced massive migration from rural to urban areas. This trend appears to have abated somewhat. Italy's largest cities are Rome (2,864,731), Milan (1,345,851), Naples (974,074), Turin (890,529), Palermo (674,435), and Genoa (586,655).[8]

Some 51.4 % of the population are women. The birthrate has been declining steadily since the mid-1980s. Individuals ages 0 to 19 account for 18 %, ages 20 to 39 for 23 %, ages 40 to 59 for 31 %, ages 60 to 79 for 21 %, and those ages 80 and above for 7 % of the total population.[9] Some 5,026,153 individuals, or approximately 8.3 % of the country's inhabitants, are foreign nationals (2,381,487 males; 2,644,666 females). The majority of these are from Romania (1,151,395), Albania (467,687), Morocco (437,485), the People's Republic of China (271,330), Ukraine (230,728), and the Philippines (165,900).[10]

b) Language

The official language is Italian. Regional official languages are French (in the region of the Aosta Valley), Slovene (in the provinces of Trieste and Gorizia), and German and Ladin (in the province of Bolzano). These linguistic minorities are protected under Art. 6 Cost. Since 1999, the following historical minority languages have enjoyed special protection in the areas where they are spoken: Albanian, Catalan, Croatian, Franco-Provencal, French, Friulian, German, Greek, Ladin, Occitan, Sardinian, and Slovene.[11] In 2015, 507,845 illiterates were counted in Italy, constituting less than 1 % of the population; of these, 184,630 were men, 323,215 women.[12]

---

5 Istituto nazionale di statistica – annuario statistico italiano 2016, p. 77.

6 Istituto nazionale di statistica – annuario statistico italiano 2016, p. 12.

7 CIA World Factbook: Italy, People and Society.

8 As of 2015, Fischer Weltalmanach 2017, p. 229.

9 As of 1 Jan. 2016, Istituto nazionale di statistica.

10 As of 1 Jan. 2016, Istituto nazionale di statistica.

11 See L. 15 Dec. 1999, n. 482.

12 UNESCO Institute for statistics.

c) Religion

The predominant religion is Roman Catholicism (89 %).[13] In addition, there are 1.3 million Muslims, 550,000 Protestants, some 230,000 Jehovah's Witnesses, 200,000 Buddhists, 110,000 Hindus, and 40,000 Jews in Italy.[14]

3. Economy

Italy is an industrial state with a social market economy. Numerous privatizations have reduced the share of state-run enterprises, which was originally very high. The gross domestic product is 1.636 trillion Euro[15] (27,044 Euro per capita[16]), 2 % of which are generated in agriculture, 24 % in industry, and 74 % in the service sector.[17] Employment sectors are agriculture (4 %), manufacturing (27 %), and service (69 %).[18] The gross national income per capita is 25,400 Euro.[19] The official currency is the Euro. Many private companies are headquartered in the highly-developed north, whereas agriculture is predominant in the less-developed south.

Italy is the third largest economy in the Eurozone.[20] The country was hard hit by the financial crisis and continues to struggle with the consequences. Many economic recovery plans were created to boost the economy. In 2015, Italy's annual economic output rose for the first time in three years: the growth rate was 0.8 %. Germany is Italy's top trading partner. In 2015, the inflation rate was 0.1 %.[21]

While unemployment hovered around 10 % throughout the 1990s and sank to 6 % by 2007, the number of unemployed persons rose continuously as a result of the financial crisis 2007/2008 and reached more than 12 % by 2013/2014. As the strong regulation of the labor market was seen to be another factor contributing to this increase, the "Jobs Act" was enacted in 2014.[22] Among other things, this legislation loosened protections against dismissal. Beginning in 2015, a positive change

---

13 As of 2016, Fischer Weltalmanach 2017, p. 229.

14 As of Aug. 2017, Foreign Office.

15 As of 2015, Fischer Weltalmanach, p. 229.

16 As of 2015, Istituto nazionale di statistica.

17 As of 2016, Fischer Weltalmanach 2017, p. 229.

18 As of 2014, Fischer Weltalmanach 2017, p. 229.

19 As of 2014, Istituto nazionale di statistica.

20 CIA World Factbook: Italy, Economy.

21 Auswärtiges Amt, Fischer Weltalmanach 2017, p. 229.

22 D.L. 20 March 2014, n. 34, converted with amendments into L. 16 May 2014, n. 78. and L. 10 Dec. 2014, n. 183; this legislation provided the authorization for numerous legislative decrees *(decreto legislativo)* that were enacted in 2015 and 2016.

became apparent and unemployment fell slowly but constantly. In the second quarter of 2015, unemployment was 12.2 %; in the second quarter of 2016, it was 11.6 %; and in the second quarter of 2017, it was 11.2 % (10.4 % of men and 12.4 % of women were unemployed).[23] While the number of unemployed youth ages 15 to 24 also decreased, youth unemployment is still at 35.4 % (second quarter 2017).[24] It should be noted that there are significant regional differences in this context: whereas the unemployment rate in northern Italy was 6.8 % in the second quarter of 2017, it was 10.0 % in the center of the country, and 19.6 % in the south.[25]

4. System of government

– System of government

The unification of Italy in 1861 gave rise to a nation state, the Kingdom of Italy *(Regno d'Italia)*, with a monarch as head of state. In 1922, fascists under the leadership of *Benito Mussolini* took over, turned the monarchy into a totalitarian state, and entered World War II on Hitler's side. After the fall of the government in autumn of 1943, Italy switched sides and declared war on its former allies. After World War II, Italians were asked to vote in a referendum on the form of government. On 2 June 1946, the monarchists lost (54.3 % to 47.7 %), and the Italian Republic *(Repubblica Italiana)* was proclaimed. King *Vittorio Emanuele III* had abdicated shortly before, and his son *Umberto II* ascended the throne. When the old and the new king went into exile on 13 June 1946, Umberto II temporarily passed the function of head of state to Prime Minister *Alcide De Gasperi*.[26] Ever since, Italy has been a parliamentary republic based on the principle of separation of powers (Arts. 1, 5, and 94 Cost.).[27]

– President

The president *(presidente della Repubblica)* is the head of state (Arts. 83–91 Cost.). Elected in a secret ballot for a seven-year term by parliament in a joint session *(seduta comune)* and by three representatives of each of the regions (due to its size, Valle d'Aosta has only one representative), the president represents national unity *(unità nazionale)*. His role is not merely representational, however, he or she is also the guarantor of the Constitution, in the sense that it is the president's role to

23 Based on persons ages 15 years and above. Istituto nazionale di statistica.

24 Istituto nazionale di statistica.

25 Istituto nazionale di statistica.

26 See also *Onida/Pedrazza Gorleo*, Compendio, p. 9.

27 See also *Onida/Pedrazza Gorleo*, Compendio, p. 164.

ensure, during a governmental crisis, for example, that the constitutional organs function and that they cooperate with one another. While the president has a special position vis à vis the three branches of power – legislature, executive, and judiciary – he or she does not actively participate in national policy making.[28]

– Legislature

Legislative powers are exercised primarily by the national parliament. The regions and autonomous provinces have no power to make criminal law (Art. 117 para. 2l Cost.); they can only provide for administrative sanctions. An exception of sorts applies to the region of Trentino-Alto Adige and the provinces of Trento and Bolzano. They are authorized to provide criminal punishments so as to protect the provisions of their own laws; however, these must conform to those included in the corresponding offense definitions in the national law.[29] In certain cases, the government may also make criminal laws in the form of decree laws *(decreto legge)* and legislative decrees *(decreto legislativo)*.[30] A law may be repealed by referendum *(referendum)*. A referendum is conducted if 500,000 voters so request. Referendums may not be called regarding tax and budgetary laws, laws governing amnesty and remission, or laws ratifying international conventions (Art. 75 Cost.).

The bicameral parliament *(parlamento bicamerale)* consisting of the Chamber of Deputies *(Camera dei Deputati)* and the Senate *(Senato)* is elected in general and direct elections to a five-year term (Arts. 55–82 Cost.). The two chambers have the same powers, and they legislate together (Art. 70 Cost.). They differ only in terms of the number and composition of their members and how they are elected. There are 630 deputies in the Chamber of Deputies (including 12 representatives of expatriates). There are 315 senators who are elected by region and a number of senators who are appointed for life. Former presidents of the Republic and a maximum of five individuals appointed by the president for their special achievements in society, science, the arts, or literature (Art. 59 Cost.) are senators for life.

For more than 40 years, the Italian election system was purely proportional. This led to the fragmentation of parties, promoted instability, and generated a total of 47 governments from 1948 to 1993. In 1993,[31] a referendum triggered a change in the electoral system. Accordingly, three-quarters of the seats in both chambers were allocated on the basis of the plurality system and one-quarter of the seats on the basis of proportional representation, and a threshold clause – that is, the minimum share of the vote that a political party must receive in order to obtain a seat – of

---

28 *Onida/Pedrazza Gorleo*, Compendio, p. 240; *Riz/Happacher*, Grundzüge, pp. 113–114.

29 Art. 23 Statuto Speciale per il Trentino-Alto Adige, D.P.R 31 Aug. 1972, n. 670.

30 See I.F.2.

31 By the so-called *Legge Mattarella*, L. 4 Aug. 1993 n. 276 and n. 277.

4 % was introduced.[32] In 2005,[33] proportional representation was reinstated because the reform failed to meet expectations in terms of government stability. This time, however, there was a majority bonus and a threshold clause (except for the Valle d'Aosta region).[34] In 2013, the Constitutional Court ruled some aspects of the election process unconstitutional and called for a new election law.[35] In response, a reform concerning the election of the Chamber of Deputies was enacted in 2015;[36] this reform was modified in January 2017 by the Constitutional Court.[37] Accordingly, the electoral threshold was a mere 3 %, and a party that garners at least 40 % of the vote got a plurality bonus in order to reach 340 (= 54 %) seats. The electoral lists were made up of an equal number of men and women.

There had been plans in the context of a further constitutional reform to abolish the bicameral system of the Italian parliament so as to reduce gridlock in the legislative process. The idea was to make significant cuts in the competencies of the Senate and to reduce the number of senators from 315 to 100. The law reforming the Constitution was approved in early 2016 by an absolute majority but not by a qualified majority of two-thirds in each house. Thus, pursuant to Art. 138 Cost., a referendum was required.[38] Held on 4 December 2016, the referendum resulted in a clear (60 %) rejection of the reform so that, initially, the old election law remained in effect. In November 2017, a new election system was finally passed.[39] Consequently, in both houses, 37 % of seats are allocated via the first-past-the-post system (directly elected) and 61 % are allocated using a proportional method (indirectly elected based on party lists). In addition, twelve deputies and six senators (2 %) are elected by Italians living abroad. There is a 3 % threshold for parties and 10 % for coalitions.[40]

The legislative process is regulated in Arts. 70–82 Cost. Typically, bills are introduced by the government (legislative initiative); the presentation to parliament of bills initiated by the government must be authorized by the president of the Republic (Art. 87 para. 4 Cost.), who can only evaluate the bill's constitutionality. The following parties also enjoy the right of legislative initiative: members of par-

---

32 *Becchi/Palma*, I sistemi elettorali, pp. 21–29; *Onida/Pedrazza Gorleo*, Compendio, pp. 167–168; *Riz/Happacher*, Grundzüge, p. 89.

33 By the so-called *Porcellum*, L. 21 Dec. 2005, n. 270.

34 *Becchi/Palma*, I sistemi elettorali, pp. 31–36; *Onida/Pedrazza Gorleo*, Compendio, pp. 189–176; *Riz/Happacher*, Grundzüge, pp. 89–91.

35 Corte Cost. 13 Jan. 2014, n. 1, Giur.Cost. 2014, pp. 1–63. *Becchi/Palma*, I sistemi elettorali, pp. 36–40.

36 By the so-called *Italicum*, L. 6 May 2015, n. 52.

37 Corte Cost. 9 Feb. 2017, n. 35, Giur. Cost. 2017, pp. 225–327.

38 Fischer Weltalmanach 2017, p. 231; *Magnoli Bocchi*, EconoMonitor, 1 Dec. 2016, footnote 18.

39 The so-called *Rosatellum-bis*, L. 3 Nov. 2017, n. 165

40 *Becchi/Palma*, I sistemi elettorali, pp. 69–74.

liament (Art. 71 para. 1 Cost.), Regional Councils (Art. 121 para. 2 Cost.), the National Council for Economics and Labor (*Consiglio nazionale dell'economia e del lavoro*, CNL, Art. 99 para. 3), and the people by way of a legislative proposal signed by a minimum of 50,000 eligible voters (Art. 71 para. 2 Cost.).

In parliament, bills are first debated in committee. In proceedings involving rapporteur committees *(commissione in sede referente)*, which is the regular procedure for particularly important bills, the final vote takes place in the plenum (Art. 72 para. 4 Cost.). In contrast, each chamber has rules establishing when the examination and approval of bills can be deferred to a committee acting in a legislative capacity *(commissione in sede deliberante)*. In such cases, the final vote of the committee – whose membership mirrors the proportions of the parties in the respective chamber – takes the place of a plenary vote. Proceedings may be moved to the full assembly at any time, however, if the government, one-tenth of the members of the chamber, or one-fifth of the members of the committee so request (Art. 72 para. 3 Cost.).[41]

Before promulgating a law, which the president of the Republic must do within one month of its approval by parliament (Art. 73 para. 1 Cost.), the president may send it back to the chambers for a new debate with an explanation of why he or she is doing so (e.g., the belief that it is unconstitutional).[42] If the chambers pass it again, the president must promulgate it (Art. 74 Cost.). Immediately after their promulgation, laws are published in the *Gazzetta Ufficiale della Repubblica Italiana* and – provided there is nothing to the contrary in the laws themselves – enter into force on the 15th day following publication (Art. 73 Cost.).

Laws that amend the Constitution must be approved in each chamber after two successive votes at intervals of not less than three months. If the second vote results in a two-thirds majority of the members of each chamber, the constitutional law *(legge costituzionale)* is forwarded directly to the president of the Republic for promulgation. If only an absolute majority in one or both of the chambers is obtained, the law can enter into force only if it is submitted to a popular referendum and approved by a majority of votes (Art. 138 Cost.).[43]

There is no institutionalized lobbying of the legislative process by social or religious groups; however, the informal influence of Catholicism must not be underestimated. For instance, the Catholic Church regularly calls into question the laws on abortion and had a significant influence on the legislation governing in-vitro fertilization.[44]

---

41 See also *Riz/Happacher*, Grundzüge, p. 103. See also Chamber of Deputies, The Passage of a Law Through Parliament. http://en.camera.it/4?scheda_informazioni=15.

42 *Riz/Happacher*, Grundzüge, pp. 104–105.

43 See also I.C.1.

44 L. 19 Feb. 2004, n. 40.

– *Executive*

The highest executive organ is the government (*governo*, Arts. 92–100 Cost.). The principal organ of the government is the Council of Ministers *(Consiglio dei ministri)*, which consists of the prime minister *(presidiente del Consiglio)* and the ministers *(ministri)*, who are proposed by the prime minister. Both chambers of parliament must confirm the ministers in a vote of confidence within ten days of their nomination by the president of the Republic (Art. 94 Cost.). The prime minister conducts and is responsible for the government's general policy (Art. 95 para. 1 Cost.).

– *Judiciary*

The judiciary is within the exclusive legislative competence of the (national) state (Art. 117 let. l Cost.).[45] Justice is administered in the name of the people and judges are subject only to the law (Art. 101 Cost.). Judicial independence is both personal and organizational in nature.[46] The prohibition of extraordinary and special courts *(principio di unità della giurisdizione)* is a basic principle in Italy; however, specialized sections for specific issues (such as employment) may be established within ordinary judicial bodies (Art. 102 Cost.).[47] The Constitution also provides for a number of specialized courts, such as the Council of State *(Consiglio di Stato)* in Rome, which serves as second instance administrative court, the Court of Accounts *(Corte dei Conti)*, the military tribunals *(tribunali militari)*, as well as first instance regional administrative courts (Arts. 103 and 125 Cost.). Finally, there are the tax commissions of the provinces (first instance) and the regions (second instance) and the public water tribunals (*Tribunali delle acque pubbliche*, R.D. 11 Dec. 1933, n. 1755).

The following are courts of ordinary jurisdiction: offices of the justices of the peace *(giudice di pace)*, district courts *(tribunale)*, courts of appeals *(Corte d'Appello)*, and the Court of Cassation *(Corte di Cassazione)*.[48] The ordinary courts are subject to their own court constitution (Judicature Act, *ordinamento giudiziario* = o.g.);[49] their self-governing body, the Superior Council of the Judiciary (*Consiglio Superiore della Magistratura*, CSM), is responsible for ensuring compliance with the court constitution.

---

45 For the judicial system, see also *Livingston* et al., The Italian legal system, pp. 66–71; *Di Amato/Fucito*, Criminal Law in Italy, pp. 27–33, 157–159 (nos. 18–35, 422–431.

46 See *Riz/Happacher*, Grundzüge, p. 150.

47 *Onida/Pedrazza Gorleo*, Compendio, pp. 367–368.

48 On their jurisdiction in criminal matters, see below 5.c.

49 R.D. 30 Jan. 1941, n. 12.

– *Constitutional Court*

The Constitution places the Constitutional Court *(Corte Costituzionale)*, like the president of the Republic, outside the three traditional branches of government. The Constitutional Court monitors compliance with the Constitution. Its most important function is to rule on the constitutionality of laws and of acts with the force of law (such as decree laws and legislative decrees[50]). There are two ways of bringing a complaint to the Constitutional Court: directly and indirectly. A direct constitutional complaint *(giudizio in via principale)* can be brought by the government in a challenge to the constitutional validity of a regional law or, vice versa, by a region in a challenge to the constitutional validity of a state law or a law of another region. Such complaints must be brought within 60 days of the entry into force of the challenged law (Art. 127 Cost.). Direct constitutional complaints cannot be initiated by private individuals. An indirect constitutional complaint *(giudizio in via incidentale)* arises in the context of a proceeding pending in court when the constitutionality of a law is questioned. In such a situation, the judge submits the complaint to the Constitutional Court, either on the request of a party or ex officio.[51] The Constitutional Court also rules on conflicts between the various branches of the state, between the state and the regions, and between individual regions, on accusations against the president of the Republic (Art. 134 paras. 2 and 3 Cost.), and on questions involving the legitimacy of a referendum (Art. 2 L. cost. 11 marzo 1953, n. 1).

– *Political structure*

The Italian Republic is divided into 20 regions (*regioni*, Piedmont, Valle D'Aosta, Lombardy, Trentino-Alto Adige, Veneto, Friuli-Venezia Giulia, Liguria, Emilia-Romagna, Tuscany, Umbria, Marche, Latium, Abruzzi, Molise, Campania, Apulia, Basilicata, Calabria, Sicily, Sardinia, Art. 131 Cost.).[52] The regions constitute an intermediate political administrative level. Although their position was significantly strengthened in 2001,[53] their legislative power is still considerably less than that of, say, the German states. While they are now entitled to enact concurrent legislation in many areas, Italy still cannot be described as a federal state; rather, it can be described as a decentralized unitary state. In 2009, parliament passed

---

[50] See I.F.2.

[51] Details are governed by L. cost. 9 Feb. 1948, n. 1 and L. cost. 11 March 1953, n. 87. See also *Onida/Pedrazza Gorleo*, Compendio, pp. 386–392; *Riz/Happacher*, Grundzüge, pp. 240–243.

[52] For the role of the regions within Italy's political system, see also *Livingston* et al., The Italian legal system, pp. 61–66.

[53] By L. cost. 18 Oct. 2001, n. 3, see also *Livingston* et al., The Italian legal system, p. 62.

a law on so-called tax federalism *(federalismo fiscale)*.[54] In an attempt to undercut separatist movements, five of the regions (Valle D'Aosta, Trentino-Alto Adige, Friuli-Venezia Giulia, Sicily, and Sardinia) were granted special status (*statuto speciale*, Art. 116 para. 1 Cost.) with far-reaching autonomy.

The administrative level below the regions consists of metropolitan cities *(città metropolitane)* and provinces *(province)*. In 2017, there were 93 provinces and 14 metropolitan cities. The smallest number of provinces in a region is one; the largest twelve. For fiscal reasons, neither provinces nor metropolitan cities have had directly elected governing bodies since 2015.[55] The provinces are divided, in turn, into municipalities (*comuni*, see Art. 114 Cost.). The smallest number of municipalities in a region is six; the largest 316. The governing bodies of municipalities are the municipal council *(consiglio comunale)* and the mayor *(sindaco)*, both directly elected, as well as the municipal executive board *(giunta comunale)*.

5. Crime and criminal prosecution

a) Investigating authorities

Pursuant to Art. 327 Code of Criminal Procedure (*codice di procedura penale*, c.p.p.[56]), preliminary proceedings, known as preliminary investigations *(indagini preliminari)*, are led by the Office of the Public Prosecutor *(pubblico ministero)*, which is in charge of the proceedings. This office is also responsible for conducting investigations in favor of the suspect (Art. 358 c.p.p.). Investigations are carried out by the judicial police *(polizia giudiziaria)* in accordance with the prosecutor's instructions. Certain investigative measures require the permission of an examining judge (*giudice per gli indagini preliminari*, Art. 328 c.p.p). The offices of the public prosecutor *(procure della Repubblica)* are located in and attached to the district courts, the courts of appeals, and the Court of Cassation (Art. 51 c.p.p.; Art. 2 o.g.).

Pursuant to Art. 57 c.p.p, the judicial police include officials of the following police forces: the state police *(Polizia di Stato)*, the Carabinieri Corps *(Arma dei carabinieri)*, the border and tax-control police *(Guardia di finanza)*, prison guards *(Polizia penitenziaria)*, and the national forest guard *(Corpo forestale dello stato)*. In terms of responsibilities, Art. 57 c.p.p. distinguishes between police agents *(agenti)* and police officials *(ufficiali)*. Only police officials are authorized to take reports of criminal activity or to receive complaints filed by injured parties. The

---

[54] L. 5 May 2009, n. 42.

[55] L. 7 Apr. 2014, n. 56.

[56] For an introduction to Italian Law of Criminal Procedure, see *Di Amato/Fucito*, Criminal Law in Italy, pp. 157–221; for the historical development of the Italian Criminal Procedure, see I.G.3.

educational requirement for leadership positions (beginning, e.g., in the *Polizia di Stato*, with the rank of *commissari*) is a degree in law or political science (Art. 3 para. 2 D.Lgs. 5 Oct. 2000, n. 334).

The Anti-Mafia Investigation Department *(Direzione Investigativa Antimafia)* was established in 1991 to combat organized crime. This department has preventive as well as repressive policing functions; the judicial police are required to cooperate with it. The National Anti-Mafia Department *(Direzione Nazionale Antimafia)*, which is located at the Court of Cassation[57] and led by the national anti-mafia prosecutor *(procuratore nazionale antimafia)*, is responsible for coordinating investigations at the national level.

In 2014, 3,466,658 serious offenses[58] were recorded by the offices of the public prosecutor, which amounts to 5,700 offenses per 100,000 inhabitants. 61.6 % of these involved complaints against persons unknown; another 19.5 % of preliminary proceedings were dropped (of these, 9 % were dropped because the statute of limitations had run).[59]

b) Prosecuting authorities

The Office of the Public Prosecutor *(pubblico ministero)* is the only prosecutorial authority (Art. 50 c.p.p.). Like judges, public prosecutors *(procuratori della repubblica)* are judicial officers *(magistratura)* and, pursuant to Art. 104 Cost., belong to the league or "order" of the judiciary *(ordine giudiziario)*, which is autonomous and independent of the other branches of government (Art. 4 para. 1 o.g.). Nonetheless, due to the fact that the Office of the Public Prosecutor is the representative of the prosecution, it remains outside the courts, even though it is also bound to be impartial, which is why it must also investigate for the benefit of the suspect.[60] Furthermore, since 2006,[61] the option of bringing charges both in person and by referring them to a colleague has created a certain hierarchy that has invited some criticism.[62] The Office of the Public Prosecutor is organized along the lines of the courts; as such, prosecutorial offices are located at the Court of Cassation, in the appellate courts, at the general district courts, and at the juvenile courts (Art. 2 o.g.).[63]

The duties of the Office of the Public Prosecutor as defined in Art. 73 para. 1 o.g. include monitoring compliance with the law, ensuring the prompt and con-

---

57 D.L. 20 Nov. 1991, n. 367.

58 On the distinction between serious criminal offenses and infractions, see II.C.1.b.

59 Istituto nazionale di statistica – annuario statistico italiano 2016, pp. 183 and 208.

60 *Fantacchiotti/Fiandanese*, Il nuovo ordinamento giudiziario, pp. 143–144.

61 Art. 2 D.Lgs. 20 Feb. 2006, n. 150.

62 See, e.g., *Fantacchiotti/Fiandanese*, Il nuovo ordinamento giudiziario, pp. 39 and 149.

63 On the individual courts, see below 5.c.

sistent administration of justice, combatting crime, and implementing coercive measures. In the criminal process, this means first and foremost the bringing of charges and the mandatory participation in criminal proceedings (Art. 74 paras. 1 and 2 o.g.). The principle of mandatory prosecution *(principio di obbligatorietà dell'azione penale)*, which is enshrined in Art. 112 Cost., is of major importance. This absolute duty to prosecute is a manifestation of the general principle of equality (Art. 3 Cost.) and serves, on the one hand, to prevent arbitrary inactivity on the part of the office of the prosecutor, and, on the other hand, to protect against pressure from the outside not to prosecute in certain cases.[64] In practice, it is almost impossible to adhere to a principle of mandatory prosecution as strict as this one. In view of the huge number of reports of criminal activity, it is obvious that not all criminally relevant acts can be prosecuted. In many cases, particularly those involving trivial offenses, the unofficial instrument of "time will take care of cases" is applied. In other words, the acts are "allowed" to become time-barred before charges can be brought.[65] So as not to leave everything up to chance, criteria for prioritizing criminal matters have been set (Art. 227 D.Lgs. 19 Feb. 1998, n. 51 and Art. 132-*bis* disp. att. c.p.p.).[66] However, the Office of the Public Prosecutor does not always have the sole right to bring charges. In proceedings before a justice of the peace involving offenses prosecuted on complaint *(reati procedibili a querela)*, for example, the injured person may also initiate criminal proceedings by filing an immediate application *(ricorso immediato)* with the court.[67]

To be admitted as a judicial officer (judge or prosecutor), a candidate must pass an entrance exam (*concorso per magistrato ordinario*, Art. 106 para. 1 Cost.). In order to sit for this exam, candidates must have completed their legal studies and must prove additional experience (such as postgraduate studies, a doctorate, passage of the bar exam, or six years as an honorary judge).[68] Honorary judges and prosecutors *(magistrati onorari)* may also be appointed by election (Art. 106 para. 2 Cost.).

In 2014, 636,045 persons were charged with a crime; of the persons charged, 23.2 % were foreign-born and 3.0 % were minors at the time the crime was committed.[69] 69.9 % of serious criminal offenses were handled by ordinary courts; other offenses were dealt with by means of orders of summary punishment *(decreto di condanna)*, plea bargains *("patteggiamento")*, or other types of alternative proceedings.[70]

---

64 See *Chiavario*, Diritto processuale penale, p. 141.

65 On this issue, see also *Chiavario*, Diritto processuale penale, p. 147.

66 *Chiavario*, Diritto processuale penale, p. 149–150; *Peri*, Obbligatorietà, p. 4.

67 *Jarvers*, Massen- und Kleinkriminalität, pp. 30–32. On the jurisdiction of the justice of the peace courts, see below 5.c.

68 Arts. 1 and 2 D.Lgs. 5 Apr. 2006, n. 160.

69 Istituto nazionale di statistica – annuario statistico italiano 2016, pp. 183, 208.

70 Istituto nazionale di statistica – annuario statistico italiano 2016, pp. 184, 208.

c) Criminal courts

Italy has a three-tiered court system.[71] Depending on the type and gravity of the criminal offense, proceedings begin either at the level of the justice of the peace, the district court or the court of assize. Courts of the justice of the peace *(giudice di pace)* have jurisdiction over selected widespread or so-called "mass" crime and petty crime.[72] Justices of the peace always sit alone. The district courts *(tribunale,* Art. 48 o.g.*)*, sitting as panels of three professional judges ("collegial" court, *tribunale in composizione collegiale*), have jurisdiction over all criminal offenses subject to more than ten years' imprisonment as well as the many serious criminal offenses listed in Art. 33-*bis* c.p.p. Single judges at the district courts *(tribunale in composizione monocratica)* have jurisdiction over all other offenses, unless the courts of assize *(Corte di assise)* have jurisdiction. The courts of assize sit in panels composed of two professional judges and six lay judges *(giudici popolari)*[73] and have jurisdiction over particularly serious criminal offenses. Particularly serious offenses are offenses for which the law provides life imprisonment or imprisonment for a maximum term of at least 24 years, certain homicide offenses, other serious intentional offenses that resulted in the death of one or more persons, and, finally, serious offenses against the existence of the state (Art. 5 c.p.p).

Juvenile courts *(tribunale per i minorenni)* are responsible for offenders who were under the age of 18 at the time the crime was committed. Juvenile courts sit in panels of two professional judges and two lay judges (one male, one female) with expertise in social work. Juvenile courts are located at the courts of appeals.[74]

Most judgments of courts of first instance can be appealed to second-instance courts on points of facts (Art. 596 c.p.p.): Decisions of a justice of the peace are appealed to a single judge at the district court. The general courts of appeals on issues of fact *(Corte di appello)* sit in panels of three professional judges (Art. 56 o.g.) and have jurisdiction over appeals from first-instance decisions of the district courts (both panel decisions as well as decisions of single judges, Art. 53 o.g.). Courts of appeals are located, for the most part, in the regional capitals. The juvenile division of the courts of appeals hears appeals from decisions of the juvenile courts.[75] Appeals on issues of fact *(appello)* from the courts of assize are heard by the appeals courts of assize *(Corte di assise di appello)*, which sit in panels of two professional judges and six lay judges.[76]

---

71 For the judicial system, see also *Livingston* et al., The Italian legal system, pp. 66–71; *Di Amato/Fucito*, Criminal Law in Italy, pp. 27–33, 157–159 (nos. 18–35, 422–431).

72 See Art. 4 D.Lgs. 28 Aug. 2000, n. 274; see also *Jarvers*, Massen- und Kleinkriminalität, pp. 14–26.

73 Art. 3 L. 10 Apr. 1951, n. 287.

74 Art. 50 o.g., Art. 2 R.D.L. 20 July 1934, n. 1404.

75 Art. 5 R.D.L. 20 July 1934, n. 1404.

76 Art. 4 L. 10 Apr. 1951, n. 287.

The third and highest tier is the Court of Cassation *(Corte di Cassazione)*. It is responsible for reviewing decisions of the courts of appeals on points of law *(ricorso per cassazione)*. This court also hears direct appeals on points of law *(ricorso immediato)* from first-instance decisions. Each of the seven criminal divisions *(sezioni)* is composed of five professional judges; the combined divisions *(sezioni unite)* are composed of nine professional judges (Art. 67 o.g.).

Individuals may apply to the European Court of Human Rights (ECtHR) to contest alleged violations of the European Convention on Human Rights.[77] A conviction of Italy in such a proceeding may be reason for a new national trial under Art. 630 c.p.p.[78] This explains the widespread perception among Italians that for all intents and purposes the European Court has evolved into a court of fourth instance because it can be called on after all procedural possibilities on the national level have been exhausted and because it affects the final decision.[79] Others, like the Court itself, consider the term "fourth instance" incorrect in this context.[80] In 2016, Italy was one of the four European countries with the most judgments against them – 2,351 or 12 % – since the establishment of the European Court of Human Rights in 1959. Of these, 1,791 or 76 %, were convictions for at least one violation of the European Convention on Human Rights. The vast majority of these convictions (1,190 or 66 %) were due to the excessive length of proceedings.[81]

The International Criminal Court in The Hague, created by the Rome Statute, has jurisdiction over genocide, crimes against humanity, and war crimes. The Court supplements national court systems to the extent that it acts only if the offense in question is not prosecuted domestically.[82] Since Italy has not yet enacted legislation enabling it to prosecute these crimes in its own courts, however, they remain subject to the exclusive jurisdiction of the International Criminal Court.[83]

In times of peace, the jurisdiction of the military court system is limited to criminal offenses provided in the Military Penal Code for Times of Peace (*codice penale militare di pace*, c.p.m.p.) allegedly committed by members of the armed forces (Art. 103 para. 3 Cost., Arts. 262, 263 c.p.m.p.).[84] The three military courts *(tribunale militare)* in Verona, Rome, and Naples are courts of first instance;[85] the Military Court of Appeals *(corte militare di appello)* in Rome is the court of second

77 See I.B.2.b.

78 Corte Cost. 7 Apr. 2011, n. 113, Giur. Cost. 2011, pp. 1523–1565.

79 *Iacoviello*, Cass. pen. 2011, 800.

80 See *Giunchedi*, Arch. pen, 2013, 113–139; ECtHR *Mirilashvili v. Russia*, 11 Dec. 2008, (6293/04), 161.

81 1959 to 2016, European Court of Human Rights.

82 *Padovani*, Diritto penale, pp. 12–13.

83 *Marinucci/Dolcini*, Manuale, p. 55. See I.B.2.b.

84 R.D. 20 Feb. 1941, n. 303.

85 See Art. 2 para. 603 L. 24 Dec. 2007, n. 244.

instance (appeals on points of fact). Appeals on points of law of decisions of the military court system are heard by the (general) Court of Cassation.[86]

The educational requirements for professional judges and prosecutors *(magistrati)* are the same; both are members of the "order" of the judiciary *(ordine giudiziario).*[87]

There is lay participation only at the courts of assize and the appeals courts of assize. Both of these courts sit in panels of six lay judges *(giudici popolari)* and two professional judges *(giudici togati)*. It should be noted that justices of the peace, who are trained lawyers and members of the judiciary and who must complete a six-month practical training course before taking up their duties, are not included in either the category of lay judge or the category of professional judge.[88] Similarly, honorary judges at the district courts *(giudici onorari di tribunale)* who, in certain cases, may fill in for professional judges (Arts. 42-*ter* und 43-*bis* o.g.) must also have a law degree.

In 2015, a total of 314,550 persons were convicted, 93,585 (29.8 %) for infractions and 220,965 (70.2 %) for serious criminal offenses. 265,628 (84.4 %) of convicted persons were male; for some offenses (such as intentional homicide, drug offenses, and robbery), the percentage of male convicts exceeded 90 %. 53.6 % of convicted persons were ages 25 through 44; 1.04 % were minors (i.e., under the age of 18). Convictions for each type of offense were as follows: intentional homicide, 964 (0.34 %); negligent homicide, 1,918 (0.6 %), bodily injury, 9,178 (42.9 %); theft, 34,301 (10.9 %); robbery, 7,323 (2.3 %); drug offenses, 21,955 (6.9 %); driving under the influence of alcohol, 44,957 (14.3 %); violation of immigration provisions, 4,503 (1.4 %); violation of weapons and explosives provisions, 6,507 (2.06 %); and environmental offenses, 4,114 (1.3 %).[89] The number of acquittals is unknown.

d) Criminal penalties

The Italian Penal Code (*codice penale*, c.p.) employs a dual-track system of criminal punishments: penalties and security measures.[90] Penalties *(pene)* can only be imposed on offenders with criminal capacity. The main penalties *(pene principali)* for serious criminal offenses[91] are life imprisonment (*ergastolo*, Art. 22 c.p.), term imprisonment (*reclusione*, Art. 23 c.p.) for terms of 15 days to 24 years, and fines for serious offenses (*multa*, Art. 24 para. 1 c.p.) that range from € 50 to € 50,000. Many criminal offense definitions prescribe a fine along with a custodial

86 Art. 6 L. 7 May 1981, n. 180.

87 See also above 5.b.

88 *Jarvers*, Massen- und Kleinkriminalität, pp. 9–11.

89 Istituto nazionale di statistica – annuario statistico italiano 2016, pp. 184 and 209.

90 For details about the sanctioning system, see *Di Amato/Fucito*, Italian Criminal Law, pp. 131–150.

91 On the distinction between serious criminal offenses and infractions, see II.C.1.b.

sentence. If the offense was based on greed, the judge may impose an additional fine of from € 50 to € 25,000, even if the law only prescribes imprisonment (Art. 24 para. 2 c.p.). Fines are not imposed as day fines but as lump sums. If the individual in question is unable to pay, the fine may be converted to so-called controlled liberty *(libertà controllata)* or to so-called substitute work *(lavoro sostitutivo)*.[92] In the case of life imprisonment, conditional release is possible after the person has served 26 years (Art. 176 para. 3 c.p.). Infractions are subject to a custodial sentence (*arresto*, Art. 25 c.p.) of from five days to three years and a special fine for infractions (*ammenda*, Art. 26 c.p.) of from € 20 to € 10,000.

For many criminal offenses, collateral or accessory penalties *(pene accessorie)*, such as the prohibition on practicing one's profession or the termination of parental rights, may be imposed in addition to the main penalties (Arts. 28–38 c.p.). So-called substitute sanctions *(sanzioni sostitutive)*, introduced in 1981,[93] may be imposed on first-time offenders instead of short custodial sentences. Substitute sanctions include part-time detention *(semidetenzione)*, that is, incarceration in prison for at least ten hours a day; controlled liberty *(libertà controllata)*, during which time convicted persons may not leave their residences without special permission and must register with the authorities on a daily basis; and fines *(pena pecuniaria)*.

Security measures *(misure di sicurrezza)* may be imposed as an alternative or in addition to penalties. In this context, what matters is not the culpability of but rather the risk posed by the criminal offender. There are personal and property-related security measures. Personal custodial security measures *(misure di sicurezza personali detentive)* include admission to a prison farm or a workhouse (Arts. 216–218 c.p.), placement of offenders with diminished capacity or without criminal capacity in psychiatric hospitals (Arts. 219–222 c.p.),[94] and placement of juvenile offenders regardless of their capacity in reform schools (Arts. 223–227 c.p.). Personal non-custodial security measures *(misure di sicurezza personali non detentive)* are supervised liberty (*libertà vigilata*, Arts. 228–232 c.p.), various bans on staying in or frequenting certain places (Arts. 233–234 c.p.), and the deportation of foreign nationals (Art. 235 c.p.). Property-related security measures *(misure di sicurezza partrimoniali)* include the requirement to pay a deposit to ensure good conduct (Arts. 237–239 c.p.) and the confiscation of property (Art. 240 c.p.).

Of the 314,550 persons convicted of an infraction in 2015, 50,964 (16.2 %) were sentenced to a fine for infractions, 42,333 (13.5 %) to imprisonment for up to one year, 284 (0.09 %) to imprisonment for one to five years, and 4 (0.001 %) to imprisonment for more than five years (penalties for infractions). Regarding serious criminal offenses, 51,789 (16.5 %) were sentenced to a fine for serious offenses,

---

[92] Art. 136 c.p. in conjunction with Art. 102 L. 24 Nov. 1981, n. 689.

[93] L. 24 Nov. 1981, n. 689.

[94] See I.G.4.

117,564 (37.4 %) to imprisonment for up to one year, 29,721 (9.45 %) to imprisonment for a term of one to two years, 16,334 (5.19 %) to imprisonment for a term of two to five years, 3,781 (1.20 %) to imprisonment for a term of five to ten years, and 1,776 (0.56 %) to imprisonment for more than ten years (penalties for serious criminal offenses).[95]

e) Execution of custodial penalties

Italy has various types of penal institutions *(istituti penitenzari)*. Art. 59 Prison Act (*ordinamento penitenziario*, o.p.) provides for the incarceration of adults as follows: in centers for pre-trial detention *(istituti di custodia cautelare)*, in correctional facilities for the execution of custodial penalties *(istituti per l'esecuzione delle pene)*, in facilities for the implementation of security measures *(istituti per le misure di sicurezza)*, and in observation centers *(centri di osservazione)*. There are additional facilities for persons suffering from physical or mental illnesses or disabilities (*istituti per infermi e minorati*, Art. 65 o.p.).[96]

Pre-trial detention facilities (Art. 60 o.p.) include county prisons *(case mandamentali)*, which house individuals who are to be tried by a single judge at district courts. All other suspects are confined *(custodia)* in remand prisons *(case circondariali)*. However, both of these pre-trial facilities may also serve as correctional facilities.

There are two types of correctional facilities for persons sentenced by the authorities to a custodial sentence (Art. 61 o.p.): arrest centers *(case di arresto)* for persons convicted of infractions and prisons *(case di reclusione)* for persons convicted of serious criminal offenses. It should be noted, however, that while the law provides for arrest centers, they do not yet exist in practice, which means that de facto there are only prisons available for the execution of custodial sentences.

Facilities for the execution of security measures (Art. 62 o.p.) include prison farms *(colonie agricole)*, workhouses *(case di lavoro)*, treatment and custody centers *(case di cura e di custodia)*, and psychiatric hospitals (REMS).[97]

The observation centers (Art. 63 o.p.) do not actually serve as correctional facilities but as research centers aimed at determining the treatment best suited for a convict, whereas facilities for the mentally and physically ill and disabled (*istituti per infermi e minorati*, Art. 65 o.p.) house individuals who are unable to function within the disciplinary and work-related system of regular correctional facilities.

---

95 Istituto nazionale di statistica – annuario statistico italiano 2016, pp. 184 and 209.

96 For details about the execution of punishment, see *Di Amato/Fucito*, Italian Criminal Law, pp. 223–233; for the historical development of the execution of punishment, see I.G.4.

97 See I.G.4.

Altogether, there are 190 detention facilities *(istituti penitenziari)*, 48 of which are prisons *(case di reclusione)*, 139 remand prisons *(case circondariali)*, and 18 juvenile prisons *(istituti penali per minorenni)*.[98]

On 30 June 2017, 56,919 adults were incarcerated; of these, 19,690 were in pre-trial facilities, 36,946 in prisons, and 283 in psychiatric hospitals. Females accounted for 4.22 %, foreign nationals for 34.14 %.[99] Of these inmates, 1.6 % were ages 18 to 19, 18.6 % ages 20 to 29, 29.7 % ages 30 to 39, 26,8 % ages 40 to 49, 15.7 % ages 50 to 59, 6,2 % ages 60 to 69 years, and 1.3 % over 70 years old.[100]

Persons convicted by final judgment were incarcerated for the following types of offenses: 31,883 for offenses against property, 22,608 for offenses against persons, 19,752 for drug-related offenses, 10,072 for violations of the weapons law, 7,854 for offenses against the public administration, 4,650 for offenses against the public faith, 7,048 for mafia-like associations, 6,552 for offenses against the administration of justice, 3,942 for infractions, and 3,134 for offenses against the public order.[101] 24.3 % received custodial sentences of up to three years, 28.7 % sentences of from three to six years, 18.3 % sentences of from six to ten years, 17.6 % sentences of from 10 to 20 years, and 11 % sentences of more than 20 years or life sentences.[102]

With a prison population rate of 95 per 100,000 inhabitants, Italy ranks 153rd globally and about average in Europe.[103] However, the prison population rate has fluctuated greatly in recent decades. Since the turn of the millennium, the situation in Italian prisons has again and again been on the verge of collapse. The 190 penal institutions currently in operation are designed for 50,241 inmates.[104] Whereas the number of inmates remained more or less constant at this level in the 1990s, the number subsequently climbed steadily – due to excessive use of the criminal law – before peaking at 61,264 in the summer of 2006. The high level of overcrowding in the detention facilities triggered a comprehensive remission of punishment *(indulto)*[105] by L. 31 July 2006, n. 41, which reduced the number of inmates to approximately 39,000 by the end of the year. In the following years, this number almost doubled, among other reasons due to the rigid criminal policy at the time,[106] and when it peaked at 68,258 at the end of 2010, it was higher than before the remis-

---

98 Ministero della Giustizia – number of penal institutions – number of juvenile prisons.

99 Ministero della Giustizia – inmates 1991–2017.

100 Ministero della Giustizia – inmates by age.

101 As of 30 June 2017, Ministero della Giustizia – inmates by imputed offenses.

102 As of 31 Dec. 2016, Ministero della Giustizia – inmates by duration of sentence imposed.

103 As of 31 Aug. 2017, International Centre for Prison Studies.

104 As of 30 June 2017, Ministero della Giustizia – inmates and prison capacity.

105 On the details of remission of punishment, see II.K.3.

106 See I.G.1.

sion was granted. While some measures were taken to empty the prisons, at the same time more persons were taken into custody; as a result, by mid-2013 the total number of inmates had only decreased by 2,230.[107]

The tipping point came in 2013 following Italy's conviction by the European Court of Human Rights in the *Torreggiani* case[108] thanks to numerous more successful reforms in substantive criminal law, in criminal procedure, and in the execution of punishment.[109] In fact, the number of inmates began a steady decrease in mid-2013, reaching 62,536 at the end of 2013, 53,623 at the end of 2014, and 52,164 at the end of 2015. Unfortunately, in 2016, the numbers began to rise again (reaching 54,072 in mid-2016, 54,653 at the end of 2016, and 56,919 in mid-2017).[110] It remains to be seen whether this increase was only a temporary phenomenon.

Bibliography and further reading

General references:

Brütting, Richard (ed.), Italienlexikon (Encyclopedia of Italy). Berlin 1995.

Grundmann, Stefan/Zaccaria, Alessio (eds.), Einführung in das italienische Recht (Introduction to Italian law). Frankfurt a.M. 2007.

Maiwald, Manfred, Einführung in das italienische Straf- und Strafprozessrecht (Introduction to Italian criminal law and law of criminal procedure). Frankfurt a.M. 2009.

Geography:

CIA World Factbook: Italy, https://www.cia.gov/library/publications/the-world-factbook/geos/it.html [last visited Sept. 2017].

Istituto nazionale di statistica (National Italian Statistical Institute), Annuario statiscico italiano 2016 (Italian statistical yearbook 2016): https://www.istat.it/it/files/2016/12/Asi-2016.pdf [last visited Sept. 2017].

Population:

CIA World Factbook: Italy, https://www.cia.gov/library/publications/the-world-factbook/geos/it.html [last visited Sept. 2017].

Der neue Fischer Weltalmanach 2017. Zahlen, Daten, Fakten (The New Fischer World Almanac 2017). Frankfurt a.M. 2016, pp. 229–232.

---

107 Ministero della Giustizia – inmates 1991–2016.

108 *Torreggiani and Others v. Italy*, App. 32517/09, 8 Jan. 2013.

109 For details, see I.G.1., I.G.2., I.G.3., and I.G.4.

110 Ministero della Giustizia – inmates 1991–2016.

Istituto nazionale di statistica (National Statistical Institute of Italy):

– Annuario statiscico italiano 2016 (Italian statistical yearbook 2016): https://www.istat.it/it/files/2016/12/Asi-2016.pdf [last visited Sept. 2017].

– Population in Italy on 1 Jan. 2016 by age, sex, and marital status: http://demo.istat.it/pop2016/index.html [last visited Sept. 2017].

– Foreign nationals:

Foreign population resident on 1 Jan. 2016: http://demo.istat.it/strasa2016/index.html [last visited Sept. 2017].

Resident population by sex and citizenship on 31 Dec. 2015: http://demo.istat.it/str2015/index.html [last visited Sept. 2017].

Language:

UNESCO Institute for statistics

– Illiterate Population (Italy): http://uis.unesco.org/country/it [last visited Feb. 2017].

Religion:

Der neue Fischer Weltalmanach 2017. Zahlen, Daten, Fakten. (The New Fischer World Almanac 2017). Frankfurt a.M. 2016, pp. 229–232.

Auswärtiges Amt (German Foreign Office):

– Religionen in Italien (Religions in Italy), January 2017: http://www.auswaertiges-amt.de/DE/Aussenpolitik/Laender/Laenderinfos/01-Nodes_Uebersichtsseiten/Italien_node.html [last visited Sept. 2017].

Economy:

Der neue Fischer Weltalmanach 2017. Zahlen, Daten, Fakten (The New Fischer World Almanac 2017). Frankfurt a.M. 2016, pp. 229–232, 631–632.

Auswärtiges Amt (German Foreign Office):

– Inflation rate http://www.auswaertiges-amt.de/sid_6DB11286A2614D9B24EDC5236727CEF0/DE/Aussenpolitik/Laender/Laenderinfos/Italien/Wirtschaft_node.html [last visited Sept. 2017].

Istituto nazionale di statistica (National Statistical Institute of Italy):

– value per capita http://dati.istat.it/Index.aspx?DataSetCode=DCCN_PILT [last visited Aug. 2017].

– Gross national income (2014): https://www.google.de/url?sa=t&rct=j&q=&esrc=s&source=web&cd=4&cad=rja&uact=8&ved=0ahUKEwiZ0YOe9MzVAhUFsxQKHTEhC1YQFghEMAM&url=http%3A%2F%2Fdati.istat.it%2FIndex.aspx%3FDataSetCode%3DDCCN_VALPROCAPN&usg=AFQjCNFTOMeAp1i9r3MmVmcBAAr3Kl26-g [last visited Aug. 2017].

Seasonally adjusted quarterly unemployment rate: http://dati.istat.it/Index.aspx?DataSetCode=DCCV_TAXDISOCCUDE1&Lang=# (last visited Sept. 2017)

System of government:

Becchi, Paolo/Palma, Giuseppe, I sistemi elettorali dal dopoguerra ad oggi (Electoral systems from post-war to today). Vicalvi 2017.

Chamber of Deputies, The Passage of a Law Through Parliament, http://en.camera.it/4?scheda_informazioni=15 [last visited Aug. 2017].

Di Amato, Astolfo/Fucito, Federica, Criminal Law in Italy. 3d ed. Alphen aan den Rijn 2016.

Livingston, Michael A./Monateri, Pier Giuseppe/Parisi, Francesco, The Italian legal system: An introduction. 2d ed. Stanford, CA 2015.

Magnoli Bocchi, Alessandro, Italy: Willingness to Reform Is the Issue, Not the Referendum, EconoMonitor, 1 Dec. 2016, http://www.economonitor.com/blog/2016/12/italy-willingness-to-reform-is-the-issue-not-the-referendum [last visited Aug. 2017].

Onida, Valerio/Pedrazza Gorlero, Maurizio (eds.), Compendio di Diritto Costituzionale (Outline of constitutional law). 3d ed. Milan 2014, pp. 161–407.

Riz, Roland/Happacher, Esther, Grundzüge des italienischen Verfassungsrechts (Fundamentals of Italian constitutional law). 4th ed. Innsbruck 2013.

Crime and criminal prosecution:

Chiavario, Mario, Diritto processuale penale (Code of Criminal Procedure). 7th ed. Turin 2017.

Della Casa, Franco, Approvata la legge c.d. svuota-carceri: un'altro "pannicello caldo" per l'ingravascente piaga del sovrafollamento carcerario? (The so-called "empty prison law" has been passed: One more bandage for the growing sore of prison overcrowding). Dir. pen. e proc. 2011, 5–9.

Di Amato, Astolfo/Fucito, Federica, Criminal Law in Italy. 3d ed. Alphen aan den Rijn 2016.

Di Ronza, Paolo, Manuale di diritto dell'esecuzione penale (Textbook on the execution of punishment). 5th ed. Padua 2003, pp. 112–117.

Fantacchiotti, Mario/Fiandanese, Franco, Il nuovo ordinamento giudiziario (The new Judicature Act). Padua 2008.

Giunchedi, Filippo, La tutela dei diritti fondamentali previsti dalla CEDU: la Corte europea dei diritti dell'uomo come giudice di quarta istanza? (The protection of fundamental rights by the ECtHR: The European Court of Human Rights as judge of fourth instance?). Archivio penale 2013, pp. 113–139.

Iacoviello, Francesco Mauro, Il quarto grado di giurisdizione: la corte europea dei diritti dell'uomo (The court of fourth instance: The European Court of Human Rights). Cass. pen. 2011, pp. 794–283.

Jarvers, Konstanze, Das italienische Strafvollstreckungs- und -vollzugssystem. Historische Entwicklung, Überblick und gerichtliche Kontrolle (The Italian system of execution of punishment and prison regime. Historical development, overview, and judicial control). In: C.D. Spinellis/Nikolaos Theodorakis/Emmanouil Billis/George Papadimitrakopoulos (eds.), Europe in Crisis: Crime, Criminal Justice, and the Way Forward. Festschrift für Nestor Courakis, vol. II. Athens 2017, pp. 817–845, available at http://crime-in-crisis.com/en/ and http://crime-in-crisis.com/en/?cat=8 [last visited Oct. 2017]).

Jarvers, Konstanze, Landesbericht Italien (Country report Italy). In: Hans-Georg Koch (ed.), Wegsperren? – Freiheitsentziehende Maßnahmen gegen gefährliche, strafrechtlich verantwortliche (Rückfall-)Täter im internationalen Vergleich (Lock them up? – Custodial measures against dangerous, criminally responsible [recidivist] offenders – An international comparison). Berlin 2011, pp. 123–157.

– Massen- und Kleinkriminalität vor dem italienischen Friedensrichter. Neue Wege durch alternative Erledigungsmöglichkeiten und Sanktionsformen (Widespread and petty crime and the Italian justice of the peace. New approaches through alternative disposition measures and new forms of sanction). Berlin 2007.

Livingston, Michael A./Monateri, Pier Giuseppe/Parisi, Francesco, The Italian legal system: An introduction. 2d ed. Stanford, CA 2015.

Maiwald, Manfred, Einführung in das italienische Strafrecht und Strafprozessrecht (Introduction to Italian criminal law and the law of criminal procedure. Frankfurt a.M. 2009.

Marinucci, Giorgio/Dolcini, Emilio, Manuale di diritto penale. Parte generale (Textbook on criminal law. General part). 6th ed. Milan 2017.

Padovani, Tullio, Diritto penale (Criminal law). 11th ed. Milan 2017.

Pisani, Mario/Molari, Alfredo/Perchinunno, Vincenzo/Corso, Piermaria/Dominioni, Oreste/Gaito, Alfredo/Spangher, Giorgio, Manuale di procedura penale (Textbook on criminal procedure). 8th ed. Bologna 2008.

Siracusano, Delfino/Galati, Antonio/Tranchina, Giovanni/Zappalà, Enzo, Diritto processuale penale (The law of criminal procedure). Milan 2013.

Tonini, Paolo, Manuale di procedura penale (Textbook on criminal procedure). 16th ed. Milan 2016.

Investigating authorities:

Istituto nazionale di statistica:

– Offenses and persons reported to the judicial authorities by law enforcement officers, 2015: http://dati.istat.it/ [last visited Sept. 2017].

Prosecuting authorities:

Peri, Antonella, Obbligatorietà dell'azione penale e criteri di priorità. La modellistica delle fonti tra esperienze recenti e prospettive *de iure condendo*: un quadro ricognitivo (The principle of mandatory prosecution and priority criteria). Forum Costituzionale: http://www.forumcostituzionale.it/wordpress/images/stories/pdf/documenti_forum/paper/0225_peri.pdf [last visited Sept. 2017].

Istituto nazionale di statistica:

– Annuario statiscico italiano 2016 (Italian statistical yearbook 2016): https://www.istat.it/it/files/2016/12/Asi-2016.pdf [last visited Sept. 2017].

Criminal courts and criminal penalties:

European Court of Human Rights:

– Violation by Article and by States (1959–2016): http://www.echr.coe.int/Documents/Stats_violation_1959_2016_ENG.pdf [last visited Sept. 2017].

Istituto nazionale di statistica (National Italian Statistical Institute):

– Annuario statiscico italiano 2016 (Italian statistical yearbook 2016): https://www.istat.it/it/files/2016/12/Asi-2016.pdf [last visited Sept. 2017].

Execution of custodial penalties:

Ministero della Giustizia (Italian Ministry of Justice):

– Number of penal institutions: https://www.giustizia.it/giustizia/it/mg_form_submit.wp?uid=G_MAP&_pagina_=2&tipo_ufficio=Istituto%20penitenziario&_xml_=html&Submit=cerca [last visited Feb. 2017].

– Number of juvenile prisons: https://www.giustizia.it/giustizia/it/mg_form_submit.page [last visited Sept. 2017].

– Inmates 1991–2017:
http://www.giustizia.it/giustizia/it/mg_1_14_1.wp?facetNode_1=0_2&facetNode_2=1_5_14&previsiousPage=mg_1_14&contentId=SST165666 [last visited Sept. 2017].

– Inmates and prison capacity:

https://www.giustizia.it/giustizia/it/mg_1_14_1.page?facetNode_1=0_2&contentId=SST35918&previsiousPage=mg_1_14 [last visited Sept. 2017].

– Inmates by duration of imposed punishment:

https://www.giustizia.it/giustizia/it/mg_1_14_1.page?facetNode_1=0_2&contentId=SST674033&previsiousPage=mg_1_14 [last visited Sept. 2017].

– Inmates by offenses of conviction:

https://www.giustizia.it/giustizia/it/mg_1_14_1.page?facetNode_1=0_2&contentId=SST36902&previsiousPage=mg_1_14 [last visited Sept. 2017].

– Inmates by age:

https://www.giustizia.it/giustizia/it/mg_1_14_1.page?facetNode_1=0_2&contentId=SST37396&previsiousPage=mg_1_14 [last visited Sept. 2017].

International Centre for Prison Studies – Prison population rate:

– Italy: http://www.prisonstudies.org/country/italy [last visited Sept. 2017].

– Highest to lowest (entire world): http://www.prisonstudies.org/highest-to-lowest/prison_population_rate?field_region_taxonomy_tid=All [last visited Sept. 2017].

– Highest to lowest (Europe): http://www.prisonstudies.org/highest-to-lowest/prison_population_rate?field_region_taxonomy_tid=14 [last visited Sept. 2017].

B. Comparative legal classification and international ties

1. Comparative legal classification

Italy is traditionally considered part of the continental European or Romano-Germanic legal family, which encompasses the legal systems that evolved from Roman law. Typical of the substantive law of this legal family is extensive codification;[1] its laws are shaped primarily by scholars.[2] Criminal procedure in continental European law is characterized by inquisitorial features: prosecution is in the hands of the state and the finding of truth is the primary goal. Within the continental European legal family, Italy belongs to the family of Romanic law, which includes all legal systems influenced by French law.[3]

Italian law is characterized by very extensive codification. Its classification to the Romanic law family can be justified from a historical perspective by the significant influence of the Code Napoléon. In addition to the two major codifications, the Penal Code (*codice penale*, c.p.) and the Code of Criminal Procedure (*codice di procedura penale*, c.p.p.), there are numerous other criminal laws outside the Penal Code proper (often referred to as "secondary" or "ancillary" criminal law) that supplement or define exceptions to the two main codes.[4] Traditionally, and particularly since the 19th century, legal scholarship[5] has driven the development of the law, as evidenced by criminal scholars such as *Francesco Carrara* and *Cesare Beccaria*, but also *Cesare Lombroso*, *Enrico Ferri*, and *Raffaele Garofalo.* Today, the role of legal scholars in Italy is slowly diminishing somewhat, as is the case in other continental European countries.[6] Precedents set by high court decisions have become increasingly important and are contributing more and more to the development of the law. For criminal law, the jurisprudence of the Supreme Constitutional Court *(Corte Costituzionale)*[7] and the Court of Cassation *(Corte di Cassazione)* is of major importance. Nonetheless, academic literature continues to be the most important factor in the development of the law in Italy.[8]

Thus, it is still fundamentally correct, even today, to consider Italian law part of the continental European legal family. This is unequivocally true for many areas of

---

1 *David/Brierley*, Major Legal Systems in the World Today, p. 33.

2 *Rheinstein*, Einführung in die Rechtsvergleichung, pp. 101–102.

3 *Zweigert/Kötz*, Einführung in die Rechtsvergleichung, pp. 103–107; for a comparative account of Italian law from a common lawyer's perspective, see *Livingston* et al., The Italian Legal System.

4 See in detail, I.F.2.

5 For details, see I.G.1.

6 On the role of doctrine in the Italian legal system, see *Livingston* et al., The Italian Legal System, pp. 142–176.

7 On the jurisdiction of the Constitutional Court, see I.A.4.

8 On the sources of criminal law, see I.F.

the law, particularly the substantive criminal law. The new Code of Criminal Procedure of 1989,[9] however, marked a dramatic shift in the law of criminal procedure. It introduced, particularly in the main trial proceedings, numerous adversarial elements closely modeled on Anglo-American criminal procedure. For example, the trial judge is not privy to investigative records; evidence – for the most part – must be introduced by the parties; and witnesses are subject to cross examination by the opposing party. As far as the preliminary proceedings are concerned, the position of the investigating judge *(giudice istruttorio)* was abolished; at the same time, the position of the prosecutor, who is now in charge of this stage of the procedure, was enhanced and granted more independence.[10] Authorization from the newly introduced preliminary examining judge (*giudice per gli indagini preliminary*, GIP) is only required for those pre-trial measures that involve infringements of the defendant's fundamental rights. With these reforms, Italian criminal procedure has evolved into a blended system, although the adversarial approach *(sistema accusatorio)* predominates. As a result, Italian criminal procedure can no longer be assigned unreservedly to the continental European legal family.

2. Effects of international ties

a) Membership in international and regional organizations

On an international level, Italy is a founding member of NATO (1949) and has been a member of the United Nations (*Organizzazione delle Nazione Unite*, ONU) since 1955. In 2007/2008, Italy was one of the non-permanent members of the UN Security Council; from 2007 to 2010 and from 2011 to 2014, it was a member of the UN Human Rights Council. Italy also belongs to the G-7 and G-8 nations and has belonged to the OECD since 1962.

On a regional level, Italy is a founding member of the Council of Europe (*Consiglio d'Europa*, 1949) and of the European Communities. Standards set by the European Union (*Unione Europea*, UE) strongly influence Italian legislation, especially through the implementation of its directives *(direttive)* and – until they were abolished when the Treaty of Lisbon entered into force in 2009 – framework decisions *(decisioni quadro)*.[11] Nonetheless, in the area of criminal law, Italy delayed implementing, for example, the Council Framework Decision on the European arrest warrant *(Mandato d'arresto Europeo)* until 2005 and even then did not implement it completely.[12] Italy has been a member of the OSCE since 1973.

---

[9] D.P.R. 22 Sept. 1988, n. 447.

[10] See I.A.5.a. and I.G.3.

[11] On supranational law as source of criminal law, see I.F.2.

[12] L. 22 Apr. 2005, n. 69.

b) Signature and ratification of international treaties and conventions

Italian criminal law is also shaped by the country's participation in international treaties. Such treaties are not directly applicable; rather, they must be incorporated into national law by the legislature (dualistic principle).[13]

– *Human rights*

With regard to human rights, the European Convention on Human Rights (ECHR) of 1950[14] is paramount. Ratified by Italy in 1955,[15] its amendment, Protocol No. 6 of 1983 on the abolition of the death penalty, was ratified in 1989.[16] It was not until 2008, however, that Protocol No. 13 of 2002 completely abolishing the death penalty was ratified[17] and the Constitution amended.[18] This symbolic amendment was preceded by a law enacted in 1994 that, in practice, abolished the death penalty by removing it from the only place it still existed – the Military Wartime Penal Code.[19]

Italy is also a member state of the International Covenant on Civil and Political Rights of 1966 (ratified in 1977),[20] of the International Convention against the Taking of Hostages of 1979 (ratified in 1986),[21] and of the United Nations Convention against Torture and Other Cruel, Inhuman or Degrading Treatment or Punishment of 1984 (ratified in 1989).[22] The Treaty of Lisbon between the EU member states – and with it the Charter of Fundamental Rights of the European Union – was ratified in 2008.[23]

After the human trafficking crimes had been modified in Italy already in 2003,[24] the ratification in 2010 of the Council of Europe Convention on Action against Trafficking in Human Beings of 2005[25] and the implementation in 2014 of the directive 2011/36/EU of 2011[26] led to another broad reform of the corresponding

---

[13] See also Arts. 80 and 87 para. 8 Cost. and I.F.2.

[14] On the ECHR and the jurisprudence of the European Court of Human Rights, see I.A.5.c. and I.C.1.

[15] L. 4 Aug. 1955 n. 848.

[16] L. 2 Jan. 1989, n. 8.

[17] L. 15 Oct. 2008, n. 179.

[18] See L. cost. 2 Oct. 2007, n. 1.

[19] See L. 13 Oct. 1994, n. 589.

[20] L. 25 Oct. 1977, n. 881.

[21] L. 26 Nov. 1985, n. 718.

[22] L. 3 Nov. 1988, n. 498.

[23] L. 2 Aug. 2008, n. 130. For more on the Charter of Fundamental Rights, see also I.C.1.

[24] L. 11 Aug. 2003, n. 228.

[25] L. 2 July 2010, n. 108.

[26] D.Lgs. 4 March 2014, n. 24.

criminal offense definitions of Arts. 600 ff. c.p. Numerous amendments followed in 2012 and 2013, primarily in the Penal Code but also in the Code of Criminal Procedure, due to the implementation of the Council of Europe Convention on the protection of children against sexual exploitation and sexual abuse of 2007 (Lanzarotta Convention) and the Council of Europe Convention on preventing and combating violence against women and domestic violence of 2011 (Istanbul Convention).[27] In 2014 there were additional amendments to sex crime laws due to the implementation of the EU directive on combating the sexual abuse and sexual exploitation of children and child pornography of 2011.[28]

– International humanitarian law

As for international humanitarian law, Italy did not ratify the Hague Convention with Respect to the Laws and Customs of War on Land. It did, however, ratify (in 1951) the four Geneva Conventions[29] and their Additional Protocols I and II of 1977 (in 1986,[30] Protocol I with reservations). Additional Protocol III of 2005 was ratified in 2008.[31]

Italy is also a party to the 1948 UN Convention on the Prevention and Punishment of the Crime of Genocide (ratified in 1952). This convention was implemented in 1967 with the introduction of a detailed catalogue of statutory offenses.[32]

The Hague Convention for the Protection of Cultural Property in the Event of Armed Conflict of 1954 was ratified in 1958.[33] With the ratification of the Second Protocol of 1999, a number of criminal offenses definitions were enacted in 2009.[34] Italy is also a member state of the International Convention against the Recruitment, Use, Financing and Training of Mercenaries of 1989 (ratified in 1995).[35]

The Rome Statute *(Statuto di Roma)* of the International Criminal Court *(Corte penale internazionale)* of 1998 is particularly important;[36] Italy was one of the first states to ratify it (in 1999).[37] With the exception of a few isolated changes, however, Italian national criminal law has not yet been brought into line with the Statute's

---

27 L. 1 Oct. 2012, n. 172 and D.L. 14 Aug. 2013, n. 93, with changes amended in L. 15 Oct. 2013, n. 119.

28 D.Lgs. 4 March 2014, n. 39.

29 L. 27 Oct. 1951, n. 1739.

30 L 11 Dec. 1985, n. 762.

31 L. 15 Oct. 2008, n. 178.

32 See L. 9 Oct. 1967, n. 962.

33 L. 7 Feb. 1958, n. 279.

34 Arts. 7–12 L. 16 Apr. 2009, n. 45.

35 L. 12 May 1995, n. 210.

36 See I.A.5.c.

37 L. 12 July 1999, n. 232.

requirements. Consequently, the International Criminal Court has sole jurisdiction over genocide, crimes against humanity, and war crimes associated with Italy.[38] In contrast, the Agreement on the Privileges and Immunities of the International Criminal Court of 2002 has been implemented.[39]

– Terrorism

With regard to international anti-terrorism treaties, Italy is a party to the Hague Convention for the Suppression of Unlawful Seizure of Aircraft of 1970, the Montreal Convention for the Suppression of Unlawful Acts against the Safety of Civil Aviation of 1971,[40] the European Convention on the Suppression of Terrorism of 1977 (ratified in 1986)[41] and the UN International Convention for the Suppression of Terrorist Bombings of 1997 (ratified in 2003).[42] The UN International Convention for the Suppression of the Financing of Terrorism 1999 (ratified in 2003)[43] led to the addition of terrorism offenses to the catalogue of crimes for which legal persons can also incur criminal liability.[44]

Directive 2005/60 of the European Parliament and of the Council on the prevention of the use of the financial system for the purpose of money laundering and terrorist financing has also been transposed into national law.[45] In February 2017, two Council of Europe Conventions of 2005, the Convention on the Prevention of Terrorism and the Convention on Laundering, Search, Seizure and Confiscation of the Proceeds from Crime and on the Financing of Terrorism, were ratified.[46]

– Organized crime

To combat organized crime, Italy ratified in 1990 the UN Convention against Illicit Traffic in Narcotic Drugs and Psychotropic Substances of 1988.[47] The ratification and transposition[48] of the UN Convention against Transnational Organized Crime of 2000, including its three Protocols 12a, 12b, and 12c of 2000 and 2001,

---

38 *Marinucci/Dolcini*, Manuale, p. 55.

39 See L. 6 March 2006, n. 130.

40 Both ratified by L. 22 Oct. 1973, n. 906

41 L. 26 Nov. 1985, n. 719.

42 L. 14 Feb. 2003, n. 34

43 L. 14 Jan. 2003, n. 7.

44 Art. 25-*quater* D.Lgs. 8 June 2001, n. 231.

45 See D.Lgs. 22 June 2007, n. 109; D.Lgs. 21 Nov. 2007, n. 231; D.Lgs. 25 Sept. 2009, n. 151; D.Lgs. 11 May 2009, n. 54.

46 L. 28 July 2016, n. 153.

47 L. 5 Nov. 1990, n. 328.

48 L. 16 March 2006, n. 146.

led to a number of modifications to the Penal Code and to criminal provisions outside of the Penal Code proper. Finally, as a result of the Council of Europe Convention on Cybercrime, new criminal offenses definitions were added to the Penal Code (Arts. 495-*bis*, 635-*ter*, 635-*quater*, 635-*quinquies* c.p.) and the corresponding criminal responsibility of legal persons created (Art. 24-*bis* D.Lgs. 231/2001).[49]

– Economic and business crime

As for economic and business crime, Italy ratified the 1990 Council of Europe Convention on Laundering, Search, Seizure and Confiscation of the Proceeds from Crime in 1994.[50] Transposition of the Convention led, among other things, to amendments of the provisions on receiving stolen property and money laundering (Arts. 648–648-*ter* c.p.) and to reforms concerning the effects of foreign criminal judgments in Italy and the execution of Italian criminal judgements abroad (Arts. 730–746 c.p.p.).

Furthermore, the Convention on the Protection of the European Communities' Financial Interests of 1995 with its Protocols of 1996 and the OECD Convention on Combating Bribery of Foreign Public Officials in International Business Transactions of 1997 were ratified and transposed in 2000.[51] In this context, new criminal offense definitions were added to the Penal Code (Arts. 316-*ter*, 322-*bis*, 322-*ter*, 640-*quater* c.p.) and a hitherto unknown system providing for the liability of legal persons introduced into the legal system.[52] In 2012, the Council of Europe Criminal Law Convention on Corruption was ratified and transposed into Italian law.[53]

The transposition of the UN Convention against Corruption of 2003 in 2009[54] led to the introduction of the criminal offense of inducing false statement in the catalogue of crimes for which legal persons may also incur criminal liability as well as to the possibility of returning confiscated property to a foreign state.

– Mutual legal assistance and judicial cooperation in criminal matters

Regarding mutual legal assistance and judicial cooperation in criminal matters, Italy has entered into numerous bilateral extradition treaties. In addition to all of these separate treaties, European instruments are particularly important. For example, Italy is a party to the European Convention on Extradition of 1957 (ratified in

49 See L. 18 March 2008, n. 48.
50 L. 9 Aug. 1993, n. 328.
51 L. 29 Sept. 2000, n. 300.
52 See D.Lgs. 8 June 2001, n. 231.
53 L. 28 June 2012, n. 110.
54 L. 3 Aug. 2009, n. 116.

1963),[55] including its Second Additional Protocol of 1978 (ratified in 1985),[56] to the European Convention on Mutual Assistance in Criminal Matters of 1959 (ratified in 1961),[57] including its First Additional Protocol of 1978 (ratified in 1985),[58] and to the Council of Europe Convention on the Transfer of Sentenced Persons of 1983.[59]

In the context of police and judicial cooperation, two conventions stand out: the Schengen Convention of 1985 and the Schengen Implementation Convention of 1990, both of which Italy joined in 1990.[60] It should be noted that Art. 7 Ratification Act imposed limits on the prohibition of double jeopardy. Many are of the opinion, however, that this limitation has been nullified by the European Charter of Fundamental Rights, which entered into force via the Treaty of Lisbon, due to the Charter's provision protecting against double jeopardy (Art. 50).[61] In February 2016, a number of framework decisions of the Council of Europe[62] related to mutual recognition in criminal matters were transposed into national law.[63]

In 1998,[64] the 1995 Convention on the establishment of a European Police Office (Europol) was ratified and implemented. In addition, as an EU member state, Italy participates in the European Union's Judicial Cooperation Unit (Eurojust), seated in The Hague.

– *Other*

As for the protection of the environment, Italy ratified the Convention on International Trade in Endangered Species of Wild Fauna and Flora (Washington Convention of 1973) in 1975[65] and the International Convention for the Prevention of Pollution from Ships (MARPOL 73/78) in 1980.[66] The directive 2012/29/EU of the European Parliament and of the Council of 25 October 2012 establishing minimum standards on the rights, support and protection of victims of crime, and replacing

---

55 L. 30 Jan. 1963, n. 300.

56 L. 18 Oct. 1984, n. 755.

57 L. 23 Feb. 1961, n. 215.

58 L. 24 July 1985 n. 436.

59 See L. 27 Dec. 1988, n. 565.

60 Ratified and implemented by L. 30 Sept. 1993, n. 388.

61 See Tribunale di Milano, Uff. Ind. Prel., ud. 6 July 2011, with comments by *Vozza*, Riv. trim.-Dir. pen. cont., 2012, 143–153.

62 Framework decisions 2005/214/JI of 24 Feb. 2005, 2008/947/JI of 27 Nov. 2008, 2009/299/JI of 26 Feb. 2009, and 2009/829/JI of 23 Oct. 2009.

63 D.Lgs. 15 Feb., n. 31, 36, 37 und 38.

64 L. 23 March 1998, n. 93.

65 L 19 Dec. 1975, n. 874.

66 L. 29 Sept. 1980, n. 662.

Council Framework Decision 2001/220/JHA was transposed into the law in 2015,[67] and the rights of crime victims in the Code of Criminal Procedure were strengthened. Finally, Italy's membership in the UN Convention on the Law of the Sea of 1982 (ratified in 1995)[68] is also important for criminal law.

Bibliography and further reading

Amati, Enrico/Caccamo, Valentina/Costo, Matteo/Fronza, Emanuela/Vallini, Antonio, Introduzione al diritto penale internazionale (Introduction to international criminal law). 3d ed. Milan 2016.

Armone, Giovanni M./Cimini, Biagio Roberto/Gandini, Fabrizio/Iuzzolino, Gabriele/Nicastro, Giuseppe/Pioletti, Alberto, Diritto penale europeo e ordinamento italiano (European criminal law and Italian legal system). Milan 2006.

Bartone, Nicola (ed.), Diritto penale europeo (European criminal law). Padua 2001.

Caianiello, Michele/Orlandi, Renzo, Landesbericht Italien (Country report Italy). In: Sabine Gleß/Rainer Grote/Günter Heine (eds.), Justizielle Einbindung und Kontrolle von Europol (Judicial involvement and control of Europol). Vol. 1: Nationale und europäische Strafverfolgung (National and European prosecution). Freiburg 2001, pp. 329–382.

Certoma, G. Leroy, The Italian legal system. London 1985.

Constantinesco, Léontin-Jean, Rechtsvergleichung (Comparative law). Vol. III: Die rechtsvergleichende Wissenschaft (The science of comparative law). Cologne 1983.

David, René/Brierley, John E.C., Major Legal Systems in the World Today. 3d ed. London 1985.

Foffani, Luigi (ed.), Diritto penale comparato, europeo e internazionale: prospettive per il XXI secolo; omaggio a Hans-Heinrich Jescheck per il 92. compleanno (Comparative, European and international criminal law: Prospects for the 21st century; Festschrift for Hans-Heinrich Jescheck on his 92d birthday). Milan 2006.

Foffani, Luigi/Orlandi, Renzo, Landesbericht Italien (Country report Italy). In: Walter Gropp/Arndt Sinn (eds.), Organisierte Kriminalität und kriminelle Organisationen. Präventive und repressive Maßnahmen vor dem Hintergrund des 11. September 2001 (Organized crime and criminal organizations. Preventive and repressive measures in light of September 11, 2001). Baden-Baden 2006, pp. 221–260.

Filice, Stefania, Country report Italy. In: Sabine Gleß (ed.), Auslieferungsrecht der Schengen-Vertragsstaaten. Neuere Entwicklungen (Extradition law of Schengen Treaty countries. Recent developments). Freiburg 2002, pp. 265–295.

---

67 D.Lgs. 5 Dec. 2015, n. 212.

68 L. 2 Dec. 1994, n. 689.

Grasso, Giovanni/Sicurella, Rosaria (eds.), L'evoluzione del diritto penale nei settori d'interesse europeo alla luce del Trattato di Lisbona (The evolution of criminal law in the areas of European interest in light of the Treaty of Lisbon). Milan 2011.

Grundmann, Stefan/Zaccaria, Alessio (eds.), Einführung in das italienische Recht (Introduction to Italian law). Frankfurt a.M. 2007.

Jarvers, Konstanze/Grammer, Christoph, Grundlagen der Strafverfolgung völkerrechtlicher Verbrechen in Italien (Fundamentals of the prosecution of international crimes in Italy). In: Albin Eser/Ulrich Sieber/Helmut Kreicker (eds.), Nationale Strafverfolgung völkerrechtlicher Verbrechen (National Prosecution of International Crimes), vol. 4. Berlin 2005, pp. 337–467.

Livingston, Michael A./Monateri, Pier Giuseppe/Parisi, Francesco, The Italian legal system: An introduction. 2d ed. Stanford, CA 2015.

Manacorda, Stefano, Imputazione collettiva e responsabilità personale: uno studio sui paradigmi ascrittivi nel diritto penale internazionale (Collective imputation and personal responsibility: A study of the paradigms of impuation in international criminal law). Turin 2008.

Manes, Vittorio/Zagrebelsky, Vladimiro, La Convenzione europea dei diritti dell'uomo nell'ordinamento penale italiano (The European Convention on Human Rights in the Italian legal system). Milan 2011.

Marinucci, Giorgio/Dolcini, Emilio, Manuale di diritto penale. Parte generale (Textbook on criminal law: General part). 6th ed. Milan 2017.

Oellers-Frahm, Karin, Landesbericht Italien (Country report Italy). In: Sabine Gleß/Rainer Grote/Günter Heine (eds.), Justizielle Einbindung und Kontrolle von Europol (Judicial involvement and control of Europol). Vol. 2: Polizeiliche Ermittlungstätigkeit und Grundrechtsschutz (Police investigation and the protection of fundamental rights). Freiburg 2001, pp. 279–346.

Rheinstein, Max, Einführung in die Rechtsvergleichung (Introduction to comparative law). 2d ed. Munich 1987.

Riz, Roland/Happacher, Esther, Grundzüge des italienischen Verfassungsrechts (Fundamentals of Italian constitutional law). 4th ed. Innsbruck 2013.

Salcuni, Giandomenico, L'europeizzazione del diritto penale: problemi e prospettive (The Europeanization of criminal law: Problems and perspectives). Milan 2011.

Sotis, Carlo, Il diritto senza codice. Uno studio sul sistema penale europeo vigente (Law without a code: A study of the current European criminal law system). Milan 2007.

Vozza, Donato, Verso un nuovo "volto" del *ne bis in idem* internazionale nell'Unione europea? (Towards a new "face" of the international principle of *ne bis in idem* in the European Union?). Riv. trim.-Dir. pen. cont., 2012, 143–153.

Zweigert, Konrad/Kötz, Hein, Einführung in die Rechtsvergleichung auf dem Gebiet des Privatrechts (Introduction to comparative law in the area of private law). 3d ed. Tübingen 1996.

C. Constitutional parameters of criminal law

1. Supra-statutory rules as repositories of criminal law principles

– Constitution

The predecessor of the current Constitution was the so-called Albertine Statute (*Statuto Albertino*, also known as *Statuto del Regno*). It was issued on 4 March 1848, by King *Carlo Alberto* of Sardinia, extended to the new territories upon the founding of the Kingdom of Italy on 17 March 1861, and remained in effect throughout the fascist regime (1922–1944). On 2 June 1946, the Italian electorate voted for a Constituent Assembly *(Assemblea Costituente)* to draft a new constitution. This new Italian Constitution (*Costituzione della Repubblica italiana*, Cost.) was approved by the Constituent Assembly on 22 December 1947 and promulgated on 27 December 1947; it entered into force on 1 January 1948.[1] It can be characterized as a freely-adopted, written constitution that is rigid (i.e., not easily amended) and long.[2] Its defining features include ideas of human dignity and a state governed by the rule of law, the notion that the state exists to serve the people and not vice versa, the existence of inviolable individual, collective, and social fundamental rights, and the ideas of citizen participation in the collective decision-making process, of the equality of and reciprocal checks and balances between the branches of government, and of the justiciability of rights.[3]

The Constitution has supremacy over ordinary laws. Amendments to the Constitution must follow a special legislative procedure: They require two parliamentary readings in each Chamber within three months. The second reading must conclude, at a minimum, with an absolute majority. In the event of a two-thirds majority in both Chambers, the constitutional law *(legge costituzionale)* is forwarded directly to the president for his or her signature; otherwise, the legislative process is suspended to allow for a referendum (Art. 138 Cost.) The last such referendum was held on 4 Dec. 2016 and resulted in the rejection of the proposed constitutional law.[4] There is only one explicit barrier to a constitutional amendment: the republican form of government may not be the subject of a constitutional amendment (Art. 139 Cost.). By implication, however, the Constitutional Court has held that the "inviolable" human rights guaranteed under Art. 2 Cost. may not be amended either, as they are inherent in the supreme values on which

---

1 For the effects of the Constitution on criminal law, see below 3. and *Di Amato/Fucito*, Criminal Law in Italy, p. 60 no. 100.

2 *Riz/Happacher*, Grundzüge, p. 78. See also *Bin/Pitruzzella*, Diritto Costituzionale, pp. 127–143; G.C., The World Today, pp. 308, 316.

3 See *Onida/Pedrazza Gorleo*, Compendio, pp. 12–13.

4 See also I.A.4.

the Italian Constitution is based.[5] This is why the core values of, for example, the right to life[6] or the right to sexual self-determination[7] cannot be infringed upon by a constitutional amendment.[8]

The Constitution begins with a listing of fundamental principles (Arts. 1–12). The list is headed by the statements that Italy is a democratic republic based on labor and that the sovereignty belongs to the people, who exercise it within the framework of the Constitution (Art. 1). Other fundamental principles include the commitment to human rights (Art. 2), the principle of equality (Art. 3), the principle of the unity of the republic and of self-government (Art. 5), and the protection of linguistic minorities (Art. 6). Pursuant to the Constitution, Italian law conforms to generally accepted norms of international law (Art. 10, para. 1), and Italy rejects war as a means of conflict resolution (Art. 11).

Immediately following the fundamental principles is Part I of the Constitution, in which the rights and duties of citizens are addressed (Arts. 13–54).[9] Part II of the Constitution (Arts. 55–139) contains regulations concerning the organization of the state.[10] The Constitution ends with a section containing transitional and final provisions (Arts. I–XVIII). In addition to provisions regulating the transition from the old to the new constitutional organs and the formation of newly constituted regions, provisions concerning the abolition of the monarchy and fascism are included here. For example, Art. XII Cost. prohibits the reestablishment of the dissolved fascist party in any form whatsoever. By contrast, the initial version of Art. XIII Cost., which prohibited the former kings of the House of Savoy, their spouses, and male descendants from participating in elections and entering and sojourning in the country, was abolished in 2002.[11]

Calls for a comprehensive constitutional reform due to the difficulty of governing the country, voiced since the 1970s, have been unsuccessful but did effect a few isolated changes, particularly regarding the form of government of the regions.[12] A constitutional amendment with impact on the criminal law was the reformulation of

---

[5] Corte Cost. 29 Dec. 1988, n. 1146, Giur. Cost. 1988, p. 5566. See also *Riz/Happacher*, Grundzüge, p. 106.

[6] See Corte Cost. 27 June 1996, n. 223, Giur. Cost. 1996, pp. 1918–1937; Corte Cost. 10 Feb. 1997, n. 35, Giur. Cost. 1997, pp. 281–316.

[7] See Corte Cost. 18 Dec. 1987, n. 561, Giur. Cost. 1987, pp. 3535–3544.

[8] See *Riz/Happacher*, Grundzüge, p. 175.

[9] For more details, see below 2.

[10] See I.A.4.

[11] Art. 1 L. cost. 23 Oct. 2002, n. 1.

[12] L. cost. 22 Nov. 1999, n. 1 and L. cost. 18 Oct. 2001, n. 3. See also *Riz/Happacher*, Grundzüge, pp. 79–80.

Art. 111 Cost. in 1999.[13] In its current form, Art. 111 now includes the principle of a fair trial *(principio del giusto processo)* and associated requirements.[14]

– *Other supra-statutory rules*

Pursuant to Art. 10 para. 1 Cost., the Italian legal system abides by the generally accepted norms of international law, limited only by the fundamental principles of its own constitutional order *(principi fondamentali dell'ordinamento costituzionale).*[15] Customary international law *(diritto internazionale consuetudinario)* is directly applicable and, according to the prevailing opinion, is of constitutional rank.[16]

International treaty law *(diritto internazionale pattizio)* is not directly applicable; instead, treaties are typically incorporated into domestic law by means of a parliamentary order of execution *(ordine di esecuzione)* (dualist principle). In most cases, permission for incorporation is included in the parliamentary approval of the treaty's ratification. The status of the subject matter of the treaty is determined by the type of the execution order. Most treaties are incorporated as ordinary laws; however, a treaty with elements that amend the Constitution should be incorporated by means of a constitutional law.[17] Since the reform of 2001,[18] the constraints deriving from Italy's international obligations expressly establish the limits of the legislative powers of the state and the regions (Art. 117 para. 1 Cost.). The laws implementing the Lateran Pacts *(Patti Lateranensi)*, which govern the relationship between the Italian Republic and the Holy See are an exception. The Pacts can only be amended by laws that in turn are based on a bilateral agreement (Art. 7 para. 2 Cost.). As a result, this implementing legislation can even deviate from the Constitution as long as the deviation does not infringe upon fundamental constitutional principles.[19]

Italy ratified the Convention for the Protection of Human Rights and Fundamental Freedoms (ECHR), developed by the Council of Europe, in 1955.[20] According to the Constitutional Court, this Convention is not of constitutional rank because it does not belong to the generally recognized norms of customary international law within the meaning of Art. 10 Cost. but rather represents international treaty law. Yet, the function of the Convention – and its interpretation by the European Court

---

13 By L. cost. 23 Nov. 1999, n. 2.

14 See below 3. and I.D.4.

15 Corte Cost. 18 June 1979, n. 48, Giur. Cost. 1979 I, pp. 381–382.

16 *Riz/Happacher*, Grundzüge, S. 64; *Onida/Pedrazza Gorleo*, Compendio, p. 33. See I.F.4.

17 *Riz/Happacher*, Grundzüge, p. 64.

18 L. cost. 18 Oct. 2001, n. 3.

19 *Onida/Pedrazza Gorleo*, Compendio, pp. 38–39.

20 L. 4 Aug. 1955, n. 848. For details, see I.B.2.b.

of Human Rights – is to supplement the parameters established by the Constitution for the review of state and regional legislation. This is why Italian judges are required to interpret national norms in compliance with the Convention. Where this would exceed the limits of permitted interpretation, the judges are required to submit the issue to the Constitutional Court for review (Art. 117 para. 1 Cost.). The interpretation of the Convention must take into consideration the case law of the European Court of Human Rights.[21]

The EU Charter of Fundamental Rights,[22] which has been binding on Italy since the Lisbon Treaty of 2008 pursuant to Art. 6 of the Treaty on European Union, also provides for the upholding of human dignity, and the rights to liberty, equality, and solidarity, citizens' rights and the rights to justice. Here, too, national judges are bound to interpret national laws in compliance with the Charter. Because the Charter is ranked at treaty level, it has priority over national laws in cases of conflict (see Art. 11 Cost.).[23] Italy is also committed to the rights and freedoms laid down in the International Covenant on Civil and Political Rights of 1966 *(Patto Internazionale relativo ai Diritti civili e politici).*[24]

2. Fundamental rights and freedoms and the criminal law

The Constitution guarantees a number of fundamental rights and freedoms, some of which are granted to all individuals, others only to Italian citizens. It acknowledges the inviolability of human rights *(diritti inviolabili dell'uomo)* but at the same time requires the fulfillment of the indispensable duties of political, economic, and social solidarity (Art. 2). Constitutional amendments that change or violate the essence of these human rights are not allowed.[25]

The Constitution recognizes the principle of equality before the law *(principio di egualianza)* and establishes the duty of the state to remove any obstacles to the liberty and equality of its citizens (Art. 3).

Other constitutionally guaranteed rights and liberties include:

– the right to personal liberty (*libertà personale*, Art. 13);

---

[21] See the so-called "twin decisions" Corte Cost. 24 Oct. 2007, n. 348, Giur. Cost. 2007, pp. 3475, 3478 and Corte Cost. 24 Oct. 2007, n. 349, Giur. Cost. 2007, p. 3539, and, subsequently, Corte Cost. 26 Nov. 2009, n. 311, Giur. Cost. 2009, p. 4658 and Corte Cost. 26 March 2015, n. 49, Giur. Cost. 2015, pp. 391–432; *Marinucci/Dolcini*, Manuale, pp. 55–58. See also I.F.1. and I.F.4.

[22] On the issue of "communitization" of the European Convention on Human Rights, see also Corte Cost. 11 March 2011, n. 80, Giur. Cost. 2011, pp. 1223–1247.

[23] See also Corte Cost. 8 June 1984, n. 170, Giur. Cost. 1984, p. 1115.

[24] Ratified and transposed by L. 25 Oct. 1977, n. 881. For details, see I.B.2.b.

[25] *Riz/Happacher*, Grundzüge, p. 175.

- the inviolability of the home (*libertà di domicilio*, Art. 14);
- the inviolability of mail and telecommunications *(libertà di comunicare riservatamente*, Art. 15);
- the right to move, to reside, to leave the country, and to emigrate (*libertà di circolazione, soggiorno, espatrio ed emigrazione*, Art. 16);
- freedom of assembly (*libertà di riunione*, Art. 17);
- freedom of association (*libertà di associazione*, Art. 18);
- freedom of religion (*libertà religiosa*, Art. 19);
- freedom of expression (*libertà di manifestazione del pensiero*, Art. 21);
- right to legal capacity, citizenship, and name (*capacità giuridica, cittadinanza, nome*, Art. 22);
- freedom of the arts and sciences (*libertà dell'arte e della scienza*, Art. 33).

3. Other supra-statutory norms relevant to criminal law and criminal procedure

Art. 24 Cost.[26]

Everyone may bring cases before a court of law in order to protect their rights and lawful interests.

Defense is an inviolable right at every stage and instance of legal proceedings.

The indigent are entitled, through appropriate institutions, to proper means for action and defense in all courts.

In cases of judicial errors, the law defines the conditions and forms for reparation.

Art. 25 Cost.

No one may be removed from a court but must be heard as provided by law. No one may be punished except as provided for by a law already in force when the offense was committed.

No one may be subjected to security measures except as provided for by law.

Art. 26 Cost.

A citizen may be extradited only as expressly provided by international conventions. Extradition is not permitted for political offenses under any circumstances.

Art. 27 Cost.

Criminal responsibility is personal.

The defendant may not be considered guilty until conviction is final.

---

[26] Translations of articles of the Italian Constitution are based on the ICL translation, available at http://www.servat.unibe.ch/icl/it00000_.html [last visited Aug. 2017].

Penalties may not consist of treatment contrary to human dignity and must aim at reeducating the convict.

The death penalty is prohibited.

Art. 111 Cost.

Justice must be administered in a fair trial as defined by law.

Trials must be conducted by an independent and impartial judge in a manner guaranteeing a fair hearing. The law has to ensure reasonable time limits for the proceedings.

In criminal proceedings, the law must provide for timely and confidential information of the accused regarding the nature and reasons of charges brought against them; they are granted the time and means for their defense; they have the right to question those who testify against them or to have them questioned; those who may testify in favor of the accused must be summoned and examined under the same conditions granted to the prosecution; any evidence in favor of the accused must be acknowledged; the accused may rely on the help of an interpreter if they do not understand or speak the language used in the proceedings.

In criminal trials, evidence may only be established according to the principle of a fair hearing. No defendant may be proven guilty based on testimony given by witnesses who freely, purposely, and continuously avoided cross-examination by the defendant or defendant's counsel.

The law defines when evidence may be established without maintaining the principle of a fair hearing, either by consent of the defendant, or due to manifest and absolute impossibility, or as a result of proven unlawful conduct.

Reasons must be stated for all judicial decisions.

Appeals to the Court of Cassation are always proper for violations of the law in cases of sentences and measures concerning personal freedom issued by the ordinary or by special courts. These provisions may be waived only for sentences pronounced by military courts in time of war.

Appeals to the Court of Cassation against decisions of the Council of State and of the Court of Accounts are admissible only for reasons of jurisdiction.

Art. 112 Cost.

The public prosecutor has the duty to initiate criminal proceedings.

In addition to the fundamental rights, numerous other constitutional norms are relevant to criminal law or to criminal procedure:

- the right to take judicial action and the right to defense (*diritto di azione e di difesa*, Art. 24);
- the right to be heard by the competent judge determined by law ("natural judge," *giudice naturale*, Art. 25 para. 1);
- the principle of legality (*principio di legalità*, Art. 25 para. 2);[27]
- the prohibition of retroactivity (*principio di irretroattività*, Art. 25 para. 2);[28]

---

27 For details, see II.A.

- the principle of personal criminal responsibility (*principio della responsabilità personale in materia penale*, Art. 27 para. 1);[29]
- the presumption of innocence (*presunzione di non colpevolezza*, Art. 27 para. 2);
- the prohibition of inhuman punishments (*divieto di pene contrarie al senso di umanità*, Art. 27 para. 3);
- the principle of re-education of the convicted person (*principio di rieducazione del condannato*, Art. 27 para. 3);[30]
- the prohibition of the death penalty (*divieto della pena di morte*, Art. 27 para. 4);
- the prohibition of extradition of foreigners for political crimes (except for genocide, Art. 10 para. 4);
- the principle of legality and the requirement that all measures involving deprivation of liberty be approved by a judicial authority (Art. 13 para. 2);
- the prohibition of all forms of physical or psychological force against detainees (Art. 13 para. 4);
- the determination by law of the maximum duration of preventive detention (Art. 13 para. 5);
- the requirement that a judicial authority rule on searches and seizures of private spaces, on restrictions on the secrecy of correspondence and other forms of communication, and on seizure of printed materials (Arts. 14, 15 and 21 para. 3);
- the prohibition of extradition of Italian citizens as long as extradition is not expressly provided by international conventions (Art. 26);
- the legal status of members of parliament (Art. 68);
- the limits of responsibility of the president of the Republic (Art. 90);
- the limits of responsibility of the prime minister and ministers (Art. 96);
- amnesty, remission, and pardon (Arts. 79, 87);[31]
- judges are subject only to the law (Art. 101 para. 2);
- the principle of a fair trial (*principio del giusto processo*, Art. 111). This includes the right to adversarial proceedings, the right to a reasonable length of the proceedings, the right to question, the right to an interpreter, etc.;[32]
- the principle of mandatory prosecution (*principio dell'obbligatorietà dell'azione penale*, Art. 112).[33]

---

28 For details, see II.A.3.d.

29 See I.D.2.

30 For details, see I.D.3.

31 For further details, see II.K.

32 For further details, see I.D.4.

33 On the principle of mandatory prosecution, see also I.A.5.b. and I.D.4.

Bibliography and further reading

Antolisei, Francesco, Manuale di diritto penale. Parte generale (Textbook of criminal law. General part). 16th ed. Milan 2003.

Bin, Roberto/Pitruzzella, Giovanni, Diritto Costituzionale (Constitutional law). 17th ed. Turin 2016.

Canestrari, Stefano/Cornacchia, Luigi/De Simone, Giulio, Manuale di diritto penale. Parte generale (Textbook of criminal law. General part). 2d ed. Bologna 2017.

C. G., The New Italian Constitution, The World Today, vol. 4 no. 7 (July 1948), pp. 307–316, at http://www.jstor.org/stable/40392130 [last visited Aug. 2017].

Cocozza, Vincenzo, Voce "Costituzione (Costituzione Italiana)" (Entry "Constitution II [Italian Constitution]"). Enciclopedia giuridica Treccani (Legal Encyclopedia established by Treccani), vol. X. Rome 1999, pp. 1–9.

Di Amato, Astolfo/Fucito, Federica, Criminal Law in Italy. 3d ed. Alphen aan den Rijn 2016.

Fiandaca, Giovanni/Musco, Enzo, Diritto penale. Parte generale (Criminal law. General part). 7th ed. Bologna 2014.

Fiandaca, Giovanni/Di Chiara, Giuseppe, Una introduzione al sistema penale. Per una lettura costituzionalmente orientata (An introduction to the system of criminal law. A constitutionally-based reading). Naples 2003.

Grabenwarter, Christoph/Pabel, Katharina, Europäische Menschenrechtskonvention (The European Convention on Human Rights). 6th ed. Munich 2016.

Grundmann, Stefan/Zaccaria, Alessio (eds.), Einführung in das italienische Recht (Introduction to Italian law). Frankfurt a.M. 2007.

Leo, Guglielmo, La recente giurisprudenza della Corte Costituzionale in materia penale (Recent decisions of the Constitutional Court in penal matters). Riv. trim.-Dir. pen. cont., 1, 2012, 71–193.

Livingston, Michael A./Monateri, Pier Giuseppe/Parisi, Francesco, The Italian legal system: An introduction. 2d ed. Stanford, DA 2015.

Mantovani, Ferrando, Diritto penale. Parte generale (Criminal law. General part). 10th ed. Padua 2017.

Marinucci, Giorgio/Dolcini, Emilio, Corso di diritto penale Vol. 1. Le norme penali: Fonti e limiti di applicabilità. Il reato: nozione, struttura e sistematica (Course in criminal law vol. 1. The criminal norms: sources and limits of application. The criminal offense: concept, structure, and classification). 3d ed. Milan 2001.

– Manuale di diritto penale. Parte generale (Textbook of criminal law. General part). 5th ed. Milan 2015.

Mortati, Costantino, Voce "Costituzione della Repubblica Italiana" (Entry "Constitution of the Italian Republic"). Enciclopedia del Diritto (Encyclopedia of law), vol. XI. Milan 1962, pp. 214–231.

Onida, Valerio, Voce "Costituzione italiana" (Entry "Italian Constitution"). Digesto delle Discipline Pubblicistiche Vol. IV. Turin 1989, pp. 321–339.

Onida, Valerio/Pedrazza Gorlero, Maurizio (eds.), Compendio di Diritto Costituzionale (Outline of constitutional law). 3d ed. Milan 2014.

Riz, Roland/Happacher, Esther, Grundzüge des italienischen Verfassungsrechts (Fundamentals of Italian constitutional law). 4th ed. Innsbruck 2013.

Romano, Mario, Commentario sistematico del codice penale (Systematic commentary on the Penal Code). Vol. I: Arts. 1–84. 3d ed. Milan 2004.

Schabas, William, The European Convention of Human Rights. A commentary. Oxford 2015.

Table of cases

Corte Cost. 26 March 2015, n. 49, Giur. Cost. 2015, pp. 391–432

Corte Cost. 11 March 2011, n. 80, Giur. Cost. 2011, pp. 1223–1247

Corte Cost. 26 Nov. 2009, n. 311, Giur. Cost. 2009, pp. 4657–4679

Corte Cost. 24 Oct. 2007, n. 349, Giur. Cost. 2007, pp. 3535–3564

Corte Cost. 24 Oct. 2007, n. 348, Giur. Cost. 2007, pp. 3475–3517

Corte Cost. 10 Feb. 1997, n. 35, Giur. Cost. 1997, pp. 281–316

Corte Cost. 27 June 1996, n. 223, Giur. Cost. 1996, pp. 1918–1937

Corte Cost. 29 Dec. 1988, n. 1146, Giur. Cost. 1988 I, pp. 5565–5570

Corte Cost. 18 Dec. 1987, n. 561 Giur. Cost. 1987, pp. 3535–3544

Corte Cost. 8 June 1984, n. 170, Giur. Cost. 1984, pp. 1098–1117

Corte Cost. 18 June 1979, n. 48, Giur. Cost. 1979 I, pp. 373–382

D. Fundamentals of criminal law

1. Functions of criminal law

Criminal law is justified by the many different purposes it serves. On the one hand, it serves to protect society and the individual from criminal conduct; on the other, modern criminal law also serves as an individual guarantee for the offender by limiting the mandate of the criminal law to intervene and in so doing limiting the scope of the state's power to punish.[1] Criminal penalties severely infringe on the fundamental rights of the individual and may therefore only be imposed when absolutely necessary. Finally, criminal law helps resolve both the social conflict and the conflict between perpetrator and victim.[2]

– Criminal law as a means of social control

Criminal law exists to combat and prevent crime. To this end, it sets the limits within which the individual is free to act, and it serves as the most severe means of social control. But criminal law also protects the individual in society: it safeguards the basic conditions of human coexistence and mutual consideration, and it sets penalties that a particular society at a particular point in time believes are appropriate to protect the legal interests or values important to it. In so doing, it contributes to the preservation of peace and social order.[3]

Thus, the legislature is not entirely free in its decisions as to what types of conduct to criminalize and what types not to criminalize. In light of the fact that individual liberty is a fundamental constitutional right, lawmakers must link every criminal provision to an actual social harm and delineate as precisely as possible the scope of conduct that constitutes a criminal wrong.[4]

– Criminal law as a means of protecting recognized legal interests

Criminal law protects society by protecting individual and collective legal interests *(beni giuridici individuali e collettivi).* In Italy, adherence to the model of protected legal interests is considered an essential feature of a liberal and democratic legal system. This type of criminal law is not shaped at the whim of the legislature but rather is designed to protect authentic legal interests already present in society.[5]

---

1 *Romano*, Commentario, I, pre-Art. 1, margin no. 22. See below 2.

2 See also *Canestrari* et al., Manuale, p. 31.

3 *Canestrari* et al., Manuale, p. 30; *Fiandaca/Musco*, Parte generale, p. 4; *Romano*, Commentario, I, pre-Art. 1, margin no. 19.

4 *Romano*, Commentario, I, pre-Art. 39, margin no. 13. See also *Bricola*, "Teoria generale del reato," pp. 15–21.

5 See *Romano*, Commentario, I, pre-Art. 1, margin no. 24.

As such, a criminal act is a violation of a protected legal interest and, simultaneously, a breach of duty. It follows that, in Italy, criminal liability arises only after a protected legal interest has been violated *(principio di offensività)*.[6] A protected legal interest is an interest considered worthy of protection by means of criminal law because of its importance.[7] The question of which legal interests are worthy of protection and which are not is a dynamic one, and consequently its answer varies over time, because an individual legal interest exists only as long as it is actually effective, that is, only as long as it is useful in a given society.[8] As criminal law infringes not only on individual liberty (Art. 13 Cost.) but also on other constitutionally protected values such as "social dignity" (*dignità sociale*, Arts. 2 and 3 Cost.), some legal scholars argue that criminal law, in turn, must protect interests that are of constitutional relevance.[9]

– Criminal law as ultima ratio

Italian scholars agree that a violation of a protected legal interest, without more, is insufficient to justify recourse to criminal law. In accordance with the principle of subsidiarity *(principio di sussidiarietà)*, criminal law is but the means of last resort: First, its use must be necessary in the sense that other protective mechanisms, such as civil law or administrative law, are insufficient. Second, it must also be appropriate, that is, in fact conducive to achieving the desired goal. The legislature must therefore assess the social harm of the conduct to be criminalized as well as the effectiveness of the various types of penalties, preferably with the help of empirical studies. In this way, the principle of *ultima ratio* is related to the principle of proportionality.[10] Criminal law is also fragmentary in nature *(principio di frammentarietà)* as not all violations of protected legal interests are criminalized.

2. Limits on criminal law imposed by the rule of law

Art. 27 Cost.[11]
Criminal responsibility is personal.

---

6 *Bricola*, "Teoria generale del reato," p. 77; for details, see below 2. and II.D.5.

7 *Fiandaca/Musco*, Parte generale, p. 4.

8 *Fiandaca/Musco*, Parte generale, p. 5.

9 E.g., the theory of *Bricola*, "Teoria general del reato," p. 17. See also *Fiandaca/Musco*, Parte generale, p. 13 (with further references).

10 See *Fiandaca/Musco*, Parte generale, pp. 29–32; *Mantovani*, Parte generale, pp. XLII–XLIII.

11 Translations of articles of the Constitution are based on the ICL translation, available at http://www.servat.unibe.ch/icl/it00000_.html [last visited Aug. 2017].

The defendant may not be considered guilty until conviction is final.

Penalties may not consist of treatment contrary to human dignity and must aim at reeducating the convict.

The death penalty is prohibited.

There is broad consensus in the Italian criminal law tradition that criminal law must be guided by general principles, primarily those embodied in the Constitution. One reason for this is that the criminal code in force today, the Penal Code of 1930, retains the authoritarian features dating back to its fascist origins. But even newly enacted criminal law must be measured against these principles because it is frequently created in response to current political necessities.[12] These numerous principles include the principle of legality *(principio di legalità*, Art. 25 paras. 2 and 3 Cost.); the principle of personal responsibility *(principio della responsabilità personale*, Art. 27 para. 1 Cost.); the principle of the reeducation of the convicted person *(principio di rieducazione*, Art. 27 para. 3 Cost.),[13] and the requirement of a violation of a protected legal interest *(principio di offensività).*

– Principle of legality

The general view is that the principle of legality *(nullum crimen, nulla poena sine lege)* consists of the following four elements: the principle of legislativity *(riserva di legge, lex scripta)*, the principle of certainty (*principio di determinatezza* or *di precisione, lex certa*), the prohibition of analogy *(divieto di analogia, lex stricta)*, and the prohibition of retroactivity *(principio di irretroattività, lex praevia)*.[14]

– Principle of personal responsibility

The two-pronged principle of personal responsibility is addressed in Art. 27 para. 1 Cost.: First, it establishes responsibility for one's own actions *(responsabilità per fatto proprio)* by making it illegal to hold a person responsible for the deed of someone else *(responsabilità per fatto altrui)* based on membership in a group *(responsabilità collettiva)*, on a certain position or status *(responsabilità di posizione)*, or on coincidental circumstances *(responsabilità per il caso)*.[15]

---

[12] *Donini/Insolera*, in: Insolera (ed.), Riserva di legge, p. 13.

[13] See below 3.

[14] See, e.g., *Canestrari* et al., Manuale, pp. 110–111. For detailed discussion of the principle of legality, see II.A. See also *Di Amato/Fucito*, Criminal Law in Italy, pp. 63–64, nos. 109–113.

[15] *Canestrari* et al., Manuale, pp. 201–203.

Second, it requires the offense to have been committed culpably. Central to the criminal law systems of many countries, the principle of culpability *(principio di colpevolezza)*[16] became the linchpin of the Italian system as well when the Constitutional Court elevated it to constitutional rank in 1988. According to the Constitutional Court, for someone to be convicted of a crime, intent or negligence must be proven for all defining elements of the offense in question.[17] Nevertheless, the Italian Penal Code (*codice penale*, c.p.) still contains a number of instances of objective responsibility (strict liability), in which the actor is held responsible for the consequences of his or her conduct despite the absence of intent or negligence (Art. 43 para. 3 c.p.). This has led to criticism that the culpability principle has not yet been fully implemented.[18]

– Principle of proportionality

According to the principle of proportionality *(principio di proporzione)*,[19] the prescribed punishment must be proportionate to the severity of the prohibited act. The Constitutional Court has declared a number of criminal provisions unconstitutional because they violated this principle.[20] Punishment must reflect individual responsibility and culpability. This is why the principle – like the principle of humanity – is usually discussed in the context of purposes of punishment.[21]

– Principio di offensività

Yet another important and traditionally accepted limit on criminal law in Italy is the requirement of a violation of a protected legal interest *(principio di offensività)*, which is not explicitly regulated.[22] A criminal offense must constitute a violation of a legally protected interest; in the absence of such a violation, there can be no criminal offense. Even a concrete danger to a protected legal interest – without more – may suffice to satisfy this requirement.[23] The absence of a violation of a protected legal interest is the explanation for why both acts committed under the false as-

---

16 On this principle, see also *Di Amato/Fucito*, Criminal Law in Italy, pp. 64–65, no. 114.

17 Corte Cost. 24 March 1988, n. 364, Giur. Cost. 1988, p. 1504; Corte Cost. 13 Dec. 1988, n. 1085, Giur. Cost. 1988, p. 5271; Corte Cost. 24 July 2007, n. 322, Giur. Cost, 2007, p. 3155. Regarding the structure of the criminal offense, see II.C.2.c.

18 See, e.g., *Canestrari* et al., Manuale, p. 229. See also, Corte Cost. 8 July 1957, n. 107, Giur. Cost. 1957, p. 1005. For discussion of objective responsibility, see II.E.4.b.

19 On this principle, see also *Di Amato/Fucito*, Criminal Law in Italy, p. 65, no. 115.

20 E.g., Corte Cost. 18 July 1989, n. 409, Giur. Cost. 1989, pp. 1909–1910 and Corte Cost. 25 July 1994, n. 341, Giur. Cost. 1994, p. 2803.

21 See below 3.

22 For a detailed account of this principle, see *Manes*, ZStW 114 (2002), 720–735.

23 See *Mantovani*, Parte generale, pp. 179–207.

sumption that they are a crime and impossible attempts are not criminalized (Arts. 49 and 56 para. 1 c.p.).[24] In this context, abstract endangerment offenses are problematic and their very existence controversial.[25] The same is true of various other offense forms, such as unsuccessful incitement or the mere agreement of two or more persons to commit an offense, in which there is no violation of a protected legal interest.[26] On the one hand, the *principio di offensività* serves as a criterion for the (abstract) legislative configuration of the criminal offense definition: the legislature may only criminalize conduct that infringes on one or more protected legal interests; it can, however, be required to criminalize certain types of conduct (such as the use of force against detainees, Art. 13 para. 4 Cost.). On the other hand, the principle functions as an interpretation tool for judges: before they can conclude in a concrete case that an offense has been committed, they must ascertain that a protected legal interest has in fact been violated or endangered.[27] It follows that conduct that at first glance appears to fulfill the elements of an offense but that does not in fact endanger a protected legal interest does not satisfy the definitional elements of the offense – the same result as would be reached by means of teleological reasoning.[28]

3. Purposes of punishment

In addition to their symbolic significance, expressed in the social disapproval of criminal act and perpetrator, criminal penalties have a significant adverse effect on the convicted person, as implied by the Italian term for punishment *(pena)*[29] – which also means anguish, agony, and torment as well as compassion. Punishment is also a public sanction imposed by a court of law after a criminal trial;[30] thus, it must be especially well justified. To this end, over the years, theories aimed at identifying the purposes of punishment have developed; they are traditionally classified as "absolute" and "relative" theories.[31]

---

[24] *Romano*, Commentario, I, Art. 49, margin no. 20.

[25] See *Romano*, Commentario, I, pre-Art. 39, margin no. 114; see also II.D.6.

[26] *Cadoppi/Veneziani*, Parte generale, p. 113; *Canestrari* et al., Manuale, p. 240.

[27] For a discussion of both functions of the *principio di offensività*, see *Fiandaca/Musco*, Parte generale, p. 195 and Corte Cost. 7 July 2005, n. 265, Giur. Cost. 2005, p. 2437; Corte Cost. 24 July 1995, n. 360, Giur. Cost 1995, pp. 2668–2689; Corte Cost. 11 July 2000, n. 263, Giur. Cost. 2000, pp. 2064–2088; Corte Cost. 21 Nov. 2000, n. 519, Giur. Cost. 2000, pp. 4069–4082.

[28] *Fiandaca/Musco*, Parte generale, p. 196. For details, see II.D.5.

[29] On the differences between punishments and security measures, see I.A.5.b. and I.E.3.

[30] *Antolisei*, Parte generale, p. 675.

[31] *Antolisei*, Parte generale, p. 681.

Absolute theories *(teorie assolute)* hold that a penalty must be imposed because a criminal offense has been committed. Thus, the penalty is an end in itself: it serves as compensation and retribution *(retribuzione)* for the culpable act and as expiation *(espiazione)* for the offender.[32] Retribution as a purpose of punishment always implies proportionality: if a penalty is to compensate for the harm caused by the prohibited act, it must not be disproportionate to the seriousness of the crime.[33] An additional advantage of the absolute theory is that it does not require proof of the penalty's concrete deterrent effect. Opponents of this theory argue that it is not always easy to determine what exactly the wrong consists in; besides, it is not possible to punish all wrongs nor is it possible to punish all offenders. At times, it may make more sense not to punish a certain type of conduct, and the state ought to be at liberty not to punish in such situations.[34]

Relative theories *(teorie relative)* pose the question of how to prevent future criminal offenses. Accordingly, punishment is not an end in itself but rather is a deterrent measure. General deterrence *(prevenzione generale)* is understood as the effect of punishment on the general public, namely, deterring it from committing criminal acts. Underlying the idea of deterrence *(intimidazione)* as a purpose of punishment is the assumption that fear of its consequences will prevent criminal behavior.[35] Opponents argue that people do not always act rationally, carefully weighing pros and cons. To the contrary, criminal acts are frequently prompted by unconscious or emotional triggers that are difficult to control.[36] But general deterrence may also be viewed in a positive sense *(prevenzione generale c.d. positiva)* insofar as a symbol of public disapproval is seen in the threat of punishment, which in turn contributes to a situation in which most people identify themselves with the value system protected by law and consider it "just."[37] There is, however, no exhorting and "moralizing" effect if the threatened penalty is not followed up by the actual imposition and execution of punishment.[38]

Special or individual deterrence *(prevenzione speciale)* concentrates on the effect of punishment on individual offenders, namely, on whether punishment succeeds in deterring individual offenders from reoffending. In a negative sense, it is a means to neutralize the offender *(neutralizzazione)*; after all, an individual who is incarcerated can no longer commit certain crimes. Numerous legal prohibitions and proscriptions (e.g., suspension of driver's license), which frequently serve as supple-

---

32 *Romano*, Commentario, I, pre-Art. 1, margin no. 29.

33 *Bettiol/Petteoello-Mantovani*, Diritto penale, pp. 812–813; *Fiandaca/Musco*, Parte generale, p. 732. See also above 2.

34 *Romano*, Commentario, I, pre-Art. 1, margin no. 34.

35 *Antolisei*, Parte generale, pp. 684–686.

36 *Fiandaca/Musco*, Parte generale, pp. 747–748.

37 See *Pagliaro*, Cass. pen. 2016, 1847.

38 *Fiandaca/Musco*, Parte generale, pp. 746–749.

mentary penalties, have the same goal. In a positive sense, special deterrence is seen as a means to reform *(emenda)* and to resocialize *(risocializzazione)* the offender. The principle articulated in Art. 27 para. 3 Cost., according to which the goal of punishment must be to reeducate the convict *(principio di rieducazione)*, is the guiding principle during the execution phase of sentences; but judges must also consider the best possible options for reintegration *(recupero)* of the convict when assessing and imposing penalties.[39] Today, special deterrence is also no longer unanimously accepted.[40]

The mixed theories *(teorie miste)* attempt to combine elements of the absolute and relative theories. Punishment is inflicted to compensate for the culpable act, to deter future crimes, and to reintegrate the offender. The aim is to achieve the optimal mix of the goals of general and special deterrence by means of "appropriate" retribution.[41] This "multi-functional" *(plurifunzionale)* approach currently prevails in academic legal circles, whereby the approaches of the various scholars differ in detail.[42]

Pursuant to Art. 27 para. 3 Cost., punishments may not consist in treatment contrary to principles of humanity. The principle of humanity *(principio di umanità)* is reconfirmed in Art. 1 Prison Act *(ordinamento penitenziario)*[43] and appears in numerous international documents (e.g., in the European Convention on Human Rights). The prohibition of the death penalty (Art. 27 para. 4 Cost), of corporal punishment, and of detention in overcrowded penal institutions all flow from this principle.[44]

The goal of reeducation *(finalismo rieducativo)*, a leading purpose of punishment in Italy, is also anchored in Art. 27 para. 3 Cost. Today, the term "reeducation" is generally not understood as moral improvement. After all, a democratic state based on the rule of law should not concern itself with the conscience and state of mind of its citizens. Rather, reeducation should be understood as resocialization.[45] Its aim is – as far as possible – to promote the reintegration of convicted persons into society and to help them distance themselves from their earlier lifestyle. In addition, an effort should be made to help them gain appreciation for the fundamental values of human coexistence – at least those values protected by the criminal law

---

39 See generally *Fiandaca/Musco*, Parte generale, pp. 754–755; *Romano*, Commentario, I, pre-Art. 1, margin no. 31.

40 See *Antolisei*, Parte generale, p. 690; *Fiandaca/Musco*, Parte generale, pp. 755–756; *Pagliaro*, Parte generale, pp. 681–683.

41 *Romano*, pre-Art. 1, margin no. 36–37.

42 See *Antolisei*, Parte generale, pp. 691–693; *Pagliaro*, Parte generale, pp. 674–677.

43 L. 26 July 1975, n. 354

44 *Canestrari* et al., Manuale, p. 69.

45 *Fiandaca/Musco*, Parte generale, pp. 737, 741.

that was violated.[46] On the other hand, convicted offenders cannot be forced to reintegrate. If that were the case, reintegration would be ineffective not only because in such a situation offenders would develop even more antagonism to the system, but also because forced reintegration would violate their dignity and constrain their right to self-determination. Thus, convicts are free to decide whether or not to accept the offer of resocialization.[47]

The principle of proportionality *(principio di proporzionalità)* is another aspect of reeducation as a purpose of punishment. It is one of the guiding criteria for a state based on the rule of law and consequently a yardstick employed by theories of the function of punishment. It also inevitably follows from the idea of retribution. Furthermore, from the perspective of general deterrence, the threat of disproportionally heavy punishment might result in indifference on the part of potential offenders and may disrupt a value system that ought to reflect a proper relationship between criminal act and criminal sanction. As far as the special or individual deterrent effect of reeducation is concerned, offenders must acknowledge the wrongfulness of their actions and accept the imposed penalties as correct and proportional.[48] There must be proportionality not only with regard to the act in an objective sense but also to the degree of blameworthiness or reproachability, that is, the culpability of the offender.[49]

4. Fundamental principles of criminal procedure

In 1989, a new Code of Criminal Procedure (*codice di procedura penale*, c.p.p.)[50] based, in many key areas, on the adversarial system entered into force.[51] Since then, the criminal process has been configured largely as a party (or adversarial) process, whereby a number of inquisitorial elements (particularly in the investigative phase of the proceedings) remain in place.[52] The fundamental principles of

---

46 *Fiandaca/Musco*, Parte generale, p. 742.

47 *Fiandaca/Musco*, Parte generale, p. 742.

48 *Fiandaca/Musco*, Parte generale, p. 740.

49 See, e.g., *Canestrari* et al., Manuale, pp. 76.

50 For an English translation of the Code of Criminal Procedure as of 30 Oct. 2013, see *Gialuz* et al. (eds.), The Italian Code of Criminal Procedure, pp. 83–500; for an overview of the Code, see *Gialuz*, in: Gialuz et al. (eds.), The Italian Code of Criminal Procedure, pp. 17–52; for a more detailed account of Italian criminal procedure, see *Di Amato/Fucito*, Criminal Law in Italy, pp. 157–221; for a comparative analysis, see *Lupária*, in: Gialuz et al. (eds.), The Italian Code of Criminal Procedure, pp. 1–16.

51 See I.G.3. and, for more details, *Amodio/Selvaggi*, Temple L. Rev. 62 (1989), 1211–1224; *Pizzi/Marafioti*, Yale J. Int'l L. 17 (1992), 1–40; *Illuminati*, 4 Wash. U. Global Stud. L. Rev. 567–582 (2005); on the adjustments made in the years after the reform, see *Amodio*, Am. J. Comp. L 52 (2004), 489–500.

52 See also I.B.1.

criminal procedure are already stated in the Constitution.[53] Others are regulated only in the Code of Criminal Procedure.[54]

The Constitution lays down a general right to bring an action in a court of law to protect legitimate rights and interests (*tutela dei diritti*, Art. 24 para. 1 Cost.), the right to mount a defense (*diritto di difesa*, Art. 24 para. 2 Cost.) at every stage and instance of the proceedings, and – to ensure these rights are properly enforced – the right of the indigent to assistance (*patrocinio per i non abbienti*, Art. 24 para. 3 Cost.). As a rule, compensation must be provided for judicial errors (*errori giudiziari*, Art. 24 para. 4 Cost.).

The principle of the "natural judge" (*giudice naturale*, Art. 25 para. 1 Cost.) means that no one can be deprived of his or her competent judge, that is, the judge designated by law. In Art. 25 Cost., some aspects of the legality principle are regulated, in particular, the prohibition of retroactivity and its general applicability to punishments and security measures (Art. 25 paras. 2 and 3 Cost.).

The fair trial principle has become essential. In 1999, it was the subject of a comprehensive constitutional amendment;[55] since then, the term *giusto processo* ("just," "due," or "fair" process) has been in use. Aside from the fundamental – now constitutional – right to a fair trial (Art. 111 para. 1 Cost.), Art. 111 Cost. now contains numerous additional procedural principles flowing from the fair trial principle. These include, in para. 2, the impartiality and independence of judges *(terzietà e imparzialità del giudice)*,[56] the equality of parties *(parità tra le parti)*, and a reasonable length of procedure *(ragionevole durata)* and, in para. 3, various fundamental defense rights, including the right to an interpreter. Paras. 4 and 5 address the right to be heard by a judge and the principle of adversariness *(principio del contraddittorio)*, including exceptions to the principle. Para. 6 lays down the duty to provide reasons for all judicial decisions *(obbligo di motivazione)*. Finally, para. 7 establishes the right of appeal *(impugnazioni)* to the Court of Cassation for violations of the law regarding all measures involving deprivation of liberty.

During preliminary proceedings, the non-disclosure rule generally applies (*obbligo di segreto*, Art. 329 para. 1 c.p.p.) until the defendant is entitled to have access to the investigative actions. Prosecutors are independent (as are the courts, Arts. 104–107 Cost.) and must also remain objective, to a degree, because they are also bound to investigate facts and circumstances that favor the defendant (Art. 358 para. 1 c.p.p.). In Italy, *ex officio* offenses must be prosecuted under all circum-

[53] See I.C.3.

[54] For an extensive account of Italian law of criminal procedure, see *Di Amato/Fucito*, Criminal Law in Italy, pp. 157–221, nos. 422–607.

[55] L. cost. 23 Nov. 1999, n. 2.

[56] See also Art. 101 Cost. and *Chiavario*, Diritto processuale penale, pp. 110–114.

stances: this principle of mandatory prosecution *(principio dell'obbligatorietà)* is even of constitutional rank (Art. 112 Cost.).[57]

In the trial phase of proceedings, the following principles apply:

- principle of adversariness (*principio del contraddittorio*, also applies to the taking of evidence, Art. 498 c.p.p.);
- principle of immediacy (*principio di immediatezza*, Art. 526 para. 1 c.p.p.);
- principle of orality *(principio di oralità)*;[58]
- principle of public trial (*principio di pubblicità*, Art. 471 para. 1 c.p.p.);
- principle of reasonable time limits for trial (*ragionevole durata*, Art. 111 para. 2 Cost);
- principle of concentration of trial (*principio di concentrazione*, Art. 477 c.p.p.);
- principle of immutability of the charge and its correlation with the conviction (*immutabilità dell'accusa e correlazione con la sentenza*, Art. 521 c.p.p.);
- principle of non-return to an earlier phase of proceedings *(principio di non regressione)*;[59] and
- principle of free evaluation of evidence (*libero convincimento*, Arts. 192, 546 para. 1e c.p.p.).

Pursuant to the principle of *in dubio pro reo*, doubts are resolved in favor of the defendant (Art. 53 para. 2 c.p.p.). Until a final judgment is issued, the defendant is protected by the presumption of innocence (*presunzione d'innocenza* or *presunzione di non colpevolezza*, Art. 27 para. 2 Cost.). Following issuance of the final judgment, the defendant cannot be subject to a new prosecution for the same act (*ne bis in idem*, double jeopardy, Art. 649 c.p.p.). This is also true, as a rule, in the context of international cooperation: Thus, if a foreign judgment is recognized in Italy, the convicted person cannot, as a rule, be retried in Italy (Art. 739 c.p.p.). Also, pursuant to Art. 50 Charter of Fundamental Rights of the European Union,[60] the principle of *ne bis in idem* is applicable within the European Union. Furthermore, no one who has been tried by an Italian court can subsequently be tried by the International Criminal Court (Art. 20 para. 3 Rome Statute).[61] Other than in these exceptional circumstances, if the case falls within the jurisdiction of the Italian criminal courts, a person whose case was already adjudicated abroad can, as a rule, be retried in Italy (Art. 11 c.p.).[62]

---

57 On the principle of mandatory prosecution, see I.A.5.b.

58 *Chiavario*, Diritto processuale penale, p. 551.

59 Cass. 22 Apr. 2004, Cass. pen. 2005, p. 508.

60 On the Charter of Fundamental Rights of the European Union, see also I.C.1.

61 On the Rome Statute, see I.B.2.b.

62 *Chiavario*, Diritto processuale penale, p. 1153. On the international jurisdiction of Italian criminal law, see II.B.

The extradition of an Italian citizen is permissible only in cases expressly provided for in international conventions. In cases involving political offenses *(reati politici)*, extradition is not allowed under any circumstance (Art. 26 Cost.).

Bibliography and further reading

Amodio, Ennio, The Accusatorial System Lost and Regained: Reforming Criminal Procedure in Italy. Am. J. Comp. L. 52 (2004), 489–500.

Amodio, Ennio/Selvaggi, Eugenio, An Accusatorial System in a Civil Law Country: The 1988 Italian Code of Criminal Procedure Modern Criminal Procedure: A Comparative Law Symposium. Temple L. Rev. 62 (1989), 1211–1224.

Antolisei, Francesco, Manuale di diritto penale. Parte generale (Textbook of criminal law. General part). 16th ed. Milan 2003.

Bettiol, Giuseppe/Pettoello-Mantovani, Luciano, Diritto Penale (Penal law). 12th ed. Padua 1986.

Bricola, Franco, Voce "Teoria generale del reato" (Entry "General theory of crime"). Novissimo Digesto Italiano (New Italian digest), vol. XIX. Turin 1973, pp. 7–93.

Cadoppi, Alberto/Veneziani, Paolo, Elementi di diritto penale. Parte generale (Basic concepts of criminal law. General part). 6th ed. Padua 2015.

Canestrari, Stefano/Cornacchia, Luigi/De Simone, Giulio, Manuale di diritto penale. Parte generale (Textbook of criminal law. General part). 2d ed. Bologna 2017.

Chiavario, Mario, Diritto processuale penale (Criminal procedural law). 7th ed. Turin 2017.

Cordero, Franco, Procedura penale (Criminal procedure). 9th ed. Milan 2012.

De Francesco, Giovannangelo, Diritto penale. I fondamenti (Criminal law. The basics). 2d ed. Turin 2011.

De Vero, Giancarlo, Introduzione al diritto penale (Introduction to criminal law). Turin 2002.

Di Amato, Astolfo/Fucito, Federica, Criminal Law in Italy. 3d ed. Alphen aan den Rijn 2016.

Donini, Massimo, Teoria del reato. Una introduzione (General theory of crime. An introduction). Padua 1996.

– Verbrechenslehre. Eine Betrachtung aus der Sicht des italienischen Strafrechts (Theory of crime. Observations from the perspective of Italian criminal law). Berlin 2005.

Donini, Massimo/Insolera, Gaetano, Riserva di legge e democrazia penale: il ruolo della scienza penale – considerazioni introduttive (Principle of legislativity and democracy in criminal law: The role of criminal law science – introductory remarks). In: Gaetano Insolera (ed.), Riserva di legge e democrazia penale: il ruolo della scienza penale (Principle of legislativity and democracy in criminal law: The role of criminal law science). Bologna 2005, pp. 11–25.

Fiandaca, Giovanni/Musco, Enzo, Diritto penale. Parte generale (Criminal law. General part). 7th ed. Bologna 2014.

Gialuz, Mitja, The Italian Code of Criminal Procedure: A Reading Guide. In: Mitja Gialuz/ Luca Lupária/Federica Scarpa (eds.), The Italian Code of Criminal Procedure: Critical Essays and English Translation. Assago 2014, pp. 17–52.

Illuminati, Giulio, The Frustrated Turn to Adversarial Procedure in Italy (Italian Criminal Procedure Code of 1988). 4 Wash. U. Global Stud. L. Rev. (2005) 567–582.

Lupária, Luca, Model Code or Broken Dream? The Italian Criminal Procedure in a Comparative Perspective. In: Mitja Gialuz/Luca Lupária/Federica Scarpa (eds.), The Italian Code of Criminal Procedure: Critical Essays and English Translation. Assago 2014, pp. 1–16.

Maiwald, Manfred, Einführung in das italienische Strafrecht und Strafprozessrecht (Introduction to Italian criminal law and the law of criminal procedure). Frankfurt a.M. 2009.

Manes, Vittorio, Der Beitrag der italienischen Strafrechtswissenschaft zur Rechtsgutslehre – Terminologie und Dogmatik – Das sog. principio di offensività. ZStW 114 (2002), 720–735.

Mantovani, Ferrando, Diritto penale. Parte generale (Criminal law. General part). 10th ed. Padua 2017.

Marinucci, Giorgio/Dolcini, Emilio, Corso di diritto penale vol. 1. Le norme penali: Fonti e limiti di applicabilità. Il reato: nozione, struttura e sistematica (Lessons in criminal law vol 1. Criminal law provisions: sources and limits of application. The crime: definition, structure, and classification). 3d ed. Milan 2001.

Padovani, Tullio, Diritto penale (Criminal law). 11th ed. Milan 2017.

Pagliaro, Antonio, Principi di diritto penale. Parte generale (Principles of criminal law. General part). 8th ed. Milan 2003.

– Voce "Prevenzione generale e specifica (o speciale)" (Entry "General and special [or specific] prevention"). Enciclopedia del diritto (Encyclopedia of law), vol. I. Milan 2007, pp. 895–909.

– Funzioni della pena criminale (XYXY). Cass. pen. 2016, 1846–1852.

Palazzo, Francesco, Corso di diritto penale. Parte generale (Lessons on criminal law. General part). 6th ed. Turin 2016.

Pisani, Mario/Molari, Alfredo/Perchinunno, Vincenzo/Corso, Piermaria/Dominioni, Oreste/ Gaito, Alfredo/Spangher, Giorgio, Manuale di procedura penale (Textbook of criminal procedure). 8th ed. Bologna 2008.

Pizzi, William T./Marafioti, Luca, The New Italian Code of Criminal Procedure: The Difficulties of Building an Adversarial Trial System on a Civil Law Foundation. Yale J. Int'l L. 17 (1992), 1–40.

Pulitanò, Domenico, Diritto penale (Criminal law). 6th ed. Turin 2015.

Riz, Roland/Happacher Brezinka, Esther, Grundzüge des italienischen Verfassungsrechts (The basics of Italian constitutional law). 4th ed. Innsbruck 2013.

Romano, Mario, Commentario sistematico del codice penale (Systematic commentary on the Penal Code), I. (Art. 1–84). 3d ed. Milan 2004.

– (ed.), Teoria e prassi della prevenzione generale (Theory and practice of general prevention). Bologna 1980.

Siracusano, Delfino/Galati, Antonino/Tranchina, Giovanni/Zappalà, Enzo, Diritto processuale penale (Law of criminal procedure), vol. I. Milan 2013.

Tonini, Paolo, Manuale di procedura penale (Textbook of criminal procedure). 17th ed. Milan 2016.

Table of cases

Corte Cost. 9 Nov. 2012, n. 249, Giur. Cost. pp. 4038–4042

Corte Cost. 24 July 2007, n. 322, Giur. Cost. pp. 3144–3159

Corte Cost. 7 July 2005, n. 265, Giur. Cost. 2005, pp. 2432–2438

Cass. 22 Apr. 2004, Cass. pen. 2005, p. 508

Corte Cost. 25 July 1994, n. 341, Giur. Cost. 1994, pp. 2802–2810

Corte Cost 18 July 1989, n. 409, Giur. Cost. 1989, pp. 1906–1924

Corte Cost. 13 Dec. 1988, n. 1085, Giur. Cost. 1988, pp. 5270–5287

Corte Cost. 24 March 1988, n. 364, Giur. Cost. 1988, pp. 1504–1539

Corte Cost. 8 July 1957, n. 107, Giur. Cost. pp. 1005–1009

Corte Cost. 23 June 1956, n. 3, Giur. Cost. pp. 568–575

E. Nature, form, and boundaries of criminal law

1. Nature and form of criminal law

– Definition of criminal law

In Italy, criminal law is defined as the body of public-law norms that establish criminal penalties for certain unlawful acts.[1] These penalties vary according to the personality of the offender.[2] Hence, criminal law consists of three elements:

- The unlawful act *(fatto illecito)* is the essential and indispensable foundation of a civilized criminal law. Mere criminal intent – that is, intent that is not made manifest in a criminal act – has no legal consequences. Persons should not be prosecuted for what they think but for what they do. Because prohibited conduct is always defined by the legislature, criminal law is inevitably influenced to some extent by politics and history.[3]
- Criminal offenses are met with criminal consequences *(conseguenze penali)*, also referred to as criminal penalties. Criminal wrongdoing can be distinguished from other forms of unlawful behavior on the basis of these consequences. Criminal penalties are hardships imposed on an individual for violating a legal norm. They always involve the loss or the limitation of rights, such as of liberty or of assets, and serve the purposes of deterrence and resocialization.[4] All organized societies use penalties to combat and control crime.[5]
- Finally, the personality of the offender *(personalità dell'autore)* plays a special role both with regard to the offense, in that the unlawful act is a reflection of the offender's personality, and with regard to the determination of the criminal consequences, which must be tailored to the offender if they are to serve a reasonable purpose.[6]

The following essential features characterize the criminal law:

- Criminal law is positive law because it derives from legal norms.
- Criminal law is state law because it is a result of the state's law-making authority.
- Criminal law is public law because the goal of preventing and punishing crime is to promote peaceful coexistence in society.

---

1 For an overview, see also *Di Amato/Fucito*, Criminal Law in Italy, pp. 33–35 (margin nos. 36–40).

2 *Antolisei*, Parte generale, pp. 3–4; *Fiandaca/Musco*, Parte generale, p. 3; *Mantovani*, Parte generale, p. XXIII.

3 See *Mantovani*, Parte generale, pp. XXV–XXVIII.

4 On the purposes of punishment, see I.D.3.

5 *Mantovani*, Parte generale pp. XXXI–XXXIII. For details, see I.D.3.

6 See *Mantovani*, Parte generale, pp. XXVIII–XXXI.

– Criminal law is autonomous law because it does not simply punish conduct prohibited by other areas of the law but rather itself protects certain interests and/or values, independent of other legal regimes.

– Criminal law as a subset of public law

Criminal law is a subset of public law.[7] This is because, first, the protection afforded under criminal law is public in nature as it is typically extended independent of the will of the entity or person whose legal interest has been harmed and because, second, the power to punish is also a power under public law. On the one hand, law enforcement authorities must apply criminal norms; on the other hand, offenders are directly subordinate to these authorities.[8]

– Distinction between criminal law and civil and administrative law

Formally, criminal and civil law may be distinguished by the characterization of the sanctions they may impose. Criminal penalties include those listed in Arts. 17–20 c.p. and those that can be imposed by a justice of the peace (Arts. 52–54 D.Lgs. 28 Aug. 2000, n. 274).[9] A substantive distinction between criminal and civil law follows directly from the nature of the wrongful act. A criminal wrong *(illecito penale)* is not only more severe, but it harms society, whereas a civil wrong *(illecito civile)* entails harm between private parties that is of interest to the state only insofar as the state provides legal redress to the harmed party. Furthermore, criminal penalties are punitive in character because they consist in the loss of personal freedom or in the payment of an amount of money to the state.[10]

The characterization of the penalties also serves the formal distinction between criminal and administrative law. A substantive distinction is difficult to make because the boundaries between these two areas of law are fluid and their structures are similar.[11] Numerous decriminalization measures in Italy have converted crimes into administrative wrongs *(illecito amministrativo)*.[12] In any case, administrative offenses are usually less serious than criminal offenses,[13] but there are also important exceptions: for example, as part of the revised regulation of market abuse,[14] the prescribed administrative fines may be higher than the criminal fines in the same area.

---

7 *Di Amato/Fucito*, Criminal Law in Italy, pp. 33–34 (margin no. 36).

8 See, e.g., *Mantovani*, Parte generale, p. XXIII.

9 *Cadoppi/Veneziani*, Parte generale, p. 5. See also I.A.5.c.

10 *Cadoppi/Veneziani*, Parte generale, pp. 5–6.

11 *Pulitanò*, Diritto penale, p. 5 therefore argues for undertaking only a formal distinction.

12 See below 2.

13 For a broad discussion of this subject, see *Cadoppi/Veneziani*, Parte generale, pp. 7–8.

14 Arts. 166–170-*bis* and 184–185 D.Lgs. 24 Feb. 1998, n. 58.

– *Distinction between substantive criminal law, criminal procedure, and law of execution of punishment*

Substantive criminal law and criminal procedure are distinguishable primarily on the basis of their respective functions. Substantive criminal law *(diritto penale sostanziale)* determines the conditions that define a crime and establishes the type and modalities of the corresponding penalty, whereas the law of criminal procedure *(diritto penale processuale)* governs the mechanisms, set in motion by the (alleged) breaching of a criminal norm, that govern the application of the established penalty to the individual offender.[15] In some instances, however, it may be difficult to determine whether a given norm is a condition for criminal liability, that is, substantive in nature, or a condition of prosecutability, and thus procedural in nature. This is the case, for example, with regard to grounds for the termination of a crime *(cause di estinzione del reato)*, such as death of the accused, withdrawal of criminal complaint, expiration of the statute of limitations, etc.[16] This distinction is particularly important in two problem areas: the prohibition of analogy and the prohibition of retroactivity, both of which apply only to substantive law, not to the law of criminal procedure.[17]

Finally, the legal nature of the law of execution of punishment was a matter of controversy for a long time. Some scholars argued that it was an agglomeration of norms, some of which were substantive, others procedural in nature.[18] Other scholars saw exclusively provisions of administrative law[19] or exclusively provisions of jurisdictional[20] law or a mixture of both.[21] Today, the law of execution of punishment is increasingly viewed as an autonomous area of law.[22] With regard to the enforcement of custodial punishments and security measures that involve the deprivation of liberty, an additional distinction is made, namely, between the execution of a criminal sentence in the narrow sense and prison law. The law of execution of punishment *(diritto dell'esecuzione penale)* covers the existence, the valid adoption, the scope, and the enforceability of the sentencing order *(giudicato)*, that is, the final judgment of the court. In contrast, prison law *(diritto penitenziario)* governs prison life, for example, in terms of discipline, benefits, or rewards.[23] Thus, the law of execution of punishment and prison law are separate legal areas, although there are overlaps that sometimes make it very difficult to distinguish between them.[24]

---

15 *Antolisei*, Parte generale, p. 20; *Di Amato/Fucito*, p. 34 (margin nos. 37–39).

16 See II.K.

17 For details, see II.A.2. and II.A.3.

18 See *Di Ronza*, Manuale, p. 12 (with further references).

19 *Santoro*, L'esecuzione penale, p. 163.

20 *De Marsico*, Diritto Processuale Penale, p. 358.

21 *Falchi*, Diritto penale esecutivo, pp. 36–37.

22 See, e.g., *Di Ronza*, Manuale, p. 28.

23 *Di Ronza*, Manuale, pp. 2–3.

24 See *Di Ronza*, Manuale, p. 2.

– Core criminal law and ancillary criminal law

The core criminal law *(diritto penale fondamentale)* is the law contained in the Penal Code (*codice penale*, c.p.); ancillary or secondary criminal law *(diritto penale complementare)* comprises those numerous special laws *(leggi speciali)* located outside the Penal Code proper that also contain criminal offense definitions. Ancillary criminal law is particularly important in Italy. Many key areas of the criminal law are regulated in separate laws that cover specific subject areas, such as the consolidated law on public security *(testo unico delle leggi di pubblica sicurezza)*,[25] military criminal law,[26] abortion law,[27] criminal drug law,[28] labor and employment criminal law,[29] anti-doping law,[30] the law of data protection,[31] environmental protection law,[32] criminal law for foreign nationals,[33] and the various areas of commercial criminal law: criminal insolvency law,[34] criminal law for business organizations,[35] banking criminal law,[36] financial market criminal law,[37] criminal tax law,[38] etc.[39] Most of these laws are not primarily focused on issues of criminal law but rather provide comprehensive regulation of the pertinent subject matter. Unless regulated otherwise, the provisions of the Penal Code also apply to offense definitions located in ancillary criminal law (Art. 16 c.p.).

2. Boundaries between criminal law and other areas of law with a criminal or quasi-criminal function

Administrative criminal law *(diritto penale amministrativo)* is the first area that comes to mind when setting boundaries between criminal law and other repressive legal regimes. It, too, is a body of norms aimed – among other things – at deter-

---

25 R.D. 18 June 1931, n. 773, revised by D.Lgs. 13 July 1995, n. 480.

26 R.D. 20 Feb. 1941, n. 303.

27 L. 22 May 1978, n. 194.

28 D.P.R. 9 Oct. 1990, n. 309.

29 D.Lgs. 19 Dec. 1994, n. 758.

30 L. 14 Dec. 2000, n. 376.

31 D.Lgs. 30 June 2003, n. 196.

32 D.Lgs. 3 Apr. 2006, n. 152.

33 D.Lgs. 25 June 1998, n. 286.

34 R.D. 16 March 1942, n. 267.

35 Arts. 2621–2642 c.c.

36 D.Lgs. 1 Sept. 1993, n. 385.

37 D.Lgs. 24 Feb. 1998, n. 58.

38 D.Lgs. 10 March 2000, n. 74.

39 For a discussion of ancillary criminal law, see I.F.2. and *Di Amato/Fucito*, Criminal Law in Italy, p. 61 (margin no. 105).

rence and reform; its penalties, which are usually called administrative sanctions (*sanzione amministrativa*, e.g., disciplinary, police, or tax sanctions), are imposed by a public agency in the course of an administrative proceeding. Meanwhile, administrative sanctions can also be imposed on legal entities.[40] The legal nature of these new sanctions is the subject of fierce debate. Some legal scholars consider it a matter of genuine criminal responsibility.[41] The distinction between administrative and criminal sanctions is largely formal and is based on their characterization; however, the measure's primary objective is also an issue. In the case of administrative sanctions, the primary objective is not deterrence and reform but rather the protection of the public administration itself.[42]

The so-called decriminalized wrongdoing *(illecito depenalizzato)* is a case apart. It is the result of the transformation, in recent decades, of numerous minor criminal offenses *(contravvenzioni)* and even of some serious criminal offenses *(delitti)*[43] into administrative wrongs, particularly in 1967, 1975, 1981, 1999, and 2016.[44] These offense definitions provide for administrative sanctions, such as the payment of a fine or the revocation of a driver's license. Moreover, since the entry into force of the law of 1981, certain fundamental principles of criminal law, such as the principles of legality and of culpability, apply as well to administrative wrongs. This explains why the legal nature of this type of wrongdoing is so controversial. Some view it as a third type of responsibility, somewhere between criminal and administrative responsibility, whereas others consider it a subcategory of criminal law.[45] A third, intermediary position considers decriminalized wrongdoing a separate form entirely, a form that can be distinguished from criminal wrongdoing in that it does not protect essential values of human coexistence but rather specific and random public interests entrusted to the care of the public administration.[46]

3. Special regimes connected to the status of the offender

The Italian criminal justice system is a dual-track system *(sistema del doppio binario)*. In addition to traditional punishments *(pena)*, which are tied to the offender's culpability *(colpevolezza)*, there are also security measures *(misure di sicurez-*

---

40 For details regarding the criminal responsibility of legal entities, see II.H.

41 D.Lgs. 8 June 2001, n. 231. See, e.g., *Guerrini*, La responsabilità da reato degli enti, p. 248. See II.H.2.b.

42 *Pulitanò*, Diritto penale, p. 614.

43 On the differences between serious and less serious offenses, see II.C.1.b.

44 By L. 3 May 1967, n. 317; L. 24 Dec. 1975, n. 706; L. 24 Nov. 1981, n. 689; D.Lgs. 30 Dec. 1999, n. 507; D.Lgs. 15 Jan. 2016, n. 8.

45 See *Mantovani*, Parte generale, p. 950; *Fiandaca/Musco*, Parte generale, p. 907 (with further references).

46 *Fiandaca/Musco*, Parte generale, p. 907.

za);[47] the latter depend largely on the degree of danger the individual poses to the public *(pericolosità sociale)*. Security measures can be imposed both on persons with criminal capacity and without criminal capacity. Because these measures are aimed at resocializing the offender, the focus is on specific deterrence.[48]

Special provisions of substantive criminal law, criminal procedure, and prison law apply to juveniles ages 14 to 17 years. For example, offenders under the age of 18 must undergo a specially-tailored personality assessment to evaluate their level of capacity *(capacità)*, which is primarily determined by their mental maturity *(maturità)*. Penalties imposed on juveniles are reduced by one-third compared to adults and are more individualized and focused on deterrence and education. Special measures for juveniles include the institution of judicial pardon (*perdono giudiziale*, Art. 169 c.p.) and more options for the conditional suspension of execution of punishment (*sospensione condizionale della pena*, Art. 163 para. 2 c.p.). There is a separate juvenile court *(tribunale dei minorenni)* with specialized judges and a criminal procedure for young offenders that differs in many ways from a regular criminal proceeding.[49]

Penalties for drug and alcohol abusers can be increased by up to one-third (Art. 94 c.p.), and, in addition to a prison term, the security measure of in-patient placement in a psychiatric hospital may be imposed on these offenders (Art. 221 c.p.).

In certain circumstances, sex offenders must be sentenced to one or more of several mandatory collateral penalties, such as the loss of parental rights, a ban on assumption of guardianships, a ban on employment in schools, and the loss of the claim to maintenance from the victim (Art. 609-*nonies* c.p.).

There are also numerous special regulations in substantive criminal law, criminal procedure, and prison law for offenders and suspects in the areas of mafia- and terrorism-related offenses.[50] A conviction for membership in a mafia-related or a terrorist organization mandates the collateral penalty of confiscation of items used in commission of or constituting profits of the crime (Art. 170-*bis* para. 4 or Art. 416-*bis* para. 7 c.p.). Also, it is easier to obtain orders for special investigative measures, such as telephone, internet, or home surveillance or covert investigations.[51] This group of offenders may also be subject to preventive measures *(misure*

---

[47] On security measures, see also *Di Amato/Fucito*, Criminal Law in Italy, pp. 147–149 (margin nos. 392–397).

[48] *Fiandaca/Musco*, Parte generale, p. 734. For more on sanctions, see also I.A.5.d. and *Di Amato/Fucito*, Criminal Law in Italy, pp. 131–150 (margin nos. 331–402). On the purposes of punishment, see I.D.3.

[49] See *Mantovani*, Parte generale, p. 660. See II.J.6.

[50] See *Orlandi*, in: Gropp (ed.), Besondere Ermittlungsmaßnahmen, pp. 433–440; *Orlandi*, in: Gropp/Huber (eds.), Rechtliche Initiativen, pp. 459–477.

[51] D.L. 18 Oct. 2001, n. 374, as amended transformed by L. 15 Dec. 2001, n. 438, in association with Art. 13 D.L. 13 May 1991, n. 152, as amended transformed by L. 12 July

di prevenzione), such as the seizure and forfeiture of assets.[52] Furthermore, at trial, witness testimony may be taken by audio-visual means (Arts. 146-*bis*, 147-*bis* disp. att. c.p.p.). Finally, once in prison, only witnesses who give state's evidence are eligible for privileges or reductions in sentence.[53]

Since the reform pursuant to the so-called *ex-Cirielli* law in 2005 (L. 5 Dec. 2005, n. 251), recidivists *(recidivi)* may also be classified as a special offender group. Pursuant to this law, recidivism (particularly repeat recidivism) has been linked not only to increased penalties but also to many additional criminal and procedural consequences as well as consequences in the execution of punishment, resulting in a much harsher treatment.[54]

Bibliography and further reading

Antolisei, Francesco, Manuale di diritto penale. Parte generale (Textbook on criminal law. General part). 16th ed. Milan 2003.

Bettels, Till, Gewinnabschöpfung zur Bekämpfung Organisierter Kriminalität am Beispiel Italiens (Confiscation of profits to combat organized crime – the Italian example). Baden-Baden 2016.

Cadoppi, Alberto/Veneziani, Paolo, Elementi di diritto penale. Parte generale (Basic concepts of criminal law. General part). 6th ed. Padua 2015.

Canestrari, Stefano/Cornacchia, Luigi/De Simone, Giulio, Manuale di diritto penale. Parte generale (Textbook on criminal law. General part). 2d ed. Bologna 2017.

Certoma, G. Leroy, The Italian legal system. London 1985.

De Marsico, Alfredo, Diritto Processuale Penale (Law of criminal procedure). 4th ed. Naples 1966.

Di Amato, Astolfo/Fucito, Federica, Criminal Law in Italy. 3d ed. Alphen aan den Rijn 2016.

Di Ronza, Paolo, Manuale di diritto dell'esecuzione penale (Textbook on the law of execution of punishment). 5th ed. Padua 2003.

Falchi, Giuseppino Ferruccio, Diritto penale esecutivo, vol. I. Teoria (Handbook on the law of execution of punishment, vol. I: Theory). Padua 1934.

1991, n. 203 and Art. 25-*bis* D.L. 8 June 1992, n. 306, as amended transformed by L. 7 Aug. 1992, n. 356; Art. 9 L. 16 March 2006, n. 146.

52 E.g., Arts. 20, 24 D.Lgs. 6 Sept. 2011, n. 159. For details, see *Bettels*, Gewinnabschöpfung, pp. 176–270; *Filippi*, Il codice delle misure di prevenzione.

53 See, e.g., Art. 16-*nonies* D.L. 15 Jan. 1991, n. 8. See also *Jarvers/Kinzig*, MschrKrim 84 (2001), 444–445, 450.

54 See *Jarvers*, in: Koch (ed.), Wegsperren?, pp. 128–139.

Fiandaca, Giovanni/Musco, Enzo, Diritto penale. Parte generale (Criminal law. General part). 7th ed. Bologna 2014.

Filippi, Leonardo, Il codice delle misure di prevenzione (The Code on preventive measures). Turin 2011.

Foffani, Luigi/Orlandi, Renzo, Landesbericht Italien (Country report Italy). In: Walter Gropp/Arndt Sinn (eds.), Organisierte Kriminalität und kriminelle Organisationen. Präventive und repressive Maßnahmen vor dem Hintergrund des 11. September 2001 (Organized crime and criminal organizations. Preventive and repressive measures in light of September 11, 2001). Baden-Baden 2006, pp. 221–260.

Guerrini, Roberto, La responsabilità da reato degli enti (The responsibility of enterprises in connection with a crime). Milan 2006.

Jarvers, Konstanze, Landesbericht Italien (Country report Italy). In: Hans-Georg Koch (ed.), Wegsperren? Freiheitsentziehende Maßnahmen gegen gefährliche, strafrechtliche verantwortliche (Rückfall-)Täter (Lock them up? Liberty-infringing measures imposed on dangerous, criminally responsible [repeat] offenders). Berlin 2011, pp. 123–157.

Jarvers, Konstanze/Kinzig, Jörg, Organisierte Kriminalität und Zeugenschutz – eine vergleichende Betrachtung der italienischen und der deutschen Situation (Organized crime and witness protection – A comparative approach to the situation in Italy and Germany). MschrKrim 84 (2001), 439–452.

Mantovani, Ferrando, Diritto penale. Parte generale (Criminal law. General part). 10th ed. Padua 2017.

Marinucci, Giorgio/Dolcini, Emilio, Corso di diritto penale Vol. 1. Le norme penali: Fonti e limiti di applicabilità. Il reato: nozione, struttura e sistematica (Lessons in criminal law vol 1. Criminal law provisions: Sources and limits of application. The crime: definition, structure, and classification). 3d ed. Milan 2001.

Orlandi, Renzo, Landesbericht Italien (Country report Italy). In: Walter Gropp (ed.), Besondere Ermittlungsmaßnahmen zur Bekämpfung der Organisierten Kriminalität (Special investigative measures to combat organized crime). Freiburg 1993, pp. 407–450.

– Landesbericht Italien (Country report Italy). In: Walter Gropp/Barbara Huber (eds.), Rechtliche Initiativen gegen organisierte Kriminalität (Legal initiatives against organized crime). Freiburg 2001, pp. 443–480.

Padovani, Tullio, Diritto penale (Criminal law). 11th ed. Milan 2017.

Pagliaro, Antonio, Principi di diritto penale. Parte generale (Principles of criminal law. General part). 8th ed. Milan 2003.

Pulitanò, Domenico, Diritto penale (Criminal law). 6th ed. Turin 2015.

Romano, Mario, Commentario sistematico del codice penale (Systematic commentary on the Penal Code), I. (Arts. 1–84). 3d ed. Milan 2004.

Santoro Arturo, L'esecuzione penale (The execution of punishment). 2d ed. Turin 1953.

Legislation

Seizure and forfeiture of assets	Arts. 20, 24 D.Lgs. 6 Sept. 2011, n. 159
Criminal law of environmental protection	D.Lgs. 3 Apr. 2006, n. 152
Data protection law	D.Lgs. 30 June 2003, n. 196
Special investigative measures	D.L. 18 Oct. 2001, n. 374, as amended transformed by L. 15 Dec. 2001, n. 438, in association with Art. 13 D.L. 13 May 1991, n. 152, as amended transformed by L.12 July 1991, n. 203 and Art. 25-*bis* D.L. 8 June 1992, n. 306, as amended transformed by L. 7 Aug. 1992, n. 356; Art. 9 L. 16 March 2006, n. 146
Anti-doping law	L. 14 Dec. 2000, n. 376
Criminal tax law	D.Lgs. 10 March 2000, n. 74
Criminal law for foreign nationals	D.Lgs. 25 June 1998, n. 286
Financial market criminal law	D.Lgs. 24 Feb. 1998, n. 58
Labor and employment criminal law	D.Lgs. 19 Dec. 1994, n. 758
Banking criminal law	D.Lgs. 1 Sept. 1993, n. 385
Criminal drug law	D.P.R. 9 Oct. 1990, n. 309
Abortion law	L. 22 May 1978, n. 194
De-criminalized wrongs	L. 3 May 1967, n. 317; L. 24 Dec. 1975, n. 706; L. 24 Nov. 1981, n. 689; D.Lgs. 30 Dec. 1999, n. 507; D.Lgs. 15 Jan. 2016, n. 7; D.Lgs. 15 Jan. 2016, n. 8
Criminal insolvency law	R.D. 16 March 1942, n. 267
Criminal law for business organizations	Arts. 2621–2642 c.c., Regio Decreto 16 marzo 1942, n. 262
Military criminal law	R.D. 20 Feb. 1941, n. 303
Related to public security	R.D. 18 June 1931, n. 773, revised by D.Lgs. 13 July 1995, n. 480

F. Sources of criminal law and interpretation aids

1. Overview

The Constitution (Cost.) and constitutional laws *(leggi costituzionali)* are at the top of the Italian legal system. The second tier consists, on the one hand, of formal laws *(leggi formali)*, including state laws *(leggi statali)*, regional laws *(leggi regionali)*, and the laws of the autonomous provinces *(leggi provinciali)* Trento and Bolzano; it also includes provisions with binding force of law enacted by the government, namely, legislative decrees *(decreto legislativo)* and decree laws *(decreto legge)*. Regulations *(regolamenti)* constitute the third tier. Prevailing opinion places customary law *(consuetudine)* on the fourth level at the bottom of the hierarchy.[1] Some maintain that it does not fit comfortably into this hierarchy, however, because it also encompasses customary constitutional law and customary international law.[2] Because of the principle of legality, which is firmly established in Art. 25 paras. 2 and 3 Cost. as well as in Arts. 1 and 199 c.p., no provision ranked lower than a formal law can be a source of criminal law.[3]

2. Legislation and other written laws

– *Important national codifications*

The most important source of criminal law are formal laws passed by the national legislature.[4] Formal laws are adopted by Parliament, promulgated by the president, and published in the Official Gazette (*Gazzetta Ufficiale*, GU, Arts. 70–74 Cost.).[5] In practice, however, both Parliament and the government make regular use of legislative decrees and decree laws, also in the area of criminal law. These decrees are adopted by the Council of Ministers, enacted by the president, and published in the Official Gazette.[6]

Legislative decrees *(decreto legislative)* also known as delegated laws *(legge delegata)* are enacted by the government on the basis of an enabling act *(legge delega)*, a law in which Parliament delegates to the government the right to legislate on a particular issue. An enabling act must contain essential guidelines for the de-

---

1 *Mantovani*, Parte generale, p. 44; *Padovani*, Diritto penale, p. 29; *Pagliaro*, Parte generale, p. 35.

2 *Riz/Happacher*, Grundzüge, p. 53. See also below 3.

3 For details on the principle of legality, see II.A. and *Di Amato/Fucito*, Criminal Law in Italy, pp. 63–64 (margin nos. 109–113).

4 On national law as source of criminal law, see also *Di Amato* et al., Criminal Law in Italy, pp. 59–61 (margin nos. 100–105).

5 *Riz*, Lineamenti, p. 16.

6 *Riz/Happacher*, Grundzüge, pp. 134, 137. On the legislative procedure, see I.A.4.

cree to be promulgated and must establish the timeframe within which the government must take action. (Art. 76 Cost.). In exceptional and urgent cases, the government may issue a (provisional) statutory decree *(decreto legge)*, which Parliament must convert into a formal law within 60 days, with amendments, if necessary (Art. 77 Cost.). If Parliament does not do so, the decree law loses its effect and, pursuant to rulings of the Constitutional Court, cannot be reissued.[7] According to prevailing opinion, both types of decrees are viable sources of criminal law because, as laws in the substantive sense, these executive norms with the force of law fulfill the requirements of the principle of legislativity *(lex scripta)*: they are legitimized by Parliament either *ex ante* (through enabling acts) or *ex post* (through conversion into law).[8] Supporters of the contrary opinion, however, consider decree laws and legislative decrees questionable sources of criminal law and see in them the potential for abuse.[9]

In addition to the fundamental principles of criminal law embedded in the Constitution, which entered into force on 1 January 1948, the Penal Code (*codice penale*, c.p.[10]), which entered into force on 1 July 1931, is the main source of criminal law. The Code was supplemented by coordinating and transitional regulations in 1931 *(disposizioni di coordinamento e transitorie*[11]) and has undergone numerous modifications over time. These were necessary in order to adapt the Penal Code – which was influenced by the authoritarian principles typical of the fascist ideology of its time – to the Constitution of the Republic of Italy. The Code's basic structure, however, has remained largely unchanged, which is why there have been calls for a fundamental reform for quite some time.[12]

The Code of Criminal Procedure (*codice di procedura penale*, c.p.p.[13]), together with its implementing, coordinating, and transitional provisions (*norme di attuazione, di coordinamento e transitorie del codice di procedura penale*[14]), is the main legal foundation for the law of criminal procedure. Notwithstanding its relatively short existence, it has already undergone numerous significant changes, some as a result of legislative reforms, others based on rulings by the Constitutional Court that declared certain provisions unconstitutional, either in whole or in part.[15]

---

7 Corte Cost. 24 Oct. 1996, n. 360, Giur. Cost. 1996, pp. 3147–3148.

8 *Pagliaro*, Parte generale, p. 42.

9 *Cadoppi/Veneziani*, Parte generale, pp. 76–77; *Fiandaca/Musco*, Parte generale, p. 55; *Marinucci/Dolcini*, Manuale, p. 44; *Padovani*, Diritto penale, p. 22.

10 R.D. 19 Oct. 1930, n. 1398.

11 R.D. 28 May 1931, n. 601.

12 For details, see I.G.2.

13 D.P.R. 22 Sept. 1988, n. 447.

14 D.Lgs. 28 July 1989, n. 271.

15 For details, see I.G.3.

The Judiciary Act (*ordinamento giudiziario*, o.g.[16]) and the Prison Administration Act (*ordinamento penitenziario*, o.p.[17]) are also important national codifications.

Ancillary or secondary criminal law, that is, criminal laws outside the Penal Code proper, also play a major role as sources of Italian criminal law and criminal procedure.[18] They regulate certain issues comprehensively and often contain both substantive and procedural provisions. Penal Code provisions apply to these laws as well (Art. 16 c.p.), unless the laws provide differently. In the following, a selection of some of the more important ancillary laws is presented:

- criminal tax laws;[19]
- consolidated law on public security *(testo unico delle leggi di pubblica sicurezza)*;[20]
- juvenile criminal laws;[21]
- military criminal codes of peace and war *(codici penali militari di pace e di guerra)*;[22]
- criminal law for business organizations;[23]
- criminal bankruptcy law *(disciplina del fallimento, del concordato preventivo, dell'amministrazione controllata e della liquidazione coatta amministrativa)*;[24]
- law on genocide *(prevenzione e repressione del delitto di genocidio)*;[25]
- maternity and abortion law *(norme per la tutela sociale della maternità e sull'interruzione volontaria della gravidanza)*;[26]
- adoption law *(diritto del minore ad una famiglia)*;[27]
- consolidated drug law *(testo unico delle leggi in materia di stupefacenti e sostanze psicotrope, prevenzione, cura e riabilitazione dei relative stati di tossicodipendenza)*;[28]

---

16 R.D. 30 Jan. 1941, n. 12.

17 L. 26 July 1975.

18 On ancillary criminal law, see also *Di Amato/Fucito*, Criminal Law in Italy, p. 61 (margin no. 105).

19 L. 7 Jan. 1929, n. 4; D.Lgs. 10 March 2000, n. 74.

20 R.D. 18 June 1931, n. 773.

21 R.D.L. 20 July 1934, n. 1404; D.P.R. 22 Sept. 1988, n. 448; D.Lgs. 28 July 1989, n. 272.

22 R.D. 20 Feb. 1941, n. 303.

23 Arts. 2621–2642 c.c., R.D. 16 March 1942, n. 262.

24 Arts. 216–241 R.D. 16 March 1942, n. 267.

25 L. 9 Oct. 1967, n. 962.

26 L. 22 May 1978, n. 194.

27 L. 4 May 1983, n. 184.

28 D.P.R. 9 Oct. 1990, n. 309.

- traffic code (codice della strada);[29]
- consolidated criminal banking law (testo unico delle leggi in materia bancaria e creditizia);[30]
- consolidated regulations on financial intermediation (testo unico delle disposizioni in materia di intermediazione finanziaria);[31]
- weapons laws;[32]
- anti-doping law (disciplina della tutela sanitaria delle attività sportive e della lotta contro il doping);[33]
- code of cultural and landscape heritage (codice dei beni culturali e del paesaggio);[34]
- law on artificial fertilization (norme in materia di procreazione medicalmente assistita);[35]
- environmental law;[36]
- anti-mafia code *(codice delle leggi antimafia e delle misure di prevenzione).*[37]

As a rule, regional and provincial laws can neither create nor repeal criminal provisions, as the regions and the two autonomous provinces Trento and Bolzano lack the necessary legislative competence (Art. 117 para. 2(l) Cost.).[38] This is also true regarding the legal consequences of an offense and regarding justifications.

– International treaties

International treaties cannot take direct effect as domestic criminal law unless they are transposed into national law by way of ratification and implementation laws (dualistic principle; Arts. 80, 87 para. 8 Cost.).[39] Legislative powers must be exercised in compliance with international obligations (Art. 117 Cost.).[40] Thus, a

---

29 D.Lgs. 30 Apr. 1992, n. 285.

30 Arts. 130–143 D.Lgs. 1 Sept. 1993, n. 385.

31 Arts. 166-187 D.Lgs. 24 Feb. 1998, n. 58.

32 L. 2 Oct. 1967, n. 895; L. 18 Apr. 1975, n. 110; L. 21 Feb. 1990, n. 36; L. 9 July 1990, n. 185; L. 18 Nov. 1995, n. 496; L. 20 Dec. 2000, n. 420.

33 L. 14 Dec. 2000, n. 376.

34 D.Lgs. 22 Jan. 2004, n. 42.

35 L. 19 Feb. 2004, n. 40.

36 D.Lgs. 3 Apr. 2006, n. 152.

37 D.Lgs. 6 Sept. 2011, n. 159.

38 See Corte Cost. 13 March 2014, n. 46, Giur. Cost 59, pp. 1134–1136. See also I.C.1. and II.A.3.a.

39 *Antolisei*, Parte generale, p. 77; *Mantovani*, Parte generale, p. 56. See also I.C.2.b.

40 For Italy's international obligations in the field of criminal law, see *Di Amato/Fucito*, Criminal Law in Italy, p. 52 (margin no. 85).

law that violates such an obligation is unconstitutional.[41] In addition, Italian judges must interpret national norms in such a way that they comply with international obligations. If there is a conflict that cannot be settled by interpretation, the judges must submit the national norm at issue to the Constitutional Court. These principles also apply to the European Convention on Human Rights.[42] Thus, in the hierarchy of laws, the Convention ranks between the Constitution and ordinary laws.[43]

– *Supranational law*

Prior to the entry into force of the Treaty of Lisbon on 1 December 2009, the European Union lacked the competence to enact criminal law. At that time, EU norms, as a rule, could neither create criminal offenses nor repeal Italian criminal norms. At most, Community law could provide for administrative sanctions.[44] Under Art. 117 para. 1 Cost., amended in 2001, the legislature must comply not only with the Constitution but also with the constraints set by Community rules. In this way, EU norms could and still can influence existing Italian laws.[45] For example, the application of the Italian offense of unauthorized practice of a profession (*abusivo esercizio di una professione*, Art. 348 c.p.) is limited by Community law, which permits lawyers to practice their profession freely throughout the European Union. And conduct that is permitted by a directly applicable EU regulation must be considered justified[46] as the exercise of a right (*esercizio di un diritto*, Art. 51 c.p.).[47]

Pursuant to the Treaty on the Functioning of the European Union (*Trattato sul funzionamento dell'Unione*, TFEU), EU directives may oblige member states to harmonize their criminal law, that is, to adopt minimum rules for the definition of offenses and sanctions (Art. 83 TFEU). This competence with regard to harmonization applies, on the one hand, to particularly serious crimes with a cross-border dimension (terrorism, human trafficking, sexual exploitation of women and children, illicit drug trafficking, illicit arms trafficking, money laundering, corruption, counterfeiting of means of payment, computer crime, and organized crime). On the other hand, it applies to areas that have been subject to harmonization but where a

---

41 *Marinucci/Dolcini*, Manuale, p. 56.

42 See I.C.1.; on the influence of the ECtHR and the Council of Europe, see also *Di Amato/Fucito*, Criminal Law in Italy, pp. 57–60 (margin nos. 94–99) and below 4.

43 *Fiandaca/Musco*, Parte generale, p. 77.

44 For the relationship between domestic and EU criminal law before and after the Lisbon treaty, see also *Di Amato/Fucito*, Criminal Law in Italy, pp. 53–57 (margin nos. 86–93).

45 For a general overview on this topic, see *Grasso*, Comunità europee, pp. 255–260; *Picotti* (ed.), Possibilità e limiti, pp. XI–XIX; *Bernardi*, L'europeizzazione, pp. 20–25.

46 See II.J.3.b.

47 *Pagliaro*, Parte generale, p. 44. See also II.A.3.a.

continued approximation of criminal law is considered essential to ensure effective implementation of a Union policy. However, this competence of the European Union is still an indirect one.[48] Some scholars recognize a direct competence for the protection of the financial interests of the European Union (Arts. 86, 325 para. 4 TFEU), but this is a matter of debate.[49]

Finally, European law also binds national judges, because the priority of EU law also applies to criminal law. In addition, judges are required to interpret national laws in compliance with Community law.[50]

– Legislative materials

Legislative materials *(travaux préparatoires)* are not considered a source of law; however, they are consulted for the interpretation of laws, especially more recent laws, with regard to which there are still only a few decisions and hardly any literature.

3. Customary law

Due to the strict principle of legality (Art. 25 Cost., Art. 1 c.p.), criminal offense definitions can neither be created nor repealed by customary law. Furthermore, the position of guarantor in crimes of omission and the norms of duties of care in offenses of negligence cannot be derived from customary law.[51] In contrast, justifications can be based on customary law.[52] For example, the tradition of fireworks on New Year's Eve or a honking wedding motorcade (possibly via Art. 51 c.p.[53]) justify the criminal offense of disturbing the peace or causing work disruption (Art. 659 c.p.).

Pursuant to the requirements established by Art. 10 para. 1 Cost., customary international law is directly applicable. It offers judges criteria for interpretation and forces the legislature to safeguard internationally protected interests.[54] Art. 15 In-

---

48 See, e.g., *Marinucci/Dolcini*, Manuale, p. 49.

49 See *Cadoppi/Veneziani*, Parte generale, p. 79; *Marinucci/Dolcini*, Manuale, pp. 49–50.

50 *Marinucci/Dolcini*, Manuale, pp. 51–53; CJEU, 16.06.2005 - C-105/03, http://eur-lex.europa.eu/legal-content/EN/TXT/?uri=CELEX%3A62003CJ0105 [last visited May 2017]. For a general overview on this topic, see *Fiandaca/Musco*, Parte generale, pp. 64–75.

51 *Marinucci/Dolcini*, Manuale, p. 61.

52 *Marinucci/Dolcini*, Manuale, p. 61. Contra *Cadoppi/Veneziani*, Parte generale, p. 79. See also II.A.3.a.

53 See II.J.3. and II.J.5.

54 For details, see I.C.1.

ternational Covenant on Civil and Political Rights[55] explicitly identifies international law as a source of criminal law. This (abstract) norm can only have real impact, however, if the international law not only defines the wrongdoing that is to be criminalized but also provides for the type and extent of criminal penalties to be prescribed or at least obligates countries to enforce pertinent international treaties automatically.[56]

4. Case law and judicial opinion

In contrast to common-law countries, court decisions are not considered a source of law in Italy. Nonetheless, particularly the rulings of the highest court (the Court of Cassation) but also those of lower level courts are considered important interpretive aids. Court decisions serve the development of the law by interpreting statutes but are binding only on the individual case at issue, not generally.[57]

While even rulings of the Constitutional Court cannot extend the range of criminally relevant conduct, they can abolish or limit criminal provisions in a way that is favorable to the defendant by means of constitutional review.[58]

Decisions of the European Court of Human Rights (ECtHR) are binding both on the Italian legislature and on (constitutional court) judges. But this binding effect applies only to the case at issue.[59] The judges are also required to interpret national norms in compliance with the European Convention on Human Rights, which includes their interpretation by the European Court. Thus, to a certain extent, the decisions of the European Court do, in a way, function as a source of criminal law.[60]

5. Legal literature and academic opinion

Legal literature is not a source of criminal law; it is, however, a very important aid in the interpretation and development of the law. Criminal law science can analyze criminal law from various perspectives: in addition to technically-oriented dogmatic research, research may take historical, comparative, interdisciplinary,

---

[55] Ratified by L. 25 Oct. 1977, n. 881.

[56] *Pagliaro*, Parte generale, p. 43.

[57] *Antolisei*, Parte generale, p. 83; *Di Amato/Fucito*, Criminal Law in Italy, p. 61 (margin no. 106).

[58] *Marinucci/Dolcini*, Manuale, p. 62.

[59] *Marinucci/Dolcini*, Manuale, p. 59; on the influence of the ECtHR and the Council of Europe, see also *Di Amato/Fucito*, Criminal Law in Italy, pp. 57–60 (margin nos. 94–99).

[60] See *Fiandaca/Musco*, Parte generale, p. 78. See also I.A.5.c.

problem-oriented, critical, and principle-building approaches.[61] Italian criminal law science is strictly divided into substantive criminal law, on the one hand, and the law of criminal procedure, on the other. This division is reflected in the fact that there are separate university professorships devoted to these disciplines. In addition to publications in journals (increasingly also online), textbooks and monographs are particularly important. With a few exceptions, commentaries on the codes consist almost entirely of case comments.

Bibliography and further reading

Antolisei, Francesco, Manuale di diritto penale. Parte generale (Textbook of criminal law. General part). 16th ed. Milan 2003.

Bernardi, Alessandro, L'europeizzazione del diritto e della scienza penale (The Europeanization of criminal law and criminal law science). Turin 2004.

Bin, Roberto/Pitruzzella, Giovanni, Diritto costituzionale (Constitutional law). 17th ed. Turin 2016.

Cadoppi, Alberto/Veneziani, Paolo, Elementi di diritto penale. Parte generale (Fundamentals of criminal law. General part). 6th ed. Padua 2015.

Canestrari, Stefano/Cornacchia, Luigi/De Simone, Giulio, Manuale di diritto penale. Parte generale (Textbook of criminal law. General part). 2d ed. Bologna 2017.

Di Amato, Astolfo/Fucito, Federica, Criminal Law in Italy. 3d ed. Alphen aan den Rijn 2016.

Dolcini, Emilio/Marinucci, Giorgio (eds.), Codice penale commentato (Commentary on the Penal Code). 4th ed. Milan 2015.

Fiandaca, Giovanni/Musco, Enzo, Diritto penale. Parte generale (Criminal law. General part). 7th ed. Bologna 2014.

Forti, Gabrio/Seminara, Sergio/Zuccalà, Giuseppe (eds.), Commentario breve al codice penale (Short commentary on the Penal Code). 6th ed. Padua 2017.

Grasso, Giovanni, Comunità Europee e diritto penale (European communities and criminal law). Milan 1989.

Mantovani, Ferrando, Diritto penale. Parte generale (Criminal law. General part). 10th ed. Padua 2017.

Marinucci, Giorgio/Dolcini, Emilio, Manuale di diritto penale. Parte generale (Textbook of criminal law. General part.). 6th ed. Milan 2017.

Onida, Valerio/Pedrazza Gorlero, Maurizio (eds.), Compendio di Diritto Costituzionale (Outline of constitutional law). 3d ed. Milan 2014.

---

61 *Mantovani*, Parte generale, p. 36.

Padovani, Tullio, Diritto penale (Criminal law). 11th ed. Milan 2017.

– (ed.), Codice penale (Penal Code). 6th ed. Milan 2014.

– (ed.), Leggi penali complementari (Ancillary criminal law). Milan 2007.

Pagliaro, Antonio, Principi di diritto penale. Parte generale (Principles of criminal law. General part). 8th ed. Milan 2003.

Palazzo, Francesco Carlo/Paliero, Carlo Enrico (eds.), Commentario breve alle leggi penali complementari (Brief commentary on the ancillary criminal law). 2d ed. Padua 2007.

Picotti, Lorenzo (ed.), Possibilità e limiti di un diritto penale dell'Unione Europea (Possibilities and limits of a criminal law of the European Union). Milan 1999.

Pulitanò, Domenico, Diritto penale (Criminal law). 6th ed. Turin 2015.

Riz, Roland, Lineamenti di diritto penale. Parte generale (Fundamentals of criminal law. General part). 6th ed. Padua 2012.

Riz, Roland/Happacher, Esther, Grundzüge des italienischen Verfassungsrechts (Fundamentals of Italian constitutional law). 4th ed. Innsbruck 2013.

Romano, Mario, Commentario sistematico del codice penale (Systematic commentary on the Penal Code), I. (Arts. 1–84). 3d ed. Milan 2004.

Romano, Mario/Grasso, Giovanni, Commentario sistematico del codice penale (Systematic commentary on the Penal Code), II. (Arts. 85–149). 2d ed. Milan 1996.

Romano, Mario/Grasso, Giovanni/Padovani, Tullio, Commentario sistematico del codice penale (Systematic commentary on the Penal Code), III. (Arts. 150–240). Milan 1994.

Ronco, Mauro (ed.), Codice penale commentato (Commentary on the Penal Code). 4th ed. Turin 2012.

Table of cases

Corte Cost. 13 March 2014, n. 46, Giur. Cost 59, pp. 1134–1154

CJEU, 16.06.2005 - C-105/03, http://eur-lex.europa.eu/legal-content/EN/TXT/?uri=CELEX%3A62003CJ0105 [last visited May 2017]

Corte Cost. 24 Oct. 1996, n. 360, Giur. Cost. 1996, pp. 3147–3157

G. Developments in criminal law, criminal procedure, and the execution of punishment

1. Overview

– From Roman law to the modern era

The principal source of Roman law, the *Corpus Juris Civilis*, was a compilation of existing laws prepared by order of Emperor *Justinian I* (527–565 C.E.).[1] Published in 534, it became the foundation of continental European legal thought. The main focus of this compilation, however, was civil law: of the 50 books in the digest, only Books 47 and 48, the so-called *libri terribiles*, were devoted to criminal law. Its most important part, the *Codex Justinianus*, was kept current by the continual addition of new laws. Only the ninth of the twelve books of the Codex contained provisions of criminal law. Criminal law as a distinct area of law did not exist at that time: scholarly elaboration regarding crime was not even remotely comparable to the scholarship devoted to civil law.[2] Roman law distinguished between *delicta* and *crimina*. *Delicta* were ordinary criminal offenses between individuals, which were governed by civil procedure even if the consequences were criminal sanctions. *Crimina* were criminal offenses that violated basic social values, such as high treason *(perduellio)* and patricide *(parricidio)*. Judgment in such cases was passed by the *comitia* (assembly of Roman citizens acting as a court of law).[3]

The slow process of separation of criminal and civil law began during the Middle Ages. Legal scholars continued the work initially begun in Roman law. The first criminal law notations to the *Libri terribiles* date to sometime after the year 1000. These glosses, compiled from the multitude of regulations of the Justinian collection, provided the basic outlines of a new law in line with the changes in society that had occurred over time. Scholars of the 14th and 15th centuries subsequently followed the glosses more than the Roman texts.[4] The transition from practical treatment to dogmatic construction, which took place during these and the following two centuries, contributed to the foundation of the science of criminal law. Particularly noteworthy in this context are the principles of personal criminal responsibility, *nulla poena sine culpa*, capacity as a prerequisite for criminal liability, the necessity of a reprehensible act, and the recognition of attempt as an independent criminal offense, less serious than the completed target offense.[5] Even so, criminal

---

1 For the history of Italian law, see also *Livingston* et al., The Italian Legal System, pp. 1–52; for an extensive account of the history of criminal law until the 1920s, see *Calisse*, in: Calisse/Register (transl.), History of Italian Law, pp. 219–491.

2 *Mantovani*, Parte generale, p. 23.

3 *Aleo*, Istituzioni, p. 3.

4 *Pagliaro*, Parte generale, 8th ed., pp. 95–96.

5 *Pagliaro*, Parte generale, 3d ed., pp. 102–103.

law continued to be confusing and grim for a long time. Laws overlapped, and the distinction between criminal offenses and sins remained unclear. Corporal punishments and the death penalty dominated, and they were frequently executed with great cruelty. The inquisitorial process in its most rigorous form was practiced; torture was used to elicit confessions.[6] Prisons did not serve the purpose of executing custodial sentences but were the place where the prisoner awaited his or her trial or execution.[7]

Thanks to its primary exponents *Hugo Grotius*, *Samuel von Pufendorf*, and *John Locke*, the theory of natural law, according to which the law is derived from the human faculty of reason, was largely responsible for triggering a change of mind and a process of secularization in the 17th century that also had an impact on criminal law.[8]

– *Enlightenment*

The political and cultural roots of modern Italian criminal law can be traced to a large extent to the Enlightenment in Europe in the course of the 18th century. This movement contributed to the elaboration of fundamental principles that constituted a turnaround from the *ancien régime* and that remain valid to this day, in so far as they contribute to a balancing of the efficiency of punishment, on the one hand, and the guaranteeing of individual rights, on the other.[9] Guiding precepts in this process were legal certainty and the humanization and secularization of criminal law. The goal was to rationalize the criminal law system so as to promote effective crime prevention, combat judicial arbitrariness, and mitigate penalties by avoiding unnecessary suffering.[10] The most renowned Italian thinker of the era was *Cesare Beccaria*. He publicized the abuses and excesses of the criminal justice system of his time in the highly influential treatise *Dei delitti e delle pene*, published in Livorno in 1764, in which he demanded reforms, such as the abolition of judicial arbitrariness, torture, and capital punishment and the assessment of penalties based on the gravity of the crime.[11] This work strongly influenced the Leopoldine reforms introduced in Tuscany in 1786. These new principles, which were advocated outside of Italy as well, ultimately triumphed in the French Revolution and were incorporated into the Declaration of the Rights of Man and of the Citizen of 1789 *(Déclaration des droits de l'homme et du citoyen)*. They gained recognition in the French penal

---

6 *Aleo*, Istituzioni, p. 4; *Fiandaca/Musco*, Parte generale, pp. XII–XIV.

7 *Aleo*, Istituzioni, p. 6.

8 See also *Fiandaca/Musco*, Parte generale, p. XIV.

9 *Fiandaca/Musco*, Parte generale, p. XIII.

10 For details, see *Fiandaca/Musco*, Parte generale, pp. XVI–XVII.

11 *Aleo*, Istituzioni, pp. 7–10; *Schennach*, Rechtsgeschichte, p. 111.

codes of 1791 and 1795 and, finally, in the *Code Napoléon* (1810).[12] Under French rule, the scope of these laws was extended to large parts of Italy. Other regions first adopted the Austrian Penal Code of 1803 (in effect in Lombardy until 1859, in Veneto until 1866, and in the new provinces of Trieste, Trento, and Bolzano until 1918/1920).[13]

– Codifications

The 19th century was the century of major codifications. Beginning with the first penal and procedural codes in the individual Italian states, these laws were first harmonized following the unification of the country in 1861. Subsequently, these laws underwent a liberal reform, and the law of execution of punishment was codified.[14]

From a scholarly perspective, the following decades were characterized by a fundamental difference of opinion among the various schools of thought. The classical school *(scuola classica)*, with *Francesco Carrara* as its most important representative, was based on human self-determination and responsibility, and most of its proponents considered (proportionate) retribution the principal purpose of punishment.[15] In contrast, representatives of the positivist school *(scuola positiva)*, such as *Cesare Lombroso*, *Raffaele Garofalo*, and *Enrico Ferri*, focused less on the offense and more on the person of the offender. They linked the degree of punishment primarily to the risk posed by the offender rather than to his or her culpability and the gravity of the offense, and they incorporated other disciplines, such as anthropology, sociology, forensic medicine, and psychology, into their deliberations.[16] In the early 20th century, a new technical-legal approach *(indirizzo tecnico-giuridico)* to criminal law caught on. *Arturo Rocco*, one of its main proponents, advised criminal lawyers not to discuss disciplines other than law and urged them to limit themselves to the interpretation of the norms of criminal law.[17]

In the 1930s, during the era of Italian fascism, all the codes were rewritten and given an authoritarian bias.[18] Additional important codes were enacted in 1941. Of

---

12 *Fiandaca/Musco*, Parte generale, p. XVII; *Riz*, Lineamenti, p. 1.

13 *Riz*, Lineamenti, p. 3; *Schennach*, Rechtsgeschichte, pp. 119–120.

14 For details, see below 2., 3., and 4.

15 For detail, see, e.g., *Aleo*, Istituzioni, pp. 16–19; *Fiandaca/Musco*, pp. XIX–XXII; *Maiwald*, Einführung, p. 28; *Schennach*, Rechtsgeschichte, p. 123.

16 For an in-depth account, *Aleo*, Istituzioni, pp. 19–30; *Fiandaca/Musco*, pp. XXII–XXVII; *Maiwald*, Einführung, pp. 26–27; *Schennach*, Rechtsgeschichte, p. 123.

17 *Rocco*, in: Vormbaum (ed.), Arturo Rocco und der Rechtstechnizismus, p. 149; *Fiandaca/Musco*, Parte generale, p. XXIX; *Schennach*, Rechtsgeschichte, p. 124.

18 For details, see below 2., 3., and 4.

these, the Judiciary Act (*ordinamento giudiziario*, o.p.)[19] and the two military penal codes – one for times of peace and one for times of war *(codice penale militare di pace*, c.p.m.p. and *codice penale militare di guerra*, c.p.m.g.)[20] – remain in force to this day.

– Italian Constitution of 1948 and the new criminal law

Although the penal and procedural codes (initially) remained in effect after World War II, the enactment of the Italian Constitution of 1948[21] led to significant changes in the substantive criminal law, the law of criminal procedure, and the law of execution of punishment This was due primarily to the establishment of basic principles of criminal law, including the principle of legality, the principle of personal criminal responsibility, the notion of resocialization, the principle of an offense-based criminal law *(principio di materialità)*, the principle of requiring a violation of a protected legal interest *(principio di offensività)*, the principles of *ultima ratio* and subsidiarity, the principle of mandatory prosecution, the presumption of innocence, and the separation of the functions of prosecution, defense, and adjudication.[22] Numerous amendments ensued, in part due to rulings by the Italian Constitutional Court. But these revisions remained fragmentary and failed to bring the criminal law system automatically into line with the Constitution. This would have required a comprehensive reform, which to date has only been undertaken for the law of criminal procedure and for the law of execution of punishment.[23] In substantive law, authoritarian features remain on the books to this day.[24]

– Recent developments

Two major and essentially contrary developments can be observed in Italian criminal law. On the one hand, there is legislation characterized by rationality *(legislazione della razionalità)* that implements modernizing and humanizing international trends.[25] This legislation includes comprehensive decriminalization measures since the 1970s,[26] the abolition of local courts *(preture)*,[27] and the creation of a more modern and milder criminal law for widespread and petty crimes by outsourc-

---

19 R.D. 30 Jan. 1941, n. 12.

20 R.D. 20 Feb. 1941, n. 303.

21 For details on the Constitution, see I.C.

22 For details regarding these principles, see I.C.2. and I.C.3, and I.D.

23 See below 3. and 4.

24 See also *Mantovani*, Parte generale, pp. XLVI–XLIX and below 2.

25 See also *Mantovani*, Parte generale, p. LIV.

26 L. 24 Dec. 1975, n. 706; L. 24 Nov. 1981, n. 689: D.Lgs. 30 Dec. 1999, n. 507; D.Lgs. 15 Jan. 2016, n. 7; D.Lgs. 15 Jan. 2016, n. 8.

27 L. 16 Dec. 1999, n. 479, so-called *Legge Carotti.*

ing them to the justice of the peace *(giudice di pace)* and by establishing a corresponding system of special penalties.[28]

On the other hand, there is also a more need-based or emotional legislation *(legislazione della necessità o delle emotività)*, possibly influenced by the need for protection against crime (especially organized crime), by the survival instinct, by fear of crime, and conceivably also by the stigmatization of criminal offenders on ideological, symbolic, and emotional grounds.[29] This legislation includes many reforms of substantive and procedural laws, such as the mafia-related legislation of the 1980s and 1990s,[30] anti-terrorism legislation after 11 September 2001,[31] the anti-doping legislation of 2000 following the first scandals surrounding the Tour de France and the Giro d'Italia,[32] provisions to combat violence at sports events and the increasingly publicized clashes involving hooligans at soccer stadiums,[33] tightened regulations regarding recidivism with respect to substantive law, procedural law, and the law of execution of punishment[34] the expansion of self-defense options in cases of residential burglaries,[35] as well as tightened regulations with regard to public safety, particularly in connection with the treatment of foreign nationals[36] and sexual violence[37] in 2008 and 2009. Many of these reforms were triggered by crimes that received extensive media coverage. This implementation of the trends of the day, not infrequently prompted by "penal populism,"[38] was simultaneously evidence of a general trend towards a stricter approach to street crime.[39] More recent examples of enhanced criminal law protection include laws against corruption and gender-based violence, enhanced anti-terrorism rules, the introduction of the offense of illegal burning of trash, and self-money laundering.[40]

---

28 D.Lgs. 28 Aug. 2000, n. 274, see also *Jarvers*, Massen- und Kleinkriminalität, pp. 1–7.

29 *Mantovani*, Parte generale, p. LIV.

30 E.g., L. 13 Sept. 1982, n. 646; D.L. 15 Jan. 1991, n. 8, converted with amendments into L. 15 March 1991, n. 82; D.L. 13 May 1991, n. 152, converted with amendments into L. 12 June 1991, n. 203.

31 E.g., D.L. 18 Oct. 2001, n. 374, converted with amendments into L. 15 Dec. 2001, n. 438; D.L. 27 July 2005, n. 144, converted into L. 31 July 2005, n. 155.

32 L. 14 Dec. 2000, n. 376.

33 D.L. 24 Feb. 2003, n. 28, converted with amendments into L. 24 Apr. 2003, n. 88.

34 L. 5 Dec. 2005, n. 251, the so-called *Legge ex-Cirielli.*

35 L. 13 Feb. 2006, n. 59.

36 So-called *pacchetto sicurezza*, D.L. 23 May 2008, n. 92, converted into L. 24 July 2008, n. 125. Also, D.L. 23 Feb. 2009, converted with amendments into L. 23 Apr. 2009, n. 38 and L. 15 July 2009, n. 94. See also *Bettels*, ZStW 122 (2010), 723–740.

37 L. 23 Apr. 2009, n. 38.

38 See *Orlandi*, ZStW 127 (2015), 468 (64).

39 *Grosso*, Cinque anni di leggi penali, p. 541.

40 See in detail below 2.

Recent Italian criminal law is also shaped by the implementation of international directives, particularly by harmonization efforts within the European Union. Examples include the standards for responsibility of legal entities under administrative law,[41] legislation regarding the European arrest warrant,[42] the law ratifying the United Nations Convention against Transnational Organized Crime,[43] the norms protecting children from sexual exploitation and sexual abuse,[44] provisions protecting women against violence and domestic violence,[45] and provisions protecting victims of human trafficking and combating the sexual exploitation of minors, child pornography, and prostitution by minors.[46]

As for legislative technique, the legislature has taken to regulating selected subject areas comprehensively in special laws outside the codes proper. As a result, numerous independent microsystems or diverging subsystems have evolved, many of which incorporate substantive and procedural law and the law of execution of punishment. Examples include the system of procedures and penalties exercised by the justices of the peace, the law establishing the responsibility of legal entities, legislation concerning abortion, artificial insemination, labor and employment criminal law, environmental criminal law, and the gamut of economic and business criminal law (laws pertaining to bankruptcy, business organizations, financial markets, taxes, etc.).[47] This decodification trend *(decodificazione)* is frequently criticized in the literature.[48] Some scholars consider it an unavoidable feature of a modern criminal law system that the legislature must accept and make the best of.[49] A study conducted in 2003 counted more than 5,000 criminal provisions outside the Penal Code.[50] Since then, numerous additional provisions have been added.

The *Torreggiani* judgment of the European Court of Human Rights in 2013 marks an important stage in the development of criminal law in Italy. Due to chronic prison overcrowding, Italy was convicted in this pilot judgment of repeated violations of the prohibition of inhuman or degrading treatment (Art. 3 ECHR) and ordered to remedy the situation within one year.[51] Since then, attempts have been

---

41 D.Lgs. 8 June 2001, n. 231. See II.H.2.

42 L. 22 Apr. 2005, n. 69.

43 L. 16 March 2006, n. 146.

44 L. 1 Oct. 2012, n. 172, see also I.B.2. and below 2.

45 D.L. 14 Aug. 2013, n. 93, converted with amendments into L. 15 Oct. 2013, n. 119, see also I.B.2. and below 2.

46 D.Lgs. 4 March 2014, n. 24 and n. 39, see also I.B.2.

47 See also II.E.1. and II.F.2.

48 See, e.g., *Antolisei*, Parte generale, p. 28.

49 *Donini*, in: Donini (ed.), La riforma, p. 56.

50 See *Donini*, in: Donini (ed.), Modelli, p. X.

51 *Torreggiani and Others v. Italy* of 8 Jan. 2013, http://hudoc.echr.coe.int/fre-press?i=003-4212710-5000451 [last visited Oct. 2017]. For an explanation of the pilot judgment procedure (Rules of Court of the European Court of Human Rights, rule 61), see Factsheet

made at various levels to relax the criminal law system as a whole. In addition to two prison reform laws,[52] there was one particularly important law that amended the Penal Code by introducing the option of suspending criminal proceedings on "probation" and that, on the basis of detailed specifications, authorized the government to do three things: first, to introduce house arrest as a main penalty; second, to create a ground for excluding criminal punishment for particularly trivial offenses; and third, to decriminalize some criminal offenses and turn them into administrative or civil wrongs.[53] Whereas the deadline for the implementation of the first of these authorizations expired, a ground for excluding punishment due to the triviality of the offense was subsequently introduced into the Penal Code (Art. 131-*bis*). Also, a significant number of minor offenses were decriminalized.[54]

An additional comprehensive reform, the so-called *riforma Orlando*,[55] which had been under discussion since 2014, entered into force in August 2017. It affects substantive criminal law, the law of criminal procedure, and prison law.[56]

2. Developments in substantive criminal law

– First Italian penal codes

After a period in which either the French or the Austrian criminal codes were in force in the Italian states,[57] a number of genuinely Italian Penal Codes were enacted in the course of the 19th century:[58]

- the Code of the Kingdom of the Two Sicilies of 1819, which included a penal code as well as other important codes;
- the Penal Code of the Duchy of Parma, Piacenza, and Guastalla of 1820;[59]
- the Regulation on Crimes and Punishments of the Papal State of 1832 *(regolamento penale gregoriano)*;

of the European Court of Human Rights, Apr. 2017, available at http://www.echr.coe.int/Documents/FS_Pilot_judgments_eng.pdf [last visited June 2017].

52 See below 4.

53 See, e.g., *Jarvers*, ZStW 128 (2016), 550–551.

54 See below 2.

55 L. 23 June 2017, n. 103.

56 For details, see below 2., 3., and 4.

57 On various aspects of the Austrian penal codes in force in Italy at that time, see *Vormbaum* (ed., transl.), Beiträge zur Geschichte der habsburgischen Strafgesetzgebung in Italien.

58 For an extensive account of the history of criminal law up until the 1920s, see *Calisse*, in: Calisse/Register (transl.), History of Italian Law, pp. 219–491.

59 https://www.giustizia.it/resources/cms/documents/codice_penale_parma.pdf [last visited Feb. 2017].

- the Albertine Penal Code of the Kingdom of Sardinia of 1839 (so-called *Codice Albertino*);
- the Tuscan Penal Code of 1853;
- the Penal Code of Modena and Reggio Emilia of 1855;
- the new version of the Sardinian Penal Code of 1859.[60]

In the mid-1900s, codes were strongly influenced by legal scholarship, in particular by the classical school and its chief representative, *Francesco Carrara*, and later also by the positivist school, especially by *Cesare Lombroso*.[61]

– Unification of Italy and the Zanardelli Code of 1889

Following the unification of Italy in 1861, the jurisdiction of the Sardinian Penal Code of 1859 was extended to the entire Italian territory of the time (with the exception of Tuscany, which did not wish to reintroduce the death penalty and thus kept its Penal Code of 1853).[62] At the same time, work was begun on a new penal code. After several unsuccessful reform projects (*De Falco, Mancini, Zanardelli I, Pessina*, and *Taiani*),[63] the project *Zanardelli II* was successfully concluded and became the first Italian penal code, the *Codice Zanardelli.*[64] It was promulgated on 30 June 1889 and entered into force on 1 January 1890. A reflection of the new liberal-democratic system, this code renounced the death penalty. In addition, it was strongly influenced by the classical school and was highly regarded both at home and abroad for its great technical merits, which is why it served as a model for various penal codes in Latin America and for the Turkish Penal Code of 1926. It is still in force in the Holy See (Vatican City).[65]

Three decades later, in 1921, a reform draft of the general part of the Penal Code was introduced, prepared under the leadership of *Enrico Ferri (Progretto Ferri)* and shaped by the positivist school. Premised on the anthropological school of *Lombroso*, the criminal offender's physical and biological conditions were emphasized and punishment was replaced with security measures. The project met with strong opposition, however, and was never realized.[66]

---

60 On this topic, see *Aleo*, Diritto penale, pp. 20–22.

61 Regarding the classical and the positivist schools, see above 1.

62 *Aleo*, Istituzioni, p. 15.

63 *Riz*, Lineamenti, p. 4.

64 For a German translation of the *Codice Zanardelli* and for details about the Code, see *Vinciguerra/Vormbaum* (eds.), Strafgesetzbuch für das Königreich Italien ("Codice Zanardelli") vom 30. Juni 1889; for an early comment on the Code (when still a draft), see *von Liszt*, Der italienische Strafgesetzentwurf von 1887. For the influence of the Code on the codification of criminal law in common law countries, see *Cadoppi*, James Cook Univ. L. Rev. 7 (2000), 119–190.

65 *Cadoppi/Veneziani*, Parte generale, p. 41.

66 *Antolisei*, Parte generale, p. 23; *Riz*, Lineamenti, p. 4; for an extensive account of the *Ferri* draft, see *Garfinkel*, Criminal Law in Liberal and Fascist Italy, pp. 344–388 and *Se-*

– *Codice Rocco of 1930 and its modifications*

After the fascist takeover in 1922, a new penal code was high on the agenda.[67] To this end, a committee headed by *Arturo Rocco*, a proponent of the technical legal approach, was formed in 1925. Following statements and opinions from universities, royal commissions, the judiciary, the bar association, and the society for public prosecutors, the first draft of 1927 was succeeded by a final draft in 1929. This draft was presented to Parliament with comments by the then-minister of justice and brother of *Arturo*, *Alfredo Rocco*, and accepted by the parliamentary commission. The *Codice Rocco*, as the penal code was called, was enacted by R.D. 19 Oct. 1930, n. 1398 and entered into force on 1 July 1931. To some extent, it represented a regression to a system that was more authoritarian, more repressive, and more hostile to liberty. Many new offense definitions were introduced (particularly political offenses); the death penalty was reintroduced; and the prescribed punishments were generally very high. Following the positivist school of law, a dual system consisting of penalties (for offenders with criminal capacity) and security measures (for dangerous offenders, regardless of capacity) was introduced.[68]

After the fall of the fascist regime (1943), most offense definitions with typically fascist content were repealed. In addition, the death penalty in peacetime was abolished in 1944 and 1948[69] (abolition in time of war did not take place until 1994[70]), and in 1944, generally applicable mitigating circumstances were reintroduced (Art. 62-*bis* c.p.).[71]

– *Substantive criminal law in the Italian Republic*

The *Codice Rocco* remained in effect even after the Constitution came into force. Subsequently, however, many offenses, including the numerous crimes associated with strikes[72] and the discriminatory criminal provisions on male and female adul-

---

minara, in: Vormbaum (ed., transl.), Vorentwurf zu einem italienischen Strafgesetzbuch, pp. VII–XLI. A contemporary discussion of the *Ferri* draft can be found at *Kidd*, Cal. L. Rev. 10 (1922), 384–394.

67 For an extensive account of the development of criminal law under fascist rule, see *Garfinkel*, Criminal Law in Liberal and Fascist Italy, pp. 389–456; see also the articles by *Lacchè* (pp. 15–34), *Musumeci* (pp. 35–58), *Skinner* (pp. 59–84), and *Livingston* (pp. 85–100) in: Skinner (ed.), Fascism and Criminal Law. As a contemporaneous source, see *Battaglini*, 24 Am. Inst. Crim. L. & Criminology 278–289 (1933).

68 *Antolisei*, Parte generale, p. 23; *Cadoppi/Veneziani*, Parte generale, p. 45; *Riz*, Lineamenti, pp. 4–5.

69 D.Lgs.Lgt. 10 Aug. 1944, n. 224 and D.L. 22 Jan. 1948, n. 21.

70 L. 13 Oct. 1994, n. 589. See also Art. 27 para. 4 Cost.

71 D.Lgs.Lgt. 14 Sept. 1944, n. 288.

72 Regarding Art. 502 c.p.: Corte Cost. 4 May 1960, n. 29, Giur. Cost 1960, p. 497; Art. 504, 505 c.p.: Corte Cost. 28 Dec. 1962, n. 123, Giur. Cost 1962, p. 1506; Art. 507 c.p.: Corte Cost. 17 Apr. 1969, n. 84, Giur. Cost 1969, p. 1175; Art. 503 c.p.: Corte Cost.

tery (Arts. 559–563 c.p.),[73] were declared unconstitutional, and the entire title with the name "Offenses against the Integrity and Health of the Bloodline" was removed.[74] At the same time, there was a trend toward easing the rigorousness of the authoritarian penal code. Of note in this context are the decriminalization of offenses that were particularly minor and their transformation into administrative wrongs,[75] the reduction of the scope of some penalties, and the use of alternate penalties in place of short-term prison sentences. Other key changes include the comprehensive reform of the general part of the Penal Code (1974),[76] which moderated the penalty system; the reform of aggravating circumstances, which were brought into conformity with the principle of culpability (1990);[77] and the decision of the Constitutional Court in which the doctrine of the irrelevance of unavoidable mistakes of law was held to be unconstitutional. As a result of this decision, the principle of culpability attained constitutional rank for the first time (1988).[78]

More comprehensive, albeit fragmentary, revisions of the Penal Code were introduced to bring specific areas of the law into line with changed circumstances and new types of crime. These included the revision and relocation of abortion (1978)[79] and the creation of new offenses of money laundering (1978 and 1993),[80] subsidy fraud (1990 and 2000),[81] and membership in a terrorist (1979 and 2001)[82] or mafia-related organization (1982).[83] More criminal offenses were added to combat national and international terrorism (2005),[84] in the area of computer crime (1993),[85] and for the protection of the confidentiality of communications (1974 and 1993). Criminal offenses committed in office were redrafted (1990, 1997, and

27 Dec. 1974, n. 290, Giur. Cost 1974, p. 2984; Arts. 505, 506 c.p.: Corte Cost. 17 July 1975, n. 222, Giur. Cost 1975, p. 1669; Art. 504 c.p.: Corte Cost. 13 June 1983, n. 165, Giur. Cost 1983, p. 923.

73 Corte Cost. 19 Dec. 1968, n. 126, Giur. Cost 1968, p. 2175; Corte Cost. 3 Dec. 1969, n. 147, Giur. Cost. 1969, p. 2230.

74 L. 22 May 1978, n. 194.

75 L. 24 Dec. 1975, n. 706; L. 24 Nov. 1981, n. 689; L. 28 Dec. 1993, n. 561; D.Lgs. 13 July 1994, n. 480; D.Lgs. 19 Dec. 1994, n. 758; D.Lgs. 30 Dec. 1999, n. 507; D.Lgs. 15 Jan. 2016, n. 8.

76 D.L. 11 Apr. 1974, n. 99, converted with amendments into L. 7 June 1974, n. 220.

77 L. 7 Feb. 1990, n. 19.

78 Corte Cost. 24 March 1988, n. 364, Giur. Cost 1988, p. 1504.

79 L. 22 May 1978, n. 194.

80 D.L. 21 March 1978, n. 59, converted with amendments into L. 18 May 1978, n. 191 and revised by L. 9 Aug. 1993, n. 328.

81 L. 19 March 1990, n. 55; L. 26 Apr. 1990, n. 86; L. 29 Sept. 2000, n. 300.

82 D.L. 15 Dec. 1979, n. 625, converted with amendments into L. 6 Feb. 1980, n. 15; D.L. 18 Oct. 2001, n. 374, converted with amendments into L. 15 Dec. 2001, n. 438.

83 L. 13 Sept. 1982, n. 646.

84 D.L. 27 July 2005, n. 144, converted with amendments into L. 31 July 2005, n. 155.

85 L. 23 Dec. 1993, n. 547.

2000)[86] as were sex crimes (1996);[87] new provisions were introduced against computer crime (*reati informatici*, 1993),[88] new provisions were created for artificial insemination and the protection of embryos (2004),[89] a new title with the name "Offenses against the Feelings for Animals" (Arts. 544-*bis* to 544-*sexies* c.p.) was introduced,[90] and the rules governing the conditional suspension of sentences were reformed.[91] In 2005, the so-called *Legge ex-Cirielli*[92] led to revisions of sections in the general part of the Penal Code involving general grounds for the mitigation of sentences, recidivism, and statutes of limitation. Offense definitions pertaining to human trafficking, child prostitution, sexual exploitation of minors, and child pornography (1998, 2003, and 2006)[93] were made more stringent and supplemented, whereas those regarding freedom of expression were made significantly more lenient or even abolished (2006).[94] In the same year, the self-defense law for burglaries of private homes was appreciably expanded,[95] and the criminal offense of female genital mutilation (Art. 583-*bis* c.p.) was introduced.[96]

2008/2009 were the years of the so-called security package *(pacchetto sicurezza)*, which extended the collateral penalty of deportation for foreign nationals and introduced the general aggravating circumstance of illegal residence on national territory.[97] In the meantime, the Constitutional Court has declared the aforementioned law on aggravating circumstances unconstitutional.[98] In 2009, intentional homicide in connection with sex crimes as an aggravating factor was introduced (Art. 576 paras. 5 and 5.1 c.p.) as were several new offense definitions, such as stalking (Art. 612-*bis* c.p.),[99] falsification of geographical information and designations or of the origin of agricultural products and food products (Art. 517-*quater* c.p.),[100] the removal and detention of minors in foreign countries (Art. 574-*bis* c.p.), and the use of minors for begging (Art. 600-*octies* c.p.).[101] The same law also

---

86 L. 26 Apr. 1990, n. 86; L. 16 July 1997, n. 234; L. 29 Sept. 2000, n. 300.

87 L. 15 Feb. 1996, n. 66.

88 L. 23 Dec. 1993, n. 547.

89 L. 19 Feb. 2004, n. 40.

90 L. 20 July 2004, n. 189.

91 L. 11 June 2004, n. 145.

92 L. 5 Dec. 2005, n. 251.

93 L. 3 Aug. 1998, n. 269; L. 11 Aug. 2003, n. 228; L. 6 Feb. 2006, n. 38.

94 L. 24 Feb. 2006, n. 85.

95 L. 13 Feb. 2006, n. 59.

96 L. 9 Jan. 2006, n. 7.

97 D.L. 23 May 2008, n. 92, converted with amendments into L. 24 July 2008, n. 125.

98 Corte Cost. 5 July 2010, n. 249, Giur Cost. pp. 2996, 2997; *Bettels*, ZStW 122 (2010), 723–740.

99 D.L. 23 Feb. 2009, n. 11, converted with amendments into L. 23 Apr. 2009, n. 38. On this topic, see also above 1.

100 L. 23 July 2009, n. 99.

101 L. 15 July 2009, n. 94.

provided a further tightening of public security measures and an increase in the minimum and maximum limits of fines.[102]

Finally, a number of provisions on specific topics were moved from the Penal Code to supplementary laws (e.g., to laws on the environment and food, traffic laws, laws regulating abortion and artificial insemination).[103]

It goes without saying that the technique of piecemeal changes to the Code has caused coordination problems and upset the harmony of the system. These changes have also led to problems associated with the temporal relationships between criminal provisions that have been replaced or revised too often. The ensuing criticism focused on the claim that these reforms were introduced without a coherent plan, without a clearly established program of criminal policy, and without the coordination necessary to provide solutions tailored to the needs of a rapidly changing society.[104]

– Reform efforts

Because several decades had passed and profound political changes occurred since the adoption of the *Codice Rocco*, there was consensus that a complete reform of the Penal Code was necessary. After several unsuccessful attempts in the 1950s, 60s, and 70s, Minister of Justice *Vassalli* appointed a commission headed by *Antonio Pagliaro* in 1988. In early 1992, the commission presented a reform draft *(Progretto Pagliaro)* of the general and the special part, which earned both praise and (vehement) criticism.[105] In late 1994, the Justice Commission of the Senate formed a committee headed by *Roland Riz*, who presented his reform draft *(Progretto Riz)* in 1995, albeit only for the general part. In 2000, a commission under the leadership of *Carlo Federico Grosso* worked on a draft of the general part *(Progretto Grosso)*, which was highly praised but could not be adopted because of a change in government in 2001.[106] Under Minister of Justice *Castelli*, a new commission was installed in 2001, headed by *Carlo Nordio* in 2001, which published its draft *(Progretto Nordio)* in 2005. Nor was there time to adopt the draft published under the chairmanship of *Giuliano Pisapia (Progretto Pisapia)* in 2007 – which included the abolition of life imprisonment – while the government of *Romano Prodi* was still in power. A comprehensive reform of the Italian Penal Code is urgently needed to reverse the process of decodification and fragmenta-

---

102 L. 15 July 2009, n. 94. See also I.A.5.d.

103 See also I.F.2.

104 *Antolisei*, Parte generale, p. 27; on the problematic heritage of a criminal code originally stemming from the fascist era, see *Skinner*, 7 Int'l J. L. in Context 423–446 (2011).

105 *Antolisei*, Parte generale, pp. 24–25; *Cadoppi/Veneziani*, Parte generale, pp. 60–61. See also *Pagliaro*, Parte generale, pp. 67–74.

106 *Cadoppi/Veneziani*, Parte generale, pp. 61–62.

tion;[107] however, as shown by the developments discussed above, such a reform cannot be expected without a long-term and stable government.[108] For the time being, any hopes for a new Penal Code seem to have been shelved.[109]

– *Most recent developments*

The legislature has continued to introduce amendments in the area of substantive criminal law in recent years as well. In 2011, the crime of illegal recruitment and exploitation of workers was introduced into the Penal Code (Art. 603-*bis*).[110] In addition, the so-called Anti-Mafia Code *(codice antimafia)* was enacted, which contains most of the anti-mafia legislation and includes the measures of prevention *(misure di prevenzione)*.[111] Due in part to international requirements, an anti-corruption law containing key innovations was adopted in 2012.[112] The implementation of the Lanzarote Convention resulted in the introduction of the crimes of instigating pedophilic acts and child pornography (Art. 414-*bis* c.p.), and the crime of solicitation of minors (Art. 609-*undecies* c.p.).[113] The implementation of the Istanbul Convention triggered changes in several provisions of the Penal Code connected with the protection against gender-based violence (Arts. 61 para. 11-*quinquies*, 572, 609-*ter*, 612, and 612-*bis*).[114] In 2014, the crime of "self money laundering" (*autoriciclaggio*, Art. 648-*ter* c.p.) was introduced.[115]

In the same year, following the conviction in the *Torreggiani* judgment of the European Court of Human Rights,[116] efforts were made to make some areas of substantive criminal law more lenient in order to counteract prison overcrowding. As a result, minor narcotics offenses are now subject to a fine rather than a custodial sentence.[117] Furthermore, the option of suspending criminal proceedings on "proba-

---

107 *Antolisei*, Parte generale, pp. 28–29; *Marinucci/Dolcini*, Manuale, p. 35; *Padovani*, Diritto penale, p. 10; *Romano*, Commentario, I, pre-Art. 1, margin nos. 17–18; *Riz*, Lineamenti, p. 62.

108 See also *Mantovani*, Parte generale, p. 34.

109 *Cadoppi/Veneziani*, Parte generale, p. 62; *Palazzo*, Dir. it. dir. proc. pen. 2014, 1700.

110 D.L. 13 Aug. 2011, n. 138, converted with amendments into L. 14 Sept. 2011, n. 148.

111 D.Lgs. 6 Sept. 2011, n. 159. For an overview over the new Anti-Mafia Code, see *Militello*, in: Elsenbroich et al. (eds.), Social Dimensions of Organised Crime, pp. 79–81. On the preventive confiscation of profits, see, e.g., *Bettels*, Gewinnabschöpfung, pp. 176–270.

112 By the so-called *Legge Severino*, L. 6 Nov. 2012, n. 190. See also I.B.2.b.

113 L. 1 Oct. 2012, n. 172, see also I.B.2. and above 1.

114 D.L. 14 Aug. 2013, n. 93, converted with amendments into L. 15 Oct. 2013, n. 119, see also I.B.2. and above 1.

115 L. 15 Dec. 2014, n. 186. On this topic, see also *Palazzo*, Dir. it. dir. proc. pen. 2014, 1694–1695.

116 See above 1.

117 D.L. 20 March 2014, n. 36, converted with amendments into L. 16 May 2014, n. 79.

tion" (*sospensione del procedimento con messa alla prova*, Arts. 168-*bis* to 168-*quater* c.p.) was introduced.[118] In 2015, a ground for excluding criminal punishment for particularly trivial offenses (*tenuità del fatto*, Art. 131-*bis* c.p.)[119] was created; in 2016, far-reaching decriminalization laws were enacted. On the one hand, minor interpersonal offenses, such as forgery of a private document, insult, property damage, and keeping found property, were decriminalized; as civil wrongs, they are now subject to civil financial penalties.[120] On the other hand, minor breaches of regulations, such as indecent acts or performances, refusing assistance in case of unrest, abusing the gullibility of the people, unauthorized theater and movie presentations, conduct in breach of public decency, and numerous crimes located in laws outside the Penal Code proper, were decriminalized and converted into administrative wrongs.[121]

After the crime of illegal trash burning (Art. 256-*bis* of the environmental law)[122] was created already in 2013, a new title (VI-*bis*) containing criminal offenses against the environment was introduced into the Penal Code (Art. 452-*bis* to 452-*terdecies* c.p.) in 2015.[123] That same year also saw the tightening of terrorism legislation.[124] In 2016, crimes of negligent vehicular homicide (Art. 589-*bis* c.p.) and negligent vehicular bodily injury (Art. 590-*bis* c.p.) were introduced.[125] Compared to the basic offenses (negligent homicide, Art. 589 c.p., and negligent bodily injury, Art. 590 para. 2 c.p.), the penalties were significantly increased, even more so for certain traffic violations and if committed under the influence of alcohol or drugs. A larger reform of the criminal justice system took place in 2017 (so-called *riforma Orlando*).[126] It introduced into the Penal Code (Art. 162-*bis*) a general ground for the withdrawal of punishment if the offender engages in reparative conduct, broadly reformed the statutory time limits (prescriptions),[127] and tightened a number of criminal offense definitions, particularly those that contributed to increased feelings of insecurity among the public (e.g., robbery, blackmail, breaking and entering, and purse-snatching). In addition, it authorized the government to create additional rules, such as the expansion of the number of offenses whose prosecution requires a victim's complaint, the reform of personal security

118 L. 28 Apr. 2014, n. 67.

119 D.Lgs. 16 March 2015, n. 28. For details, see *Jarvers*, ZStW 128 (2016), 553–567. See also II.K.5.

120 D.Lgs. 15 Jan. 2016, n. 7.

121 D.Lgs. 15 Jan. 2016, n. 8. On administrative criminal law, see also I.E.2.

122 D.Lgs. 3 Apr. 2006, n. 152, introduced by D.L. 10 Dec. 2013, n. 136, converted with amendments into L. 6 Feb. 2014, n. 6.

123 L. 22 May 2015, n. 68.

124 D.L. 18 Feb. 2015, n. 7, converted with amendments into L. 17 Apr. 2015, n. 43.

125 L. 23 March 2016, n. 41.

126 L. 23 June 2017, n. 103.

127 On time limits, see II.K.3.

measures, and the reform of the criminal register. It is not yet known whether the government will make use of this authorization within the prescribed time period (by 3 August 2018).

3. Developments in criminal procedure

– First Italian codifications

A code of criminal procedure (so-called *Codice Albertino*) was produced in the Kingdom of Sardinia-Piedmont first in 1847 and again in 1859.[128] In 1865, after Italy was unified, an amended version of the Code of 1859 was adopted for the entire kingdom. This Code was based on the so-called mixed system of Napoleonic origin, which consisted of a combination of inquisitorial and adversarial elements. Reform deliberations started as early as 1866, however, whereby it took until 1892 to appoint a reform commission. In 1913, a new code of criminal procedure was produced, which retained to a great extent the mixed system but modernized it in part and introduced a number of institutions linked to the adversarial procedure. These newly introduced institutions included far-reaching rights for the accused already during the preliminary proceedings and a change in the composition of the jury, which was charged with deciding questions of fact, leaving for the court only the decision on the amount of punishment.[129]

– Codice Rocco of 1930

The abolition of the liberal system began as soon as the fascists seized power. In a first step, the government was authorized in 1923 to appoint all members of the Superior Council of the Judiciary (*Consiglio Superiore della Magistratura*, CSM) – who had previously been elected by the judges – a move that enabled the government to undermine judicial independence. In 1931, the new Code of Criminal Procedure, also called *Codice Rocco*, entered into force simultaneously with the Penal Code. Inquisitorial elements dominated in this new procedural code. The justice minister at the time, *Alfredo Rocco*, characterized it as striking a "just balance" *(giusto equilibrio)* between the state's interests and those of the accused.[130] In reality, however, the rights of the defense during the preliminary proceedings were abolished, and the criminal investigation itself was again conducted in complete secrecy. The prosecutor was given the same investigative powers as the investigating judge *(giudice istruttore)*. In simple cases, also known as summary investiga-

---

128 For the history of criminal procedure before this, see *Esmein*, History of Continental Criminal Procedure, pp. 289–295, 585–586.

129 See *Chiavario*, Diritto processuale penale, p. 31; *Tonini*, Manuale, pp. 24–25.

130 See *Tonini*, Manuale, p. 26.

tion *(istruttoria sommaria)*, prosecutors were authorized to restrict the defendant's personal liberty and to take evidence; they had, in essence, judicial powers. Investigating judges, who in other cases supervised the so-called formal criminal investigation *(istruttoria formale)* and had to decide whether or not to bring charges against the suspect were, in turn, given prosecutorial powers. The trial judge was authorized to make use of all the records in the investigation file. As a result of all this, the principle of separation of procedural functions, an achievement dating back to Napoleonic times, was abolished. The system appeared to be mixed but was in fact dominated by inquisitorial elements. Other changes included the following: the prosecutor, who reported to the Ministry of Justice, was authorized to dismiss cases independently and incontestably; the automatic release from pre-trial detention after expiration of the maximum period was repealed; and the jury as such was abolished, and the court of assize *(Corte di assise)* with two professional and five lay judges was introduced.[131]

After the return to democracy after World War II, several of the provisions adopted by the fascist regime were rescinded. Most notable among these are the restoration of judicial independence[132] and the repeal of the prosecutor's incontestable authority to dismiss cases.[133] With the adoption of the Italian Constitution in 1948 and the ratification of the European Convention on Human Rights in 1955, a number of basic principles with direct or indirect effect on criminal procedure were introduced. The most important of these include the principle of mandatory prosecution and a number of guarantees associated more closely with the adversarial principle, such as the presumption of innocence, and the separation of the functions of prosecution, defense, and adjudication. 1955 was the year of the first major reform of the Code of Criminal Procedure.[134] Subsequently, the Constitutional Court demanded changes and ruled many provisions unconstitutional. These corrections were mainly geared towards a more adversarial system. In the end, a mixed system evolved, albeit one with a predominantly adversarial character.[135]

Work on a complete reform of the Code of Criminal Procedure began in the 1960s. Because it was considered highly unlikely that Parliament would succeed in drafting an entire code on its own, it was decided to proceed by way of an enabling act *(legge delega)*. Unsuccessful attempts in 1963,[136] 1968, and 1972 ensued; when the enabling act was finally passed in 1974, it set out guidelines for a new code of

---

131 See *Chiavario*, Diritto processuale penale, p. 32; *Tonini*, Manuale, p. 26.

132 R.D.L. 31 May 1946, n. 511.

133 D.Lgs.Lgt. 14 Sept. 1944, n. 288. *Orlandi*, in: Negri/Pifferi (eds.), Diritti individuali, p. 59. On the extent of changes needed after the end of fascism, see *Ploscowe*, Colum. L. Rev. 45 (1945), 240–264.

134 With L. 18 June 1955, n. 517.

135 *Tonini*, Manuale, pp. 28–31.

136 So-called "progetto Carnelutti," see also *Orlandi*, in: Negri/Pifferi (eds.), Diritti individuali, pp. 64–66.

criminal procedure but left the details to a government-issued legislative decree (*decreto legislativo* or *legge delegata*).[137] Due to the political events of the late 1970s – the abduction of *Aldo Moro*, in particular – progress beyond the draft introduced in 1978 was impossible.[138]

– *New Code of Criminal Procedure of 1989*

In 1987, yet another enabling law was passed[139] that set out an entirely new criminal procedure based on the adversarial system. It included the taking of evidence in an adversarial trial, preceded not by investigative but by preliminary proceedings *(indagini preliminari)* now in the hands of the prosecutor. The investigating judge was to be abolished and – in order to safeguard the procedural guarantees by prosecution and police – replaced by a special judge for preliminary investigations *(giudice per le indagini preliminari)*, an examining judge of sorts, but one without investigative authority. Moreover, alternate types of procedures that would avoid the complexity of a trial were to be drawn up. Thereafter, a commission appointed by then-Minister of Justice *Giuliano Vassalli* and headed by *Gian Domenico Pisapia* drafted a new code of criminal procedure,[140] which was accepted by the government in 1988 and entered into force on 24 October 1989.[141] Special provisions for juvenile defendants were also enacted.[142]

It was not long before the new Code of Criminal Procedure was amended.[143] Several amendments were triggered by interventions of the Constitutional Court, which found quite a number of provisions unconstitutional.[144] Other changes were the result of legislative action. Reforms were introduced in the context of pre-trial detention (1989 and 1991) and in the 1990s in the area of organized crime and mafia-related crime (1992).[145] Three more reforms introduced around the turn of the millennium are noteworthy: the abolition of local courts and the creation of a unified court of first instance *(giudice unico)* at the District Courts *(tribunale)* in

---

137 L. 3 Apr. 1974, n. 108. Regarding the nature of the legislative decree, see I.F.2.

138 *Chiavario*, Diritto processuale penale, pp. 36–37; *Pisani* u.a., Manuale, pp. 3–5; *Tonini*, Manuale, pp. 31–33.

139 L. delega 16 Feb. 1987, n. 81.

140 D.P.R. 22 Sept. 1988, n. 447.

141 See *Chiavario*, Diritto processuale penale, p. 38; e.g., *Pisani* u.a., Manuale, pp. 6–8; *Tonini*, Manuale, p. 32; *Amodio/Selvaggi*, Temple L. Rev. 62 (1989), 1211–1224; *Pizzi/Marafioti*, Yale J. Int'l. L. 17 (1992), 1–40; *Illuminati*, 4 Wash. U. Global Stud. L. Rev. 567–582 (2005).

142 D.P.R. 22 Sept. 1988, n. 448.

143 On the amendments until 2004, see *Amodio*, Am. J. Comp. L 52 (2004), 489–500.

144 See *Chiavario*, Diritto processuale penale, pp. 42–43.

145 D.L. 8 June 1992, n. 306, converted with amendments into L. 7 Aug. 1992, n. 356. See also *Orlandi*, in: Negri/Pifferi (eds.), Diritti individuali, pp. 75–76.

2000;[146] the implementation of the constitutional amendment of 1999 that bore a title containing the keyword "fair trial" (*giusto processo*, enhancement of defendant's rights, right of the defense to conduct its own investigations, etc., Art. 111 Cost.);[147] and, finally, in 1999/2000, the assignment of criminal jurisdiction over certain types of offenses to the justice of the peace *(competenze penali del giudice di pace).*[148] It took until 2005 for Italy to implement the European standards regarding Eurojust and the European arrest warrant.[149] In the area of preventive coercive measures, the option of removing the suspect from the family home (Art. 282-*bis* c.p.p.) has been in effect since 2001,[150] and the prohibition of approaching places frequented by the victim (Art. 282-*ter* c.p.p.) has been in effect since 2009.[151] In 2008, the search and seizure of computer data was introduced,[152] and the option of taking DNA samples and obtaining a genetic expert opinion was introduced in 2009.[153]

The confusion caused by the many piecemeal changes quickly led to calls for a complete overhaul of the Code of Criminal Procedure.[154] To this end, a commission headed by *Andrea Dalia* was set up in 2004; its draft, however, was not followed up on. The draft submitted by the commission set up in 2006 and headed by *Giuseppe Riccio* was not implemented, either, because the government had changed in the interim. There is no other attempt on the horizon.[155]

– *Most recent developments*

The *Torreggiani* judgment of the European Court of Human Rights[156] also resulted in changes in the area of criminal procedure. In 2013, for example, the application of pre-trial detention was limited, as a rule, to criminal offenses with a minimum punishment of five years (Art. 280 para. 2 c.p.p.).[157] In 2014, additional changes in the context of preventive measures ensued, including the subordination of pre-trial detention to less drastic measures (Art. 275 para. 3 c.p.p.).[158] Also, the

---

146 L. 16 Dec. 1999, n. 479.

147 L. cost. 23 Nov. 1999, n. 2, implemented by L. 1 March 2001, n. 63. See also I.D.4.

148 D.Lgs. 28 Aug. 2000, n. 274, see above 1.

149 L. 14 March 2005, n. 41 and L. 22 Apr. 2005, n. 69, respectively.

150 L. 4 Apr. 2001, n. 154.

151 D.L. 23 Feb. 2009, converted with amendments into L. 23 Apr. 2009, n. 38.

152 L. 18 March 2008, n. 48, implementing the Budapest Convention of the Council of Europe of 23 Nov. 2001.

153 L. 30 June 2009, n. 85.

154 See, e.g., *Pisani*, Manuale, p. 9.

155 *Chiavario*, Diritto processuale penale, p. 47.

156 See above 1.

157 D.L. 1 July 2013, n. 78, converted with amendments into L. 9 Aug. 2013, n. 94.

158 L. 16 Apr. 2015, n. 47.

right of the defendant to an interpreter and to the translation of essential documents was expanded (Art. 143 c.p.p.).[159] Since 2015, the office of the prosecutor can apply for termination of proceedings for particularly trivial offenses (Art. 411 c.p.p.).[160] Other new features introduced in 2015 were designed to protect and support crime victims, for example, by informing them of their rights (Art. 90-*bis* c.p.p.) and providing them with an interpreter if they have not mastered the Italian language (Art. 143-*bis* c.p.p.).[161] Finally, in 2017, the so-called *riforma Orlando* introduced extensive changes to the law of criminal procedure.[162] These include regulations concerning the case of irreversible inability to stand trial, the shortening of deadlines applicable during the preliminary proceedings, and changes to special procedures and to the appeals process. In addition, the law authorizes the government to make extensive changes to the rules governing wiretapping by means of one or more legislative decrees; this authorization expires on 3 November 2017. Minister of Justice *Andrea Orlando* submitted a first draft in early September 2017.[163]

4. Developments in the execution of punishment

– Early Italian regulations

The question of control over the modalities of the execution of punishment was raised for the first time in 17th century Italy, then under Sardinian rule.[164] Subsequently, the Kingdom of Lombardy was the first to introduce special "courts" responsible for supervising the inner workings of penal institutions: in 1770, a provision was passed in Lombardy that obligated the so-called families of the court of Turin and its provinces (consisting of a captain and a lieutenant), to visit prisons periodically and to collect any protests of the prisoners.

In 1817, the government of Savoy (Kingdom of Sardinia-Piedmont) further stipulated that unannounced visits were to take place several times a week. The administration was responsible for the "corrective education" of prisoners, whereas the judiciary had control over the conditions in the prisons, with the specific aim of preventing arbitrariness and corruption. As a result of the confusion caused by this

159 D.Lgs. 4 March 2014, n. 32.

160 D.Lgs. 16 March 2015, n. 28, see above 2.

161 D.Lgs. 15 Dec. 2015, n. 212, see also I.B.2.b.

162 L. 23 June 2017, n. 103.

163 http://www.repubblica.it/politica/2017/09/08/news/intercettazioni_giro_di_vite_solo_riassunti_e_niente_frasi_virgolettate_e_la_privacy_fuori_dagli_atti-174894682/[last visited Oct. 2017]

164 For a more detailed account of prison reform before the Italian unification, see *Carafiello*, The Tombs of the Living, pp. 7–21.

dual responsibility, a "general inspector for penal institutions" *(Ispettore Generale degli istituti penitenziari)* was appointed in 1849, who was to report annually on prison conditions, including recommendations for changes, if necessary.

In 1853, the Grand Duchy of Tuscany also issued a provision requiring the investigating judge and the president of the court of assize to visit the prisoners at least once a month.[165]

– From the unification of Italy to the demise of fascism

The unification of Italy in 1861 created the need for standardization.[166] Thus, the execution of punishment was subsequently regulated in the Code of Criminal Procedure of 1865 and placed under the authority of the public prosecutor's office. Prison law, which addresses the treatment of convicted persons, was uniformly regulated for the first time in 1862.[167] According to these regulations, the function of prisons was to detain the inmates and secure discipline.[168]

Finally, in 1891, a new general prison regulation *(regolamento carcerario)* was issued that standardized and systematically organized this area of law.[169] The 891 articles of the regulation included both detailed duties and prohibitions for prisoners and disciplinary rules for prison guards.[170] Later, several major changes were introduced in an effort to improve the inhumane conditions to which prisoners were subjected (such as the elimination of chains for forced laborers and of punishment by means of strait jackets or confinement in dark cells). After World War I, the treatment of prisoners was further improved; however, reform attempts were brought to a sudden halt by the onset of fascism.[171]

The Code of Criminal Procedure of 1930[172] also included provisions on the execution of punishment. While the law on the execution of punishment was not considered a separate area of the law, the details of its nature were the subject of de-

[165] On this topic, see *Di Ronza*, Manuale, pp. 3–4.

[166] For details about prison reform after the Italian unification until the 1880s, see *Carafiello*, The Tombs of the Living, pp. 23–70.

[167] "General regulation for the penal institutions of the kingdom," R.D. 13 June 1862, n. 413.

[168] *Di Ronza*, Manuale, p. 6.

[169] "General regulation for detention facilities and judicial reformatories," R.D. 1 Feb. 1891, n. 260. For details about prison reform after 1887, see *Carafiello*, The Tombs of the Living, pp. 71–104; for the years until World War I, see pp. 105–117.

[170] See *Neppi Modona*, in: Picotti/Zanuso (eds.), Die Kriminalanthropologie Cesare Lombrosos, p. 103.

[171] *Di Ronza*, Manuale, p. 8; *Carafiello*, The Tombs of the Living, pp. 71–104; for the years until World War I, see pp. 119–122.

[172] See above 3.

bate.[173] A short time later, a new "Regulation for institutions of prevention and punishment"[174] was issued that was designed to improve the prisoners' conditions without reducing the painful and intimidating nature of punishment.[175]

– *Developments in the Italian Republic*

With the adoption of the Italian Constitution in 1948 and the ratification of the European Convention on Human Rights in 1955, several fundamental principles that affect the execution of punishment were introduced. For example, the Constitution emphasizes re-education, in the sense of re-socialization, as a purpose of punishment (*rieducazione*, Art. 17 para. 3 Cost.).[176] It also makes large areas of law actionable (Art. 24 Abs. 1 Cost.); from this, the Constitutional Court was quick to derive the need for judicial control over the period of execution of punishment as well.[177]

Following a number of unsuccessful reform efforts in the 1950s and 1960s, the Prison Act (*ordinamento penitenziario*, o.p.) – which is still in effect today – was enacted in 1975.[178] It is the result of a new conception of the status of convicted persons and their relationship to the enforcement agencies. Causes of action were established, and judicial bodies and procedures with procedural guarantees similar to those provided for in the trial phase were created, thus allowing for modifications of enforceable sentencing instruments. The treatment of prisoners must be humane and the dignity of the person must be respected (Art. 1 para. 1 o.p.). After serving his or her sentence, every single convicted person should be reintegrated into society.[179] Pursuant to the principle of legality in Art. 38 o.p., prisoners may only be disciplined for conduct that is expressly foreseen as a violation of prison regulations. Furthermore, alternatives to incarceration *(misure alternative)* were introduced that typically may be considered as an option after a certain portion of the sentence has been served (referral to social services for placement on probation, semi-detention, early release, and house arrest).[180]

---

173 For details, see *Di Ronza*, Manuale, p. 12.

174 R.D. 18 June 1931, n. 787.

175 *Rocco*, Rivista di diritto penitenziario 1931, 583.

176 For details about the development of the prison system in the second half of the 20th century, see *Pavarini*, in: van Zyl Smit/Dünkel (eds.), Imprisonment Today and Tomorrow, pp. 400–424.

177 See, e.g., Corte Cost. 29 May 1968, n. 53, Giur. Cost. 1968, pp. 802–831; Corte Cost. 18 May 1970, n. 69, Giur. Cost. 1970, pp. 973–981.

178 L. 26 July 1975, n. 354.

179 *Di Ronza*, Manuale, p. 19.

180 For details, in German, *Jarvers*, Das italienische Strafvollstreckungs- und -vollzugssystem, pp. 833–837.

Over time, substantial amendments to the prison law have been undertaken, including the following:

- the introduction in 1981 of alternative penalties (semi-detention, supervised freedom, and fines) in place of short prison terms;[181]
- the introduction in 1986 of comprehensive reforms by the so-called *Legge Gozzini*;[182]
- the introduction in 1991 and 1992 of the option of tightening prison conditions (including the introduction of the so-called tough prison regime, *carcere duro*, Art. 41-*bis* para. 2 o.p.) for persons convicted of organized crime;[183]
- the introduction in 1998 and 2000 of changes in the procedure for executing sentences and in alternative measures;[184]
- the introduction in 2000 of provisions promoting the resocialization of prisoners;[185]
- the introduction in 2001 of preferential treatment in prison for cooperating witnesses who turn state's evidence[186] and of alternatives to imprisonment in order to protect the relationship between prisoners and their underage children;[187] and
- the introduction in 2005 of the exclusion of repeat offenders from privileges.[188]

Since 2012, on admission to the correctional facility inmates have been issued a document *(carta dei diritti e doveri dei detenuti e degli internati)* that provides a detailed explanation of their rights and their duties.[189] That same year, the privileges of persons convicted of offenses to the detriment of minors were restricted.[190]

After a parliamentary investigation uncovered deficiencies, it was decided to close down the forensic psychiatric hospitals *(ospedali psichiatrici giudiziari)* as of 31 March 2015.[191] Since then, pertinent security measures are supposed to be

---

181 L. 24 Nov. 1981, n. 689, see I.A.5.d.

182 L. 10 Oct. 1986, n. 663.

183 D.L. 13 May 1991, n. 152, converted with amendments into L. 12 July 1991, n. 203, and D.L. 8 June 1992, n. 306, converted with amendments into L. 7 Aug. 1992, n. 356, respectively.

184 L. 27 May 1998, n. 165, the so-called *Legge Simeone* and D.L. 24 Nov. 2000, n. 341, converted with amendments into L. 19 Jan. 2001, n. 4.

185 L. 22 June 2000, n. 193 and the new Prison Act (*regolamento penitenziario* = D.P.R. 30 June 2000, n. 230).

186 L. 13 Feb. 2001, n. 45.

187 L. 8 March 2001, n. 40, reformed again by L. 21 Apr. 2011, n. 62.

188 L. 5 Dec. 2005, n. 251, so-called *Legge ex-Cirielli.*

189 Arts. 23 para. 5 and 69 para. 2 o.p., D.P.R. 30 June 2000, n. 230.

190 Art. 7 L. 1 Oct. 2012, n. 172.

191 D.L. 22 Dec. 2011, n. 211, converted with amendments into L. 17 Feb. 2012, n. 9, amended again by D.L. 31 March 2014, n. 52, converted with amendments into L. 30 May 2014, n. 81. See also I.A.5.d. and I.A.5.e.

executed in psychiatric hospitals, now called "residence[s] for the execution of security measures" (*residenza per l'esecuzione delle misure di sicurezza*, REMS). The transition, however, took place gradually.[192] Furthermore, the maximum duration of security measures was linked to the maximum punishment prescribed for the offense.[193]

– *Most recent developments*

As the extreme overcrowding in prisons led to untenable conditions following the turn of the millennium,[194] prison law in recent years has been characterized by efforts to remedy this situation. Since 2010, sentences to a prison term of up to one year and sentences with a maximum of one year of prison time remaining may also be served in the home of the convict or in another care or welfare facility or drop-in center.[195] The efforts had to be significantly increased after the conviction in the *Torreggiani* judgment of the European Court of Human Rights.[196] For example, in 2013, decisions on alternative measures and early release were expedited (Art. 656 paras. 4-*bis* and 4-*ter* c.p.p.), certain "rewards" (so-called *permessi premio)* were expanded (Art. 30-*ter* paras. 1 and 4 o.p.), and the possibility for repeat offenders to apply for and receive alternative measures for repeat offenders was increased (Art. 47-*ter* para. 1-*bis* o.p.).[197] In addition, the alternative measure of referral to social services for placement on probation was expanded (Art. 47 para. 3-*bis* o.p.), and the amount of time that must be served before early release can be granted was temporarily reduced *(liberazione anticipata speciale)*.[198] Inmates who have suffered from overcrowding in violation of Art. 3 ECHR receive compensation.[199]

In 2015, the Ministry of Justice established an interdisciplinary expert commission,[200] whose final report, published in April 2016 *(Stati generali sulla esecuzione penale)*,[201] calls attention to the most urgent issues in the area of execution of punishment and sets up guidelines for prison reforms. A complete overhaul of the Ital-

---

192 *Marinucci/Dolcini*, Manuale, pp. 771–772, 774–775.

193 D.L. 31 March 2014, n. 52, converted with amendments into L. 30 May 2014, n. 81.

194 See I.A.5.e.

195 L. 26 Nov. 2010, n. 199, amended again by D.L. 23 Dec. 2013, n. 146, converted with amendments into L. 21 Feb. 2014, n. 10.

196 See above 1.

197 With D.L. 1 July 2013, n. 78, converted with amendments into L. 9 Aug. 2013, n. 94.

198 D.L. 23 Dec. 2013, n. 146, converted with amendments into L. 21 Feb. 2014, n. 10.

199 D.L. 26 June 2014, n. 92, converted with amendments into L. 11 Aug. 2014, n. 117.

200 With D.M. 8 May 2015.

201 Published at https://www.giustizia.it/giustizia/it/mg_2_19_3.page;jsessionid=6ElC0OeA47W9ETglpZ2CQDXM?previsiousPage=mg_2_19_1 [last visited Feb. 2017].

ian system, however, which is believed to be urgently needed,[202] is not on the horizon.[203] The so-called *riforma Orlando* of 2017[204] authorizes the government to reform the Prison Act on the basis of detailed instructions; the authorization expires on 3 August 2018.

Bibliography and further reading

Aleo, Salvatore, Istituzioni di diritto penale. Parte generale (Fundamentals of criminal law. General part). Milan 2016.

Amodio, Ennio, The Accusatorial System Lost and Regained: Reforming Criminal Procedure in Italy. Am. J. Comp. L. 52 (2004), 489–500.

Amodio, Ennio/Selvaggi, Eugenio, An Accusatorial System in a Civil Law Country: The 1988 Italian Code of Criminal Procedure Modern Criminal Procedure: A Comparative Law Symposium. Temp. L. Rev., 62 (1989), 1211–1224.

Antolisei, Francesco, Manuale di diritto penale. Parte generale (Textbook on criminal law. General part). 16th ed. Milan 2003.

Battaglini, Giulio, The Fascist Reform of the Penal Law in Italy. 24 Am. Inst. Crim. L. & Criminology 278–289 (1933).

Bettels, Till, Der Ausländer als Sicherheitsrisiko (Foreign nationals as a security risk). ZStW 122 (2010), 723–740.

– Gewinnabschöpfung zur Bekämpfung Organisierter Kriminalität am Beispiel Italiens (Confiscating profits to combat organized crime – the Italian example). Baden-Baden 2016.

Cadoppi, Alberto, The Zanardelli Code and Codification in the Countries of the Common Law. James Cook U. L. Rev. 7 (2000), 119–190.

Cadoppi, Alberto/Veneziani, Paolo, Elementi di diritto penale. Parte generale (Basic concepts of criminal law. General part). 6th ed. Padua 2015.

Calisse, Carlo, Book II: Criminal Law. In: Carlo Calisse/Layton B. Register (transl.), A History of Italian Law, vol. I. Boston 1928, repr. South Hackensack 1969 and Washington 2001, pp. 219–491, available at http://heinonline.org/HOL/Page?handle=hein.beal/hisil0001&id=1&size=2&collection=beal&index=beal/hisil# [last visited Sept. 2017].

Carrafiello, Susan B., "The Tombs of the Living": Prisons and Prison Reform in Liberal Italy. New York 1998.

Chiavario, Mario, Diritto processuale penale (The law of criminal procedure). 7th ed. Turin 2017.

202 See, e.g., *Pelissero*, Dir. pen. e proc 2016, 1132.

203 For an account of the prison system as of 2016, see *Di Amato/Fucito*, Italian Criminal Law, pp. 223–233.

204 L. 23 June 2017, n. 103.

Della Bella, Angela, Il „carcere duro“ tra esigenze di prevenzione e tutela dei diritti fondamentali. Presente e futuro del regime detentivo speciale *ex* art. 41-*bis* o.p. (The "tough prison regime" between the requirements of prevention and basic rights. Present and future of the special prison system under Art. 41-*bis* o.p.). Milan 2016.

Dezza, Ettore, Beiträge zur Geschichte des modernen italienischen Strafrechts (Contributions to the history of modern Italian criminal law). Berlin 2004.

Di Amato, Astolfo/Fucito, Federica, Criminal Law in Italy. 3d ed. Alphen aan den Rijn 2016.

Di Ronza, Paolo, Manuale di diritto dell'esecuzione penale (Textbook on the law of execution of punishment. 5th ed. Padua 2003.

Donini, Massimo, Presentazione. In: Massimo Donini (ed.), Modelli ed esperienze di riforma del diritto penale complementare (Models and experiences in reforms of the penal legislation outside the Penal Code proper). Milan 2003, pp. VII–XXX.

– La riforma della legislazione penale complementare: Il suo significato "constituente" per la riforma del codice. In: Massimo Donini (ed.), La riforma della legislazione penale complementare. Studi di diritto comparato (The reform of the penal law outside the Code proper. Studies in comparative law). Padua 2000, pp. 3–59.

Esmein, A./Simpson, John (transl.), A History of Continental Criminal Procedure with Special Reference to France. Boston 1913, available at http://heinonline.org/HOL/Page?handle=hein.beal/hccp0005&div=4&start_page=ix&collection=beal&set_as_cursor=0&men_tab=srchresults# [last visited Oct. 2017].

Fiandaca, Giovanni/Musco, Enzo, Diritto penale. Parte generale (Criminal law. General part). 7th ed. Bologna 2014.

Garfinkel, Paul, Criminal Law in Liberal and Fascist Italy. Cambridge 2016.

Giarda, Angelo, Il processo penale nella XIV legislatura: buone intenzioni, qualche "dietrologia" di troppo e risultati non sempre appaganti (Criminal procedure in the 14th legislative period: Good intentions, the one or the other "political conspiracy-theory" too many, and not always satisfying results). Dir. pen. e proc. 2006, 542–544.

Grosso, Carlo Federico, Cinque anni di leggi penali: molte riforme (talune contestabili), nessun disegno organico (Five years of criminal laws: Many reforms [some vulnerable], no coherent plan). Dir. pen. e proc. 2006, 533–541.

Illuminati, Giulio, The Frustrated Turn to Adversarial Procedure in Italy (Italian Criminal Procedure Code of 1988). 4 Wash. U. Global Stud. L. Rev. 567–582 (2005).

Jarvers, Konstanze, Das italienische Strafvollstreckungs- und -vollzugssystem. Historische Entwicklung, Überblick und gerichtliche Kontrolle (The Italian system of execution of punishment and prison regime. Historical development, overview, and judicial control). In: C.D. Spinellis/Nikolaos Theodorakis/Emmanouil Billis/George Papadimitrakopoulos (eds.), Europe in Crisis: Crime, Criminal Justice, and the Way Forward. Festschrift für Nestor Courakis, vol. II. Athens 2017, pp. 817–845, available at http://crime-in-crisis.com/en/ and http://crime-in-crisis.com/en/?cat=8 [last visited Oct. 2017].

– Die „Entkriminalisierung“ von Bagatelldelikten in Italien (The "decriminalization" of petty offenses in Italy). ZStW 128 (2016), 549–577.

Jarvers, Konstanze, Die gerichtliche Kontrolle bei Vollstreckung und Vollzug von Strafen und Maßnahmen in Italien (Judicial control of the execution and enforcement of punishments and measures in Italy). In: Hark-Mo Daniel Park/Susanne Müller/Konstanze Jarvers, Gerichtliche Kontrolle bei Vollstreckung und Vollzug von Strafen und Maßnahmen (Judicial control of the execution and enforcement of punishments and measures). Seoul 2011, pp. 321–376.

– Massen- und Kleinkriminalität vor dem italienischen Friedensrichter. Neue Wege durch alternative Erledigungsmöglichkeiten und Sanktionsformen (Widespread and petty crime and the Italian justice of the peace. New approaches through alternative disposition measures and new forms of sanction). Berlin 2007.

Kidd, A.M., The Preliminary Project for an Italian Penal Code. Cal. L. Rev. 10 (1922), 384–394.

Lacchè, Luigi, The Shadow of the Law: The Special Tribunal for the Defence of the State between Justice and Politics in the Italian Fascist Period. In: Stephen Skinner (ed.), Fascism and Criminal Law: History, Theory, Continuity. Oxford 2015, pp. 15–34.

Liszt, Franz von, Der italienische Strafgesetzentwurf von 1887: (Entwurf Zanardelli); I. Buch: Allgemeiner Teil (The Italian Draft Penal Code of 1887: [Draft Zanardelli]; Book I: General part). Freiburg i.Br. 1888.

Livingston, Michael A., Criminal Law, Racial Law, Fascist Law: Was the Fascist Era Really a "Parenthesis" for the Italian Legal System? In: Stephen Skinner (ed.), Fascism and Criminal Law: History, Theory, Continuity. Oxford 2015, pp. 85–100.

Livingston, Michael A./Monateri, Pier Giuseppe/Parisi, Francesco, The Italian legal system: An introduction. 2d ed. Stanford, CA 2015.

Maiwald, Manfred, Einführung in das italienische Strafrecht und Strafprozessrecht (Introduction to Italian criminal law and the law of criminal procedure). Frankfurt a.M. 2009.

Mantovani, Ferrando, Diritto penale. Parte generale (Criminal law. General part). 10th ed. Padua 2017.

Marinucci, Giorgio/Dolcini, Emilio, Manuale di diritto penale. Parte generale (Textbook of criminal law. General part). 6th ed. Milan 2017.

Miletti, Marco Nicola, Un processo per la terza Italia. Il codice di procedura penale del 1913. Vol. I: L'attesa (A procedure for the third Italy. The Code of Criminal Procedure of 1913. Vol. I: Expectations). Milan 2003.

Militello, Vincenzo, Legal Norms Against the Italian Mafia. In: Corinna Elsenbroich/David Anzola/Nigel Gilbert (eds.), Social Dimensions of Organised Crime. Cham 2016, pp. 65–81, available at https://link.springer.com/chapter/10.1007/978-3-319-45169-5_5 [last visited Oct. 2017].

Musumeci, Emilia, The Positivist School of Criminology and Italian Fascist Criminal Law: A Squandered Legacy? In: Stephen Skinner (ed.), Fascism and Criminal Law: History, Theory, Continuity. Oxford 2015, pp. 35–58.

Neppi Modona, Guido, Das Gefängnis zur Zeit Cesare Lombrosos (Prisons in the time of Cesare Lombroso). In: Lorenzo Picotti/Francesca Zanuso (eds.), Die Kriminalanthropologie Cesare Lombrosos (Cesare Lombroso's criminal anthropology). Vienna 2015, pp. 101–116.

Orlandi, Renzo, Die präventive Wirkung strafverfahrensrechtlicher Zwangsmaßnahmen – italienische Erfahrungen im Vergleich mit dem deutschen Recht (The preventive effect of coercive measures under the law of criminal procedure – Italian experiences in comparison with German law). ZStW 127 (2015), 559–573.

– La riforma del processo penale fra correzioni strutturali e tutela "progressiva" dei diritti fondamentali (The reform of the criminal procedure between structural corrections and "progressive" protection of fundamental rights). Riv. it. dir. proc. pen. 2014, 1134–1164.

– Diritti individuali e processo penale nell'Italia repubblicana (Individual rights and criminal procedure in the Italian Republic). In: Daniele Negri/Michele Pifferi (eds.), Diritti individuali e processo penale nell'Italia repubblicana (Individual rights and criminal procedure in the Italian Republic). Milan 2011, pp. 51–83.

Padovani, Tullio, Diritto penale (Criminal law). 11th ed. Milan 2017.

Pagliaro, Antonio, Principi di diritto penale. Parte generale (Principles of criminal law. General part). 8th ed. Milano 2003.

– Principi di diritto penale. Parte generale (Principles of criminal law. General part). 3d ed. Milan 1987.

Palazzo, Francesco, Nel dedalo delle riforme recenti e prossime venture (A proposito della legge n. 67/2014) (The labyrinth of recent and forthcoming reforms [About Law No. 67 of 2014]). Riv. it. dir. proc. pen. 2014, 1693–1722.

Pavarini, Massimo, Italy – The Politics of Punishment: The Death of Prison Reform in Italy. In: Dirk van Zyl Smit/Frieder Dünkel (eds.), Imprisonment Today and Tomorrow: International Perspectives on Prisoners' Rights and Prison Conditions. 2d ed. The Hague 2001, pp. 400–424.

Pavarini, Massimo/Bertaccini, Davide, L'"altro" diritto penale (The "other" criminal law). Torino 2004.

Pelissero, Marco, Gli stati generali sull'esecuzione penale: i problemi noti messi a nudi e la necessità di risposte di sistema (General conditions in the execution of punishment: disclosure of issues and the need for answers from the system). Dir. pen. e proc. 2016, 1125–1132.

Petitto, Carlo/Sapia, Orlando, La pena tradita. Il sistema penale tra ossessione securitaria e carcerazione della povertà (Criminal punishment betrayed: The criminal justice system between the obsession with security and the incarceration of the poor). Soveria Mannelli 2017.

Pisani, Mario/Molari, Alfredo/Perchinunno, Vincenzo/Corso, Piermaria/Dominioni, Oreste/Gaito, Alfredo/Spangher, Giorgio, Manuale di procedura penale (Textbook of criminal procedure). 8th ed. Bologna 2008.

Pizzi, William T./Marafioti, Luca, The New Italian Code of Criminal Procedure: The Difficulties of Building an Adversarial Trial System on a Civil Law Foundation. Yale J. Int'l L. 17 (1992), 1–40.

Ploscowe, Morris, Purging Italian Criminal Justice of Fascism. Colum. L. Rev. 45 (1945), 240–264.

Riz, Roland, Lineamenti di diritto penale. Parte generale (Basics of criminal law. General part). 6th ed. Padua 2012.

Rocco, Alfredo, Relazione a S. M. il Re del Ministro Guardasigilli (Rocco) per l'applicazione del testo definitivo del regolamento per gli istituti di prevenzione e di pena (Report by the Minister of Justice [Rocco] to His Majesty on the application of the final text regulating institutions of prevention and punishment). Rivista di diritto penitenziario 1931, 581–699.

Rocco, Arturo, Problem und Methode der Strafrechtswissenschaft (Il problema e il metodo della scienza del diritto penale) (1910). In: Thomas Vormbaum (ed.), Arturo Rocco und der Rechtstechnizismus im italienischen Strafrecht (Arturo Rocco and legal technicalism in Italian criminal law). Berlin 2013, pp. 129–179.

Romano, Mario, Commentario sistematico del codice penale (Systematic Commentary on the Penal Code), I. (Arts. 1–84). 3d ed. Milano 2004, pre-Art. 1, margin nos. 1–18.

Schennach, Martin P., Neuere italienische Rechtsgeschichte (Modern Italian legal history). Vienna 2015.

Seminara, Sergio, Einführung: Der Vorentwurf eines italienischen Strafgesetzbuches von 1921 (Introduction: The Preliminary Draft Italian Penal Code of 1921). In: Thomas Vormbaum (ed., transl.), Vorentwurf zu einem italienischen Strafgesetzbuch über Verbrechen von 1921 („Progetto Ferri"), Text und Kommissionsbericht (Preliminary Draft Italian Penal Code on Serios Offenses of 1921 ["Project Ferri"]). Berlin 2014, pp. VII–XLI.

Skinner, Stephen, Fascist by Name, Fascist by Nature? The 1930 Italian Penal Code in Academic Commentary, 1928–46. In: Stephen Skinner (ed.), Fascism and Criminal Law: History, Theory, Continuity. Oxford 2015, pp. 59–84.

– Tainted law? The Italian Penal Code, Fascism and Democracy. 7 Int'l J. L. in Context 423–446 (2011).

Tonini, Paolo, Manuale di procedura penale (Textbook of criminal procedure). 17th ed. Milan 2016.

Vinciguerra, Sergio, Le fonti culturali del diritto penale italiano (The cultural origins of Italian criminal law). Padua 2008.

Vinciguerra, Sergio/Vormbaum, Thomas (eds.), Strafgesetzbuch für das Königreich Italien ("Codice Zanardelli") vom 30. Juni 1889 (Criminal Code of the Kingdom of Italy ["Zanardelli Code"]). Berlin 2014.

Vormbaum, Thomas (ed., transl.), Beiträge zur Geschichte der habsburgischen Strafgesetzgebung in Italien (Contributions to the history of the criminal legislation of the Habsburgs in Italy). Berlin 2010.

Table of cases

Corte Cost. 5 July 2010, n. 249, Giur. Cost. 2010, pp. 2996–3030

Corte Cost. 24 March 1988, n. 364, Giur. Cost 1988, pp. 1504–1539

Corte Cost. 13 June 1983, n. 165, Giur. Cost 1983, pp. 923–927

Corte Cost. 17 July 1975, n. 222, Giur. Cost 1975, pp. 1669–1674

Corte Cost. 27 Dec.1974, n. 290, Giur. Cost 1974, pp. 2984–2990

Corte Cost. 18 May 1970, n. 69, Giur. Cost 1970, pp. 973–981

Corte Cost. 3 Dec. 1969, n. 147, Giur. Cost 1969, pp. 2230–2249

Corte Cost. 17 Apr. 1969, n. 84, Giur. Cost 1969, pp. 1175–1194

Corte Cost. 19 Dec. 1968, n. 126, Giur. Cost 1968, pp. 2175–2208

Corte Cost. 29 May 1968, n. 53, Giur. Cost 1968, pp. 802–831

Corte Cost. 28 Dec. 1962, n. 123, Giur. Cost 1962, pp. 1506–1519

Legislation

Regulation for institutions of prevention and punishment	R.D. 18 June 1931, n. 787
Abolition of death penalty for criminal offenses of the c.p.	D.Lgs.Lgt. 10 Aug. 1944, n. 224
Reintroduction of general mitigating circumstances	D.Lgs.Lgt. 14 Sept. 1944, n. 288
Abolition of death penalty in terms of penal laws outside the Code proper	D.L. 22 Jan. 1948, n. 21
Reform Code of Criminal Procedure	L. 18 June 1955, n. 517
Guidelines Code of Criminal Procedure	L. 3 Apr. 1974, n. 108
Enactment Prison Act	L. 26 July 1975, n. 354
Decriminalization	L. 24 Dec. 1975, n. 706; L. 24 Nov. 1981, n. 689; D.Lgs. 30 Dec. 1999, n. 507
Money laundering	D.L. 21 March 1978, n. 59, converted into L. 18 May 1978, n. 191 and revised by L. 9 Aug. 1993, n. 328
Abortion	L. 22 May 1978, n. 194
Terrorist organization	D.L. 15 Dec. 1979, n. 625, converted into L. 6 Feb. 1980, n. 15; D.L. 18 Oct. 2001, n. 374, converted into L. 15 Dec. 2001, n. 438
Alternative penalties	L. 24 Nov. 1981, n. 689
Mafia	L. 13 Sept. 1982, n. 646; D.L. 15 Jan. 1991, n. 8, converted into L. 15 March 1991, n. 82; D.L. 13 May 1991, n. 152 converted into L. 12 June 1991, n. 203
Legge Gozzini	L. 10 Oct. 1986, n. 663
Proxy law criminal procedure	L. delega 16 Feb. 1987, n. 81

New Code of Criminal Procedure	D.P.R. 22 Sept. 1988, n. 447
Special provisions for juveniles	D.P.R. 22 Sept. 1988, n. 448
Aggravating circumstances	L. 7 Feb. 1990, n. 19
Subsidy fraud	L. 19 March 1990, n. 55; L. 26 Apr. 1990, n. 86; L. 29 Sept. 2000, n. 300
Offenses by officials in the course of their duty	L. 26 Apr. 1990, n. 86; L. 16 July 1997, n. 234; L. 29 Sept. 2000, n. 300
Imprisonment and Mafia	D.L. 8 June 1992, n. 306, converted into L. 7 Aug. 1992, n. 356
Computer-related criminal law	L. 23 Dec. 1993, n. 547
Abolition of the death penalty in times of war	L. 13 Oct. 1994, n. 589
Sexual offenses	L. 15 Feb. 1996, n. 66
Proceedings for executing sentences	L. 27 May 1998, n. 165, the so-called. *Legge Simeone* and D.L. 24 Nov. 2000, n. 341, converted with amendments into L. 19 Jan. 2001, n. 4
Protection of children	L. 3 Aug. 1998, n. 269; L. 11 Aug. 2003, n. 228; L. 6 Feb. 2006, n. 38
Unified court of first instance	L. 16 Dec. 1999, n. 479, so-called *Legge Carotti*
Resocialization	L. 22 June 2000, n. 193 und D.P.R. 30 June 2000, n. 230
Justice of the Peace	D.Lgs. 28 Aug. 2000, n. 274
Doping	L. 14 Dec. 2000, n. 376
Cooperative witnesses	L. 13 Feb. 2001, n. 45
Fair trial	L. 1 March 2001, n. 63
Alternatives to incarceration	L. 8 March 2001, n. 40
Removal of the suspect from the family home	L. 4 Apr. 2001, n. 154
Legal entities	D.Lgs. 8 June 2001, n. 231
International terrorism	D.L. 18 Oct. 2001, n. 374, converted into L. 15 Dec. 2001, n. 374; D. L. 27 July 2005, n. 144, converted into L. 31 July 2005, n. 155
Violence in the stadium	D.L. 24 Feb. 2003, n. 28, converted with amendments into L. 24 Apr. 2003, n. 88
Artificial insemination	L. 19 Feb. 2004, n. 40
Conditional suspension of sentence	L. 11 June 2004, n. 145

Animal protection	L. 20 July 2004, n. 189
Eurojust	L. 14 March 2005, n. 41
European arrest warrant	L. 22 Apr. 2005, n. 69
Combating terrorism	D.L. 27 July 2005, n. 144
Recidivism/Limitation of actions	L. 5 Dec. 2005, n. 251, so-called *Legge ex-Cirielli*
Female genital mutilation	L. 9 Jan. 2006, n. 7
Self-defense in burglary cases	L. 13 Feb. 2006, n. 59
Offenses involving expression of opinion	L. 24 Feb. 2006, n. 85
Organized crime	L. 16 March 2006, n. 146
Criminal offenses against the environment	D.Lgs. 3 Apr. 2006, n. 152, introduced by D.L. 10 Dec. 2013, n. 136, converted with amendments into L. 6 Feb. 2014, n. 6
Search of computer data	L. 18 March 2008, n. 48, implementing the Budapest Convention of the European Council of 23 Nov. 2001
Public safety	D.L. 23 May 2008, n. 92, converted with amendments into L. 24 July 2008, n. 125; D.L. 23 Feb. 2009, n. 11, converted with amendments into L. 23 Apr. 2009, n. 38 and L. 15 July 2009, n. 94 (so-called *pacchetto sicurezza*)
Sexual violence and stalking	L. 23 Apr. 2009, n. 38
Taking DNA samples and ordering genetic expert reports	L. 30 June 2009, n. 85
Public security	L. 15 July 2009, n. 94
Falsification of geographical information	L. 23 July 2009, n. 99
Prison reforms	L. 26 Nov. 2010, n. 199, again amended by D.L. 23 Dec. 2013, n. 146, converted with amendments into L. 21 Feb. 2014, n. 10
Exploitation at work	D.L. 13 Aug. 2011, n. 138, converted with amendments into L. 14 Sept. 2011, n. 148
Anti-mafia legislation, measures of prevention	D.Lgs. 6 Sept. 2011, n. 159
Transposition of the Lanzarote Convention	L. 1 Oct. 2012, n. 172

Anti-corruption law	L. 6 Nov. 2012, n. 190
Prison overcrowding	D.L. 22 Dec. 2011, n. 211, converted with amendments into L. 17 Feb. 2012, n. 9
Changes in criminal procedure	D.L. 1 July 2013, n. 78, converted with amendments into L. 9 Aug. 2013, n. 94
Gender-based violence	D.L. 14 Aug. 2013, n. 93, converted with amendments into L. 15 Oct. 2013, n. 119
Provisions for the protection of victims of human trafficking	D.Lgs. 4 March 2014, n. 24
Right to an interpreter	D.Lgs. 4 March 2014, n. 32
Sexual abuse of juveniles	D.Lgs. 4 March 2014, n. 39
Narcotics offenses	D.L. 20 March 2014, n. 36, converted with amendments into L. 16 May 2014, n. 79
Closing of forensic psychiatric hospitals	D.L. 31 March 2014, n. 52, converted with amendments into L. 30 May 2014, n. 81
Suspension of criminal proceedings on "probation"	L. 28 Apr. 2014, n. 67
Compensation of inmates	D.L. 26 June 2014, n. 92, converted with amendments into L. 11 Aug. 2014, n. 117
"Self money laundering"	L. 15 Dec. 2014, n. 186
Introduction of a jury	D.L. 18 Feb. 2015, n. 7, converted with amendments into L. 17 Apr. 2015, n. 43
Particular triviality of the offense	D.Lgs. 16 March 2015, n. 28.
Preventive measures	L. 16 Apr. 2015, n. 47
Establishing the committee of experts	D.M. 8 May 2015
Criminal offenses against the environment	L. 22 May 2015, n. 68
Victim protection	D.Lgs. 15 Dec. 2015, n. 212
Decriminalization and conversion into a civil wrong	D.Lgs. 15 Jan. 2016, n. 7
Decriminalization and conversion into an administrative wrong	D.Lgs. 15 Jan. 2016, n. 8
Traffic homicide	L. 23 March 2016, n. 41
Riforma Orlando	L. 23 June 2017, n. 103

List of abbreviations in country report Italy

Am. Inst. Crim. L. & Criminology	American Institute of Criminal Law and Criminology
Am. J. Comp. L.	American Journal of Comparative Law
Arch. pen.	Archivio penale (law journal)
Cal. L. Rev.	California Law Review
Cass. pen.	Cassazione penale (law journal)
c.c.	Codice civile (Civil Code)
c.d.	cosidetto (so-called)
C.E.	Common Era
CJEU	Court of Justice of the European Union
Colum. L. Rev.	Columbia Law Review
Corte Cost.	Corte Costituzionale (Constitutional Court)
Cost.	Costituzione (Constitution)
c.p.	Codice penale (Penal Code)
c.p.m.p.	Codice penale militare di pace (Military Penal Code for Times of Peace)
c.p.p.	Codice di procedura penale (Code of Criminal Procedure)
CSM	Consiglio Superiore della Magistratura (Superior Council of the Judiciary)
Dir. pen. e proc.	Diritto penale e processo (law journal)
disp. att. c.p.p.	Norme di attuazione, di coordinamento e transitorie del codice di procedura penale (implementation, coordination, and transitional provision for the Code of Criminal Procedure)
D.L.	Decreto legge (decree law)
D.Lgs.	Decreto legislativo (legislative decree)
D.Lgs.Lgt.	Decreto legislativo luogotenenziale (legislative decree of the governor)
D.M.	Decreto Ministeriale (ministerial decree)
D.P.R.	Decreto del Presidente della Repubblica (Decree of the President of the Republic)
ECHR	European Convention on Human Rights and Fundamental Freedoms
ECtHR	European Court of Human Rights
GIP	Giudice per le indagini preliminari (examining judge)
Giur. Cost.	Giurisprudenza Costituzionale (law reports for constitutional court cases)
GU	Gazzetta ufficiale (Official Gazette)

Int'l J. L. in Context	International Journal of Law in Context
James Cook U. L. Rev.	James Cook University Law Review
L.	Legge (law)
L. cost.	Legge costituzionale (Constitutional law)
let.	letter
MschrKrim	Monatsschrift für Kriminologie und Strafrechtsreform (law journal)
n.	Numero (number)
NATO	North Atlantic Treaty Organization
OECD	Organisation for Economic Co-operation and Development
o.g.	Ordinamento giudiziario (Constitution of the courts)
o.p.	Ordinamento penitenziario (Prison Act)
OSCE	Organisation for Security and Cooperation in Europe
R.D.	Regio decreto (royal decree)
R.D.L.	Regio decreto legislativo (royal legislative decree)
REMS	residenza per l'esecuzione delle misure di sicurezza (residence for the execution of security measures)
Riv. it. dir. proc. pen.	Rivista italiana di diritto e procedura penale (law journal)
Riv. trim.-Dir. pen. cont.	Rivista trimestrale-Diritto penale contemporaneo (Online-law journal)
Temp. L. Rev.	Temple Law Review
TFEU	Treaty on the Functioning of the European Union
Wash. U. Global Stud. L. Rev.	Washington University Global Studies Law Review
Yale J. Int'l L.	Yale Journal of International Law
ZStW	Zeitschrift für die gesamte Strafrechtswissenschaft (law journal)

National characteristics, fundamental principles,
and history of criminal law in

Romania

Johanna Rinceanu

Contents

A. National characteristics

1. Geography

Romania *(România)* is located in southeastern Europe. Sharing borders with Hungary, Serbia, Bulgaria, Moldova, and Ukraine as well as with the Black Sea, it holds a key geographical position in the area. Composed of three main regions, Wallachia to the south, Moldavia to the northeast, and Transylvania to the northwest, Romania (surface area 238,391 sq km) is the twelfth largest country in Europe.[1]

The Danube *(Dunărea)*, the second largest river in Europe, flows 1,075 km – over one-third of its entire length – through Romania.[2] It establishes much of the country's southern boundary with Bulgaria and Serbia and forms a delta where it leads into the Black Sea. Other large rivers are the Argeş, Ialomiţa, Mureş, Olt, Prut, Siret, and Someş. The Carpathian Mountains *(Carpaţi)* extend from the north to the southwest of the country. Most of the rivers have their source in the Carpathians and flow into the Danube.

The Romanian Constitution (*Constituţia României*, Const.) establishes the municipality of Bucharest *(municipiul Bucureşti)* as the capital of the country (Art. 14).

2. Population

a) Population and demographics

In 2016, the population of Romania was estimated at approximately 20 million, of which slightly more than half was female.[3] Life expectancy at birth for females was 78 years and for males 70 years. The infant mortality rate was 12.2 infant deaths per 1,000 live births. The fertility rate, that is, the average number of children per woman, was 1.5.[4] After the political changes in 1989, a continuous decline in birth rate took place. A decrease in the young population (0–14 years old) was accompanied by an increase in the elderly population (65 years old and older),

---

1 Permanent Representation of Romania to the EU: Geography.

2 Permanent Representation of Romania to the EU: Geography.

3 See UN country profile on Romania; see also NationMaster country profile on Romania.

4 See UN country profile on Romania.

which led to an increase in the process of demographic aging.[5] Another demographic factor that contributed both to the decrease in and the aging of the population was external migration. Between 1990 and 1995, almost 250,000 people left Romania.[6] Between 1998 and 2009, almost 10 % of the population chose to emigrate, some of them only temporarily. Emigration spiked after Romania's accession to the European Union in 2007. The main destination countries were Italy, Spain, and Germany.[7]

The population density in 2016 was 83 inhabitants per square kilometer.[8] In 2016, only 14.7% of the population was 0–14 years old whereas 22.2 % of the population was 60 years old or older.[9] Bucharest, the largest city, had 1,883,425 inhabitants in 2011; in the same year, the population of other large cities was Cluj-Napoca (324,576), Timişoara (319,279), Iaşi (290,422), and Constanţa (283,872).[10] In 2016, 56.3 % of the population lived in urban areas.[11]

Approximately 10 % of the population belongs to a minority group. The most numerous minority group are Hungarians (6.5 %), followed by Roma people (3.2 %), Ukrainians, Germans, Lippovan Russians, Turks, Tartars, Serbs, Slovaks, Bulgarians, Croatians, Greeks, Jews, Czechs, Poles, Italians, and Armenians.[12]

b) Language

Pursuant to Art. 13 Const., the official language of Romania is Romanian *(limba română)*. There are six main dialects: *Ardelenesc*, *Bănăţean*, *Maramureşean*, *Moldovenesc*, *Muntenesc*, and *Oltenesc*. Romanian is, however, not the only language spoken in the country. Romanian citizens belonging to national minorities have the right to express themselves in their mother tongue before the courts of law, under the terms specified by an organic law (Art. 128(2) Const.). Languages spoken by minorities in Romania include Hungarian, Romany, and German.[13]

Romanian is a Latin language that can be traced back to the time before Emperor *Trajan* conquered King *Decebalus* and Geto-Dacia in 106 C.E.[14] The Dacians

---

5 See *Lazăr/Lazăr*, Revista Română de Statistică no. 8/2011, 75.

6 See *Lazăr/Lazăr*, Revista Română de Statistică no. 8/2011, 76.

7 *Ciocănescu*, Revista Română de Statistică no. 7/2011, 77.

8 Der neue Fischer Weltalmanach 2017, p. 368.

9 National Institute of Statistics, Romania in Figures, p. 11.

10 Der neue Fischer Weltalmanach 2017, p. 368 (figures based on the 2011 census).

11 National Institute of Statistics, Romania in Figures, p. 11.

12 See Romanian Government – Department for Interethnic Relations; see also Population and Housing census 2011 in Romania.

13 On the use of minority language in communications with local authorities, see *Selejan-Guţan*, The Constitution of Romania, pp. 154–155.

14 *Carageani*, in: Letteratura della Romania, p. 49.

spoke a little-known language; it is possible that a few hundred words derived from their language – such as *copil* (child), *prunc* (baby), and *copac* (tree) – survived and became part of modern Romanian.

Already before the conquest of Geto-Dacia, some Romanization of the language occurred due to trading between Daciens and Romans. At that time, the Latin alphabet was known to only a few Daciens; after 106 C.E. a strong Romanization of the language began and lasted until 271 when the Romans retreated from Dacia Felix. The Romans left behind a Latin Vulgate *(latina vulgata)*, which was spoken by both Daciens and Romans and which continued to develop into Romanian.[15] A second Latinization took place during the 18th century and the beginning of the 19th century with the assimilation of French words.

The estimated literacy rate as measured by the reading and writing capabilities of the population ages 15 and over was 98.8 % in 2015: 99.1 % of males and 98.5 % of females were literate.[16]

c) Religion

Christianity is the major religion in Romania. In 2011 81.9 % of the population was Romanian Orthodox, 6.4 % Protestant, and 4.3 % Roman Catholic; 0.9 % of the population belonged to another religion; 0.2 % had no religion or were atheist.[17]

Freedom of religious belief may not be restricted in any form whatsoever. No one may be compelled to embrace a religion contrary to his or her own convictions. All religions are free and are organized in accordance with their own statutes, under the terms laid down by law (Art. 29 Const.).

3. Economy

After the fall of communism in 1989, Romania joined the free market economy. Due to reforms in 2000 and accession to the European Union in 2007, which led to immediate international trade liberalization, the country experienced strong economic growth. By the end of 2008, however, Romania's gross domestic product (GDP) dropped as the country began to feel the effects of a global downturn in financial markets and trade. In 2009, the GDP fell more than 7 %, prompting the country to seek a USD 26 billion emergency assistance package from the International Monetary Fund (IMF), the European Union, and other international lenders. Drastic austerity measures, which were part of Romania's IMF-led agreement, led

---

15 *Carageani*, in: Letteratura della Romania, p. 49.

16 CIA – The World Factbook.

17 CIA – The World Factbook; Der neue Fischer Weltalmanach 2017, p. 368.

to a further 1.9% GDP contraction in 2010. In 2014 (est.), the GDP-real growth rate was 3 %, in 2015 (est.) 3.8 % and in 2016 (est.) 5 %. The GDP composition by sector according to a 2016 estimate was 3.3 % agriculture, 35.4 % industry, and 61.3 % services; the inflation rate was -1.1 %.[18]

In 2017, Romania had a developing, upper-middle income market economy. The unemployment rate in 2016 (est.) was 6.7 %, falling from 6.8 % in 2015 (est.).[19] In 2016, the monthly net average wage was 2,088 RON[20] (app. USD 559).[21]

4. System of government

Romania is a republic (Art. 1(2) Const.) and a democratic and social state, governed by the rule of law: human dignity, the rights and freedoms of citizens, the free development of the human personality, justice, and political pluralism represent supreme values and are guaranteed (Art. 1(3) Const.). From 1965 until December 1989, Romania was a socialist people's republic.[22]

Today, the organization of the state is based on the principle of separation and balance of powers – legislative, executive, and judicial – within the framework of constitutional democracy (Art. 1(4) Const.).[23] It is mandatory to uphold the Constitution and its supremacy and to observe the laws (Art. 1(5) Const.).

– *Legislature*

Legislative power is vested in Parliament *(Parlament)*, which is the supreme representative body of the Romanian people and the sole legislative authority (Art. 61 Const.). Parliament is divided into two chambers: the Chamber of Deputies *(Camera Deputaţilor)*, with 346 members, and the Senate *(Senat)*, with 140 members. The Chamber of Deputies and the Senate are elected by universal, equal, direct, secret, and free suffrage in accordance with the election law (Art. 62 Const.). Both chambers are elected for a four-year term; the term may, however, be extended by

---

18 See CIA – The World Factbook, Romania.

19 CIA – The World Factbook, Romania.

20 National Institute of Statistics, Romania in Figures, p. 32.

21 Treasury Reporting Rates of Exchange (exchange rate as of 27 Feb. 2018).

22 For a short overview of the constitutional history, see *Selejan-Guţan*, The Constitution of Romania, pp. 2–30. For an extensive account of the history of Romanian communism, see *Tismaneanu*, Stalinism for All Seasons.

23 For further details, see *Tomescu/Levai*, The USV Annals of Economics and Public Administration, vol. 11, issue 1 (15), 2012, 284–293.

law in the event of a mobilization, war, siege, or emergency until such event has ceased to exist (Art. 63 Const.).[24]

The Chamber of Deputies and the Senate pass laws and carry resolutions and motions in the presence of the majority of their members (Art. 67 Const.). More precisely, Parliament passes constitutional laws *(legi constituţionale)*, organic laws *(legi organice)*, and ordinary laws *(legi ordinare)*.[25] The government, deputies, senators, and groups of at least 100,000 citizens entitled to vote have the right to initiate legislation; citizens may not initiate legislation on matters concerning taxation, international affairs, amnesty, or pardon (Art. 74(1) and (2) Const.). Legislative proposals must first be submitted to the chamber with primary competence *(primă Cameră sesizată)*. The Chamber of Deputies, for example, has primary competence with regard to bills and legislative proposals concerning the ratification of treaties and other international agreements, concerning legislative measures deriving from the implementation of such treaties and agreements, and for bills concerning organic laws. The Senate has primary competence with regard to all other bills and legislative proposals (Art. 75(1) Const.). As a rule, the chamber with primary competence must adopt or repeal a legislative proposal within 45 days (or, where the laws are complex, within 60 days, Art. 75(2) Const.); subsequently the legislative proposal is sent to the other chamber, which will make a final decision. Finally, the law is submitted to the president for promulgation and published in the Official Gazette of Romania *(Monitorul Oficial al României)*. It enters into force three days after its publication date or on a subsequent date as stipulated in its text (Art. 78 Const.).

– *Executive*

Executive power is vested in the president of Romania *(Preşedintele României)* together with the Romanian government *(Guvernul)*. The president and the government are coequal and generate a dualistic executive *(executic bicefal)* with a head of state and a head of government.[26]

The president[27] represents the state and is responsible for safeguarding the national independence, unity, and territorial integrity of the country. He or she oversees the protection of the Constitution and the proper functioning of the public authorities. To this effect, he or she acts as a mediator between the various branches of state power as well as between the state and society (Art. 80 Const.). The presi-

---

24 For details about the Romanian Parliament, see *Selejan-Guţan*, The Constitution of Romania, pp. 65–99.

25 See I.F.2 and *Selejan-Guţan*, The Constitution of Romania, pp. 34–35.

26 *Muraru/Tănăsescu*, Constituţia României, p. 807; *Kerek*, Verfassungsgerichtsbarkeit in Ungarn und Rumänien, pp. 86–87.

27 For details about the president of Romania, see *Selejan-Guţan*, The Constitution of Romania, pp. 102–126.

dent is elected by universal, equal, direct, secret, and free suffrage for a term of five years and can be reelected once; the maximum term of office is ten years. During his or her term of office, the president cannot be a member of any political party, nor can he or she hold any other public or private office (Art. 84(1) Const.). The president has the duty to designate a candidate to the office of prime minister and appoint the government on the basis of the vote of confidence of Parliament. The president can consult with the government on urgent or extremely important matters (Art. 86 Const.) and has the right to participate in government meetings on matters of national interest with regard to foreign policy, the defense of the country, and the assurance of public order as well as on other matters on request of the prime minister (Art. 87 Const.). The president has the power to conclude on behalf of Romania international treaties negotiated by the government and to submit them subsequently to Parliament for ratification within a reasonable period of time. Other treaties and international agreements must be concluded, approved, or ratified according to the procedures set up by law (Art. 91 Const.).

The president is commander-in-chief of the armed forces *(comandantul forţelor armate)* and presides over the Supreme Council of the National Defense *(Consiliu Suprem de Apărare a Ţării)*. Besides many other rights and duties, the president can confer decorations and titles of honor, make promotions to the ranks of marshal, general, and admiral, make appointments to public offices under the terms provided by law, and grant individual pardons (Art. 94 Const.). Finally, he or she enjoys immunity.

The government[28] ensures – in accordance with the program accepted by Parliament – the implementation of the domestic and foreign policy of the country and carries out the general management of public administration. The government consists of the prime minister *(Primul-ministru)*, ministers *(miniştrii)*, and other members as established by means of an organic law. Appointed by the president (Art. 85(1) Const.), the prime minister directs actions taken by the government and coordinates activities of its members. The prime minister must also submit reports and statements on government policy to the Chamber of Deputies or the Senate to be debated with priority (Art. 107 Const.). The president appoints the government on the basis of the vote of confidence of Parliament (Art. 85(1) Const.).

The government has the authority to adopt decisions *(hotărâri)* and ordinances *(ordonanţe)*. It is politically responsible only to Parliament. Each member of the government is politically and jointly liable with the other members for the activities and acts of the government (Art. 109(1) Const.). Members of the government are entitled to attend the proceedings of Parliament. If they are requested to be present, participation is compulsory (Art. 111(2) Const.). The government exercises its term of office until the next general parliamentary election is validated (Art. 110(1) Const.).

[28] For details about the government of Romania, see *Selejan-Guţan*, The Constitution of Romania, pp. 126–139; for the public administration, see pp. 139–146.

– Judiciary

Judicial power is vested in the High Court of Cassation and Justice *(Înalta Curte de Casaţie şi Justiţie)*, the courts of appeal *(Curţi de apel)*, the tribunals *(Tribunale)*, specialized tribunals *(Tribunale specializate)* and district courts *(Judecătorii)*, which judge in first instance *(judecata în primă instanţă)*, in appeal *(judecata în apel)*, or in recourse *(judecata în recurs)*.[29] The organization of the judicial system is regulated by Law no. 304/2004 on the organization of the judiciary (Law no. 304/2004).[30] The establishment of extraordinary courts is prohibited (Art. 126 Const.).

The Constitutional Court *(Curtea Constituţională)*, which is designed to be separate from the judiciary, is the country's highest court and serves as the guarantor of the supremacy of the Constitution (Art. 142 Const.). It consists of nine judges appointed for a term of nine years, with no possibility of prolongation or renewal. Three of the judges are appointed by the Chamber of Deputies, three by the Senate, and three by the president. One-third of the judges are replaced every three years in accordance with the provisions of the Court's organic law.[31]

– Administrative divisions

Romania is divided into 41 counties *(judeţe)* and the municipality of Bucharest. Most counties are named after a major river – such as *Alba*, *Argeş*, *Dâmbovita*, and *Mureş*; some are named after notable cities. Counties, in turn, are subdivided into cities, municipalities, and communes, which are the lowest level of administrative subdivision. The administrative division is similar to that of France.[32]

5. Crime and criminal prosecution

a) Investigating authorities

The Public Ministry *(Ministerul Public)*, organized under the authority of the minister of justice together with other criminal investigation organs *(organe de cercetare penală)*, is the criminal investigating authority in Romania. The role of

---

29 For details about the judicial system, see *Selejan-Guţan*, The Constitution of Romania, pp. 181–201.

30 Legea nr. 304/2004 privind organizarea judiciară, republished in M. Of. I no. 827 of 13 Sept. 2005.

31 For details about the Constitutional Court, see *Selejan-Guţan*, The Constitution of Romania, pp. 163–181.

32 For details on the system of local government, see *Selejan-Guţan*, The Constitution of Romania, pp. 147–160.

the Public Ministry is to represent the general interests of society and to defend the legal order and the rights and freedoms of citizens (Art. 131 Const.). The tasks of the Public Ministry are carried out by (public) prosecutors *(procurorii)*, organized in numerous offices of the prosecutor located around the country (Art. 131(2) Const.). As a rule, prosecutors are responsible for coordinating and supervising criminal investigations carried out by the police. In cases involving certain serious offenses, however, such as murder *(omorul)*, homicide on request *(uciderea la cererea victimei)*, and torture *(tortura)*, the investigation must be carried out by a prosecutor (Art. 56 Code of Criminal Procedure [*Codul de procedură penală*, C.p.p.]). The offices of the prosecutor are attached to courts of law.[33]

The organization of the Public Ministry is regulated in detail by Law no. 304/2004. The Ministry is organized on the basis of a strict hierarchy: On the top of the hierarchy is the office of the prosecutor affiliated with the High Court of Cassation and Justice; it is represented by the public prosecutor general. Immediately thereunder are offices of the prosecutor attached to the courts of appeal, followed by offices attached to the tribunals, and, finally, offices attached to the district courts. Prosecutors must carry out their activities in accordance with the principle of legality *(principiul legalității)*,[34] impartiality *(principiul imparțialității)*, and hierarchical control *(principiul controlului ierarhic)*, under the authority of the minister of justice (Art. 132(1) Const.).[35] The office of the prosecutor is incompatible with any other public or private office, except for academic activities (Art. 132(2) Const.).

The Public Ministry is responsible, through offices of the prosecutor, for criminal investigation in cases and under conditions provided by law and participates in conflict resolution by alternative means (Art. 63 Law no. 304/2004). Furthermore, it leads and coordinates investigative activities carried out by the judicial police *(poliția judiciară)* and leads and controls the activities of other investigative bodies. The Public Ministry, in addition to being a prosecuting authority, undertakes civil action in cases provided by law, participates in court trials, appeals court decisions, protects the rights and legitimate interests of minors, disappeared persons, and other persons, contributes to preventing and fighting crime under the direction of the Ministry of Justice *(ministrului justiției)*, analyses factors that generate or favor criminality, elaborates and presents drafts to the Ministry of Justice regarding decriminalization, verifies the observance of the law in pre-trial detention, and performs other duties provided by law (Art. 63 Law no. 304/2004).[36]

---

33 For the controversy surrounding the constitutional and legal status of prosecutors, see *Selejan-Guțan*, The Constitution of Romania, pp. 185–189. *Ciopec*, J. E.-Eur. Crim. L. no. 1/2014, 33–52.

34 On the principle of legality, see II.A.

35 See also Art. 62(2) Law no. 304/2004.

36 *Otavă*, in: Yordanova/Markov (eds.), Judicial Reform, pp. 130–132.

There are several additional investigating authorities, known as criminal investigation organs. They are, pursuant to Art. 55 C.p.p., the criminal investigation organs of the judicial police *(organele de cercetare penală ale poliţiei judiciare)* and the special criminal investigation organs *(organele de cercetare penală speciale)*. The judicial police is composed of specialized employees of the Ministry of Administration and Interior *(Ministerul Administraţiei şi Internelor)* who are appointed by the minister of administration and interior with the approval of the public prosecutor general at the High Court of Cassation and Justice. The responsibilities of the judicial police are to investigate committed offenses, collect data with regard to the initiation of criminal proceedings, and effectuate criminal investigations.[37]Criminal investigations are generally performed by the judicial police; in special cases, they are carried out by special criminal investigation organs. Special criminal investigation organs include officers appointed by commanders of military units or so-called frontier police officers (Art. 55 C.p.p.). Criminal investigation organs carry out investigation activities only under the supervision of the office of the prosecutor.

Prosecutors are selected on the basis of a national competition for admission to the National Institute for Magistracy *(Institutul Naţional al Magistraturii)*. Pursuant to Law no. 303/2004 concerning the status of judges and prosecutors *(Lege Nr. 303/2004 privind statutul judecătorilor si procurorilor)*, the prerequisites for participating in the national competition are as follows (Art. 14 Law no. 303/ 2004): applicants must be Romanian nationals, reside in Romania, and be capable of holding rights; they must hold a law degree, not have a criminal record, and have knowledge of the Romanian language (Art. 14 Law no. 303/2004). Once admitted to the national competition, applicants must sit for a very difficult written law exam.[38]

In 2015, the police resolved 342,118 cases. This corresponds to an offense rate of 1,538 per 100,000 inhabitants. 1.63% of the cases involved serious crimes committed with violence *(infracţiuni grave săvârşite cu violenţă)*, such as murder, attempted murder, assault leading to death, rape, and robbery; 18.5 % of the cases involved other crimes committed with violence *(alte infracţiuni săvârşite cu violenţă)*, such as assault and negligent homicide; 42.5 % of the cases involved offenses against property *(infracţiuni contra patrimoniului)*, such as theft, damage to property, and fraudulent management; and 37.3% of the cases involved other crimes.[39]

---

[37] *Neagu*, Tratat de Procedură Penală, p. 168.

[38] For details, see the National Institute for Magistracy.

[39] General Inspectorate of the Romanian Police within the Ministry of Administration and Interior.

b) Prosecuting authorities

The prosecuting authority is the Public Ministry,[40] which consists of numerous offices of the prosecutor *(procurori constituiţi în parchete)* throughout the country. Prosecutors are responsible for bringing actions against defendants – with the exception of cases of private action, where the injured party takes on the role of the prosecuting authority *(partea vătămată)*.

c) Criminal courts

The organization of the judicial system is regulated by the Constitution, the Code of Criminal Procedure, and Law no. 304/2004. The following courts have jurisdiction over criminal matters (Art. 2(2) Law no. 304/2004): the High Court of Cassation and Justice, courts of appeal, tribunals and specialized tribunals *(tribunale şi tribunale specializate)*, military courts *(instanţe militare)*, and district courts *(judecătorii)*.

District courts *(Judecătorii)* are exclusively courts of first instance and have jurisdiction over all offenses except those assigned by law to the competence of other courts, that is, military courts, tribunals and specialized tribunals, courts of appeal, or the High Court of Cassation and Justice (Art. 35 C.p.p.). District courts are composed of one judge (Art. 54 Law no. 304/2004). There are 188 district courts.

Tribunals *(Tribunale)* are also exclusively courts of first instance. They have jurisdiction over offenses such as murder, aggravated murder, homicide on request, manslaughter, slavery, human trafficking, child trafficking, aggravated property damage, migrant trafficking, torture, and offenses such as acceptance of benefits by a public official, granting of an undue advantage, influence trafficking, purchase of influence, acts committed by members of arbitration organs or in connection with such acts, acts committed by foreign office workers or in connection with such acts. Tribunals also have jurisdiction over offenses committed with praeter-intention *(praeterintenţie)* that have led to the death of a person, offenses prosecuted by the Directorate for Investigating Organized Crime and Terrorism[41] or by the National Anticorruption Directorate[42] if no other higher organ is responsible by law, offenses regarding money laundering and fiscal evasion, and other offenses that, by law, come under their jurisdiction. Tribunals are composed of one judge (Art. 54 Law no. 304/2004). There are 42 tribunals.

Courts of appeal *(Curti de apel)* can be courts of first or second instance. Courts of appeal have jurisdiction as courts of first instance over offenses against the safe-

---

40 On the educational requirements of prosecutors, see above 5.a.

41 Directorate for Investigating Organized Crime and Terrorism.

42 National Anticorruption Directorate.

ty of the state, such as treason, treason by transmission of state secrets, treason by assisting the enemy, acts against the constitutional order, hostile acts against the state, espionage, attacks that endanger the national security, attacks against the collective, acts of diversion, communication of false information, and genocide, crimes against humanity, and war crimes (Arts. 438–445 C.p.). Courts of appeal also have jurisdiction as courts of first instance over *inter alia* offenses concerning national security regulated in special laws, offenses committed by district court and tribunal judges and by prosecutors working at these courts, as well as offenses committed by attorneys, notaries public, marshals, and others. As courts of first instance, courts of appeal are composed of one judge (Art. 54 Law no. 304/2004). As courts of second instance, they are composed of two judges (Art. 54(2) Law no. 304/2004) and hear appeals *(apeluri)* against decisions taken by district courts and tribunals. The appeal is a fact control. There are 15 courts of appeal.

The High Court of Cassation and Justice *(Înalta Curte de Casaţie şi Justiţie)* is the highest court in criminal matters. It can be a court of first, second, or third instance. Sitting as a court of first instance composed of three judges (Art. 31(1a) Law no. 304/2004), it has jurisdiction over offenses of high treason and all offenses allegedly committed by senators, deputies, or Romanian members of the European Parliament, all offenses allegedly committed by members of the government, by judges of the Constitutional Court, by members of the Supreme Council of the Judicial Magistracy *(Consiliul Superior al Magistraturii)*, by judges working at the High Court of Cassation and Justice, and by prosecutors working at that court (Art. 40 C.p.p.). Sitting as a court of second instance, it hears appeals against decisions of courts of appeal and appeals against first-instance decisions issued by the criminal law division of the High Court of Cassation and Justice. The appeal is a fact control. As a court of second instance, it is composed of three (Art. 31(1c) Law no. 304/2004) or five judges. As a court of third instance composed of three judges, it deals with recourses *(recursuri)* against decisions issued by courts of appeal in the second instance. Whereas an appeal is a completely new trial, recourse is based exclusively on legal grounds and is therefore a legal control. Finally, the High Court of Cassation and Justice rules on specified conflicts of jurisdiction (Art. 40(4) C.p.p.).

There are specialized tribunals *(Tribunale specializate)* for civil cases, criminal cases, cases involving minors and family *(Tribunal pentru Minori şi Familie)*, cases involving administrative and fiscal disputes *(Tribunal administrativ-fiscal)*, and cases involving employment and social insurance *(Tribunal de muncă şi asigurări sociale)*; finally, there is a tribunal for maritime and river-related cases *(cause maritime şi fluviale)* (Art. 36(3) Law no. 304/2004). The special tribunals for minors and family have jurisdiction over criminal offenses committed by or against minors (Art. 40 Law no. 304/2004).[43]

---

[43] See *Păroşanu*, Jugendstrafrecht in Rumänien, pp. 167–168.

Romanian law also provides for military jurisdiction in criminal matters. There are three kinds of military tribunals: military tribunals *(Tribunal militar)*, military courts of appeal *(Curţea militară de apel)*, and the High Court of Cassation and Justice.

Military tribunals are exclusively courts of first instance. They have jurisdiction over offenses committed by members of the military up to the grade of colonel with the exception of those cases assigned by law to other courts (Art. 37 C.p.p.). Military tribunals are composed of one military judge.

Military courts of appeal can sit either as courts of first instance or as courts of appeal (Art. 39 C.p.p.). As courts of first instance, they have jurisdiction over offenses against national security (Arts. 394–397 and Arts. 399–412 C.p.) and genocide, crimes against humanity, and war crimes (Arts. 438–445 C.p.) if the offense was committed by a member of the military. They also have jurisdiction over offenses concerning the national security that are codified in special laws and committed by a member of the military, offenses committed by judges of military tribunals or by military prosecutors at those courts, and offenses committed by generals *(generali)*, marshals *(mareşali)*, and admirals *(amirali)*; finally, they have jurisdiction over applications for transfer *(strămutare)* in cases stipulated by law. Military courts of appeal in the first instance are composed of one military judge. As courts of second instance (hearing appeals against decisions of military tribunals), military courts of appeal are composed of two military judges.

The High Court of Cassation and Justice is a court of second instance in military cases (Art. 40 C.p.p.). It judges appeals against decisions taken by military courts of appeal in the first instance. The court is composed of three judges in the second instance.

The Code of Criminal Procedure provides only for the participation of professional judges[44] in criminal trials. No provision is made for the participation of lay judges or for a jury system.

In 2016, 32,720 persons were definitively convicted: 5,744 of these convictions were for offenses against persons *(infracţiuni contra persoanei)*, such as murder, severe bodily injury, homicide, and rape; 7,661 for offenses against property *(infracţiuni contra patrimoniului)*, such as theft, robbery, speculation, and fraud; 455 for forest offenses *(infracţiuni silvice)*; 949 for offenses committed in public office *(infracţiuni de serviciu)*, such as bribery, taking a bribe, and selling influence; 357 for offenses against authorities *(infracţiuni contra autorităţilor)*, such as assault; 1,368 for economic offenses *(infracţiuni economice)*; 1,509 for offenses causing damage to social relations *(infracţiuni care aduc atingere unor relaţii privind convieţuirea social)*, such as offenses against morality; and 10,839 for of-

[44] On the educational requirements, see *Lefterache*, AUB Drept 2013–II, 184–193 and 5.a. above.

fenses against the public traffic system *(infracţiuni la regimul circulaţiei pe drumurile publice)*.[45] There are no statistics available concerning acquittals.

d) Criminal penalties

The Romanian Penal Code (*Codul penal*, C.p.), which entered into force on 1 February 2014, provides for a three-pronged system of criminal sanctions *(sistemul sancţiunilor penale)* that consists of punishment *(pedepsele)*, security measures *(măsurile de siguranţă)*, and educational measures *(măsurile educative)*.

– Punishment

The previous penal code provided a general definition of punishment and of the function of penal sanctions *(scopul pedepsei)*. According to that definition, penal sanctions had a coercive side *(caracter coercitiv)* and a corrective side *(caracter corectiv)*.[46] This definition was struck out without any explanatory statement by the new penal code. The new code, which envisages comprehensive provisions concerning punishment (Arts. 53–106 C.p.), contains three separate categories of penal sanctions against physical persons: main penal sanctions, accessory penal sanctions, and complementary penal sanctions (Arts. 53–55 C.p.),[47] and two categories of penal sanctions against legal entities: main penal sanctions and complementary penal sanctions (Art. 136 C.p.).

• Punishment of physical persons

Main penal sanctions *(pedepsele principale)* against physical persons are life sentence *(detenţiune pe viaţă)*, imprisonment *(închisoare)* from 15 days to 30 years, and fine *(amenda)* (Art. 53 C.p.). The institution of a fine system imposed in daily units is new. The minimum fine consists of thirty and the maximum fine four hundred daily units (Art. 61(2) C.p.). The amount of the daily unit, which takes into consideration the personal and financial circumstances of the offender, varies from 10 to 500 RON (app. 3 to 155 USD, Art. 61(2) C.p.). A main penal sanction can be the only sanction the court imposes on a particular defendant.

Accessory penal sanctions (*pedepsele accesorie*, Art. 54 C.p.) consist in a ban on the exercise of certain rights, such as the right to be elected to the ranks of public authorities or other public office, the right to vote, parental rights, the right to be a legal guardian or a curator, the right to hold a position involving state authority, the

---

45 See National Institute of Statistics, Romania in Figures, p. 84.

46 *Dongoroz*, Explicaţii teoretice ale codului penal român, p. 4. On the purposes of punishment, see I.D.3.

47 For the new Penal Code, see *Paşca*, Drept penal. Partea generală, pp. 430–483.

right to hold a position or to carry out a profession or to follow an activity of the same kind as the committed offense, the right to leave Romanian territory, and the right to be at a certain location (Art. 65 in conjunction with Art. 66(1) C.p.). An accessory penal sanction is – as the term illustrates – accessory to a main penal sanction of life sentence or imprisonment. Courts do not always have to impose accessory penal sanctions explicitly, as the imposition of a life sentence or term imprisonment as a main penal sanction automatically entails certain accessory penal sanctions.

Complementary penal sanctions (*pedepsele complementare*, Art. 55 C.p.) consist in a ban on the exercise of certain rights *(interzicerea exercitării unor drepturi)* from one to five years, military demotion *(degradarea militară)*, and public disclosure of the conviction *(publicarea hotărârii de condamnare)*. The latter sanction was first introduced in 2014. A complementary penal sanction can only be imposed as an additional sanction.

- Punishment of legal entities

There are two categories of penal sanctions against legal entities:[48] main penal sanctions and complementary penal sanctions (Art. 136 C.p.).

The main penal sanction (*pedepsele principale*, Art. 136(2) C.p.) is a fine. The institution of a fine system imposed in daily units was introduced in 2014. The minimum fine consists of 30 and the maximum fine consists of 600 daily units. The amount of the daily unit taking into consideration the personal and financial circumstances of the offender varies from 100 to 5,000 RON (app. 26 to 1,322 USD, Art. 137(2) C.p.).[49]

Complementary sanctions are the dissolution of the legal entity, if the latter was constituted for the purpose of committing offenses, the complete or partial suspension of the legal entity's activity for a period of three months up to three years, the closing of certain branches of the legal entity for a period of three months up to three years, the prohibition on participating in any tender procedure for a period of one to three years, judicial oversight of the legal entity, and publication of the conviction (Art. 136(3) C.p.).[50]

There are no statistics available concerning how often each type of criminal penalty is imposed against natural and legal persons.

---

[48] For the new Penal Code, see *Paşca*, Drept penal. Partea generală, pp. 469–483. For details on legal entities, see II.H.

[49] Exchange rate as of March 2018, see https://www.fiscal.treasury.gov/fsreports/rpt/treasRptRateExch/treasRptRateExch_home.htm

[50] See II.H.2.

– Security measures

Security measures *(măsurile de siguranţă)* are criminal sanctions that can be imposed either in addition to a punishment or an educational measure or independently of any other sanction (Arts. 108–112 C.p.). Their aim is to eliminate an individual state of danger or to avoid the perpetration of criminal acts.[51] Security measures include the obligation to undergo medical treatment *(obligarea la tratament medical)*, confinement in a medical facility *(internarea medicală)*, a ban on holding a certain office or exercising a certain profession *(interzicerea ocupării unei funcţii sau a exercitării unei profesii)*, special confiscation *(confiscarea specială)*, and expanded confiscation *(confiscarea extinsă)*. Security measures have a preventive character.[52]

– Educational measures

The new Penal Code provides two different types of educational measures for minors: measures without and measures with custody.[53]

Educational measures without custody (*măsurile educative neprivative de libertate*, Art. 115(1) no. 1 C.p.) are civic training courses *(stagiul de formare civică)*, supervision *(supravegherea)*, curfew on weekends *(consemnarea la sfârşit de săptămână)*, and assistance on a daily basis *(asistarea zilnică)*. They can only be imposed on minors from their 14th up to their 18th birthdays (Art. 114 para. 1 C.p.).[54]

Educational measures with custody (*măsurile educative privative de libertate*, Art. 115(1) no. 2 C.p.) are confinement in an education center *(internarea într-un centru educativ)* and confinement in a so-called custody center *(internarea într-un centru de detenţie)*. In exceptional cases, an educational measure with custody can be imposed if the youth has already committed an offense for which an educational measure was imposed or if the penalty required by law for the committed offense is a term of imprisonment of at least seven years or lifelong imprisonment (Art. 114(2) C.p.).[55]

---

51 Art. 107 C.p.

52 *Teişanu*, RDP vol. XIX, issue 4/2012, 109–116.

53 For an overview, see *Ioan* et al., Revista medico-chirurgicală a Societă ţii de Medici şi Naturalişti din Iaşi 119, no. 1 (2015), 211–212.

54 For details, see *Păroşanu*, Jugendstrafrecht in Rumänien, pp. 145–150, 259–265.

55 For details, see *Păroşanu*, Jugendstrafrecht in Rumänien, pp. 150–153, 209–258, 266–305.

e) Execution of custodial penalties

The two main penal sanctions of imprisonment for life *(detenţiunea pe viaţă)*, and imprisonment for a term of years *(închisoarea)* are executed in penitentiaries *(penitenciare)* pursuant to Law no. 275/2006 concerning the execution of penalties and measures imposed by judicial organs during the criminal trial.[56] Penitentiaries are established by the government (Art. 11(2) Law no. 275/2006). They are subordinate to the National Administration of Penitentiaries *(Administraţia Naţională a Penitenciarelor)*, which is responsible for guaranteeing security in each facility.

There are two types of penitentiaries: general and special. There are special penitentiaries for minors and young adults and for women, and there are hospital penitentiaries (Art. 12(2) Law no. 275/2006). Law no. 83/2010 has modified and supplemented Law no. 275/2006. As of 31 January 2017, there were 45 penitentiaries with a total of 27,308 prisoners, including pre-trial detainees. The incarceration rate at that time was 139 inmates per 100,000 residents (based on an estimated national population of 19.64 million).[57] Given the official capacity of the prison system of 27,744 prisoners, the occupancy level was 98.4 %. At the end of December 2016, 5.1 % of the prison population was female and 1.4 % were juveniles; foreigners made up 1.1 % of the prison population.[58]

Bibliography and further reading

General references:

CIA World Factbook:
https://www.cia.gov/library/publications/the-world-factbook/geos/ro.html [last visited March 2018].

De la Cuesta, Jose Luis, Noul Cod Penal român. Consideraţii generale şi preliminare prin prisma principiilor cheie ale politicii penale (The new Romanian Penal Code. General and preliminary considerations through the prism of the key principles of criminal policy). RDP vol. XX, issue 3/2013, 152–160.

Der neue Fischer Weltalmanach 2017 (The new Fischer World Almanac 2017). Frankfurt am Main 2016.

Doss, Marion T./Bowers, Stephen R./Hanganu, Cristina, The transformation of the Romanian criminal justice system. 3 Int'l J. Police Sci. & Mgmt. 226–245 (2001).

---

56 Legea nr. 275/2006 privind executarea pedepselor şi a măsurilor dispuse de organele judiciare în cursul procesului penal, published in M. Of. no. 627 of 20 July 2006. On developments in the execution of punishment, see I.G.4.

57 World Prison Brief: Romania.

58 World Prison Brief: Romania.

Gâdiuţă, Filip, The Romanian Constitutional Court's Relationship with the Ordinary Courts: What Are Some of the Causes of Its High Caseload? 37 Rev. Cent. & E. European L. 53–93 (2012).

Juler, Caroline, Romania. National Geographic Traveler. Washington, D.C. 2010.

Permanent Representation of Romania to the EU: Romania; Romania, an overview; Geography, http://ue.mae.ro/en/romania/312 [last visited March 2018].

Population:

Ciocănescu, Eduard Andrei, The external migration with Romania as country of origin and destination countries in the European Union – Brief analysis for 1998–2009 period. Revista Română de Statistică no. 7/2011, 71–80.

Lazăr, Cornel/Lazăr, Mirela, Number and structure of Romania's employed population – Evolutions and perspectives at national and regional level. Revista Română de Statistică no. 8/2011, 75–84.

National Institute of Statistics, Romania in Figures 2017, http://www.insse.ro/cms/en/content/romania-figures-%E2%80%94-statistical-abstract-0 [last visited March 2018].

NationMaster country profile on Romania, http://www.nationmaster.com/country-info/profiles/Romania/People [last visited March 2018].

Population and Housing census 2011 in Romania, http://www.insse.ro [last visited March 2018].

Romanian Government – Department for Interethnic Relations, http://www.dri.gov.ro [last visited March 2018].

UN country profile on Romania, http://data.un.org/CountryProfile.aspx?crName=ROMANIA [last visited March 2018].

Language:

Carageani, Gheorghe, Breve profilo di storia della lingua romena (Short outline of the history of the Romanian language). In: Pubblicazione annuale dell`Associazione Giuseppe Acerbi. Letteratura della Romania (Romanian Literature). San Pietro in Cariano 2005, pp. 49–54.

Selejan-Guţan, Bianca, The Constitution of Romania: A Contextual Analysis. Oxford 2016.

Economy:

România National Institute of Statistics: Monthly average wage, http://www.insse.ro/cms/files/statistici/comunicate/castiguri/a12/cs02e12.pdf [last visited March 2018].

Treasury Reporting Rates of Exchange, https://www.fiscal.treasury.gov/fsreports/rpt/treasRptRateExch/treasRptRateExch_home.htm [last visited March 2018].

System of government:

Constitution of Romania, http://www.cdep.ro/pls/dic/site.page?id=371&idl=1 [last visited March 2018]; English version, http://www.cdep.ro/pls/dic/site.page?id=339&idl=2 [last visited March 2018].

Hein, Michael, Politik und Recht in den Verfassungsordnungen Bulgariens und Rumäniens. Strukturprobleme, Verfassungskonflikte und Konsolidierung seit 1991 (Politics and law in the constitutional systems of Bulgaria and Romania. Structural problems, constitutional conflicts and consolidation since 1991). JOR 54/2 (2013), 301–332.

Kerek, Angela, Verfassungsgerichtsbarkeit in Ungarn und Rumänien – Ein Vergleich der Verfassungsgerichtsbarkeiten zweier osteuropäischer Transformationsstaaten auf ihrem Weg zum konsolidierten Rechtsstaat (Constitutional jurisdiction in Hungary and Romania – A comparison of the constitutional jurisdiction of two eastern European transformational countries on their way to a consolidated constitutional state). Berlin 2010.

Muraru, Ioan/Tănăsescu, Elena Simina (eds.), Constituţia României – Comentariu pe articole (The Romanian Constitution – Annotation of articles). Bucharest 2008, pp. 783–934.

Selejan-Guţan, Bianca, The Constitution of Romania: A Contextual Analysis. Oxford 2016.

Tismaneanu, Vladimir, Stalinism for All Seasons: A Political History of Romanian Communism. Berkeley 2003.

Tomescu, Camelia/Levai, Mihaela Codrina, The principles of equilibrium and separation of powers under the Romanian Constitution. The USV Annals of Economics and Public Administration, vol. 11, issue 1 (15), 2012, 284–293.

Crime and criminal prosecution:

Dianu, Tiberiu, The Romanian Criminal Justice System. In: Stanislaw Frankowski/Paul B. Stephan III (eds.), Legal Reform in Post-Communist Europe. The View from Within. Dordrecht 1995, pp. 257–273.

General Inspectorate of the Romanian Police within the Ministry of Administration and Interior, http://andromeda.rutgers.edu/~wcjlen/WCJ/stats/romania.html [last visited March 2018].

Neagu, Ion, Tratat de procedură penală. Partea generală. (Treatise on the law of criminal procedure. General part). 3d ed. Bucharest 2013.

Investigating authorities:

Law no. 303/2004, http://www.mmuncii.ro/pub/imagemanager/images/file/Legislatie/LEGI/L303-2004_act.pdf [last visited March 2018].

National Institute for Magistracy, http://www.inm-lex.ro/index.php?MenuID=35&DetailID=1638 [last visited March 2018].

Neagu, Ion, Tratat de procedură penală. Partea generală. (Treatise on the law of criminal procedure. General part). 3d ed. Bucharest 2013.

Novac, Iulian Mihai, Structure and Responsibilities of the Investigation Authorities of the Romanian Police as Part of the Judicial System. In: Maria Yordanova/Dimitar Markov (eds.), Judicial Reform: The Prosecution Office and Investigation Authorities in the Context of EU Membership. Sofia 2005, pp. 133–138, http://www.csd.bg/fileSrc.php?id=1693 [last visited March 2018].

Otavă, Monica, Prosecution and Investigative Authorities in Romania: Current Status and Future Reforms. In: Maria Yordanova/Dimitar Markov (eds.), Judicial Reform: The Prosecution Office and Investigation Authorities in the Context of EU Membership. Sofia 2005, pp. 130–132, http://www.csd.bg/fileSrc.php?id=1694 [last visited March 2018].

Prosecuting authorities:

Banu, Cristiana Ecaterina, Consideraţii teoretice şi practice privind punerea în mişcare a acţiunii penale (Theoretical and practical considerations with regard to bringing an action). In: Gheorghe Bică et al. (eds.), George Antoniu – in honorem: culegere de studii juridice (George Antoniu – in honorem: collection of judicial studies). Craiova 2009, pp. 26–29, https://de.scribd.com/document/37796767/Culegere-de-studii-juridice [last visited March 2018].

Neagu, Ion, Tratat de procedură penală. Partea generală (Treatise on the law of criminal procedure. General part). 3d ed. Bucharest 2013.

Schroth, Peter W./Bostan, Ana Daniela, International Constitutional Law and Anti-Corruption Measures in the European Union's Accession Negotiations: Romania in Comparative Perspective. 52 Am. J. Comp. L. 625–711 (2004).

Superior Council of Magistracy, http://www.ejtn.eu/About-us/Members/Romania/ [last visited March 2018].

Criminal courts:

Directorate for Investigating Organized Crime and Terrorism, www.diicot.ro [last visited March 2018].

Julean, Dorel L., Drept procesual penal – partea generală (Law of criminal procedure – general part). Timişoara 2010, pp. 135–188.

Lefterache, Lavinia Valeria, Recrutarea judecătorilor în România (Recruitment of judges in Romania). AUB Drept 2013-II, 184–193.

National Anticorruption Directorate, www.pna.ro [last visited March 2018].

Neagu, Ion, Tratat de procedură penală. Partea generală (Treatise on the law of criminal procedure. General part). 3d ed. Bucharest 2013.

Theodoru, Grigore, Tratat de Drept procesual penal (Treatise on the law of criminal procedure). 3d ed. Bucharest 2013.

Penal sanctions:

Dongoroz, Vintilă, Explicaţii teoretice ale codului penal român. Partea generală (Theoretical explanatory notes on the Romanian Penal Code. General part), vol. II. 2d ed. Bucharest 2003.

Ioan, Beatrice/Damian, Simona/Scripcaru, C./Neagu, Marius/Chirilă, B., From punishment to education – juvenile delinquency in Romanian criminal law. Revista medico-chirurgicală a Societă ţii de Medici şi Naturalişti din Iaşi 119, no. 1 (2015), 207–213.

Ivan, Gheorghe, Criteriile speciale de individualizare a pedepsei amenzii (Special criteria for the individualization of the fine). RDP vol. XIX, issue 2/2012, 27–32.

Păroşanu, Andrea, Jugendstrafrecht in Rumänien: historische, kriminologische, rechtliche und rechtspolitische Aspekte (Juvenile criminal law in Romania: historical, criminological, legal, and legal policy aspects). Mönchengladbach 2016.

Paşca, Viorel, Drept penal. Partea generală (Criminal law. General part). 3d ed. Bucharest 2014.

Teişanu, Florentin, Măsurile de siguranţă. Concept. Importanţă (Security measures. Concept. Importance). RDP vol. XIX, issue 4/2012, 109–116.

Execution of custodial penalties:

Barbu, S.G./Daczo, C.A./Goga, Alexandru, Recent considerations on the institution of probation. In: Mihaela Tomiţă (ed.), The Fourth International Conference Psycho-Social Perspectives in the Quasi-Coercive Treatment of Offenders Social Control and Vulnerable Groups SPECTO 2013. Pianoro 2013, pp. 147–150.

Carbunaru, I.E., Probation in Romania between social control and rehabilitation. In: Mihaela Tomiţă (ed.), The Fourth International Conference Psycho-Social Perspectives in the Quasi-Coercive Treatment of Offenders Social Control and Vulnerable Groups SPECTO 2013. Pianoro 2013, pp. 5–8.

Damboeanu, Cristina/Antonescu, F., The practice of conditional release from prison in Romania. In: Mihaela Tomiţă (ed.), The Fourth International Conference Psycho-Social Perspectives in the Quasi-Coercive Treatment of Offenders Social Control and Vulnerable Groups SPECTO 2013. Pianoro 2013, pp. 221–226.

Statistics of the Ministry of Justice – National Administration of Penitentiaries, http://anp.gov.ro [last visited March 2018].

World Prison Brief: Romania, http://www.prisonstudies.org/country/romania [last visited March 2018].

B. Comparative legal classification and international ties

1. Comparative legal classification

Legal systems are traditionally classified either as a civil (or continental) law system or as a common law system. Countries that belong to the civil law system rely mainly on statutes passed by Parliament whereas countries that belong to the common law system rely mainly on judge-made law. This distinction has, however, lost significance in the area of criminal law and criminal procedure.[1]

The Romanian legal system can be classified nonetheless as a civil law system as it relies mainly on statutes passed by Parliament. This was not always the case, however: From the 14th to the 18th centuries, in the territory of the principalities Wallachia *(Principatul Valahiei)* and Moldova, customary law along with Byzantine and Canonical law and written Baronial law were predominant.[2]

Beginning in the 16th century, a tendency to codify Baronial (feudal) law emerged. 16th century law is intrinsically tied to the sovereign *Vasile Lupu* (1595–1661) in Moldova and the sovereign *Matei Basarab* (1580–1654) in Wallachia, both of whom introduced codified laws for their territories.

During the 18th century, the idea of central authority was strengthened at the expense of feudal law and, in parallel, the ideology of natural law spread;[3] simultaneously, the adoption of Canonical and Byzantine sources of law increased.[4] Diverse collections of customary law for example by *Petru Manega* in 1825–1826[5] (who studied jurisprudence in France) – and legislative codes in Romanian and Greek, such as the Code Ypsilanti of 1780[6] and the Code Caragia of 1818 in Wallachia and the Code Callimachis of 1817 in Moldova, were composed.[7] During the 18th century, Greek became the language of government.[8] With the collections of customary law and legislative codes, the era of partial local codification was accomplished.[9] These written laws, which had an educational and didactical function, were the historical premise for the classification of Romania as a civil law system.[10]

---

1 *Weigend*, in: Smits (ed.), Elgar Encyclopedia of Comparative Law, p. 267.

2 *Gambaro/Sacco*, Sistemi Giuridici Comparati, p. 319. For more details see I.G.

3 *Gambaro/Sacco*, Sistemi Giuridici Comparati, p. 319.

4 *Gambaro/Sacco*, Sistemi Giuridici Comparati, p. 319.

5 *Bocşan*, in: Giaro (ed.), Modernisierung durch Transfer, p. 35.

6 *Zachariä*, Kritische Zeitschrift für Rechtswissenschaft und Gesetzgebung des Auslands, vol. 12. 1840, 411.

7 *Gambaro/Sacco*, Sistemi Giuridici Comparati, p. 319.

8 *Maksimovič*, in: Giaro (ed.), Modernisierung durch Transfer, p. 25.

9 *Gambaro/Sacco*, Sistemi Giuridici Comparati, p. 319.

10 *Bocşan*, in: Giaro (ed.), Modernisierung durch Transfer, p. 37.

By the end of the 19th century, Romania – independent and partially unified – was strongly influenced by France and its legislative codifications. French legislative models not only had an impact on civil law but also on criminal law. The first Romanian Penal Code (1864) was basically a translation of the *Code Napoléon* of 1810. The second Romanian Penal Code (1936), in turn, was strongly influenced by Italian doctrine and the *Codice Rocco* of 1930; this second Penal Code was modified and amended, more precisely adapted to the social changes and the "socialist legal order,"[11] and republished in 1948. Written law did not replace customary law entirely, however, until the second half of the 20th century.[12] During the 19th and early 20th centuries, Romanian criminal lawyers – most notably *Ioan Tanoviceanu* (1858–1917) and *Traian Pop* (1885–1960) – developed a Romanian doctrine of criminal law. The third Romanian Penal Code (1969) was influenced by the socialist criminal model. Since the fall of the communism in 1989, Romanian criminal law as well as the entire legal system can be classified as a civil law system. This can also be said of the new Penal Code adopted in 2009 (*Codul penal*, C.p.), which entered into force on 1 February 2014.

The evolution of the Romanian law of criminal procedure is similar to that of the substantive criminal law: The first Romanian Code of Criminal Procedure (1864) was based on the French *Code d'Instruction Criminelle* of 1808. The second Romanian Code of Criminal Procedure (1936) was influenced primarily by the Italian Code of Criminal Procedure *(Codice Rocco "di rito")* of 1930 and the Italian doctrine and was modified several times during the period 1936 to 1943.[13] The third Romanian Code of Criminal Procedure (1969) was influenced by the socialist model until the fall of communism in 1989. Like the new Penal Code, the current Code of Criminal Procedure (*Codul de procedură penală*, C.p.p.) entered into force on 1 February 2014. Romanian criminal procedure is inquisitorial in nature and can be classified as a civil law system. Characteristic of the inquisitorial system, investigation and trial are undertaken by one and the same institution; that is, the judge conducts the investigation; questions the accused, the witnesses, and the official experts in order to find the substantive truth; decides on the penalty; and declares the verdict.

---

[11] *Dianu*, in: Frankowski/Stephan (ed.), Legal Reform in Post-Communist Europe, p. 258.

[12] *Bocşan*, in: Giaro (ed.), Modernisierung durch Transfer, p. 39.

[13] *Dianu*, in: Frankowski/Stephan (eds.), Legal Reform in Post-Communist Europe, p. 265.

2. Effects of international ties

a) Membership in international and regional organizations

Romania is member of numerous international and regional organizations relevant to criminal law. In the following, some of the most important international and regional organizations are mentioned.

At the international level, Romania has been a member of the United Nations (UN) since 1955. It was a member of the Security Council in 1962, 1976–1977, 1990–1991, 2004–2005 and 2007–2009, a member of the Economic and Social Council (ECOSOC) in 1965–1967, 1974–1976, 1978–1980, 1982–1987, 1990–1998, and 2001–2003, and it is a member of a number of specialized agencies such as the UN High Commissioner for Refugees (UNHCR), the International Labour Organization (ILO), the UN Educational, Scientific and Cultural Organization (UNESCO), the World Health Organization (WHO), the International Bank for Reconstruction and Development (IBRD), and the International Monetary Fund (IMF).

In addition, Romania has been a member of the International Criminal Police Organization, also known as INTERPOL, since 1923. The INTERPOL National Central Bureau for Romania in Bucharest is made up of two units: the International Wanted Persons and Extradition Unit, which is responsible for the international search for wanted persons, extraditions, arrest warrants, and the transfer of convicted persons, and the Identification and Documentation Unit, which is responsible for organized crime, serious criminal offences, letters rogatory, identification of persons, identity and travel documents, and the identification of unidentified bodies.

Romania is a founding member of the Organization for Security and Co-operation in Europe (OSCE), which is the successor of the Conference on Security and Co-operation in Europe (CSCE) founded in the early 1970s. Since 2004, Romania has been a member of the political and military alliance North Atlantic Treaty Organization (NATO). Romania is not yet a member of the Organisation for Economic Co-operation and Development (OECD), but it has expressed its wish to join.

On a regional level, Romania has been a member of the Council of Europe since 1993, where it held the chairmanship of the Committee of Ministers in 2005–2006, and a member of the European Court of Human Rights (ECtHR) since 1994. Since 2007, Romania has been a member of the European Union. Romania also participates in a number of Black Sea regional organizations with a security focus. It is, for example, a member of the Southeastern Europe Brigade (SEEBRIG). SEEBRIG is responsible for stability and security in Southeastern Europe and routinely conducts exercises with NATO; in addition, it has assisted throughout the region with various engineering projects.[14] Romania founded, together with Albania, Armenia,

---

[14] *Moroney/Hogler*, The DISAM Journal, 2006, 28.

Azerbaijan, Bulgaria, Georgia, Greece, Moldova, Russia, Turkey, and Ukraine the Organization of the Black Sea Economic Cooperation (BSEC) in 1992, which was joined by Serbia at a later stage. The BSEC is a political and economic organization whose primary function is to foster interaction and harmony among its member states; it also serves the function of ensuring peace, stability, and prosperity in the Black Sea region. The BSEC obtained the status of observer in the UN General Assembly in 1999.

The objectives of the international and regional organizations often overlap, and this leads to cooperative actions: a key objective of both NATO and OSCE is to combat terrorism; an aim of NATO, OSCE, and BSEC is to improve border security and management; NATO, OSCE, and SEEBRIG promote defense and military reform.[15]

b) Signature and ratification of international treaties and conventions

Romania has signed and ratified a plethora of international treaties relevant to criminal law. Art. 11 of the Constitution deals with the relationship between international law and national law and states that the Romanian State pledges to fulfill its obligations deriving from treaties to which it is a party. International treaties ratified by Parliament, according to the law, are part of national law (Art. 11(2) Const.). If a treaty Romania is to become a party to contains provisions contrary to the Constitution, its ratification cannot take place until after the Constitution has been amended. (Art. 11(3) Const.). In the following, some of the most important international treaties relevant to criminal law in the fields of human rights law, international humanitarian law, terrorism, organized crime, drug trafficking, doping, and white collar crime are specified. The new Penal Code and the new Code of Criminal Procedure implemented many of the international treaties.

– *Human rights*

Romania signed the Convention for the Protection of Human Rights and Fundamental Freedoms (ECHR, 1950)[16] in 1993 and ratified it in 1994. In 1993, it signed the first Protocol to the Convention (1952), Protocols nos. 2–4 (1963), and Protocol no. 5 (1966); all five Protocols were ratified in 1994. It also signed Protocol no. 6 (1983), Protocol no. 7 (1984), Protocol no. 8 (1985), Protocol no. 9 (1990), and Protocol no. 10 (1992) in 1993; Protocols nos. 6–10 were ratified in 1994. (Protocol no. 10 has not yet entered into force.) Protocol no. 11 (1994) was signed and ratified in 1995; Protocol no. 12 (2000) was signed in 2000 and ratified in 2006; Protocol no. 13 (2002) was signed in 2002 and ratified in 2003; and Protocol no. 14

---

[15] *Moroney/Hogler*, The DISAM Journal, 2006, 31.

[16] All dates concerning conventions in parentheses are dates of opening for signature.

(2004) was signed in 2004 and ratified in 2005. Protocol no. 14 did not enter into force until 2010, following ratification by Russia. Protocol no. 15 (2013) was signed in 2013 and ratified in 2015. Protocol no. 16 (2013) was signed in 2014 but has not yet been ratified.[17]

Romania signed the International Covenant on Economic, Social and Cultural Rights (ICESCR, 1966) in 1968 and ratified it in 1974. It acceded to the Slavery Convention (1926) in 1957 and to the UN Convention against Torture and Other Cruel, Inhuman or Degrading Treatment or Punishment (1984) in 1990 and to the International Convention Against the Taking of Hostages (1979) in 1990.[18] In 2005, Romania signed the Council of Europe Convention on Action against Trafficking in Human Beings (2005) and ratified it in 2006. It signed the Council of Europe Convention on the Protection of Children against Sexual Exploitation and Sexual Abuse (2007) in 2007 and ratified it in 2011.

– *International humanitarian law*

In 1954, Romania acceded to the Convention for the Amelioration of the Condition of the Wounded and Sick in Armed Forces in the Field (Geneva Convention I, 1949), the Convention for the Amelioration of the Condition of Wounded, Sick and Shipwrecked Members of Armed Forces at Sea (Geneva Convention II, 1949), the Convention relative to the Treatment of Prisoners of War (Geneva Convention III, 1949), and the Convention relative to the Protection of Civilian Persons in Time of War (Geneva Convention IV, 1949). In 1990, it acceded to the Additional Protocol relating to the Protection of Victims of International Armed Conflicts (Protocol I, 1977) and the Additional Protocol relating to the Protection of Victims of Non-International Armed Conflicts (Protocol II, 1977).[19] Romania acceded to the Convention on the Prevention and Punishment of the Crime of Genocide (1948) in 1950 and signed the UN Convention on the Non-Applicability of Statutory Limitations to War Crimes and Crimes against Humanity (1968) in 1969 and ratified it in 1969.[20] Romania signed the International Convention Against the Recruitment, Use, Financing and Training of Mercenaries (1989) in 1990 but has not yet ratified it. In 1999, it signed the Rome Statute of the International Criminal Court (1998)

---

[17] Council of Europe Portal, http://www.coe.int/en/web/conventions/search-on-treaties/-/conventions/treaty/results/subject/3 [last visited March 2018].

[18] For the status of the ICESCR and the Torture Convention, see UNTC, Status of Treaties: Chapter IV (Human Rights); for the status of the Slavery Convention and the Hostage Convention, see UNTC, Status of Treaties: Chapter XVIII (Penal Matters) (https://treaties.un.org/Pages/ParticipationStatus.aspx?clang=_en [last visited March 2018]).

[19] For the status of the Geneva Conventions and Additional Protocols, see https://ihl-databases.icrc.org/applic/ihl/ihl.nsf/vwTreaties1949.xsp [last visited March 2018].

[20] For the status of the Genocide Convention and the War Crimes Convention, see UNTC, Status of Treaties: Chapter IV (Human Rights), https://treaties.un.org/Pages/ParticipationStatus.aspx?clang=_en [last visited March 2018].

and ratified it in 2002. Finally, it signed the Agreement on the Privileges and Immunities of the International Criminal Court (2002) in 2004 and ratified it in 2005.[21]

– *Terrorism*

Romania has acceded to numerous international counter-terrorism conventions that are deposited with the secretary-general of the UN,[22] including the Convention on the Prevention and Punishment of Crimes against Internationally Protected Persons, including Diplomatic Agents (1973) in 1978 and the International Convention against the Taking of Hostages (1979) in 1990. In addition, it signed the International Convention for the Suppression of Terrorist Bombings (1997) in 1998 and ratified it in 2004, the International Convention for the Suppression of the Financing of Terrorism (1999) in 2000 and ratified it in 2003, and the International Convention for the Suppression of Acts of Nuclear Terrorism (2005) in 2005 and ratified it in 2007.

Romania has also acceded to many multilateral anti-terrorism conventions that are deposited elsewhere, including the following: the Convention for the Suppression of Unlawful Seizure of Aircraft (1970) in 1972, which is deposited with the governments of the Russian Federation, the United Kingdom, and the United States of America; the Convention on Offenses and Certain Other Acts Committed on Board Aircraft (Tokyo Convention, 1963) in 1974, which is deposited with the secretary-general of the International Civil Aviation Organization; the Convention for the Suppression of Unlawful Acts against the Safety of Civil Aviation (1971) in 1975, which is deposited with the governments of the Russian Federation, the United Kingdom, and the United States of America.[23]

On a regional level, Romania signed the European Convention on the Suppression of Terrorism (1977) in 1995 and ratified it in 1997.[24] It also acceded to the Council of Europe Convention on the Prevention of Terrorism (2005) in 2007.[25]

---

[21] For the status of the Mercenaries Convention and Conventions surrounding the International Criminal Court, see UNTC, Status of Treaties: Chapter XVIII (Penal Matters), https://treaties.un.org/Pages/ParticipationStatus.aspx?clang=_en [last visited March 2018].

[22] For the status of conventions mentioned in this paragraph, see UNTC, Status of Treaties: Chapter XVIII (Penal Matters), https://treaties.un.org/Pages/ParticipationStatus.aspx?clang=_en [last visited March 2018].

[23] For the status of conventions mentioned in this paragraph, see ICAO, Status of Romania (Sept. 1999), www.icao.int/secretariat/legal/Status%20of%20individual%20States/romania_en.pdf [last visited March 2018].

[24] For the status of this convention, see https://www.coe.int/en/web/conventions/full-list/-/conventions/treaty/090/signatures?p_auth=WHduX8kz [last visited March 2018].

[25] For the status of this convention, see https://www.coe.int/en/web/conventions/full-list/-/conventions/treaty/196/signatures?p_auth=WHduX8kz [last visited March 2018].

These international conventions on terrorism have been implemented to a great extent in the new Penal Code. For example, mitigating circumstances *(circumstanţe atenuante)* are not applicable in cases of terrorism (Art. 75(1)(d) C.p.), extended confiscation *(confiscarea extinsă)* is applicable to acts of terrorism (Art. 112^1(1)(f) C.p.), and an offense relating to the establishment of an organized criminal group *(constituirea unui grup infracţional organizat)* has been created (Art. 367 C.p.).

– *Organized crime, drug trafficking, doping*

In order to combat organized crime, drug trafficking, doping, etc., Romania has acceded to several international conventions, such as the UN Convention against Illicit Traffic in Narcotic Drugs and Psychotropic Substances (1988) in 1993.[26] In 2000, it signed the UN Convention against Transnational Organized Crime (2000) and its two Protocols – the Protocol to Prevent, Suppress and Punish Trafficking in Persons, Especially Women and Children (2000) and the Protocol against the Smuggling of Migrants by Land, Sea and Air (2000); it ratified the Convention and the two Protocols in 2002. In 2004, Romania acceded to the Protocol against the Illicit Manufacturing of and Trafficking in Firearms, Their Parts and Components and Ammunition (2001), which also supplements the UN Convention against Transnational Organized Crime.[27] It signed the Convention on Cybercrime (2001) in 2001 on the very day it was opened for signature and was one of the first countries to ratify the Convention in 2004.[28] Romania signed the Council of Europe Convention on Laundering, Search, Seizure and Confiscation of the Proceeds from Crime and of the Financing of Terrorism (2005) in 2005 and ratified it in 2007.[29]

– *White collar crime*

While Romania has not yet acceded to the OECD Convention on Combating Bribery of Foreign Officials in International Business Transactions (1997), it signed the UN Convention against Corruption (2003) in 2003 and ratified it in 2004.[30] This international convention on white collar crime was implemented mainly in Arts. 289–292 C.p.

---

26 For the status of this convention, see UNTC, Status of Treaties: Chapter VI (Narcotic drugs and Psychotropic Substances), https://treaties.un.org/Pages/ParticipationStatus. aspx?clang=_en [last visited March 2018].

27 For the status of the Conventions against Organized Crime and Its Protocols, see UNTC, Status of Treaties: Chapter XVIII (Penal Matters), https://treaties.un.org/Pages/ParticipationStatus.aspx?clang=_en [last visited March 2018].

28 For the status of the Cybercrime Convention, see COE, https://www.coe.int/en/web/conventions/full-list/-/conventions/treaty/185 [last visited March 2018].

29 For the status of this convention, see COE, https://www.coe.int/en/web/conventions/full-list/-/conventions/treaty/198 [last visited March 2018].

30 For the status of the OECE Convention, see http://www.oecd.org/daf/anti-bribery/WGBRatificationStatus.pdf [last visited March 2018]; for the status of the Convention

– *Mutual legal assistance and judicial cooperation*

With respect to international conventions on mutual legal assistance and judicial cooperation in criminal matters, Romania signed the European Convention on Extradition (1957) in 1995 and ratified it in 1997. Other important international conventions signed and ratified by Romania in this regard are the European Convention on Mutual Assistance in Criminal Matters (1959), which was signed in 1995 and ratified in 1999 and the Council of Europe Convention on the Transfer of Sentenced Persons (1983), which was signed in 1995 and ratified in 1996.[31] With its accession to the European Union in 2007, it acceded to the European Arrest Warrant Framework Decision (2002), the Schengen Agreements (1985), the Convention Implementing the Schengen Agreement (1990), and the Europol Convention (1995).[32] It has implemented these international conventions mainly through Law no. 302/2004, republished in 2011,[33] on international judicial cooperation in criminal matters. Law no. 302/2004 applies to the following forms of mutual legal assistance and international judicial cooperation in criminal matters: extradition, surrender under a European arrest warrant, transfer of proceedings in criminal matters, recognition and enforcement of judicial decisions, transfer of sentenced persons, legal assistance in criminal matters, and other forms of international judicial cooperation in criminal matters (Art. 1 Law no. 302/2004). The main authorities for the realization of mutual legal assistance are the Ministry of Justice *(Ministerul Justiției)* with respect to requests formulated during the trial and execution phase, the office of the prosecutor of the High Court of Cassation and Justice *(parchetul de pe langă Inalta Curte de Casație si Justiție)* with respect to requests formulated during the investigation and criminal prosecution phase, and the Ministry of Internal Affairs *(Ministerul Administratiei si Internelor)* for requests referring to criminal records (Art. 10 Law no. 302/2004).

– *Other international conventions*

Romania signed the UN Convention on the Law of the Sea (UNCLOS, 1982) in 1982 and ratified it in 1996.[34] In 1994, it acceded to the Convention on International Trade in Endangered Species of Wild Fauna and Flora (CITES, 1973).[35]

---

against Corruption, see UNTC, Status of Treaties: Chapter XVIII (Penal Matters), https://treaties.un.org/Pages/ParticipationStatus.aspx?clang=_en [last visited March 2018].

[31] For the status of these COE conventions, see https://www.coe.int/en/web/conventions/full-list [last visited March 2018].

[32] Romania is a member state of Europol, see https://www.europol.europa.eu/partners-agreements/member-states/romania.

[33] Legea nr. 302/2004 privind cooperarea judiciara internationala in materie penala, republished 2011 in Monitorul Oficial, Part I no. 377/31 May 2011.

[34] For the status of the Convention on the Law of the Sea, see UNTC, Status of Treaties: Chapter XXI (Law of the Sea), https://treaties.un.org/Pages/ParticipationStatus.aspx?clang=_en [last visited May 2018].

Bibliography and further reading

Antonesco, Michel, La vie internationale de la Roumanie – Ses relations extérieures, son droit international public (International life of Romania – Its external relations, its international public law). In: Henri Lèvy-Ullmann/Boris Mirkine-Guetzévitch (eds.), La vie juridique des peuples (The legal life of peoples). Paris 1933, pp. 388–428.

Bocşan, Mircea-Dan, L'œuvre de codification – enjeu de la modernisation du droit roumain (The œuvre of codification – issue of modernization of Romanian law). In: Tomasz Giaro (ed.), Rechtskulturen des modernen Osteuropa, Bd. 1, Modernisierung durch Transfer im 19. und frühen 20. Jahrhundert (Legal cultures of modern Eastern Europe, vol. 1, Modernization through transfer in the 19th and early 20th centuries). Frankfurt am Main 2006, pp. 33–46.

Constantinesco, Léontin-Jean, Rechtsvergleichung. Die rechtsvergleichende Wissenschaft – Die theoretischen Grundlagen (Comparative law. The comparative legal science – Theoretical foundations), vol. III. Cologne 1983.

Delmas-Marty, Mireille, Les grands systèmes de politique criminelle (The grand systems of criminal policy). Paris 1992.

Dianu, Tiberiu, The Romanian criminal Justice system. In: Stanislaw Frankowski/Paul B. Stephan III (eds.), Legal reform in Post-Communist Europe. The view from within. Dordrecht 1995, pp. 257–273.

Gambaro, Antonio/Sacco, Rodolfo, Sistemi Giuridici Comparati (Comparative legal systems). 3d ed. Milanofiori Assago 2011.

Giaro, Tomasz, Modernisierung durch Transfer – Schwund osteuropäischer Rechtstraditionen (Modernization through transfer – Loss of Eastern European legal traditions). In: Tomasz Giaro (ed.). Rechtskulturen des modernen Osteuropa, Bd. 1, Modernisierung durch Transfer im 19. und frühen 20. Jahrhundert (Legal cultures of modern Eastern Europe, vol. 1, Modernization through transfer in the 19th and early 20th centuries). Frankfurt am Main 2006, pp. 275–344.

Glenn, Patrick H., Legal traditions of the world. Sustainable diversity in law. Oxford 2000.

Goga, Lucian, Politik und Rechtskultur der Zwischenkriegszeit in Rumänien (Politics and legal culture of the interwar period in Romania). In: Tomasz Giaro (ed.). Rechtskulturen des modernen Osteuropa, Bd. 2, Modernisierung durch Transfer zwischen den Weltkriegen (Legal cultures of modern Eastern Europe, vol. 2, Modernization through transfer between the World Wars). Frankfurt am Main 2007, pp. 31–68.

Jung, Heike, Recht und kulturelle Identität – Anmerkungen zur Rezeption, Transplantation und Diffusion von Recht (Law and cultural identity – Comments on the reception, transplantation and diffusion of law). ZStW 121 (2009), 467–500.

Legeais, Raymond, Grands systèmes de droit contemporains – Approche comparative (Grand systems of contemporary law – Comparative approach). Paris 2004.

---

[35] For the status of this convention, see CITES, https://www.cites.org/eng/disc/parties/chronolo.php [last visited May 2018].

Maksimovič, Kirill, Byzantinische Rechtsbücher und ihre Bedeutung für die Rechtsgeschichte Osteuropas (Byzantine law books and their significance for the legal history of Eastern Europe). In: Tomasz Giaro (ed.), Rechtskulturen des modernen Osteuropa, Bd. 1, Modernisierung durch Transfer im 19. und frühen 20. Jahrhundert (Legal cultures of modern Eastern Europe, vol 1, Modernization through transfer in the 19th and early 20th centuries). Frankfurt am Main 2006, pp. 1–32.

Moroney, Jennifer D.P./Hogler, Joe, Romania's role in the Black Sea region. The DISAM Journal, 2006, 27–34.

Pop, Traian, Drept penal comparat. Partea generală (Comparative criminal law. General part.). Cluj 1923.

Rinceanu, Johanna, Völkerstrafrecht in Rumänien (International criminal law in Romania). Berlin 2008.

Sacco, Rodolfo, Einführung in die Rechtsvergleichung (Introduction to comparative law). 2d ed. Baden-Baden 2011.

Weigend, Thomas, Criminal law and criminal procedure. In: Jan M. Smits (ed.), Elgar encyclopedia of comparative law. 2d ed. Cheltenham 2012, pp. 261–278.

Zachariä, E., Rechtsquellen in der Walachei (Sources of law in Walachia). Kritische Zeitschrift für Rechtswissenschaft und Gesetzgebung des Auslands 12 [1840], 408–434.

C. Constitutional parameters of criminal law

1. Supra-statutory rules as repositories of criminal law principles

– Constitution

Romania's first written constitution, adopted in 1866, consisted of 133 articles; it was – for the most part – a translation of the Belgian Constitution of 1831.[1] Art. 1 of the Constitution of 1866 proclaimed the establishment of one single, indivisible state, made up of the United Romanian Principalities *(Principatele Unite Române)*, to be known as Romania *(România)*. This constitution introduced representative governmental institutions and established numerous principles, such as those of sovereignty, hereditary monarchy, inviolability of the monarch, representative government, ministerial responsibility, separation of powers, and rigidity and supremacy of the constitution.[2] In addition, it proclaimed rights and freedoms of citizens, such as freedom of conscience, academic freedom, and freedom of association, of the press, and of assembly.[3] All citizens were equal before the law.[4] This constitution was amended three times: in 1879, 1884, and 1917.[5]

Due to social and political changes and territorial enlargement after the First World War, a second constitution was adopted in 1923. Romania became a constitutional monarchy. The second constitution illustrates the transformation of liberalism into neo-liberalism: state power was introduced in social life, individual property was limited in the interest of society, and the concept of citizen rights *(drepturile cetăţeneşti)* as a social function was introduced.[6] Several of the new principles introduced by this constitution include the recognition of a centralized state, universal suffrage and consolidation of a parliamentary democracy, institution of senators, the concept of property as a social function, engagement of the state for social protection, and the principle of legality.[7] Legislative power was entrusted to the king and Parliament, which consisted of a Senate and an Assembly of Deputies;[8] executive power was entrusted to the king;[9] and judicial power was entrusted to the central and local judicial organs.[10] The Constitution of 1923 recog-

---

1 *Ionescu*, Drept constituţional şi instituţii politice, vol. II, p. 36; *Selejan-Guţan*, The Constitution of Romania, p. 11. For the constitutional history of the years 1866 through 1938, see *Selejan-Guţan*, The Constitution of Romania, pp. 10–15.

2 *Ionescu*, Drept constituţional şi instituţii politice, vol. II, p. 36.

3 *Ionescu*, Drept constituţional şi instituţii politice, vol. II, p. 38.

4 Art. 10 Constitution of 1866.

5 *Ionescu*, Drept constituţional şi instituţii politice, vol. II, p. 44.

6 *Ionescu*, Drept constituţional şi instituţii politice, vol. II, p. 55.

7 *Ionescu*, Drept constituţional şi instituţii politice, vol. II, p. 56.

8 Art. 34 Constitution of 1923.

9 Art. 39 Constitution of 1923.

10 Arts. 101–107 Constitution of 1923.

nized rights and freedoms for all Romanian citizens, regardless of ethnicity, language, religion, or social class. The right to vote was expanded beyond the regulations of the Constitution of 1866: the Constitution of 1923 established a universal, equal, direct, compulsory, and secret vote for all male citizens beginning at the age of 21; it established furthermore that special laws should specify the conditions under which women could exercise political rights;[11] however, the right to vote for women was introduced only 16 years later, in 1939.

The third constitution was adopted in 1938.[12] It strengthened the principle of the supremacy of the king and abolished the separation of powers and a series of citizen rights and freedoms.

In the course of time, Romania experienced three additional constitutions, which by comparison with those of the era and policy which preceded them, were socialist:[13] the fourth constitution (1948),[14] the fifth constitution (1952),[15] and the sixth constitution (1965).[16] The Constitution of 1948 was the first communist constitution; it proclaimed the "Romanian People's Republic" *(Republica Populară Română)*. The Constitution of 1965 proclaimed the "Socialist Republic of Romania" *(Republica Socialistă România)*. The three socialist constitutions were marked by the abandonment of the separation of powers, the abandonment of political pluralism, the subordination of the entire organization of the state to a one-party system, the restriction of citizen rights and freedoms, and the subordination of the individual to the state.[17] These constitutions were influenced, among other things, by the pursuit of a policy of absolute class conflict *(luptea de clasă)*, by the broad use of the epithet "opponent of the working class" (which stigmatized persons so designated as opponents of the country's sole political party), and by the treatment of group interests as the social interests of the entire society.[18]

The political changes in 1989 led to the breakdown of socialism. Changes in the political system and in ideology necessitated a new constitution. The new Romanian Constitution (*Constituţia României*, Const.), which is still in force today, entered

---

[11] *Ionescu*, Drept constituţional şi instituţii politice, vol. II, p. 57–58; Art. 6 Constitution of 1923.

[12] Published in M. Of., no. 48/27 Feb. 1938. On the period of right-wing (partly royal) dictatorships from 1938–1944, see *Selejan-Guţan*, The Constitution of Romania, pp. 15–16.

[13] For an overview of the constitutional history of the socialist period, see *Selejan-Guţan*, The Constitution of Romania, pp. 17–19.

[14] Published in M. Of., no. 87 *bis*/13 Apr. 1948; *Zakrzewska*, Revue d'études comparatives Est-Ouest, vol. 9, 1978, no. 2, 151.

[15] Published in B. Of., no. 1/27 Sept. 1952; *Zakrzewska*, Revue d'études comparatives Est-Ouest, vol. 9, 1978, no. 2, 151.

[16] Published in B. Of., no. 1/21 Aug. 1965; *Zakrzewska*, Revue d'études comparatives Est-Ouest, vol. 9, 1978, no. 2, 151.

[17] *Ionescu*, Drept constituţional şi instituţii politice, vol. II, p. 83.

[18] *Ionescu*, Drept constituţional şi instituţii politice, vol. II, p. 83.

into force in 1991.[19] As a supra-statutory law, it embodies fundamental human rights and freedoms as well as principles concerning the organization and functioning of the powers of the state.

Pursuant to the Constitution of 1991, the individual is regarded as a citizen with human rights but also with obligations *vis-à-vis* the state. Fundamental rights *(drepturi fundamentale)* are defined as the "subjective" rights of citizens, that is, rights that are essential for their life, freedom, and human dignity and that are indispensable for the free development of the citizen's personality.[20] These fundamental rights are laid down in the new Constitution. At the same time, the new Constitution lays down fundamental obligations *(îndatori fundamentale)* of citizens *vis-à-vis* the state.[21] Fundamental rights together with fundamental obligations form the "juridic state" *(statutul juridic)* of the citizen.[22]

Since its entry into force, the Constitution has only been revised once, in 2003,[23] in order to meet the requirements of the European Union. It contains 156 articles divided into eight titles: Title I contains general principles *(Principii generale)* concerning, for example, the state, sovereignty, territory, unity of the people and equality among citizens, citizenship, the right to identity, pluralism, and political parties, national symbols, and the official language. Title II contains fundamental rights, liberties, and duties *(Drepturile, libertăţile şi îndatoririle fundamentale)*.[24] Title III establishes the public authorities *(Autorităţile publice)*. Title IV regulates the economy and public finance *(Economia şi finanţele publice)*. Title V provides for the Constitutional Court *(Curtea Constituţională)*. Title VI regulates Romania's integration into the European Union and NATO. Title VII regulates revisions of the Constitution *(Revizuirea Constituţiei)*. Accordingly, revisions may be initiated by the president of Romania on the proposal of the government, by at least one quarter of the number of Deputies or Senators, as well as by at least 500,000 citizens with the right to vote (Art. 150(1)). The proposal for revision must be adopted by the Chamber of Deputies and the Senate by at least two-thirds of the members of each Chamber (Art. 151(1)). Title VIII contains final and transitional provisions *(Dispoziţii finale şi tranzitorii)*.

---

19 For details concerning the Constitution, see I.A.4. and I.A.5.c.

20 *Muraru/Tănăsescu*, Drept constituţional şi instituţii politice, vol. I, pp. 147–148. For details about the fundamental rights in the Romanian Constitution, see *Selejan-Guţan*, The Constitution of Romania, pp. 216–230.

21 *Selejan-Guţan*, The Constitution of Romania, pp. 230–231.

22 *Muraru/Tănăsescu*, Drept constituţional şi instituţii politice, vol. I, p. 148.

23 Published in M. Of., no. 767/31 Oct. 2003.

24 See below 2.

– *Other supra-statutory rules*

As additional supra-statutory rules, international (human rights) conventions guarantee fundamental human rights and freedoms. International conventions are part of national law once they are ratified by Parliament (Art. 11 Const.).[25] All citizens enjoy not only the rights and freedoms granted them by the Constitution but also by other laws (Art. 15 Const.). By ratification of or accession to an international convention, Romania assumes its obligation to fulfill the rights and freedoms specified in these conventions. Constitutional provisions concerning citizen rights and freedoms must be interpreted and enforced in conformity with the Universal Declaration of Human Rights and with the covenants and other treaties to which Romania is a party (Art. 20 Const.).[26] Romania has signed and ratified the Convention for the Protection of Human Rights and Fundamental Freedoms (ECHR) as well as all Protocols thereto. It is also a party to the International Covenant on Economic, Social and Cultural Rights (ICESCR) and the International Covenant on Civil and Political Rights (ICCPR). These international conventions are part of national law and are a supra-statutory source of principles of criminal law and procedure.

2. Fundamental rights and freedoms and the criminal law

Under the Constitution, all citizens enjoy the rights and freedoms granted to them by the Constitution and other laws (Art. 15 Const.). The following fundamental rights, freedoms, and duties *(drepturile, libertăţile şi îndatoririle fundamentale)* are listed in the Constitution (Arts. 22–57):

- right to life and to physical and mental integrity (*dreptul la viaţă şi la integritate fizică şi psihică*, Art. 22),
- individual freedom (*libertatea individuală*, Art. 23),[27]
- right to defense (*dreptul la apărare*, Art. 24); this includes the right to a defense attorney in the criminal context,
- freedom of movement (*libera circulaţie*, Art. 25),
- personal and family privacy (*viaţa intimă, familială şi privată*, Art. 26),[28]
- inviolability of domicile (*inviolabilitatea domiciliului*, Art. 27),
- secrecy of correspondence (*secretul corespondenţei*, Art. 28),
- freedom of conscience (*libertatea conştiinţei*, Art. 29),[29]

[25] For details, see *Selejan-Guţan*, The Constitution of Romania, pp. 36–37.

[26] *Selejan-Guţan*, The Constitution of Romania, pp. 211–214.

[27] For details, see *Selejan-Guţan*, The Constitution of Romania, pp. 222–223.

[28] For details, see *Selejan-Guţan*, The Constitution of Romania, p. 223.

[29] For details, see *Selejan-Guţan*, The Constitution of Romania, pp. 221–222.

- freedom of expression (*libertatea de exprimare*, Art. 30),[30]
- right to information (*dreptul la informaţie*, Art. 31),[31]
- fight to education (*dreptul la învăţătură*, Art. 32),
- access to culture (*accesul la cultură*, Art. 33),
- right to protection of health (*dreptul la ocrotirea sănătăţii*, Art. 34),
- right to a healthy environment (*dreptul la mediu sănătos*, Art. 35),
- right to vote (*dreptul de vot*, Art. 36),
- right to stand for public office (*dreptul de a fi ales*, Art. 37),
- right to stand for election to the European Parliament (*dreptul de a fi ales în Parlamentul European*, Art. 38),
- freedom of assembly (*libertatea întrunirilor*, Art. 39),[32]
- right of association (*dreptul de asociere*, Art. 40),[33]
- labor and social protection of labor (*munca şi protecţia socială a muncii*, Art. 41),
- prohibition of forced labor (*interzicerea muncii forţate*, Art. 42),
- right to strike (*dreptul la grevă*, Art. 43),
- right to private property (*dreptul de proprietate privată*, Art. 44),[34]
- economic freedom (*libertatea economică*, Art. 45),
- right of inheritance (*dreptul la moştenire*, Art. 46),
- living standard (*nivelul de trai*, Art. 47),
- family (*familia*, Art. 48),
- protection of children and young people (*protecţia copiilor şi a tinerilor*, Art. 49),
- protection of disabled persons (*protecţia persoanelor cu handicap*, Art. 50),
- right of petition (*dreptul de petiţionare*, Art. 51),
- right of a person aggrieved by a public authority (*dreptul persoanei vătămate de o autoritate public*, Art. 52), and
- restriction on the exercise of certain rights or freedoms (*restrângerea exerciţiului unor drepturi sau al unor libertăţi*, Art. 53).[35]

---

30 For details, see *Selejan-Guţan*, The Constitution of Romania, pp. 218–219.

31 For details, see *Selejan-Guţan*, The Constitution of Romania, p. 220.

32 For details, see *Selejan-Guţan*, The Constitution of Romania, p. 220.

33 For details, see *Selejan-Guţan*, The Constitution of Romania, p. 220.

34 For details, see *Selejan-Guţan*, The Constitution of Romania, pp. 228–230.

35 For details, see *Selejan-Guţan*, The Constitution of Romania, pp. 214–216.

Art. 16 Const. enshrines the principle of equality before the law *(egalitatea în drepturi)*. Accordingly, all citizens are equal before the law and before public authorities, without any privilege or discrimination. No one is above the law.[36]

Constitutional provisions with reference to citizen rights and freedoms must be interpreted and enforced in conformity with international human rights law (Art. 20(1) Const.). If there are any inconsistencies between the covenants and treaties on fundamental human rights to which Romania is a party, on the one hand, and the national laws, on the other, the international regulations take precedence unless the national law is more favorable to the individual's rights (Art. 20(2) Const.).[37]

The exercise of certain rights or freedoms may be restricted if absolutely necessary for the defense of national security, of public order, health, or morals, of citizen rights and freedoms, or if absolutely necessary in order to conduct a criminal investigation or to prevent the consequences of a natural calamity, disaster, or an extremely severe catastrophe (Art. 53(1) Const.). Such restrictions must be proportional to the gravity of the situation, must be applied without discrimination, and may not affect the existence of the right or freedom in question (Art. 53(2) Const.).[38]

The Constitution lists the following duties (Arts. 54–57):

– loyalty to the country (*fidelitatea faţă de ţară*, Art. 54),
– defense of the country (*apărarea ţării*, Art. 55),
– financial contributions (*contribuţii financiare*, Art. 56),
– exercise of rights and freedoms (*exercitarea drepturilor şi a libertăţilor*, Art. 57).

3. Other supra-statutory norms relevant to criminal law and criminal procedure

In addition to the fundamental rights, freedoms, and duties listed in Arts. 22–57, the Constitution contains a number of supra-statutory norms relevant to criminal law and criminal procedure. For example, except for criminal or administrative laws more favorable, laws do not have retroactive effect but rather apply prospectively (Art. 15(2)).

Pursuant to constitutional rules on extradition and expulsion *(extrădarea şi expulzarea)*, no Romanian citizen may be extradited or expelled from Romania

36 For details, see *Valea*, Curentul Juridic (2013), 65–67.

37 *Selejan-Guţan*, The Constitution of Romania, pp. 211–214.

38 For details, see *Savenco*, 9 EIRP Proceedings (2014); *Selejan-Guţan*, The Constitution of Romania, pp. 214–216.

(Art. 19 Const.). In exceptional cases, Romanian citizens can be extradited on the basis of international agreements to which Romania is a party, subject to the law, and provided that there is reciprocity. Aliens and stateless persons may only be extradited on the basis of an international agreement or on terms of reciprocity. Expulsion or extradition is determined by the courts.[39]

Free access to the courts *(accesul liber la justiţie)* is guaranteed (Art. 21 Const.). All persons have access to the courts in order to defend their rights, freedoms, and legitimate interests. No law can restrict the right of free access to the courts. Parties are entitled to a fair trial and to have their cases resolved within a reasonable period of time.[40]

Other norms relevant to criminal law and criminal procedure are found in Art. 73 Const., which provides that organic laws regulate criminal offenses, penalties, and the execution thereof. Organic laws are special laws of great importance that regulate essential issues and that supplement the Constitution; the parliamentary majority required for their adoption is greater than that required for ordinary legislation. The right to a translator in criminal proceedings, free of charge, is guaranteed (Art. 128(4) Const.).

In addition to the Constitution, the Convention for the Protection of Human Rights and Fundamental Freedoms and its Protocols provide supra-statutory rights relevant to criminal law and criminal procedure, such as the prohibition of torture (Art. 3 ECHR), the right to liberty and security (Art. 5 ECHR), the right to a fair trial (Art. 6 ECHR), no punishment without law (Art. 7 ECHR), the right to an effective remedy (Art. 13 ECHR), the prohibition of imprisonment for debt (Art. 1 Protocol No. 4), the abolition of the death penalty (Art. 1 Protocol No. 6), the right to appeal in criminal matters (Art. 2 Protocol No. 7), and the right not to be tried or punished twice for the same offense (Art. 4 Protocol No. 7). The Convention for the Protection of Human Rights and Fundamental Freedoms is part of national law (Art. 11(2) Const.).

Bibliography and further reading

Balan, Marius, La souveraineté d'État et l'intégration européenne (The sovereignty of the state and European integration). In: Genoveva Vrabie (ed.), L'Évolution des concepts de la doctrine classique de droit constitutionnel (The evolution of the concepts of the classical doctrine of constitutional law). Iaşi 2008, pp. 33–54.

---

[39] *Valea*, Curentul Juridic (2013), 68.

[40] For details, see *Selejan-Guţan*, The Constitution of Romania, pp. 217–218; *Valea*, Curentul Juridic (2013), 67.

Balan, Marius, L'enjeu politique de la fidélité du juge envers la Constitution et la loi (The political challenge of the judge's loyalty to the Constitution and the law). In: Genoveva Vrabie (ed.), Le pouvoir judiciaire (The judiciary). Iaşi 2011, pp. 171–183.

Constantinescu, Mihai/Iorgovan Antonie/Muraru, Ioan/Tănăsescu, Elena Simina, Constituţia României revizuită – comentarii şi explicaţii (The Romanian Constitution reviewed – Commentaries and explanations). Bucharest 2004.

Dianu, Tiberiu, The Romanian Criminal Justice System. In: Stanislaw Frankowski/Paul B. Stephan III (ed.), Legal reform in post-Communist Europe. The view from within. Dordrecht 1995, pp. 257–273.

Duculescu, Victor, La réforme constitutionnelle en Roumanie et les exigences de l'intégration européenne (The constitutional reform in Romania and the requirements for European integration). Revue internationale de droit comparé 1–2004, 193–202.

Guţan, Manuel, Building the Romanian modern law – Why is it based on legal transplant? ACTA Universitatis Lucian Blaga 2005, pp. 130–143.

Iancu, Bogdan, Romania under EU influence: Note on the constitutive limits of external constitutional interventions. Romanian Journal of Political Science, vol. 12, no. 2, 2012, 53–76.

– Constitutionalism in Perpetual Transition: The Case of Romania. In: Bogdan Iancu (ed.), The Law/Politics Distinction in Contemporary Public Law Adjudication. Utrecht 2009, pp. 187–211.

Ifrim, Dumitru D., La Constitution, entre tradition et innovation (The Constitution, between tradition and innovation). Revue Roumaine des Sciences Juridiques. vol. VI (XXXIX), no. 1, 1995, 47–52.

Ionescu, Cristian, Drept constituţional şi instituţii politice – Curs sinteză (Constitutional law and political institutions – course synthesis). Bucharest 2012.

– Drept constituţional şi instituţii politice – Teoria generală a instituţiilor politice (Constitutional law and political institutions – General theory of political institutions), vol. I. Bucharest 2001.

– Drept constituţional şi instituţii politice – Sistemul constituţional românesc (Constitutional law and political institutions – The Romanian constitutional system), vol. II. Bucharest 2001.

Kerek, Angela, Verfassungsgerichtsbarkeit in Ungarn und Rumänien – Ein Vergleich der Verfassungsgerichtsbarkeiten zweier osteuropäischer Transformationsstaaten auf ihrem Weg zum konsolidierten Rechtsstaat (Constitutional jurisdiction in Hungary and Romania – A comparison of the constitutional jurisdiction of two eastern European transformational countries on their way to a consolidated constitutional state). Berlin 2010.

Lucian, Mihai, Constitutional Law of Romania. In: Stanislaw Frankowski/Paul B. Stephan III (ed.), Legal Reform in Post-Communist Europe. The View from Within. Dordrecht 1995, pp. 51–69.

Muraru, Ioan/Tănăsescu, Elena Simina, Drept constituţional şi instituţii politice (Constitutional law and political institutions), vol. II. 15th ed. Bucharest 2017.

– Drept constituţional şi instituţii politice. (Constitutional law and political institutions), vol. I. 15th ed. Bucharest 2016.

Parker, Jill, West meets East: A discussion of European Union enlargement and human rights. 11 Tulsa. J. Comp. & Int'l L. 603–640 (2003).

Pop, Traian, Drept penal. Întroducere. Chestiuni de istorie şi filosofie penală. Criminologie (Criminal law. Introduction. Questions of history and penal philosophy. Criminology), vol. I. Orăştie 1921.

Popescu, Corneliu-Liviu, La révision de la Constitution de la Roumanie (The revision of the Constitution of Romania). Revue Roumaine des Sciences Juridiques, vol. VI (XXXIX), no. 1, 1995, 53–67.

Razi, G.-M., La Constitution de la République populaire de Roumanie (The Constitution of the People's Republic of Romania). Revue internationale de droit comparé 1951, 262–298.

Rinceanu, Johanna, Völkerstrafrecht in Rumänien (International criminal law in Romania). Berlin 2008.

Savenco, Iulian, Restriction of Certain Rights and Freedoms in the Romanian Constitution. 9 EIRP Proceedings (2014), http://www.proceedings.univ-danubius.ro/index.php/eirp/article/view/1528/1404 [last visited March 2018].

Selejan-Guţan, Bianca, The Constitution of Romania: A Contextual Analysis. Oxford 2016.

Siani-Davies, Peter, Romanian revolution or coup d'état? A theoretical view of the events of December 1989. 29 Communist & Post-Communist Stud. (1996), 453–465.

Tănăsescu, Elena Simina, The constitutionalization of EU law in Romanian jurisprudence. In: Topidi Kyriaki/Alexander Morawa (ed.), Constitutional Evolution in Central and Eastern Europe. Burlington 2011, pp. 43–64.

– Roumanie – un système judiciaire entre formalisme excessif et excès de pouvoir (Romania – a judicial system between excessive formalism and abuse of power). In: Genoveva Vrabie (ed.), Le pouvoir judiciaire (The judiciary). Iaşi 2011, pp. 89–104.

Valea, Daniela Cristina, General principles of fundamental rights and freedoms in the light of the Romanian constitution, republished. Curentul Juridic (2013), 63–70, http://www.upm.ro/facultati_departamente/ea/RePEc/curentul_juridic/rcj13/recjurid134_7F.pdf [last visited March 2018].

Walsworth, Lynn M., Moving towards the rule of law: Romanian democracy and human rights. 44 U. New Brunswick L.J. 263–285 (1995).

Zakrzewska, Janina, Les révisions de la Constitution de la République socialiste de Roumanie (The revisions to the Constitution of the Socialist Republic of Romania). Revue d'études comparatives Est-Ouest vol. 9, 1978, no. 2, 151–169.

D. Fundamentals of criminal law

1. Functions of criminal law

Criminal law is marked, on the one hand, by an ongoing attempt to control human acts of aggression with an offensive character against social values and, on the other hand, by a corresponding attempt to control, humanize, and subordinate to the law the state's aggressive reaction to such acts.[1] This reaction, however, which takes the form of criminal sanctions, should always be the *ultima ratio*. The function of criminal law varies, depending on the criminal policy adopted by the state at any given point in time.[2] This is one of the reasons why there is no unanimous scholarly opinion on what the functions of criminal law are.[3] In the following, the main functions of contemporary Romanian criminal law are presented.

– Protective function

One of the main functions of criminal law is its protective function *(funcţia protectoare)*. On the one hand, criminal law protects essential social values *(protecţia valorilor sociale fundamentale)*, that is, values of the society as a whole, against criminal offenses; on the other hand, it protects the individual offender *(protecţia persoanei care a încălcat legea penală)* against a disproportionate reaction or abuse of power by the state. The protection of social values is based on the assumption that criminal law has a preventive aspect *(aspectul preventiv)* as well as a repressive aspect *(aspectul represiv)*. The preventive aspect, that is, the prevention of acts that could harm protected values, and the repressive aspect, that is, the punishing of individuals who have committed such acts, are considered to be intrinsically linked.[4]

The function of criminal law, however, consists not only in the protection of essential values of the society against criminal offenses but also in the protection of the individual offender against a disproportionate or abusive reaction by the state. The purpose of criminal law is not only to legitimate the state's prerogative to punish – it also serves to determine the conditions under which that prerogative may be exercised: The right to punish *(ius puniendi)* is not discretionary, as punishment can only be imposed within the limits of the law. The offender may not be obliged to submit to a punishment that is not foreseen by law, and he or she cannot be held criminally responsible for an offense committed by someone else. The punishment imposed may neither cause physical suffering nor may it be humiliating for the convicted person.

---

1 *Paşca*, Curs de drept penal – Partea generală, p. 8.

2 *Streteanu*, Tratat de drept penal – Partea generală, p. 3.

3 *Streteanu*, Tratat de drept penal – Partea generală, p. 3.

4 *Streteanu*, Tratat de drept penal – Partea generală, p. 6.

– *Educational function*

In addition to its protective function, criminal law also has an educational function *(funcţia educativă)*. Criminal law should motivate members of society to respect the social values protected by the law beyond the threat of criminal sanctions. The scholarship refers in this context to the symbolic effects *(efectele simbolice)* of criminal law or to a symbolic criminal law *(drept penal simbolic)*. Symbolic criminal law is characterized by its capacity to provide society with certain messages that appeal to the conscience of each individual and produce effects only on the level of conscience, beyond the protective function.[5] The educational function is, however, only a secondary or auxiliary one.[6]

– *Ultima ratio function*

According to the scholarship,[7] criminal law has a subsidiary character *(caracter subsidiar)*: Criminal norms are the *ultima ratio* and thus a last resort if other reactions are inadequate to protect social values. An intervention by way of criminal law is legitimated not solely by the importance of the protected social values but rather by the fact that recourse to criminal law for the protection of these social values is inevitable because other sanctions are impracticable or inefficient.[8]

2. Limits on criminal law imposed by the rule of law

The limits on the form and content of criminal law emanate from the rule of law *(stat de drept)*, which is anchored in various provisions of the Penal Code (*Codul penal*, C.p.) and the Constitution as well as in international and supranational laws.

Romania declares itself a democratic and social state, governed by the rule of law (Art. 1 para. 3 Const.). "Rule of law" is understood as a legal-political regime under which the law restrains the state and its authorities – legislative, executive, and judicial – by promoting certain individual liberties and creating order and predictability in terms of the administration of state matters. In the most basic sense, "rule of law is a system that attempts to protect the rights of citizens from arbitrary and abusive use of government power."[9] Additional limits on criminal law, including the principle of legality, the principle of personal responsibility, the principle of proportionality, and the principle of humanity are discussed in the following.

---

5 For details, see *Streteanu*, Tratat de drept penal – Partea generală, p. 7.

6 *Streteanu*, Tratat de drept penal – Partea generală, p. 7.

7 *Streteanu/Niţu*, Drept penal – Partea generală, p. 19.

8 *Streteanu*, Tratat de drept penal – Partea generală, pp. 16–17; *Streteanu/Niţu*, Drept penal – Partea generală, pp. 19–20.

9 *Roos*, in: Vukadinovic (ed.), Šipan Yearbook 2007, p. 2.

– *Principle of legality*

The principle of legality *(principiul legalităţii incriminării)* states that an individual can only be prosecuted and punished for a conduct that is defined by law as an offense that is under threat of penalty at the time it occurs.[10] As one of the most important restrictions of the *ius puniendi*, the principle of legality (i.e., *nullum crimen sine lege scripta, certa, stricta*, and *praevia*) is laid down in Art. 1 C.p. *(nullum crimen)* and Art. 2 C.p. *(nulla poena)* and is complemented by various articles in the Constitution (Arts. 15 (2), 23 (12), 126 (5), and 115 (6)). Moreover, it embodies an internationally recognized human right anchored in Art. 7 European Convention of Human Rights (ECHR) and Art. 15 International Covenant on Civil and Political Rights (ICCPR).

– *Principle of personal responsibility*

Criminal law is based on the principle of personal responsibility *(principiul răspunderii subiective)*, also known as the principle of culpability or *nulla poena sine culpa*. This principle can be deduced from Art. 15 C.p., which states that an "offense" is an act defined by criminal law that is committed culpably, is unjustified, and can be attributed to the person who committed the act. Culpability is a *conditio sine qua non* for the punishability of the offender. In other words, it is not enough to ascertain the completion of the objective side of an offense; rather, in order to attribute criminal responsibility, it must be ascertained that the person who acted was in fact culpable. Under the former penal code (in force until 31 January 2014), culpability was considered by a majority of scholars to consist of the psychological relationship between the offender and the act – the so-called psychological doctrine of culpability *(teoria psihologică a vinovaţiei)*. In contrast, the promoters[11] of the new Penal Code as well as more and more scholars are of the opinion that culpability may not be resolved in psychological categories but consists of blame *(reproş)* addressed to the offender's will-building process. Seen in this light, the principle of personal responsibility places a limit on criminal law.

– *Principle of proportionality*

The *principle of proportionality* governs the judicial individualization of punishment *(individualizarea pedepselor)* pursuant to Arts. 74–106 C.p. and is as such a limit on criminal law. General criteria for the judicial individualization of punishment include the limits of punishment specified in the special part of the Penal Code, the level of the social threat *(gradul de pericol social)* of the committed of-

[10] On the principle of legality in Romania, see in detail II.A.

[11] *Paşca*, Drept penal – Partea generală, p. 122.

fense, the offender, and the mitigating or aggravating circumstances relating to his or her criminal responsibility.

– *Principle of humanity*

An additional limit on criminal law is the principle of humanity, which is manifested in the principle of rehabilitation *(reabilitarea)* pursuant to Arts. 165–171 C.p. In accordance with these articles, punishment must be designed to rehabilitate the offender and may not to be used as an instrument of revenge by the state.

3. Purposes of punishment

The current penal code, which entered into force in 2014, does not provide a definition of punishment. However, the scholarship follows the definition of punishment that was provided in Art. 52 of the previous penal code. In this article, punishment was defined as a measure of constraint *(măsură de constrângere)* and a means of reeducation *(mijloc de reeducare)* of the convicted person. Its purpose was to prevent the commission of new offenses *(prevenirea săvârşirii de noi infracţiuni)* and to reestablish the legal order *(restabilirea ordinii de drept)*, thereby protecting both the state and its inhabitants.[12]

The commission of new offenses is prevented by imposing punishment on the offender, a step that simultaneously serves as a means of reeducation. "Special prevention" *(prevenţie specială)*, which applies to the specific offender, is supplemented by "general prevention" *(prevenţie generală)*, that is, by the abstract threat of punishment that applies to all members of society as the addressees of criminal norms.[13] As of late, there is an increased tendency to reconsider the retributive aspects of punishment.[14] In this respect, it can be said that the theory of punishment in Romania tends to include all relevant aspects of the main theories of punishment; in other words, it integrates retributive as well as general and special preventive aspects.

4. Fundamental principles of criminal procedure

The fundamental principles of criminal procedure, that is, the basic rules on which criminal procedure is based and which determine the entire structure of criminal procedure, are found primarily in the Constitution and in the Code of

---

12 *Hotca*, Codul Penal, pp. 628–629.

13 *Mitrache/Mitrache*, Drept penal român – Partea generală, pp. 189–190.

14 For a discussion on the aspects of punishment, see *Rotaru*, Fundamentul pedepsei.

Criminal Procedure (*Codul de procedură penală*, C.p.p.). However, a series of fundamental procedural principles is also established in Law no. 304/2004 of 28 June 2004 on the organization of the judiciary.

– *Due process and procedural safeguards for the accused*

The presumption of innocence *(prezumţia de nevinovăţie)* requires the prosecution – and hence the state – to prove the guilt of an accused person and relieves the accused of the burden of proving his or her innocence (Art. 23 (11) Const., Art. 4 C.p.p.).[15]

The principle of legality *(legalitatea procesului penal)* applies not only to substantive criminal law but also to the law of criminal procedure. In the domain of criminal procedure, it corresponds to the fundamental principle *nulla justitia sine lege* (no justice without law).[16] In this regard, Art. 23 (12) Const. stipulates that "[p]enalties shall be established or applied only in accordance with and on the grounds of the law" and Art. 2 C.p.p. stipulates that criminal trials must take place in accordance with the provisions of the law.

The right to a fair trial *(dreptul la un proces echitabil)* is another fundamental principle of criminal procedure. It is anchored in Art. 6 ECHR, which is directly applicable in Romania (Art. 11 (1) in conjunction with Arts. 20 and 21 (3) Const.).[17] Accordingly, all parties are entitled to a fair trial and to the resolution of their cases within a reasonable period of time *(termen rezonabil)*. As to the concept "within a reasonable time," no exact period of time is stipulated within which a case must be decided. However, the idea that justice should be done without delay so that its efficiency and credibility are not discredited leads to the speedy resolution of individual cases. This idea is also expressed in the phrase "justice delayed, justice denied" *(o justiţie întârzită, o justiţie negată)* and in the French "justice rétive, justice fautive" *(o justiţie lentă, o justiţie greşită)*.[18] In addition, Art. 10 Law no. 304/2004 stipulates that all persons are entitled to a fair trial and to the resolution of their cases within a reasonable period of time by an impartial, independent, and legally constituted court of law.

---

15 For details on the presumption of innocence, see *Tascu*, in: Universitatea Titu Maiorescu (ed.), International Conference: Law between modernization and tradition, pp. 944–947.

16 On the principle of legality, see II.A. See also *Neagu*, Tratat de procedură penală, pp. 73–76; *Theodoru*, Tratat de Drept procesual penal, p. 78; *Muraru/Tănăsescu*, Constituţia României, pp. 225–226.

17 For further details, see *Neagu*, Tratat de procedură penală, pp. 115–119; *Damaschin*, LESIJ no. XVIII, vol. 2/2011, 23–33; *Tascu*, in: Universitatea Titu Maiorescu (ed.), International conference: Law between modernization and tradition, pp. 943–944. See also I.B.2.b. and I.C.1.

18 *Muraru/Tănăsescu*, Constituţia României, pp. 181–182.

The right to a fair trial is supplemented by the right to an open, public trial *(dreptul la judecarea cauzei sale în mod echitabil, în mod public)* as well as by the right to a speedy trial (*în termen rezonabil,*[19] Art. 6 para. 1 ECHR). The right to a speedy trial is also anchored in Art. 21 (3) Const. and in Art. 10 Law no. 304/2004. The right to a fair trial is supplemented by the presumption of innocence (*prezumţia de nevinovăţie, in dubio pro reo,*[20] Art. 6 (2) ECHR, Art. 23 (11) Const.,[21] Arts. 4, 66 C.p.p.). Accordingly, everyone is presumed innocent until proven guilty by a final court decision.

The fundamental principle of the search for the truth *(principiul aflării adevărului)*[22] stipulates that a criminal trial must lead to the discovery of the truth with regard to the facts and circumstances of the case as well as with regard to the offender (Art. 5 C.p.p.). According to the principle of official investigation *(principiul oficialităţii),*[23] the investigation of criminal matters is a function of the state. Any acts necessary for carrying out a criminal trial must be performed *ex officio*, unless otherwise provided by law (Art. 7 C.p.p.). This requirement is supplemented by a plethora of articles in the Code of Criminal Procedure, of which only a few will be mentioned here. For example, after being informed of a complaint of an offense, the criminal investigation body *(organul de urmărire penală)* carries out, *ex officio*, the act of initiating the criminal investigation (Art. 305 C.p.p.). If the prosecutor *(procuror)* has returned the files to the criminal investigators, the latter must initiate or continue the criminal investigation. In accordance with the principle of mandatory prosecution, the prosecutor is required to bring a case against a suspect if the legal conditions for doing so are met (Art. 327 C.p.p.). The principle of the active role of the criminal investigation body *(rolul activ al organelor judiciare penale)* falls within the ambit of the principle of official investigation.[24] Accordingly, criminal investigators and courts must take an active part in the criminal trial in terms of initiating and conducting the criminal investigation.

The right to defense *(dreptul la apărare)*[25] is guaranteed (Art. 6 (3) ECHR, Art. 24 Const., Art. 10 C.p.p., Art. 15 Law no. 304/2004). The accused has the right to be assisted by a lawyer of his or her own choice or appointed *ex officio* throughout the entire trial. The judicial bodies must inform the suspect or the ac-

---

19 For details on the right to a speedy trial, see *Neagu*, Tratat de procedură penală, pp. 110–113.

20 For details on the presumption of innocence, see *Neagu*, Tratat de procedură penală, pp. 76–81; *Tascu*, in: Universitatea Titu Maiorescu (ed.), International conference: Law between modernization and tradition, pp. 944–947.

21 *Muraru/Tănăsescu*, Constituţia României, pp. 223–225.

22 *Neagu*, Tratat de procedură penală, pp. 81–84.

23 *Neagu*, Tratat de procedură penală, pp. 84–87.

24 *Neagu*, Tratat de procedură penală, pp. 87–89.

25 *Neagu*, Tratat de procedură penală, pp. 98–107; *Muraru/Tănăsescu*, Constituţia României, pp. 226–235.

cused before the hearing of the reason why he or she is under investigation and of the accusations made against him or her; the judicial bodies have to assure him or her of the possibility of defense.

Within the ambit of the right to defense falls the guaranteed right of the accused to the free assistance of an interpreter *(interpret gratuit)* if he or she does not understand or speak the language used in court.[26] A further fundamental principle of criminal procedure as far as language is concerned is the principle of conducting a criminal trial in Romanian (*limba română în care se desfăşoară procesul penal*, Art. 128(1) Const., Art. 12 C.p.p., Art. 14 Law no. 304/2004). Accordingly, legal proceedings are conducted in Romanian. Foreign citizens and stateless persons who do not understand or speak the language are entitled "to take cognizance of all the file papers and proceedings, to speak in court and draw conclusions, by means of an interpreter; in criminal law suits, this right is ensured free of charge" (Art. 128(4) Const.).

– *Principles relating to the judiciary and criminal justice administration*

The principle of equality of treatment during a criminal trial *(egalitatea persoanelor în procesul penal)*[27] stipulates that all accused persons are equally subject to the same rules of criminal procedure without any privilege or discrimination (Art. 16(1) and (2) Const.). No one is above the law. Additional aspects of the principle of equality of treatment include the statement that "[j]ustice shall be one, impartial, and equal for all" (Art. 124(2) Const.) and the statement that "[j]ustice shall be done according to the law, it is unique, impartial and equal for all" (Art. 2 Law no. 304/2004). Finally, "[a]ll citizens are equal before the law, without any privilege or discrimination" and "[j]ustice is done equally to all people, no matter what race, nationality, ethnic origin, language, religion, sex, sexual orientation, opinion, political orientation, fortune, origin, or social condition or of any other discriminatory criteria" (Art. 7 (1) and (2) Law no. 304/2004).

– *Other principles of criminal procedure*

The principle of respect for human dignity *(respectare demnităţii umane)*[28] stipulates that every person who is the subject of a criminal investigation must be treated respectfully with regard to human dignity (Art. 11 C.p.p.). Submitting someone to torture or to cruel, inhuman, or degrading treatment is punishable by law. Fur-

---

[26] *Muraru/Tănăsescu*, Constituţia României, p. 231; for details, see *Danisor*, Agora Int'l J. Jurid. Sci. 2013, 26–31.

[27] *Neagu*, Tratat de procedură penală, pp. 107–110; *Muraru/Tănăsescu*, Constituţia României, pp. 149–161.

[28] *Neagu*, Tratat de procedură penală, pp. 95–98.

thermore, no one may be subjected to torture or to any kind of inhuman or degrading punishment or treatment (Art. 22(2) Const.).

The principle of individual freedom *(garantarea libertăţii persoanei)*[29] specifies, among other things, that the individual freedom and security of a person are inviolable; the search, detention, or arrest of a person are permitted only in the cases and under the procedure provided by law; detention may not exceed 24 hours; preventive custody must be ordered by a judge and may only be imposed in the course of criminal proceedings; and a person in preventive custody has the right to apply for provisional release, under judicial control or on bail (Art. 23 Const.). The principle of individual freedom states that the freedom of a person is guaranteed throughout the entire criminal trial (Art. 9 C.p.p.).

Bibliography and further reading

Antoniu, George, Vinovăţia penală (Criminal guilt). 2d ed. Bucharest 2003.

– Vinovăţia, în perspectiva reformei penale şi a aderării la Uniunea Europeană (Guilt, in the light of the criminal reform and the accession to the EU). Revista de drept penal no. 2/2003, 9–28.

Avrigeanu, Tudor, Trăsăturile esenţiale ale infracţiunii. Sedes materiae (Essential characteristics of the infraction. Sedes materiae). Revista de drept penal no. 1/2010, 28–47.

Damaschin, Mircea, The juridical nature of the right to a fair trial. LESIJ no. XVIII, vol. 2/2011, 23–33.

Danisor, Diana-Domnica, The Right to a Fair Trial: The Role of the Translator-Interpreter in the Criminal Trial. Agora Int'l J. Jurid. Sci. 2013, 26–31.

– Guarantees specific to a fair trial in criminal matters. Harmonization of Jurisprudence. LESIJ no. XVII, vol. 1/2010, 72–83.

Deleanu, Ion, Instituţii şi proceduri constituţionale – în dreptul român şi în dreptul comparat (Constitutional institutions and procedures – in Romanian and comparative law). Bucharest 2006.

Dianu, Tiberiu, The Romanian Criminal Justice System. In: Stanislaw Frankowski/Paul B. Stephan III (eds.), Legal Reform in Post-Communist Europe. The View from Within. Dordrecht 1995, pp. 257–273.

Hotca, Mihai Adrian, Codul Penal – Comentarii şi explicaţii (Penal Code – Commentaries and explanations). Bucharest 2007.

Lauterwein, Carl Constantin, The Limits of Criminal Law – A Comparative Analysis of Approaches to Legal Theorizing. Farnham 2010.

Mitrache, Constantin/Mitrache, Cristian, Drept penal român – Partea generală (Romanian criminal law. General part). 8th ed. Bucharest 2010.

---

[29] *Neagu*, Tratat de procedură penală, pp. 90–95; *Muraru/Tănăsescu*, Constituţia României, pp. 211–226.

Muraru, Ioan/Tănăsescu, Elena Simina (eds.), Constituţia României – Comentariu pe articole (The Romanian Constitution – Annotation of Articles). Bucharest 2008.

Neagu, Ion, Tratat de procedură penală. Partea generală (Treatise on the law of criminal procedure. General part). 3d ed. Bucharest 2013.

Neagu, Ion/Mateuţ, Gheorghiţă/Damaschin, Mircea, Special procedural measures adopted and the observance of the human rights – Romania's report. Lex et Scientia, no. XV vol. 2/2008, http://lexetscientia.univnt.ro/archive/?dir=&download=2008_LESIJ_XV_2.pdf [last visited May 2018], pp. 7–43.

Paraschiv, Elena, Despre legitimitatea unor legi penale (About the legitimacy of some criminal laws). In: Gheorghe Bică/Doinel Dinuică/Gavril Paraschiv/Cezar Tită/Constantin Pletea/Elena Paraschiv/Dana Tită/Daniel Paraschiv (eds.), George Antoniu – in honorem: culegere de studii juridice (George Antoniu – in honorem: Collection of judicial studies). Craiova 2009, pp. 274–279, http://www.spiruharet.ro/facultati/drept-valcea/cercetare/65ea39eacdb9b8d9fbf5423de35ee20c.pdf [last visited May 2018].

Paşca, Viorel, Drept penal. Partea generală (Criminal law. General part). Bucharest 2014.

Rinceanu, Johanna, Analiza trăsăturilor esenţiale ale infracţiunii în legea penală română (Analysis of the essential characteristics of the infraction in Romanian criminal law). Revista de drept penal no. 1/2010, 14–27.

Roos, Stefanie Ricarda, The "Rule of Law" as a Requirement for Accession to the European Union. In: Lidija Cehulic Vukadinovic (ed.), Šipan Yearbook 2007, pp. 1–13, http://www.kas.de/wf/doc/kas_15604-544-1-30.pdf [last visited May 2018].

Rotaru, Cristina, Fundamentul pedepsei. Teorii moderne (Fundamentals of punishment. Modern theories). Bucharest 2006.

Streteanu, Florin, Proiectul noului Cod penal şi reconfigurarea teoriei infracţiunii în dreptul român (Project of the new Penal Code and reconfiguration of the theory of the infraction within Romanian law). CDP 2/2009, 50–57.

– Tratat de drept penal – Partea generală (Treatise on criminal law – General part), vol. 1. Bucharest 2008.

Streteanu, Florin/Niţu, Daniel, Drept penal – Partea generală. Curs universitar (Criminal law – General part), vol. 1. Bucharest 2014.

Tascu, Simona-Elena, Right to a Fair Trial in Criminal Matter. Presumption of Innocence. In: Universitatea Titu Maiorescu (ed.), International Conference: Law between modernization and tradition. Implications for the legal, political, administrative and public order organization. Bucharest 2015, pp. 943–948.

Theodoru, Grigore, Tratat de Drept procesual penal (Treatise on criminal procedural law) 3d ed. Bucharest 2013.

E. Nature, form, and boundaries of criminal law

1. Nature and form of criminal law

There is no legal definition of criminal law in the new Penal Code, which entered into force on 1 February 2014. The previous penal code, however, defined the purpose of criminal law *(scopul legii penale).* According to this definition, the objective of criminal law was to protect Romania (its sovereignty, independence, unity, and indivisibility), the individual and his or her rights, freedoms, and property, as well as the entire legal order against offenses (Art. 1 C.p. 1969).[1] Although this definition was not retained in the current penal code, the doctrine follows the definition as it appeared in the former code.

– *Definition*

Drept penal – penal law – derives from the Latin word "directus," which means right, straight, or straightforward.[2] The legal literature also uses as a synonym for *drept penal* the term *drept criminal* – criminal law – which derives from the Latin word "crimen," meaning accusation or crime.[3] There is, however, no single definition of criminal law accepted by all scholars. In 1912, *Ioan Tanoviceanu*, an eminent criminal lawyer and father of Romanian criminal law doctrine, analyzed various definitions of criminal law, including those of *Joseph-Louis-Elzéar Ortolan, Immanuel Kant, Paul Johann Anselm von Feuerbach*, and *Francesco Carrara. Tanoviceanu* criticized *Ortolan's* definition for the idea that society should be able to punish an individual for all kinds of violation of law; in his opinion, society should rather be able to punish only for grave violations.[4] He criticized *Kant's* definition because it considered penalization a right – exercised in accordance with a "vocation" – but not a duty of the sovereign.[5] His main objection to the *Feuerbach* and *Carrara* definitions of criminal law is that they, too, ultimately, consider penalization a right or a "vocation" of the sovereign rather than its social obligation.[6] *Tanoviceanu* defines criminal law as that part of public law that deals with "infractions" and with penalties that must be imposed on offenders.[7] *Traian Pop*, also an eminent Romanian criminal lawyer, finds *Tanoviceanu's* definition too narrow, as "penalty" in the strict sense means only "repressive measure" whereas criminal law

---

[1] On the purpose of criminal law, see I.D.3. and *Babu*, 4 Contemp. Readings L. & Soc. Just. (2012), 595–598.

[2] *Paşca*, Drept penal. Partea generală, p. 11.

[3] *Paşca*, Drept penal. Partea generală, p. 11.

[4] *Tanoviceanu*, Curs de drept penal, vol. I, p. 2.

[5] *Tanoviceanu*, Curs de drept penal, vol. I, p. 2.

[6] *Tanoviceanu*, Curs de drept penal, vol. I, pp. 2–3.

[7] *Tanoviceanu*, Curs de drept penal, vol. I, p. 3.

encompasses not only repressive measures but also other kinds of measures for social protection.[8] *Pop*, in 1921, defined criminal law in the strict sense as "law that deals with antisocial acts, avowed 'infractions,' and means of social defense against such antisocial acts."[9] In the same year, however, *Pop* extended his definition to include procedural, penological, and correctional aspects. Correspondingly, criminal law in the wider sense comprises rules according to which the criminal justice system functions in order to prosecute offenses and execute punishments.[10]

There is a plethora of definitions of criminal law by current scholars. Some of these are based on older definitions; others are newly created. According to a more recent definition, criminal law is a collection of norms that criminalizes offenses and punishes dangerous acts against social values with the goal of protecting those values, either by preventing the commission of offenses or by punishing those who have committed them.[11]

– *Classification*

All branches of law can be categorized either as public law *(dreptul public)* or as private law *(dreptul privat)*. Public law, which deals with the relationship between the state and individuals, is characterized by a hierarchical system of superiority and subordination. Private law, in contrast, which regulates the relationship between individuals, is characterized by equality. Criminal law belongs to the realm of public law, alongside administrative law and constitutional law.[12] Administrative law is the law that governs the essential tasks of the state; constitutional law encompasses all norms that address the organization of the state; and criminal law is the law through which the government exercises its repressive power.

With regard to the duration of the law, criminal law can be categorized as permanent criminal laws *(legi penale permanente)*, temporary criminal laws *(legi penale temporare)*, ordinary criminal laws *(legi penale ordinare)*, and exceptional criminal laws *(legi penale excepţionale)*.

– *Components of criminal law*

Criminal law in a broader sense is composed of substantive criminal law *(dreptul penal)* and the law of criminal procedure *(dreptul procesual penal)*. Substantive criminal law specifies the requirements of criminal liability, that is, the elements of

---

[8] *Pop*, Drept penal. Întroducere, vol. I, p. 3.

[9] *Pop*, Drept penal. Întroducere, vol. I, p. 4.

[10] *Pop*, Drept penal. Întroducere, vol. I, p. 5.

[11] See *Bulai/Bulai*, Manual de drept penal, p. 7; *Streteanu*, Tratat de drept penal, vol. I, p. 2.

[12] *Paşca*, Drept penal. Partea generală, p. 14.

an offense, and the legal consequences. It is mainly regulated in the Penal Code as well as in numerous secondary or ancillary laws *(legi penale complimentare)*. The law of criminal procedure comprises the legal norms concerning the formal course of the criminal procedure as well as the enforcement of judgments *(executarea hotărârilor penale)*. It is mainly regulated in the Code of Criminal Procedure (*Codul de procedură penală*, C.p.p.).[13] The Penal Code, the Code of Criminal Procedure and Law no. 254/2013 on law enforcement *(legea privind executarea pedepselor)*,[14] taken together, are considered criminal law in a broader sense.

– *Location*

The Penal Code is the main source of criminal law. Other sources of criminal law are the Constitution, ancillary laws *(legi penale complimentare)*, such as the law on international judicial cooperation in criminal matters,[15] special criminal laws *(legi speciale penale)*, such as the law on preventing and combating trafficking and illicit drug use,[16] and non-criminal laws that contain penal provisions *(legi nepenale care conţin dispoziţii penale)*. Environmental law is an example of a non-criminal law that contains penal provisions. International treaties and conventions become a source of criminal law as soon as they are ratified.[17]

– *Legal disciplines related to criminal law*

A number of legal disciplines are related to criminal law. They include criminology *(criminologia)*;[18] penology *(penologia)*, which is the study of the punishment of crime in both its deterrent and its reformative aspects; criminalistics *(criminalistica)*; legal medicine *(medicina legală)*;[19] judicial psychology *(psihologia judiciară)*; and scientific police law *(poliţia ştiinţifică)*.[20]

---

13 For an overview over the law of criminal procedure, see II.D.4.

14 Legea nr. 254/2013 privind executarea pedepselor şi a măsurilor privative de libertate dispuse de organele judiciare în cursul procesului penal.

15 Legea nr. 302/2004 privind cooperarea judiciara internationala in materie penala.

16 Legea nr. 143/2000 privind prevenirea şi combaterea traficului şi consumului ilicit de droguri.

17 For details, see I.F.2.

18 On criminology in Romania, see *Simion*, 2 Rivista di Criminologia, Vittimologia e Sicurezza (2008), 78–87; on the development of Romanian criminology in the 19th century, see *Constantinescu*, 19 Philobiblon (2014), 194–217.

19 On forensic medicine in Romania, see *Scripcaru* et al., 5 Int'l J. Med. Dentistry (2015), 20–22. *Dettmeyer/Jung*, Rechtsmedizin 27 (2017), 124–126.

20 *Mitrache/Mitrache*, Drept penal român, pp. 30–31.

2. Boundaries between criminal law and other areas of law with a criminal or quasi-criminal function

Criminal law is not the only area of law with a repressive function. The imposition of administrative, disciplinary, and civil sanctions can also have a repressive and therefore a quasi-criminal function.

– *Nature of sanction*

A criterion that distinguishes criminal law from other areas of law with a quasi-criminal function is the nature of the sanction. The law recognizes two types of sanctions: penal or punitive sanctions, which are part of criminal law, and other types of sanctions (e.g., administrative, disciplinary, and civil), which are not.[21]

- Penal or punitive sanctions

The punitive sanctions of the criminal law are based on culpability. Primary punitive sanctions are known as punishments; the two categories of so-called additional punitive sanctions are educational measures *(măsurile educative)* and security measures *(măsurile de siguranță)*.

Punishments that can be imposed on natural persons include main penal sanctions (*pedepsele principale*, Art. 53 C.p.), complementary penal sanctions (*pedepsele complementare*, Art. 55 C.p.), and accessory penal sanctions (*pedepsele accesorie*, Art. 54 C.p.). There are three kinds of main penal sanctions: life sentence *(detențiune pe viață*, Arts. 56–59 C.p.), term imprisonment *(închisoare*, Art. 60 C.p.), and fine *(amenda*, Arts. 61–64 C.p.). There are three kinds of complementary penal sanctions: the ban on the exercise of certain rights *(interzicerea unor dreptur*, Arts. 66–68 C.p.), military demotion *(degradarea militară*, Art. 69 C.p.), and publication of the final judgment (*publicarea hotărârii definitive de condamnare*, Art. 70 C.p.). Finally, there is one kind of accessory penal sanction: ban on the exercise of the rights anchored in Art. 66 C.p. (*interzicerea unor dreptur*, Art. 65 C.p.)[22] Main penal sanctions are punitive in character whereas complementary and accessory penal sanctions are primarily preventive or remedial in character. Accessory penal sanctions can be imposed in addition to main penal sanctions.[23]

Educational measures (*măsurile educative*, Art. 115 C.p.) are generally imposed on minors ages 14, 15, 16 and 17 (Art. 114(1) C.p.) if it can be shown that they had criminal capacity when they committed the offense. There are two types of educational measures: non-custodial *(măsurile educative neprivative de libertate)*, such

---

[21] *Fodor*, Fiat Iustitia, no. 1/2007, 2; *Bulai*, Manual de drept penal, pp. 278–279.

[22] For details, see I.A.5.d.

[23] *Fodor*, Fiat Iustitia, no. 1/2007, 2.

as a civic traineeship, supervision, curfew on weekends, and assistance on a daily basis, and custodial *(măsurile educative privative de libertate)*, such as referral to an educational center and referral to a detention center.[24]

Security measures (*măsurile de siguranţă*, Arts. 107–112¹ C.p.) are criminal sanctions that are imposed in addition to a punishment or an educational measure. Their aim is to eliminate a state of danger or to prevent the perpetration of criminal acts.[25] Security measures include the obligation to undergo medical treatment, referral to a medical facility, a ban on employment in or practice of a certain profession, special confiscation, and extended confiscation (Art. 108 C.p.).

• Administrative sanctions

Administrative law provides for the imposition of administrative sanctions for administrative infringements or contraventions *(contravenţii)*. There are two types of administrative sanctions: contraventional sanctions *(sancţiuni contravenţionale)* and other administrative sanctions.[26] The former are regulated by Government Ordinance no. 2/2001.[27] Art. 5 thereof specifies main and complementary contraventional sanctions:

Art. 5 Gov. Ord. no. 2/2001[28]

(1) Contraventional sanctions are main and complementary sanctions.

(2) Main contraventional sanctions are:

a) warning;

b) contraventional fine;

c) performance of an activity for the collective.

(3) Complementary contraventional sanctions are:

a) confiscation of goods intended for, used or arisen from contraventions;

b) adjournment or annulment, as the case may be, of the approval, agreement, or the permit of exercising an activity;

c) closure of a unity;

d) blocking of a banking account;

e) adjournment of the activity of a salesman *(agent economic)*;

f) retraction of a license or an approval for certain operation or for foreign trade activities, temporarily or definitively;

g) dissolution of work and return to the initial status.

(4) Other main or complementary sanctions can be regulated by special laws.

---

24 For details, see I.A.5.d.

25 For details, see I.A.5.d.

26 *Fodor*, Fiat Iustitia, no. 1/2007, 2.

27 Gov. Ord. no. 2/12 July 2001, published in M. Of. no. 410/ 25 July 2001.

28 Translation by the author.

(5) The stipulated sanction has to be proportionate to the degree of social danger of the committed offense.

(6) Complementary sanctions are applied in accordance with the nature and the gravity of the offense.

(7) For one and the same contravention, one can apply only one main contraventional sanction and one or more complementary sanctions.

Other administrative sanctions include administrative fines, surcharges, and the removal of an illegally obtained advantage.[29] Administrative sanctions can be imposed in addition to a penal sanction.

- Disciplinary sanctions

Labor Law provides for the dismissal *(concedierea)* of an employee by an employer as a disciplinary sanction for grave malfeasance, grave malpractice, and against repeated malfeasance concerning labor rules.[30]

- Civil sanctions

The most important civil sanctions are the contractual penalty (*clauza penală*, Arts. 1538–1546 *Codul civil*, C.civ.) and the absolute nullity *(nulitatea absolută)* or relative nullity *(nulitatea relativă)* of contracts (Arts. 1246–1248 C.civ.).

– Sanctioning body

The body imposing the sanctions is a further criterion that distinguishes criminal law from other areas of law with a quasi-criminal function. Penal or punitive sanctions are imposed by a criminal court, whereas contraventional sanctions are generally imposed by an administrative authority.[31] Disciplinary sanctions are generally imposed by private persons or by public entities acting as private persons; civil sanctions are likewise imposed by private persons.

– Subject of sanctions

The question of who (or what) can be the subject (or addressee) of a sanction is no longer a distinguishing criterion between criminal law and other areas of law with a quasi-criminal function. Both natural persons as well as legal entities can be the subject of penal or punitive sanctions as well as of contraventional sanctions (in

---

[29] *Fodor*, Fiat Iustitia, no. 1/2007, 5.

[30] For more details, see *Beligrădeanu*, Competența statornicirii regulilor referitoare la cercetarea disciplinară obligatorie, pp. 67–79 and *Cosma*, 10 J. Crim. Investigations (2016), 25–32.

[31] *Fodor*, Fiat Iustitia, no. 1/2007, 5.

2006, Law no. 278[32] introduced legal norms establishing the criminal responsibility of legal entities[33]).

– Means of appeal

Penal or punitive sanctions can be contested in criminal courts, administrative sanctions in administrative courts, and disciplinary sanctions and civil sanctions in civil courts.

– Judicial safeguards

The most important judicial safeguards are anchored in the Constitution and are therefore equally applicable to criminal law, administrative law, and civil law. They include the principle of non-retroactivity and the *lex mitior* principle *(legea mai favorabilă)*, which state that "[t]he law shall only act for the future, except for the more favorable criminal or administrative law" (Art. 15(2) Const.);[34] the principle of equality *(egalitatea în drepturi)*, according to which all "[c]itizens are equal before the law and public authorities, without any privilege or discrimination" (Art. 16(1) Const.); free access to justice *(accesul liber la justiţie)*, according to which "[e]very person is entitled to bring cases before the courts for the defense of his legitimate rights, liberties, and interests." (Art. 21(1) Const.); the fair trial principle *(proces echitabil)*, which provides that "[a]ll parties shall be entitled to a fair trial and a solution of their cases within a reasonable period of time (Art. 21(3) Const.); and the right to defense *(dreptul la apărare*, Art. 24(1) Const.).[35]

Additional safeguards include the principle of legality *(principiul legalităţii incriminării)*,[36] which has separate regulations for criminal matters (Arts. 2 and 10–16 C.p.) and administrative matters (Gov. Ord. no. 2/2001). The application of the *ne bis in idem* principle in the context of administrative law is limited when compared to its application in the criminal law context.[37] If an illicit form of conduct constitutes concurrently a criminal offense and an administrative offense, it can be sanctioned only as one or the other.[38] However, if an illicit form of conduct is punished with a main criminal sanction, a complementary contraventional sanction may also be imposed.[39]

---

32 Published in M. Of. no. 601 of 12 July 2006.

33 See *Rinceanu*, in: Fiorella/Stile (eds.), Corporate criminal liability and compliance programs, pp. 387–405. On corporate criminal liability, see II.F.

34 For an English translation of the Constitution, see http://www.cdep.ro/pls/dic/site.page?id=339&idl=2 [last visited March 2018].

35 For details, see I.C.

36 For details, see II.A.

37 *Fodor*, Fiat Iustitia, no. 1/2007, 9.

38 *Fodor*, Fiat Iustitia, no. 1/2007, 9.

39 *Fodor*, Fiat Iustitia, no. 1/2007, 9.

3. Special regimes connected to the status of the offender

– *Juvenile offenders*

Minors *(minori)* under the age of 14 cannot be held criminally liable according to the Penal Code.[40] In exceptional cases, minors ages 14 and 15 years can be held criminally liable if it is proven by an expert that the offense was committed with the requisite discernment *(discernământ)*. Juveniles ages 16 and 17 years can be held criminally liable (Art. 113 C.p.).[41] The Penal Code contains special provisions for juvenile offenders (Arts. 113–134). This special regime provides for educational measures (*măsurile educative*, Art. 115 C.p.), such as civic traineeship *(stagiul de formare civică)*, supervision *(supravegherea)*, curfew on weekends *(consemnarea la sfârşit de săptămână)*, assistance on a daily basis *(asistarea zilnică)*, referral to an educational center *(internarea într-un centru educativ)* and referral to a detention center *(internarea într-un centru de detenţie)*.[42] Important considerations in choosing a sanction for a juvenile offender are the degree of the social danger of the committed offense, the intellectual and moral development of the juvenile, as well as the conditions in which he or she grew up.[43]

– *Recidivists*

The Penal Code provides a special regime for recidivists *(recidivă*, Arts. 41–43). Art. 41 C.p. defines the circumstances under which an offender will be considered a recidivist, namely, an offender who commits an offense with direct intent *(intenţie)* or conditional intent *(intenţie depăşită)* after he or she was already sentenced to at least one year imprisonment by a final decision. The newly committed offense must be subject to at least one year imprisonment (Art. 41 C.p.). Juvenile offenses, offenses of negligence, amnestied offenses, and acts that are no longer offenses are not taken into consideration in the determination of whether a person is a recidivist (Art. 42 C.p.). Recidivists are punished more severely than non-recidivist offenders.[44]

---

40 For an extensive account, see *Păroşanu*, Jugendstrafrecht in Rumänien.

41 See II.J.6.

42 For details, see I.A.d.; see also *Puscasu*, Challenges of the Knowledge Society, pp. 115–123; *Ioan* et al., Revista medico-chirurgicală a Societă ţii de Medici şi Naturalişti din Iaşi 119, no. 1 (2015), 211–212.

43 *Gheorghe/Sandu*, in: Bică et al. (eds.), George Antoniu in honorem, p. 176.

44 For more details, see *Simionescu*, 2011 Annals Constantin Brancusi U. Targu Jiu Juridical Sci. Series (2011), 149–162.

– Offenders who are mentally ill or addicted to drugs

For offenders who are mentally ill or addicted to drugs,[45] the Penal Code provides two security measures *(măsurile de siguranţă)*, namely, the obligation to undergo medical treatment *(obligarea la tratament medical*, Art. 109) and commitment to a hospital *(internarea medicală*, Art. 110). Both measures have a medical-curative character with the goal of healing the offender or at least ameliorating his or her pathological condition.[46] Both measures can be imposed on their own as a stand-alone sanction or in addition to a main penal sanction.[47] The manner of medical treatment is determined by a physician.

– Sex offenders

The Penal Code contains numerous sex offenses (*infracţiuni contra libertăţii şi integrităţii sexuale*, Arts. 218–223), such as rape *(violul)*, sexual aggression *(agresiunea sexuală)*,[48] sexual intercourse with a minor *(actul sexual cu un minor)*,[49] sexual corruption of minors *(coruperea sexuală a minorilor)*, recruitment of minors for sexual purposes *(racolarea minorilor în scopuri sexuale)*, and sexual harassment *(hărţuirea sexuală)*.[50] The Penal Code does not, however, provide a special regime for sex offenders.

Bibliography and further reading

Babu, Vasile, Criminal Policy in Constitutional Democracy – Terminology and Concept. 4 Contemp. Readings L. & Soc. Just. (2012), 595–598.

Bulai, Costică/Bulai, Bogdan, Manual de drept penal. Partea generală (Handbook of criminal law. General part). Bucharest 2007.

Bulai, Costică/Bulai, Bogdan Nicolae, Minoritatea (Minority), Arts. 113–134. In: Antoniu George/Toader Tudorel (eds.), Explicaţiile noului cod penal (Explanations of the new Penal Code), vol. II: Articles 53–187. Bucharest 2015, pp. 336–378.

Constantinescu, Gabriel, Criminology and Modernization in Romania during the Second Half of the Nineteenth Century. 19 Philobiblon (2014), 194–217.

---

45 See II.J.7.

46 *Paşca*, Drept penal. Partea generală, p. 461.

47 *Paşca*, Drept penal. Partea generală, pp. 462 and 464.

48 For details, see *Vidrighin*, 2013 Acta Universitatis Lucian Blaga, pp. 222–233.

49 For details, see *Radu*, 20 Valahia University Law Study (2012), 47–52.

50 For details, see *Radu*, 58 Curentul Juridic – Juridical Current (2014), 79–86.

Cosma, Camelia Valentina, Public Dismissal – Disciplinary Sanctions. 10 J. Crim. Investigations (2016), 25–32.

Dettmeyer, R./Jung, H., Die Forensische Obduktion in Rumänien. Rechtsmedizin 27 (2017), 124–126.

Dongoroz, Vintilă, Explicaţii teoretice ale codului penal român. Partea generală (Theoretical explanatory notes on the Romanian Penal Code. General part), vol. II. 2d ed. Bucharest 2003.

Fodor, Elena-Mihaela, Administrative Sanctions and the Concept of the "Criminal Charge". Romanian Perspective in a Comparative Law Study. Acta Universitatis Danubius, no. 2/2011, pp. 16–30.

– General principles of administrative sanctions in the Romanian law. Fiat Iustitia, no. 1/2007, 1–10.

Gheorghe, Isabela Maria/Sandu, Ana-Maria, Delicvenţa juvenilă (Juvenile delinquency). In: Gheorghe Bică/Doinel Dinuică/Gavril Paraschiv/Cezar Tită/Constantin Pletea/Elena Paraschiv/Dana Tită/Daniel Paraschiv (eds.), George Antoniu – in honorem: culegere de studii juridice (George Antoniu – in honorem: Collection of judicial studies). Craiova 2009, pp. 171–178, http://www.spiruharet.ro/facultati/drept-valcea/cercetare/65ea39eacdb9b8d9fbf5423de35ee20c [last visited May 2018].

Ioan, Beatrice/Damian, Simona/Scripcaru, C./Neagu, Marius/Chirilă, B., From punishment to education – Juvenile delinquency in Romanian criminal law. Revista medicochirurgicală a Societă ţii de Medici şi Naturalişti din Iaşi 119, no. 1 (2015), 207–213.

Ivan, Gheorghe, Recidiva, Arts. 41–43. In: Antoniu George/Toader Tudorel (eds.), Explicaţiile noului cod penal (Explanations of the new Penal Code), vol. I: Articles 1–52. Bucharest 2015, pp. 443–501.

– Criteriile speciale de individualizare a pedepsei amenzii (Special criteria for the individualization of the fine). RDP vol. XIX, issue 2/2012, 27–32.

Lefterache, Lavinia, Executarea măsurilor educative prevăzute în noul Cod penal (The execution of educative measures according to the new Penal Code). AUB Drept vol. 2012-II, 165–192.

Lupu, Liviu, Unele consideraţii privind aplicarea în timp a legii penale în cazul minorilor, determinate de intrarea în vigoare a noului Cod penal (The new Penal Code on the operative period of a criminal law in case of minors). Caiete de drept penal, no. 1/2012, 101–143.

Mitrache, Constantin/Mitrache, Cristian, Drept penal român. Partea generală (Romanian criminal law. General part). 8th ed. Bucharest 2010.

Niculeanu, Costel, Tratat de drept penal. Partea generală, vol. I: Infracţiunea şi răspunderea penală în noul cod penal (Treaty of criminal law. General part, vol. I: Criminal offenses and criminal responsibility within the new Penal Code). Craiova 2011.

Paşca, Viorel, Drept penal. Partea generală (Criminal law. General part). 3d ed. Bucharest 2014.

Pop, Traian, Drept penal. Întroducere. Chestiuni de istorie şi filosofie penală. Criminologie (Criminal law. Introduction. Questions of history and penal philosophy. Criminology), vol. I. Orăştie 1921.

Popescu, Traian/Bîrzan, Loredana, Aplicarea sancţiunilor cu caracter administrativ in cazul faptelor care nu prezintă pericolul social al unei infracţiuni. In: Gheorghe Bică/ Doinel Dinuică/Gavril Paraschiv/Cezar Tită/Constantin Pletea/Elena Paraschiv/Dana Tită/ Daniel Paraschiv (eds.), George Antoniu – in honorem: culegere de studii juridice (George Antoniu – in honorem: Collection of judicial studies). Craiova 2009, pp. 386–388, http://www.spiruharet.ro/facultati/drept-valcea/cercetare/65ea39eacdb9b8d9fbf5423de35 ee20c [last visited May 2018].

Puscasu, Andrei-Lucian, Legal Framework of Educational Measures Involving Non-Deprivation of Liberty in Romanian Criminal Law. Challenges of the Knowledge Society 2015, 115–123.

Radu, Mariana Narcisa, Considerations on sexual harassment. 58 Curentul Juridic – Juridical Current (2014), 74–86.

– The incrimination of sexual intercourse with a minor along time. 20 Valahia University Law Study (2012), 44–53.

Rinceanu, Johanna, Criminal responsibility of legal entities in Romania. In: A. Fiorella/ A.M. Stile (eds.), Corporate criminal liability and compliance programs. First Colloquium. Naples 2012, pp. 387–405.

Scripcaru, Andrei/Iliescu, Diana Bulgaru/Scripcaru, Calin, The Past, Present and Future of Legal Medicine in Romania. 5 Int'l J. Med. Dentistry (2015), 20–22.

Simion, Raluca, Criminology in Romania. A controversial discipline? 2 Rivista di Criminologia, Vittimologia e Sicurezza (2008), 78–87.

Simionescu, Elena-Giorgiana, Sanctioning System of the Natural Person's Second Offence in the Regulations of the New Criminal Code. 2011 Annals Constantin Brancusi U. Targu Jiu Juridical Sci. Series (2011), 149–162.

Streteanu, Florin, Tratat de drept penal. Partea generală (Treaty of criminal law. General part). Bucharest 2008.

Streteanu, Florin/Niţu, Daniel, Drept penal. Partea generală (Criminal law. General part), vol. I. Bucharest 2014.

Tanoviceanu, Ioan, Curs de drept penal (Criminal law course), vol. I. Bucharest 1912.

Teişanu, Florentin, Măsurile de siguranţă. Concept. Importanţă (Security measures. Concept. Importance). RDP vol. XIX, issue 4/2012, 109–116.

Vidrighin, Vasile, The Crime of Sexual Agression. 2013 Acta Universitatis Lucian Blaga, pp. 222–233.

Vlad, Barbu/Dumitrache, Ştefania, Considerations on replacing and suspending disciplinary sanctions. The issue of granting compensation for ungrounded or unlawful disciplinary sanctions. Juridical Tribune, vol. 1, issue 1, June 2011, 52–57.

Table of cases

Mihai Toma v. Romania, Application no. 1051/06, Eur. Ct. H.R. Final Judgment 24.04.2012

F. Sources of criminal law and interpretation aids

1. Overview

"Sources of criminal law" *(izvoarele dreptului penal)* are generally understood as the collection of judicial norms that determine which facts constitute offenses and that establish the legal reaction and the applicable sanctions for such offenses.[1] These sources can take a written or (according to a minority of scholars) unwritten form;[2] they can be enacted by internal or external authorities; and they can have a direct or an indirect impact.[3] The definition of "sources of criminal law" and "criminal law" *(legea penală)* is in this respect very similar. Criminal law is defined by law (Art. 173 C.p.) as a provision with penal character that is located in an organic law, emergency ordinance, or other normative act that had legal force by the time of adoption of the Constitution in 1991 and does not violate constitutional provisions.[4]

The sources of criminal law are the Constitution, organic laws *(legile organice)* and normative acts assimilated to organic laws *(actele normative assimilate acestora)*, emergency ordinances *(ordonanțele de urgență)*, decisions of the Constitutional Court *(deciziile Curții Constituționale)*, international conventions *(convențiile internaționale)* that have been ratified by Romania, and acts *(acte)* that have been adopted within the European Union. The last two sources are external, whereas the other sources are internal.[5]

The sources of criminal law are hierarchically structured: precedence is given to European law, followed by the Constitution, organic laws, emergency ordinances, presidential decrees, decisions of the Constitutional Court, and certain decisions of the High Court of Cassation and Justice. The principle of *lex superior derogat legi inferiori* applies.

2. Legislation and other written laws

– *National legislation*

The Constitution is the most important internal source of criminal law and – after European law – is located at the top of the hierarchy of legal norms.[6] After the po-

---

[1] *Paşca*, Drept penal – Partea generală, p. 18; *Streteanu*, Tratat de drept penal – Partea generală, p. 99; *Streteanu/Nițu*, Drept penal – Partea generală, p. 73.

[2] See discussion of customary law at below 3.

[3] *Streteanu*, Tratat de drept penal – Partea generală, p. 99; *Streteanu/Nițu*, Drept penal – Partea generală, p. 73.

[4] *Duvac*, in: Antoniu/Toader (ed.), Explicaţiile noului Cod penal, p. 516.

[5] See *Streteanu*, Tratat de drept penal – Partea generală, p. 100.

[6] For details on the Constitution, see I.C.1.; *Streteanu/Nițu*, Drept penal – Partea generală, p. 74. For the hierarchy between the Constitution and EU law, see *Selejan-Guțan*, The Constitution of Romania, pp. 38–40.

litical changes in Romania in 1989 and the breakdown of socialism, a new constitution entered into force, the Constitution of 1991 (Const.). Since then, it has been revised only once, in 2003,[7] in order to meet the requirements of the European Union. The Constitution contains a number of provisions that are relevant to the criminal law.[8]

In addition to constitutional laws, Parliament also issues organic and ordinary laws (Art. 73 Const.). The issuance of organic laws requires a majority vote of the members of each Chamber (Art. 76(1) Const.), whereas the issuance of ordinary laws *(legile ordinare)* requires only a majority vote of the members present in each Chamber (Art. 76(2) Const.).[9] Furthermore, organic laws cannot be amended, and they cannot be repealed, except by organic law. Organic laws, such as the Penal Code[10] and the Code of Criminal Procedure[11] – both of which entered into force on 1 February 2014 – and special laws that provide criminal norms, are the main sources of criminal law. Other important organic laws include the Law on the organization of the judiciary,[12] the Law on the prevention and sanctioning of money laundering as well as on the formation of measures of prevention and suppression of terrorist financing (last modified in 2012);[13] the Law on the prevention and suppression of human trafficking;[14] the Law on the prevention, detection and sanctioning of corruption;[15] the Law on the prevention and suppression of drug-trafficking and illegal drug consumption;[16] the Law on the prevention and suppression of fiscal evasion;[17] the Law on the prevention and suppression of organized crime;[18] the Law on measures for the assurance of transparency in the exercise of public offices, public functions, and, in the field of business, prevention and sanctioning of cor-

---

7 Published in M. Of. no. 767/31 Oct. 2003.

8 See I.C.2. and I.C.3.

9 On the legislative procedure, see I.A.4. On the distinction between organic and ordinary laws, see *Selejan-Guțan*, The Constitution of Romania, pp. 34–35.

10 Published in M. Of. no. 510/24 July 2009.

11 Published in M. Of. no. 486/15 July 2010.

12 Legea nr. 304/2004 privind organizarea judiciară, republished in M. Of. no. 827/13 Sept. 2005.

13 Legea nr. 656/2002 pentru prevenirea şi sancționarea spălării banilor, precum şi pentru instituirea unor măsuri de prevenire şi combatere a finanțării actelor de terrorism, published in M. Of. no. 702/12 Oct. 2012.

14 Legea nr. 678/2001 privind prevenirea şi combaterea traficului de persoane, published in M. Of. no. 783/11 Dec. 2011.

15 Legea nr. 78/2000 pentru prevenirea şi sancționarea faptelor de corupție, published in M. Of. no. 219/18 May 2000.

16 Legea nr. 143/2000 privind prevenirea şi combaterea traficului şi consumului ilicit de droguri, published in M. Of. no. 362/3 Aug. 2000.

17 Legea nr. 241/2005 pentru prevenirea şi combaterea evaziunii fiscale, published in M. Of. no. 672/27 July 2005.

18 Legea nr. 39/2003 privind prevenirea şi combaterea criminalității organizate, published in M. Of. no. 50/29 Jan. 2003.

ruption;[19] the Law on the prevention and suppression of terrorism;[20] and the Law on the prevention and suppression of pornography.[21]

Normative acts considered equivalent to organic laws are ordinary written laws that were enacted before the adoption of the Constitution in 1991. Before 1991, there was no distinction between organic laws and ordinary laws. Normative acts enacted before 1991 remain in force insofar as they do not violate constitutional provisions (Art. 154(1) Const.). As such normative acts are considered equivalent to organic laws, they are not modifiable and cannot be abrogated other than by an organic law.[22]

Ordinances issued by the government are generally not considered a source of criminal law. Provisions regarding criminal offenses, penalties, and the execution thereof must be issued by organic laws (Art. 73(3)(h) Const.). In exceptional cases, however, such as a disaster *(calamităţi)*, state of emergency *(stare de necesitate)*, or state of war *(stare de război)*, the government can adopt emergency ordinances *(ordonanţe de urgenţă)* that are considered sources of criminal law (Art. 115(5) Const.).[23] Emergency ordinances can only be issued in situations that call for immediate regulatory action; the government must set forth reasons that support its claim of urgency. They must be submitted to Parliament for approval, according to the legislative procedure, and Parliament can either approve or reject the emergency ordinance by means of a law.

All written laws must be published in the Official Gazette of Romania *(Monitorul Oficial al României)* otherwise they will not enter into force.[24] The Chamber of Deputies is the publisher of the Official Gazette.

– *International treaties and conventions*

International treaties and conventions *(tratate şi convenţii internaţionale)* are sources of criminal law as soon as they are ratified by the Parliament. Ratified treaties and conventions are part of national law (Art. 11(2) Const). The scholarly literature distinguishes between international treaties and conventions that constitute

---

[19] Legea nr. 161/2003 privind unele măsuri pentru asigurarea transparenţei în exercitarea demnităţilor publice, a funcţiilor publice şi în mediul de afaceri, prevenirea şi sancţionarea corupţiei, published in M. Of. no. 279/21 Apr. 2003.

[20] Legea nr. 535/2004 privind prevenirea şi combaterea terorismului, published in M. Of. no. 1161/6 Dec. 2004.

[21] Legea nr. 196/2003 privind prevenirea şi combaterea pornografiei, published in M. Of. no. 87/4 Feb. 2008.

[22] *Streteanu*, Tratat de drept penal – Partea generală, p. 106.

[23] *Paşca*, Drept penal. Partea generală, p. 23; *Streteanu*, Tratat de drept penal – Partea generală, p. 108.

[24] Legea nr. 24/2000 privind normele de tehnica legislativa pentru elaborarea actelor normative, republished in M. Of. no. 260/21 Apr. 2010.

direct sources of criminal law and those that constitute indirect sources of criminal law. The former are directly applicable whereas the latter must be implemented by means of an act of Parliament. The European Convention on Human Rights is a direct source of criminal law in Romania. Other important international treaties and conventions that are direct sources of criminal law include the International Covenant on Civil and Political Rights and the Convention on the Rights of the Child. International treaties and conventions that are indirect sources of criminal law include the Convention on the Prevention and Punishment of the Crime of Genocide and the Convention against Torture and Other Cruel, Inhuman or Degrading Treatment or Punishment.[25]

– *Supranational law*

Romania joined the European Union (EU) in 2007.[26] The country's integration into the EU requires a constant adaptation of its criminal law to the legislation of the EU. In accordance with the accession act, provisions of the constituent treaties of the EU and other mandatory community regulations take precedence over conflicting provisions of national law (Art. 148(2) Const.). These EU provisions have a direct effect and constitute a source of criminal law. A distinction must be made between constituent treaties – known as primary laws of the EU – and other mandatory community regulations – known as secondary laws of the EU – which derive from primary laws, on the one hand, and secondary laws that are not mandatory (such as recommendations and opinions), on the other. Non-mandatory secondary laws do not constitute sources of criminal law.

3. Customary law

According to the scholarly literature, customary law *(cutuma, obiceiul, consuetudinea)* exists if compliance with a certain unwritten standard within a precise social or territorial environment is uniform, consistent, and general and if the standard is treated as a legal requirement *(opinio juris)*.[27] Given the principle of legality,[28] it seems daring to refer to customary law as a source of criminal law. Indeed, there is disagreement among scholars concerning the status of customary law. Some argue that the purpose of the principle of legality is to guarantee legal certainty for citizens *(cetăţeanul)* and to protect citizens from abusive acts by judicial organs in

---

25 See also I.B.2.b.

26 See I.B.2.a.

27 *Streteanu*, Tratat de drept penal – Partea generală, p. 109.

28 On the principle of legality, see II.A.

criminal matters.[29] According to the prevailing opinion, however, customary law cannot create criminal norms and therefore cannot constitute a source of criminal law.[30] Customary law is generally recognized as an aid to be considered in the interpretation of criminal law.[31]

International customary law *(cutuma internaţională)* consisting of general practice and *opinio juris* is – alongside international treaties – a source of public international law. This does not mean, however, that it is also a source of national criminal law. The Constitution does not mention international customary law at all. This is an indication that it is not considered a source but merely an aid to be considered in the interpretation of criminal law.

4. Case law and judicial opinion

Judicial decisions are generally not considered a source of criminal law. They are simply a means to interpret criminal legislation. Decisions of the Constitutional Court, however, can be regarded as sources of criminal law insofar as they ascertain the unconstitutionality of a legal norm or ordinance. These decisions are binding, and even though they cannot create criminal norms, they can force the suspension of such norms. Therefore, decisions of the Constitutional Court can be regarded as "direct formal sources of criminal law with a negative character" *(izvoare formale directe cu caracter negativ)*.[32] These decisions must be published in the Official Gazette (Art. 147(4) Const.). As soon as they are published, they are binding on all courts with prospective effect *(ex nunc)*. They are generally available on the Court's homepage.[33]

Decisions of the High Court of Cassation and Justice *(Înalta Curte de Casaţie şi Justiţie)* – like decisions of other courts – are generally not regarded as sources of criminal law. The role of these decisions and judicial opinions is the assurance of the uniform interpretation and application of norms.[34] Some scholars argue, however, that decisions of the Court on appeal of law *(recurs în interesul legii)* do constitute sources of criminal law.[35] Their main argument is that it can be clarified by means of an appeal of law whether a particular criminal norm was implicitly abro-

---

[29] *Streteanu*, Tratat de drept penal – Partea generală, pp. 109–114.

[30] *Paşca*, Drept penal. Partea generală, pp. 24–25.

[31] *Paşca*, Drept penal. Partea generală, p. 25.

[32] See *Streteanu*, Tratat de drept penal – Partea generală, p. 101.

[33] See https://www.ccr.ro [last visited May 2018].

[34] *Paşca*, Drept penal. Partea generală, p. 26; *Selejan-Guţan*, The Constitution of Romania, p. 38.

[35] *Streteanu*, Tratat de drept penal – Partea generală, pp. 114–117.

gated by the legislature.[36] Decisions of the Court are generally not binding on courts, as judicial independence must be preserved. Nevertheless, for the purpose of a correct application of law, courts are expected to comply with them voluntarily. Scholars who argue that the decisions of the Court on appeal of law constitute sources of criminal law consider these decisions binding on courts. These decisions are published in the Official Gazette of Romania and are generally available on the Court's homepage.[37]

5. Legal literature and academic opinion

Legal literature and academic opinion *(doctrina)* are not considered a source of criminal law. The role of the scholarly literature is a theoretical and explanatory one; it serves to inspire the legislature and the judiciary.[38]

In fact, the influence of scholarly literature ranges far beyond the theoretical. Before a new law is adopted, scholars are frequently consulted; this was the case with regard to the new Penal Code, and the new Code of Criminal Procedure.[39]

6. Other

Presidential decrees *(decretele prezidențiale)* in criminal matters, such as acts of grace,[40] do not constitute sources of criminal law as the president has no legislative power. Such decrees are administrative acts in individual cases.[41]

Bibliography and further reading

Agheniței, Mihaela/Flămînzeanu, Ion, Jurisprudența ca izvor de drept (Jurisprudence as a source of law). RDP vol. XX, issue 1, 111–116.

Boghirnea, Iulia, Scurt istoric al jurisprudenței ca izvor al dreptului (Short history of jurisprudence as source of law). In: Gheorghe Bică/Doinel Dinuică/Gavril Paraschiv/Cezar Tită/Constantin Pletea/Elena Paraschiv/Dana Tită/Daniel Paraschiv (eds.), George Antoniu

36 *Streteanu,* Tratat de drept penal – Partea generală, p. 116.
37 See http://www.scj.ro [last visited May 2018].
38 *Selejan-Guțan,* The Constitution of Romania, p. 38.
39 *Selejan-Guțan,* The Constitution of Romania, p. 38.
40 For details on pardon, see II.K.2.
41 *Pașca,* Drept penal. Partea generală, p. 24.

– in honorem: culegere de studii juridice (George Antoniu – in honorem: collection of judicial studies). Craiova 2009, pp. 62–69, http://www.spiruharet.ro/facultati/drept-valcea/cercetare/65ea39eacdb9b8d9fbf5423de35ee20c [last visited March 2018].

Brînza, William, Drept penal. Partea generală. Curs universitar (Criminal law. General part. University course). Bucharest 2012, pp. 21–31.

Bulai, Costică/Bulai, Bogdan, Manual de drept penal. Partea generală (Handbook of criminal law. General part). Bucharest 2007.

Duvac, Constantin, Art. 173. In: George Antoniu/Tudorel Toader (eds.), Explicaţiile noului Cod penal (Explanations of the new Penal Code), vol. II, Arts. 53–187. Bucharest 2015.

Kerek, Angela, Verfassungsgerichtsbarkeit in Ungarn und Rumänien – Ein Vergleich der Verfassungsgerichtsbarkeiten zweier osteuropäischer Transformationsstaaten auf ihrem Weg zum konsolidierten Rechtsstaat (Constitutional jurisdiction in Hungary and Romania – A comparison of the constitutional jurisdiction of two eastern European transformational countries on their way to a consolidated constitutional state). Berlin 2010.

Lefterache, Lavinia Valeria, Drept penal. Partea generală. Curs pentru studenţii anului II (Criminal law. General part. Course for students of the second year). 3d ed. Bucharest 2011.

Mitrache, Constantin/Mitrache, Cristian, Drept penal român. Partea generală (Romanian criminal law. General part). 8th ed. Bucharest 2010.

Paşca, Viorel, Drept penal. Partea generală (Criminal law. General part). 3d ed. Bucharest 2014.

– Romania's New Penal Code and the Saga of Its Adoption. Journal of Eastern-European Criminal Law no. 1/2014, 9–22.

Popa, Nicolae, Consideraţii generale privind conceptul de izvor al dreptului (General considerations regarding the concept of sources of law). In: Gheorghe Bică/Doinel Dinuică/Gavril Paraschiv/Cezar Tită/Constantin Pletea/Elena Paraschiv/Dana Tită/Daniel Paraschiv (eds.), George Antoniu – in honorem: culegere de studii juridice (George Antoniu – in honorem: collection of judicial studies). Craiova 2009, pp. 350–371, http://www.spiruharet.ro/facultati/drept-valcea/cercetare/65ea39eacdb9b8d9fbf5423de35ee20c [last visited May 2018].

Selejan-Guţan, Bianca, The Constitution of Romania: A Contextual Analysis. Oxford 2016.

Streteanu, Florin, Tratat de drept penal. Partea generală (Treatise on criminal law. General part). Bucharest 2008.

Streteanu, Florin/Niţu, Daniel, Drept penal. Partea generală (Criminal law. General part), vol. I. Bucharest 2014.

Tănăsescu, Elena-Simina, Cour Constitutionnelle et système judiciaire: des rapports de force? (Constitutional Court and judicial system: power politics?). AUB Drept 2012-II, 240–251.

Toarder, Tudorel/Safta, Marieta, Evolutions of the constitutional review in the context of integration into the European Union. The role of the Constitutional Court of Romania in the process of reception of European Law into the national legal order. In: Florea Măgureanu/George Măgureanu/Silvia Tăbuşcă (eds.), Instituţii juridice contemporane în contextul integrării României în Uniunea Europeană (Contemporary legal institutions in the context of Romania's integration in the European Union). 6th ed. Bucharest 2012, pp. 23–33, http://ijc.rau.ro/documents/2012-IJC-ed6.pdf [last visited March 2018].

G. Developments in criminal law, criminal procedure, and the execution of punishment

1. Overview

Today, the Romanian legal system can be assigned to the civil or continental law system[1] as it is mainly based on statutes passed by Parliament. This was not always the case, however: from the 14th to the 18th centuries, customary law along with Byzantine and Canonical law as well as written feudal law predominated in the territory of the principalities of Moldova and Wallachia *(Valahiei)*.[2] Among other sources of law, customary law was particularly important, although the significance of written law increased steadily[3] as customary law lost the ability to respond in a satisfactory way to changes attributable to the processes of modernization and social change.[4] The Orthodox Church affected the policy of the sovereigns during the 15th and 16th centuries.[5]

From the 16th century onwards, there was a trend to codify feudal law. The 16th century is intrinsically tied to the sovereign *Vasile Lupu* (1595–1661) in Moldova and the sovereign *Matei Basarab* (1580–1654) in Wallachia, both of whom introduced codified laws for their territories. Although the penal codes of *Vasile Lupu* (1646) and *Matei Basarab* (1652) were harsh and barbaric in terms of punishment, they were written in Romanian – and not in Greek or Slavic – and thereby contributed to the development of a national culture.[6]

Beginning in the 18th century, the idea of authority began to take hold. During this century, Wallachia and Moldova were ruled by Greek nationals (Phanariotes) selected by the Ottomans. Consequently, the adoption of Canonical and Byzantine[7] sources of law increased.[8] By the end of the Phanariot era in 1820, the first codification of laws had taken place. Legislative codes issued in the principality of Wallachia included the Code *Ypsilanti* of 1780[9] and the Code *Caragea* of 1818; legislative codes issued in the principality of Moldova included the Code *Callimachis* of 1817.[10] The Code *Callimachis* was strongly inspired by the Austrian Code of 1811 and was superior to the Code *Caragea*, which was less complete and less struc-

---

1 On the comparative legal classification of Romanian criminal law, see I.B.1.

2 *Gambaro/Sacco*, Sistemi Giuridici Comparati, p. 319.

3 *Gambaro/Sacco*, Sistemi Giuridici Comparati, p. 319.

4 *Bocşan*, in: Giaro (ed.), Rechtskulturen des modernen Osteuropa, p. 34.

5 *Bocşan*, in: Giaro (ed.), Rechtskulturen des modernen Osteuropa, p. 34.

6 *Rosen*, De la Récidive dans le Droit Pénal Roumain, p. 21.

7 On the influence of Byzantine law, see also *Cront*, 7 Balkan Stud. (1966), 188–193.

8 *Gambaro/Sacco*, Sistemi Giuridici Comparati, p. 319.

9 *Zachariä*, Kritische Zeitschrift für Rechtswissenschaft und Gesetzgebung des Auslandes 12 (1840), 411.

10 *Gambaro/Sacco*, Sistemi Giuridici Comparati, p. 319.

tured. During the 18th century, Greek became the language of government;[11] as a result, the Code *Callimachis* and the Code *Caragea* – both of which dealt with both civil and criminal matters – were written in Greek.[12] In addition to these two codes, diverse collections of customary law, such as the one by *Petru Manega* in 1825–1826[13] (who studied jurisprudence in France) were composed. These collections of customary law and the legislative codes completed the era of partial local codification.[14] All these written laws, which have also played an educational role, contributed to the historical premise for the classification of Romania to the civil or continental law system.[15]

2. Developments in substantive criminal law

– United principalities of Romania and Kingdom of Romania

Following the Treaty of Paris in 1857, Wallachia and Moldova began a process of unification that resulted in the proclamation of the new State of Romania by *Alexandru Ioan Cuza* in 1862.[16] Romania – independent and partially unified – was strongly influenced by France and its legislative codifications. French legislative models had an impact not only on civil law but on criminal law as well.[17]

The first Romanian penal code, the Penal Code of 1864 *(Codice Penale)*, was basically a translation of the *Code Napoléon* of 1810;[18] however, the Code also displayed features of the Prussian Penal Code of 1851.[19] It was divided into three books or volumes and a preliminary section. The preliminary section (*Disposiţiunĭ preliminarie*, Arts. 1–6) contained general provisions concerning punishment and jurisdiction. The first book (*Cartea I*, Arts. 7–65) contained regulations relating to the general part of criminal law. Like its French legislative model, this code divided offenses into three categories: crimes *(crimă)*, delicts *(delict)*, and contraventions *(contravenţiune)*. This tripartite division *(diviziune tripartită)* or trichotomy

---

[11] *Maksimovič*, Byzantinische Rechtsbücher und ihre Bedeutung für die Rechtsgeschichte Osteuropas, p. 25.

[12] *Rosen*, De la Récidive dans le Droit Pénal Roumain, p. 25.

[13] *Bocşan*, in: Giaro (ed.), Rechtskulturen des modernen Osteuropa, p. 35.

[14] *Gambaro/Sacco*, Sistemi Giuridici Comparati, p. 319.

[15] *Bocşan*, in: Giaro (ed.), Rechtskulturen des modernen Osteuropa, p. 37.

[16] See *Selejan-Guţan*, The Constitution of Romania, pp. 7–10.

[17] For the history of and reasons for this French influence, see *Gutan*, Acta Universitatis Lucian Blaga 2005 (Supp. 2005), pp. 133–135.

[18] *Gutan*, Acta Universitatis Lucian Blaga 2005 (Supp. 2005), p. 138; *Avrigeanu*, ZStW 129 (2017), 826.

[19] *Missir*, in: Franz von Liszt (ed.), Die Strafgesetzgebung der Gegenwart in rechtsvergleichender Darstellung, p. 344.

(trichotomia) was based on the gravity of the offense. The second book (*Cartea II*, Arts. 66–380) and the third book (*Cartea III*, Arts. 381–400) contained regulations concerning concrete offenses. In accordance with the principle *societas delinquere non potest*, the Penal Code of 1864 did not provide for the criminal liability of corporations.[20] In contrast to the *Code Napoléon* of 1810, the Penal Code of 1864 did not provide for capital punishment and was therefore more lenient than its French model.[21] The following punishments were provided for crimes: lifelong daily work *(munca silnică)*, incarceration *(reclusiunea)*, imprisonment *(detenţiunea)*, and civic degradation *(degradaţiunea civică)*. For delicts, the Code provided the punishments of corrective penitentiary *(închisorea corecţionale)*, loss of certain political, civil, or family rights *(interdicţiunea unora din drepturile politice, civile ori de familiă)*, and fine *(amendă)*. Finally, as punishment for contraventions, the Code provided detention in a police penitentiary *(închisorea poliţienească)* and fine. This code was eminently liberal, an attitude that was criticized by Romanian scholars for not being appropriate for Romanian society, whose level of modernization was less than that of French society.[22]

In 1881, Romania became a monarchy. The Penal Code of 1864 continued to apply with several amendments.

Romanian criminal law scholars, most notably Professor *Ioan Tanoviceanu* (1858–1917) and Professor *Traian Pop* (1885–1960), developed a Romanian doctrine of criminal law during the 19th and early 20th centuries. *Ioan Tanoviceanu* deserves most of the credit for decoupling Romanian criminal law from French criminal law and for developing an independent criminal law doctrine.[23] Another important criminal law scholar who contributed to the formation of a distinctly Romanian criminal law was Professor *Vespasian V. Pella* (1897–1960). He became internationally well known for his early call – already in 1926 – for the adjudication of war crimes by a permanent international criminal tribunal.[24]

– *Greater Romania and military dictatorship*

The main task for Romanian criminal lawyers beginning in the 1920s was the unification of the criminal law applied within the boundaries of the Romanian states. After the First World War, with the acquisition of Bessarabia, Bukovina,

---

20 On the historical development of corporate criminal liability, see II.H.2.a.

21 *Frankowski*, in: Hodgkinson/Rutherford (eds.), Capital Punishment, p. 216.

22 *Tanoviceanu*, România sub raportul moral, pp. 209, 223, 277, 278, 283.

23 *Theodoru*, Tratat de Drept processual penal, p. 37.

24 *Pella*, in: Pella (ed.), La Guerre-Crime et les Criminels de Guerre (1946), pp. 129–144; *Friedlander*, 15 Case W. Res. J. Int'l L. (1983), 5. See also the contemporary review of *Kane*, 18 J. Am. Inst. Crim. L. & Criminology (1927), 126–132.

and Transylvania, Romania became "Greater Romania" *(România Mare)*.[25] These provinces were subject to foreign penal legislation, which continued to apply even after unification. As a result, different laws applied on the same territory: in Bessarabia, Russian criminal law applied; in Bukovina, Austrian criminal law applied; and in Transylvania, Hungarian criminal law applied. These laws co-existed with the Romanian Penal Code of 1864. A unification of the criminal rules was necessary in order to achieve the legal expression of the new politically-unified state of the entire Romanian nation. The adoption of a new penal code was deemed necessary.[26]

In contrast to the Penal Code of 1864, the second Romanian penal code, the Penal Code of 1936, was strongly influenced by Italian doctrine and the Italian *Codice Rocco* of 1930.[27] The Penal Code of 1936 consisted of a general part and a special part. It abandoned the tripartite division of the offense and divided criminal offenses into two categories, crimes and delicts, according to the punishment provided by law. The Penal Code of 1936 introduced corporate criminal liability in the broad sense. As a general feature, this Code – in contrast to the liberal Penal Code of 1864 – was authoritarian. It paid tribute to the political context of the 1930s, which was characterized by a succession of crises, which progressively weakened the democratic parliamentary regime. A royal dictatorship was introduced by a new constitution in 1938, only two years after the entry into force of the Penal Code of 1936. Capital punishment was introduced by that dictatorship, including its imposition for political crimes.[28] Written law, however, did not replace customary law entirely until the second half of the 20th century.[29] Authoritarian policy continued during the military dictatorship (1940–1944), which replaced the royal dictatorship.[30]

– Communist era

During the turbulent years following the Second World War and preceding the abolition of the monarchy and the establishment of the communist political system in 1947,[31] authoritarian tendencies increased. In 1948, the Penal Code of 1936 was

---

25 For an overview, see *Cercel*, in: Skinner (ed.), Fascism and Criminal Law, pp. 104–112.

26 *Cercel*, in: Skinner (ed.), Fascism and Criminal Law, p. 113.

27 For more details on the 1936 code, see *Cercel*, in: Skinner (ed.), Fascism and Criminal Law, pp. 112–126. For a German translation of the code, see *Isopescul-Grecul* (transl.), Das rumänische Strafgesetzbuch Carol II.

28 *Frankowski*, in: Hodgkinson/Rutherford (eds.), Capital Punishment, p. 217.

29 *Bocşan*, in: Giaro (ed.), Rechtskulturen des modernen Osteuropa, p. 39.

30 On these dictatorships, see *Selejan-Guţan*, The Constitution of Romania, pp. 15–16.

31 For a short overview, see *Selejan-Guţan*, The Constitution of Romania, pp. 17–19. For an extensive account of the history of Romanian communism, see *Tismaneanu*, Stalinism for All Seasons.

modified and amended, that is, adapted to the social changes and the "socialist legal order."[32] These modifications had to meet the challenges posed by the difficult economic and social situation of Romania after the Second World War, on the one hand, and the challenges posed by the desiderata of the new political ruler, on the other. The criminal law became a "weapon" to be used against the political resistance and to assist in the replacement of the old bourgeois society. A new political, social, and economic communist program was introduced. In 1969, a third Romanian penal code was adopted. Although this code was the penal code of a socialist state and therefore had to exhibit socialistic features, it was nevertheless the work of the prestigious scholar *Vintilă Dongoroz*, whose previous experience as a "bourgeois scholar" helped create a genuinely Romanian legislative work.

The Penal Code of 1969[33] was divided into a general part and a special part. Characteristic of the general part was the definition of the purpose of criminal law (Art. 1) and the definition of the offense (Art. 17) as any act that constitutes a social threat *(pericol social)*, that is willingly perpetrated *(săvârşită cu vinovăţie)*, and that is prohibited by criminal law *(prevăzută de legea penală)*. This code no longer contained the distinction between crime and delict, as the classification of the criminal offense according to the gravity of the punishment was regarded as scientifically baseless;[34] instead, it recognized only one category of criminal offenses: criminal acts *(infractiuni)*. The Penal Code of 1969 provided for capital punishment.[35] Its entire approach was based on the principle of legality *(nullum crimen sine lege, nulla poena sine lege)* and rejected the analogy *in malam* as well as *in bonam partem*, a characteristic feature of the Soviet-inspired criminal law. It did not show significant structural differences when compared to western codes. This does not mean, however, that there were no significant differences at all; indeed this code regulated political offenses against the state and offenses against societal property, and it abolished corporate criminal liability. In sum, the Penal Code of 1969 was similar to western codes, despite the existence of these kinds of socialistic regulations. As a result, the Penal Code of 1969 remained in force – with many amendments – until 2014 (some 25 years after the fall of communism).

– *Post-communist era*

In 1989, communism fell. This development led to several changes to the Penal Code of 1969, such as the elimination of the difference between public and private

---

[32] *Dianu*, in: Frankowski/Stephan (eds.), Legal Reform in Post-Communist Europe, p. 258; see also *Cojocariu*, Subordinating Justice in Communist Romania System. For a German translation of the amended code (as of 1960), see *Tiefenthaler/Provasi* (transls.), Rumänisches Strafgesetzbuch.

[33] For a translation of this code including an introduction, see *Vrăbiescu Kleckner* (transl.), The Penal Code of the Romanian Socialist Republic.

[34] *Dongoroz* (ed.), Explicaţii teoretice ale codului penal român, p. 116.

[35] *Frankowski*, in: Hodgkinson/Rutherford (eds.), Capital Punishment, p. 222.

property, the elimination of regulations on state protection, and the elimination of capital punishment.[36] Some years later, in 2006, the criminal liability of legal persons was (re)introduced. At the beginning of the 21st century, efforts to create and enact a new penal code were begun. In 2004, a new penal code was adopted by Parliament. The Penal Code of 2004 reintroduced the tripartite categorization of criminal acts, namely, crimes, delicts, and contraventions. This code, however, was too rooted in the previous code and was therefore considered a failure by the new government, which came into power in 2005. As a result, the Penal Code of 2004 never entered into force. In 2005, the new government appointed a commission to create a new penal code. This commission presented a new code in 2009, which was adopted immediately. The Penal Code of 2009 entered into force on 1 February 2014.

A goal of the Penal Code of 2009, Romania's fourth penal code, was to preserve the criminal law tradition of the country to the greatest extent possible while at the same time implementing specific requirements of European Union law. This balancing act took almost five years from the date of the adoption and publication of the Penal Code in the Official Journal in 2009.[37] Like its predecessor, the Penal Code of 2009 contains a general part and a special part. The configuration of the general part (especially the general theory of crime) was influenced by Italian and Spanish doctrine, which, in turn, were influenced by the prevailing German doctrine. It is remarkable that the Penal Code of 2009 maintained in its general part a legal definition of the offense – albeit in a modified form – despite the fact that neither the Penal Code of 1864 nor the Penal Code of 1936 provided such a definition and despite the fact that most European penal codes do not contain one, either.[38] According to the new definition, an act is a criminal offense if it is prohibited by criminal law and is unlawful and imputable.[39] Like its predecessor, the Penal Code of 2009 recognizes only one category of criminal offenses. Criminal liability of legal persons has been maintained.[40] The special part contains the main offenses.

---

36 *Doss* et al., 3 Int'l J. of Police Sci. & Mgmt. (2001), 226–245.

37 For an overview of the new Romanian Penal Code, see *Paşca*, J. E.-Eur. Crim. L. no. 1/2014, 9–22.

38 *Paşca*, J. E.-Eur. Crim. L. no. 1/2014, 11.

39 *Streteanu*, CDP 2/2009, 50; for details, see *Avrigeanu*, ZStW 129 (2017), 825–850.

40 *Stănilă*, J. E.-Eur. Crim. L. no. 1/2014, 109–121. For details, see II.H.2.b.

3. Developments in criminal procedure

– United principalities of Romania and Kingdom of Romania

The evolution of the Romanian law of criminal procedure[41] was similar to that of the criminal law: The *Codice de Procedură Criminală* of 1864, which entered into force on 30 April 1865, was the first Romanian code of criminal procedure. It consisted of 603 articles and was strongly inspired by the French *Code d'Instruction Criminelle* of 1808, even though the French code was strongly criticized by French scholars for its lack of accuracy and specificity, its lack of general rules and definitions, and its lack of logical divisions.[42]

The Code of Criminal Procedure of 1864 provided for an oral and public hearing *(judecată orală şi publică)* and was for the most part adversarial in nature *(judecată contradictorie)*. Only the pre-trial phase was inquisitorial in nature. Criminal proceedings were divided into two parts: the pre-trial phase *(premergătoare judecăţii)* – which consisted of detection *(descoperirea)*, investigation *(urmărirea)*, and charging *(instrucţia)* – and the trial phase *(judecată)*.[43] Finally, sentences were executed *(executarea)*. This code of criminal procedure provided for courts of first instance *(judecătoriile de plasă)*, district courts *(tribunalele de judeţ)*, jury courts *(curţile cu juri)*, and the High Court of Cassation and Justice *(Înalta Curte de Casaţie şi Justiţie)*. Courts of first instance and district courts had jurisdiction over delicts and contraventions whereas jury courts had jurisdiction over crimes.[44] The jury had to answer two questions with yes or no during each trial: the first question concerned the defendant's guilt; the second concerned extenuating circumstances *(circumstanţe atenuante)*.[45] The Code of Criminal Procedure of 1864 was modified in 1867, 1868, 1875, 1877, and 1902. Some of the most important amendments were made in 1902 with the strengthening of the rights of the accused (e.g., addition of the right to a defense attorney during the pre-trial phase). Additional modifications were made in 1907, 1909, 1913, and 1919.

– Greater Romania and military dictatorship

The *Codul de Procedură Penală Carol al II-lea* of 1936 was Romania's second code of criminal procedure. Consisting of seven parts and 673 articles, it entered into force on 1 January 1937. Part One contained general provisions; Part Two

---

[41] See *Mitica*, The Public Ministry's Historical Evolution (2014), pp. 45–53. On the judicial organization during the second half of the 19th and the beginning of the 20th century, see *Ghitulescu*, 4 Contemp. Readings L. & Soc. Just. (2012), 687–694.

[42] *Tanoviceanu*, Tratat de drept şi procedură penală, p. XII.

[43] *Negoiţă*, Istoria statului şi dreptului românesc, p. 228.

[44] On the distinction between petty and more serious offenses, see above 2.

[45] *Negoiţă*, Istoria statului şi dreptului românesc, p. 228.

dealt with the initial investigation and instructions *(instructie)*; Part Three set regulations concerning the courts; Part Four contained provision on appellate remedies; Part Five consisted of regulations on the execution of sentences; Part Six incorporated special procedures and measures of public interest; and Part Seven was devoted to temporary regulations. The Code was mainly influenced by its predecessor (the Penal Code of 1864), by the Italian Code of Criminal Procedure of 1930 *(Codice Rocco "di rito")*, and by Italian scholarship.[46] In addition to simplifying and accelerating the criminal process, it was meant to maintain an equilibrium between the interests of the individual and the interests of society. The Code of Criminal Procedure of 1936 was modified several times between its entry into force and 1943: on the way to an authoritarian state (beginning with the royal dictatorship in 1938 and followed by the military dictatorship in 1940), the Code was amended in order to eliminate jury courts *(curţile cu juraţi)*, to introduce criminal sections within the courts of appeal, and to provide for the transfer of cases involving political – and during the war also non-political – offenses to military tribunals.[47]

– *Communist period and fall of communism*

The *Codul de Procedură Penală al Republicii Socialiste România* of 1968 was Romania's third code of criminal procedure. It entered into force on 1 January 1969 and consisted of 524 articles. The Code was divided into a general part (with general provisions, provisions on jurisdiction, rules of evidence, preventive measures, and rules on procedural files) and a special part (with provisions on penal action, courts, and execution of sentences and rules governing special procedures). It showed clear socialistic traits. Characteristic of this third code was the introduction of a definition of the purpose of criminal procedure (Art. 1). Accordingly, the purpose of criminal procedure was to determine the exact time an offense was committed *(constatarea la timp)* and all facts that constitute a criminal offense, so that every person who commits an infraction is punished according to his or her own degree of culpability and no innocent person is held criminally liable. In addition, criminal procedure was designed to contribute to the protection of social and state order *(apărarea orînduirii sociale şi de stat)*, to the strengthening of legality *(întărirea legalităţii)*, to the prevention of criminal offense *(prevenirea infracţiunilor)*, and to the education of citizens *(educarea cetăţenilor)* in the spirit of respecting the laws and rules of social co-existence. After the fall of communism, the Code of Criminal Procedure of 1968 was subject to a plethora of amendments: it became more liberal, and the protection of the interests of individuals and their fundamental human rights took on a role of central importance.

---

[46] *Dianu*, in: Frankowski/Stephan (eds.), Legal Reform in Post-Communist Europe, p. 265.

[47] *Theodoru*, Tratat de Drept procesual penal, p. 16.

– *Post-communist era*

The fourth and current Romanian code of criminal procedure, the Code of Criminal Procedure of 2010, entered into force on 1 February 2014. It was intended to create a modern legislative framework for criminal proceedings and to implement specific requirements as handed down by the European Court of Human Rights in several cases against Romania. Today, Romanian criminal procedure is inquisitorial in nature and can be assigned to the civil or continental law system.[48]

The Code of Criminal Procedure of 2010 consists of 603 articles and is divided into a general part and a special part. Important procedural principles, which are anchored in the general part, are the principle of legality (*legalitatea procesului penal*, Art. 2), separation of judicial offices (*separarea funcţiilor judiciare*, Art. 3), presumption of innocence (*prezumţia de nevinovăţie*, Art. 4), the principle of finding the truth (*aflarea adevărului*, Art. 5), the principle of *ne bis in idem* (Art. 6), the accusatory principle (*obligarea punerii în mişcare şi a exercitării acţiunii penale*, Art. 7), the right to a fair trial within a reasonable period of time (*caracterul echitabil şi termenul rezonabil al procesului penal*, Art. 8), the right to liberty and security (*dreptul la libertate şi siguranţă*, Art. 9), the right to defense (*dreptul la apărare*, Art. 10), and the respect of human dignity and private life (*respectarea demnităţii umane şi a vieţii private*, Art. 11).[49] Additional provisions in the general part concern the criminal process, penal action and civil action, participants in the trial, evidence, preventive measures, and rules concerning procedural files. The special part contains provisions on prosecution, tribunals, special procedures, and rules on the enforcement of judgments.[50]

4. Developments in the execution of punishment

No written records can be found concerning the promulgation and execution of punishment in the Middle Ages. The first legal regulations regarding the application of punishment were elaborated during the 17th century.[51]

---

[48] For the post-communist transformation of the justice system, see generally *Coman*, Reformer la justice dans un pays post-communiste: le cas de la Roumanie.

[49] See *Ciopec/Roibu*, The New Romanian Code of Criminal Procedure, p. 3. For details, see I.D.4.

[50] On amendments to the new Code of Criminal Procedure due to Constitutional requirements, see *Teodorescu*, in: Universitatea Titu Maiorescu (ed.), Law between modernization and tradition, pp. 989–993.

[51] *Chiş*, Drept executional penal, p. 17.

– General features of punishment from the 17th to the 19th centuries

During the 17th century, a distinction was made between the despotic era, the humanitarian era, and the contemporary era. During the early despotic era *(epoca despotică)*, corporal punishment was barbaric and particularly cruel. Despotism was considered the most suitable form of government for a society without social and legal tradition.[52] The goal of barbaric punishment during the despotic era was intimidation of the masses in order to restrain them from committing offenses. Mutilation *(mutilaţiunea)* and torture *(tortura)* – in the form of the amputation of a leg, arm, ear, nose, or tongue or the putting out of an eye – were common during this period.[53] The death penalty *(pedeapsa cu moarte)* was imposed by impaling, hanging, burning on a pyre, decapitation, pouring molten lead into the throat, or burning alive.[54] Punishment was not proportional to the offense, and it was not equal for all citizens but varied, depending on the social status of the offender. During this early despotic era, imprisonment as a punishment was unknown.[55] The penal code of *Vasile Lupu* (1646), in force in the territory of the principality of Moldova, and the penal code of *Matei Basarab* (1652), in force in the territory of the principality of Wallachia, introduced similar systems of sentencing and punishment. Although punishment pursuant to those two penal codes was cruel, it was no longer arbitrary.[56] Both penal codes provided for the death penalty. The penal code of *Vasile Lupu* provided, for example, for the mutilation of a person who killed his or her mother: the hand with which the mother was slain was cut off; subsequently, the offender was tied to the tail of a horse and dragged through the streets; finally, the offender was decapitated.[57] The penal code of *Matei Basarab* contained very similar forms of punishment; it was, however, more detailed and better structured.

The despotic era was followed by the humanitarian era *(epoca umanitară)* in the second half of the 18th century. This was the era of the rebirth of criminal law *(epoca renaşterii dreptului penal)*.[58] The French Revolution of 1789 led to the collapse of the structures of despotism. Along with the central ideas of the French Revolution – *liberté*, *egalité*, and *fraternité* – came the concept of equal penalties for everyone. Torture was abolished. The fundamental principle of *nullum crimen sine lege, nulla poena sine lege* was proclaimed.[59] The system of corporal punish-

---

52 *Pop*, Drept penal. Întroducere, p. 47.

53 *Pop*, Drept penal. Întroducere, p. 49.

54 *Rosen*, De la Récidive dans le Droit Pénal Roumain, p. 13; *Tanoviceanu*, Curs de drept penal, p. 144; *Pop*, Drept penal. Întroducere, pp. 48–49.

55 *Pop*, Drept penal. Întroducere, p. 49.

56 *Rosen*, De la Récidive dans le Droit Pénal Roumain, pp. 15–16.

57 *Rosen*, De la Récidive dans le Droit Pénal Roumain, p. 16.

58 *Pop*, Drept penal. Întroducere, p. 50.

59 *Pop*, Drept penal. Întroducere, p. 55.

ment was replaced by a system of imprisonment[60] and fine.[61] The main ideas of the humanitarian era inspired the classical school of criminal law *(şcoala penală clasică)*, which, in turn, was the source of inspiration for the so-called classical penal codes, such as the first Romanian penal code (the Penal Code of 1864).[62]

At the end of the 19th century, developments in biology, psychology, and sociology revolutionized the classical criminal law with their naturalistic, realistic spirit.[63] It became clear that criminal law had to be reformed and put on an anthropological, psychological, and sociological fundament.[64] The contemporary era *(epoca contimporană)* supplanted the humanitarian era. The main ideas of the contemporary era inspired the positive criminal law school *(şcoala penală pozivită)*. Important principles established during this time period include the principle of individualization of punishment *(individualizarea pedepsi)*, the principle of suspended sentence for first offenders *(condamnarea condiţională a infractorilor primari)*, the principle of probation for a rehabilitated offender *(liberarea condiţională a condamnatului îndreptat)*, and the establishment of special rules regarding the responsibility and punishment of persons who have committed minor offenses.[65]

– *Forms of punishment provided for in the Romanian penal codes of 1865, 1936, and 1968 and regulation of the penitentiary system*

Both the Penal Code of 1864 and the Penal Code of 1936 provided for two kinds of punishment – criminal punishment *(pedepse criminale)* and correctional punishment *(pedepse corecţionale)*. The choice to impose the one or the other depended on the gravity of the committed offense; however, both were imposed for common offenses.[66] The specific punishment for political crimes – the so-called political punishment *(pedepse politice)*[67] – was served in fortress custody. By the middle of the 19th century, fortress custody was served in monasteries as none of the fortresses were in good condition.[68] A regulation for a penitentiary system was adopted in 1862. Twelve years later, in 1874, a special law concerning prisons

---

60 For the development of imprisonment as a penalty, see *Goga*, 56 Int'l Letters of Soc. & Humanistic Sci. (2015), 58–63. On the prison system in the first half of the 19th century, see *Merei*, IV Contemp. Readings L. & Soc. Just. (2012), 653–659.

61 *Pop*, Drept penal. Întroducere, p. 55.

62 *Pop*, Drept penal. Întroducere, p. 57.

63 *Pop*, Drept penal. Întroducere, p. 59.

64 *Pop*, Drept penal. Întroducere, p. 59.

65 *Pop*, Drept penal. Întroducere, pp. 59–60.

66 See above 2.

67 *Dongoroz* (ed.), Explicaţii teoretice ale codului penal roman, p. 22.

68 *Missir*, in: Franz von Liszt (ed.), Die Strafgesetzgebung der Gegenwart in rechtsvergleichender Darstellung, p. 344.

(Legea închisorilor) that reorganized the penitentiary system was adopted.[69] The reorganization required the construction of prison cells for more than one prisoner and the construction of juvenile prisons. In 1929, an additional law concerning prisons *(Legea pentru organizarea penitenciarelor şi instituţiilor de prevenţie)* was adopted. According to this 1929 law, the goal of the execution of punishment was personal rehabilitation.[70] When a person began to serve his or her sentence, the penitentiary regime was severe; over time, however, privileges were granted.[71]

Both the Penal Code of 1864 and the Penal Code of 1936 provided for imprisonment and fines as main punishments, for a ban on the exercise of certain rights as ancillary penalties *(pedepse complimentare)*, such as the publication of the conviction, and for accessory punishments *(pedepse accesorii)*, such as deprivation of parental responsibility, in cases in which imprisonment was imposed. In 1938, capital punishment and the confiscation of assets were introduced into the Penal Code of 1936: capital punishment was carried out by means of the firing squad.

In 1969, Law no. 23/1969 concerning the execution of punishment made the Ministry of Internal Affairs responsible for the general administration of prisons. The Ministry chose to structure penitentiaries as military units. In many prisons, working factories were set up.[72] Prisoners were obligated to work. The Penal Code of 1968 retained the same basic forms of punishment, including capital punishment. Capital punishment could be imposed for particularly aggravated homicide as well as for certain political crimes and particularly serious harms to the property of the socialist state. Capital punishment[73] was not abolished until 1989, after *Nicolae Ceauşescu* was sentenced to death and executed during the political system change in Romania.[74] Prison sentences could be imposed with or without suspension since 1936. The regime of suspension was increasingly diversified during the 1990s and early 2000s. In 2004, Law no. 294/2004 concerning the execution of punishment and measures contained the prohibition of torture during imprisonment and the prohibition of discrimination. Two years later, Law no. 275/2006 concerning the execution of punishment and measures required respect for further human rights. New forms of execution, such as probation, were introduced, whereby the

---

69 *Chiş*, Drept execuţional penal, p. 60.

70 *Chiş*, Drept execuţional penal, p. 80.

71 *Chiş*, Drept execuţional penal, pp. 81–82.

72 *Chiş*, Drept execuţional penal, pp. 124–125.

73 On the use of capital punishment in the communist era, see *Stancu*, in: Hodgkinson (ed.), Capital Punishment: New Perspectives, pp. 337–358; *Stancu*, 66 Revista Economică (2014), 112–135.

74 *Frankowski*, in: Hodgkinson/Rutherford (eds.), Capital Punishment, pp. 226–227. On the *Ceauşescu* trial, see *Falciola*, Contemporanea (2010), pp. 53–78; *Kozinski*, 77 A.B.A. J. (1991), 70–73; For its display in the media, see *Schneider*, in: von Amelunxen/Ujica (eds.), Television/Revolution: das Ultimatum des Bildes, pp. 133–146; for a (German) transcript of the trial, see Olschewski, Der Conducator Nicolae Ceausescu: Phänomen der Macht, pp. 185–240.

concrete implementation of probation continues to be difficult. This trend continued following the entry into force of the fourth penal code (the Penal Code of 2009).

– *Forms of punishment provided for by the Penal Code of 2009*

Romania's current penal code, the Penal Code of 2009 (which entered into force on 1 February 2014), provides the following main penalties (Art. 53 C.p.): life imprisonment *(detenţiunea pe viaţă)*, term imprisonment *(închisoarea)*, and fine *(amenda)*. Life imprisonment consists of the deprivation of freedom for an indeterminate period of time and is served in accordance with the Law on the Service of Penalties (Art. 56 C.p.). A prison sentence, which consists of the deprivation of freedom for a determined period of time (15 days to 30 years), is also served in accordance with the Law on the Service of Penalties (Art. 60 C.p.). A fine is an amount of money a convicted individual is compelled to pay to the state. The amount of a fine is established in accordance with the system of day-fines. The amount for one day-fine ranges from 10 RON (app. 2.60 USD) to 500 RON (app. 131 USD);[75] this number is multiplied by the number of day-fines imposed, which ranges from 30 to 400 (Art. 61 C.p.). The Penal Code of 2009 also provides for the accessory penalty (*pedeapsa accesorie*, Art. 54 C.p.) of a ban on the exercise of certain rights – beginning when the conviction becomes final and lasting until the sentence of imprisonment has been fully served (or deemed as served) – as well as for ancillary penalties (*pedepsele complementare*, Art. 55 C.p.), such as a ban on the exercise of certain rights *(interzicerea exercitării unor drepturi)*, military demotion *(degradarea militară)*, and publication of judgment to convict *(publicarea hotărârii de condamnare)*.[76]

In 2013, Law no. 254/2013 concerning the execution of punishment and measures replaced Law no. 275/2006. Among other things, it introduced compensation for detention conditions (e.g., insufficient space) that are not consistent with European prison standards.

– *Enforcement of sentences*

Beginning in the Middle Ages, the traditional form of imprisonment was forced labor in a salt mine *(ocnă)*. This form of imprisonment was gradually replaced by detention in penitentiaries.[77] The Penal Code of 1936 provided for forced labor and severe dungeon *(temniţă grea)* as well as for prison. The Penal Code of 1968 unified all different types of imprisonment and stipulated just one form of imprison-

---

75 Exchange rate as of March 2018. For the exchange rate, see the US treasury at https://www.fiscal.treasury.gov/fsreports/rpt/treasRptRateExch/currentRates.htm.

76 On the criminal sanctions, see I.A.4.d.

77 *Goga*, 56 Int'l Letters of Soc. & Humanistic Sci. (2015), 58.

ment, namely, detention *(inchisoare)*. Capital punishment was abolished and replaced by life imprisonment *(detenţiune pe viaţă)*. Recent trends, embodied by the current Penal Code of 2009, aim to increase flexibility in the execution of sentences by means of regimes of closed prisons, semi-open prisons, and open prisons. Inmates have the possibility to work in prison, thereby reducing the duration of their incarceration.

Bibliography and further reading

Antoniu, George, The New Criminal Law. Tradition and Reform. In: Mircea Duţu/Mihaela Tomiţă (eds.), New Criminal Legislation – Important phase in the development of Romanian law. Bucharest 2014, pp. 7–9.

– Contribuţiile profesorului Vintilă Dongoroz la dezvoltarea dreptului penal român (Contributions of Professor Vintilă Dongoroz to the development of the Romanian criminal law). RDP no. 3/2013, 9–26.

Avrigeanu, Tudor, Hat man in Rumänien einen Straftatbegriff gefunden? Wege und Irrwege einer missglückten Rezeption (Did one find a criminal offense concept in Romania? Ways and wrong ways of a failed reception). ZStW 129 (2017), 825–850.

– Constants of Criminal Law? In: Mircea Duţu/Mihaela Tomiţă (eds.), New Criminal Legislation – important phase in the development of Romanian law. Bucharest 2014, pp. 31–34.

Bocşan, Mircea-Dan, L'œuvre de codification – enjeu de la modernisation du droit roumain (The œuvre of codification – issue of modernization of Romanian law). In: Tomasz Giaro (ed.), Rechtskulturen des modernen Osteuropa (Legal cultures of modern Eastern Europe), vol. 1: Modernisierung durch Transfer im 19. und frühen 20. Jahrhundert (Modernization through transfer in the 19th and early 20th centuries). Frankfurt am Main 2006, pp. 33–46.

Cercel, Cosmin S., The Enemy Within: Criminal Law and Ideology in Interwar Romania. In: Stephen Skinner (ed.), Fascism and Criminal Law: History, Theory, Continuity. Oxford 2015, pp. 101–126.

Chiş, Ioan, Drept execuţional penal (Penitentiary law). Bucharest 2009.

Ciopec, Flaviu, The New Romanian Code of Criminal Procedure. J. E.-Eur. Crim. L. no. 1/2014, 33–52.

Ciopec, Flaviu/Roibu, Magdalena, The New Romanian Code of Criminal Procedure: Cosmetics or Surgery? La legislazione penale, 2016, 1–12.

Ciucă, Liviu Bogdan, Some Considerations Regarding the New Criminal Legislation in the Context of the National and European Legislative Reform. In: Mircea Duţu/Mihaela Tomiţă (eds.), New Criminal Legislation – Important phase in the development of Romanian law. Bucharest 2014, pp. 279–283.

Cojocariu, Maria Andreea, Subordinating Justice in Communist Romania: The Sovietization of the Romanian Criminal Justice System. Budapest 2011.

Coman, Ramona, Reformer la justice dans un pays post-communiste: le cas de la Roumanie (Reforming justice in a post-communist country: The case of Romania). Brussels 2009.

Cront, Georges, Le droit Byzantin en Roumanie. Nouvelles éditions des anciennes sources juridiques (Byzantine law in Romania. New editions of old legal sources). 7 Balkan Stud. (1966), 188–193.

Dianu, Tiberiu, The Romanian Criminal Justice System. In: Stanislaw Frankowski/Paul B. Stephan III (eds.), Legal Reform in Post-Communist Europe. The View from Within. Dordrecht 1995, pp. 257–273.

Dongoroz, Vintilă (ed.), Explicaţii teoretice ale codului penal român. Partea generală (Theoretical explanatory notes on the Romanian Penal Code. General part), vol. I. 2d ed. Bucharest 2003.

Doss, Marion T./Bowers, Stephen R./Hanganu, Cristina, The Transformation of the Romanian Criminal Justice System. 3 Int'l J. Police Sci. & Mgmt. 226–245 (2001).

Duţu, Mircea, De la comentarii exegetice ale codurilor, la explicaţii sistematice ale dreptului român (From exegetical comments of the codes to systematic explications of the Romanian law). DREPTUL no. 8/2014, 154–170.

Falciola, Luca, Hit One to Save One Hundred. The Ceausescus' Trial and the Transition Strategies in Post-Communist Romania. Contemporanea (2010), 53–78.

Frankowski, Stanislaw, Post-Communist Europe. In: Peter Hodgkinson/Andrew Rutherford (eds.), Capital Punishment: Global Issues and Prospects. Winchester 1996, pp. 215–242.

Friedlander, Robert A., The Foundations of International Criminal Law: A Present-Day Inquiry. 15 Case W. Res. J. Int'l L. (1983), 13–26.

Gambaro, Antonio/Sacco, Rodolfo, Sistemi giuridici comparati (Comparative legal systems). 3d ed. Milanofiori Assago 2011.

Ghitulescu, Bogdan, Judicial Organization in Romanian Principalities during the Second Half of the Nineteenth and the Beginning of the Twentieth Century. 4 Contemp. Readings L. & Soc. Just. (2012), 687–694.

Goga, Cristina Ilie, The Transformation of Detention in Romania: from Exile to Main Punishment. 56 Int'l Letters of Soc. & Humanistic Sci. (2015), 58–63.

Griga, Ioan, Relevant Issues of Criminal Procedural Law Resulting from the New Criminal Procedure Code. In: Mircea Duţu/Mihaela Tomiţă (eds.), New Criminal Legislation – important phase in the development of Romanian law. Bucharest 2014, pp. 175–179.

Gutan, Manuel, Building the Romanian Modern Law – Why Is It Based on Legal Transplant. Acta Universitatis Lucian Blaga 2005 (Supp. 2005), pp. 130–143.

Isopescul-Grecul, Constatin von (transl.), Das rumänische Strafgesetzbuch Carol II: in deutscher Übertragung mit einer rechtsgeschichtlichen Einführung und rechtsvergleichenden Texthinweisen (The Romanian Penal Code Carol II: German translation with a historical introduction and comparative annotations). Berlin 1942.

Julean, Dorel, Evolution of the Law on the Execution of Criminal Penalties and Related Acts post 1989. J. E.-Eur. Crim. L. no. 1/2014, 163–170.

Kane, Francis Fisher, Review of la Criminalité Collective des États et le Droit Pénal de L'Avenir. 18 J. Am. Inst. Crim. L. & Criminology (1927), 126–132.

Kozinski, Alex, Death, Lies & Videotape – The Ceausescu Show Trial and the Future of Romania. 77 A.B.A. J. (1991), 70–73.

Maksimovic, Kirill, Byzantinische Rechtsbücher und ihre Bedeutung für die Rechtsgeschichte Osteuropas (Byzantine law books and their significance for the legal history of Eastern Europe). In: Tomasz Giaro (ed.), Rechtskulturen des modernen Osteuropa. Modernisierung durch Transfer im 19. und frühen 20. Jahrhundert (Legal cultures of modern Eastern Europe. Modernization through transfer in the 19th and early 20th centuries). Frankfurt am Main 2006, pp. 1–32.

Merei, Luminiţa Eleni, The organization of prisons in the Romanian principalities (1831–1862). IV Contemp. Readings L. & Soc. Just. (2012), 653–659.

Missir, P.Th., Rumänien (Romania). In: Franz von Liszt (ed.), Die Strafgesetzgebung der Gegenwart in rechtsvergleichender Darstellung (Current criminal legislation in a comparative legal context), vol. I: Das Strafrecht der Staaten Europas (Criminal law of the states of Europe). Berlin 1894, pp. 343–351.

Mitică, Ruxandra, The Public Ministry's Historical Evolution. Challenges of the Knowledge Society (2014), 45–53.

Muţiu, Florentina Olimpia, Probation Services and Their Role in the Execution of Criminal Sanctions. J. E.-Eur. Crim. L. no. 1/2014, 122–127.

Negoiţă, Florin, Istoria statului şi dreptului românesc (History of the Romanian State and Law). Bucharest 2011.

Olschewski, Malte, Prozeß und Exekution: Das historische Video (Trial and execution: The historical video). In: Malte Olschewski, Der Conducator Nicolae Ceausescu: Phänomen der Macht (The Conducator Ceausescu: A phenomenon of power). Vienna 1990, pp. 185–240.

Paşca, Viorel, Romania's New Penal Code and the Saga of Its Adoption. J. E.-Eur. Crim. L. no. 1/2014, 9–22.

Pavel, Nicolae, The Conformity of the New Criminal Code and of the New Code of Criminal Procedure with the Constitution of Romania. In: Mircea Duţu/Mihaela Tomiţă (eds.), New Criminal Legislation – important phase in the development of Romanian law. Bucharest 2014, pp. 239–243.

Pella, Vespasian V., Projet de Statut pour la création d'une chambre criminelle au sein de la cour permanente de justice international (Draft Statute for the establishment of a Criminal Chamber in the Permanent Court of International Justice). In: Vespasian V. Pella (ed.), La Guerre-Crime et les Criminels de Guerre (War crime and war criminals). Geneva 1946, pp. 129–144.

– Les infractions pénales; leur répression; leur réparation (The criminal offenses; their repression; their reparation). In: H. Lèvy-Ullmann/B. Mirkine-Guetzévitch, La vie juridique des peuples (The legal life of peoples). Paris 1933, pp. 179–225.

Pop, Traian, Drept penal. Întroducere. Chestiuni de istorie şi filosofie penală. Criminologie (Criminal law. Introduction. Questions of history and penal philosophy. Criminology), vol. I. Orăştie 1921.

Răileanu, Ruxandra-Paula, Principiile fundamentale ale procesului penal român în lumina noului cod de procedură penală (Fundamental principles of the Romanian penal procedure in the light of the new Code of Criminal Procedure). DREPTUL no. 6/2014, 98–111.

Rosen, Jacques, De la récidive dans le Droit Penal Roumain (Recidivism in Romanian criminal law). Paris 1907, pp. 1–56.

Schneider, Manfred, Das Gericht im Off. Der Prozeß gegen die Ceauşescus (The Court in the off. The trial against the Ceauşescus). In: Hubertus von Amelunxen/Andrei Ujica (eds.), Television/Revolution: das Ultimatum des Bildes. Rumänien im Dezember 1989 (Television/Revolution: The ultimatum of images. Romania in December 1989). Marburg 1990, pp. 133–146.

Selejan-Guţan, Bianca, The Constitution of Romania: A Contextual Analysis. Oxford 2016.

Stan, Lavinia, Transitional Justice in Post-Communist Romania: The Politics of Memory. Cambridge 2013.

Stancu, Radu, The Political Use of Capital Punishment in Communist Romania Between 1969 and 1989. In: Peter Hodgkinson (ed.), Capital Punishment: New Perspectives. Abingdon 2016, pp. 337–358.

– Ideology and Repression in Romania in the Decade Before the Adoption of the Penal Code of 1969. Case Study: The Economic Criminality and the Application of Capital Punishment. 66 Revista Economică (2014), 112–135.

Stănilă, Laura, Criminal Liability of Legal Persons. History, Evolution and Trends in Romanian Criminal Law. J. E.-Eur. Crim. L. no. 1/2014, 109–121.

Streteanu, Florin, Proiectul noului Cod penal şi reconfigurarea teoriei infracţiunii în dreptul roman (Project of the new penal code and reconfiguration of the theory of the infraction within Romanian law). CDP 2/2009, 50–57.

Streteanu, Florin/Niţu, Daniel, Drept penal. Partea generală. Curs universitar (Criminal law. General part. University lecture), vol. I. Bucharest 2014.

Tanoviceanu, Ioan, Tratat de drept şi procedură penală (Treatise on criminal law and criminal procedure), vol. IV – procedura penală (Criminal procedure). 2d ed. Bucharest 1927.

– Curs de drept penal (Criminal law lecture), vol. I. Bucharest 1912.

– România sub raportul moral (Romania from a moral point of view). Analele Academiei Române. Memoriile Secţiunii Istorice vol. 24 (1902), 209–287.

– Rumänien (Romania). In: Franz von Liszt (ed.), Die Strafgesetzgebung der Gegenwart in rechtsvergleichender Darstellung (Current criminal legislation in a comparative legal context), vol. II: Das Strafrecht der außereuropäischen Staaten (Criminal law of non-European states). Berlin 1899, pp. 498–500.

Teodorescu, Maria-Georgiana, Amendments in the New Code of Criminal Procedure in the Light of the Solutions Provided by the Constitutional Court of Romania (CCR) and the High Court of Cassation and Justice (HCCJ). In: Universitatea Titu Maiorescu (ed.), International Conference: Law Between Modernization and Tradition. Implications for the Legal, Political, Administrative and Public Order Organization. Bucharest 2015, pp. 989–993.

Theodoru, Grigore, Tratat de Drept procesual penal (Treatise on criminal procedure law). 3d ed. Bucharest 2013.

Tiefenthaler, Paula/Provasi, Alois (transls.), Rumänisches Strafgesetzbuch: amtlicher Text, mit den Abänderungen bis zum 1. Dezember 1960 (The Romanian Penal Code: official text including amendments until 1 December 1960). Berlin 1964.

Tismaneanu, Vladimir, Stalinism for All Seasons: A Political History of Romanian Communism. Berkeley 2003.

Vrăbiescu Kleckner, Simone-Marie (transl.), The Penal Code of the Romanian Socialist Republic. South Hackensack, N.J. 1976.

Zachariä, E., Rechtsquellen in der Walachei (Sources of law in Wallachia). Kritische Zeitschrift für Rechtswissenschaft und Gesetzgebung des Auslandes 12 (1840), 408–434.

List of abbreviations in country report Romania

A.B.A. J.	American Bar Association Journal
Am. J. Comp. L.	American Journal of Comparative Law
AUB	Analele Universităţii din Bucureşti (law journal)
Balkan Stud.	Balkan Studies
B. Of.	Buletinul Oficial (Official Gazette)
BSEC	Organization of the Black Sea Economic Cooperation
Case W. Res. J. Int'l L.	Case Western Reserve Journal of International Law
C.civ.	Codul civil (Civil Code)
CDP	Caiete de Drept Penal / Criminal Law Writings (law journal)
C.E.	Common Era
CITES	Convention on International Trade in Endangered Species of Wild Fauna and Flora
Const.	Constitution
Contemp. Readings L. & Soc. Just.	Contemporary Readings in Law & Social Justice
C.p.	Codul penal (Penal Code)
C.p.p.	Codul de proceduă penală (Code of Criminal Procedure)
DISAM	Defense Institute of Security Assistance Management

ECHR	European Convention on Human Rights
Eur. Ct. H.R.	European Court of Human Rights
GDP	Gross Domestic Product
Gov. Ord.	Government Ordinance
ICCPR	International Covenant on Civil and Political Rights
ICESCR	International Covenant on Economic, Social and Cultural Rights
INTERPOL	International Criminal Police Organization
IMF	International Monetary Fund
Int'l J. Jurid. Sci.	International Journal of Juridical Sciences
Int'l J. Police Sci. & Mgmt.	International Journal of Police Science and Management
Int'l Letters of Soc. & Humanistic Sci.	International letters of Social and Humanistic Sciences
J. Am. Inst. Crim. L. & Criminology	Journal of the American Institute of Law & Criminology
J. Crim. Investigations	Journal of Criminal Investigations
J. E.-Eur. Crim. L.	Journal of Eastern-European Criminal Law
JOR	Jahrbuch für Ostrecht (law journal)
Jurid. Trib.	Juridical Tribune
LESIJ	Lex ET Scientia International Journal
MLA	Mutual Legal Assistance
M. Of.	Monitorul Oficial (Official Gazette)
NATO	North Atlantic Treaty Organization
OECD	Organisation for Economic Co-operation and Development
OSCE	Organization for Security and Co-operation in Europe
RDP	Revista de drept penal (law journal)
Rev. Cent. & E. European L.	Review of Central and East European Law
RON	Leu românesc (symbol of Romanian currency)
SEEBRIG	Southeastern Europe Brigade
Stud.	Studies
Tulsa. J. Comp. & Int'l L.	Tulsa Journal of Comparative & International Law
UNCLOS	UN Convention on the Law of the Sea
U. New Brunswick L.J.	University of New Brunswick Law Journal
USD	United States Dollar
ZStW	Zeitschrift für die gesamte Strafrechtswissenschaft (law journal)

National characteristics, fundamental principles, and history of criminal law in

Spain*

Teresa Manso Porto

---

* This country report first appeared in the German version of the project as "Rahmenbedingungen, Vorgaben, Grundlagen und Entwicklung des Strafrechts in Spanien." In: Ulrich Sieber/Karin Cornils (eds.), Nationales Strafrecht in rechtsvergleichender Darstellung, vol. 1. Berlin 2009, pp. 663–730. It was translated, revised, and updated for this publication.

Contents

A. National characteristics

1. Geography

The Kingdom of Spain *(Reino de España)* occupies the greater part of the Iberian Peninsula in southwestern Europe and, with a total area of 505,944 sq km,[1] is the fourth largest country on the European continent.[2] Spanish sovereign territory also includes two archipelagos – the Balearic Islands in the Mediterranean and the Canary Islands in the Atlantic – as well as five exclaves on the Moroccan coast: two autonomous cities, Ceuta and Melilla, and the Chafarinas Islands, the Peñón (rock) de Alhucemas, and the Peñón de Vélez de la Gomera. The Spanish part of the Iberian Peninsula is bordered by France and Andorra to the north, Portugal to the west, and the British territory of Gibraltar to the south. Spain's external possessions share maritime and land borders with Morocco.[3] The capital of Spain is Madrid.

2. Population

a) Population and demographics

In 2018, Spain was the fifth most populous country in the European Union.[4] The population has been increasing since the last census *(censo de población)* in 2001: in January 2017, it was estimated at 46.529 million, an increase of around 88,867 persons over the previous year.[5] Population density, however, at 92.5 persons per sq km (2015), is lower than in most western European countries.[6] Unlike the coastal areas and metropolitan Madrid, the country's interior is sparsely populated. Almost half of the population resides in seven of the country's 50 provinces: all of these highly populated provinces – except for Madrid – are located on the coast. In contrast, of the 22 provinces with the least population, none has coastal access.[7] In

---

1 Der neue Fischer Weltalmanach 2018, p. 426.

2 CIA World Factbook: Spain: Geography.

3 CIA World Factbook: Spain: Geography.

4 Eurostat, Population and Population Change Statistics, Table 1 (Demographic balance, 2016).

5 Eurostat, Population and Population Change Statistics, Table 1 (Demographic balance, 2016); INE, Notas de Prensa, 29 June 2017, p. 1.

6 Eurostat, Population density.

7 Eurostat, Population grids, figures 1 (2011) and 3 (2012).

addition to Madrid, with nearly six million inhabitants, and Barcelona, with five million, there are 13 more metropolitan areas with more than 500,000 inhabitants.[8]

In 2017, there were slightly more women than men in Spain.[9] The two largest age groups, persons ages 30 to 44 and 45 to 59, make up nearly one-fourth each, that means together half of the total population whereas the younger generation, age groups 0 to 14 and 15 to 29, make up only 15 % each, that means together one-third of the total population.[10]

According to statistical data from 2017, foreigners make up 9.5 % of Spain's inhabitants.[11] In comparison, in 1998 foreigners made up only 1.6 % of the population.[12] This increase dates to the mid-1990s, and the rate of increase has accelerated in the beginning of the 21th century until the financial crisis in 2008–2011 which stopped this development and even led to emigration.[13] In absolute numbers, Spain still ranks position 13 worldwide, with one of the higher immigration rates in the world (7.8 migrants/1,000 population in 2017 [est.][14]). In January 2017, the total number of foreigners living in Spain was estimated at 4.424 million, 1.845 million of whom were EU citizens, especially from Romania (largest population), the UK, Italy, and Germany. The majority of foreigners from non-member countries were from Ibero-American countries (Ecuador, Columbia, Bolivia) and the Maghreb (Morocco, second largest population).[15]

b) Language

The official language *(idioma oficial)* is Spanish *(español, castellano)*. Three other languages have "official" status *(lenguas cooficiales)* in their respective autonomous communities:[16] Catalan, Galician, and Basque.[17] In 2006, Occitan or Aranese (a Gallo-Romance language that is also spoken in parts of France and Italy) was declared an official language in Catalonia.[18]

---

[8] Ministerio de Fomento, Las Grandes Áreas Urbanas y sus municipios, pp. 1–7.

[9] INE, Population resident in Spain.

[10] INE, Notas de Prensa, 29 June 2017, p. 3.

[11] INE, Notas de Prensa, 29 June 2017, p. 1.

[12] INE, Residential variations statistics.

[13] Banco de España (Bank of Spain), Boletín Económico, Los flujos migratorios en España durante la crisis; El País, España perderá medio millón de habitantes en la próxima década si se mantiene la tendencia demográfica.

[14] CIA World Factbook: Spain: People and Society.

[15] INE, Notas de Prensa, 29 June 2017, pp. 3–4.

[16] Regarding the autonomous regions, see below 4.

[17] Der neue Fischer Weltalmanach 2018, p. 426.

[18] Generalitat de Catalunya, Catalan, language of Europe, p. 29.

Although Spanish is not yet an official language of the European Union, its importance around the world continues to grow. Spoken by almost 500 million people, it was the world's second most common language (after Chinese) in terms of the number of native speakers in 2017, and it is the second most studied language (after English) in the world.[19] The *Instituto Cervantes*, a Spanish cultural organization with branches in more than 40 countries worldwide, promotes both the Spanish language and Spanish culture, including the culture of Spanish-speaking Latin American countries *(Hispanoamérica)*.[20]

The historically high illiteracy rate has declined dramatically in recent decades. In 2017, 98.2 % of the population as a whole was literate (98.8 % of men and 97.7% of women).[21] In 2016, illiteracy increased as age increased. Basically, only adults over the age of 70 suffer from significant illiteracy.[22]

c) Religion

Spain is a secular state. The Constitution guarantees both freedom of religion as well as cooperation between the state and the various religious communities. Catholicism, the religion of 67.8 % of the population (2016 est.), dominates. In 2016, only 2.2 % of the population belonged to other religions.[23] According to a survey undertaken in July 2017, the number of practicing Catholics was relatively small, and there is a continuing downward trend in this area. In that year, only about 16 % of members of a religion attended services or performed their religious duties on a regular basis; 26 % of those surveyed described themselves as non-believers or atheists.[24]

In 2016, Muslims made up the second largest religious denomination, followed by Jehovah's Witnesses and Protestants. These religions, as well as Judaism, Mormonism, and, most recently, Buddhism, have the status of a well-known and deeply-rooted religion *(religión de notorio arraigo)*, which confers tax benefits and allows for presence in schools, hospitals, prisons, and military barracks.[25]

---

[19] Instituto Cervantes, El español, una lengua viva, informe 2017, p. 5.

[20] Instituto Cervantes, Quiénes somos.

[21] INE, Population of 16 years old and over by educational level reached.

[22] Agencia EFE, Día alfabetización.

[23] CIA World Factbook: Spain: People and Society.

[24] CIS, Barómetro de Julio 2017, p. 20.

[25] Ministerio de Justicia (Ministry of Justice), Annual report on the status of religious freedom in Spain 2016, pp. 15–25.

3. Economy

Spain's economic system is a hybrid form that combines attributes of both free market capitalism and social market economy. This is evident from two contrasting provisions in the Constitution of 1978 (*Constitución Española*, CE): while Art. 38 CE recognizes free enterprise within the framework of a market economy, according to Art. 128 para. 1 CE, the entire wealth of the country "in its different forms, irrespective of ownership" is subordinate to the general interest, and Art. 128 para. 2 recognizes public initiative in economic activity. Numerous additional norms address the economic system.

Prior to democratization, recovery from the economic disaster left by civil war and 40 years of dictatorship was slow. In the 1960s, the economy slowly began to open to the outside. During this time, the country profited from thriving tourism, increasing foreign investment, European growth, and the emigration of one million Spaniards to wealthier countries. Free trade could not take hold, however, due to the continued existence of high tariffs. The fundamental economic changes of the past decades did not take place until after Spain joined the European Union in 1986.

Strong domestic consumption profiting from growing revenues in the tourism sector was the engine of the dynamic development of the economy in 2016. Spain was host to more than 75 million visitors that year, a new peak as a result of the political crises in Turkey and Egypt as well as the threat of terrorism in France.[26]

The continuing economic growth, measured at an annual rate of 3.2 % in 2016, was one of the highest in the Eurozone and for the first time reached the level it had had in 2008, before the financial crisis. The inflation rate in 2016 was -0.3 %, which, due to a higher real income, stimulated demand for consumer goods. In addition, private investments made an important contribution to growth (3.1 %). Impulses came from a cheap money policy and rising corporate profits, profiting especially from subsidies that provided inexpensive long-term loans and favored the internationalization of medium-sized companies. Nonetheless, this stimulation did not have much of an effect on the still very tense situation on the job market in 2016. The unemployment rate at 19.6 % stayed continuously on a very high level. The situation is even more serious for young job seekers: 43 % of persons ages 15 to 24 were registered as unemployed.[27] Trade data from 2016 shows imports at 309.3 billion EUR (slightly higher than exports: 287.5 billion EUR).[28]

Spain was particularly hard hit by the consequences of the global financial crisis of 2007–2008. The effects of these consequences continue to be felt in 2018. Even

---

26 Der neue Fischer Weltalmanach 2018, p. 632.

27 Der neue Fischer Weltalmanach 2018, p. 632.

28 Der neue Fischer Weltalmanach 2018, p. 427.

if the economic growth rate in 2016 exceeded the pre-crisis level, the crisis has not yet been overcome with regard not only to the very high overall unemployment rate but also with regard to the national debt (99.4 % of the gross national product [GNP] in 2016 as a result of the high outlays for social services and other subsidies).[29]

The GDP in 2016 amounted to 1,114 billion EUR, 74 % of which was generated by the service sector, 23 % by manufacturing, and 3 % by agriculture. This distribution is mirrored in the employment structure: in 2016, 76 % of the population was employed in the service sector, 20 % in manufacturing, and 4 % in agriculture.[30]

Among the members of the World Bank and according to its estimates, Spain was ranked 47th in 2016, with a gross national income (GNI) of 36,450 International Dollars per capita (based on purchasing power parity; an International Dollar has the same purchasing power over GNI as a USD has in the United States).[31]

4. System of government

Spain, a social and democratic state under the rule of law, is a parliamentary monarchy.[32] King *Felipe VI* has been the head of state since 2014. Spain has a bicameral, asymmetric parliament *(Cortes Generales)* that is comprised of a lower house, the Congress of Deputies *(Congreso de los Diputados)*, and an upper house, the Senate *(Senado)*; more power is vested in the lower house.[33]

The current system of government is the result of a long and peaceful transition from the *Franco* dictatorship – which began at the end of the civil war of 1936–1939 and continued until *Franco's* death in 1975 – to democracy. This historic transition, whose precise time frame is disputed, is known as *Transición Española*.[34] Two days after *Franco's* death, *Juan Carlos* became king. Following a referendum on 15 December 1976, the Law on Political Reform *(Ley para la Reforma Política)* abolishing the dictatorial system was passed. The first democratic elections followed on 15 June 1977. The Constitution was approved in a referendum on 6 December 1978.

Important questions regarding the territorial organization of the state and the separation of powers – particularly the independence of the judiciary – are regulated not only in the Constitution of 1978 but in many organic laws *(leyes orgánicas)*

---

29 Der neue Fischer Weltalmanach 2018, p. 427.

30 Der neue Fischer Weltalmanach 2018, p. 427.

31 World Bank, Gross national income per capita 2016, p. 1.

32 *Ferreres Comella*, The Constitution of Spain, pp. 26–35, 71–89; Der neue Fischer Weltalmanach 2018, p. 426.

33 For details on the Parliament, see *Ferreres Comella*, The Constitution of Spain, pp. 91–125.

34 *Ferreres Comella*, The Constitution of Spain, pp. 8–12. See also I.B.1.

as well. Taken together, these laws form the so-called constitutional block *(bloque de constitucionalidad)*. This situation is attributed to the lack of political consensus regarding significant constitutional issues at the time the Constitution was drafted. As a result of this lack of consensus, these controversial issues were "reserved" and delegated to future lawmakers to be addressed by means of organic laws *(reserva de ley orgánica)*.

The territorial organization and, in particular, the decentralization and distribution of competences between the (central) state and the various autonomous communities were highly contested issues during the transition process and could not be conclusively regulated in the Constitution. In the scholarly literature, the constitutional system of autonomy is referred to as a federal state *sui generis*. There are several reasons for this: first, the various competences are devolved asymmetrically among the autonomous communities; second, the distribution of competences has not been finalized; and third, there is (still) no second federal chamber:[35] Spain's upper chamber, the Senate, does not really work as a body representing the interests of the autonomous communities.[36]

Only a few of the autonomous communities (Andalusia, Basque Country, Galicia, and Catalonia) adopted a federal model from the outset, while the others assumed their competences over time. Currently, all 17 autonomous communities and both autonomous cities have implemented their constitutional "right" to self-government, albeit to differing degrees, and have enacted statutes of autonomy *(Estatutos de Autonomía)*.[37] The status of Navarra, officially known as *Comunidad Foral de Navarra* (Regional Community of Navarra), is special. Navarra has no need for a statute of autonomy because its constitutional status is linked to older legislation, which granted it autonomy and its own institutions at an earlier date. All of the autonomous communities have their own government and their own legislative bodies. Their competences encompass the areas of public health and education, and each community may establish its own court of auditors *(tribunal de cuentas)* and Ombudsman *(defensor del pueblo)*, among other things. Some of the communities administer their own public budgets virtually independently; some have their own police force – which carries out the functions of the national police force in its stead. In addition to the autonomous communities, there are two autonomous cities: Ceuta and Melilla. Other administrative units are the provinces *(provincias)* and municipalities *(municipios)*.[38]

---

35 See *García de Enterría*, La Revisión del Sistema de Autonomías Territoriales, pp. 23–39.

36 *Zapata-Barrero*, in: Joppke/Seidle, Immigrant Integration in Federal Countries, p. 137; *Ferreres Comella,* The Constitution of Spain, pp. 122–124.

37 On the statutes of autonomy, see *Ferreres Comella*, The Constitution of Spain, pp. 47–48, 161–200.

38 For a summary of the territorial organization, see *Bachmaier Winter/del Moral García*, Criminal Law in Spain, pp. 21–24 (nos. 6–13); *Ferreres Comella*, The Constitution of Spain, pp. 47–48, 161–200.

The separation of powers as implemented in Spain differs in a number of ways from its implementation in other European countries. The controversial constitutional question regarding the independence of the judicial branch (called the "judicial power" – *del poder judicial* – in the Constitution) was solved by the creation of a body responsible for the governance of the courts – the General Council of the Judiciary *(Consejo General del Poder Judicial)* – members of which are elected by Parliament. Another typical feature is the enhanced parliamentary support of the executive through strict parliamentary regulations and the Law on Political Parties *(Ley Orgánica 6/2002 de Partidos Políticos)*.

Legislative powers are vested in the Parliament (Art. 66. para. 2 CE). Pursuant to Art. 82 CE, Parliament can delegate legislative authority to the government with regard to specific matters by means of a basic or "framework" law *(ley de bases)*, a law that sets out major guidelines and leaves the details up to the government, or with regard to the consolidation of laws *(refundición)* by means of an ordinary law *(ley ordinaria)*. Additional government powers include the authority to enact temporary legislation in times of urgent need (Art. 86 CE); from time to time, generous use is made of this option. For example, this is how the major criminal law reform of 1983 was enacted, a reform that reflected the profound impact of the Constitution of 1978 on the criminal law system in force at the time.

The government, the Congress, and the Senate are all entitled to initiate legislation. The Constitution also provides for popular initiatives and allows the parliaments of the autonomous communities to initiate legislation (Art. 87 CE).

There are no statutory provisions that allow social or religious groups to influence the law directly – for example, at hearings during the legislative process – but in practice such influence is exercised. In the case of legislative reforms concerning issues with strong ethical implications, such as abortion, efforts are made to engage in dialogue with representatives of the Catholic Church. The same applies to reform of the financing model of the church and to the issue of religious instruction in schools. Nevertheless, fundamental institutional reforms have been enacted despite the direct opposition of the church. A clear example of this was the introduction of same-sex marriage in 2005. In sum, attempts to achieve consensus in a particular case always depend on the willingness of those concerned to communicate and, ultimately, on political decisions. In the area of criminal law, individual scholars have raised the issue of the need for new, rational criteria for criminal legislation. In this context, the lack of opportunity for input by groups who are affected by draft legislation has been sharply criticized.[39]

---

[39] For information on these issues, see *Díez Ripollés*, La Racionalidad de las Leyes Penales, pp. 50–58.

5. Crime and criminal prosecution

a) Investigating authorities

In Spain, the investigating authorities comprise the police, the public prosecution service *(Ministerio Fiscal)*, and, most importantly, the examining judge *(Juez de Instrucción)*.[40] Independent action by the police and the public prosecution service is permitted only during the preliminary investigation *(instrucción preliminar)*, whereby certain actions, even in this phase of the proceedings, require judicial authorization. If telephone surveillance, for example, is necessary during the preliminary investigation, the judge must be kept apprised of the ongoing investigation.[41] To be sure, the examining judge is in charge of the investigation. In July 2011, however, a preliminary draft of a law to reform criminal procedure was presented that would have made the public prosecutor alone responsible for conducting investigations. In exchange, the competences of the judge as a "guarantor" of the proceedings would have been strengthened. As the general elections were moved forward to December 2011, however, it was not possible for Parliament to pass the preliminary draft prior to the conclusion of the legislative period. The draft was never discussed again and was not adopted in the reform of 2015.

Due to the principle of mandatory prosecution, these authorities are required to prosecute all criminal offenses brought to their attention.[42] Nevertheless, given the need to allocate limited resources, various priorities are set. In contrast, the principle of discretionary prosecution applies in the context of juvenile crime.[43]

The organization of the police forces in Spain is rather complicated.[44] At the national (state) level, there are two forces: the National Police *(Policía Nacional)* and the Civil Guard *(Guardia Civil)*. The Civil Guard is a paramilitary police force un-

---

[40] *Montero Aroca* et al., Derecho Jurisdiccional III, pp. 133–148. For details, see *Bachmaier Winter/del Moral García*, Criminal Law in Spain, pp. 27–30 (nos. 23–28) (police), pp. 30–32 (nos. 29–31) (public prosecution), and p. 32 (no. 32) (examining judge). For an overview of the investigative stage of the proceedings and the roles of the various actors, see *Aebi/Balcells,* 14 Eur. J. on Crim. Policy & Res. (2008), 317–321.

[41] For an in-depth view, see *Moreno Catena/Cortés Domínguez*, Derecho Procesal Penal, pp. 259–263, 282–286; *Bachmaier Winter/del Moral García*, Criminal Law in Spain, pp. 27–32 (nos. 23–32).

[42] *Merino-Blanco*, Spanish Law and Legal System, p. 141; *Bachmaier Winter/del Moral García*, Criminal Law in Spain, p. 224 (445). On the discussion concerning the introduction of the opportunity principle in Spain, see *Aebi/Balcells*, 14 Eur. J. on Crim. Policy & Res. (2008), 329.

[43] See *Rechea Alberola/Fernández Molina*, 19 J. Contemp. Crim. Just., (2003), 403; for an overview of proceedings in juvenile cases, see *Aebi/Balcells*, 14 Eur. J. on Crim. Policy & Res. (2008), 326–328.

[44] For a brief introduction to the police, see *Bachmaier Winter*, Criminal Law in Spain, pp. 27–30 (nos. 23–28); *Canabat/Dulin*, in: Kurian (ed.), World encyclopedia of police forces and correctional systems, pp. 846–847; *Aebi/Jar-Couselo*, in: World Police Encyclopedia, pp. 774–780.

der the authority of both the Ministry of Interior and the Ministry of Defense. In its role as provider of public security and as judicial police *(Policía Judicial)*, the Civil Guard is under the authority of the Ministry of Interior. The distribution of competences between these two police forces is based partly on territory and partly on subject matter. In the area of law enforcement, the role of the police forces of the autonomous communities (the *Mossos d'Esquadra* in Catalonia, the *Ertzaintza* in Basque Country, and the *Policía Foral* in Navarra) is only to provide support in cooperation with the state police. Local police *(Policía Local)* may also act as judicial police, take preventive measures, and assist in other ways.[45]

Investigations are conducted either by the examining judge or by the public prosecutor. Educational requirements are similar for judges and public prosecutors. After completing their studies in law, candidates must pass a special theoretical examination that requires two to five years of preparation. Selected candidates must then complete two years of practical training. When they are hired, they become civil servants for life.[46]

The public prosecution service is not integrated into the judiciary. Structured hierarchically, it is under the authority of the state prosecutor general *(Fiscal General del Estado)*, who is appointed by the government.[47]

Recent statistics show that there has not been a significant overall change in criminality over the past few years. In 2010, the number of registered criminal offenses, both serious and less serious offenses *(delitos)* and minor offenses *(faltas)*,[48] was 2,297,353 (including, e.g., 103,155 crimes against life, limb, and liberty as well as 590,444 crimes against property, excluding minor offenses). The total number of criminal offenses in 2016 (2,011,586) amounted to 43.2 criminal offenses per 1,000 inhabitants (a decrease of 0.5 % from 2015).[49] Thus, developments in Spain reflected a general tendency in the EU, namely, a decrease in the level of crime. Whereas the number of crimes increased in ten EU Member States during the period 2007 to 2012, Spain was in the group of the remaining 16 EU Member

---

45 *Bachmaier Winter/del Moral García*, Criminal Law in Spain, pp. 27–30 (nos. 23–28); *Montero Aroca* et al., Derecho Jurisdiccional III, pp. 137–138.

46 *Poblet/Casanovas*, in: Guiseppe Di Federico (ed.) Recruitment, Professional Evaluation and Career of Judges and Prosecutors in Europe, pp. 192–194, 196–199. See also *Damián Moreno*, Introducción a la organización judicial española, pp. 118–123.

47 For details, see *del Moral García*, in: Jueces para la Democracia, no. 43, p. 21; for an overview, see *Bachmaier Winter/del Moral García*, Criminal Law in Spain, pp. 30–32 (29–31); *Aebi/Balcells,* 14 Eur. J. on Crim. Policy & Res. (2008), 311–331.

48 For the distinction between *delitos* and *faltas* (which was revoked by Organic Law 1/2015), see II.C.1.b.

49 MIR, Estadisticas de Criminalidad 2016, p. 5.

States in which a decrease in the number of crimes was recorded.[50] To be sure, these figures only reflect offenses that were officially reported.[51]

During the last ten years (2006–2016), the death toll from domestic violence offenses *(delitos de violencia doméstica)* was between 44 and 73 per year, all in all declining.[52] This area of crime, comprised primarily of cases of violence against women by their partners or spouses *(violencia machista)* but also of cases involving violence against children, has been the focus of numerous reforms in recent years and has become a top-priority issue in society and for criminal policymakers. The growing number of reports to the police indicates that victims are becoming less and less willing to tolerate such offenses. Police statistics point to other areas of focus as well. In the area of money laundering, for example, the number of detected offenses rose from 46 in 2000 to 175 in 2010 while the number of cases of child pornography rose from 45 to 862 in the same time period.[53] Similar developments were recorded with regard to violations of the controlled substances act, the seduction of minors, and possession of illegal weapons.[54]

In 2016, of the 2,009,690 committed crimes, 641,353 were solved, corresponding to a detection rate of 32 %; 367,936 individuals were arrested, corresponding to an arrest rate of 183 arrests per 1,000 offenses.[55]

b) Prosecuting authorities

The prosecuting authority is generally the public prosecution service.[56] In the case of so-called private prosecution offenses (*delitos privados*, Art. 215 Penal Code, *Código Penal*, CP), however, the right to initiate charges lies with the victim. In such cases, the offense must be prosecuted and the case must be pursued for

---

50 Eurostat, Archive: Crime statistics (1/2014), Table 1 Crimes recorded by the police, 2002–12.

51 See *Díez Ripollés*, Revista Española de Investigación Criminológica, Art. 1, no. 4 (2006), 17–18; Eurostat, Archive: Crime statistics (1/2014) Table 1 Crimes recorded by the police, 2002–12.

52 INE, Delito y violencia: Víctimas mortales por violencia de género por periodo.

53 MIR, Balance de Criminalidad 2010, Gráfico 17, p. 18 (child pornography); Gráfico 25, p. 26 (money laundering).

54 MIR, Balance de Criminalidad 2010, Gráfico 18, p. 19 (seduction of minors): Gráfico 19, p. 20 (crimes against the "patrimony"); Gráfico 26, p. 27 (assault); Gráfico 27, p. 28 (theft); Gráfico 31, p. 32 (plans re drugs near schools); Gráfico 32, p. 33 (possession of weapons); Gráfico 33, p. 34 (police); Gráfico 34, p. 35 (police).

55 MIR, Delitos, faltas, detenciones e imputaciones, y victimizaciones 2016, Table 3-1-0.

56 *Montero Aroca* et al., Derecho Jurisdiccional III, pp. 75–79; *De la Oliva Santos*, Derecho Procesal Penal, pp. 192–193; *Moreno Catena/Cortés Domínguez*, Derecho Procesal Penal, pp. 106–107; for details, see *Bachmaier Winter/del Moral García*, Criminal Law in Spain, pp. 30–32 (nos. 29–31); *Aebi/Balcells*, Eur. J. on Crim. Policy & Res. (2008), 311–331.

as long as the victim *(acusador privado)* asserts his or her right. In any event, the public prosecutor is not involved in this type of action. In the case of so-called semi-public offenses (*delitos semipúblicos*, e.g., Arts. 226–228 CP), the victim must at a minimum report the offense in order for it to be prosecuted. Spanish law also recognizes the instrument of non-public accusation *(acusación particular)*, which allows the victim to appear as a party in all proceedings; this instrument should not, however, be confused with the procedure for private prosecution discussed above. Another special feature of criminal proceedings is the procedural device known as a popular accusation *(acción popular)*, according to which every citizen (as well as every legal entity) has a constitutional right to initiate charges (Art. 125 CE).[57]

c) Criminal courts

Criminal courts are organized on the basis of various territorial entities. At the lowest level is the examining judge *(juez de instrucción)*, who is assigned to a judicial district *(partido judicial)*, that is, a town or several towns. For smaller municipalities or villages that do not have an examining judge, a justice of the peace *(Juzgados de Paz)*, a lay judge with jurisdiction over a limited number of minor criminal offenses is appointed by the city council every four years. At the provincial level, the criminal courts *(Juzgado de lo Penal)* have jurisdiction over criminal offenses subject to penalties of less than five years of imprisonment. The Civil and Criminal Chambers of the Provincial Courts *(Audiencia Provincial)* are the courts of second instance for such cases and also serve as courts of first instance for more serious criminal offenses. The Superior Courts of Justice *(Tribunal Superior de Justicia)* are the courts of the autonomous regions. The criminal divisions of the Superior Courts of Justice have jurisdiction over criminal cases against judges as well as over appeals of fact of decisions of the Provincial Courts. A special feature of the Spanish judiciary is the National Court *(Audiencia Nacional)*, which hears criminal cases of national importance (such as criminal offenses against the crown, forgery, drug crimes, and terrorism) from all over the country. The Supreme Court *(Tribunal Supremo)* is at the top of the court system; it is primarily responsible for appeals on matters of law *(casación)*; it does not hear appeals on matters of fact.[58]

As a rule, cases involving minor offenses *(delitos leves)* as well as cases involving offenses subject to penalties of less than five years of imprisonment are heard

---

[57] For a summary of the right to initiate charges, see *Armenta Deu*, Lecciones de Derecho Procesal Penal, pp. 97–103; *Gimeno Sendra*, Manual de Derecho Procesal Penal, pp. 161–163; *Bachmaier Winter/del Moral García*, Criminal Law in Spain pp. 224–226 (nos. 446–452); *Moreno Catena/Cortés Domínguez*, Derecho Procesal Penal, pp. 110–115; see I.C.3.

[58] *Bachmaier Winter/del Moral García*, Criminal Law in Spain, pp. 32–33 (nos. 33–34); *Montero Aroca* et al., Derecho Jurisdiccional III, pp. 54–55, 56–64.

by judges sitting alone *(juzgados unipersonales)*; cases involving criminal offenses punishable by imprisonment of more than five years and appeals are heard by a (collegial) panel of judges *(órganos colegiados)*. A judicial panel can be either a chamber or a section (*Sala* or *Sección*). Such panels are generally comprised of a minimum of three judges. There are, however, numerous exceptions to these rules. For example, appeals of decisions by examining judges in proceedings involving minor offenses *(juicios por delitos leves)* are decided by an individual judge of the Provincial Court, which usually is a court with judicial panels. Appeals of law involving offenses punishable by imprisonment of 12 years or more are heard by a section of the Supreme Court composed of a panel of five judges. In addition, certain cases are decided by a full panel (15 judges) of the Supreme Court.[59]

Since the introduction of the Law on Jury Trials in 1995 (Organic Law 5/1995), some criminal offenses are decided by a jury. Such trials take place at the seat of the Civil and Criminal Chambers of the Provincial Court. The jury court is composed of nine lay jurors and is presided over by a professional judge.[60] There are no lay judges in Spain, with the exception of justices of the peace.

According to the annual report of the General Council of the Judiciary *(Consejo General del Poder Judicial)*, on 1 January 2016, there were 1,130 judges sitting alone with jurisdiction over criminal matters *(jurisdicción penal)* and 1,046 judges sitting alone with jurisdiction over both civil and criminal matters *(jurisdicción mixta civil-penal)*. At that time, there were also 106 courts composed of judicial panels with jurisdiction over criminal matters and 44 courts composed of judicial panels with jurisdiction over both civil and criminal jurisdiction. This amounts to 12.2 judicial bodies per 100,000 residents (these statistics did not take into account justices of the peace – of which there were 7,687 on 1 Jan. 2016).[61]

---

[59] For a summary, see *Montero Aroca* et al., Derecho Jurisdiccional I, pp. 158–163; *Gimeno Sendra*, Manual de Derecho Procesal Penal, pp. 110–120.

[60] For details, see *Moreno Catena/Cortés Domínguez*, Derecho Procesal Penal, pp. 511–528; *Montero Aroca* et al., Derecho Jurisdiccional III, pp. 589–592; *Bachmaier Winter/del Moral García*, Criminal Law in Spain, pp. 33, 308–311 (nos. 33, 647–651); *Jimeno-Bulnes*, 148 Studia Iuridica Auctoritate Universitatis Pecs Publicata (2011), 135–166; *Grande*, in: Ross/Thaman (eds.), Comparative Criminal Procedure, pp. 365–395. For an extensive account of Spain's return to a jury system, see *Thaman*, 21 Hastings Int'l & Comp. L. Rev. (1997), 241–538.

[61] Consejo General del Poder Judicial, La justicia dato a dato, Año 2016, pp. 9–12, 51.

d) Criminal penalties

Spanish criminal law recognizes three types of penalties: deprivation of liberty, other penalties involving the deprivation of rights, and fines.[62] It also recognizes security measures.

– Criminal penalties

• Penalties involving deprivation of liberty (*penas privativas de libertad*, Arts. 35–38, 53 CP):

– reviewable life imprisonment (*prisión permanente revisable*, Arts. 35, 36 para. 1 and 92 CP);
– imprisonment (Art. 36 para. 2 CP);
– continuous tracking (up to six months, Art. 37 CP);
– "subsidiary" imprisonment due to non-payment of fines (*responsabilidad personal subsidiaria*, Art. 53 CP).

• Penalties involving deprivation of rights (*penas privativas de derechos*, Arts. 39–49 CP):[63]

– declaration of absolute disqualification: this entails the permanent loss of all official honors, employment, and positions held by the penalized person; such a person may not obtain these or any other honors, employment, or post nor may he or she be elected to public office during the term of the sentence;
– declaration of special disqualification from public employment or public office, certain professions or professional activities, certain commercial or business activities, parental rights, guardianship, custody or curatorship, eligibility for election, or any other right specifically set forth in the judgment;
– suspension from public employment or from public office;
– revocation of driver's license for motor vehicles and mopeds;
– revocation of firearm license;
– revocation of the right to live at or to visit certain places;
– prohibition on approaching the victim, the victim's family, or certain other individuals named by the judge;

---

[62] *Gracia Martín* (ed.), Tratado de las consecuencias jurídicas del delito, pp. 79–88; for an extensive account in German, see *Arroyo Zapatero*, ZStW 110 (2009), 438–460.

[63] On alternative sanctions (sanctions excluding imprisonment and fines), see *Ortiz Pradillo*, in: Hilgendorf/Valerius (eds.), Alternative Sanktionsformen zu Freiheits- und Geldstrafe im Strafrecht ausgewählter europäischer Staaten, pp. 93–116; *Dianiška* et al., 5 Societas and iurisprudentia (2017), 38–49.

– prohibition on contacting the victim, the victim's family, or other individuals named by the judge or by the court;
– pro bono community service;
– revocation of custody.

• Fines (*pena de multa*, Arts. 50–53 CP): A daily rate is set for the calculation of fines.

Based on their nature and duration, penalties are classified as serious, less serious, or minor (Art. 33 CP). This classification has no immediate consequences on jurisdiction, however, which is otherwise regulated by the laws of criminal procedure.

The maximum possible term of imprisonment or duration of a declaration of disqualification is 20 years (Arts. 36 para. 2 and 40 CP) unless otherwise provided for in the special part of the Penal Code. For certain offenses – aggravated murder (Art. 140 CP), rebellion (Art. 473 CP), and offenses against the crown (Art. 485 CP) – a term of imprisonment of up to 25 years may be imposed, and in some cases involving multiple serious offenses or terrorism, a term of imprisonment of up to 30 or 40 years may be imposed (Art. 76 CP).

Penalties involving the deprivation of rights can be imposed as principal penalties *(penas principales)* or as accessory penalties *(penas accesorias)*. Principal penalties, which are provided for in the special part of the Penal Code, are linked to specific forms of criminal conduct by means of offense definitions. Accessory penalties, in contrast, are not directly linked to specific forms of criminal conduct but may be associated with principal penalties and may in some instances be imposed in accordance with rules in the general part of the Penal Code. Depending upon the situation, the imposition of an accessory penalty may be mandatory or discretionary.[64]

– Security measures

In addition to criminal penalties, there are security measures *(medidas de seguridad)* (multi-track system, Arts. 95–108 CP). As a rule, these measures may only be imposed on persons without capacity or those with diminished capacity and only for the maximum duration of the corresponding penalty potentially applicable for the offense.[65] If penalties involving a deprivation of liberty and security measures are imposed at the same time, the security measure is served first. Subsequently, the criminal penalty – minus the amount of time spent serving the security measure – is served. If execution of the remaining criminal penalty would jeopardize the

---

[64] *Muñoz Conde/García Arán*, Derecho Penal, Parte General, pp. 537–539; *Bachmaier Winter/del Moral García*, Criminal Law in Spain, p. 163.

[65] *Gracia Martín*, Tratado de las consecuencias jurídicas del delito, pp. 434–455.

success of the security measure, execution can be suspended or an alternative security measure that does not involve a deprivation of liberty can be imposed (Art. 99 CP). The following is a list of potential security measures:

- Measures that involve a deprivation of liberty (Arts. 101–104 CP):
  - involuntary commitment to a psychiatric facility;
  - involuntary commitment to a detoxification facility;
  - involuntary commitment to an educational institution.
- Measures that do not involve a deprivation of liberty (Arts. 105–108 CP):
  - declaration of disqualification from a profession;
  - deportation of foreigners residing illegally in Spain;
  - supervised liberty *(libertad vigilada)*;
  - release to the custody of a family member;
  - revocation of driver's license for motor vehicles and mopeds;
  - revocation of firearm license.

Supervised liberty, which was introduced in the 2010 reform by Organic Law 5/2010, is a form of supervision that subjects the convicted person to judicial control through the imposition of conditions (Art. 106 CP). Some of the conditions that may be imposed were previously imposed as independent measures that did not involve a deprivation of liberty. Since the reform took effect, supervised liberty is the only security measure that, in cases involving sexual offenses or acts of terrorism, can also be imposed on persons with full criminal capacity.

A third type of penalty, in the broad sense, are the so-called collateral or accessory consequences (*consecuencias accesorias*, Arts. 127–129 bis CP). These include the forfeiture of items derived from the criminal offense, of tools used in the commission of the offense, and of gains realized from the offense as well as the forfeiture of other assets belonging to the offender that are of corresponding value (Art. 127 para. 3 CP). With regard to criminal offenses committed by a criminal or terrorist organization or group, there has been a presumption since the reform of 2010 that the assets of each individual participant stem from illegal activity if their value appears disproportionate in relation to assets lawfully obtained by that individual (Art. 127 para. 1 CP).[66]

The reform of 2010 also introduced the possibility of imposing criminal liability on legal entities. Legal consequences previously imposed on legal entities as accessory consequences (such as the closure of a company or the liquidation of corporations, associations, or foundations) are now – in addition to other new penalties –

---

66 See *Quintero Olivares*, in: Quintero Olivares (ed.), La Reforma Penal de 2010, pp. 107–110.

(also) classified as genuine penalties (Art. 129 paras. 1 and 2 in conj. with Art. 33 para. 7 a. through g. CP).[67]

e) Execution of custodial penalties

The law governing execution of custodial penalties addresses only the execution of sentences involving a deprivation of liberty in a prison facility.[68] The system of custodial penalties is based on the idea of reeducation and social reintegration, which is expressly set forth in the Constitution as the goal of punishment.[69] The Law on the Execution of Custodial Penalties (*Ley Orgánica General Penitenciaria* 1/1979) was enacted in 1979. Together with the corresponding regulations *(reglamentos)*, the law regulates a flexible and multi-leveled prison regime. The first level is closed prison, the second and third levels are open prisons in designated facilities (inmates in the third level are only required to spend certain times of the day in the facility), and the final level is early release on probation. The fundamental maxim is that no prisoner should be held at a level lower than the one that is appropriate for him or her. The system does not require an inmate to pass through all levels; for example, an inmate may transition directly from the first to the third level.

There are 69 penal institutions *(Centros Penitenciarios)* that are suitable for inmates serving a closed prison sentence.[70] Open prison sentences are executed either in a special "open section" *(sección abierta)* of such a penal institution or, preferably, in a so-called social integration center *(Centro de Inserción Social)*. As of 2017, there were 21 open prison sections and 32 social integration centers.[71]

According to data from the Council of Europe, there were 64,017 prisoners in Spain in September 2015, including pre-trial detainees. This amounts to about 138 inmates per 100,000 residents.[72] About one-third of all prisoners were foreigners,[73] and almost 8 % were women.[74] The number of inmates increased steadily until the reform of 2010. Since then, there has been a steady decline.[75] This may be because previous criminal law reforms generally led to longer prison terms. The average

---

[67] See *Zugaldía Espinar*, La Ley penal, 76, 2010, pp. 11–12; *Bacigalupo Saggese*, Diario La Ley no. 7541, 2011, 1292–1300; *Cuesta*, 84 Revue internationale de droit pénal (2013), 143–179. See also II.H.

[68] For a summary, see *Bachmaier Winter/del Moral García*, Criminal Law in Spain, pp. 33–34 (no. 35).

[69] See I.C.3.

[70] MIR, Establecimientos penitenciarios: Tipo-Centros Penitenciarios.

[71] MIR, Establecimientos penitenciarios: Tipo-Centros de Inserción Social.

[72] CoE: SPACE I – 2015, Table 1, p. 34.

[73] CoE: SPACE I – 2015, Table 4, p. 70.

[74] CoE: SPACE I – 2015, Table 3.A., p. 63.

[75] World Prison Brief: Spain.

annual increase in the number of inmates between the years 2000 and 2010 was 5.2 (113 inmates per 100,000 residents in 2000; 165 in 2010).[76] The reform of 2010, which created new alternatives to imprisonment and provided for a reduced sentencing range for drug-related offenses, has brought about a reduction in the number of prison inmates in recent years. Data from January 2018 estimate the number of prison inmates at 58,950 and the incarceration rate at 126 per 100,000 residents.[77] Given these figures, Spain is in the upper third in European and in the upper half in global comparisons.[78]

According to the most recent statistics from the Council of Europe in January 2016, prisons are no longer overcrowded. In 2015, about 82 inmates occupied 100 spaces.[79] As recently as 2009, 100 spaces were occupied by 153 inmates, whereas one year later 100 spaces were occupied by only 97 inmates.[80] This is because, in addition to the effects of the reform of 2010, a construction plan decided upon in 2005 called for the building of 18 new prison facilities and 32 social integration centers in order to increase capacity by 18,000 spaces.[81]

Bibliography and further reading

General references:

Armenta Deu, Teresa, Lecciones de Derecho Procesal Penal (Lessons on the law of criminal procedure). 9th ed. Madrid 2016.

Bachmaier Winter, Lorena/del Moral García, Antonio, Criminal Law in Spain. 2d ed. Alphen aan den Rijn 2012.

Damián Moreno, Juan, Introducción a la organización judicial española (Introduction to the organization of the Spanish judiciary). Madrid 2004.

de la Oliva Santos, Andrés, Derecho Procesal Penal (Law of criminal procedure). 5th ed. Madrid 2007.

del Moral García, Antonio, Ministerio Fiscal y reforma de la Justicia (The prosecutor's office and judicial reform). Jueces para la Democracia, no. 43, March 2002, 19–27, available at https://dialnet.unirioja.es/descarga/articulo/232230.pdf [last visited March 2018].

---

76 World Prison Brief: Spain.

77 World Prison Brief: Spain.

78 World Prison Brief, Prison Population Rate (Highest to lowest: Europe); World Prison Brief, Prison Population Rate (Highest to lowest: Entire world).

79 CoE: SPACE I – 2015, Table 1, p. 34.

80 For comparison, see CoE: SPACE I – 2009, Table 1, p. 26 (excluding Catalonia) and CoE: SPACE I – 2010, Table 1, p. 37 (excluding Catalonia).

81 MIR, Notas de Prensa, 18 Nov. 2005.

Der neue Fischer Weltalmanach 2018. Zahlen, Daten, Fakten (New Fischer World Almanac 2018. Numbers, data, facts). Frankfurt am Main 2017.

Díez Ripollés, José Luis, Algunos rasgos de la delincuencia en España a comienzos del siglo XXI (Some characteristics/features of criminal delinquency in Spain at the beginning of the 21st century). Revista Española de Investigación Criminológica, Art. 1, no. 4 (2006), 1–19, available at https://dialnet.unirioja.es/descarga/articulo/2083343.pdf [last visited March 2018].

Díez Ripollés, José Luis, La racionalidad legislativa penal: contenidos e instrumentos de control (The legislative rationality in criminal law). In: José Luis Díez Ripollés/Ana María Prieto del Pino/Susana Soto Navarro (eds.), La política legislativa penal en occidente. Una perspectiva comparada (The legislative policy in criminal law in the Occident. A comparative perspective). Valencia 2005, pp. 272–322.

– La racionalidad de las leyes penales (The rationality of the criminal laws). 2d ed. Madrid 2013.

García de Enterría, Eduardo, La Revisión del Sistema de Autonomías Territoriales. Reforma de Estatutos, Leyes de Transferencia y Delegación, Federalismo (The revision of the system of autonomous territories. Reform of the statutes, laws on transfer and delegation, federalism). Madrid 1988.

Gimeno Sendra, Vicente, Manual de Derecho Procesal Penal (Handbook of the law of criminal procedure). 3d ed. Madrid 2015.

Hoffmann, Markus (trans.), Das spanische Strafgesetzbuch vom 23. November 1995 nach dem Stand vom 31. Dezember 2001 (The Spanish Penal Code of 23 November 1995 as of 31 December 2001). Freiburg 2002.

Merino-Blanco, Elena, Spanish Law and Legal System. 2d ed. London 2006.

Montero Aroca, Juan/Gómez Colomer, Juan Luís/Montón Redondo, Alberto/Barona Vilar, Silvia, Derecho Jurisdiccional III – Proceso Penal (Law of jurisdiction III – Criminal procedure). 25th ed. Valencia 2017.

– Derecho Jurisdiccional I – Parte General (Law of jurisdiction I – General part). 25th ed. Valencia 2017.

Moreno Catena, Víctor/Cortés Domínguez, Valentín, Derecho Procesal Penal (Law of criminal procedure). 7th ed. Valencia 2015.

Oliva Santos de la, Andrés, Derecho Procesal Penal (Law of criminal procedure). 8th ed. Madrid 2007.

Geography:

CIA World Factbook: Spain: Geography, https://www.cia.gov/library/publications/resources/the-world-factbook/geos/sp.html [last visited March 2018].

Der neue Fischer Weltalmanach 2018 (The New Fischer World Almanac 2018). Frankfurt am Main 2017.

Population:

Banco de España (Bank of Spain), Boletín Económico, Los flujos migratorios en España durante la crisis (Economic report, The migratory flows in Spain during the crisis). Available at: https://www.bde.es/f/webbde/SES/Secciones/Publicaciones/InformesBoletines Revistas/BoletinEconomico/14/Sep/Fich/be1409-art5.pdf [last visited March 2018].

CIA World Factbook: Spain: People and Society, https://www.cia.gov/library/publications/resources/the-world-factbook/geos/sp.html [last visited March 2018].

El País, España perderá medio millón de habitantes en la próxima década si se mantiene la tendencia demográfica (Spain is going to lose half a million of inhabitants in the next decade if it maintains the demographic tendency), 7 Oct. 2011, https://elpais.com/sociedad/2011/10/07/actualidad/1317938404_850215.html [last visited March 2018].

Eurostat:

– Population and Population Change Statistics, http://ec.europa.eu/eurostat/statistics-explained/index.php/Population_and_population_change_statistics [last visited March 2018].

– Population density, http://ec.europa.eu/eurostat/tgm/table.do?tab=table&init=1&language=en&pcode=tps00003&plugin=1 [last visited March 2018].

– Population grids, http://ec.europa.eu/eurostat/statistics-explained/index.php/Population_grids [last visited March 2018].

Instituto Nacional de Estadística, INE (National Institute for Statistics):

– Notas de Prensa (press release), Cifras de Población a 1 de enero de 2017 Estadística de Migraciones 2016 (Population figures as of 1 Jan. 2017 Migration statistics 2016), 29 June 2017, http://www.ine.es/prensa/cp_2017_p.pdf [last visited March 2018].

– Population resident in Spain, http://www.ine.es/dyngs/INEbase/es/operacion.htm?c=Estadistica_C&cid=1254736176951&menu=ultiDatos&idp=1254735572981.

– Residential variations statistics, http://www.ine.es/jaxiPx/Datos.htm?path=/t20/e245/p08/l0/&file=01004.px [last visited March 2018].

Ministerio de Fomento (Ministry of public works), Las Grandes Áreas Urbanas y sus municipios (Large urban reas and their Municipalities), https://www.fomento.gob.es/NR/rdonlyres/416CE7FD-A6B0-431D-881B-D1F07664795E/146838/listado__2017.pdf [last visited March 2018].

Language:

Agencia EFE (Spanish international news agency), Día alfabetización: En España hay casi 700.000 personas analfabetas (International Literacy Day: In Spain there are almost 700,000 illiterate people), 8 Sept. 2016, https://www.efe.com/efe/espana/sociedad/en-espana-hay-casi-700-000-personas-analfabetas/10004-3034673 [last visited March 2018].

Der neue Fischer Weltalmanach 2018 (The New Fischer World Almanac 2018). Frankfurt am Main 2017.

Generalitat de Catalunya (Government of Catalonia), Catalan, language of Europe, http://llengua.gencat.cat/permalink/91192f76-5385-11e4-8f3f-000c29cdf219 (no publication date) [last visited March 2018].

Instituto Cervantes (Cervantes Institute):

– El español, una lengua viva, informe 2017 (Spanish, a living language, report 2017), https://cvc.cervantes.es/lengua/espanol_lengua_viva/pdf/espanol_lengua_viva_2017.pdf [last visited March 2018].

– Quiénes somos (About us), http://www.cervantes.es/sobre_instituto_cervantes/informacion.htm [last visited March 2018].

Instituto Nacional de Estadística, INE (National Institute for Statistics), Population of 16 years old and over by educational level reached, http://www.ine.es/jaxiT3/Tabla.htm?t=6369 [last visited March 2018].

Religion:

Centro de Investigaciones Sociológicas, CIS (Center for Sociological Research), Barómetro de Julio 2017, Estudio n° 3183 (Barometer of July 2017, Study no. 3183), http://datos.cis.es/pdf/Es3183mar_A.pdf [last visited March 2018].

CIA World Factbook: Spain People and Society, https://www.cia.gov/library/publications/resources/the-world-factbook/geos/sp.html [last visited March 2018].

Ministerio de Justicia (Ministry of Justice), Annual report on the status of religious freedom in Spain 2016), 2017, http://www.mjusticia.gob.es/cs/Satellite/Portal/1292428604097?blobheader=application%2Fpdf&blobheadername1=Content-Disposition&blobheadername2=Grupo&blobheadervalue1=attachment%3B+filename%3DInforme_anual_sobre_la_situacion_de_la_libertad_religiosa_en_Espana_2016_Ingles.PDF&blobheadervalue2=Docs_Libertad+religiosa [last visited March 2018].

Economy:

Der neue Fischer Weltalmanach 2018. Zahlen, Daten, Fakten (New Fischer World Almanac 2018. Numbers, data, facts). Frankfurt am Main 2017.

World Bank, Gross national income per capita 2016, http://databank.worldbank.org/data/download/GNIPC.pdf [last visited March 2018].

System of government:

Bachmaier Winter, Lorena/del Moral García, Antonio, Criminal Law in Spain. 2d ed. Alphen aan den Rijn 2012.

Der neue Fischer Weltalmanach 2018. Zahlen, Daten, Fakten (New Fischer World Almanac 2018. Numbers, data, facts). Frankfurt am Main 2017.

Díez Ripollés, La Racionalidad de las Leyes Penales. 2d ed. Madrid 2013.

Ferreres Comella, Victor, The Constitution of Spain. Oxford 2013.

García de Enterría, Eduardo, La Revisión del Sistema de Autonomías Territoriales. Reforma de Estatutos, Leyes de Transferencia y Delegación, Federalismo (The revision of the system of autonomous territories. Reform of the statutes, laws on transfer and delegation, federalism). Madrid 1988.

Zapata-Barrero, Ricard, Spain. In: Christian Joppke/F. Leslie Seidle (eds.), Immigrant Integration in Federal Countries. Montreal 2012, pp. 135–160.

Investigating authorities:

Aebi, Marcelo F./Balcells, Marc, The Prosecution Service Function within the Spanish Criminal Justice System. 14 Eur. J. on Crim. Policy & Res. (2008), 311–331.

Aebi, Marcelo F./Jar-Couselo, Gonzalo, Spain. In: Dilip K. Das (ed.), World Police Encyclopedia. New York 2006, pp. 773–780.

Bachmaier Winter, Lorena/del Moral García, Antonio, Criminal Law in Spain. 2d ed. Alphen aan den Rijn 2012.

Canabata, Josep/Dulin, Adam, Spain. In: George Thomas Kurian (ed.), World encyclopedia of police forces and correctional systems. 2d ed. Detroit, Mich. 2006, pp. 846–849.

Damián Moreno, Juan, Introducción a la organización judicial española (Introduction to the organization of the Spanish judiciary). Madrid 2004.

del Moral García, Antonio, Ministerio Fiscal y reforma de la Justicia (The Prosecutor's office and judicial reform). Jueces para la Democracia, no. 43, March 2002, 19–27, available at https://dialnet.unirioja.es/descarga/articulo/232230.pdf [last visited March 2018].

Díez Ripollés, José Luis, Algunos rasgos de la delincuencia en España a comienzos del siglo XXI (Some characteristics/features of criminal delinquency in Spain at the beginning of the 21st century). Revista Española de Investigación Criminológica (Spanish Journal of Criminological Research), Art. 1, no. 4 (2006), 1–19, available at https://dialnet.unirioja.es/descarga/articulo/2083343.pdf [last visited March 2018].

Eurostat, Archive: Crime statistics (1/2014) Table 1 Crimes recorded by the police, 2002–12 (2012), http://ec.europa.eu/eurostat/statistics-explained/index.php/Archive:Crime_statistics#Total_recorded_crime [last visited March 2018].

Instituto Nacional de Estadística, INE (National Institute for Statistics), Delito y violencia: Víctimas mortales por violencia de género por period, http://www.ine.es/jaxi/Datos.htm?path=/t00/mujeres_hombres/tablas_1/l0/&file=v02001.px [last visited March 2018].

Merino-Blanco, Elena, Spanish Law and Legal System. 2d ed. London 2006.

Ministerio del Interior, MIR (Ministry of the Interior):

– Estadisticas de Criminalidad 2016 (Crime statistics), http://www.interior.gob.es/documents/10180/6865255/Presentacion+ministro_Balance+de+Criminalidad+2016.pdf [last visited March 2018].

– Delitos, faltas, detenciones e imputaciones, y victimizaciones 2016 (Offenses, minor offenses, detentions and charges, and victimizations 2016), www.interior.gob.es/documents/642317/7696854/Delitos%2C%20faltas%2C%20detenciones+e+imputaciones%2C%20y+victimizaciones+2016.zip/a82edd92-96e8-4bcf-99ac-56a8e6fc05fe [last visited March 2018].

– Balance de Criminalidad 2010 (Criminality balance sheet 2010), http://www.interior.gob.es/documents/642317/1204780/Informe+Nacional+Evoluci%C3%B3n+Criminalidad+(Senado).pdf/689da2c2-6a52-4527-9b46-b1c82206e0e8 [last visited March 2018].

Montero Aroca, Juan/Gómez Colomer, Juan Luís/Montón Redondo, Alberto/Barona Vilar, Silvia, Derecho Jurisdiccional III – Proceso Penal (Law of jurisdiction III – Criminal procedure). 25th ed. Valencia 2017.

Moreno Catena, Víctor/Cortés Domínguez, Valentín, Derecho Procesal Penal (Law of criminal procedure). 7th ed. Valencia 2015.

Poblet, Marta/Casanovas, Pompeu, Recruitment, Professional Evaluation and Career of Judges and Prosecutors in Spain. In: Guiseppe Di Federico (ed.) Recruitment, Professional Evaluation and Career of Judges and Prosecutors in Europe: Austria, France, Germany, Italy, The Netherlands and Spain. Bologna 2005, http://www.difederico-giustizia.it/wp-content/uploads/2010/09/recruitment-evaluation-and-career.pdf [last visited March 2018].

Rechea Alberola, Cristina/Fernández Molina, Esther, Juvenile Justice in Spain: Past and Present. 19 J. Contemp. Crim. Just. 403 (2003).

Prosecuting authorities:

Aebi, Marcelo F./Balcells, Marc, The Prosecution Service Function within the Spanish Criminal Justice System. 14 Eur. J. on Crim. Policy & Res. (2008), 311–331.

Armenta Deu, Teresa, Lecciones de Derecho Procesal Penal (Lessons on the law of criminal procedure). 9th ed. Madrid 2016.

Bachmaier Winter, Lorena/del Moral García, Antonio, Criminal Law in Spain. 2d ed. Alphen aan den Rijn 2012.

de la Oliva Santos, Andrés, Derecho Procesal Penal (Law of criminal procedure). 5th ed. Madrid 2007.

Gimeno Sendra, Vicente, Manual de Derecho Procesal Penal (Handbook of the law of criminal procedure). 3d ed. Madrid 2015.

Montero Aroca, Juan/Gómez Colomer, Juan Luís/Montón Redondo, Alberto/Barona Vilar, Silvia, Derecho Jurisdiccional III – Proceso Penal (Law of jurisdiction III – Criminal procedure). 25th ed. Valencia 2017.

Moreno Catena, Víctor/Cortés Domínguez, Valentín, Derecho Procesal Penal (Law of criminal procedure). 7th ed. Valencia 2015.

Criminal courts:

Bachmaier Winter, Lorena/del Moral García, Antonio, Criminal Law in Spain. 2d ed. Alphen aan den Rijn 2012.

Consejo General del Poder Judicial (Spanish General Council of the Judiciary), La justicia dato a dato, Año 2016 (Data on the judiciary, 2016), http://www.poderjudicial.es/cgpj/es/Temas/Estadistica-Judicial/Estudios-e-Informes/Justicia-Dato-a-Dato [last visited March 2018].

Gimeno Sendra, Vicente, Manual de Derecho Procesal Penal (Handbook of the law of criminal procedure). 3d ed. Madrid 2015.

Grande, Elisabetta, Rumba justice and the Spanish jury trial. In: Jacqueline E. Ross/Stephen C. Thaman (eds.), Comparative Criminal Procedure. Cheltenham 2016, pp. 365–395.

Jimeno-Bulnes, Mar, Jury Selection and Jury Trial in Spain: Between Theory and Practice. 148 Studia Iuridica Auctoritate Universitatis Pecs Publicata (2011), 135–166.

Montero Aroca, Juan/Gómez Colomer, Juan Luís/Montón Redondo, Alberto/Barona Vilar, Silvia, Derecho Jurisdiccional III – Proceso Penal (Law of jurisdiction III – Criminal procedure). 25th ed. Valencia 2017.

Moreno Catena, Víctor/Cortés Domínguez, Valentín, Derecho Procesal Penal (Law of criminal procedure). 7th ed. Valencia 2015.

Criminal penalties:

Arroyo Zapatero, Luis, Grunderfordernisse des Allgemeinen Teils für ein europäisches Sanktionenrecht. Landesbericht Spanien (Basic requirements of the general part for a European law of sanctioning. Country report Spain). ZStW 110 (2009), 438–460.

Bacigalupo Saggese, Silvina, Los criterios de imputación de la responsabilidad penal de los entes colectivos y de sus órganos de gobierno (arts. 31 bis y 129 CP) (Criteria of attribution of criminal liability of public corporations and their governing bodies). Diario La Ley, no. 7541, 2011, 1292–1300.

Cuesta, José Luis de la, Criminal Responsibility of Legal Persons in Spanish Law, Criminal Responsibility of Legal Persons in Spanish Law. 84 Revue internationale de droit pénal (2013), 143–179.

Dianiška, Gustáv/Strémy, Tomáš/Laciak, Ondrej, Alternative Sanctions in the Spanish Criminal Law. 5 Societas and iurisprudentia (2017), 38–49.

Gracia Martín, Luis (ed.), Tratado de las consecuencias jurídicas del delito (Treatise on the legal consequences of crimes). Valencia 2006.

Muñoz Conde, Francisco/García Arán, Mercedes, Derecho Penal, Parte General (Criminal law, general part). Valencia 2015.

Ortiz Pradillo, Juan Carlos, Alternative Sanctions in Spanish Criminal Law, Excluding Imprisonment and Fines: Present and Future. In: Eric Hilgendorf/Brian Valerius (eds.), Alternative Sanktionsformen zu Freiheits- und Geldstrafe im Strafrecht ausgewählter europäischer Staaten (Alternative sanctions to imprisonment and fines in selected European countries). Berlin 2015, pp. 93–116.

Quintero Olivares, Gonzalo, La reforma del comiso (art. 127 CP) (The reform of confiscation). In: Gonzalo Quintero Olivares (ed.), La Reforma Penal de 2010: Análisis y Comentarios (The criminal law reform 2010: Analysis and commentary). Navarra 2010, pp. 107–110.

Thaman, Stephen C., Spain Returns to Trial by Jury. 21 Hastings Int'l & Comp. L. Rev. (1997), 241–538.

Zugaldía Espinar, José Miguel, Societas delinquere potest, análisis de la reforma operada en el Código Penal español por la LO 5/2010, de 22 de junio (Societas delinquere potest, analysis of the reform operated in the Spanish Penal Code by the Organic Law 5/2010 of 22nd of June). La Ley penal: Revista de derecho penal, procesal y penitenciario, 76, 2010, 5–16.

Execution of custodial penalties:

Bachmaier Winter, Lorena/del Moral García, Antonio, Criminal Law in Spain. 2d ed. Alphen aan den Rijn 2012.

Council of Europe, Council of Europe Annual Penal Statistics (CoE):

– SPACE I – 2015 (updated 25 Apr. 2017), http://wp.unil.ch/space/files/2017/04/SPACE_I_2015_FinalReport_161215_REV170425.pdf [last visited March 2018].

– SPACE I – 2010, http://wp.unil.ch/space/files/2014/04/SPACE1_2010_English.pdf (excluding Catalonia) [last visited March 2018].

– SPACE I – 2009, http://wp.unil.ch/space/files/2011/02/SPACE-1_2009_English2.pdf (excluding Catalonia) [last visited March 2018].

Ministerio del Interior, MIR (Ministry of the Interior):

– Establecimientos penitenciarios: Tipo-Centros Penitenciarios, http://www.institucionpenitenciaria.es/web/portal/centrosPenitenciarios/localizacion.html?ep=&ept=pen&epp= [last visited March 2018].

– Establecimientos penitenciarios: Tipo-Centros de Inserción Social, http://www.institucionpenitenciaria.es/web/portal/centrosPenitenciarios/localizacion.html?ept=ins [last visited March 2018].

– Notas de Prensa (Press release), Interior invertirá más de 1.647 millones de euros en la construcción de 46 nuevas infraestructuras penitenciarias (Interior will invest more than 1,647 million euros in the construction of 46 new peniticiaries), 18 Nov. 2005, http://www.institucionpenitenciaria.es/web/portal/Noticias/Noticias/noticia_0153.html?fototeca=n [last visited March 2018].

World Prison Brief:

– Spain, http://www.prisonstudies.org/country/spain [last visited March 2018].

– Prison Population Rate (Highest to lowest: Europe), http://www.prisonstudies.org/highest-to-lowest/prison-population-total?field_region_taxonomy_tid=14 [last visited March 2018].

– Prison Population Rate (Highest to lowest: Entire world), http://www.prisonstudies.org/highest-to-lowest/prison_population_rate?field_region_taxonomy_tid=All [last visited March 2018].

B. Comparative legal classification and international ties

1. Comparative legal classification

Spain belongs to the continental European legal family and, within this family, it is a representative of the Roman-canonical tradition. The importance attached to both of these elements for the understanding of current Spanish law – namely, Romanization until the 5th century, on the one hand (which led to the initial standardization of almost all the legal systems in existence at that time on the Iberian peninsula), and the power of church authority and canonical law, on the other – has given rise to the controversial claim that other elements, such as the codifications since the 19th century and Spain's current self-image as a social and democratic state under the rule of law, are incidental to rather than essential or integral components of the Spanish system.[1]

The invasion by the Germanic peoples in 415 did not lead to a break with Roman law. Indeed, the most significant codifications of the Visigoth kings (*Codex Euricianus*, *Breviary of Alaric* or *Lex Romana Visigothorum*, and *Liber Iudiciorum*) did not contain Germanic law but rather "vulgar" Roman law (i.e., laws not imposed by Rome), although a few Germanic practices were adopted.[2] In any event, the impact of Germanic elements on the law in Spain has remained a topic of debate to this day.[3]

Likewise, the invasion by the Moors at the beginning of the 7th century did not result in a significant Islamic impact on future Spanish law. However, beginning with the division of the country into Christian and Muslim territories and continuing throughout the *Reconquista*, the incipient process of standardization of law did in fact stagnate until the 11th century. During this period, there were numerous Christian kingdoms, each with its own legal system, and the Christianization of the law reached one of its peaks.[4]

In the 12th century, a new era of unification of law began – not only in Spain – thanks to the creation and reception of the *ius commune*, a combination of Justinian, canonical, local, and feudal laws, which was revised in accordance with Roman-canonical methods and ultimately implemented in practice. This development is also closely linked to the emergence of the sciences of law and of universities.[5]

---

[1] *Ibán*, Einführung in das spanische Recht, p. 27; *Neumayer*, in: David/Grasmann (eds.), Einführung in die großen Rechtssysteme der Gegenwart, pp. 56–57; *Górriz Royo*, Institutions of Criminal Law, p. 16.

[2] See *Ibán*, Einführung in das spanische Recht, p. 24; *Merino-Blanco*, The Spanish Legal System, p. 4.

[3] *Alvarado Planas*, El problema del germanismo en el Derecho español, pp. 15–24.

[4] *Ibán*, Einführung in das spanische Recht, p. 24; *Merino-Blanco*, Spanish Law and Legal System, p. 5; *David/Brierley*, Major Legal Systems in the World Today, pp. 36–37.

[5] *Ibán*, Einführung in das spanische Recht, p. 24.

Nevertheless, it remains difficult for Spain to characterize the reception of the *ius commune* in general terms because its integration into both royal and traditional law varied by region, and details of the process are still the subject of debate today.[6] From the 13th century onward, the law code *Siete Partidas* (The Seven Parts of Law), which was strongly influenced by Roman law, gained prominence; promulgated as law in Castile, its application in other regions was subsidiary.[7]

A truly national law did not emerge until the 15th century after the unification of the crowns of Castile and Aragon and the expulsion of the Muslims in 1492.[8] In addition to the generally-applicable Castilian law, which can be considered the foundation of Spanish law, numerous additional legal systems with regional applicability remained in force. Although the further implementation of Castilian law in the Spanish kingdom contributed to the unification of the law until well into the 18th century, for certain issues of civil law, rules with regional (or "particular") applicability *(Fueros)* are still in force today.

An additional element that links Spain to the continental European legal family is the codification of law that took place in the 19th century.[9] Following the War of Independence, provoked by the Napoleonic invasion in 1808, and continuing throughout the century, Spain experienced major political fluctuations (proclamation of the First Republic in 1873, restoration of the monarchy in 1874). During this period, there was a "Frenchification" of Spanish law, including among other things the strengthening of the position of a codified law that called for judges to be bound by the law and prescribed the subsidiarity of customary law. The first Commercial Code *(Código de Comercio)*, based on French law, was enacted in 1829. This was followed in 1848 by the Penal Code *(Código Penal)*, which represented the first renunciation of the criminal law system of the *ancien régime*; in 1855 by the Code of Civil Procedure *(Ley de Enjuiciamiento Civil)*; in 1883 by the Code of Criminal Procedure *(Ley de Enjuiciamiento Criminal)*; and, finally, in 1889 by the Civil Code *(Código Civil)*.[10]

The 20th century began with a weakened monarchical system. The Second Spanish Republic was proclaimed in 1931; however, it did not last long enough to realize its planned reforms.[11] The Spanish Civil War, which gave rise to the *Franco*

---

[6] *Lalinde Abadía*, El derecho común en los territorios ibéricos, pp. 150, 172–178; *Bachmaier Winter/del Moral García*, Criminal Law in Spain, pp. 35–36 (no. 39).

[7] *Zweigert/Kötz*, An Introduction to Comparative Law, p. 107.

[8] *Ibán*, Einführung in das spanische Recht, p. 25; see *Masferrer*, 4 J. Civ. L. Stud. 432 (2011).

[9] For details on the codification of criminal law through the criminal codes of 1822, 1848, 1870, 1928, 1944, and 1995 and their major amendments, see *Bachmaier Winter/del Moral García,* Criminal Law in Spain, pp. 37–44 (nos. 42–52).

[10] *Merino-Blanco*, Spanish Law and Legal System, pp. 17–24.

[11] *Ibán*, Einführung in das spanische Recht, p. 26.

dictatorship, broke out in 1936. A new political model was not introduced until after *Franco's* death, 40 years later. The transition to this new model took place over a two-year period, called the *Transición Española*, which can be described as a shift from an autocratic to a democratic constitutional system using mechanisms provided for in the first system. The fruits of the search for a constitutional law framework based upon the broadest possible consensus can be seen in the Constitution of 1978, which is still in force today. The goal was a framework within which the conflicts in Spanish society, rooted in the 19th century, could be resolved peacefully for the future. While the Constitution provided for a new territorial organization of the state and for the independence of the judiciary, the core issue of religion and the relationship between church and state continues to be a controversial aspect of the new constitutional order.[12] In the years following adoption of the Constitution, comprehensive legal reforms in all areas of the law were introduced. Especially crucial was the change in judicial practice, which was primarily the result of decisions of the Constitutional Court *(Tribunal Constitucional)* and the Supreme Court *(Tribunal Supremo)* – to some extent through application of the same laws.

Another defining characteristic of the Spanish legal system is its link to the law in Latin America as a result of colonization in the 15th century. In the course of time, however, the individual Latin American countries have developed in different ways and been subject to different influences.

2. Effects of international ties

a) Membership in international and regional organizations

The cornerstones of Spain's international relationships are Europe, the Atlantic region, Latin America, and the Mediterranean region. It is a member of many international organizations with long traditions, such as the UNESCO (since 1953), the United Nations (since 1955), the International Monetary Fund (since 1958), and the Organization for Economic Co-operation and Development (OECD; since 1961). It was not until the last quarter of the 20th century, particularly since the second democratic elections in 1982, that Spain entered a phase of opening up to the outside world, as a result of which its relationships with western European countries and its international presence were significantly strengthened. In 1977, it joined the Council of Europe; in 1986, it entered (together with Portugal) the European Economic Union (today the European Union); since 1988 it has been a member of NATO; and in 1990 it entered (again together with Portugal) the Western European Union (which ceased to exist in 2011). Spain has held a seat as a non-permanent

---

[12] See *López Guerra/Rodríguez Mourullo* et al., El Derecho Constitucional Español del siglo XX, pp. 24–30; *Merino-Blanco*, Spanish Law and Legal System, pp. 24–25.

member of the UN Security Council five times; it has been a member of the World Trade Organization since 1995.

In the context of its relationship to Latin America, Spain has joined the following organizations: member of the Economic Commission for Latin America and the Caribbean *(Comisión Económica para América Latina y el Caribe)*, founded in 1948; permanent observer to the Organization of American States; observer to the Andean Community (*Comunidad Andina*, called the Andean Pact until 1996), which came into existence upon the signing of the Cartagena Agreement in 1969; and observer to the Latin American Integration Association *(Asociación latino-americana de integración)*, founded in 1980.

b) Signature and ratification of international treaties and conventions

Spanish criminal law is increasingly shaped by supranational instruments. Ratified international treaties do not become part of the domestic legal order until they have been published in the official state gazette (Art. 96 para. 1 CE). The primary objective of significant developments in the criminal law over the past two decades has been the implementation of European and international law requirements.

As far as the protection of human rights is concerned, Spain did not commit itself to granting the fundamental guarantees of the European Convention for the Protection of Human Rights and Fundamental Freedoms (ECHR, 1950) until 1979. Subsequent additional protocols, such as Protocols nos. 6 and 13 regarding the abolition of the death penalty (the latter was signed in 2002 *ad referendum*) are also binding. The International Covenant on Civil and Political Rights of 1966 was ratified in 1977, one year prior to the Constitution of 1978. Additional instruments in the area of human rights are the Council of Europe Convention on Action against Trafficking in Human Beings of 2005 (entered into force in 2009), and the Council of Europe Convention on the Protection of Children against Sexual Exploitation and Sexual Abuse of 2007 (entered into force in 2010). The Council of Europe Convention on Preventing and Combating Violence against Women and Domestic Violence – a problem area that has achieved high priority in national criminal policy in recent years[13] – was signed in 2011 *ad referendum*.

Also related to human rights is the UN Convention against Torture and Other Cruel, Inhuman or Degrading Treatment or Punishment of 1984, ratified in 1987, and its optional Protocol, which entered into force in 2006, that establishes a system of regular visits to prison undertaken by independent observers. The European Convention for the Prevention of Torture and Inhuman or Degrading Treatment or Punishment of 1987 was ratified in 1989. Spain's involvement in international instruments against torture triggered intense debate on the legal regulation of such

[13] See I.A.5.a.

practices in Spanish law. The introduction of an offense of torture based on the international model (as an *ex officio* offense) was followed in 1995 by the recognition of a new legally protected interest, namely, that of moral integrity, and the introduction of a new offense that encompasses similar abuses committed by private persons.

In the area of international humanitarian law, all four of the Geneva Conventions (1949) were ratified in 1952. The additional protocols were also ratified (I–II, 1989; III, 2010). The same is true of the UN Convention on the Prevention and Punishment of the Crime of Genocide of 1948 (ratified in 1968), which led to the introduction of the offense of genocide in the Spanish Penal Code early on. Further important additions in the area of international criminal offenses were made following ratification of the Rome Statute of the International Criminal Court (1998) in 2000: In 2003, provisions concerning crimes against humanity were implemented and the provisions on war crimes were reformed so as to comply to some extent with the Rome Statute. Organic Law 18/2003 of 10 December 2003 governs cooperation with the International Criminal Court. Similar procedural laws governing cooperation with the ICTY (1994) and the ICTR (1998) were enacted earlier.

The fight against terrorism is a top priority and is one of the areas in which Spain is particularly dependent on international assistance. In addition to domestic legislation – which is fully sufficient – and to EU instruments, all of the UN counterterrorism conventions are applicable. More recently ratified treaties include, in 2006, the Treaty of Prüm on the stepping up of cross-border cooperation, particularly in combating terrorism and cross-border crime, which provides contracting parties certain rights to access national data on DNA, fingerprints, and vehicle registration, and, in 2007, the UN Convention for the Suppression of Acts of Nuclear Terrorism of 2005.

Spain is party to several major UN instruments in the area of organized crime. These include the UN Convention against Transnational Organized Crime (New York 2000, ratified in 2002), its Additional Protocols on Human Trafficking and on Smuggling of Migrants (also ratified in 2002), and the Additional Protocol against the Illicit Manufacturing of and Trafficking in Firearms, Their Parts and Components and Ammunition, as well as against their illegal trade (New York 2001, accession in 2007).

Significant instruments in the fight against economic crime – money laundering, in particular – include the United Nations Convention against Illicit Traffic in Narcotic Drugs and Psychotropic Substances (Vienna 1988, ratified in 1990), the Council of Europe Convention on Laundering, Search, Seizure and Confiscation of the Proceeds from Crime (1990) ratified and entered into force in 1998, and the Council of Europe Convention on Laundering, Search, Seizure and Confiscation of the Proceeds from Crime and on the Financing of Terrorism (2005) ratified and entered into force in 2010. Spain acceded to the OECD Convention on Combating

Bribery of Foreign Public Officials (Paris 1997) in 2000. In 2005, it acceded to the Convention on the fight against corruption involving officials of the European Communities or officials of Member States of the European Union (1997), and in 2006 it ratified the UN Convention against Corruption (New York 2003). The Council of Europe Criminal Law Convention against Corruption (1999) and its Additional Protocol (2003) entered into force in 2010 and 2011, respectively.

Spanish criminal law is strongly influenced by European legal instruments.[14] In the area of international mutual legal assistance within the context of the Council of Europe, the European Convention on Extradition of 1957 and the European Convention on Mutual Assistance in Criminal Matters of 1959 were ratified in 1982. The Protocols to the Convention on Extradition were ratified in 1985, the First Protocol to the Convention on Mutual Assistance in 1991. In addition, the Convention on the Transfer of Sentenced Persons of 1983 was ratified in 1985 (the Additional Protocol of 1987 was ratified in 1992); the European Convention on the Transfer of Proceedings in Criminal Matters of 1972 was ratified in 1988; and the European Convention on the International Validity of Criminal Judgments of 1970 was ratified in 1994. Within the context of European criminal law,[15] the Schengen Agreement of 1985 and the Convention implementing the Schengen Agreement of 1990 (both ratified in 1993) are particularly important. In addition, there are the Convention on the establishment of a European Police Force (Europol) of 1995, which entered into force in 1998, the Convention relating to extradition between Member States of the European Union of 1996 (also in force since 1998), and the Convention on simplified extradition procedure between the Member States of the European Union of 1995, which entered into force in 1999. However, the Council Framework Decision 2002/584/JHA of 13 June 2002 on the European arrest warrant and the surrender procedure between Member States was implemented in 2003 (Law 3/2003), replacing the previous extradition procedure. The Convention on Mutual Assistance in Criminal Matters between the Member States of the European Union was signed in 2000 and came into effect provisionally in 2004. In 2006, the Council Framework Decision 2003/577/JHA of 22 July 2003 on the execution in the European Union of orders freezing property or evidence was also implemented (Law 18/2006).

---

14 For an overview, see *Arroyo/Nieto*, Código de Derecho Penal Europeo e Internacional, pp. 702–704.

15 For an overview of the EU's impact on Spanish criminal law, see *Bachmaier Winter/ del Moral García*, Criminal Law in Spain, pp. 49 and 50–51 (nos. 62–63, 66).

Bibliography and further reading

Alvarado Planas, Javier, El problema del germanismo en el Derecho español (The problem of Germanism in Spanish law). Madrid 1997.

Arroyo Zapatero, Luis/Nieto Martin, Adán, Código de Derecho Penal Europeo e Internacional (European and international criminal law code). Madrid 2008.

Bachmaier Winter, Lorena/del Moral García, Antonio, Criminal Law in Spain. 2d ed. Alphen aan den Rijn 2012.

David, René/Brierley, John E.C., Major Legal Systems in the World Today. 3d ed. London 1988.

Górriz Royo, Elena Maria, Institutions of criminal law: General part. Valencia 2012.

Ibán, Ivan C., Einführung in das spanische Recht (Introduction to Spanish law). Baden-Baden 1995.

Lalinde Abadía, Jesús, El derecho común en los territorios ibéricos (The ius commune in the Iberian territories). In: Antonio Pérez Martín (ed.), España y Europa, un pasado jurídico común. Actas del I Simposio Internacional del Instituto de Derecho Común (Spain and Europe, a common legal past. Records of the 1st International Symposium of the Institute of Ius Commune). Murcia 1986.

López Guerra, Luis/Rodríguez Mourullo, Gonzalo et al., El Derecho Constitucional Español del siglo XX (The Spanish constitutional law of the 20th century). In: Luis María López Guerra/M. Carmen Chinchilla Marín et al. (eds.), El Derecho español en el siglo XX (Spanish law in the 20th century). Madrid 2000, pp. 3–30.

Masferrer, Aniceto, Plurality of Laws, Legal Traditions and Codification in Spain. 4 J. Civ. L. Stud. 2011, 419–448.

Merino-Blanco, Elena, Spanish Law and Legal System. London 2006.

Neumayer, Heinz, Erster Teil: Grundriß der Rechtsvergleichung (First part: Outline of comparative law). In: René David/Günther Grasmann (eds.), Einführung in die großen Rechtssysteme der Gegenwart (Introduction to the major legal systems of today). 2d ed. Munich 1988, pp. 1–78.

Zweigert, Konrad/Kötz, Hein, An Introduction to Comparative Law. 3d ed. Oxford 1998.

C. Constitutional parameters of criminal law

1. Supra-statutory rules as repositories of criminal law principles

– Constitution

The current Constitution of 1978 is the product of a political transition from an authoritarian system to a constitutional system that was undertaken without a formal break from the prior system.[1] The *Franco* regime was based on seven Fundamental Laws *(Leyes Fundamentales)* that provided, among other things, for a single legislative chamber (whose members were not elected by popular vote) and for the use of referendums to settle important points. After *Franco's* death, the Law for Political Reform (*Ley para la Reforma Política*, LRP)[2] was drafted by the successor government, passed by the legislative chamber and submitted to a referendum. This law, which was adopted in accordance with provisions of the Fundamental Laws and which had the same status as the other seven of these laws, established the substantive foundation for the transition to a constitutional system. In Art. 1 LRP, the state expressed its commitment to democracy and human rights. Pursuant to Art. 2 LRP, the (future) legislature would comprise two chambers and its members would be elected directly by the people. Art. 3 LRP set forth the important elements of the process of constitutional reform. Following the first democratic elections on 15 June 1977, the new Constitution was passed by Parliament, approved by referendum, sanctioned by the king, and ultimately published on 29 December 1978.[3]

Pursuant to the Constitution of 1978, Spain is a social[4] and democratic[5] state subject to the rule of law (Art. 1 para. 3 CE).[6] The individual is viewed as a citizen with both rights and obligations. The position as a rights holder is emphasized by the express recognition of the dignity of the person, the inviolable rights inherent to all people, and the free development of personality as the foundation of political order and social peace (Art. 10 para. 1 CE). On the other hand, citizens are bound by the Constitution and the rest of the legal order (Art. 9 para. 1 CE) and are obligated to respect the law and the rights of others (Art. 10 para. 1 CE).

---

1 On the transition to democracy, see *Ferreres Comella*, The Constitution of Spain, pp. 8–15.

2 On the LRP, see *Ferreres Comella*, The Constitution of Spain, pp. 9–10.

3 See *López Guerra* et al., Derecho Constitucional I, pp. 22–23; *Pérez Royo*, Curso de Derecho Constitucional, pp. 91–94; *Labastida*, Las constituciones españolas, pp. 89–90, 120–121.

4 See *Ferreres Comella*, The Constitution of Spain, pp. 29–32.

5 See *Ferreres Comella*, The Constitution of Spain, pp. 32–34.

6 *Pérez Luño*, Derechos humanos, pp. 239–243; *Pérez Royo*, Curso de Derecho Constitucional, pp. 140–147; *Ferreres Comella*, The Constitution of Spain, p. 26. See I.A.4.

The Constitution is at the top of the legal order, and its core provisions cannot be modified by the legislature.[7] If significant amendments are sought, a new parliament must first be elected (Art. 168 CE). Other reforms, too, can only be implemented by means of special procedures (Art. 167–169 CE). As a rule, a bill involving a constitutional amendment requires a qualified majority of three-fifths of members of both chambers. The superior status of the Constitution is also maintained in that international treaties that contradict its provisions in any way cannot be ratified until the Constitution has been amended (Art. 95 para. 1 CE).[8]

– *Other supra-statutory norms*

The Constitution confers supra-statutory status on international agreements that address issues of fundamental rights. The Universal Declaration of Human Rights (UDHR) is mentioned by name in the Constitution. All norms that affect constitutionally recognized fundamental rights and liberties[9] must be interpreted in conformity with human rights law so that they do not contradict the provisions of the UDHR or any other international agreement on human rights that Spain has ratified (Art. 10 para. 2 CE).[10]

2. Fundamental rights and freedoms and the criminal law

Broadly speaking, almost one-third of all constitutional provisions are associated with fundamental rights, fundamental liberties, or fundamental duties, institutions that are regulated – for the most part – in the first title of the Constitution (*De los derechos y deberes fundamentales*, Arts. 10–54 CE). In addition to the "ordinary" fundamental rights found in most human rights instruments, the Constitution guarantees numerous social, economic, and cultural rights, such as the right to the protection of health, the right to a livable environment, consumer rights, the right to access culture, and the right to state promotion of sports and leisure activities. The fundamental rights anchored in the Constitution can be grouped according to operative criteria, namely, they can be viewed, on the one hand, according to how they can be regulated by law or, on the other, according to how they can be enforced (Art. 53 CE).[11] For example, as a rule, the rights contained in Title I, Chapter Two

---

[7] *López Guerra* et al., Derecho Constitucional I, pp. 50–52; *Pérez Royo*, Curso de Derecho Constitucional, pp. 107–109.

[8] For details on the process of amending the Constitution, see *Ferreres Comella*, The Constitution of Spain, pp. 55–62.

[9] See below 2.

[10] For details on the relationship between the Constitution and international and European law, see *Ferreres Comella*, The Constitution of Spain, pp. 62–69.

[11] *Peces-Barba*, Derechos Fundamentales, pp. 92–99.

(Arts. 14–38 CE) can only be regulated by means of a parliamentary law *(reserva de ley*, Art. 53 para. 1 CE) – whereby the rights that appear in Title I, Chapter Two, Section One (Arts. 15–29 CE) can only be regulated by means of an organic law (*reserva de ley orgánica*, Art. 81 CE).[12] Claims based on the latter rights – as well as those based on the fundamental right of equality before the law (Art. 14 CE) and the fundamental right to conscientious objection to military service (Art. 30 para. 2 CE) – can be enforced by means of a fast-track summary proceeding *(recurso preferente y sumario)* in courts of ordinary jurisdiction or by filing an appeal to the Constitutional Court (*recurso de amparo*, Art. 53 para. 2 CE).[13] The remaining fundamental rights and liberties of Title I, Chapter One and Chapter Two, Section Two are enforced by the legal system in the same way as all other "subjective" rights. Finally, the provisions in Title I, Chapter Three (Arts. 39–52 CE) contain some "fundamental" rights that are not directly actionable but that consist primarily of economic and socio-political principles, the protection of which is the obligation of the entire legal order (protection of the family, protection of the social and economic rights of Spanish workers outside the country, right to accommodation fit for human habitation, and the right to protection of health mentioned above).[14]

As a rule, the fundamental rights and obligations set forth in Title I CE – with the exception of the right to vote in Art. 23 – also apply to foreign citizens, subject to any relevant provisions set out in national laws or international treaties and taking into account special circumstances that apply to European citizens (Art. 13 paras. 1 and 2 CE).[15]

A list of significant fundamental rights and liberties follows:

- the right to equality and the prohibition of discrimination based on origin, race, sexual orientation, religion, opinion, or other personal or social conditions (Art. 14 CE);[16]
- the right to life and to physical and moral integrity. From these rights derive the prohibition of torture and of inhuman or degrading punishment or treatment as well as the abolition of the death penalty, except as provided for by military law in times of war (Art. 15 CE);[17]

---

[12] On the restriction and suspension of fundamental rights, see *Ferreres Comella*, The Constitution of Spain, pp. 245–251.

[13] *Pérez Royo*, Curso de Derecho Constitucional, p. 208.

[14] *Pérez Royo*, Curso de Derecho Constitucional, pp. 209, 438.

[15] *López Guerra* et al., Derecho Constitucional I, pp. 151–153; *Ferreres Comella*, The Constitution of Spain, pp. 251–254.

[16] *Pérez Royo*, Curso de Derecho Constitucional, pp. 211–238.

[17] *Pérez Royo*, Curso de Derecho Constitucional, pp. 243–250.

- freedom of ideology, religion, and worship and the related prohibition against compelling a person to make statements about his or her world view, religion, or beliefs (Art. 16 para. 1 CE);[18]
- the right to liberty and security (Art. 17 para. 1 CE). In addition to the right to liberty, the Constitution also establishes minimum prerequisites that must be satisfied in order for the state to infringe on this right in the context of the commission of criminal offenses: First, preventive police detention is restricted to a maximum of 72 hours, after which time the detained person must either be released or brought before a judge (Art. 17 para. 2 CE). Second, in this context, the Constitution also recognizes the right of a suspect to be informed of his or her rights, the right to remain silent, and the right to legal counsel (Art. 17 para. 3 CE). Third, legislation regulating *habeas corpus* proceedings is called for. The institution of *habeas corpus* guarantees that every person who has been illegally detained be immediately brought before a judge (Art. 17 para. 4 CE);[19]
- the right to honor, the right to a sphere of privacy for the individual and the family, and the right to one's own image (Art. 18 para. 1 CE). The Constitution also states that the use of electronic data-processing techniques must be restricted by law in order to guarantee the full exercise of these rights (Art. 18 para. 4);[20]
- the right to the inviolability of one's domicile. Searches without the permission of the person concerned or a court order are not permitted. This only refers to physical entry into the home, however, and does not include external surveillance by acoustical or optical means. Exceptions are allowed in the case of imminent danger *(delito flagrante)*;[21]
- the right to maintain the secrecy of communications, particularly postal, telegraphic, and telephonic communications (Art. 18 para. 3 CE). A court order is required for the infringement of the secrecy of communications;[22]
- the right to travel freely and to choose one's place of residence (Art. 19 sen. 1 CE) as well as the right to leave and return to Spain freely in accordance with the conditions established by law; the latter right may not be restricted on political or ideological grounds (Art. 19 sen. 2 CE);[23]
- the right to freedom of opinion (Art. 20 CE), which encompasses the following rights: the right freely to express and disseminate thoughts, ideas, and opinions verbally, in writing, or by any other means; the right to produce technical, scientific, artistic, and literary works; freedom of teaching; the right to send and re-

---

[18] *Pérez Royo*, Curso de Derecho Constitucional, pp. 255–262.

[19] *Pérez Royo*, Curso de Derecho Constitucional, pp. 267–289.

[20] *Pérez Luño*, Derechos humanos, pp. 344–350; *Pérez Royo*, Curso de Derecho Constitucional, pp. 296–310, 318–319.

[21] *Pérez Royo*, Curso de Derecho Constitucional, pp. 305–308.

[22] *Pérez Royo*, Curso de Derecho Constitucional, pp. 308–311.

[23] *Pérez Royo*, Curso de Derecho Constitucional, pp. 315–319.

ceive truthful information by any means of dissemination (freedom of the press). Freedom of opinion is guaranteed by a prohibition on all forms of censorship (Art. 20 para. 2 CE). A court order is required for the seizure of documents, data, and other information media (*secuestro de publicaciones*, Art. 20 para. 5 CE). Finally, limits on the exercise of freedom of opinion set by the Constitution include respect for the fundamental rights and liberties of others, particularly the right to honor, to privacy, to one's own image, and to the protection of juveniles and children (Art. 20 para. 4 CE);[24]

- the right to assemble peacefully without weapons with no requirement of prior registration or authorization (Art. 21 para. 1 CE). While gatherings and demonstrations in public places require prior notification of the authorities, they may only be prohibited for cause, that is, if they present a danger to people or property due to disturbances of the public order (Art. 21 para. 2 CE);[25]
- the right of association (Art. 22 para. 1 CE). However, the Constitution prohibits associations formed in pursuit of illegal aims (Art. 22 para. 2 CE), secret organizations, and organizations that are paramilitary in nature (Art. 22 para. 4 CE). A court order is required to dissolve a registered association or to force it to suspend its activities;[26]
- the right to participate in public life, which includes the right to vote and the right to run for public office (Art. 23 CE);[27]
- judicial rights, namely, the rights to effective legal protection (Art. 24 para. 1 CE), to a judge determined by law ("natural judge"), to mount a defense and to the assistance of legal counsel, to be informed of pending charges, to a public trial and one without undue delay, to the use of evidence, not to make self-incriminating statements, and the right to be presumed innocent (Art. 24 para. 2 CE);[28]
- the right not to be convicted or punished for actions or omissions that did not constitute a criminal offense *(delito)* or an administrative infraction *(infracción administrativa)* under the law in force at the time they were committed (principle of legality, Art. 25 para. 1 CE);[29]
- the right of prisoners, while in custody, to social reintegration and occupational training, to be paid for their work, to social security benefits (particularly health insurance, social insurance, social security benefits), to education, and to the development of personality (Art. 25 para. 2 CE). Of these rights, the express mention of reeducation and social reintegration *(reeducación y reinserción social)* as

---

[24] *Pérez Royo*, Curso de Derecho Constitucional, pp. 320–338.

[25] *Pérez Royo*, Curso de Derecho Constitucional, pp. 338–347.

[26] *Pérez Royo*, Curso de Derecho Constitucional, pp. 347–358.

[27] *Pérez Royo*, Curso de Derecho Constitucional, pp. 361–373.

[28] *Pérez Royo*, Curso de Derecho Constitucional, pp. 373–399.

[29] *Pérez Royo*, Curso de Derecho Constitucional, pp. 399–402. See II.A.

goals of custodial sentences and security measures (Art. 25 para. 2 CE) – a legacy of the influence of correctionalism in Spain in the 19th century – is particularly noteworthy.[30] The goal of social reintegration as an aspect of specific deterrence does not, however, preclude other goals of punishment. Indeed, social reintegration is most prominent during the execution of sentence, where it plays a major role in the determination of the amount of time a convict actually spends in custody;[31]

- the right to education and freedom of teaching (Art. 27 CE);[32]
- the right to form and join trade unions (Art. 28 para. 1 CE) and the right to strike (Art. 28 para. 2 CE);[33]
- the right to petition (Art. 29 paras. 1 and 2 CE).[34]

3. Other supra-statutory norms relevant to criminal law and criminal procedure

In addition to the principle of legality[35] – which, as formulated in Art. 25 CE emphasizes the requirement of clarity *(nulla poena sine lege certa)* – the Preliminary Title of the Constitution (Arts. 1–9) contains a provision that emphasizes the prohibition of retroactivity with regard to legislation that increases the scope or intensity of criminal penalties (Art. 9 para. 3).[36]

Other constitutionally guaranteed rights relevant (not only) to criminal law and the law of criminal procedure include the right to be reimbursed by the state for damages caused by judicial error or by improper operation of the administration of justice (Art. 121 CE), the right to represent the public interest in the prosecution of public crimes (*acción popular*, Art. 125 CE),[37] judicial independence (Art. 117 paras. 1–3 CE), indemnity of deputies and senators for opinions expressed in the exercise of their functions (Art. 71 para. 1 CE), immunity of deputies and senators from criminal prosecution (Art. 71 para. 2 CE), and inviolability of the king (Art. 56 para. 3 CE).

---

30 See I.D.3. and I.G.4.

31 *Pérez Royo*, Curso de Derecho Constitucional, pp. 402–404.

32 *Pérez Royo*, Curso de Derecho Constitucional, pp. 404–412.

33 *Pérez Royo*, Curso de Derecho Constitucional, pp. 412–417.

34 *Pérez Royo*, Curso de Derecho Constitucional, pp. 417–420.

35 For details, see *Górriz Royo*, Institutions of Criminal Law, pp. 69–72.

36 *Bachmaier Winter/del Moral García*, Criminal Law in Spain, pp. 66–67 (nos. 93–97).

37 *Bachmaier Winter/Gómez-Jara Díez/Ruda-González*, Blurred Borders in Spanish Tort and Crime, p. 239. See I.A.5.b.

Many other principles have gained constitutional status due to the normative nature of constitutional court rulings (Art. 5.1 LOPJ) or because they are derived from the Constitution and its basic norms and principles. For example, the principle of *ne bis in idem*, derived from the principle of legality, has been recognized by the Constitutional Court *(Tribunal Constitucional)*.[38] In addition, in a 1991 decision, the Constitutional Court recognized the principle of culpability as a constitutional principle anchored in human dignity.[39]

Bibliography and further reading

Bachmaier Winter, Lorena/del Moral García, Criminal Law in Spain. 2d ed. Alphen aan den Rijn 2012.

Bachmaier Winter, Lorena/Gómez-Jara Díez, Carlos/Ruda-González, Albert, Blurred Borders in Spanish Tort and Crime. In: Matthew Dyson, Comparing Tort and Crime. Cambridge 2015, pp. 223–270.

Ferreres Comella, Viíctor, The Constitution of Spain. A Contextual Analysis. Oxford 2013.

Górriz Royo, Elena, Institutions of Criminal Law, General Part. Valencia 2012.

Labastida, Horacio, Las constituciones españolas (The Spanish Constitutions). Mexico City 1994.

López Guerra, Luis/Espín, Eduardo/García Morillo, Joaquín, Derecho Constitucional (Constitutional law), vol. 1. 10th ed. Valencia 2016.

Peces-Barba, Gregorio, Derechos Fundamentales (Fundamental rights). 4th ed. Madrid 1983.

Pérez Luño, Antonio Enrique, Derechos humanos, Estado de Derecho y Constitución (Human rights, rule of law, and Constitution). 10th ed. Madrid 2010.

Pérez Royo, Javier, Curso de Derecho Constitucional (Constitutional law course). 15th ed. Madrid 2016.

Table of cases

STC 150/1991

STC 2/1981

---

38 STC 2/1981.

39 STC 150/1991.

D. Fundamentals of criminal law

1. Functions of criminal law

– Criminal law as a means of social control

The function of criminal law is closely related to the purpose of punishment because penalties and security measures are the criminal law's most important means of intervention. Thus, according to Spanish legal doctrine, every theory of punishment constitutes a theory of the function of criminal law, and, conversely, the function of criminal law depends on the purpose accorded punishment and security measures.[1] A discussion of the function of criminal law necessarily encompasses a discussion of the function of all criminal norms taken together – not just legal consequences – including the theory of the criminal offense. At the same time, the function of criminal law changes, depending on what tasks the state is expected to carry out. These tasks, in turn, legitimize the existence of the state and its actions. From this perspective, the function of criminal law can only be explained in terms of the specific social system in which it is embedded. Penalties and security measures cannot be analyzed in isolation but rather must be seen in the context of the corresponding system of government and in historical and cultural perspective.[2]

In keeping with Spain's self-image as a social and democratic state, criminal law, according to the majority opinion in Spanish legal doctrine, fulfills a number of functions. The traditional confrontation between absolute or retributive theories, on the one hand, and relative or preventive theories, on the other, which led to the so-called doctrinal dispute in Germany, was resolved for the most part in favor of the theory of limited deterrence.[3] According to this theory, the purpose of criminal law is to maintain and to protect society; at the same time, however, in enforcing the criminal law, the state must respect the limits placed on its ability to act. Seen in this light, the deterrent function of criminal law is to unite and to reconcile the attributes of retribution, general deterrence, and special deterrence.[4]

Criminal law in its role as a means of social control is viewed critically by the majority of Spanish legal scholars. Some argue that "social control" is a term of socio-criminological origin that – from a legal perspective – is difficult to grasp and that is too vague and therefore not by itself suited to legitimize the exercise of

---

[1] *Bacigalupo*, Principios de derecho penal, p. 7; *Pérez del Valle*, Estudios sobre los fundamentos del Derecho Penal, p. 22; *Zugaldía Espinar*, Fundamentos de Derecho Penal, p. 41; for a similar analysis, see *Morillas Cueva*, Derecho penal, p. 31.

[2] See *Cuello Contreras*, El derecho penal español, pp. 36–37.

[3] *Mir Puig*, Derecho Penal, p. 101; *Cuello Contreras*, El derecho penal español, pp. 106–107, 36–37; *Bacigalupo*, Principios de derecho penal, pp. 8, 15–18.

[4] See *Antón Oneca*, Discurso leído en la apertura del curso académico de 1944 a 1945, pp. 99–104; *Zugaldía Espinar*, Derecho Penal, pp. 56–70, 62; *Zugaldía Espinar*, Fundamentos de Derecho Penal pp. 62–64; see below 3.

penal power.[5] Others stress that the motivating effect of criminal norms has yet to be empirically proven and that motivation can only be successfully influenced if other mechanisms of social control are effective. As a result, criminal law is regarded as a mere secondary – albeit indispensable – means of social control.[6]

– *Criminal law as a means to protect legal interests*

Criminal law scholars generally agreed that criminal law, as a system for the protection of society, may only protect "legal interests," more precisely, "criminal legal interests."[7] As a result, one of the recognized functions of the concept "protected legal interests" is a criminal-political one. It follows from the principle of legally protected interests in a social democratic state under rule of law that criminal law may not protect mere moral interests. Rather, only those legal interests may be protected that are conditions of social life associated with an individual's chances to participate in the social system.[8] These kinds of legal interests should be of fundamental relevance, that is, only those legal interests whose violation would have a serious negative impact on the workings of the social system may be the subject of criminal law protection.[9]

In addition to the social dimension of protected (criminal) legal interests – in relation to which interests, to be sure, the perspective of the individual should be present – the determination of what should be protected by the criminal law is largely linked to the Constitution.[10] Principles and values of constitutional law should provide guidance for criminal law when new individual or collective legal interests are recognized.[11] In particular, it cannot be the duty of the criminal law to protect legal interests that do not enjoy constitutional recognition. Still, in the legal literature it is often stated that, in practice, the principle of protected legal interests is of little use as far as the effective restriction of criminal law interventions is concerned and that

---

5 *Polaino Navarrete*, Derecho penal, pp. 138–139; *Zugaldía Espinar*, Derecho Penal, pp. 42–43; see *Morillas Cueva*, Derecho penal, pp. 27–28.

6 *Muñoz Conde/García Arán*, Derecho Penal, pp. 61–65; *Bustos Ramírez/Hormazábal Malaré*, Lecciones de derecho penal, p. 49; *Prieto del Pino*, Scope of application of the Spanish substantive criminal law, pp. 21–22.

7 *Romeo Malanda*, Intervenciones genéticas sobre el ser humano y derecho penal, p. 37; *Gracia Martín*, Fundamentos de la dogmática penal, pp. 166–167; see *Borja Jiménez*, Acerca de lo universal y lo particular del Derecho Penal, p. 143–146; *Prieto del Pino*, Scope of application of the Spanish substantive criminal law, p. 24.

8 *Mir Puig*, Derecho Penal, pp. 174–175.

9 See *Muñoz Conde/García Arán*, Derecho Penal, pp. 59–61; *Polaino Navarrete*, Derecho Penal, p. 134; *Cuello Contreras*, El derecho penal español, p. 54; *Cuello Contreras/Mapelli Caffarena*, Curso de derecho penal, pp. 39–42.

10 *Arroyo Zapatero*, Fundamento y función del sistema penal; *Cuello Contreras*, El derecho penal español, pp. 59–60, with further references; see in particular *Álvarez García*, Bien jurídico y Constitución, pp. 30, 37, 42–44.

11 *Zugaldía Espinar*, Derecho Penal, p. 197.

the lawmaker has ample space within which to act.[12] Specifically, the current trend to expand criminal law, which is often tied to the creation of new, supra-individual legal interests, could not be stopped. On the one hand, many of the theories of the (aspired to) concept of protected legal interests are formulated very generally. On the other, there are complaints that the lawmaker often embarks on reforms without engaging in the necessary preparations and without prior academic debate. From this perspective, it appears justified to question the legitimacy of criminal norms on the basis of purely formal criteria.[13] But it is evident that compensation for shortcomings such as these in process of norm creation cannot take place at the level of theory building.

– Criminal law as ultima ratio

The principle of *ultima ratio* or the subsidiarity of criminal law is shaped by utilitarian considerations that combine the maximum possible utility for potential victims (deterrence) with the minimum necessary infringement on the rights of criminal offenders.[14] The utilitarian approach emphasizes that the maximization of deterrence is not the only goal of criminal law; rather, criminal law should be the means of last resort (i.e., it should be applied only in the absence of other, less intrusive means).[15] This requirement and the requirement of the fragmentary nature of criminal law are closely related. The phrase "fragmentary nature" means that criminal law is not supposed to offer comprehensive legal protection but rather protection from certain types of offenses that are particularly serious or dangerous.[16] The two postulates are frequently viewed as aspects of the principle of minimal intervention *(principio de intervención mínima)*.[17] The argument against the principle of minimal intervention is that a minimalist position risks neglecting many legal interests that are worthy of protection merely because criminal law should only be minimally active. This is why there is another opinion, namely, that for the intervention of criminal law the minimalist standard ought to be replaced by the necessity standard.[18]

---

12 *Romeo Malanda*, Intervenciones genéticas sobre el ser humano y derecho penal, pp. 114–115.

13 See *Zugaldía Espinar*, Derecho Penal, pp. 194–202; *Muñoz Conde/García Arán*, Derecho Penal, pp. 78–83; *Díez Ripollés*, La racionalidad de las leyes penales, pp. 139–140; *Portilla Contreras*, CPC 1989, 735.

14 *Mir Puig*, Derecho Penal, pp. 128–129; *Gómez-Jara Díez/Chiesa*, in: Heller/Dubber (eds.), The handbook of comparative criminal law, pp. 491–492.

15 *Bustos Ramírez/Hormazábal Malaré*, Lecciones de derecho penal, p. 95.

16 *Zugaldía Espinar*, Derecho Penal, p. 203; *Gimbernat Ordeig*, Concepto y método de la ciencia del derecho penal, pp. 28–31; *Prieto del Pino*, Scope of application of the Spanish substantive criminal law, pp. 25–26.

17 *Mir Puig*, Derecho Penal, pp. 128–129; *Prieto del Pino*, Scope of application of the Spanish substantive criminal law, pp. 24–25.

18 *Zugaldía Espinar*, Derecho Penal, pp. 204–205.

2. Limits on criminal law imposed by the rule of law

The key principles of Spanish criminal law, which are also seen as limits on the state's exercise of *ius puniendi*, are the principles of legality,[19] culpability, and proportionality. These principles provide concrete doctrinal criteria that enable them to be implemented by law and that facilitate constitutional oversight of criminal law. In addition, there are numerous principles or postulates that serve as guidelines for the criminal law system and the academic debate on criminal law; they can be categorized in different ways.[20]

The principle of culpability[21] serves to maintain the dignity of the individual and to avoid instrumentalizing the offender.[22] Punishment may only be imposed if the offender could have chosen to act differently (act-based principle of culpability).[23] In contrast, the offender's personality and lifestyle should not come into play or should at least not play a fundamental role. According to a decision of the Spanish Constitutional Court *(Tribunal Constitucional)* in 1991, an actor-based criminal law *(derecho penal de autor)*, namely, one that punishes on the basis of the offender's personality and not according to his or her culpability would be considered unconstitutional.[24]

According to the principle of culpability, culpability is both a prerequisite to as well as a quantitative limit on punishment. Its role as a prerequisite of punishment can be seen in the requirement of intent or negligence as a condition of criminal liability and in the exclusion of strict liability (Art. 5 CP), in the recognition of the relevance of mistake to criminal law (Art. 14 CP), and in the requirement of a subject (i.e., potential offender) who is able to respond to motivation (Arts. 19, 20 paras. 1, 2, and 3 CP).[25] The effects of the principle of culpability on sentencing are, first, that the severity of punishment must be proportional to the severity of culpability, and second, that purely deterrent goals (whether general or special)

---

19 See I.C.2., I.C.3., and II.A. See also *Bachmaier Winter/del Moral García*, Criminal Law in Spain, pp. 59–63 (nos. 80–89); *Gómez-Jara Díez/Chiesa*, in: Heller/Dubber (eds.), The handbook of comparative criminal law, pp. 490–491; *Prieto del Pino*, Scope of application of the Spanish substantive criminal law, pp. 71–77.

20 See *Pérez del Valle*, Estudios sobre los fundamentos del Derecho Penal, pp. 36–41; see above 1.

21 Regarding the culpability principle and its constitutional foundation, see I.C.3. See also *Bachmaier Winter/del Moral García*, Criminal Law in Spain, p. 64 (no. 90); *Gómez-Jara Díez/Chiesa*, in: Heller/Dubber (eds.), The handbook of comparative criminal law, p. 491; *Prieto del Pino*, Scope of application of the Spanish substantive criminal law, pp. 23–24.

22 *Zugaldía Espinar*, Derecho Penal, p. 311; *Mir Puig*, Derecho Penal, pp. 135–136.

23 *Bacigalupo*, Principios de derecho penal, pp. 108–111; *Polaino Navarrete*, Derecho Penal, pp. 155–156.

24 STC 150/1991; see *Jaén Vallejo*, Los principios superiores del derecho penal, pp. 43–44.

25 See *Muñoz Conde/García Arán*, Derecho Penal, pp. 92–94; *Mir Puig*, Derecho Penal, pp. 136–138; *Zugaldía Espinar*, Derecho Penal, pp. 309–310.

cannot justify punishment that exceeds culpability.[26] From this perspective, the Spanish provision that treats recidivism as an aggravating factor (Art. 20 para. 8 CP) is problematic.

But the principle of culpability is not without its critics. Building on the debate in Germany, scholars emphasize that the existence of free will – the very basis of the principle of culpability – cannot be proven. This position is countered by the argument that empirical proof of the deterministic approach is equally absent. Others argue that the concept of culpability is morally fraught. However, alternatives such as attempts to replace the principle of culpability with the principle of proportionality or to replace the term culpability with some other term (such as responsibility) in the criminal law doctrine have been unsuccessful – whereby the Spanish Penal Code refers primarily to criminal responsibility.[27]

The principle of proportionality and the principle of humanity are viewed by some as consequences of the principle of minimal intervention with regard to the severity of the legal consequences. They are not explicitly addressed in the Constitution. The principle of proportionality in the narrow sense requires that punishment be proportionate to the severity of offenses committed.[28] This principle was initially drafted with security measures in mind, as these measures are not assessed on the basis of the culpability of the offender. But it should also apply to penalties, especially according to those authors who would even replace the principle of culpability with the principle of proportionality or who would like to treat culpability merely as an upper limit. Opponents point out that the principle of culpability also calls for a relationship between punishment and the generally applicable requirements of criminal liability.[29] The constitutional doctrine concerning the requirement of proportionality between the offense committed and the response of criminal law is very restrictive.[30]

The principle of humanity has an impact on the type and duration of punishment and on the conditions under which punishment is executed as well as on criminal procedure.[31] As far as the type of punishment is concerned, the Constitution prohibits both the death penalty and inhumane or degrading punishment (Art. 15). Although the Penal Code of 1995 introduced alternatives to incarceration, such as

---

26 *Bacigalupo*, Principios de derecho penal, p. 109.

27 On the status of the dispute, see *Bacigalupo*, Principios de derecho penal, pp. 110–111; *Bustos Ramírez/Hormazábal Malaré*, Lecciones de derecho penal, pp. 427–428.

28 See STC 66/1995; *Bachmaier Winter/del Moral García*, Criminal Law in Spain, pp. 64–65 (nos. 91–92).

29 See *Mir Puig*, Derecho Penal, p. 139; *Zugaldía Espinar*, Derecho Penal, p. 220; in detail *Aguado Correa*, El principio de proporcionalidad en Derecho penal, pp. 275–307.

30 See in detail *Lamarca Pérez*, El principio de proporcionalidad y el control de constitucionalidad de las leyes penales, pp. 33–36, 41, 47–48.

31 *Muñoz Conde/García Arán*, Derecho Penal, p. 84.

public service, and replaced short prison terms with fines, the length of sentences is open to criticism when measured against humanitarian standards.[32] Maximum penalties for certain types of criminal offenses were significantly increased, and the option of prison remission through work was abolished. Even though life imprisonment does not exist on paper, Spanish criminal law is a long way from the desired maximum sentence of 15 years. The maximum prison term is generally 20 years. Sometimes, however, prison terms of 25, 30, or 40 years can be imposed and, in certain cases, must actually be served. This situation, which arose in the wake of the introduction of the Penal Code of 1995 and was aggravated by subsequent reforms, is also criticized from the perspective of the principle of social reintegration.[33] With regard to prison conditions, even though much has improved and additional reforms are planned, legal scholars are critical of the fact that the reality of the Spanish prison regime does not yet conform to the minimum standards of the UN. As a consequence of the principle of humanity, torture is prohibited in criminal procedure (Art. 15 CE).

Other principles also considered limits on the government's *ius puniendi* include the principle of legally protected interests,[34] the principle of minimal intervention,[35] the prohibition of exemplary penalties, the principle of necessity and utility of criminal law interventions,[36] the principle of social reintegration,[37] and the principle of subjective liability,[38] which, as one of the requirements of culpability, prohibits all types of objective criminal responsibility.

3. Purposes of punishment

Combined theories of punishment, according to which punishment must fulfill a deterrent/preventive (future-oriented) function while at the same time retaining its retributive nature, dominate in Spain. The various combined theories weight these two aspects differently. From relative theories they borrow the idea that punishment must serve a social purpose by deterring the public from committing crimes (public deterrence, negative general deterrence), on the one hand, and by having an effect on the offender (deterrence and – in particular – social reintegration), on the other. They adopt from theories of retribution the idea that punishment should be tailored to the offender's culpability and that it should not exceed the limit estab-

32 *Zugaldía Espinar*, Derecho Penal, pp. 215–216.

33 *Zugaldía Espinar*, Derecho Penal, pp. 223–228.

34 See above 1.

35 See above 1.

36 *Zugaldía Espinar*, Derecho Penal, pp. 219–220.

37 See below 3.

38 See *Mir Puig*, Derecho Penal, pp. 136–137.

lished by culpability, regardless of any deterrence-based considerations. Some authors recognize these two goals by distinguishing between the foundation of punishment (namely, retribution) and the goal of punishment (namely, prevention/ deterrence) or by distinguishing between the concept and the justification of punishment. From a socio-political perspective, the favored position should be one that considers illegitimate any punishment that is proportionate to the culpability of the offender but that is useless from the perspective of society.[39]

Throughout history, various combined theories have fallen in and out of favor, among them conceptions of criminal law propounded by Spanish theologians and jurists of the 16th and 17th centuries and the Spanish Correctionalist School, which dates to the late 19th century.[40] The main representative of this school – whose fundamental principles, oddly enough, were adopted by the (few) 19th century German authors who did not subscribe to a retributive theory *(Krause, Ahrens, Röder)* – was *Dorado Montero*, author of "El derecho protector de los criminales" (The law in protection of the criminal offender), written in 1925. Additional impulses in support of a criminal policy favoring special deterrence came from the Italian positivist school.[41] At that time, the impact of German idealism, which based criminal law on the idea of free will and emphasized culpability as a prerequisite of criminal liability and as the standard by which to measure sentencing, was minimal.[42] Still, this reform effort failed to generate comprehensive modifications of the legal consequences and the sentencing system. The level of danger posed by offenders continued to play a limited role in sentencing. It was not until the reform of 1944 that a sentencing rule (Art. 61 para. 4 CP) was introduced that mandated punishment based on the offender's personality; however, forms of criminal conduct deemed dangerous were regulated outside the Penal Code by the Vagrancy Act *(Vagos y Maleantes)* of 1933, which prescribed indeterminate preventive detention for recidivists and habitual offenders and in some circumstances for dangerous first-time offenders as well. This law was replaced in 1970 by a similar law on dangerousness and social reintegration.[43] After the entry into force of the democratic constitution in 1978, these kinds of measures were phased out as part of the ensuing criminal law reform. The Penal Code of 1995 restored recidivism as an

---

[39] For a summary of the various theories, see *Muñoz Conde/García Arán*, Derecho Penal, pp. 46–51; *Mir Puig*, Derecho Penal, p. 95; *Cerezo Mir*, Curso de derecho penal español, pp. 22–38; *Polaino Navarrete*, Derecho penal, pp. 78–81; *Cid Moliné*, ¿Pena justa o pena útil?, pp. 225, 231; *Zugaldía Espinar*, Derecho Penal, p. 67; *Gracia Martín*, Fundamentos de la dogmática penal, pp. 171–199; *Gómez-Jara Díez/Chiesa*, in: Heller/Dubber (eds.), The handbook of comparative criminal law, pp. 496–497; *Prieto del Pino*, Scope of application of the Spanish substantive criminal law, pp. 36–45.

[40] For an overview, see *Cerezo Mir*, Curso de derecho penal español, pp. 26–38.

[41] See *Mir Puig*, Derecho Penal, p. 91.

[42] *Bacigalupo*, Principios de derecho penal, pp. 48–50.

[43] *Cerezo Mir*, Curso de derecho penal español, pp. 39–40; *Muñoz Conde/García Arán*, Derecho Penal, p. 53.

aggravating factor (Art. 22 no. 8); in 2003, a provision on multiple recidivism (Art. 66 para. 1 no. 5) was reintroduced.[44]

Current trends favor combined theories that integrate several purposes.[45] In contrast, retributive theories, according to the legal literature, are incompatible with the tenets of a social and democratic state under rule of law.[46] Models inspired by the theory of positive general deterrence developed in Germany beginning in the 1980s are gaining momentum in Spain as well. They shift the focus away from the potential criminal offender to society and the law-abiding citizen; for them, the primary purpose of punishment is to affirm the validity of norms.[47] In terms of its communicative meaning, punishment is seen as a response to the offender's act, which constitutes a challenge to norm validity. This function, which is temporally linked to the imposition of punishment, does not exclude other purposes of punishment, particularly social reintegration.

According to the legal scholarship,[48] there are clear indications in the current Penal Code of 1995 that it is not based on an absolute theory of punishment. These include the option of the conditional suspension of sentence (Art. 80–89 CP) as well as the power of pardon, the institute of statutory limitations, and the effect of forgiveness by the victim (Art. 130 CP). Still, criminal theorists are critical of the fact that the Penal Code has not managed to strike a satisfactory balance between the various purposes of punishment.[49] On the one hand, the penalties, which are much too stiff, cannot be reconciled with the theory of social reintegration and therefore disproportionately favor general deterrence. On the other hand, some regulations favoring individual deterrence are seen as too far-reaching. For example, the Penal Code offers the option of suspension for sentences of up to five years' imprisonment if the offenses were committed by intoxicated offenders (habitual offenders included); this includes serious criminal offenses. In addition, critics hold that these regulations do not sufficiently meet general deterrence requirements.[50]

From the point of view of the combined theories, the relationship between penalties and security measures is particularly difficult. The legal scholarship emphasizes that a strict differentiation between penalties and security measures is possible

---

44 On dealing with dangerousness in Spain, see *Manso Porto*, in: Koch (ed.), Wegsperren?, pp. 321–348.

45 In summary, see *Polaino Navarrete*, Derecho penal, pp. 78–81.

46 See *Polaino Navarrete*, Derecho penal, p. 67; *Bustos Ramírez/Hormazábal Malaré*, Lecciones de derecho penal, p. 60.

47 *Cerezo Mir*, Curso de derecho penal español, p. 29; *Cuello Contreras*, El derecho penal español, pp. 134–138; *Gracia Martín*, Fundamentos de la dogmática penal, p. 208; see *Bustos Ramírez/Hormazábal Malaré*, Lecciones de derecho penal, pp. 75–77.

48 *Mir Puig*, Derecho Penal, p. 102; *Zugaldía Espinar*, Derecho Penal, p. 65.

49 *Cerezo Mir*, Curso de derecho penal español, p. 34.

50 See *Zugaldía Espinar*, Derecho Penal, pp. 65–70.

only from the perspective of absolute theories. The relationship between act-based culpability and dangerousness is particularly problematic.[51] One explanation for why penalties are too high – they are not only anathema to the idea of social reintegration but are also an impediment to a clean distinction between (act-based) culpability as a prerequisite of criminal liability, on the one hand, and dangerousness as prerequisite for the imposition of security measures *(medidas de seguridad)*, on the other – could lie in the fact that the problem of dangerousness has not been satisfactorily resolved in the Spanish multi-track system of penalties and security measures.[52] The multi-track system introduced in 1995 does not reserve penalties for offenders with criminal capacity and security measures for dangerous offenders (with or without criminal capacity). Liberty-depriving security measures may only be imposed on offenders who lack criminal capacity entirely or whose capacity is diminished. Until recently, however, the criminal law has not recognized such a security measure for individuals with full criminal capacity or for individuals who exhibit a tendency to commit crime *(delincuente "por tendencia")*. A liberty-depriving measure for offenders with criminal capacity was not introduced until the reform of 2010; however, this measure only applies to terrorists and sexual offenders. Moreover, recidivism is still treated as an aggravating circumstance (Art. 22 no. 8 CP); as a result, dangerous offenders whose capacity is diminished and dangerous offenders with full criminal capacity are treated very differently.[53]

4. Fundamental principles of criminal procedure

The following are fundamental principles of the Spanish law of criminal procedure:[54]

– the right to a judge determined by law ("natural judge," Art. 24 para. 2 CE);
– the right to effective legal protection (Art. 24 para. 2 CE);
– the principle of nemo tenetur (Art. 24 para. 2 CE);

---

[51] See *Bacigalupo*, Principios de derecho penal, pp. 21–27; see *Mir Puig*, Derecho Penal, pp. 98–99; in summary (including a historical overview), *Cuello Contreras*, El Derecho Penal Español, pp. 139–154.

[52] For a critical approach, see, e.g., *Cerezo Mir*, Curso de derecho penal español, pp. 38–44.

[53] *Bacigalupo*, in: Hoffmann (transl.), Das spanische Strafgesetzbuch, pp. 3–4.

[54] The following principles can be found in *Cobo del Rosal*, Tratado de derecho procesal español, pp. 53–148; *López Barja de Quiroga*, Tratado de derecho procesal penal, pp. 187–194. For an overview over the law of criminal procedure, see *Gómez-Jara Díez/Chiesa*, in: Heller/Dubber (eds.), The handbook of comparative criminal law, pp. 494–496; *Bachmaier Winter/del Moral García*, Criminal Law in Spain, pp. 205–318 (nos. 409–673); *Merino-Blanco*, The Spanish law and legal system, pp. 137–176; *Ibán*, Einführung in das spanische Recht, pp. 154–162.

- the right to mount a defense and to the assistance of legal counsel (Art. 24 para. 2 CE);
- the accusatory principle (principio acusatorio);
- the principle of public prosecution (principio de oficialidad);
- the presumption of innocence (Art. 24 para. 2 CE);
- the principle of mandatory prosecution (Art. 55 para. 1 CE); juvenile criminal law is subject to the principle of discretionary prosecution (Art. 19 LO 5/2000);
- the principle of confrontation and of fair hearing (principio de contradicción, principio de audiencia);
- the principle of equality of arms;
- the principle of concentration (of trial), direct consequences of this principle in Arts. 749 and 788 para. 1 LECrim; Art. 47 LO 5/1995;
- the principle of trial without undue delay (principio del plazo razonable) (Art. 24 para. 2 CE);
- the principle of public trial (Arts. 24 para. 2 and 120 para. 1 CE);
- the right to appeal;
- the right to refuse to give evidence (witness privilege) (Art. 24 para. 2, 2d part CE);
- the principle of ne bis in idem;
- the principle of in dubio pro reo;
- the principle of orality (Art. 120 para. 2 CE);
- the principle of immediacy.

Bibliography and further reading

Aguado Correa, Teresa, El principio de proporcionalidad en Derecho penal (The principle of proportionality in criminal law). Madrid 1999.

Álvarez García, Francisco Javier, Bien jurídico y Constitución (Legally protected interest and Constitution). CPC 43, 1991, 5–44.

Antón Oneca, José, Discurso leído en la apertura del curso académico de 1944/1945 (Speech given at the opening of the academic year of 1944/45). Salamanca 1944.

Arroyo Zapatero, Luis Alberto, Fundamento y función del sistema penal: el programa penal de la Constitución (Foundation and function of the criminal system: The criminal program of the Constitution). RJCLM, 1, 1987.

Bachmaier Winter, Lorena/del Moral García, Antonio, Criminal Law in Spain. 2d ed. Alphen aan den Rijn 2012.

Bacigalupo, Enrique, Principios de derecho penal. Parte general (Principles of criminal law. General part). 4th ed. Madrid 1997.

– Einführung (Introduction). In: Markus Hoffmann (transl.), Das spanische Strafgesetzbuch vom 23. November 1995 nach dem Stand vom 31. Dezember 2001 (The Spanish Penal Code of 23 November 1995 as of 31 December 2001). Freiburg 2002, pp. 1–14.

Borja Jiménez, Emiliano, Acerca de lo universal y lo particular del Derecho Penal (About the universal and the particular of the criminal law). Valencia 2012.

Bustos Ramírez, Juan/Hormazábal Malaré, Hernán, Lecciones de derecho penal. Parte general (Criminal law lectures. General part). Madrid 1997.

Cerezo Mir, José, Curso de derecho penal español. Parte general (Spanish criminal law course. General part), vol. I: Introducción (Introduction). 6th ed. Madrid 2007.

Cid Moliné, José, ¿Pena justa o pena útil? El debate contemporáneo en la doctrina penal Española (Just punishment or useless punishment? The contemporary debate in the criminal law doctrine). Madrid 1994.

Cobo de Rosal, Manuel, Tratado de derecho procesal español (Treatise on the Spanish law of criminal procedure). Madrid 2008.

Cuello Contreras, Joaquín, El derecho penal español. Parte general (The Spanish criminal law. General part). 3d ed. Madrid 2002.

Cuello Contreras, Joaquín/Mapelli Caffarena, Borja, Curso de derecho penal, Parte general (Criminal law course, general part). 3d ed. Madrid 2015.

Díez Ripollés, José Luis, La racionalidad de las leyes penales (The rationality of the criminal laws). 2d ed. Madrid 2013.

Gimbernat Ordeig, Enrique, Concepto y método de la ciencia del derecho penal (Concept and method of the science of criminal). Madrid 1999.

Gómez-Jara Díez, Carlos/Chiesa, Luis E., Spain. In: Kevin Jon Heller/Markus Dirk Dubber (eds.), The handbook of comparative criminal law. Stanford, Cal. 2011, pp. 488–530.

Gracia Martín, Luis, Fundamentos de la dogmática penal. Una introducción a la concepción finalista de la responsabilidad penal (Foundations of criminal law doctrine. An introduction to the goal-directed theory of criminal liability). Barcelona 2006.

Ibán, Iván C., Einführung in das spanische Recht (Introduction to Spanish law). Baden-Baden 1995.

Jaén Vallejo, Manuel, Los principios superiores del derecho penal (The higher principles of criminal law). Madrid 1999.

Lamarca Pérez, Carmen, El principio de proporcionalidad y el control constitucional de las leyes penales (The principle of proportionality and the constitutional review of criminal laws). Madrid 2011.

López Barja de Quiroga, Jacobo, Tratado de derecho procesal penal (Treatise on the law of criminal procedure), vol. I. 6th ed. Cizur Menor 2014.

Manso Porto, Teresa, Landesbericht Spanien (Country report Spain). In: Hans-Georg Koch (ed.), Wegsperren? Freiheitsentziehende Maßnahmen gegen gefährliche, strafrechtlich verantwortliche (Rückfall-)Täter (Lock them up? Liberty-infringing measures against dangerous, criminally responsible [repeat] offenders). Berlin 2011, pp. 321–348.

Merino-Blanco, Elena, Criminal Procedure. In: Elena Merino-Blanco, The Spanish law and legal system. 2 ed. London 2006, pp. 137–176.

Mir Puig, Santiago, Derecho Penal. Parte General (Criminal law. General part). 10th ed. Barcelona 2011.

– Función de la pena y teoría del delito en el Estado social y democrático de derecho (The function of punishment and the theory of the criminal offense in a social and democratic state). Barcelona 1979.

Moreno Catena, Víctor/Cortés Domínguez, Valentín, Derecho Procesal Penal (Criminal procedure law). 7th ed. Valencia 2015.

Morillas Cueva, Lorenzo, Sistema de Derecho Penal, Parte General. Fundamentos conceptuales y metodológicos del Derecho Penal. Ley Penal (The system of criminal law, general part. Conceptual and methodological foundations of criminal law. Criminal law). 3d ed. Madrid 2016.

Muñoz Conde, Francisco/García Arán, Mercedes, Derecho Penal. Parte General (Criminal law. General part). 8th ed. Valencia 2010.

Pérez del Valle, Carlos, Estudios sobre los fundamentos del Derecho Penal (Studies on the foundations of criminal law). Madrid 2006.

Polaino Navarrete, Miguel (with cooperation of *Polaino-Orts, Miguel*), Derecho Penal. Parte General (Criminal law. General part), vol. I: Fundamentos científicos del Derecho penal (Scientific foundations of criminal law). 6th ed. Barcelona 2008.

Portilla Contreras, Guillermo, Principio de intervención mínima y bienes jurídicos colectivos (The principle of minimal intervention and protected collective legal interests). CPC 39, 1989.

Prieto del Pino, Ana María, General Part I. Scope of application of the Spanish substantive criminal law. Cizur Menor 2017.

Romeo Malanda, Sergio, Intervenciones genéticas sobre el ser humano y derecho penal (Genetic interventions on the human being and criminal law). Bilbao 2006.

Sánchez Martínez, Olga, Los principios en el derecho y la dogmática penal (The principles in criminal law and the criminal law doctrine). Madrid 2004.

Silva Sánchez, Jesús M., El nuevo Código penal: cinco cuestiones fundamentales (The new Penal Code: Five fundamental questions). Barcelona 1997.

Zugaldía Espinar, José Miguel, Derecho Penal. Parte General (Criminal law. General part). 2d ed. Valencia 2004.

– Fundamentos de Derecho Penal. Parte general (Foundations of criminal law. General part). 4th ed. Valencia 2010.

Table of cases

STC 66/1995 (principle of proportionality)

STC 246/1991 (ne bis in idem and legality principle)

STC 150/1991 (culpability principle)

E. Nature, form, and boundaries of criminal law

1. Nature and form of criminal law

In Spain, it is still common to link the concept of criminal law, systematically, with the distinction between criminal law as a normative system (objective criminal law or *ius poenale*) and criminal law as a "subjective" right of the state (subjective criminal law or *ius puniendi*).[1] Criminal law in an objective sense encompasses only substantive law. Substantive law is formally defined as a compilation of the legal norms and provisions of the state that define criminal offenses and infractions and their consequences, namely, penalties *(penas)* and security measures *(medidas de seguridad)*.[2] Today, most scholars see the law of criminal procedure and prison law as autonomous areas of law, separate from substantive criminal law. The law of criminal procedure is a subset of procedural law, which is traditionally separated from substantive law, both from a conceptual perspective and in the academic world.[3] It was not until recently that isolated attempts have been made to emphasize the close connections between substantive criminal law and the law of criminal procedure; at the same time, efforts to draft general theories of procedural law continue.[4]

Prison law consists entirely of norms that address the execution of custodial sentences and security measures *(Derecho penitenciario)*.[5] Today, it is governed by its own statute (*Ley Orgánica 1/1979 General Penitenciaria*, plus its regulation) and is under the jurisdiction of special prison judges *(Jueces de Vigilancia Penitenciaria)*.[6] An argument in favor of the independent status of this area of law *ratione materiae* is that it regulates a specific legal relationship – namely, a relationship characterized by subjugation *(relación de sujeción especial)*[7] – of persons with concrete rights and obligations within a specific institution *(Institución Penitenciaria)*.[8]

---

1 *García-Pablos de Molina*, Introducción al Derecho Penal, p. 457; *Górriz Royo*, Institutions of criminal law, pp. 19–20.

2 *García-Pablos de Molina*, Introducción al Derecho Penal, p. 48.

3 *Bachmaier Winter/del Moral García*, Criminal Law in Spain, pp. 25–26 (nos. 17 and 19); *Górriz Royo*, Institutions of criminal law, p. 18.

4 See *Cobo del Rosal*, Tratado de Derecho Procesal Penal, pp. 45–47; *García-Pablos de Molina*, Introducción al Derecho Penal, pp. 121–125; *Fairén Guillén*, Doctrina general del derecho procesal, pp. 267–274.

5 *Berdugo Gómez de la Torre/Zúñiga Rodríguez*, Manual de Derecho Penitenciario, p. 107. For details, see *Bachmaier Winter/del Moral García*, Criminal Law in Spain, pp. 319–335 (nos. 674–703); *Górriz Royo*, Institutions of criminal law, p. 19.

6 For a critical view, see *Cuello Contreras*, La autonomía del Derecho penitenciario frente al Derecho penal y procesal, p. 1614.

7 See STC 2/1987; STC 175/2000.

8 *Fernández Arévalo/Nistal Burón*, Manual de Derecho Penitenciario, pp. 183–184; see also *Rodríguez Alonso*, Lecciones de Derecho Penitenciario, p. 2; *Mapelli Caffarena*, La autonomía del Derecho Penitenciario, p. 457.

2. Boundaries between criminal law and other areas of law with a criminal or quasi-criminal function

The establishment of boundaries between criminal law and other repressive systems, in particular the law of administrative sanctions *(Derecho administrativo sancionador)*,[9] has largely been settled in Spain, at least as far as institutions are concerned. In the past, the exercise of sanctioning power by administrative authorities was criticized as an unlawful exception to criminal jurisdiction and regarded as an area subordinate to criminal law. Today, the law of administrative sanctions is considered an independent area of public law, albeit one strongly influenced by criminal law, and acts undertaken by administrative authorities *(los actos administrativos)*, including the imposition of sanctions, are subject to the jurisdiction of administrative – not criminal (or any other) – courts *(juzgados y tribunales del orden contencioso administrativo)*. Thus, the administration – which retained its sanctioning power throughout the 19th century – and the criminal courts are no longer viewed, as they were traditionally, as independent sanctioning powers of equal rank; instead, sanctioning power in a broad sense is original to the courts. This is now true also of the sanctioning power of the administration, which was first expressly recognized by the Constitution of 1978 (Art. 25 para. 1).[10]

Nevertheless, there is still no comprehensive legislation (such as the Regulatory Offenses Act, *Ordnungswidrigkeitengesetz* in Germany) in this area.[11] The most important substantive and procedural principles of the law of administrative sanctions (including the principle of culpability) are regulated in Chapter III of Preliminary Title of the Law 40/2015 of 1 October on the Legal Regime of Public Sector (*Ley 40/2015, de 1 de octubre, de Régimen Jurídico del Sector Público*, LRJSP).

The current debate centers primarily on the extent to which principles of criminal law should apply in the context of the law of administrative sanctions, a legal regime that is still incomplete and generally less well-developed than criminal law.[12] Issues such as the consequences of the principle of *ne bis in idem* and the principle of culpability are the subject of debate.[13] The statutory period of limitations for administrative law sanctions was not recognized by law until 1992 (Law 30/1992,

9 For details, see also *Bachmaier Winter/del Moral García*, Criminal Law in Spain, pp. 160–161 (nos. 314–316); *Arroyo Zapatero*, ZStW 110 (1998), 457–460; *Prieto del Pino*, Scope of application of the Spanish substantive criminal law, pp. 55–57.

10 See *Nieto García*, Derecho Administrativo Sancionador, pp. 47–55.

11 For a critical view, see *Nieto García*, Derecho Administrativo Sancionador, pp. 18–19.

12 See *Carretero Pérez/Carretero Sánchez*, Derecho Administrativo Sancionador, pp. 110–113; *Gómez Tomillo/Sanz Rubiales*, Derecho Administrativo Sancionador, pp. 115–120.

13 *Cerezo Mir*, Curso de Derecho Penal Español, pp. 61–64; *Gómez Tomillo/Sanz Rubiales*, Derecho Administrativo Sancionador, pp. 210–241, 373–380; for detailed information on the consequences of the culpability principle, see *Pemán Gavín*, El sistema sancionador español, pp. 292–336.

rescinded by Law 40/2015); prior to 1992 the limitations period was established by judicial decisions.[14]

Prevailing opinion negates an essential qualitative distinction between the law of administrative sanctions and criminal law;[15] on a theoretical level this lack of difference supports the argument that principles of criminal law should apply in both areas. Thus, the only distinguishing factor is a formal one, namely, the decision of the legislature,[16] whereby in some areas the administrative wrong *(ilícito administrativo)* and the corresponding criminal wrong *(ilícito penal)* are virtually identical. In this environment of competing jurisdiction of administrative and criminal courts, the latter have priority.[17] While administrative sanctions may be considered milder than criminal penalties, this is true only because administrative authorities are constitutionally barred from imposing liberty-depriving sanctions (Art. 25 para. 3 CE). Otherwise, administrative sanctions may be quantitatively much higher than the corresponding criminal penalties. In practice, the imposition of sanctions by administrative authorities and the position taken by administrative courts, which have control over administrative acts (Art. 106 CE), are perceived as rather restricted and restrained, whereby sanctioning policy is viewed critically.[18]

Sanctioning powers are vested not only in the central, autonomous, and local administrations but also in other administrative institutions, agencies, and entities, which, in the case of professional associations, can be derived from a comprehensive code (*Ley de Colegios Profesionales* of 13 Feb. 1974). Other entities – which cannot (or not without raising questions) be called "administration" – also exercise certain sanctioning powers, such as the chamber of a court that has jurisdiction over judicial administration and disciplinary matters *(Sala de Gobierno)*.[19]

The boundary between criminal law and disciplinary law is difficult to draw from a substantive perspective. In Spain, disciplinary law has never been considered a part of criminal law. Still, in modern society, the disputed differences between criminal penalties and disciplinary law sanctions are gradually disappear-

---

[14] STS 7.3.1981 (RJ 1981\934); *Nieto García*, Derecho Administrativo Sancionador, pp. 533–535, 539–542; *Gómez Tomillo/Sanz Rubiales*, Derecho Administrativo Sancionador, pp. 613–649.

[15] *Cerezo Mir*, Curso de Derecho Penal Español, p. 60; *Carretero Pérez/Carretero Sánchez*, Derecho Administrativo Sancionador, pp. 103–107; *Mir Puig*, Derecho Penal, p. 43; *Morillas Cueva*, Derecho penal, p. 61; *Bachmaier Winter/del Moral García*, Criminal Law in Spain, p. 160 (no. 315).

[16] *Carretero Pérez/Carretero Sánchez*, Derecho Administrativo Sancionador, p. 107; *Nieto García*, Derecho Administrativo Sancionador, p. 128.

[17] *Carretero Pérez/Carretero Sánchez*, Derecho Administrativo Sancionador, p. 192.

[18] *Nieto García*, Derecho Administrativo Sancionador, pp. 34–40.

[19] See *Nieto García*, Derecho Administrativo Sancionador, pp. 96–98.

ing.[20] Criminal penalties have a number of aims, some of which have to do with the guarantee of an optimal administrative law organization,[21] whereby it is frequently difficult to distinguish between questions of internal organization and their external effects. Disciplinary law sanctions are no longer limited to the area of hierarchical relationships or special relationships based on power.[22]

Disciplinary law today is made up of norms of prison law, juvenile criminal law, military criminal law (including prison law), university law, the law of sports, and the law of professional organizations as well as norms regulating civil service employees. In addition, there are disciplinary law provisions of a private law nature in business law.[23] The rapprochement of disciplinary and criminal law does not, however, give rise to the suggestion to combine the two areas of law, something that is not considered viable in practice. Rather, the question is how to provide disciplinary law with an acceptable level of legal guarantees.[24]

There are few formal requirements placed on norms of disciplinary law. Most such provisions appear in administrative regulations.[25] Delegating laws *(leyes de transferencia o delegación)* do not meet the requirements that must be fulfilled by referring or blank-form laws *(leyes penales en blanco)*. Neither the description of conduct that comprises an offense nor the prescribed sanctions are subject to the requirement of clarity *(nulla poena sine lege certa)*. The principle of *ne bis in idem* and other principles of the law of sanctions do not apply to disciplinary law (Art. 127 para. 3 LRJAP-PAC).[26] Legal scholars (some more broadly than others) have called for the application of the principle of *ne bis in idem* to penalties and to disciplinary law sanctions.[27]

---

[20] See *Cerezo Mir*, Curso de Derecho Penal Español, p. 64; *Nieto García*, Problemas capitales del Derecho disciplinario, pp. 30, 32; *Prieto del Pino*, Scope of application of the Spanish substantive criminal law, pp. 57–58.

[21] *Cerezo Mir*, Curso de Derecho Penal Español, p. 66.

[22] *Nieto García*, Problemas capitales del Derecho disciplinario, p. 39.

[23] *Cerezo Mir*, Curso de Derecho Penal Español, p. 67.

[24] For details, see *Gómez Tomillo/Sanz Rubiales*, Derecho Administrativo Sancionador, pp. 251–277.

[25] See *Cerezo Mir*, Curso de Derecho Penal Español, pp. 66–67.

[26] *Nieto García*, Problemas capitales del Derecho disciplinario, pp. 30–31; *Linde Paniagua*, in: Julio Díaz-Maroto y Villarejo (ed.), Derecho y justicia penal en el siglo XXI, pp. 312–314.

[27] See *Gómez Tomillo/Sanz Rubiales*, Derecho Administrativo Sancionador, pp. 265–277.

3. Special regimes connected to the status of the offender

The main legal consequences are penalties *(penas)* and security measures *(medidas de seguridad)*.[28] Spain employs a multi-track system that allows for the imposition of security measures both instead of and in addition to penalties. Security measures, which are based on the danger posed by the offender, are subject to strict limits:[29] First, the duration of security measures may not exceed the duration of the corresponding penalties; they may not be imposed for an indeterminate duration; nor may they be imposed retroactively.[30] Second, under current criminal law, security measures may only be imposed for offenses that would have carried a prison sentence for an offender with full criminal capacity (Art. 95. no. 2 CP). As a result, the distinction between security measures and criminal penalties remains unclear.[31] Until the reform in 2010, when the security measure of supervised liberty *(libertad vigilada)* was introduced for sexual offenders and terrorists,[32] there were no security measures for offenders with full criminal capacity whose actions and personal circumstances indicate a propensity for crime *(delincuente "por tendencia")*.[33] This means that the issue of danger posed by the offender is mainly an issue of punishment – at least in the case of offenders with criminal capacity. This is generally reflected in the severity of penalties but also in the fact that recidivism retains its status as an aggravating circumstance (Art. 22 no. 8 CP).

Criminal law distinguishes between liberty depriving and non-liberty depriving security measures. Under Arts. 101–103 CP, the following liberty-depriving measures may be imposed on individuals lacking criminal capacity pursuant to Art. 20 nos. 1–3 CP:

- in the case of a mental abnormality or disorder, the measure of commitment for the purpose of medical treatment or for special education to a facility specifically designed to address the exhibited mental abnormality or disorder may, if necessary, be imposed;

28 Compare I.A.5.d. See in detail *Silva Sánchez*, El nuevo Código penal, pp. 15–49; *Requejo Rodríguez*, Peligrosidad criminal y Constitución, p. 13; *Pujol Robinat/Puig Bausili*, CPC 94, 2008, 255–284 (260); *Encinar del Pozo*, Circunstancia: Revista de ciencias sociales del IUIOG, vol. VI, no. 16, 2008; *Bachmaier Winter/del Moral García*, Criminal Law in Spain, pp. 174–180 (nos. 349–360); *Prieto del Pino*, Scope of application of the Spanish substantive criminal law, pp. 47–49.

29 *Guanarteme Sánchez Lázaro*, Un problema de peligrosidad postdelictual, pp. 145–150.

30 See *Berdugo Gómez de la Torre/Zúñiga Rodríguez*, Manual de Derecho Penitenciario, pp. 43–44.

31 For a critical view, see *Terradillos Basoco*, In: Santiago Delgado Bueno (Dir.), Psiquiatría legal y forense, p. 108; see *Morales Prats/García Alvero*, Doctrina del Tribunal Constitucional sobre medidas de seguridad, pp. 1152–1154.

32 See I.A.5.d.

33 *Manso Porto*, in: Koch (ed.), Wegsperren?, pp. 321–336; see *Encinar del Pozo*, Circunstancia: Revista de ciencias sociales del IUIOG, vol. VI, no. 16, 2008.

– in the case of full-fledged intoxication due to consumption of alcoholic beverages, drugs, narcotics, psychotropic, or other substances, the measure of commitment to a public or duly accredited or approved private detoxification center may, if necessary, be imposed;
– in the case of a cognitive ability disorder present since birth or childhood that has led to a severely distorted sense of reality, the measure of commitment to a special educational facility may, if necessary, be imposed.

In addition to these measures or if, in the scenarios mentioned above, there is a partial defense, additional non-liberty depriving measures may be ordered (in the second case, in addition to liberty-depriving punishment), such as the prohibition on staying or living in certain places, the prohibition on visiting certain places or seeking out premises for the purpose of consuming alcohol, and the requirement to attend out-patient therapy, accept family welfare service, or participate in educational or job training programs.

Criminal law consequences in the form of measures *(medidas)* can be imposed on minors ages 14 and above.[34] Measures against underage criminal offenders (that is, offenders ages 14 through 17) appear in the Organic Law 5/2000 (*Ley Orgánica 5/2000, reguladora de la responsabilidad de los menores*, in the version of Organic Law 8/2012 of 27 December) and in the regulations, which were not passed until 2004. These measures are defined as interventions of an educational nature. The severest measure is placement in a special facility *(centro)* for eight years (ten years in some cases of multiple offenses), followed by release and another five years of supervision.[35]

Bibliography and further reading

Arroyo Zapatero, Luis, Grunderfordernisse des Allgemeinen Teils für ein europäisches Sanktionenrecht. Landesbericht Spanien (Basic requirements of the general part for a European law of sanctioning. Country report Spain). ZStW 110 (1998), 438–460.

Bachmaier Winter, Lorena/del Moral García, Antonio, Criminal Law in Spain. 2d ed. Alphen aan den Rijn 2012.

Berdugo Gómez de la Torre, Ignacio/Zúñiga Rodríguez, Laura (coord.), Manual de Derecho Penitenciario (Handbook of prison law). Salamanca 2001.

---

34 For details, see *de la Cuesta*, 14 Chronicle (2005), 11–15; *Källman*, Das neue Jugendstrafrecht in Spanien; *Bachmaier Winter/del Moral García*, Criminal Law in Spain, pp. 180–182 (nos. 361–365); *Rechea Alberola/Fernández Molina*, 19 J. Contemp. Crim. Just. (2003), 384–412.

35 See *Cruz Márquez*, La medida de internamiento y sus alternativas en el derecho penal juvenil, pp. 38–40.

Carretero Pérez, Adolfo/Carretero Sánchez, Adolfo, Derecho Administrativo Sancionador (Law of administrative sanctions). 2d ed. Madrid 1995.

Cerezo Mir, José, Curso de derecho penal español. Parte general (Course of Spanish criminal law. General part), vol. I: Introducción (Introduction). 6th ed. Madrid 2007.

Cobo del Rosal, Manuel, Tratado de Derecho Procesal Penal Español (Treatise of the law of Spanish criminal procedure). Madrid 2008.

Cruz Márquez, Beatriz, La medida de internamiento y sus alternativas en el derecho penal juvenil (The measure of commitment and its alternatives in juvenile criminal law). Madrid 2007.

Cuello Contreras, Joaquín, La autonomía del Derecho penitenciario frente al Derecho penal y procesal (The autonomy of prison law from penal and procedural law). La Ley: Revista jurídica española de doctrina, jurisprudencia y bibliografía, no. 1, 1999, 1613–1619.

Cuesta, José Luis de la, The new Spanish criminal law for minors and juvenile delinquents. 14 Chronicle (2005), 11–15, https://www.ehu.eus/documents/1736829/2010409/A+59+The+new+spanish+criminal+law+for+minors+and+juvenile+delinquents.pdf [last visited March 2018].

Encinar del Pozo, Miguel Ángel, Discusión sobre las medidas a adoptar en función de la peligrosidad del autor (Discussion of adopting measures based on the dangerousness of the offender). Circunstancia: Revista de ciencias sociales del IUIOG, vol. VI, no. 16, 2008.

Fairén Guillén, Víctor, Doctrina general del derecho procesal (General doctrine of the law of criminal procedure). Barcelona 1990.

Fernández Arévalo, Luis/Nistal Burón, Javier, Manual de Derecho Penitenciario (Handbook of prison law). Cizur Menor (Navarra) 2011.

García-Pablos de Molina, Antonio, Introducción al Derecho Penal (Introduction to criminal law), vol. I. 5th ed. Madrid 2005.

Gómez Tomillo, Manuel/Sanz Rubiales, Íñigo, Derecho Administrativo Sancionador (Law of administrative sanctions). 4th ed. Cizur Menor 2017.

Górriz Royo, Elena Maria, Institutions of criminal law: General part. Valencia 2012.

Guanarteme Sánchez Lázaro, Fernando, Un problema de peligrosidad postdelictual: reflexiones sobre las posibilidades y límites de la denominada custodia de seguridad (A problem of post-offense dangerousness: Reflections on the possibilities and limits of so-called security custody). Revista Penal no. 17, 2006, 142–165.

Källman, Eva, Das neue Jugendstrafrecht in Spanien – ley orgánica 5/2000 reguladora de la responsabilidad penal de los menores – Vorbild für ein 2. JGGÄndG? (The new juvenile criminal law in Spain – ley orgánica 5/2000 reguladora de la responsabilidad penal de los menores – A model for a 2d law amending the Juvenile Court Act?). Berlin 2006.

Linde Paniagua, Enrique, El régimen disciplinario de la función pública y la penetración en el mismo de los principios que rigen el Derecho penal (The disciplinary regimen of the public function and the penetration in it of the principles that rule criminal law). In: Julio Díaz-Maroto y Villarejo (ed.), Derecho y justicia penal en el siglo XXI: liber amicorum en homenaje al profesor Antonio González-Cuéllar García (Law and criminal justice in the 21st century: Festschrift in honor of Professor Antonio González-Cuéllar García). Madrid 2006, pp. 301–324.

Manso Porto, Teresa, Landesbericht Spanien (Country report Spain). In: Hans-Georg Koch (ed.), Wegsperren? Freiheitsentziehende Maßnahmen gegen gefährliche, strafrechtlich verantwortliche (Rückfall-)Täter (Lock them up? Liberty-infringing measures against dangerous, criminally responsible [repeat] offenders). Berlin 2011, pp. 321–348.

Mapelli Caffarena, Borja, La autonomía del Derecho Penitenciario (The autonomy of prison law). In: Estudios de Derecho Penal en Homenaje al Profesor Luis Jiménez de Asúa (Criminal law studies in honor of Professor Luis Jiménez de Asúa). RFDUC, 11, 1986, 453–461.

Mir Puig, Santiago, Derecho Penal. Parte general. (Criminal law. General part). 10th ed. Barcelona 2016.

Morales Prats, Fermín/García Alvero, Ramón Miguel, Doctrina del Tribunal Constitucional sobre medidas de seguridad: ¿Réquiem por la Ley de Peligrosidad y Rehabilitación Social? (Doctrine of the Constitutional Court on security measures: Requiem for the Law of Social Dangerousness and Reintegration?). La Ley: Revista jurídica española de doctrina, jurisprudencia y bibliografía, no. 1, 1991, 1142–1154.

Morillas Cueva, Lorenzo, Derecho penal. Parte general. Fundamentos conceptuales y metodológicos del Derecho Penal, Ley Penal (Criminal law. General part. Conceptual and methodological foundations of criminal law). 2d ed. Madrid 2010.

Nieto García, Alejandro, Problemas capitales del Derecho disciplinario (Main problems of disciplinary law). Revista de administración pública, no. 63, 1970, 39–84 https://dialnet.unirioja.es/descarga/articulo/2111728.pdf [last visited 14 May 2018].

– Derecho Administrativo Sancionador (The law of administrative sanctions). 5th ed. Madrid 2017.

Pemán Gavín, Juan María, El Sistema Sancionador Español. Hacia una teoría general de las infracciones y sanciones administrativas (The Spanish sanctions system: Towards a general theory of administrative infractions and sanctions). Barcelona 2000.

Prieto del Pino, Ana María, General Part I. Scope of application of the Spanish substantive criminal law. Cizur Menor 2017.

Pujol Robinat, Amadeo/Puig Bausili, Lluïsa, Concepto de peligrosidad criminal: evolución histórica del concepto (Concepts of criminal dangerousness: Historical evolution of the concept). CPC 94, 2008, 255–284.

Rechea Alberola, Cristina/Fernández Molina, Esther, Juvenile Justice in Spain: Past and Present. 19 J. Contemp. Crim. Just. (2003), 384–412.

Requejo Rodríguez, Paloma, Peligrosidad criminal y Constitución (Criminal dangerousness and the Constitution). Indret: Revista para el Análisis del Derecho, no. 3, 2008.

Rodríguez Alonso, Antonio, Lecciones de Derecho Penitenciario (Lessons on prison law). 4th ed. Granada 2011.

Silva Sanchez, Jesús María, El nuevo Código Penal: cinco cuestiones fundamentales (The new Penal Code: Five fundamental questions). Barcelona 1997.

Sola Reche, Esteban, La peligrosidad de la conducta como fundamento de lo injusto penal (The dangerousness of conduct as a basis of criminal wrongdoing). ADPCP, vol. 47, 1994, C. 167–186.

Terradillos Basoco, Juan María, Enfermedad mental, peligrosidad social y derecho penal (Mental illness, social dangerousness, and criminal law). In: Santiago Delgado Bueno (dir.), Psiquiatría legal y forense (Legal and forensic psychiatry), vol. I. Madrid 1994, pp. 95–112.

Table of cases

STC 175/2000 (special legal relationship in execution of custodial sentence)

STC 2/1987 (special legal relationship in execution of custodial sentence)

STS 7.3.1981 (RJ 1981\934) (statutory period of limitations for administrative law sanctions)

F. Sources of criminal law and interpretation aids

1. Overview

Written (parliamentary) law is the preeminent source of Spanish criminal law.[1] The Constitution establishes both the general principle of legality (Art. 9 para. 3) and the principle of legality for criminal law (Art. 25 para. 1).[2] Accordingly, no one may be punished or sanctioned for an act or omission that did not constitute a criminal offense *(delito)* or an administrative infraction *(infracción administrativa)* at the time of commission.[3] Provisions concerning other sources of law, namely, customary law *(costumbre)* and the general principles of law *(los principios generales del derecho)*, can be found in the Civil Code (Art. 1 paras. 3 and 4 Código Civil, CC). Compared to written law, their role in criminal law is secondary or limited to marginal or supplementary aspects.[4] Nevertheless, the role of the general principles must be examined more carefully, particularly because many principles are enshrined in legal norms or in the Constitution.[5] Court decisions are excluded as a source of law in the strict sense (Art. 1 para. 6 CC). Still, they provide vitally important support in the interpretation of statutes, and, although judges are not legally bound by prior decisions, they do in fact take them into consideration.[6]

The primacy of written law as a source of law is also evident in the fact that a number of issues can only be regulated by means of an organic law (law of constitutional rank, *ley orgánica*). Pursuant to Art. 81 para. 1 CE, provisions that have an impact on the fundamental rights and liberties listed in Art. 15 CE must be embedded in organic laws.[7] Such laws require an absolute majority in Parliament. Thus, neither regulations *(reglamentos)* nor decree laws *(decretos leyes)* nor legislative decrees *(decretos legislativos)* can serve as sources of law in these areas. The prevailing opinion in the legal literature is that the establishment of criminal offense definitions and penalties infringe on the right to liberty or, at a minimum, on the right to honor, which is why they can only be established by means of organic laws.[8] Still, it is disputed whether the requirement of an organic law should apply across the board for all criminal matters or whether exceptions should be made, for instance, for penalties that do not affect fundamental rights.[9]

---

1 *Polaino Navarrete*, Derecho Penal, p. 213.

2 For information on the principle of legality, see II.A.

3 See *Cerezo Mir*, Curso de Derecho Penal Español, pp. 184–185.

4 *Luzón Peña*, Curso de Derecho Penal, p. 156.

5 See I.D.2.

6 *Ferreres Comella*, El Principio de Taxatividad en Materia Penal y el Valor Normativo de la Jurisprudencia, pp. 159–160.

7 See I.C.2.

8 See, e.g., *Polaino Navarrete*, Derecho Penal, pp. 242–244; *Bacigalupo*, Principios de Derecho Penal, pp. 81–82.

9 See *Luzón Peña*, Curso de Derecho Penal, pp. 139–140; *Bachmaier Winter/del Moral García*, Criminal Law in Spain, pp. 51–52 (no. 68); *Gómez-Jara Díez/Chiesa*, in: Heller/Dubber (eds.), The handbook of comparative criminal law, p. 493; for details, see II.A.3.a.

Nevertheless, due to the legislative technique of so-called referring or blank form criminal laws *(leyes penales en blanco)*, ordinary laws *(leyes ordinarias)*, decree laws, legislative decrees, and the legislation of the autonomous regions (on subjects such as environmental laws or health) ultimately do count at least as supplemental or complementary sources of criminal law.[10] Indeed, some offense definitions in the Penal Code refer expressly to regulations, stating, for instance, that certain conduct in violation of statutory or regulatory rules is subject to penalty.[11] The Spanish Constitutional Court *(Tribunal Constitucional)* has upheld the constitutionality of referring laws if the following conditions are met:[12]

– the reference is explicit and justified in view of the legal interest protected by criminal law;
– the referring law prescribes the penalty;
– the referring law defines the essential core of the prohibition and satisfies the principle of clarity *(nulla poena sine lege certa)* so that, taken together with the indispensable supplemental material in the referred-to norm, the definition of the prohibited conduct is sufficiently concrete.

The Penal Code instructs judges to apply the provisions of the law strictly.[13] A judge who, in the course of exercising his or her judicial responsibilities, learns of conduct worthy of punishment that has not been criminalized must refrain from engaging in any proceedings against it and must explain to the government why it ought to be the subject of a criminal penalty (Art. 4 para. 2 CP).

Conversely, if the strict application of the law would lead to the punishment of an act or omission that, in the opinion of the court, should not be punishable or if punishment seems too severe, the court – regardless of whether or not the sentence is soon to be executed – is likewise required to approach the government to request the repeal or amendment of the pertinent provision or to request a pardon (Art. 4 para. 3 CP).[14] This provision, which has never been applied, is criticized as outdated in that it limits judicial authority in favor of the executive and because it compels the court, for all intents and purposes, to impose an unfair punishment.[15] Instead, after exhausting all possible methods of interpretation, judges in such cases are obligated to submit the issue to the Constitutional Court *(cuestión de inconstitucionalidad)*, because every court is subject to the constitu-

---

10 *Bustos Ramírez*, Manual de Derecho Penal, pp. 146–147; *Gómez-Jara Díez/Chiesa*, in: Heller/Dubber (eds.), The handbook of comparative criminal law, p. 493.

11 See, e.g., Arts. 320, 360, 361, 363, 364, 441 CP.

12 STC 127/1990 of 5 July 1990.

13 *Bacigalupo*, Principios de Derecho Penal, p. 59; cf. *Cerezo Mir*, Curso de Derecho Penal Español, p. 204.

14 *Cerezo Mir*, Curso de Derecho Penal Español, p. 205.

15 On the separation of powers, see below 2.

tional requirement of Art. 117 para. 1 CE (namely, the administration of justice emanating from the people).[16]

2. Legislation and other written laws

In addition to the establishment of written law as the only source of criminal law and the establishment of the principle of legislativity *(nulla poena sine lege scripta)* is the question concerning the hierarchy of norms, an issue that arises less in the context of criminal law and more as a general problem inherent to the state's system of norms. Traditionally, the principle of hierarchy and the system of sources of law were issues of civil law and became matters of public law by way of the Constitution. Today, it is primarily a subject of constitutional debate. For the most part, however, the principle of the hierarchy of norms has lost its traditional significance as the organizing principle of a legal system in a liberal state under rule of law. The relationship among new "types of norms" that have evolved due to the territorial organization of the state and the distribution of competences is not – or is not only – hierarchical. Consequently, attempts have been made to reformulate the principle of hierarchy for a constitutional state and a more complex system of norms.[17] The hierarchy of the legal system is no longer regarded as the starting point but merely as a desirable objective.[18]

As far as the creation of criminal law norms is concerned, the Constitutional Court has expressly ruled that criminal laws that prescribe liberty-depriving penalties must have the rank of organic law.[19] The question of whether other criminal legislation also requires an organic law is disputed; however, the use of organic laws has become the rule.[20] Ultimately, due to the availability of referring or blank-form laws (which pose their own set of problems),[21] ordinary laws and regulations also play a significant role in criminal law.[22]

Criminal law is regulated, for the most part, in the Penal Code of 1995. There are also quite a few special criminal laws *(leyes penales especiales)*, some of which predate the Constitution. Notwithstanding, most of the individual criminal offense definitions are found in Books II and III of the Penal Code. Special criminal laws that criminalize certain activities include the Organic Law 12/1995 of 12 December

---

[16] STC 65/1986; *Bacigalupo*, Principios de Derecho Penal, pp. 64, 73–74; for details, see II.A.3.c.

[17] See *Requena López*, El Principio de Jerarquía Normativa, pp. 26–39; *Pérez Luño*, El Desbordamiento de las Fuentes del Derecho, pp. 73–98.

[18] *Pérez Luño*, El Desbordamiento de las Fuentes del Derecho, p. 77.

[19] STC 140/86.

[20] See above 1. and II.A.3.a.

[21] See *Cerezo Mir*, Curso de Derecho Penal Español, pp. 187–193.

[22] See above 1. and II.A.3.a.

1995 to combat smuggling *(Ley Orgánica de Represión del Contrabando)*, the Military Penal Code (Organic Law 13/1985 of 9 December 1985), the law on jury trial (Organic Law 5/1995 of 22 May 1995), and the Law 209/1964 of 24 December 1964 on air traffic *(Ley penal y procesal de la Navegación Aérea)*.[23] The clemency law of 18 June 1870 (last amended by Law 1/1988 of 14 Jan. 1988) is another special criminal law.[24]

Legislation is officially disseminated by publication in the Official State Gazette *(Boletín Oficial del Estado)*. Since 1 January 2009, the online version of the Official State Gazette has been considered official and authentic.[25]

Aside from the problem of the internal hierarchy of norms, which does not raise any particular issues in criminal law, there are a number of terms denoting or "preference" that are associated with hierarchy *(supremacía, prevalencia, primacía, preferencia)* and that are often used ambiguously. Some of them, such as "primacy" *(primacía)*, are used to characterize the relationship between international (European, in particular) and national law. Given that these legal orders do not share a common, hierarchically-superior legal order, the discussion should not in fact be framed in terms of hierarchy but rather – for instance – in terms of the integration of European law into the national legal system.[26]

International treaties may not be applied immediately but only after they have been published in their entirety in the Official State Gazette (see Art. 1 para. 5 CC and Art. 96 para. 1 CE).[27] The assertion that this causes them to be incorporated into the domestic legal system is regarded by some scholars as a fiction insofar as international law – regardless of its applicability – is a legal order separate from the state's legal system.[28] As far as matters of criminal law are concerned, new offenses based on international agreements can only be created by domestic criminal laws. With regard to exemptions from punishment, decriminalization, and mitigation of punishment, however, international agreements are afforded the status of a legal source akin to customary law or to the general principles of law. In addition, some scholars affirm the possibility of an immediate repeal of criminal norms by international agreements as long as the agreement is directly applicable, that is, does not require the creation of additional norms.[29] Others emphasize that the repeal of domestic laws by international law is not the issue; rather, the issue is that

23 See *Cerezo Mir*, Curso de Derecho Penal Español, pp. 179–183.

24 *Luzón Peña*, Curso de Derecho Penal, p. 128.

25 Agencia Estatal Boletín Oficial del Estado, http://www.boe.es [last visited 15 May 2018].

26 *Requena López*, El Principio de Jerarquía Normativa, pp. 303–314.

27 *Polaino Navarrete*, Derecho Penal, p. 225.

28 *Requena López*, El Principio de Jerarquía Normativa, pp. 329–332.

29 See *Cerezo Mir*, Curso de Derecho Penal Español, p. 196; *Luzón Peña*, Curso de Derecho Penal, p. 159.

domestic norms are not applicable if they conflict with international law, a situation that indirectly obligates the state to repeal or amend them.[30]

The same is true for European law, which is important for criminal law as a "legal source" in the sense mentioned above. To date, criminal law (except for environmental law) is not within the competence of the Union; still, European directives and regulations in the area of criminal law may apply where criminal offense definitions in special areas contain referring norms or normative elements that are regulated by European law (such as smuggling or currency offenses). This is the case, in particular, in the context of directly applicable law.[31]

Finally, there are a number of criminal offense definitions that expressly refer to international norms: for example, motives for crimes against humanity (Art. 607 bis para. 1 no. 1 CP), deprivation of liberty in violation of international norms on arrest (Art. 607 bis para. 2 no. 7 CP), and the definition of the term "protected persons" (Art. 608 no. 7 CP).

3. Customary law

Customary law is part of the traditional system of sources of law and is applicable without statutory regulation (Art. 1 para. 3 CC).[32] Nevertheless, due to the criminal principle of legality and, more specifically, to the mandate of *lex scripta*, which only recognizes written legislation as a source of law, customary law is generally excluded as a formal source of criminal law in Spain. This means that customary law may not establish punishability and may not create criminal offenses. Still, its inclusion in the general part at least *in bonam partem* is not prohibited. Both national and international customary law play important supplementary roles and serve as interpretational aids.[33] For example, in judgements of 2003 and 2004, the Supreme Court *(Tribunal Supremo)* relied on international customary law to limit the application of universal jurisdiction.[34]

---

[30] *Requena López*, El Principio de Jerarquía Normativa, pp. 332–335; *Luzón Peña*, Curso de Derecho Penal, p. 158; *Zugaldía Espinar*, Derecho Penal, p. 67; for a summary of the "proliferation" of the sources of law, see *Pérez Luño*, El Desbordamiento de las Fuentes del Derecho, pp. 86–101.

[31] *Luzón Peña*, Curso de Derecho Penal, p. 160; for an overview of the EU's impact on Spanish criminal law, see *Bachmaier Winter/del Moral García*, Criminal Law in Spain, pp. 49, 50–51 (nos. 62–63, 66).

[32] See *Polaino Navarrete*, Derecho Penal, pp. 214–215.

[33] *Luzón Peña*, Curso de Derecho Penal, p. 137; *García-Pablos de Molina*, Introducción al Derecho Penal, pp. 522–523; *Cerezo Mir*, Curso de Derecho Penal Español, p. 195.

[34] See STS 327/2003 of 25 Feb. 2003 and STS 319/2004 of 8 March 2004.

4. Case law and judicial opinion

Case law in a narrow sense evolves only through repeated decisions of the Supreme Court (*Tribunal Supremo*, Art. 1 para. 6 CC).[35] It is not accepted as an official source of law (with the exception of rulings of the Constitutional Court);[36] still, it plays a very important supplementary role in the interpretation and application of law.[37] Thus, for the sake of the certainty of the law, there is great interest in court decisions being as consistent as possible; in this regard, criminal law is no exception. It is the responsibility of the Supreme Court (as ordered by the Constitutional Court) to achieve the greatest possible degree of consistency in the application of the law,[38] a goal whose realization is brought about primarily by means of Supreme Court rulings in cases involving appeals on issues of law *(recurso de casación)*.[39] Opinions written by individual judges may be included in published rulings. It is also possible to call for a judicial conference at which to standardize the criteria for judicial decisions and procedural practice (Art. 264 LOPJ).

While higher court decisions are not legally binding on lower courts, lower courts usually consider them in their decision-making process.[40] Defense counsel are not alone in relying on previous decisions of higher courts; the Supreme Court regularly refers to its own prior rulings, often quoting them verbatim. In fact, some scholars are of the opinion that Supreme Court decision should (also) be officially binding on lower courts. This would have the advantage of highlighting the Supreme Court's job of standardizing judicial opinions, and any deviations from earlier guidelines would always have to be explicit and justified.[41]

Opinions of international courts are generally viewed as supplemental or as interpretational aids and not as a source of law in the formal sense. Their impact in a particular case depends on the relationship between the international norm in question and domestic law. The Constitution requires provisions concerning fundamental rights and freedoms to be interpreted in accordance with the provisions of the Universal Declaration of Human Rights and other international agreements on these matters ratified by Spain (Art. 10 para. 2 CE); this is the source of the binding

---

35 *Luzón Peña*, Curso de Derecho Penal, pp. 157–158.

36 *Bustos Ramírez*, Manual de Derecho Penal, p. 151; *Luzón Peña*, Curso de Derecho Penal, p. 158.

37 *Polaino Navarrete*, Derecho Penal, p. 222; *Bachmaier Winter/del Moral García*, Criminal Law in Spain, p. 53 (no. 71); *Gómez-Jara Díez/Chiesa*, in: Heller/Dubber (eds.), The handbook of comparative criminal law, pp. 493–494.

38 STC 2/1983.

39 *Ferreres Comella*, El Principio de Taxatividad en Materia Penal y el Valor Normativo de la Jurisprudencia, p. 160.

40 *Cerezo Mir*, Curso de Derecho Penal Español, pp. 196–197.

41 See *Ferreres Comella*, El Principio de Taxatividad en Materia Penal y el Valor Normativo de la Jurisprudencia, pp. 160–182.

nature of decisions of the European Court of Human Rights when questions concerning the interpretation of fundamental rights and liberties arise.[42]

Decisions of the Court of Justice of the European Union cannot repeal national law that violates European law. Because European law takes precedence over national law, however, the effect of a ruling by the European Court of Justice may be that a domestic law is no longer applied.[43] It should be noted that Spanish law does not provide specific guidelines on how to handle a potential conflict between European and domestic law.

5. Legal literature and academic opinion

Legal literature is not considered a source of law. It provides a theoretical foundation of the legal system, functions as a critical observer of legal education, and – to the extent that the formation of concepts and theories aims for the greatest possible objectivity in the application of the law – delivers important guidance to those who apply the law.[44] Its specific content is not binding, however, nor do courts customarily refer to it in their decisions (at least not expressly).

Bibliography and further reading

Bachmaier Winter, Lorena/del Moral García, Antonio, Criminal Law in Spain. 2d ed. Alphen aan den Rijn 2012.

Bacigalupo, Enrique, Principios de Derecho Penal. Parte General (Principles of criminal law. General part). 5th ed. Madrid 1998.

Baeza Avallone, Vicente, La jurisprudencia como fuente del derecho penal (Jurisprudence as source of criminal law). In: Anales del Centro de Alzira de la Universidad Nacional de Educación a Distancia (Yearbook of the Alzira Center of the National Open University of Education), no. 6, 1992, 221–248.

Bustos Ramírez, Juan, Manual de Derecho Penal. Parte General (Handbook of criminal law. General part). 4th ed. Barcelona 1994.

Cerezo Mir, José, Curso de Derecho Penal Español. Parte General (Course of Spanish criminal law. General part), vol. I: Introducción (Introduction). 6th ed. Madrid 2007.

---

42 STC 114/1984, FJ 3.

43 See *Zugaldía Espinar*, Derecho Penal, pp. 66–67.

44 See *Polaino Navarrete*, Derecho Penal, p. 211; *Gómez-Jara Díez/Chiesa*, in: Heller/Dubber (eds.), The handbook of comparative criminal law, p. 494.

Ferreres Comella, Víctor, El Principio de Taxatividad en Materia Penal y el Valor Normativo de la Jurisprudencia. Una Perspectiva Constitucional (The principle of clarity in criminal law and the normative value of jurisprudence. A constitutional perspective). Madrid 2002.

García-Pablos de Molina, Antonio, Introducción al Derecho penal (Introduction to criminal law). 3d ed. Madrid 2005.

Gómez-Jara Díez, Carlos/Chiesa, Luis E., Spain. In: Kevin Jon Heller/Markus Dirk Dubber (eds.), The handbook of comparative criminal law. Stanford, Calif. 2011, pp. 488–530.

Luzón Peña, Diego Manuel, Curso de Derecho Penal. Parte General I (Course of criminal law. General part I). Madrid 1996.

Pérez Luño, Antonio Enrique, El Desbordamiento de las Fuentes del Derecho (The proliferation of the sources of law). Madrid 2011.

Polaino Navarrete, Miguel, Derecho Penal. Parte General I (Criminal law. General part I). 6th ed. Barcelona 2008.

Requena López, Tomás, El Principio de Jerarquía Normativa (The principle of normative hierarchy). Madrid 2004.

Zugaldía Espinar, José, Lecciones de Derecho Penal, Parte General (Lessons on criminal law, general part). 3d ed. Valencia 2016.

Table of cases

STS 319/2004 of 8 March 2004 (limiting the principle of universality)

STS 327/2003 of 25 Feb. 2003 (limiting the principle of universality)

STC 127/1990 (requirements for referring (blank-form) laws)

STC 65/1986 (judges bound by the law)

G. Developments in criminal law, criminal procedure, and the execution of punishment

1. Overview

Current criminal law builds on the codification process, completed in the 19th century, that in the past had been viewed as a "break" *(ruptura)*[1] but more recently is seen as a "bridge" *(puente)*[2] between the criminal law of the *ancien régime* and the reformed criminal law. On the one hand, the 19th century saw an important renewal of Spanish law; on the other hand, codification as seen from a modern perspective constitutes (not only) a break with the past.[3] The codification also contains elements of a European *ius commune* that evolved on a supranational level beginning in the late Middle Ages by way of the reception of Roman-canonical law and that has largely been forgotten today.[4] From this perspective, it is possible to engage in a balanced evaluation of both the foundations of modern criminal law and of the scope of the reforms of the new regime.[5]

Spanish legal historians date the concept of a public system of justice to the 13th century.[6] The reception of the *ius commune* favored the idea of justice as a task intrinsic to public authorities. The principles and legal concepts of Roman-canonical law provided a framework that facilitated the introduction of a criminal justice system in Castile.[7]

Within the *ius commune*, the influence of canonical doctrine on the criminal law of the modern era and the contributions of Spanish legal philosophers of the 16th and 17th centuries were particularly important. This was also the period when criminal law doctrine began to develop.[8]

In the 18th century, the influence of Enlightenment thought was smaller in Spain than in other European countries. First, in the absence of a bourgeois society, Spain lacked the social underpinning necessary to translate the new ideas into a political agenda. Second, the teachings of *Beccaria* were received with an array of reservations, even within the small circle of enlightened Spanish philosophers. Still, a few

---

1 *Gracia Martín*, in: Díez Ripollés et al. (eds.), La ciencia del derecho penal ante el nuevo siglo, p. 353.

2 *Masferrer Domingo*, Tradición y reformismo en la codificación española, p. 24.

3 *Masferrer Domingo*, Tradición y reformismo en la codificación española, pp. 24, 31, 105.

4 *Masferrer Domingo*, Tradición y reformismo en la codificación española, pp. 35, 36–41.

5 *Masferrer Domingo*, 4 J. Comp. L. 96–139 (2009).

6 For the evolution of Spanish/Hispanic law from antiquity until the end of the Middle Ages, see *Kleffens*, Hispanic law until the end of the Middle Ages.

7 *Alonso Romero*, Historia del proceso penal ordinario en Castilla, pp. 15–17; *Tomás y Valiente*, El Derecho penal de la monarquía absoluta, pp. 25–27.

8 *Masferrer Domingo*, Tradición y reformismo en la codificación española, p. 35.

traces of the philosophy of the Enlightenment are evident in monarchic legislation prior to codification.[9]

The change in the political system did indeed allow for the introduction into legislation of Enlightenment teachings on criminal law and criminal procedure; however, the codification of criminal law in the 19th century in Spain also mirrored the political instability of the time as well as the development of crime. It should be noted, however, that individual laws and reforms have not yet been sufficiently studied from a legal-historical perspective. In the 20th century, too, the impact of the European reform movement on Spanish reforms was not significant. Furthermore, legislation must be viewed independently of the development of doctrine and theological-philosophical thought; traditionally, legal norms and legal doctrine are treated separately. Also, the law in practice must be evaluated independently, within the context of each era, and compared with legislation.[10]

In the last quarter of the 20th century, Spain underwent a process of democratization, opened up to Europe, and strengthened its ties to the international community, which led to fundamental legal reforms. Still, some view even the democratic Penal Code of 1995 as closely linked to its predecessors, despite the fact that it incorporates important elements of modern criminal law.[11] However, the term "modern criminal law" has yet to be precisely defined and is interpreted in the Spanish literature from a variety of perspectives. In contrast to the liberal criminal law of the Enlightenment (sometimes also called "classic" criminal law), the defining features of modern criminal law are, first, that it comprises a quantitatively growing catalogue of criminal offenses that addresses new aspects of society. With respect to these aspects of society, which were not addressed by the traditional system, criminal law is no longer limited to the protection of individual legal interests. Second, under modern criminal law, which is increasingly regarded as a public safety instrument *(derecho penal de la seguridad ciudadana)*, traditional criminal offenses are punished more severely than in the past and far-reaching criminal investigation powers have been introduced. New areas include groups of offenses that can be subsumed under the keyword "preventive criminal law" (abstract endangerment offenses, in particular); economic and environmental criminal law; corporate criminal law; and other new (or conventional) offenses that have taken on previously unknown forms as a result of globalization, such as criminal offenses for the protection of the EU's financial interests, internet crime, human trafficking, international drug trafficking, and money laundering. The major developments in criminal

---

9 *Silva Forné*, RDPC 2001, 239–241, 246–249, 256–257.

10 *Masferrer Domingo*, Tradición y reformismo en la codificación española, pp. 31–66.

11 See *Bacigalupo*, Principios de Derecho Penal, Parte General, p. 54; *Bacigalupo*, in: Hoffmann (transl.), Das spanische Strafgesetzbuch, pp. 1–2; *Quintero Olivares/Morales Prats*, Parte General del Derecho Penal, pp. 224–233.

law in the 21st century were associated with the implementation of European and international standards.[12]

Complaints about this development include the claim that, to this day, criminal law scholarship has failed to exert a measurable influence on legislation and that from time to time criminal law scholars distance themselves from problems confronting the law in practice. Moreover, there is a serious lack of empirical findings that could provide a solid foundation for certain trends in criminal policy – a situation that further increases the risk in contemporary society of populism and mass media exerting undue influence on criminal policy.[13]

Spanish legal scholarship displays widely differing views on the phenomenon of the expansion of criminal law.[14] Traditionalists insist on the ideal of a liberal and minimalist criminal law; for them, current developments conflict with basic principles of criminal law (minimal intervention, protection of legal interests, and *ultima ratio*).[15] Opponents of the traditionalist position welcome this development as a departure from a system that, while providing formal safeguards for all citizens, has been instrumentalized from a substantive perspective to oppress the lower classes. According to these scholars, the goal of a modern criminal law that reflects the guarantees of a social and democratic state under the rule of law ought to be the criminalization of the socially and morally reproachable behavior patterns of a powerful social elite. In their view, however, this expansion does not conflict with the requirements of a rule-of-law state.[16] Moderates view the expansion critically

---

[12] On these developments, see *Gracia Martín*, Prolegómenos, pp. 57–60; *Gracia Martín*, in: Díez Ripollés et al. (eds.), La ciencia del derecho penal ante el nuevo siglo, p. 358; *Silva Sánchez* et al., in: da Agra et al. (eds.), La seguridad en la sociedad del riesgo, p. 113; *Cancio Meliá*, in: Jakobs/Cancio Meliá (eds.), El sistema functionalista del derecho penal, pp. 26–27. For special emphasis on economic crime, see *Martínez-Buján Pérez*, in: Díez Ripollés et al. (eds.), La ciencia del derecho penal ante el nuevo siglo, pp. 402–403; *Mendoza Buergo*, in: Díaz-Maroto y Villarejo (ed.), Derecho y justicia penal en el siglo XXI, pp. 352–356.

[13] *Díez Ripollés*, in: Cuadernos penales José María Lidón, no. 1, Las recientes reformas penales: algunas cuestiones, pp. 11–38; *Díez Ripollés*, RECPC no. 06-03 (2004), 10–12; for information on the fundamentals of criminal law, see *Silva Sánchez*, in: Cerezo Mir (ed.), El nuevo Código Penal: presupuestos y fundamentos, pp. 209–217; on the various interpretations of the term "criminal policy," see *Ortiz de Urbina Gimeno*, in: de Toledo y Ubieto et al. (eds.), Estudios penales en recuerdo del Profesor Ruiz Antón, pp. 879–888; on the aspect of prevention, see *Herrero Herrero*, in: Guzmán Dálbora et al. (eds.), Derecho penal y criminología como fundamento de la política criminal, pp. 1237–1251; for the perspective of court decisions, see *Redondo Hermida*, La Ley Penal, 40, 2007, 76–82; on the relationship to the legal scholarship and criminology, see *Sanz Morán*, in: Pérez Álvarez et al. (eds.), Universitas vitae: homenaje a Ruperto Núñez Barbero, pp. 729–740.

[14] On the status of the dispute, see *Gracía Martín*, Prolegómenos, pp. 155–160; *Faraldo Cabana*, in: Rivera Beiras (ed.), Política Criminal y Sistema Penal, pp. 399–400; *Silva Sánchez*, La expansión del Derecho penal, pp. 150–157; *Díez Ripollés*, RECPC no. 06-03 (2004), 7.

[15] See I.D.1.

[16] *Gracia Martín*, Prolegómenos, pp. 155, 161–167.

but recognize its irreversibility as a trend and suggest an alternative model: namely, a criminal law of "two speeds." Accordingly, the rules governing the attribution of criminal responsibility and the criminal policy guarantees *(garantías político-criminales)* would be upheld for "classical criminal law" and especially for criminal offenses carrying custodial sentences, whereas in the second area, both these rules and the guarantees would be handled more flexibly. A fourth position argues that most criminal law scholars analyze recent developments on the basis of the criteria of a failed – that is, outmoded – model; as a result, so the argument, they can neither properly comprehend such developments nor can their conclusions meet with comprehension in the society as a whole. The expansion, the claim continues, is the result of two different phenomena: on the one hand, the modernization of criminal law, which is principally directed against the crimes of the powerful, and on the other hand, society's growing demand for security, which mainly affects classical criminal activity.[17]

2. Developments in substantive criminal law

– Criminal law of the Middle Ages

Criminal law as a system public in nature evolved along with the consolidation of royal power. For centuries, kings had to wrestle with the local, autonomous, and custom-based criminal law of the Middle Ages. In the early Middle Ages, during which time there was a return to primitive forms of communal living and – according to scholars – a certain amount of Germanic influence, the twin concepts of offense-vengeance *(ofensa-venganza)* belonged to the private sphere. Over time, local laws assumed the task of guaranteeing the protection of certain private individuals or certain locales, such as the home. Later, kings guaranteed protection in specific areas, such as in the markets and on the streets, and, with the gradual increase in royal power, the phenomenon of "court cases" *(casos de corte)* – cases within the scope of the king's laws and tried by royal judges – came into existence. By the late Middle Ages, royal and local laws existed side by side. Even in the modern era, each region had its own interpretation of royal law, and local customs in combination with judicial arbitrariness gave rise to a myriad of criminal laws.[18]

– Criminal law in the early modern era and during the Enlightenment

The authoritarian implementation of royal criminal law enjoyed a significant surge during the reign of the Catholic monarchs (1474–1516), who not only enacted criminal laws but also applied them in a way that reflected their strong political

---

[17] *Díez Ripollés*, RECPC no. 06-03 (2004), 7, n. 7.

[18] *Tomás y Valiente*, El derecho penal de la monarquía absoluta, pp. 24–25.

will. Criminal law became the tool of a political agenda, namely, consolidation of royal power, peacemaking within the kingdom (including the countryside), subjugation of the nobility to royal authority, and religious unity.[19] For the monarchs, religious unity was a mechanism with which to achieve the integration and consolidation of royal power, and thus ecclesiastical and secular politics merged. The Spanish inquisition was the most patent evidence of this symbiosis.[20]

Beginning with the influence of Spanish legal philosophers and theologians in the 16th century (*Francisco de Vitoria*, 1483–1546; *Domingo de Soto*, 1494–1560; *Alfonso de Castro*, 1495–1558; *Luis de Molina*, 1535–1600; *Francisco Suárez*, 1548–1617), criminal law was increasingly seen as a function of the state. Spanish criminal law scholarship emerged around the same time. *Castro*, with his drive for systematization, is considered by some the founder of criminal law, although this position is not uncontroversial.[21] *Suárez* and *Soto*, for instance, argued for the exclusion of criminal responsibility in the case of ignorance of the law. *Diego de Covarrubias* (1512–1577), the dominant ecclesiastical legal scholar, contributed to the systematization of the concept of the criminal offense and to the gradual implementation of the concept of culpability in secular criminal law.[22]

In the last third of the 18th century, one group of thinkers in Spain was strongly influenced by Enlightenment authors from France, England, and Italy. They were criminal law scholars who were well-versed in court practices and who sought to achieve fundamental reforms in criminal justice on the basis of the new ideas in legal philosophy. *Manuel de Lardizábal*, for instance, was of the opinion that nothing could be of greater interest to a nation than good criminal laws, because civil liberties and, to a large extent, a good constitution and the security of the state depend on them.[23] Regardless, the criminal law reform with which he was charged by *Charles III* could not be realized in a time of absolute monarchy and within a feudal system.[24]

---

19 *Cuello Contreras*, El derecho penal español, pp. 292–293; *Tomás y Valiente*, El derecho penal de la monarquía absoluta, pp. 26–32.

20 See *Tomás y Valiente*, El derecho penal de la monarquía absoluta, pp. 155–157.

21 But see *Tomás y Valiente*, El derecho penal de la monarquía absoluta, pp. 91–92.

22 *Cuello Contreras*, El derecho penal español, pp. 321–322; *Masferrer Domingo*, Tradición y reformismo en la codificación española, p. 96; *Cerezo Mir*, Curso de derecho penal español, p. 93.

23 *Lardizábal y Uribe*, Discurso sobre las penas, p. 5.

24 *Cerezo Mir*, Curso de derecho penal español, pp. 98–102.

– The criminal law of the codification movement in the 19th century

From the 19th century onwards, criminal legislation developed parallel to the emerging constitutional orders and subject to major political fluctuations.[25] The Penal Code of 1822, a code of little practical import, followed in the wake of the liberal Constitution of 1812.[26] The Constitution of 1845 was followed by the major Penal Code of 1848 and the authoritarian reform of 1850 – which was a result of concerns raised by the revolutionary movements in Europe. The liberal Constitution of 1869 and the Constitution of the Second Spanish Republic of 1931 were followed by the criminal law reforms of 1870 and 1932, respectively.[27]

The Penal Code of 1848 is regarded as the most important codification of criminal law in the 19th century, not only because of its much-lauded technical perfection but also because of its lasting influence on later developments in criminal law that endure to this day. This code was based on the *Código criminal* of Brazil of 1830, which in turn was influenced by the *Code Napoléon*.[28]

This new criminal law was based on a retributive theory of punishment. It established the principle of legality, rejected the criminalization of acts undertaken in preparation of the commission of a criminal offense, and limited judicial discretion. The result was a rigid, almost mathematical sentencing system, which became the foundation of the current (simplified) system. On the other hand, penalties for criminal offenses against religion and political crimes were exceedingly harsh.[29]

The Penal Code of 1848 was the subject of several reforms throughout the decades (1850, 1870, 1932, 1944), most of which reflected the political changes of the day.[30] A short-lived penal code was introduced in 1928 during the last years of General *Primo de Rivera's* dictatorship; it was replaced by a reintroduction of the Penal Code of 1848 (in the version of 1870), shortly after the proclamation of the Second Spanish Republic in 1931.

– The 20th century and recent trends in criminal policy

Following the installation of the *Franco* regime after the Spanish Civil War (1936–1939), the Penal Code of 1944 – officially known as the so-called recast text

---

25 For details on the codification of Spanish criminal law in the 19th century, see *Masferrer Domingo*, 4 J. Comp. L. 96–139 (2009).

26 *Bachmaier Winter/del Moral García*, Criminal Law in Spain, p. 37 (no. 42).

27 *Ibán*, Einführung in das spanische Recht, pp. 139–141; *Silva Forné*, RDPC 2001, 233–309 (273–277).

28 *Silva Forné*, RDPC 2001, 233–309 (299–302).

29 *Cerezo Mir*, Curso de derecho penal español, p. 132; *Bachmaier Winter/del Moral García*, Criminal Law in Spain, pp. 37–38 (no. 43).

30 *Bacigalupo*, in: Hoffmann (transl.), Das spanische Strafgesetzbuch, p. 1.

(texto refundido) of 1944 – was introduced;[31] this text was subsequently amended numerous times and remained in force until well after the introduction of the democratic Constitution of 1978. Major reforms since introduction of the Constitution include those of 1983 (which brought the Penal Code into conformity with the requirements of the principle of culpability[32]), and those of 1988. After several drafts and preliminary drafts of a "new" democratic penal code,[33] the Penal Code was ultimately enacted in 1995.[34] Still in force, it has been amended more than 25 times since its enactment.[35]

The Penal Code of 1995 represented a renunciation of a criminal policy position held since the entry into force of the Constitution of 1978, elements of which were codified in the reform of 1983. In the following years, an increasingly repressive approach led to the large-scale abandonment of the goal of social reintegration anchored in the Constitution. Indicators of this evolving trend, which also extends to conventional forms of crime, include tightened rules on the application of penalties, increased punishment ranges, and the treatment of petty offenses committed by repeat or habitual offenders.[36]

Recidivism as an aggravating circumstance had been phased out in the reform of 1986, only to be reintroduced in the Penal Code of 1995 (Art. 22 para. 8). Grounds for aggravated penalties for multiple recidivism (so-called *multireincidencia*) that had been repealed in 1983 were reintroduced in 2003 (Art. 66 para. 6 CP). Types of crime deemed particularly dangerous have been periodic targets of reforms that increase the penalty range. For example, penalty ranges for drug offenses that were reduced in 1983 were increased as early as 1988 to up to 23 years (during the *Franco* dictatorship, the maximum penalty was 20 years). In the new Penal Code, particularly serious drug offenses are subject to a maximum penalty of 20 years and three months and higher fines. In the same time period, the treatment of drug-dependent offenders improved significantly.[37]

---

31 *Bachmaier Winter/del Moral García*, Criminal Law in Spain, pp. 39–40 (no. 47); *Tamarit Sumalla*, Historical memory and criminal justice in Spain, pp. 49–60. A German translation of the code including an introduction is provided by *Quintano-Ripollés* et al. (transl.), Das Spanische Strafgesetzbuch vom 23. Dezember 1944.

32 *Strien*, Einflüsse des deutschen Strafrechts auf die jüngere Strafrechtsreformbewegung in Spanien, pp. 25–26.

33 *Strien*, Einflüsse des deutschen Strafrechts auf die jüngere Strafrechtsreformbewegung in Spanien, pp. 20–29.

34 For a German translation (including an introduction by *Enrique Bacigalupo*), see *Hoffmann* (transl.), Das spanische Strafgesetzbuch.

35 For an overview, see *Cuello Contreras*, El derecho penal español, pp. 300–307; *Mir Puig/Gómez Martín*, Derecho penal. Parte general, p. 54.

36 For an overview of the development until 2005, see *Rebollo Vargas*, RdPP no. 14, 2005, 103–110.

37 *Miró Miquel*, in: Rivera Beiras (ed.), Política Criminal y Sistema Penal, pp. 307–311; see also *de la Cuesta Arzamendi*, in: Díez Ripollés/Laurenzo Copello (eds.), La actual política criminal sobre drogas: una perspectiva comparada, pp. 63, 67–70.

The trend toward repression can also be seen in the rules governing the application of penalties and in the reforms of these rules (1999, 2003, 2004, 2015).[38] The Penal Code of 1995 repealed the possibility of a prison remission through work, which led to an increase in the number of prisoners because even if sentences are shorter, convicted persons generally stay in prison longer.[39] Aside from the abovementioned rules for recidivists, penalties increased by one degree can be imposed for continuing serious offenses or infractions (*delito continuado*, Art. 74 para. 1 CP). In some cases involving multiple offenses, the actual time served may be as much as 40 years – instead of 20 (Art. 76 CP). Moreover, the rule in Art. 78 CP leads, *de facto*, to actual life imprisonment because pursuant to this Article, prison privileges *(beneficios penitenciarios)* and the amount of time to be served prior to conditional discharge from custody can, in some cases involving multiple offenses, be calculated on the basis of the total sum of the penalties imposed in the sentences rather than on the effective – that is, the adjusted aggregate or cumulative – sentence. For serious offenses, this means that offenders convicted of multiple offenses may actually have to serve 40-year prison terms, particularly if offenses of terrorism are involved.[40]

Two additional features characteristic of current substantive criminal law include the introduction of offenses in new areas where the primary aim is to protect supraindividual (i.e., collective) legal interests and the expansion of traditional forms of crime to cover conduct not previously considered relevant from a criminal law perspective: offenses against the environment (1983, 1995, 2003, 2010, 2015) and against land-use regulations (1995); crimes against public security (1995), including those involving the risk of a catastrophic event (1995); drug crimes (1995, 2003, 2010, 2015) and doping (2006); traffic crimes (1989, 1995, 2007); corporate crimes (1995); crimes associated with intellectual property (1995, 2003, 2015), with commercial property (1995, 2003), and with the market place and consumers (1995, 2003, 2010, 2015); illegal party funding (2015); criminal insolvencies (1995, 2003, 2015); illegal migration (2000, 2003, 2007, 2015); and the expansion of crimes of personal injury and abuse through the introduction of a new category of criminal offenses against moral integrity (1995, 2003), the introduction of new sex offenses (1995, 1999, 2003, 2010, 2015), and new offenses of coercion, such as stalking, forced marriage, and coercion intended to prevent the legitimate enjoyment of housing (2015). The expansion of criminalization to new forms of conduct often involves the creation of so-called anticipatory liability, that is, liability incurred even earlier than previously possible in the run-up to criminal conduct. This kind of "preponement" of criminal liability can be seen in abstract endangerment

---

38 For an overview of the reforms of the 1995 Penal Code, see *Bachmaier Winter/ del Moral García*, Criminal Law in Spain, pp. 42–44 (no. 52).

39 See I.A.5.e.

40 *Faraldo Cabana*, in: Rivera Beiras (ed.), Política Criminal y Sistema Penal, pp. 411–427.

offenses and in so-called possession-based offenses, such as the possession of computer software that can be used to commit fraud (Art. 248 para. 2(b) CP 2003), an offense that is subject to the range of punishment prescribed for the basic form of the offense of fraud.[41]

The following issues have been at the top of the legal policy agenda in recent years: domestic violence, terrorism, sex crimes, and crimes committed by foreigners. Even the previous penal code contained a special provision for personal injury or abuse within the family. After the entry into force of the Penal Code of 1995 and following several reforms in this area (1999, 2003, 2015), a comprehensive law *(Ley integral)* was passed in 2004 that included provisions in the areas of criminal and civil law, the law of procedure, and employment law and that also provided for special protective measures for women in the sectors of health and education. The reform includes the establishment of special police units and a special court with jurisdiction over cases involving so-called gender-based violence *(violencia de género)*.[42]

As far as protection from terrorism – which was already comprehensive – is concerned, a reform passed in 2000 included expanded criminalization of so-called street terrorism, a reform with regard to the glorification of terrorism, increased sentences for property damage, and protection of community facilities.[43]

Changes to sex offenses include increased penalties; additions in the areas of sexual harassment, sexual exploitation, and child pornography; the reintroduction of the offense of corruption of morals of minors as an addition to child prostitution; and new regulations regarding time limitations (i.e., statutes of limitations/ prescriptions) and the application of the principle of universality (1999, 2003, 2010, 2015).

As for criminal offenses committed by foreigners, the option of extradition was expanded and simplified in 2003.[44]

3. Developments in criminal procedure

– *Development of a public procedure*

The unification of law that began in Spain in the 12th century and the continuing reception of the *ius commune* facilitated the development of a public justice system

[41] See *Pastor Muñoz*, Los delitos de posesión y los delitos de estatus, pp. 53, 66–77, 88–89.

[42] For a critical overview, see *Laurenzo Copello*, RECPC no. 7 (2005), 1–23.

[43] See *Aranada Ocaña*, in: Rivera Beiras (ed.), Política Criminal y Sistema Penal, pp. 381–382.

[44] See *Miró Llinares*, RECPC no. 10-05 (2008), 22–26; *Monclús Masó*, in: Rivera Beiras (ed.), Política Criminal y Sistema Penal, pp. 337–348.

that required a formalized, public process. At the same time, one form of private justice remained, namely, the earlier accusatory process *(proceso acusatorio)* within the ambit of municipal laws *(fueros municipales)*, a process that was clearly contrary to the interests of royal power. In order to maintain the public peace and to free prosecution from its dependence on private accusations, this procedure between private individuals was later largely reformed or replaced by new systems of criminal procedure that favored state authority. The church introduced the inquisitorial process at the same time. As a result, two different procedures of royal justice existed side by side, each of which borrowed from and lent principles and features to the other. Both types of procedures are set out in the code of *Alfonso X* (1252–1284) known as *Las Siete Partidas* (Seven-Part Code).[45]

– The criminal procedure of the absolute monarchy

Beginning in the 16th century, the earlier inquisitorial and accusatory processes evolved into a single mixed procedure that reconciled both public and private interests, even if not in equal measure. Royal legislation in criminal proceedings decreased, and the procedure continued to evolve – sometimes in ways contrary to the formally established law – based on the judges' style and the works disseminated by legal practitioners.[46]

The procedure was basically divided into two stages: investigation *(fase sumarial)* and trial *(fase plenaria)*. The first stage was secret, inquisitorial *(inquisitiva)*, and partisan and was conducted without the participation of the defendant. The judge himself conducted this investigation, assisted by the public prosecutor *(fiscal)* and the private prosecutor. The second phase consisted in the fixing of the positions taken by the parties and the presentation, in writing, of the corresponding evidence. Reasons for judgments were not given because judicial decisions were purely discretionary.

In addition to this standard procedure *(proceso ordinario)*, which was highly complex and slow, another simpler and quicker procedure *(proceso simplificado)*, also based on the *ius commune*, evolved. Furthermore, in cases of so-called atrocious crimes *(delitos atroces)*, such as treason or sodomy, judicial discretion also extended to the rules of procedure. In order to make punishment more efficient, judges would drastically curtail the procedural guarantees of the defendant. As a result, during the monarchy of the *ancien régime*, criminal procedure evolved into a repressive weapon against crime, whose individual elements were primarily geared

---

45 *Alonso Romero*, El Proceso Penal en Castilla, pp. 39–41; *Alonso Romero*, Historia del proceso penal ordinario en Castilla, pp. 15–19; *Bachmaier Winter/del Moral García*, Criminal Law in Spain, pp. 35–36 (no. 39).

46 *Alonso Romero*, El Proceso Penal en Castilla, pp. 91–95; on criminal procedure in the 16th–18th centuries, see also *Esmein*, A History of Continental Criminal Procedure with special reference to France, pp. 295–301.

to rendering guilty verdicts. The excesses were attributed to a system in which judges, whose remuneration from the royal coffers was meager, received a portion (generally one-third) of the court costs and of each fine imposed. There were also discretionary fines *(penas pecuniarias arbitrarias)*, of which – it is estimated – the judge pocketed half.[47]

– The modernization of criminal procedure in the 19th century

Inquisitorial elements (secrecy, written form, confessions extracted under torture) dominated criminal procedure well into the 19th century. This long tradition presented a major hurdle along the way to the establishment of a modern criminal procedure.[48]

A first step was attempted with the liberal Constitution of 1812. Torture was abolished (Art. 303), the requirement of bringing a prisoner before a judge within 24 hours of arrest was introduced (Art. 290), and the position of the accused during preliminary proceedings was strengthened. However, during the era of the Napoleonic invasions, this constitution never fully entered into effect, and after the return of *Ferdinand VII* in 1814 and the reintroduction of the *ancien regime*, it was abolished. It was subsequently reinstated twice – and repealed both times. In the following years, the country's political climate was characterized by social tensions and conflict between liberal and conservative forces. The implementation of many legislative proposals based on French or English models failed, either due to political or to financial difficulties.[49]

It was not until the rather conservative Constitution of 1876 that Spain achieved some degree of political stability, which made possible the establishment of a new criminal procedure. Following numerous drafts and contentious parliamentary debates, a new law of criminal procedure (*Ley de Enjuiciamiento Criminal*, LECrim) was enacted; it entered into force in September 1882. The law was the result of a political compromise between liberals and conservatives and was lauded as a balanced mix of inquisitorial procedure in preliminary proceedings and adversarial procedure in trial. It continued Spanish legal tradition, on the one hand, and mirrored influences of foreign (French, English, Austrian, and German) laws of criminal procedure, on the other. In 1888, a law on jury courts was passed; these courts did not, however, work well.[50] They were abolished in 1923 under the dictatorship

---

[47] See *Alonso Romero*, Historia del proceso penal ordinario en Castilla, pp. 20–33.

[48] *Volkmann-Schluck*, Der spanische Strafprozeß zwischen Inquisitions- und Parteiverfahren, p. 26; *Esmein*, A History of Continental Criminal Procedure with special reference to France, pp. 584–585.

[49] *Volkmann-Schluck*, Der spanische Strafprozeß zwischen Inquisitions- und Parteiverfahren, pp. 27–33.

[50] *Thaman*, 21 Hastings Int'l & Comp. L. Rev. (1997), 248.

of *Miguel Primo de Rivera*, reintroduced in 1931 at the beginning of the Second Republic, and abolished again in 1936 until the introduction of democracy.[51] During the *Franco* dictatorship, the continued development of criminal procedure according to the ideals of democracy and the rule of law was impossible. But a few reforms were initiated in 1967, such as the introduction of a special procedure for less serious criminal offenses.[52]

– The Constitution of 1978 and current reforms

The Constitution of 1978 introduced new institutional and criminal-procedural guidelines that provided a major impetus for the continued development of the law of criminal procedure.[53]

An independent judiciary was created. The independence of individual judges was safeguarded by abolishing all regulations that permitted influence-taking on the part of the executive (such as granting or rejecting promotion). The *Consejo General del Poder Judicial* (LO 6/1985), a governmental body for judges, was established to strengthen the independence of the judiciary.[54]

But a comprehensive reform of the law of criminal procedure post-1978 – along the lines of the Penal Code of 1995 for substantive criminal law – has not yet been achieved. The system of 1882, which remains in effect to this day, is brought into conformity with democratic principles mainly by means of decisions of the Constitutional Court and partial reforms that are subject to broad criticism due to their patchwork nature.[55]

The goal of some of these reforms (1988, 1994, 2002, 2003) was to strengthen and simplify the abbreviated or summary procedure *(procedimiento abreviado)* and to introduce the so-called speedy trial *(juicio rápido)* as a special procedural feature of summary procedures for criminal offenses punishable by imprisonment of up to five years. Since 1988, all criminal offenses punishable by prison terms of up to nine years have been subject to the "abbreviated procedure." Thus, *de facto*, this procedure has become the ordinary procedure, whereas the conventional and complex "ordinary procedure" *(procedimiento ordinario)*, which is used much less frequently, is fading into the background. Additional reforms designed to speed up criminal proceedings include those that recognized new modes of achieving con-

[51] *Thaman*, 21 Hastings Int'l & Comp. L. Rev. (1997), 249; for an extensive account on its reintroduction under the 1978 Constitution, see 250–538.

[52] *Gimeno Sendra*, Introducción al Derecho Procesal, p. 174; *Volkmann-Schluck*, Der spanische Strafprozeß zwischen Inquisitions- und Parteiverfahren, pp. 27–35.

[53] *Volkmann-Schluck*, Der spanische Strafprozess zwischen Inquisitions- und Parteiverfahren, p. 35.

[54] *Gimeno Sendra*, Introducción al Derecho Procesal, pp. 50–51.

[55] See, e.g., *Barona Vilar*, Seguridad, celeridad y justicia penal, p. 60.

sensus within the criminal process (1988, 1992, 2002, 2003), particularly the admission on the part of the defendant of the facts against him or her *(reconocimiento de los hechos)* and the plea agreement *(conformidad)*.[56]

Other reforms are linked to the aforementioned criminal-political trend whose goal is to satisfy growing demands for security. The reforms of pre-trial detention (2003) were intended to bring these regulations into compliance with the doctrine of the Constitutional Court. Prerequisites for and purposes of pre-trial detention were defined more clearly. At the same time, the circle of persons authorized to order pre-trial detention and the maximum duration of detention (which depends on the duration of the prescribed penalty) were increased. Different regulations apply to the ordering of pre-trial detention in the context of domestic violence. The introduction of video surveillance in public venues (1997) is yet another reform designed to increase security.[57]

Special treatment for terrorism-related offenses exists in the procedural arena as well, in the areas, for example, of arrest and detention in solitary confinement.[58]

4. Developments in the execution of punishment

– *Prison law in the Middle Ages*

Imprisonment as a true punishment in Spain dates back to the late Middle Ages. With the reception of Roman and canonical law and the rise in royal power, criminal law was understood as a duty of the state, and incarceration, which until then was employed preventively (*cárcel de custodia*; to secure the proceedings), became a real penalty. However, even before then, there was incarceration for debts, confinement in cloisters (for religious offenses), forced labor, banishment, and detention as punishment (for serfs). These penalties are referred to not only in the body of rules of the *Siete Partidas* (specifically in *Partida* no. 7) but also in regional law. Their purpose was to punish and to deter by instilling fear of punishment. Private prisons were abolished at that time and detailed regulations introduced on issues

---

[56] See *Barona Vilar*, Seguridad, celeridad y justicia penal, pp. 142–160, 185–189, 213–245.

[57] On the regulation of video surveillance, see the following critical approach *Díez Ripollés/Cerezo Domínguez*, Política Criminal 2007, pp. 7–14.

[58] *Catalina Benavente*, in: Faraldo Cabana et al. (eds.), Derecho penal de excepción: terrorismo e inmigración, pp. 171–218; see *Llobet Anglí*, Derecho penal del terrorismo, pp. 202–204; for an overview of substantive reforms, see *Cancio Meliá*, in: Álvarez García/González Cussac (eds.), Comentarios a la Reforma Penal de 2010, pp. 521–532; *Cancio Meliá*, Los delitos de terrorismo, pp. 200–286; see *Llobet Anglí*, Derecho penal del terrorismo, pp. 160–192.

such as chains and stocks, the classification of prisoners, rules of hygiene, communication, pay, responsibility in the case of an escape, etc.[59]

– *Prison law in the modern era*

Beginning with the era of the Catholic monarchs (late 15th century), the difference between preventive *(cárcel)* and punitive *(presidio)* incarceration, carried out primarily in castles and fortresses, solidified. Because the king was considered God's representative on earth, religious heterodoxy was punished as high treason and the punishment level was increased dramatically, for next to the idea of justice was that of Christian love: punishment was aimed at the eternal salvation of the offender's soul as well as at his or her physical destruction. On the other hand, as the economic value of human labor was recognized, it became the dominant factor behind forced labor and galley service (the latter served as a custodial sentence from 1530 to 1748 and from 1784 to 1803).[60] In the 16th century, several thinkers notable for their writings and suggestions for prison reform emerged – such as *Tomás Cerdán de Tallada* with his treatise "Visita a la cárcel y los presos" (Visit in prison and the prisoners), Valencia 1754, and *Bernardino de Saldoval* with his "Tractado del cuydado que se debe tener de los presos pobres" (Tractate on the care to be taken of poor prisoners), Toledo 1564. The 16th and 17th century saw the establishment of a number of facilities with Christian background that championed social work with prisoners and minors.[61]

The inquisition was a special chapter in Spanish criminal law. It was introduced to protect the purity of faith at a time when religious and political powers were merging. The infamous torture method *(tormento)* for pre-trial detention notwithstanding, prisons of the inquisition were considered better than others. Innovative regulations were introduced at these facilities, such as the possibility of cohabitation for married people, temporary permission to leave for work, and the conversion of life imprisonment to house arrest for life.[62]

In the second half of the 18th century, there were several humanizing trends as a result of the Enlightenment; for instance, houses of correction *(casa de corrección)* were introduced, military prisons replaced galleys, and institutions for the protec-

---

59 *Berdugo Gómez de la Torre/Zúñiga Rodríguez* (eds.), Manual de Derecho Penitenciario, p. 59; *Bueno Arús*, Lecciones de Derecho Penitenciario, pp. 11–13; *Tomás y Valiente*, El Derecho penal de la monarquía absoluta, p. 381.

60 *Pike*, 58 Hisp. Am. Hist. Rev. (1978), 21–40; *Pike*, Penal servitude in early modern Spain.

61 See *Bueno Arús*, Lecciones de derecho penitenciario, pp. 14–16; *Berdugo Gómez de la Torre/Zúñiga Rodríguez* (eds.), Manual de Derecho Penitenciario, p. 60.

62 *Bueno Arús*, Lecciones de derecho penitenciario, p. 15.

tion of minors and prisoners in general were established. In 1771, life sentences were prohibited, except for dangerous offenders.[63]

In the 19th century, the death penalty was curtailed and torture and corporal punishment were abolished. Incarceration became the most important penalty and, under the influence of several different theories (enlightened pedagogy, Romantic philanthropy, Krausism, Freemasonry), its purpose was seen in the correction of the offender *(correccionalismo)*, primarily in a moral sense. The new anthropological and sociological insights of criminology were incorporated into the execution of custodial sentences. Some legislation was very progressive: adults and minors were housed separately in prison; there was the option to serve part of the sentence by working. But disciplinary law in serious cases was extremely harsh (corporal punishment, gagging, chaining, etc.). Prisons were part of the civil and no longer part of the military administration. Nevertheless, at the end of the century, prison conditions were described as abominable.[64]

The first prison law, a precursor of the progressive system, is the Ordinance of the Arsenals Prisons *(Ordenanza de los Presidios de Arsenales)* of 20 May 1804. After several other models were tried, the progressive system of Irish origin prevailed in the early 20th century. More laws were passed in the 20th century, and a complex system of liberty-depriving penalties based on the principles of culpability and proportionality (i.e., retributive principles) was retained. At the same time, institutions of crime prevention were introduced, including security measures and probation; in fact, the tug of war between retribution and prevention continues to this day.[65]

On 5 May 1913, the first prison law, the so-called *Código penitenciario español*, incorporating all prior legislation, was passed by royal decree. During the Second Republic (1931–1939), a number of major reforms and improvements were introduced within a short period of time (e.g., the prohibition of chains, shackles, and similar devices; freedom of conscience, access to the news media, and conditional release for prisoners who reach the age of 70).[66]

---

63 *Bueno Arús*, Lecciones de derecho penitenciario, p. 16; see also *García Valdés*, Derecho penitenciario, pp. 27–28.

64 *Berdugo Gómez de la Torre/Zúñiga Rodríguez* (eds.), Manual de derecho penitenciario, p. 117; *Bueno Arús*, Lecciones de derecho penitenciario, pp. 17–23. On the abolition of torture, see *Tomás y Valiente*, La tortura en España, pp. 156–160.

65 *Bueno Arús*, Lecciones de derecho penitenciario, pp. 17–23; *García Valdés*, Derecho penitenciario, p. 247.

66 *García Valdés*, Derecho penitenciario, p. 249; *García Valdés*, in: Bueno Arús (ed.), Lecciones de derecho penitenciario, p. 37.

Following the Civil War (1936–1939) and the *Franco* dictatorship (1939–1975),[67] the General Prison Act (*Ley Orgánica General Penitenciaria*, LOGP) was passed in 1979; its regulations followed in 1981. The Act covers only the execution of prison sentences and, in its mission statement, defines prison as a "necessary evil," thereby reflecting the goal of social reintegration enshrined in the Constitution. It creates for the first time the position of a special prison judge *(Juez de Vigilancia Penitenciaria)*, whose competences include counseling, supervision, and decision-making. Another important new feature is a very detailed regulation concerning the treatment of prisoners. Treatment is defined by law as a goal towards whose achievement all other aspects of the prison system must be geared (Art. 71 LOGP).[68]

To this day, prison law covers nothing but the execution of custodial sentences in prison facilities.[69] The prison system is inspired by the idea of social reintegration, which is expressly recognized as the purpose of punishment in the Constitution of 1978.[70] The prison law and the pertinent regulations have generated a flexible, step-by-step prison regime: the first step is closed prison, the second and third steps are open prison in corresponding facilities, and the last step is early release on probation.[71] The basic premise is that no prisoner may be held at a lower level than appropriate for him or her. The system does not require a prisoner to pass through every single level; for instance, prisoners may be transferred directly from the first to the third level (Art. 72 para. 2 LOGP).

The regulations provide for a whole range of therapeutic measures, professional and vocational training, and participation in different types of programs. Private initiatives for the development of activities for the social reintegration of prisoners are also permitted.[72] Unfortunately, funds for these statutory programs are not always available. And there may be other problems as well, such as an increase in the number of prisoners or in organized gangs, both of which have serious negative impacts on life in prison.

---

67 On the prison situation in these years, see *Cid/Larrauri*, in: Ruggiero et al. (eds.), The New European Criminology, pp. 146–148.

68 *Berdugo Gómez de la Torre/Zúñiga Rodríguez* (eds.), Manual de derecho penitenciario, p. 123; *García Valdés*, Derecho penitenciario, pp. 44–46, 251.

69 For details on today's prison system, see *Bachmaier Winter/del Moral García*, Criminal Law in Spain, pp. 323–335 (nos. 680–703).

70 See I.C.2. and I.D.3.; *Berdugo Gómez de la Torre/Zúñiga Rodríguez* (eds.), Manual de derecho penitenciario, p. 37.

71 For more information, see *Berdugo Gómez de la Torre/Zúñiga Rodríguez* (eds.), Manual de derecho penitenciario, pp. 319–332.

72 *García Valdés*, in: Bueno Arús (ed.), Lecciones de derecho penitenciario, pp. 51–58; *Berdugo Gómez de la Torre/Zúñiga Rodríguez* (eds.), Manual de derecho penitenciario, pp. 122–123.

A major tenet of prison law has been (at least until recently) to treat prisoners equally, regardless of the type of crime they committed; however, reforms triggered by efforts to combat terrorism and serious crime have significantly weakened this principle.[73]

– *Current trends*

Regulations in the Prison Law that impact persons convicted of terrorist or other serious offenses have been tightened, primarily as a result of the 2003 reform of the Penal Code. New, stricter admission requirements for access to level three of the prison regime and restrictions on early release on probation have permanently laid to rest the spirit – and in particular the flexibility – of the earlier prison system.[74]

For prison sentences of five years or more, a so-called safety period has been introduced, similar to those in other European countries. This safety period bars transfers to level three of the prison regime until half the sentence has been served (Art. 36 para. 2 CP). In justified cases with a positive prognosis, the new regulation offers the prison judge the option of ordering the application of the general execution rule. This provision cannot, however, conceal the fact that the so-called general execution rule for offenses punishable by prison terms of five or more years has in fact become the exception. It does not apply to terrorist or other offenses carried out within the framework of a criminal organization; in other words, in cases involving terrorism or organized crime, the safety period must be observed without exception.[75]

General restrictions aside, in order to transition to level three of the prison regime, inmates must have complied with additional conditions. Prisoners must have satisfied their civil liabilities (Art. 72 para. 5 LOGP). In terrorism or organized crime cases, offenders must prove beyond a doubt that they have renounced terrorist goals and means. Furthermore, offenders must actively collaborate with the justice system to prevent further criminal offenses on the part of the organization, to minimize the consequences of the criminal offense, to identify, arrest, and sentence terrorist offenders, to gain evidence, etc. Offenders can comply with these requirements by means of a declaration in which they state explicitly that they have distanced themselves from the criminal offense and from any violence, and by seeking forgiveness from the victims of their crimes. Expert opinions confirming that the individual in question is no longer a member of the organization, has distanced

73 See immediately below.

74 See *Faraldo Cabana*, in: Rivera Beiras (ed.), Política Criminal y Sistema Penal, pp. 411–432; *Aranda Ocaña*, in: Rivera Beiras (ed.), Política Criminal y Sistema Penal, pp. 387–388.

75 See *Faraldo Cabana*, in: Rivera Beiras (ed.), Política Criminal y Sistema Penal, pp. 414–416.

him- or herself from that environment, and has dissociated him- or herself from jointly committed offenses may also be submitted (Art. 72 para. 6 LOGP).

In the literature, some scholars criticize the requirement that offenders must renounce not only the organization's violent means but also its goals. After all, a region's aspiration to independence is in itself not an illegitimate goal. The new regulation is criticized in as much as correctional facilities are used not only for the social reintegration and the free development of the inmate's personality but beyond this are misused as an instrument to enforce the dominant concept of the state. Furthermore, the aforementioned condition requiring convicted offenders to ask their victims for forgiveness is criticized not only because it is morally questionable but also because from a victimological perspective it confers on some victims a privileged status – based on the criminal offense – that is unwarranted.[76]

As for the general conditions for early release, the following are general requirements for the ordering of conditional release: inmates must be in level three of the prison regime; they must have completed three-fourths of their sentence (or – in exceptional cases – two-thirds); and their prognosis must be favorable (Arts. 90 and 91 CP). For inmates convicted of terrorism and organized crime, there are specific rules detailing when a prognosis may be viewed as favorable; in any event, a favorable prognosis requires, again, renunciation of the means and goals of the criminal organization and active collaboration with the justice system. The exception that allows for the conditional release of inmates who have served two-thirds of their sentence if they have a favorable prognosis and participate in job-related programs, cultural activities, and occupational courses does not apply to individuals convicted of acts of terrorism or organized crime.[77]

Convicted individuals on conditional release who fail to comply with the applicable rules of conduct are returned to prison. Furthermore, in terrorism cases, time spent on conditional release is not counted as time served.[78]

Additional effects of the reform of 2003 are increases in the severity of the prison regime that are not expressly limited to terrorism and organized crime. If pursuant to Art. 76 para. 1 CP the application of the rules limiting the maximum term of imprisonment lead to a punishment that amounts to less than half of the sum of all imposed penalties, the judge may order prison privileges to be determined on the basis of the sum of the imposed penalties in the judgment and not on the basis of the maximum term of imprisonment pursuant to Art. 76 para. 1 CP.

---

[76] For more on this criticism, see *Faraldo Cabana*, in: Rivera Beiras (ed.), Política Criminal y Sistema Penal, pp. 419–422.

[77] For a critical view, see *Faraldo Cabana*, in: Rivera Beiras (ed.), Política Criminal y Sistema Penal, p. 426.

[78] See *Faraldo Cabana*, in: Rivera Beiras (ed.), Política Criminal y Sistema Penal, p. 427.

Similarly, according to a Supreme Court decision of 2006, credits due to work, studies, etc. should be applied against each individual punishment and not against the maximum term of imprisonment. Accordingly, terrorists who had been sentenced in accordance with the Penal Code of 1973 were prevented from being released after 30 years in prison. In July 2012, the European Court of Human Rights held that this decision, which served as the basis of the "*Parot* doctrine" (named after the convicted terrorist), represented a violation of the Convention for the Protection of Human Rights and Fundamental Freedoms.[79] The Spanish government appealed this decision.

As a result of the reform of 2015, the punishment of reviewable life imprisonment *(prisión permanente revisable)* was introduced into the Penal Code for more serious crimes. This penalty is of indeterminate duration; the status of the prisoner must be reviewed after he or she has served a portion of the sentence (Arts. 36 para. 1 and 92 CP).

Bibliography and further reading

Alonso Romero, María Paz, El proceso penal en Castilla. Siglos XIII–XVIII (The criminal process in Castile. 13th–18th centuries). Salamanca 1982.

– Historia del proceso penal ordinario en Castilla. Siglos XIII–XVIII (History of ordinary criminal procedure in Castile. 13th–18th centuries). Salamanca 1979.

Aranda Ocaña, Mónica, La Política criminal en materia de terrorismo (Criminal policies with regard to terrorism). In: Iñaki Rivera Beiras (ed.), Política Criminal y Sistema Penal. Viejas y nuevas racionalidades punitivas (Criminal policies and criminal system. Old and new punitive rationales). Barcelona 2005, pp. 367–394.

Bachmaier Winter, Lorena/del Moral García, Antonio, Criminal Law in Spain. 2d ed. Alphen aan den Rijn 2012.

Bacigalupo, Enrique, Principios de Derecho Penal, Parte General (Principles of criminal law, general part). 4th ed. Valencia 2004.

– Einführung (Introduction). In: Markus Hoffmann (transl.), Das spanische Strafgesetzbuch vom 23. November 1995 nach dem Stand vom 31. Dezember 2001 (The Spanish Penal Code of 23 November 1995 as of 31 December 2001). Freiburg 2002, pp. 1–14.

Barona Vilar, Silvia, Seguridad, celeridad y justicia penal (Security, speed, and criminal justice). Valencia 2004.

Berdugo Gómez de la Torre, Ignacio/Zúñiga Rodríguez, Lauram (eds.), Manual de derecho penitenciario (Handbook of prison law). Salamanca 2001.

[79] *Del Río Prada v. Spain*, App. no. 42750/09, Judgment of the ECtHR (Third Section) (10 July 2012).

Bueno Arús, Francisco, Lecciones de derecho penitenciario (Lessons of prison law). Alcalá de Henares 1985.

Cancio Meliá, Manuel, Dogmática y política criminal en una teoría funcional del delito (Criminal doctrine and policies in a functional theory of the offense). In: Günther Jakobs/ Manuel Cancio Meliá (eds.), El sistema funcionalista del derecho penal: ponencias presentadas en el II Curso Internacional de Derecho Penal (Lima, 29–31 de agosto y 1 de septiembre de 2000) (The functionalist system of criminal law: Lectures given in the 2d International Criminal Law Course [Lima, 29–31 August and 1 September 2000]). Lima 2000, pp. 17–42.

– Delitos de terrorismo (arts. 571, 572, 574, 576, 576 bis y 579) (Terrorism offenses). In: Francisco Javier Álvarez García/José Luis González Cussac (eds.), Comentarios a la Reforma Penal de 2010 (Comments on the criminal law reform of 2010). Valencia 2010, pp. 521–532.

– Los delitos de terrorismo: estructura típica e injusto (The terrorism offenses: typical structure and injustice). Madrid 2010.

Catalina Benavente, María Ángeles, Los supuestos de detención en los casos de terrorismo: propuestas para una reforma (Criteria for detention in the terrorism cases: Suggestions for a reform). In: Patricia Faraldo Cabana/Luz María Puente Aba/Eva María Souto García (eds.), Derecho penal de excepción: terrorismo e inmigración (Exceptional criminal law: Terrorism and immigration). Valencia 2007, pp. 171–218.

Cerezo Domínguez, Ana Isabel, La prevención de la delincuencia callejera mediante videocámaras. Regulación jurídica y eficacia (The prevention of street crime by means of video cameras. Legal regulation and efficiency). Política Criminal: Revista Electrónica Semestral de Políticas Públicas en Materias Penales 2007, 1–25, available at http://www.politicacriminal.cl/n_07/a_6_7.pdf [last visited 25 Jan. 2018].

Cerezo Mir, José, Curso de derecho penal español, Parte general I (Course of Spanish criminal law, general part I), vol. I: Introducción (Introduction). 6th ed. Madrid 2007.

Cid, José/Larrauri, Elena, Prison and Alternatives to Prison in Spain. In: Vincenzo Ruggiero/Nigel South/Ian Taylor (eds.), The New European Criminology: Crime and Social Order in Europe. London 2002, pp. 146–155.

Cuello Contreras, Joaquín, El derecho penal español, Parte general (Spanish criminal law, general part). 3d ed. Madrid 2002.

De la Cuesta Arzamendi, José Luis, Características de la cultura política criminal española en materia de drogas (Characteristics of the culture of Spanish criminal policy with regard to drugs). In: Luis Díez Ripollés/Patricia Laurenzo Copello (eds.), La actual política criminal sobre drogas: una perspectiva comparada (Current criminal policy on drugs: A comparative perspective). Díez Ripollés/Laurenzo Copello (coord.). Valencia 1993, pp. 37–82.

Díez Ripollés, Luis, Algunos rasgos de la delincuencia en España a comienzos del Siglo XXI (Some characteristics of delinquency in Spain at the beginning of the 21st century). REIC, no. 4, 2006, art. 1, 1–19, available at http://reic.criminologia.net/pdf/reic/ano4-2006/ a42006art1.PDF [last visited 31 Jan. 2018].

– El nuevo modelo penal de la seguridad ciudadana (The new criminal law model of public security). RECPC no. 6 (2004), artículo 3, 1–34, available at http://criminet.ugr.es/ recpc/06/recpc06-03.pdf [last visited 31 Jan. 2018].

Díez Ripollés, Luis, La nueva política criminal Española (The new Spanish criminal policy). In: Cuadernos penales José María Lidón, no. 1, Las recientes reformas penales: algunas cuestiones (The recent criminal law reforms: some questions). Bilbao 2004, pp. 11–40, available at http://www.deusto-publicaciones.es/deusto/pdfs/lidon/lidon01.pdf [last visited 31 Jan. 2018].

Esmein, Adhémar (author)/*Simpson, John* (transl.), A History of Continental Criminal Procedure with special reference to France. Boston 1913, pp. 295–301; 584–585.

Faraldo Cabana, Patricia, Un derecho penal de enemigos para los integrantes de organizaciones criminales. La Ley Orgánica 7/2003, de 30 de junio, de medidas de reforma para el cumplimiento íntegro y efectivo de las penas (A criminal law of the enemy for members of criminal organizations. Organic Law 7/2003, from 30 June about measures of the reform for the complete and effective fulfilment of the sentences). In: Iñaki Rivera Beiras (ed.), Política Criminal y Sistema Penal. Viejas y nuevas racionalidades punitivas (Criminal policy and criminal system. Old and new punitive rationales). Barcelona 2005, pp. 395–433.

García Valdés, Carlos, Derecho penitenciario español: Notas sistemáticas (Prison law: Systematic notes). In: Francisco Bueno Arús (ed.), Lecciones de Derecho Penitenciario (Lessons of prison law). Alcalá de Henares 1985, pp. 33–58.

– Derecho Penitenciario (Prison law). Madrid 1989.

Gimeno Sendra, Vicente, Introducción al derecho procesal (Introduction to the law of criminal procedure). 9th ed. Madrid 2014.

Gómez Martín, Víctor, Cultura del control, sociedad del riesgo y política criminal (Culture of control, risk society, and criminal policy). In: Víctor Gómez Martín/Santiago Mir Puig/Mirentxu Corcoy Bidasolo (eds.), Política criminal y reforma penal (Criminal policy and reform of criminal law). Madrid 2007, pp. 55–103.

Gracia Martín, Luis, ¿Qué es la modernización del derecho penal? (What is the modernization of criminal law?). In: José Luis Díez Ripollés/Carlos Maria Romeo Casabona/Luis Gracia Martín/Juan Felipe Higuera Gimerá (eds.), La ciencia del derecho penal ante el nuevo siglo. Libro homenaje al Prof. Dr. Don José Cerezo Mir (Criminal law science at the threshold of the new century. Festschrift for Prof. Dr. Don José Cerezo Mir). Madrid 2002, pp. 349–394.

– Prolegómenos para la lucha por la modernización y expansión del derecho penal y para la crítica del discurso de resistencia (Foreword for the fight for the modernization and expansion of criminal law and for the criticism of the resistance discourse). Valencia 2003.

Hartwig, Alfredo (transl.), Spanisches Strafgesetzbuch vom 17. Juni 1870 (The Spanish Penal Code of 17 June 1870). Berlin 1909.

Herrero Herrero, César, La prevención, principal vía realizadora de la política criminal (Prevention, The principal way of realizing criminal policy). In: José Luis Guzmán Dálbora/Francisco Bueno Arús/Alfonso Serrano Maíllo (eds.), Derecho penal y criminología como fundamento de la política criminal: estudios en homenaje al profesor Alfonso Serrano Gómez (Criminal law and criminology as foundation of criminal policy: Studies in honor of Professor Alfonso Serrano Gómez). Madrid 2006, pp. 1237–1251.

Hoffmann, Markus (transl.), Das spanische Strafgesetzbuch vom 23. November 1995 nach dem Stand vom 31. Dezember 2001 (The Spanish Penal Code of 23 November 1995 as of 31 December 2001). Freiburg 2002

Ibán, Iván C., Einführung in das spanische Recht (Introduction to Spanish law). Baden-Baden 1995.

Kleffens, Eelco Nicolaas van, Hispanic law until the end of the Middle Ages. Edinburgh 1968.

Lardizábal y Uribe, Manuel, Discurso sobre las penas: contraído a las leyes criminales de España para facilitar su reforma (Discourse concerning punishments: The obligation of Spanish criminal laws to facilitate their reform). Madrid 1916.

Laurenzo Copello, Patricia, La violencia de género en la Ley Integral: valoración políticocriminal (Gender-based violence in the "Ley Integral" [integrity protection law]: criminal policy evaluation). RECPC no. 7 (2005), available at http://criminet.ugr.es/recpc/07/recpc07-08.pdf [last visited 25 Jan. 2018].

Llobet Anglí, Mariona, Derecho penal del terrorismo. Límites a su punición en un Estado democrático (Criminal law in terrorism legislation. Limits of punishment in a democratic state). Madrid 2010.

Magnol, Joseph/Moulins, Charles de (transls.), Le Code pénal espagnol du 8 septembre 1928 suivi du décret-loi du 3 février 1929 sur les tribunaux tutélaires pour mineurs et des règlements pénitentiaires (The Spanish Penal Code of 8 September 1928 followed by the décret-loi of 3 February 1929 on the juvenile courts and prison regulations). Paris 1931.

Martínez-Buján Pérez, Carlos, Algunas reflexiones sobre la moderna teoría del big crunch en la selección de bienes jurídico-penales (especial referencia al ámbito económico) (Some reflections on the modern theory of the "big crunch" in the selection of protected legal interests [special reference to economic sector]). In: José Luis Díez Ripollés/Carlos Maria Romeo Casabona/Luis Gracia Martín/Juan Felipe Higuera Gimerá (eds.), La ciencia del derecho penal ante el nuevo siglo. Libro Homenaje al Prof. Dr. Don José Cerezo Mir (Criminal law science at the threshold of the new century, Festschrift for Prof. Dr. Don José Cerezo Mir). Madrid 2002, pp. 395–431.

Masferrer Domingo, Aniceto, Codification of Spanish Criminal Law in the Nineteenth Century: A Comparative Legal History Approach. 4 J. Comp. L. 96–139 (2009).

– Tradición y reformismo en la codificación española (Tradition and reformism in the Spanish codification). Jaén 2003.

Mendoza Buergo, Blanca, Gestión de riesgo y política criminal de seguridad en la sociedad de riesgo (Risk management and criminal security policy in the risk society). In: Julio Díaz-Maroto y Villarejo (ed.), Derecho y justicia penal en el siglo XXI: liber amicorum en homenaje al profesor Antonio González-Cuéllar García (Criminal law and criminal justice in the 21st century. Liber amicorum for Professor Antonio González-Cuéllar García). Madrid 2006, pp. 351–372.

Mir Puig, Santiago/Alcácer Guirao, Rafael, Cambio de orientación en la política criminal española: últimas reformas del código penal (Change of orientation in Spanish criminal policy: Recent reforms of the Penal Code). In: Víctor Gómez Martín/Santiago Mir Puig/Mirentxu Corcoy Bidasolo (eds.), Política criminal y reforma penal (Criminal policy and reform of criminal law). Madrid 2007, pp. 107–120.

Mir Puig, Santiago/Gómez Martín Victor, Derecho penal. Parte general (Criminal law. General part). 9th ed. Barcelona 2011.

Miró Llinares, Fernando, Política comunitaria de inmigración y política criminal en España. ¿Protección o "exclusión" penal del inmigrante? (Communitarian policy of immigration and criminal policy in Spain. Protection or criminal exclusion of the immigrant?) RECPC no. 10-5 (2008), available at http://criminet.ugr.es/recpc/10/recpc10-05.pdf [last visited 25 Jan. 2018].

Miró Miquel, Gabriel, La Política criminal del problema droga. Etapas del problema y consecuencias de las soluciones adoptadas (The criminal policy of the drug problem. Stages of the problem and consequences of the adopted solutions). In: Iñaki Rivera Beiras (ed.), Política Criminal y Sistema Penal. Viejas y nuevas racionalidades punitivas (Criminal policy and criminal system. Old and new punitive rationales). Barcelona 2005, pp. 303–318.

Monclús Masó, Marta, Hacia una política criminal diferenciada para los extranjeros: la consolidación de la expulsión como sanción penal especial (Towards a differentiated criminal policy for foreigners: The consolidation of expulsion as a specific criminal sanction). In: Iñaki Rivera Beiras (ed.), Política Criminal y Sistema Penal. Viejas y nuevas racionalidades punitivas (Criminal policy and penal system. Old and new punitive rationales). Barcelona 2005, pp. 330–348.

Ortiz de Urbina Gimeno, Iñigo, La referencia político-criminal en el derecho penal contemporáneo: ¿es el derecho penal la barrera infranqueable de la política criminal, o se orienta por ella? (The political-criminal reference in contemporary criminal law: Is the criminal law the insuperable barrier, or does it serve as an orientation?). In: Emilio Octavio de Toledo y Ubieto/Manuel Gurdiel Sierra/Emilio Cortés Bechiarelli (eds.), Estudios penales en recuerdo del Profesor Ruiz Antón (Criminal law studies in memory of Professor Ruiz Antón). Valencia 2004, pp. 859–894.

Pastor Muñoz, Nuria, Los delitos de posesión y los delitos de estatus: una aproximación político-criminal y dogmática (Possession offenses and status offenses: A politico-criminal and doctrinal approximation). Barcelona 2005.

Pérez Cepeda, Ana Isabel, El código penal de la seguridad: una involución en la política criminal de signo reaccionario (The Penal Security Code: A comeback of the reactionary sign in criminal policy). In: María José Bernuz Benéitez/Ana Isabel Pérez Cepeda (eds.), La tensión entre libertad y seguridad: una aproximación socio-jurídica (The tension between liberty and security: A socio-legal approximation). Logroño 2006.

Pike, Ruth, Penal servitude in early modern Spain. Madison, Wis. 1983.

– Penal servitude in the Spanish Empire: Presidio Labor in the Eighteenth Century. 58 Hisp. Am. Hist. Rev. (1978), 21–40.

Quintano-Ripollés, Antonio/Heilpern Quintano, Johanna/Scharff, Helmut (transl.), Das Spanische Strafgesetzbuch vom 23. Dezember 1944 (The Spanish Penal Code of 23 December 1944). Berlin 1955.

Quintero Olivares, Gonzalo/Morales Prats, Fermín, Parte General del Derecho Penal (General part of criminal law). 4th ed. Cizur Menor 2010.

Rebollo Vargas, Rafael, Rasgos actuales de la política criminal (Current characteristics in criminal policy). RdPP no. 14, 2005, 103–110.

Redondo Hermida, Alvaro, La función de la Política Criminal en la más reciente Jurisprudencia del Tribunal Supremo (The function of criminal policy in the latest judgments of the Supreme Court). La ley penal: revista de derecho penal, procesal y penitenciario, no. 40, 2007, 76–82.

Ross, Friso, Justiz im Verhör: Kontrolle, Karriere und Kultur während der Diktatur von Primo de Rivera (1923–1930) (Justice interrogated: Control, career, and culture during the dictatorship of Primo de Rivera). Frankfurt am Main 2006.

Sanz Morán, Ángel José, Algunas consideraciones en torno a la política criminal (Some considerations about criminal policy). In: Fernando Pérez Álvarez/Miguel Ángel Núñez Paz/Isabel García Alfaraz (eds.), Universitas vitae: homenaje a Ruperto Núñez Barbero (Universitas vitae: homage to Ruperto Núñez Barbero). Salamanca 2007, pp. 729–740.

Silva Forné, Diego, La Codificación penal y el surgimiento del estado liberal en España (The criminal codification and the rise of the liberal state in Spain). RDPC 2001, 233–309.

Silva Sánchez, Jesús María, Reflexiones sobre las bases de la Política Criminal (Reflections on the fundamentals of criminal policy). In: José Cerezo Mir (ed.), El nuevo Código Penal: presupuestos y fundamentos (libro homenaje al profesor Doctor Don Angel Torío López) (The new Penal Code: Prerequisites and foundations [Festschrift for Prof. Dr. Don Angel Torío López]). Granada 1999, pp. 209–220.

– La expansión del derecho penal: aspectos de la política criminal en las sociedades postindustriales (The expansion of criminal law: Aspects of criminal policy in post-industrial societies). Madrid 1999.

Silva Sánchez, Jesús María/Felip i Saborit, David/Robles Planas, Ricardo/Pastor Muñoz, Nuria, La ideología de la seguridad en la legislación penal española presente y futura (The ideology of security in present and future Spanish criminal legislation). In: Cândido da Agra/José Luis Domínguez/Juan Antonio García Amado/Patrick Hebberecht/Amadeu Recasens (eds.), La seguridad en la sociedad del riesgo. Un debate abierto (Security in a risk society. An open debate). Barcelona 2003, pp. 113–135.

Strien, Andrea, Einflüsse des deutschen Strafrechts auf die jüngere Strafrechtsreformbewegung in Spanien (Influences of German criminal law on the recent criminal law reform movement in Spain). Berlin 1992.

Tamarit Sumalla, Josep Maria, Historical memory and criminal justice in Spain: a case of late transitional justice. Cambridge 2013.

Thaman, Stephen C., Spain Returns to Trial by Jury. 21 Hastings Int'l & Comp. L. Rev. (1997), 241–538.

Tomás y Valiente, Francisco, La tortura en España – Estudios históricos (Torture in Spain – Historical studies). Barcelona 1973.

– El derecho penal de la monarquía absoluta (The criminal law of the absolute monarchy). 2d ed. Madrid 1992.

Volkmann-Schluck, Thomas, Der spanische Strafprozeß zwischen Inquisitions- und Parteiverfahren (The Spanish criminal trial between inquisitorial and adversarial procedure). Baden-Baden 1979.

Table of cases

Del Río Prada v. Spain, App. no. 42750/09, Judgment of the ECtHR (Third Section) (10 July 2012) (Parot doctrine)

STS of 28 Feb. 2006 (Parot doctrine)

List of abbreviations in country report Spain

ADPCP	Anuario de Derecho Penal y Ciencias Penales (law journal)
CC	Código civil (Civil Code)
CE	Constitución Española (Spanish Constitution)
CIS	Centro de Investigaciones Sociológicas (Center for Studies in Sociology)
CP	Código penal (Penal Code)
CPC	Cuadernos de política criminal (law journal)
dir.	director
DNA	Desoxyribonucleic acid
ECtHR	European Court of Human Rights
EU	European Union
EuGH	Court of Justice of the European Union
Eur. J. on Crim. Policy & Res.	European Journal on Criminal Policy and Research
GNP	Gross National Product
Hastings Int'l & Comp. L. Rev.	Hastings International & Comparative Law Review
Hisp. Am. Hist. Rev.	Hispanic American Historical Review
ICTR	International Criminal Tribunal for Rwanda
ICTY	International Criminal Tribunal for the Former Yugoslavia
IUIOG	Instituto Universitario de Investigación Ortega y Gasset
INE	Instituto Nacional de Estadística (National Institute for Statistics)
J. Civ. L. Stud.	Journal of Civil Law Studies
J. Comp. L.	Journal of Comparative Law
J. Contemp. Crim. Just.	Journal of Contemporary Criminal Justice
LECrim	Ley de Enjuiciamiento Criminal (Code of Criminal Procedure)
LO	Ley Orgánica (Constitutional Law, Organic Law)
LOGP	Ley Orgánica General Penitenciaria (General Organic Law regarding the execution of custodial sentences)
LOPJ	Ley Orgánica del Poder Judicial (Organic Law on judicial power)

LRJP-PAC	Ley de Régimen Jurídico de las Administraciones Públicas y del Procedimiento Administrativo Común (Law on public administration and on administrative proceedings)
LRP	Ley para la Reforma Política (Law for political reform)
MIR	Ministerio del Interior (Ministry of the Interior)
NATO	North Atlantic Treaty Organization
OECD	Organization for Economic Cooperation and Development
RdPP	Revista de derecho y proceso penal (law journal)
REIC	Revista Española de Investigación Criminológica (law journal)
RECPC	Revista electrónica de ciencia penal y criminología (law journal)
RFDUC	Revista de la Facultad de Derecho de la Universidad Complutense (law journal)
RDPC	Revista de Derecho Penal y Criminología (law journal)
RJCLM	Revista jurídica de Castilla-La Mancha (law journal)
TC	Tribunal Constitucional (Constitutional Court)
STC	Sentencia del Tribunal Constitucional (Judgment of the Constitutional Court)
STS	Sentencia del Tribunal Supremo (Judgment of the Supreme Court)
UNESCO	United Nations Educational, Scientific, and Cultural Organization
UDHR	Universal Declaration of Human Rights
USD	United States Dollar
ZStW	Zeitschrift für die gesamte Strafrechtswissenschaft (law journal)

Editors and authors

Jain, Neha

Prof. Dr. *Neha Jain* is an associate professor of law and a McKnight Land-Grant Professor (2016 to 2018) at the University of Minnesota Law School (USA). She received her B.A., LL.B. (Hons.) from the National Law School of India University and her B.C.L. and D.Phil. in law from Oxford University, where she was a Rhodes Scholar and Jowett Senior Scholar at Balliol College. Prior to joining the Minnesota faculty, she was a law research fellow at Georgetown University Law Center (2010 to 2012) and worked at the Max Planck Institute for Foreign and International Criminal Law in Freiburg, Germany (2008 to 2010). Prof. *Jain* has served as a visiting professional with the Chambers Division of the International Criminal Court and has held visiting fellowships at the Stellenbosch Institute for Advanced Study, the Danish National Research Foundation's Centre of Excellence for International Courts, and the Lauterpacht Centre for International Law. She has published numerous research articles on international law in leading journals, including the American Journal of International Law, Harvard International Law Journal, and European Journal of International Law.

Jarvers, Konstanze

Dr. *Konstanze Jarvers* has been head of the section "Italy and Greece" at the Max Planck Institute for Foreign and International Criminal Law since 1999. In this capacity, she has written country reports on substantive as well as procedural criminal law for numerous Institute projects, and she co-led a study on the criminalization of incest (with Prof. *Hans-Jörg Albrecht* and Prof. *Ulrich Sieber*). She is the author of country report Italy for the International Max Planck Information System for Comparative Criminal Law. After completing both German state exams in law, Dr. *Jarvers* worked in the legal department of a private bank before joining the Institute. She was awarded a doctorate from the University of Freiburg in 2007 for her dissertation on widespread and petty crime as dealt with by Italian justices of the peace *(Massen- und Kleinkriminalität vor dem italienischen Friedensrichter)*.

Manso Porto, Teresa

Dr. *Teresa Manso Porto*, Mag. iur. comp., completed her legal studies at the CEU San Pablo (Complutense University of Madrid). From 1997 to 1999, she was a researcher at the University of Bonn, where she was awarded a Master of Comparative Law, and from 2000 to 2004, she was a researcher at the University of Freiburg and the Max Planck Institute for Foreign and International Criminal Law. In 2003, she was appointed acting head of the section "Spain and (intermittently) Portugal" at the Institute and has been head of the section since 2005. She earned her doctorate in 2009 for a dissertation on inculpatory ignorance of the law *(Normunkenntnis aus belastenden Gründen)*. She was a guest lecturer at the University Pompeu Fabra in Barcelona (2009 to 2010) and at the University of A Coruña (2011). She has been a guest lecturer at the UOC in Barcelona (distance learning) and in various masters-of-laws programs in Spain, Argentina, and Bolivia since 2011. Dr. *Manso Porto* is the author of publications in Spain, Latin America, and Germany, on mistake of law, the legality principle, environmental offenses, money laundering, corruption, etc. She has written country reports on Spain for Institute projects on the general part of criminal law, the role of honor in criminal law, preventive detention, and incest.

Rinceanu, Johanna

Dr. *Johanna Rinceanu*, LL.M. (GWU), studied law in Freiburg from 1993 to 1998. In 1998, she was awarded a Fulbright scholarship to study at the George Washington University Law School in Washington D.C. (USA). From 2000 to 2002, she absolved her legal clerkship *(Referendariat)* in Germany. In 2007, she completed her dissertation *(Völkerstrafrecht in Rumänien)* at the Humboldt University in Berlin. From 1999 to 2000, Dr. *Rinceanu* was employed as a consultant at the World Bank's legal department in Washington D.C. Since 2002, she has worked as an attorney in Freiburg, with a focus on criminal law and human rights law. She worked as a researcher and senior researcher at the Max Planck Institute for Foreign and International Criminal Law from 2002 to 2008 and has been head of the section "Romania" since 2009. She began lecturing at the University of Freiburg in 2007. Dr. *Rinceanu* is the author of numerous publications on German and Romanian criminal law and human rights law that have been published in Brazil, Germany, Greece, Italy, Romania, Spain, Turkey, and the USA.

Sieber, Ulrich

Prof. Dr. Dr. h.c. mult. *Ulrich Sieber*, director at the Max Planck Institute for Foreign and International Criminal Law and scientific member of the Max Planck Society for the Advancement of Science since 2003, is an honorary professor and faculty member at the law faculties of the University of Freiburg and the University of Munich. He is also an advisory professor at the law departments of Renmin University, Beijing Normal University, and Wuhan University (all China). His main areas of interest encompass the changing face of crime, criminal law, and legal policy in today's "global risk society." His research focuses primarily on the territorial and functional limits of criminal law in the prosecution of new types of transnational and complex crime. Major project areas include organized crime, terrorism, economic crime, and cybercrime as well as comparative criminal law, European criminal law, and international criminal law. He is also the initiator and spokesperson of the International Max Planck Research School for Comparative Criminal Law (IMPRS-CC), a cooperative venture of the Max Planck Institute and the law faculty of the University of Freiburg. In addition to his academic work, Prof. *Sieber* is active as an expert consultant and legal counsel, especially in the areas of computer law and international criminal law.

Silverman, Emily

Emily Silverman, J.D. (Berkeley Law), LL.M., has served for many years as head of the sections "United States and Canada," "Israel," and "Translation (German to English)" at the Max Planck Institute for Foreign and International Criminal Law. She is the author of the country report USA for the International Max Planck Information System for Comparative Criminal Law and has written country reports for numerous other Institute projects, including preventive detention, incest, the liability of leaders of criminal groups and networks, national prosecution of international crimes, and restitution. A 1991 graduate of the Boalt Hall School of Law (University of California, Berkeley), her LL.M. from the University of Freiburg for a comparative thesis on the role of crime victims in criminal procedure in Germany and the United States was supported by grants from the German Academic Exchange Service (DAAD) and the Max Planck Society. She writes and translates in the areas of criminal law and criminal policy.

Schriftenreihe des Max-Planck-Instituts für ausländisches und internationales Strafrecht

The main research activities of the Max Planck Institute for Foreign and International Criminal Law are published in the following six subseries of the "Schriftenreihe des Max-Planck-Instituts für ausländisches und internationales Strafrecht" (Research Series of the Max Planck Institute for Foreign and International Criminal Law), which are distributed in cooperation with the publisher Duncker & Humblot:

- "Strafrechtliche Forschungsberichte" (Reports on Research in Criminal Law)
- "Kriminologische Forschungsberichte" (Reports on Research in Criminology)
- "Interdisziplinäre Forschungen aus Strafrecht und Kriminologie" (Reports on Interdisciplinary Research in Criminal Law and Criminology)
- "Publications of the Max Planck Partner Group for Balkan Criminology"
- "Series of the Max Planck Institute for Foreign and International Criminal Law and Bahçeşehir University Joint Research Group"
- "Sammlung ausländischer Strafgesetzbücher in Übersetzung" (Collection of Foreign Criminal Laws in Translation)

These publications can be ordered from the Max Planck Institute at <www.mpicc.de> or from Duncker & Humblot at <www.duncker-humblot.de>. Two additional subseries are published: "research in brief" contains short reports on results of research activities, and "Arbeitsberichte" (working materials) present preliminary results of research projects. These publications are available at the Max Planck Institute.

Detailed information on all publications of the Max Planck Institute for Foreign and International Criminal Law can be found at <www.mpicc.de>.

Die zentralen Veröffentlichungen des Max-Planck-Instituts für ausländisches und internationales Strafrecht werden in Zusammenarbeit mit dem Verlag Duncker & Humblot in den folgenden sechs Unterreihen der „Schriftenreihe des Max-Planck-Instituts für ausländisches und internationales Strafrecht" vertrieben:

- „Strafrechtliche Forschungsberichte"
- „Kriminologische Forschungsberichte"
- „Interdisziplinäre Forschungen aus Strafrecht und Kriminologie"
- „Publications of the Max Planck Partner Group for Balkan Criminology"
- „Series of the Max Planck Institute for Foreign and International Criminal Law and Bahçeşehir University Joint Research Group"
- „Sammlung ausländischer Strafgesetzbücher in Übersetzung"

Diese Publikationen können direkt über das Max-Planck-Institut unter <www.mpicc.de> oder über den Verlag Duncker & Humblot unter <www.duncker-humblot.de> erworben werden. Darüber hinaus erscheinen in der Unterreihe „research in brief" zusammenfassende Kurzbeschreibungen von Forschungsergebnissen und in der Unterreihe „Arbeitsberichte" Veröffentlichungen vorläufiger Forschungsergebnisse. Diese Veröffentlichungen können über das Max-Planck-Institut bezogen werden.

Detaillierte Informationen zu den einzelnen Publikationen des Max-Planck-Instituts für ausländisches und internationales Strafrecht sind unter <www.mpicc.de> abrufbar.

Max-Planck-Institut für ausländisches und internationales Strafrecht

Other volumes of this project:

S 128.**1**.1 *Ulrich Sieber / Konstanze Jarvers / Emily Silverman* (eds.)
National Criminal Law in a Comparative Legal Context
Volume 1.1: Introduction to National Systems
2013 • 314 Seiten • ISBN 978-3-86113-822-8 € 40,00

S 128.**1**.2 Volume 1.2: Introduction to National Systems
2013 • 363 Seiten • ISBN 978-3-86113-826-6 € 43,00

S 128.**1**.3 Volume 1.3: Introduction to National Systems
2014 • 297 Seiten • ISBN 978-3-86113-818-1 € 40,00

S 128.**1**.4 Volume 1.4: Introduction to National Systems
2014 • 391 Seiten • ISBN 978-3-86113-810-5 € 43,00

S 128.**2**.1 *Ulrich Sieber / Susanne Forster / Konstanze Jarvers* (eds.)
Volume 2.1: General limitations on the application of criminal law
2011 • 399 Seiten • ISBN 978-3-86113-834-1 € 43,00

S 128.**2**.2 *Ulrich Sieber / Konstanze Jarvers / Emily Silverman* (eds.)
Volume 2.2: General limitations on the application of criminal law
2017 • 272 Seiten • ISBN 978-3-86113-798-6 € 35,00

S 128.**3**.1 *Ulrich Sieber / Susanne Forster / Konstanze Jarvers* (eds.)
Volume 3.1: Defining criminal conduct
2011 • 519 Seiten • ISBN 978-3-86113-833-4 € 46,00

S 128.**3**.2 *Ulrich Sieber / Konstanze Jarvers / Emily Silverman* (eds.)
Volume 3.2: Defining criminal conduct
2017 • 370 Seiten • ISBN 978-3-86113-790-0 € 43,00

S 128.**4**.1 *Ulrich Sieber / Konstanze Jarvers / Emily Silverman* (eds.)
Volume 4.1: Special forms of criminal liability
2015 • 401 Seiten • ISBN 978-3-86113-803-7 € 43,00

S 128.**5**.1 Volume 5.1: Grounds for rejecting criminal liability
2016 • 410 Seiten • ISBN 978-3-86113-800-6 € 43,00

S 114.1 *Ulrich Sieber / Karin Cornils* (Hrsg.)
Nationales Strafrecht in rechtsvergleichender Darstellung
– Allgemeiner Teil –
Band 1: Grundlagen
2009 • 790 Seiten • ISBN 978-3-86113-849-5 € 55,00

S 114.2 Band 2: Gesetzlichkeitsprinzip – Internationaler Geltungsbereich – Begriff und Systematisierung der Straftat
2008 • 470 Seiten • ISBN 978-3-86113-860-0 € 41,00

S 114.3 Band 3: Objektive Tatseite – Subjektive Tatseite – Strafbares Verhalten vor der Tatvollendung
2008 • 490 Seiten • ISBN 978-3-86113-859-4 € 41,00

S 114.4 Band 4: Tatbeteiligung – Straftaten in Unternehmen, Verbänden und anderen Kollektiven
2010 • 527 Seiten • ISBN 978-3-86113-842-6 € 45,00

S 114.5 Band 5: Gründe für den Ausschluss der Strafbarkeit – Aufhebung der Strafbarkeit – Verjährung
2010 • 718 Seiten • ISBN 978-3-86113-841-9 € 55,00

Additional criminal law publications:

S 160 *Mandy Vetter*
Verteidigerkonsultation im Ermittlungsverfahren
Eine rechtsvergleichende Untersuchung zum deutschen und englischen Strafverfahrensrecht im Lichte der Europäischen Menschenrechtskonvention
2018 • 760 Seiten • ISBN 978-3-86113-787-0 € 50,00

S 159 *Johannes Schäuble*
Strafverfahren und Prozessverantwortung
Neue prozessuale Obliegenheiten des Beschuldigten in Deutschland im Vergleich mit dem US-amerikanischen Recht
2017 • 477 Seiten • ISBN 978-3-86113-791-7 € 44,00

S 158 *Hannes Schrägle*
Das begehungsgleiche Unterlassungsdelikt
Eine rechtsgeschichtliche, rechtsdogmatische und rechtsvergleichende Untersuchung und die Entwicklung eines Systems der Garantietypen
2017 • 339 Seiten • ISBN 978-3-86113-793-1 € 35,00

S 156 *Ulrich Sieber / Nicolas von zur Mühlen* (eds.)
Access to Telecommunication Data in Criminal Justice
A Comparative Analysis of European Legal Orders
2016 • 771 Seiten • ISBN 978-3-86113-796-2 € 58,00

S 155 *Jennifer Schuetze-Reymann*
International Criminal Justice on Trial
The ICTY and ICTR Case Referral Practice to National Courts and Its Possible Relevance for the ICC
2016 • 232 Seiten • ISBN 978-3-86113-797-9 € 35,00

Max-Planck-Institut für ausländisches
und internationales Strafrecht

Selected criminological, interdisciplinary, and Balkan Criminology Group publications:

K 179 *Michael Kilchling*
Opferschutz innerhalb und außerhalb des Strafrechts
Perspektiven zur Übertragung opferschützender Normen aus dem Strafverfahrensrecht in andere Verfahrensordnungen
Berlin 2018 • 165 Seiten • ISBN 978-3-86113-267-7 € 32,00

K 177 *Tillmann Bartsch, Martin Brandenstein, Volker Grundies, DieterHermann, Jens Puschke, Matthias Rau* (Hrsg.)
50 Jahre Südwestdeutsche und Schweizerische Kriminologische Kolloquien
Berlin 2017 • 312 Seiten • ISBN 978-3-86113-265-3 € 35,00

K 175 *Michael Kilchling*
Täter-Opfer-Ausgleich im Strafvollzug
Wissenschaftliche Begleitung des Modellprojekts Täter-Opfer-Ausgleich im baden-württembergischen Justizvollzug
Berlin 2017 • 218 Seiten • ISBN 978-3-86113-262-2 € 35,00

K 174 *Min Kyung Han*
The Effectiveness of Electronic Monitoring in Korea
Berlin 2017 • 210 Seiten • ISBN 978-3-86113-261-5 € 35,00

K 173 *Jing Lin*
Compliance and Money Laundering Control by Banking Institutions in China
Self-Control, Administrative Control, and Penal Control
Berlin 2016 • 222 Seiten • ISBN 978-3-86113-260-8 € 35,00

K 172 *Julia Kasselt*
Die Ehre im Spiegel der Justiz
Eine Untersuchung zur Praxis deutscher Schwurgerichte im Umgang mit dem Phänomen der Ehrenmorde
Berlin 2016 • 495 Seiten • ISBN 978-3-86113-255-4 € 42,00

K 171 *Rita Haverkamp, Harald Arnold* (Hrsg.)
Subjektive und objektivierte Bedingungen von (Un-)Sicherheit
Studien zum Barometer Sicherheit in Deutschland (BaSiD)
Berlin 2015 • 384 Seiten • ISBN 978-3-86113-254-7 € 38,00

I 25 *Chenguang Zhao*
The ICC and China
The Principle of Complementarity and National Implementation of International Criminal Law
Berlin 2017 • 245 Seiten • ISBN 978-3-86113-266-0 € 35,00

BC 2 *Sunčana Roksandić Vidlička*
Prosecuting Serious Economic Crimes as International Crimes
A New Mandate for the ICC?
Berlin 2017 • 530 Seiten • ISBN 978-3-86113-264-6 € 44,00